The

Secret Path

Beyond Ego

Ascended Master Teachings, Volume 1

Kim Michaels

More to Life Publishing

The

Secret Path

Beyond Ego

Ascended Master Teachings, Volume 1

Kim Michaels

More to Life Publishing

The Secret Path Beyond Ego
Ascended Master Teachings, Volume 1
by Kim Michaels.
Copyright © 2012 by Kim Michaels

Published by More to Life Publishing, owned by More to Life OÜ, Estonia. To contact the publisher, use the contact information on *www.morepublish.com*.

All rights reserved.

No part of this book may be reproduced, translated or transmitted by any means except by written permission from the publisher. A reviewer may quote brief passages in a review.

ISBN 978-9949-9251-3-1 (paperback)

ISBN 978-9949-9251-4-8 (hardcover)

ISBN 978-9949-9251-5-5 (series)

Cover design by Helen Michaels.

Contents

Introduction: About This Book   **13**

Chapter 1:
Introducing the Ascended Masters?   **15**
The hierarchy of ascended beings   17
How are the teachings in this book brought forth?   23

Chapter 2:
Introducing the Components of Self   **28**
What is the very core of your being?   28
Your spiritual self   31
Your Christ self   32
A deeper understanding of the soul   33
The container of self and your four lower bodies   36
The human ego   38

Chapter 3:
Ego Teachings, 2004-05   **40**
Awaken and BE the light of the world!   40
Help me consume the conflict in the Middle East   43
God's Will is your will   45
If you love me, give my Rosary of God's Will   54
Wake up—NOW!   59
Why on earth are you here on Earth?   64
What is true healing?   67
You cannot give away what you do not own   70
Transcend time and space!   74

Victory Is All That Is Real	80
I call the Guardians of the Mother Light!	85
Form a nucleus for world change	88
Hypocrites need not apply!	92
Know the Eternal Silence!	96
I am overjoyed in the company of saints	98
Will you BE with us in the Golden Age Consciousness?	99
If you want to BE with me, become more—as I AM	104
Mercy is setting life free	111
Claim Your Freedom from Religion!	112
The Living Christ is ALWAYS more than you think	118
I release a flood tide of unconditional love	124
Non-attachment is the Master Key to the Ascension	125
I Claim South America for the Cause of Freedom!	130
See the Living Christ in yourself—and let the Living Word flow through you	134
The Master Key to the Success of Spiritual Movements	135
It is time to understand my true message of oneness	136
Why the Ascended Masters Sponsor Organizations	141
Reach for the One Vision—the Vision of Oneness	142
We look to establish the true Sangha of the Buddha	143

Chapter 4:
Ego Teachings, 2006 — **148**

Always look for the practical solution—not the ideal solution	148
There is only one test of chelaship—will you pass it?	150
It is time to purify the heart	154
The inevitable decision to let the ego die	160
I need those who will walk the Path of Peace	166
The true alchemy of the heart	174

Dare to let your light shine!	178
Why difficulties can be blessings in disguise	180
I will send you to bear witness to Christ truth in this age	183
Dare to disturb people	185
Find centeredness in the heart	187
Become the open door for the Living Christ	192
The Key to establishing the Mystery School on Earth	196
Anchoring the Mother Light in the base chakra of America	198
Those who start wars cannot stop war	200
Be spiritual regardless of outer conditions	209
God government versus human government	212
Let the people of Europe choose the Living Christ!	214
Allow yourself to enjoy the journey	221
All I want is constantly growing chelas	223
The spiritual path should make you more free, not less free	227
Keeping your peace while letting your light shine	228
The master key to growth is integration between your Higher and lower Being	235
Are you awake?	244
Let your vision be MORE	252
When your forgiveness is unconditional, your joy will be full	258

Chapter 5:
Ego Teachings, 2007 — **268**

Let 2007 be the year of unconditional peace	268
Leave the eternal struggle and find freedom in the Eternal NOW	272
Overcoming the planetary momentum of death	277
Why you will be justified or condemned by the WORD	280
Are you serving a dead god or the Living God?	287
Why you are not forgiven for rejecting the INNER WORD	289

Reconnecting to the love that brought you to this world	296
Passing through the screen door to heaven	302
Going beyond a dualistic view of God's Will	306
A Buddhic perspective on how America can represent Christ in the world	307
Find bliss beyond your expectations	313
Unconditional acceptance leads to unconditional surrender of all conditions	317
Let us rise above the fighting over land!	325
The key to the ultimate victory is ultimate surrender	329
A special dispensation to help Europeans rise above the past	332
Be MORE than normal!	336
I challenge you to rethink the concept of ownership	337
There IS MORE to Life!	338
The Living Christ is the true King of Britain	351
Project a new vision of the world upon the Ma-ter light	355
Reconnect to your highest love and fulfill your divine plan	360
Poverty is hatred of the Mother	362
Freedom means surrender into oneness	369
Integrating the teachings on the Eighth Ray	374

Chapter 6:
Ego Teachings, 2008 — **380**

Let 2008 be a year of positive change	380
The kingdom of God is at hand—through the union of the Divine Father and the Divine Mother	382
Overcome your grand illusions to find a higher level of service	387
NOW is the time to embrace the Golden Age consciousness!!!	395
Remembering your own sins no more—by being MORE	398
You cannot overcome the past without looking at the past	408

How can Europe be free when the minds of the people are imprisoned by illusions?	413
Choose ye this day the parallel universe in which you want to abide	416
Can any man-made system bring the Promised Land to Earth?	427
Dare to communicate from the heart	430

Chapter 7:
Ego Teachings, 2009 — 438

Wisdom is more than intellectual knowledge	438
Do not try to understand love — let it flow!	443
Your real self is still pure	449
Communicate that life is MORE	453
Serve fully by being at peace	456
Let the Holy Spirit speak through you	459
A non-linear view of karma	464
Wisdom is a vital force of healing	473
You are always worthy of love	479
Acceleration is the key to wholeness	485
Closing the gap on the spiritual path	494
The unconditional joy of true service	504
Balancing the scales of life	511
The eighth ray of integration	520
The ninth ray of equilibrium	526
The tenth ray of transparency	533
The eleventh ray of transcendence	541
The twelfth ray of rebirth	552
The thirteenth ray of creative flow	562
The fourteenth ray of sharing your Presence	564

Knowing your divine plan through the crystalline structure of divine direction — 566

There is no room for judgment in the ascension spiral — 572

Chapter 8:
Ego Teachings, 2010-11 — 574

How a limited imagination blocks peace in the Middle East — 574

I, Jesus, withdraw my light from Christianity — 576

The Roman Empire symbolizes your personal struggle with the structures you have created — 580

Don't be like the Romans—be the Christ in you — 585

Hatred of the mother – unwillingness to face changing conditions on Earth — 590

I withdraw space from the consciousness of anger against women — 593

I officially inaugurate the Aquarian age—catch my enthusiasm — 601

How you can come to "know" ultimate truth — 602

Can the Islamic world – starting with Turkey – be accelerated into the golden age consciousness? — 607

Entering the ascension spiral requires you to overcome the great projection game — 609

Let the cosmic wrecking ball shatter the structures that limit your Spirit — 620

Imagination, acceptance, oneness: A new formula for alchemy in the Golden Age — 621

The choice is yours: increased resistance or increased transcendence — 625

Beginning to understand Hatred of the Mother — 629

Putting Satan behind you or putting Satan between you and God — 634

Knowing the will of God in the Year of the Mother — 638

Is there any injustice in the universe? — 644

Make matter real—either by materializing your perception or by seeing that all life is ONE — 658

See yourself together with the Elohim as part of the Consciousness of the Divine Mother 662

Shattering the serpentine lie of freeing the people through Communism 664

Glossary **666**

Introduction: About This Book

The teachings in this book were all given by the ascended masters in dictations. They were given between 2004 and 2011. The masters have given a huge amount of teachings through me, but in this book I have selected only teachings that talk about the ego and the path of overcoming that separate self and reclaiming your true identity.

In most cases, what you see here is an excerpt from a longer dictation. I have taken only the teachings relating to the topic of this book. However, a dictation is always a spherical work of art, so if you find that a particular excerpt speaks to you, it is a good idea to read the full dictation. It will be available for free on our website *www.ascendedmasterlight.com*. You can easily find it by using the name of the master and the date.

I also want to mention that Jesus has given a series of discourses on the ego that complement the teachings in this book. They have been published in the book *Unmasking the Ego*.

The first two chapters of this book will give you a brief introduction that will help you get a greater benefit from the teachings on the ego. The first chapter will introduce ascended masters and explain how the teachings in this book were brought forth. The second chapter will introduce the components of your self, which will help you get a framework for seeing the ego and how it affects your life and spiritual growth.

Chapter 1:
Introducing the Ascended Masters?

This is a brief description of what an ascended master is and how they give us their teachings. We will approach this from two vantage points:

Beings who took embodiment and ascended:
Let us first explain this from our point of view as human beings in embodiment on earth. The material universe is truly a sophisticated feedback "device" that is designed to facilitate our growth in self-awareness.

Many people don't really like the word school, but there is one aspect of the concept of a school that applies here. Most schools have a final exam, and when we pass it, we are free to move on with our lives without looking back. So if we keep raising our consciousness and transcending our self-awareness, what happens?

Well, at some point we reach the final "exam," meaning we enter a process that leads to our "graduation" from the schoolroom of the material universe. This is a profound and complex process, that involves us dis-identifying from the ego, the separate self, and embracing a new self-awareness as one with the spiritual realm above and one with all life in this world. It also involves letting go of all desires or attachments related to this world.

This process is often called the spiritual path, but the final stages of it are called the ascension spiral, leading to the ascension. After we ascend, we are permanently free from earth and the material universe. And given that the only way to complete the ascension process is to gain mastery over our own minds, we have now earned the title: "Ascended Master."

Throughout the long history of planet earth (far longer than recorded in official history), many lifestreams have ascended. A newly ascended master faces a choice: Will it move on in the almost infinite rungs of the spiritual realm, or will it remain with earth and seek to help other beings ascend?

Many ascended masters have made the vow to stay with earth in order to help those of us who have not yet ascended. So technically, these are what we call ascended masters, because they have experienced what it is like to be in embodiment on earth (or other planetary systems) and then ascend from this very dense realm. Given that they have experienced what we are going through, they have a unique ability to help us pass the same initiations that they have passed.

Beings who did not take embodiment:

The universe is created as a hierarchical structure. The realm, or sphere, in which we live was created by beings in the sphere immediately above ours. Yet their realm was created by beings in a higher realm, and so forth, forming a hierarchical structure that leads back to our Creator.

The important point to grasp is that the beings who are able to create a new – unascended – realm have earned this power by coming into oneness with the beings that created them and the entire hierarchical structure above them. In other words, the essential difference between the material realm and the spiritual realm is that in the material world, we tend to see ourselves as separate beings living in a separate world. In order to ascend to the spiritual realm, you must overcome this illusion and truly merge into oneness with all life.

So when beings in a higher realm create a new – unascended – realm, they do so out of their own beings. In other words, they don't see the new sphere as being separated from themselves. However, the new sphere is created with a lower or denser vibration than the spiritual realm. The purpose is that the beings who create the new sphere will now send extensions of themselves down into the new sphere to take embodiment in bodies made from the energies of the sphere.

This has a two-fold purpose. One is to raise the vibration of the new sphere until it ascends and becomes part of the spiritual realm. Yet the real purpose for this process is that the beings in the spiritual realm create individualized extensions of themselves, who then grow in self-awareness by helping their sphere ascend.

So in one sense, we can say that the beings who created our sphere have not taken embodiment in their fullness. Yet in a sense they have taken embodiment through the individualized extensions they have sent down. These individualized extensions are not some mysterious or perfect beings that are fundamentally different from the rest of us. They are us!

Even though we have been programmed to look at ourselves as human beings, who are limited, perhaps even sinners, we are extensions of the very beings who created our sphere. In fact, the very purpose of the spiritual path and the ascension is for us to truly accept our identity as individualized extensions of the entire spiritual hierarchy above us.

The important point to grasp here is that even though there are many beings among the Ascended Host who have not taken embodiment in their fullness, they have indeed taken embodiment through us—the extensions of themselves. Thus, ascended beings simply do not fit into the traditional image of the remote – and often angry – God in the sky. They are not seeking to judge or condemn us; they are ONLY seeking to raise us up.

For even though we have forgotten that we are extensions of ascended beings, they have not forgotten. And obviously, you only want to raise up what you know is part of your own being. Yet being raised up does not mean we lose our individuality. On the contrary, it means we merge with our spiritual individuality and transcend the limitations of our human "individuality," the separate self. This is not a loss but a gain

The hierarchy of ascended beings

Let us begin with our vantage point here on earth. The material universe is made from energies that vibrate within a certain spectrum. Right above this spectrum is the lowest level of the spiritual realm. There are other realms above this, stretching through 6 spheres (ours being the seventh) to the Creator. In each of these spheres, there is a hierarchy of spiritual beings.

The material realm was created by beings in the realm right above us in vibration. Thus, these beings are what we normally call ascended masters. The masters also use the name "Ascended Host," and this refers to all beings in all spheres above us. However, many of these beings do interact with us here on earth.

Newly ascended masters
When a being ascends from the material world, it usually takes some time to explore its new self-awareness and the spiritual realm to which it now has conscious access. Yet some masters have already been involved with teaching human beings before they ascended, so they may indeed immediately begin to fill a teaching position.

The Chohans
There are seven spiritual rays, which are the basic energy spectra from which the material universe is made. In order to walk the spiritual path and qualify for the ascension, we must attain mastery on all seven rays. Thus, we can see the spiritual path as a structured process, where we learn from each of the seven rays.

To facilitate this learning, each ray has several ascended masters who are seeking to help us pass the initiations represented by their ray. The leaders of this group of teachers is called the "Chohan." Thus, each ray has a Chohan, who is kind of like the headmaster of a particular school.

The Chohans normally present themselves as masculine or feminine. Not all chohans have a counterpart of the compimentary polarity. For example, a masculine chohan may not have a feminine counterpart, either because the feminine counterpart has not yet ascended or because it has moved on to other realms and is not directly working with earth.

The Archangels
Some ascended beings are not created to take embodiment, namely the angels. Angels have many different assignments, but from our vantage point, the most helpful are the angels assigned to helping us grow. These angels are also organized according to the seven rays.
Groups of angels are often referred to as "bands," and each band has a leader, with the title of "Archangel." Thus, there is an archangel for each of the seven rays. The archangels are always masculine, but they

also have feminine polarities, called the "Archeia." For example, the feminine polarity of Archangel Michael is Archeia Faith.

The Elohim
The material universe is created from the energies of the seven rays, and this is done by reducing the vibration of the rays by a certain factor. A mental blueprint is then superimposed upon this energy in order to form the basic structures that make up the material universe.

The beings who initiated and oversee this process are often called the "Elohim," but they can also be called "God and Goddesses." Again, there is a masculine/feminine polarity at this level. For example, the Elohim Hercules has a feminine polarity named Amazonia.

The Central Sun
The highest level of ascended beings known to us is represented by two beings, called Alpha and Omega. It is sometimes said that they reside in the "Central Sun," but this is not a physical sun in the material universe. It is a "place" in the spiritual realm.

As explained, there are six spheres above our level. Each of these spheres forms a hierarchical structure, somewhat comparable to a pyramid. In each sphere, there is a central sun in which resides two beings, named Alpha and Omega. In the very first sphere, there is the ultimate level of Alpha and Omega, namely the beings who are direct expressions of the Creator.

However, it is important to understand that what is given here is a linear representation, and the linear mind is not capable of grasping the non-linear reality of the spiritual realm. Thus, it is important not to place too great importance on the words or their interpretation. To truly grasp the non-linear reality of the spiritual realm, one must experience it directly.

Gods and Goddesses
Although the Elohim are sometimes called Gods and Goddesses, there are other ascended beings who have attained to the level represented by a God. For example, there is a Goddess of Liberty, a Goddess of Justice (Portia) and a Goddess of Mercy (Kuan Yin).

Solar Logoi

Each planetary system has a sun and each physical sun has a polarity of two solar hierarchs, who are actually making it possible for the sun to be the open door between the material and the spiritual realm. If energy was not constantly streaming into a planetary system from the spiritual ream, no life would be possible in that system. The hierachs of our physical sun are named Helios and Vesta.

Lord of the World

For each planet, there is a being who holds the office of Lord of the World. This is a being with Buddhic attainment, meaning it has mastered space. Thus, this being literally holds the spiritual balance for the earth to exist in space. The Lord of the World for earth is Gautama Buddha.

Planetary or Individual Christ

For each planet there is a being who holds the office of Christ. Regardless of the sectarian nature of the Christian religion "Christ" is a universal word that signifies oneness between the Creator and its creation. Thus, you can ascend only by attaining the Christ consciousness and overcoming the illusion of separation. When Jesus said, "I am the way, the truth and the life, no one comes to the father save by me," he was not talking about his outer person but the Christ consciousness. Currently, Jesus is holding the office of Planetary Christ for earth.

Cosmic Christ

For each planet, a master holds the office that represents the universal Christ consciousness for that planet. Lord Maitreya holds this office for earth. He was also the master depicted (in distorted and primitive form) as the "God" in the Garden of Eden. The reality behind the myth is that Lord Maitreya was and is the overseer of the spiritual schoolroom (sometimes called a Mystery School) in which lifestreams are prepared to take embodiment on earth and deal with the initiations represented by the density of this realm.

For profound teachings from Lord Maitreya, especially concerning the fall in the Garden of Eden, see the book *Master Keys to Spiritual Freedom*.

World Teachers
These are beings who oversee the general progression of humankind's consciousness and determine how to best teach people the universal lessons. They also determine which new teachings to release, based on the progress (or lack of it) in the collective consciousness. This office is currently held by Jesus and Kuthumi.

The Karmic Board, Lords of Karma
The ascended masters seek to teach us at two levels. One is that they give us spiritual teachings and encourage us to use them for self-observation, leading to self-transcendence. The other is what is called the "School of Hard Knocks," where they allow us to experience the physical consequences of our state of consciousness. This is what is popularly called "bad karma."

Overseeing the karmic aspects of teaching is a board consisting of 8 ascended masters. It is important to realize that despite the popular concept of "bad karma," karma never has the purpose of punishing anyone. The purpose is only to teach those who have made themselves unreachable for a spiritual teaching.

As a result, the Karmic Board can withhold the descent of a person's karma, if they estimate the person has learned or is close to learning the associated lesson. On the other hand, they can also accelerate the descent of karma for a person who is in a negative spiral and is abusing other people.

The Karmic Board performs a very complex task of not only looking at each individual lifestream embodied on earth but also looking at groups and humanity as a whole. They determine who is allowed to take embodiment on earth, and they sometimes decide that a certain lifestream has misused its opportunity and will no longer be allowed to embody here.

The Karmic Board also teaches in a more direct way when we are in between embodiments. Along with other spiritual teachers, members of the Karmic Board help each lifestream determine the specifics of its next embodiment, based on an evaluation of which circumstances best help that lifestream learn its lessons and express its divine plan (the gift we came to bring).

The current members of the Karmic Board are: The Great Divine Director, The Goddess of Liberty, Pallas Athena, Nada, Portia (Goddess of Justice), Kuan Yin (Goddess of Mercy), Elohim Cyclopea and Vajrasattva.

Dhyani Buddhas

In traditional Buddhism, these are considered "primordial" Buddhas, meaning they have never taken embodiment as did Gautama. There are six of these in the ascended realm, and they each represent the anti-dote to a specific spiritual poison. By invoking the Presence of the Dhyani Buddha, you receive help in transcending the anti-dote.

NOTE: In terms of all of the above positions in hierarchy, it is important to keep in mind, that these are offices. As it is on earth, an office is held by a specific person, but that person can be replaced by another person over time. Thus, the Archangel of the First Ray is an office and has throughout time been held by various beings. The same is true for all other offices. In fact, as we ascend, we have the potential to fill some of these offices. This might explain why various spiritual teachings associate different names with these offices.

How are the teachings in this book brought forth?

If you want to understand how the ascended masters communicate with those of us who are still in embodiment, you need to understand the Law of Free Will. The purpose of our existence is to grow in self-awareness, and this can happen only when we make choices and experience the consequences of them. Thus, we might say that planet earth is like a cosmic classroom in which we – the students – have the potential to learn certain lessons.

There are many such classrooms throughout the material universe, and each has certain characteristics. Planet earth still belongs to a category in which it is possible to have a very specific experience, namely that one is a separate being – separated from God and separated from other humans – and then awakening from that experience.

This experience is made possible by the density of the energies that make up planet earth. There are planets in the universe that have risen to a higher level, in which "matter" is not as dense, meaning one can directly perceive that it is made from a finer substance, namely spiritual light. On such planets it is no longer possible to have the illusion that one is a separate being, but on earth this is still a possibility.

Why plausible deniability must be maintained
According to the Law of Free Will, the density of the energies that make up a planet is a product of the consciousness of the inhabitants of the planet. It is quite possible that the earth will be raised in vibration, so that it one day becomes impossible to believe that matter is separated from Spirit. In fact, the ascended masters – along with many of us in embodiment – are working towards that point. Yet until a critical mass of people voluntarily raise their consciousness to the level where this shift can occur, the masters will respect the Law of Free Will.

This means (among other things) that the masters cannot simply appear in the sky or through some undeniable manifestation. Instead, they can communicate with humankind only in such a way that the basic illusion of separation can be maintained by those who still want to see themselves as separate beings. In other words, the basic principle that the masters must follow is that plausible deniability must be maintained. It must be possible to deny God's existence, to deny that there is a spiritual reality beyond the material world, to deny that ascended masters exist and to deny that they can communicate with us.

This goal is attained by the masters communicating with humans in very specific ways, so that it is easy to overlook or deny this communication. Up until the mid 1800s the masters were not actually allowed to make their existence know through any public means of communication, such as books that could be found by anyone. Instead, they worked exclusively with so-called secret societies in which the existence of the masters was revealed only to people who had passed certain initiations.

Yet in the second half of the 19th century, the masters were allowed to make their existence known through public forms of communication, such as books and organizations that openly proclaimed to be receiving communication from the masters. Since then, there has been a string of books and tools published by single authors or organizations. Yet in each case, there was no undeniable proof that this was coming from beings beyond the material realm.

How the masters communicate with us

The ascended masters can communicate with human beings in various ways. Truly, it is important not to be too intellectual in wanting to confine the ascended masters to categories that can be grasped by the human intellect (the reason being that the masters can help us only if we are willing to rise above the linear mind). Yet it can be helpful to talk about two different types of communication: direct and indirect.

Indirect communication can be compared to what a radio or television station is doing. The ascended masters are constantly broadcasting certain energies and messages from the ascended realm. Yet it is important to realize that these signals cannot be received by people in what is currently the "normal" or common state of consciousness. The minds of all of us do have the ability to tune in to these signals, but it can only be done by raising one's consciousness beyond what is currently normal. However, anyone willing to raise his or her consciousness can indeed tune in to what is being broadcast by the masters.

Throughout history, many people have made use of this ability. In many cases, people were not even consciously aware of where the ideas came from, which has given rise to the classical idea of muses or inspiration. Some people have been able to receive an idea only once in a lifetime, whereas others have had a higher degree of attunement. Nevertheless, through such general broadcasts, the masters have been able to bring into the physical realm many ideas that had a positive impact on the evolution of humankind.

Yet beyond this indirect or non-specific communication, the masters can also communicate in a more direct manner. This happens only to people who acknowledge that ascended masters exist. In some cases people receive direct communication and put it into books without exposing the source. Yet in other cases, people do expose that the messages they receive come from ascended masters. And for such people it is possible to receive communication, where an ascended master can speak directly through a person in embodiment. This has traditionally been called "a dictation" or a message. Some people write such messages, while others speak them aloud, even in front of a group of people.

The teachings and tools on this website are brought forth as a link in this tradition of the ascended masters giving more direct forms of communication. Since 2002 I, Kim Michaels, have been receiving both dictations and tools from the ascended masters. My wife, Helen, has been doing this since 2009. Yet despite the fact that I have been doing this for some time, I feel I am still in training. I think it is wise to recognize that earth is a schoolroom, and as long as we are here, we have more to learn.

In some organizations, the person receiving dictations has been called a "messenger." Personally, I feel that this should be seen as a very humble position. Unfortunately, some organizations have idolized the position of being a messenger, making the person more important than the members, almost as if the messenger was the only link between people and the masters. Therefore, I prefer to refer to myself as simply an "open door." And I recognize that all people have the ability to tune in to the ascended masters. In fact, if the teachings in this book are successful, they will empower many people to attain such attunement.

What is a dictation?

For many spiritual people, the process of communicating with the masters will be what they know as channeling. However, "channeling" is a word that has been used to describe a wide range of phenomena. So I will describe how I receive my material from the masters. This is not to in any way put down what others are doing; it is simply to clarify what I am doing.

A dictation is where I attune my mind to the Presence of a specific ascended master. I do not go into a trance, because it is my understanding that the ascended masters do not work with trance channels. The reason is that this is a violation of free will, as the channeler is not aware of what the channeling entity will do or say during the trance. So I am fully conscious during the process, but I have been trained to go into a neutral or pure state of mind, where my personal thoughts or feelings are not engaged.

In most cases, I have no advance conscious awareness of what a master will say during a dictation. In some cases I have an awareness of the topic, and I often have a beginning thought that has been given to me ahead of time—just to get me started. Yet once the dictation starts, it is my task to stay attuned to the master without being distracted by external noise or my own internal noise (I have taken dictations in front of groups up to 100 people and also in public places). I have often started a dictation without having any idea of what the master will say, and the dictation has lasted for over an hour, giving a perfectly consistent message—something my outer mind simply would not be capable of doing.

What the master releases to me is not words that I hear in my mind and repeat. Nor do I see them in flaming letters and repeat them. What I tune in to is a stream of consciousness that is beyond the linear vehicle of words. This stream of consciousness is then "translated" into words in my mind. I literally hear the words as they are being spoken, but I could, of course, choose to interrupt the process at any time.

However, the most important element of a dictation is not the audible words, but the stream of spiritual light that is carried by the words. A dictation always has a message that can be grasped by the linear, intellectual mind. Yet if you read or hear a dictation only with the mind, you will miss the most important part, namely the light. Because I have taken dictations for so long, I am used to the process, but I recently had an interesting experience. I took a dictation during a conference. In the audience was a person who was new to the concept and somewhat skeptical. After the dictation, he made the remark that it simply wasn't possible for a human being to speak for nearly an hour with such power in his voice, and even to increase that power towards the end of the dictation. I realized this is true, and it brings up an important point.

My dictations often last an hour or more, and in most cases I am standing up the entire time. Yet I never feel physically, mentally or emotionally tired afterwards. Instead, I feel energized and feel my consciousness has been raised to a new level of clarity. I would be concerned if I felt depleted afterwards, because that would mean the being dictating had taken energy from me. Instead, the ascended masters give me light during a dictation, and at the same time they release light to the audience. If you want the full benefit from a dictation, tune in to the light (which is best done by listening to the recording).

Chapter 2: Introducing the Components of Self

The purpose of this chapter is to give you a brief introduction to the components of your self. Having this understanding will give you a greater benefit from the teachings about the ego that you will find in the following chapters.

What is the very core of your being?

Consider this statement: "In reality, you are who you are. In the here and now, you are who you think you are. There is currently a gap between who you really are and who you think you are. The ultimate goal of the spiritual path is to close that gap."

The implication is simple: Right now, you are seeing everything – including yourself – through a perception filter, a sense of self. Yet this self is not who you really are. It is simply an outer persona, that the real you is using as a way to experience the world from a certain perspective.

Jesus made a very interesting statement: "And no man hath ascended up to heaven, but he that came down from heaven." The implication is profound: We descended from the spiritual realm in a certain state. While down here on earth, we have taken on an outer self, a perception filter. Yet the *only* way to ascend back to the spiritual realm is to transcend *all* of the perception filters found on earth.

How your perception filter limits you
Let us look at your current situation. You may be seeing yourself as a limited being, because you are convinced that there are certain external conditions that limit you. In other words, you think these material

conditions have power over you. Yet, is it possible, that the way you currently experience the world is a product of the fact, that the original "you" has chosen to take on a particular sense of self? This self acts as a perception filter, and as long as you look at life through the filter, it seems absolutely real that certain external conditions have power over you?

In other words, at some point in the past (perhaps in a previous lifetime long forgotten), the original "you" chose to take on a limited sense of self. This limited self was developed precisely by defining certain material conditions as having absolute reality and thus having power over you. This may sound theoretical, so let us relate it to a historical fact. About 500 years ago, most people in Europe were firmly and absolutely convinced that the earth was flat. Ask yourself this question: "Was the earth really flat 500 years ago, or was it as round then as it is today?"

Obviously, the earth has not changed shape, so what has changed is the way we human beings look at the earth. It was a specific perception filter that caused people to believe – as an unquestionable fact – that the earth was flat. And that perception filter limited them in many ways, because they thought it was dangerous to sail across the ocean to look for new land.

As long as you look at life through the perception filter that defines your current sense of self, there is absolutely no way you can question the belief that material conditions are real and have power over you. The *only* way you might transcend these conditions is to question the very perception filter that makes them seem real. Yet you can *never* do this as long as you look at life from inside the perception filter. This is the human enigma, the existential catch-22.

You are NOT your current self

Is there a way out? Of course, and it is to realize that you are *not* your current sense of self. In reality, you are a being that descended from the spiritual realm, and as such you cannot be permanently affected by anything on earth. This being has simply taken on a limited self, and as long as you see yourself through the filter of that self, you think this is who you are. Yet regardless of your current perception, you are still the same being that descended.

The next step is to consider how the pure "you" took on your current self? It did so by projecting itself into that self, much like an actor who puts on a certain costume and make-up in order to play a part in a theater. Your current self is simply a role, that you have chosen to play in the theater of life. Yet if you are beginning to have had enough of playing this part, you can take off the costume.

How do you transcend your current self? By realizing that the pure "you" projected itself into this self, which means it also has the potential to extricate itself from the self it has taken on. The way to do this is to realize that the real you has the potential to attain a state of pure consciousness, meaning you have *no* perception filter. You simply look at conditions in the material realm without labeling or judging them. The labeling and judging is a product of your perception filter.

The ascended masters have named the "you" that originally descended the "Conscious You." Yet it is important not to be hung up on the name, because the same concept is found in other mystical teachings, simply given different names. For example, the founder of Tibetan Buddhism, PadmaSambhava, called it "pure awareness" or "naked awareness." Zen Buddhism calls it "beginner's mind" and Jesus talked about us becoming as little children in order to enter the kingdom of heaven.

The important thing to realize is that the Conscious You has not been permanently changed by your current self—any more than your eyes would be changed if you put on a pair of yellow glasses. Thus, the Conscious You is perfectly capable of attaining a state of pure awareness, where you do not have any of the perception filters defined on earth. You see things as they really are.

This is what the Buddha called pure perception, and it is what Jesus talked about when he said: "When thine eye be single, thy whole body shall be full of light." Think about that last statement. When your vision is "single," meaning it is not divided by any perception filters, then you see that everything in the material universe is made from light.

The Conscious You in its pure state, sees that all appearances in the material realm are just that: appearances. Thus, they have no power over you as pure Spirit. Returning to this pure perception is the only way to avoid giving material conditions power over you.

Introducing the Components of Self

Your spiritual self

Most spiritual people realize we are more than our physical bodies. Many believe we are a soul that is only abiding in this particular body for a time, but has resided in other bodies in the past. Many believe we originally came from the spiritual realm and that we have the potential to return there. Many also believe that what sent us into this world was a higher part of our beings.

We might call this part of our beings for the spiritual self or higher self. Since the 1930s, the ascended masters have also called it the "I AM Presence." This is partly to signify that it is what gives us our basic sense of being or existence, the sense that "I am." It is also to signify that the I AM Presence is our link to God, who gave Moses the name "I AM."

The I AM Presence is in the spiritual realm, which is a realm of higher vibrations. Your lower being is connected to the I AM Presence with a tube of light or crystal cord. In between the two is your Christ self, which is a mediator, a connecting link, between your Presence and your soul.

Your divine blueprint

Your I AM Presence contains the divine blueprint for your individuality, all of the characteristics that make you a unique expression of God's Being. This blueprint was created by your spiritual parents – spiritual Beings existing in one of the spiritual realms – and it is permanent and immutable.

It is precisely to express this divine blueprint as a gift to planet earth, that your I AM Presence created you, the Conscious You that is meant to be an open door through which the Presence can express its gift and also experience the material world. In other words, your highest potential is to be an open door, through which the individuality anchored in the Presence can be freely expressed. This is what Jesus described when he said "I can of my own self do nothing" and "It is the father within me who is doing the works."

Because the I AM Presence resides in a realm of vibration that is above the material universe, it cannot be negatively affected by any mistake you make in this realm. No matter what mistakes you might have made, it has not impacted your true identity. Therefore, regardless of how miserable you might feel, or what mistakes you think you have made, you *always* have the potential to reconnect to your I AM Presence and unlock your true spiritual potential.

This is a safety mechanism built into God's design of the universe, and you can *never* lose your ability to establish a sense of oneness with your higher Being. However, the ego works against this connection and seeks to keep you in a state of mind in which you feel separated from God.

Your Christ self

Your Christ self is the mediator between the I AM Presence and the lower being lost in duality, specifically the Conscious You. We might say that your Christ self is a spiritual teacher that is sent to you after you lost contact with your higher Being. It is inside your container of self, and thus you can reach it at any time by focusing on your heart and activating your intuitive faculties. Jesus talked about the Christ self in the following quotes:

> And I will pray the Father, and he shall give you another Comforter, that he may abide with you for ever; (John 14:16)

> But the Comforter, which is the Holy Ghost, whom the Father will send in my name, he shall teach you all things, and bring all things to your remembrance, whatsoever I have said unto you. (John 14:26)

It does not take any superhuman or psychic abilities to hear the still, small voice of your Christ self. However, take note that your Christ self does *not* look at you or your life through your current perception filter. In fact, the purpose of your Christ self is to – in any situation – offer you an alternative to your current perception filter.

This does not mean that your Christ self offers you some absolute or ultimate truth, because your Christ self knows exactly what you can and cannot accept based on your current perception filter. Thus, the goal of your Christ self is to offer you a frame of reference that is one step above your current perception.

A deeper understanding of the soul

There are certain words that are used by different people to mean so many different things, that the words almost become useless. One example of this is the word "soul." It has been used for centuries by different religious and spiritual teachings to mean many different things. And it is often used without clearly defining it, based on the assumption that people know what it means.

In previous teachings, the ascended masters used the word "soul" pretty much like most other teachings use it, meaning without defining it clearly. Yet, today they offer us a more nuanced understanding by breaking the soul, or the lower being, into different components.

Many spiritual people accept the concept of reincarnation, and it is commonly assumed that it is the soul that reincarnates. This also leads to the common assumption that the soul was created in a higher realm and then descended into the material realm. Which means it is the soul that ascends back to the spiritual realm.

This then leads to two common ideas about what you need to do in order to get your soul to qualify for reentry into the spiritual realm:

- The soul has "fallen" or descended into a lower state, so it no longer qualifies. Thus, you need to compensate for the errors you have made and purify or raise the soul.

- The soul is meant to be perfected, thus it is your task to raise your soul to a state of perfection (however it is defined).

What can revolutionize your understanding of the soul is the concept of the Conscious You. The core understanding is that it was the Conscious You that originally descended and started the process of you being in embodiment in the material world. Thus, it is the Conscious You that has the potential to ascend back to the spiritual realm.

Yet this ascension process does *not* happen by the Conscious You compensating for an imperfect state or seeking to attain a state of perfection based on earthly or man-made criteria. On the contrary, the Conscious You can ascend *only* by fulfilling its highest potential, which is to be in a state of pure awareness, where it can function as an open door for the Presence.

This has two aspects. First, the Presence can express itself through the open door of the Conscious You, by letting its light flow into the material realm. Secondly, the Presence can experience the material world through the clear pane of glass of the Conscious You.

In other words, in its highest state the Conscious You has no individuality or sense of self as a separate being. It sees itself as nothing more and nothing less than an open door for the Presence to express itself in this world and as a clear pane of glass for the Presence to experience this world.

The Conscious You in its highest state has no perception filter. Thus, it does not block or hold back any expression from the Presence and it does not block anything it experiences from reaching the Presence. The Conscious You does not judge after appearances, but allows the Presence to evaluate its experiences, and then learn from them, storing the results in the causal body. Compare this to how often we evaluate our intuitive insights to see whether they are appropriate according to an earthly standard and how often we seek to hide something from God. It is now important to understand that the Conscious You did not originally descend in this state.

How the Conscious You descended

The material world is created from spiritual light that was reduced in vibration by a certain reduction factor. This means that the material world was originally at a certain level of vibration, meaning it was made from energies that had a greater density than the spiritual realm. This accounts for the fact that we do not directly perceive the spiritual realm through our physical senses. The senses are attuned to the vibrations in the material frequency spectrum, and they are currently so much lower than the spiritual vibrations that our senses cannot bridge the gap and "see" the spiritual realm (many spiritual people can sense spiritual energies intuitively, but generally not through the physical senses).

The purpose of creating the material realm with a higher density is to facilitate the growth of self-aware beings—us. By descending into a realm where there is no direct perception of the spiritual, we have the opportunity to gradually raise our consciousness, until we can serve as an open door between the spiritual and the material realm. By going through this process, we also help to raise the vibrations of the material realm, until it vibrates at the level of the spiritual realm.

The Conscious You does not descend with its highest self-awareness. The Conscious You is created with a point-like sense of self that it has the potential to raise through many levels, until it attains the same omni-present sense of self as the Creator.

In order to descend into the denser vibrations of the material universe, the Conscious You needs a vehicle, meaning a sense of self that is made from the same vibrations as the material realm. Here is the important realization: the Conscious You takes on this vehicle; it does *not* become the vehicle. The Conscious You is *not* changed by this process; it is only its sense of self – its perception – that is changed. Again, it is like an actor who puts on a costume and makeup in order to play a role in a theater performance—meaning that the actor can take off the costume as easily as it is put on.

Originally, the Conscious You descended into a sense of self that was made from the same base vibrations out of which the material universe was first created. It is this self, this vehicle, that is what we – from a higher perspective – can call the soul.

Yet take note that this soul was *not* created in the spiritual realm, nor was it created from the vibrations of the spiritual realm. It was, as the Bible says, created from dust, meaning material energies. Thus, the soul – according to this definition – did not descend and consequently cannot ascend. It is the Conscious You that can ascend, but only when it stops identifying itself with or as the soul and instead attains its highest potential—the state of pure awareness in which it sees itself as one with the Presence.

However, there is a subtle distinction to be made. The soul has what most people call individuality or personality. Yet this was created based on the conditions found in the material universe when the Conscious You first descended. The personality and individuality you have today is a product of the experiences you have had during your sojourn in the material world. So things have likely been added to the original soul into which the Conscious You descended.

Yet all of this outer personality and individuality is *not* who you are. You truly are the individuality anchored in your I AM Presence. This individuality can potentially be expressed through the Conscious You, but the outer personality you have created as a reaction to conditions in the material world will block or color this expression.

The outer personality and individuality – the outer self – that you currently have was created over many lifetimes as a reaction to the imperfect conditions in the material world. Thus, it can *never* be perfected so that it can ascend to the spiritual realm. What can ascend is the Conscious You that first descended. Yet the Conscious You can ascend only by coming to disidentify itself from the outer self.

It does so by transcending the limiting beliefs and raising the energies that make up the soul. Thus, in a sense one can say that the soul is raised, but it is not raised as a separate self. The limiting beliefs are dissolved and the lower energies are accelerated to a higher vibration. If you put a pot of water on the stove and let it boil until all the water is gone, would you say the water was raised into a higher realm? Or would you say the water was accelerated to a higher state—steam?

The container of self and your four lower bodies

A part of your soul or lower being is what the ascended masters call your "four lower bodies" or the four levels of the mind. These are interpenetrating energy bodies that co-exist in the same space because they vibrate at different levels of frequencies:

- The identity body, also called the etheric body. The contents of your identity body define your sense of identity. How do you see yourself, how do you see God, how do you see the world and how do you see the interaction between them? Do you see yourself as a spiritual being who is here to take dominion over the Earth or do you see yourself as a material being, a product of the Earth with no power to change it?

• The mental body contains your thoughts. It is here you form a mental image of the specific things you want to do in the material world and how to accomplish them. This mental image will be based upon your sense of identity, which defines parameters for what you think you can or cannot do. Thus, if you identify yourself as a human being, you will limit what you think you can do.

• The emotional body is obviously the seat of your feelings. Emotion means Energy in **MOTION**. Your thoughts are mental images, but in order to become actions or manifest forms, they must be set in motion, and this happens at the level of the emotional body. However, this body also contains your desires, and they can conflict with your higher goals. Ideally, your emotions should be reflections of your thoughts that are reflections of your sense of identity that again is a reflection of your Divine individuality. Yet it is common that the emotions take on a life of their own and seek to run your life instead of being controlled by your thoughts.

• The physical brain and the carnal mind. Many materialistic scientists believe all of our thoughts and feelings are products of the physical brain. And while this is not correct, it is indeed correct that the physical brain is a very complex computer that is fully capable of producing many of our thoughts and sensations However, the physical brain is only the hardware for a level of the mind that the ascended masters call the carnal mind. This is the mind that is in charge of taking care of the needs of the physical body, such as the need for protection, food and propagation.

The essential question now becomes: which of your four lower bodies is your conscious mind centered upon? For a large percentage of humankind, their conscious awareness is centered on the physical body and the material world. This does mean that many of their thoughts and feelings are products of the physical brain and carnal mind. For example, many people focus most of their attention on the basic bodily needs of protection, food, clothing and sex.

Yet most spiritual people have expanded their conscious awareness to encompass at least parts of the three higher bodies. Continuing to expand this conscious awareness is the key to attaining mastery over your four lower bodies, so that they become vehicles that support your spiritual mission in this wold.

The human ego

As is the case with the word "soul," the word "ego" has been used differently by various spiritual teachings, psychologists and self-help experts. The ascended masters teach that we can all walk a systematic path, whereby we raise our consciousness until we can ascend. On each level of this path, there is a corresponding aspect of the ego. It is this ego that makes a particular level of consciousness seem real and seem like it has some power to hold the Conscious You at that level. In other words, the ego will seek to make the Conscious You believe that it cannot, is not allowed to or does not need to rise beyond its current level. Thus, in order to rise from one level of consciousness to the next, the Conscious You will have to transcend the corresponding aspect of the ego.

While this may sound difficult, it really isn't so hard, once you begin to intuitively "see" how the ego works. The ego only has a limited number of options, and some "tricks" are used at each level of consciousness, so they can be recognized.

The primary trick used by the ego is to divert your attention away from looking inside yourself. Jesus made an interesting statement, when he asked us why we so often look at the splinter in the eyes of our brothers but fail to see the beam in our own eyes. The primary reason for this is that the ego is so good at diverting our attention by making us believe that we have to do something, solve some problem or pay attention to something outside ourselves.

The basic key to rising from one level of consciousness to the next is to look inside ourselves and realize two things:

- My current level of consciousness is limiting me, and I no longer want to be at this level.

Introducing the Components of Self

- I, meaning the Conscious You, am more than my current level of consciousness, meaning that I can extricate myself from my current sense of self and rise – or be reborn – into a new sense of self.

Yet for you to come to the point of being willing to leave the old self behind, you need to see it for what it is. And you simply cannot do that as long as you are looking outside yourself, seeking to change other people or the world according to the perception you have at your current level of consciousness.

Your current level of consciousness forms a perception filter. As long as you are looking at the world through that filter, you will see the world a certain way, and your ego will seek to make you believe that what you see is ultimate reality, absolute truth or the only way to look at life. Meaning that your current perception is something you cannot question, are not allowed to question or do not need to question.

Compare this to a chess game, where the rules have been altered in such a way, that no move you make will make your opponent checkmate. In other words, no matter what you do, you cannot win the game. You will either play the game indefinitely, or you will come to a point where you realize this and thus refuse to continue playing. No matter what you do, you cannot transcend your current level of consciousness until you begin to question your perception filter—and your ego will do everything it can to prevent you from doing this.

The ego has created a false path, which we might call the outer path. It makes you think that you can qualify for the ascension by doing something to change other people or change the world. The real path is an inner path, where you realize that the *only* way that *you* can qualify for *your* ascension is to change yourself—your sense of self. And the only way to rise to a higher sense of self is to let the old self die. But in order to do that, you must come to see it as a limitation, see it as unreal and see that the Conscious You is more than the self, meaning that the Conscious You will not die when the self dies. And in order to come to that point, you must see through the smokescreen created by the ego.

Obviously, the rest of the book will give you teachings about the many subtle aspects of the ego, so let us move on from this brief introduction.

Chapter 3: Ego Teachings, 2004-05

Awaken and BE the light of the world!

The Presence of Infinite Light, September 29, 2004

The illusion of matter

Think about the fact that without your physical sun no life would be possible on Earth. Yet what drives the physical sun is that the sun serves as a portal, whereby the spiritual light of my Presence can stream into the material universe and be lowered in vibration, until it is radiating as the life-giving rays of the sun.

This then is your potential as a self-conscious being. You can eventually become a self-luminous being and radiate light that can nourish and sustain life in the ever-expanding chain of God's creation. Yet at some point in the distant past, human beings gradually became more and more enveloped in and focused upon their own creations. They forgot that they could not create anything lasting by using the Ma-ter light that had already taken on form. They forgot that they could create something lasting only by using the Alpha light of my Presence, allowing it to stream through their conscious minds and superimpose the perfect vision of God upon the passive substance of the Ma-ter light.

After they forgot this, and were lost in the consciousness of duality that caused them to see themselves as separated from the Father light, they began to believe that all that is real, all that exists, is the Ma-ter light which has already taken on form. They began to believe they could create only by using their physical bodies, eking out a living by the sweat of their brow. They thought they could build only by using matter itself, by manipulating that matter through the very limited powers of their physical bodies. They forgot the immense powers of their minds and became trapped in the matter universe.

They now began to see the contracting force of the Mother as their enemy, because it would break down and destroy their creations. They had forgotten that the Ma-ter light will blindly contract, and it will destroy all structures until it becomes spiritualized and can consciously maintain the form that is in harmony with God's law. And they forgot that they were sent here to spiritualize the Ma-ter light by endowing it with my Alpha light, streaming through their minds and blessing everything in this world.

Human beings are not sent here to forever be locked in a struggle against the contracting force of the Mother. They are here to bless all matter until the contracting force finds a perfect equilibrium and maintains the perfect forms of the kingdom of God that will last forever and ever because the Ma-ter light has now become the Word incarnate. When the Mother light becomes spiritualized, it can self-transcend instead of changing only as a result of being acted upon by self-aware beings.

After human beings forgot their reason for being, they began to believe that the matter universe is a prison. They felt lost and limited, so they began to resent the Mother, to be angry with the Mother and to hate the Mother. And ever since then, they have shown their contempt for the Mother by misusing her creation in the form of their own physical bodies and the very planet itself. And thus human beings have created imbalances in the physical body that have led to the current very restricted life span and the many diseases you see on Earth. They have created imbalances in Mother Nature that have led to many imperfect conditions, from famine and a limited food supply to natural disasters.

Human beings have forgotten why they came here, namely that they came to multiply their God-given talents and to take dominion over the Earth by imposing the perfect vision of God, seen through their God-given individuality, upon the Ma-ter substance. Instead, they have superimposed an imperfect vision, seen through the human ego and the individuality they have built based on that ego.

I am the Presence of Infinite Light, and I am come this day to awaken those on planet Earth, those who can be awakened, to their original calling and their reason for being on this planet. I am come to call those who are willing to see beyond their human egos, their human individualities and their dualistic beliefs and world view. I am come to awaken those who are willing to gradually rise above this limited sense of identity and reconnect with their true, divine individuality, so that they can rise and claim their God-given right to be the sons and daughters of God in the Earth, to be the co-creators with God in the Earth. I am here to call those who are willing to rise above their fears, their lack of worthiness, their sense that they have no right to be here on Earth or to exercise their Christhood. I am come to awaken those who are willing to consciously make the decision to take back their dominion over themselves and then exercise that dominion of the self by taking dominion over the Earth.

I am come to call those who are willing to come apart from the mass consciousness, to be a separate and chosen people who have elected to worship the one true God who resides in the kingdom of God that is within them. I am come to awaken those who are willing to be the open doors, whereby the perfect vision of God can once again be held in he conscious minds of the inhabitants of the Earth. And through those minds, this vision can be superimposed upon matter itself so that this planet can shed the imperfect images, the imbalances, that have been forced upon it for eons. Thereby, this planet can quickly right itself on its axis and once again spin off the imperfections and outpicture the harmony, the balance, the peace and the perfection of God. This action will truly bring the abundant life to all people on Earth and manifest God's kingdom on Earth, as that kingdom is already manifest in Heaven in the form of a perfect vision held in the minds of the Ascended Host.

I am come to awaken you to your inner calling, to awaken those of you who volunteered to come to Earth long ago to raise this planet and its inhabitants out of the darkness and into the light, the light of God, the light of the Father, stirring the ocean of the light of the Mother and materializing God's perfect vision in the Ma-ter universe.

Help me consume the conflict in the Middle East

Mother Mary, January, 23, 2005

Understanding why the Middle East is such a focus for conflict

How can it be that this particular region of the Earth has been the source of so much conflict? How can it be that this particular region has been allowed by God to play such an important role in terms of having control over so much of the world's oil reserves? How could God allow this to happen?

Well, as always, God did not allow it to happen. Humankind has allowed it to happen because despite the fact that three major religions have been started in that region, the vast majority of the inhabitants of that region have refused to embody the true inner teachings of any of these religions. Truly, any person who embodies the mystical teachings of Islam, the mystical teachings of Judaism or the mystical teachings of Christianity will not be cattle for the fodder of those who want nothing but bloodshed and warfare. Truly, such a person would refuse to participate in these ceaseless conflicts and quests for revenge, fueled by the insane belief that human beings must meter out justice because God is not doing so. Or the belief that God has commanded human being to administer justice by killing their fellow humans.

So because of the widespread refusal to embody either of these three religions, we now have a situation in the Middle East, where a group of souls, who are almost completely dedicated to warfare and revenge, can control a large part of the world's oil reserves and can thereby intimidate the rest of the world. We might say that the general population in the area have refused the means given to them by God to raise themselves above the warring in their own members, and because of this refusal they have fallen prey to the warmongers in their midst. You see my beloved, when you do not defeat the enemy within, you become easy prey for the enemy without.

We might call these souls the laggard souls because they came to Earth after the fall of man, and they came because they had been engaged in warfare on other planets. And ever since they came, they have continued this ceaseless and – seen with the eyes of mature souls – groundless warfare. And this is what you see in the Middle East today, namely those, even some in leadership positions, who talk about peace, but they never talk honestly about peace. They only talk about peace on their terms and they simply pay lip service to world opinion as a means to get their way. These souls are so consumed by their pride that getting their way is more important to them than anything else. Thus, they are ready to kill their own people, even die themselves and blow up the planet upon which they live, in order to get their way. And in this they truly stand apart from most of the people on this Earth.

Precisely because these souls refuse to let go of their pride, their egos and their never-ending demands for human justice and revenge, they are today lagging far behind the spiritual development of humankind in general. And thus it is indeed time to call forth the judgment of Heaven upon such laggard souls and the dark spirits that support and imprison them. It is high time for these souls to be removed from the Earth and taken to other systems of worlds, where they might be given another opportunity to grow, or where they can self-destruct without pulling down so many of the good souls that are currently embodied on Earth.

Yet for these souls to be taken, a critical mass of people must come apart from the laggard souls and their laggard philosophy of revenge and of the necessity to wash clean the sins of the past through the spilling of human blood. And despite the fact that these laggard leaders have showed their colors any number of times, the world has yet to rise up and denounce them and their philosophy. In fact, the world keeps tiptoeing around these Middle Eastern leaders, refusing to call out as the little child, "But the emperor has got nothing on!" And likewise the world has yet to make itself independent of the oil reserves controlled by these people.

God's Will is your will

Presence of God's Will, February 20, 2005

I AM the Presence of God's Will, and I come to give you the truth about God's will, so that you have the option to choose to free yourself from the lies about God's will that have been programmed into your soul for so long that you never even think to question them. You have been taught by beloved Mother Mary and beloved Jesus about the process that caused your souls to descend into the consciousness of duality, in which you see yourself as separated from God. Therefore, it is inevitable that you see God's will as outside of, as separate from even as being in opposition to your own will.

I am come to dispel this dualistic ego-illusion. For truly, without Him was not anything made that was made, and therefore without His will was not anything made that was made. So you see that God's will is embedded within all life. Therefore, God's will is not outside of or apart from you. It is truly the law that God has written in your inward parts because God's will is the will of your I AM Presence, which is your true identity.

Your I AM Presence is an individualization of God, and therefore the will of your I AM Presence is an individualization of the will of God. Your lifestream was born out of that will, and you must understand that God has no desire to restrict or control you. However, neither does God desire to see you destroy yourself, your brothers and sisters or the universe in which you live. Therefore, God's will, expressed as the laws that guide the unfoldment of the world of form, are meant to protect you from self-destruction by guiding your creative expression.

God only desires you to express your individuality, your God-given individuality, in full measure. And yet God knows that because you have free will, you have the potential to go against the laws that guide the growth of this universe. And if you do go against these laws of growth, you will inevitably begin to separate yourself from God. You will begin to separate yourself from the consciousness of God, which is constantly transcending itself. Therefore, you will sink into a consciousness in which you refuse to transcend yourself and refuse to grow. This consciousness of anti-growth will not self-transcend but self-contract, and thereby you will limit your ability to express your individuality and your God-given creativity. Thus, you will confine your soul to a box that will become narrower and narrower, until you can no longer move and cry out for deliverance.

Pandora's box of the anti-will

God has no desire to see you suffer in this self-created box of limitations, this Pandora's box. God has the desire to see you grow in creativity and love in the universe of unlimited possibilities that He has formed as a platform for the creative expression of his sons and daughters, his co-creators. And thus you see that God's will truly is for you to be who you are, to be who you were created to be. God even desires you to transcend what you were created to be and be more of yourself and more of God.

Your lifestream, your I AM Presence, was born out of the will of God and God's desire to be more through you. And your soul was formed out of the will of your I AM Presence to be more of God through the soul that can descend into the lower vibrations of the material universe. And thus you see that your soul sprang from the will of the I AM Presence and the I AM Presence sprang from the will of God. And so how can the will of God possibly be alien to, apart from or outside the true will of your I AM Presence and your soul?

You now see that if you think God's will is outside of your will, is in opposition to your will or that God's will restricts your creativity and freedom, then there is only one explanation, which is that you have become trapped in an ego-illusion. You have come to identify yourself with a will that is not your own. And it is truly this lower will, this dualistic will, this self-centered will, that is alien to your soul and in opposition to your true will. It is this lower will that seeks to restrict your freedom and creativity by preventing you from being all that you are and becoming more of God. It is this lower will, this will of the ego, that seeks to confine you to a box in which it has your soul under its complete control and domination, so that you dare not even move or consider a new idea or a possibility beyond what the ego has defined as your dualistic identity.

I am moved by compassion

Oh my beloved hearts, as the Presence that focuses the flame of the will of God, I am moved by compassion for those on Earth who are trapped in this limited will of their egos. I am moved by compassion because I know the truth that nothing happens without will. I know that the very beginning of creation was an act of will. Your Creator could create only by beginning with an act of will, the will to create. And yet the will to create is truly the Omega polarity to the Alpha polarity of the will to Be. And so your Creator has the will to Be. And out of that will to Be, came the will to Be more. It is this will to Be more that gave rise to the will to create the world of form, of which your lifestream is a part. And so you see that creation itself started with an act of will because God had the will to Be more than He was before creation began.

When you understand the nature of the will of God as the will to Be more, you suddenly see through one of the lies that have been programmed into your soul, namely, that the will of God is static and never-changing. This lie claims that God's unchanging will leaves you no room for growth but only restricts you into a mold, where you have no freedom and creativity. When you expose this illusion, you see that God's will is not static. It does not stand still because God's will is the will to be more. And therefore God's will is constantly and perpetually transcending itself.

God is transcending Itself because without God was not anything made that was made. God simply could not create something that was outside of or apart from himself, and thus God created the world of form out of His own Being. And in doing so, God had only one option, namely to Be more. God can create in only one way, namely by Being more. And out of that more, the world of form is created. And so you see that God is not the angry and controlling old man in the sky who seeks to beat you into submission to his restrictive will. God is truly the source of all creativity, the source of all joy, and God is constantly transcending Itself.

God has no desire but to see you transcend yourself and become more. And that drive to become more is the saving grace that is embedded so deep within your soul that you can never lose it, although you can cover it over by a veil of ego-illusions. And so you see that God's will for you is that you transcend yourself and become more than even God envisioned you to be. And you become more by exercising your own

God-given creativity and transcending your present sense of identity, that is a product of your imagination and your vision.

What restricts your freedom?

If God's will does not restrict your freedom, what does restrict your freedom? It is the lower will of the ego, which truly wants to control you because it knows that if you engage in the process of life, the process of transcending your limited sense of identity and becoming more of who you are in God, then one day you will transcend the ego and the ego will be no more. So out of its self-centered survival instinct, the ego must seek to restrict your creativity and prevent you from transcending the limited sense of identity that it has defined for you and programmed into your soul for so many lifetimes that your soul has come to accept these limitations as being real and being absolute. And thus you believe in the illusion of time and space, the illusion of the material world and you think that it sets limitations for your soul.

Oh, my beloved hearts, my heart truly goes out in compassion to those who have been trapped by this lower will of their egos and the lower will of the forces of this world. These souls have come to believe in various illusions that portray them as limited, mortal human beings. Perhaps they even believe they are nothing more than the physical body, nothing more than a collection of cells that are destined to die and disappear into nothingness after such a short life span that truly any soul that has any spark of life in it must rebel against this restriction of its life force.

Thus, you see that most people, in fact humankind as a whole, is a house divided against itself because from the outside, from the forces of this world and their own egos, people have been programmed to believe in a set of limitations that have boxed them in and restricted their creativity and their life force. Yet from deep within themselves they have some spark of remembrance of the truth that their souls are unlimited, God-free, spiritual beings who have the potential to transcend any limitation in this world and become more of who they truly are in God. And this then is the central dynamic on planet Earth today. The spiritual people are going through an awakening, whereby they become more attuned to the will of God within them, the will to self-transcend and overcome the limitations in this world, seeking to turn them into material beings.

People have a desire to break that mold of materialism and be the spiritual beings that they truly are, while they are still here on Earth. And yet, so many of those who are partially awakened do not understand the central dynamic that they are being torn in opposite directions by the false will of their egos and by the true will of their souls and I AM Presence.

Imagine a new day
Imagine what could happen if millions of people on Earth, those who feel the spark of light within their souls, could come to understand the central dynamic that I have just explained to you. Imagine what could happen if these people suddenly saw through the illusions of their egos and therefore realized that by accepting these ego-illusions they have chosen to place themselves inside a very small mental box. In this box they are restricted by a set of beliefs that spring from the dualism and the separation of the ego, reinforced by the dualism and separation of the forces of this world. And these forces, in their rebellion against God, are seeking to imprison every soul on Earth in order to prove that God was wrong in giving souls free will.

Imagine what could happen if people suddenly saw the unreality, the complete illusion, of their egos and the forces of this world. Imagine what could happen if people realized the central illusion that they are not separated from God, that God is not an angry and judgmental God who seeks to impose his will upon them. Imagine what could happen if these spiritual souls realized that they only turned away from God because they came to believe in one of the dualistic illusions. And thus they have the power to, at any point in time, expose the fallacy and the contradictions of that illusion. They have the power to, at any moment, look their egos straight in the eye and say, "I will no longer allow you to trap me in the consciousness of death, and I now choose the consciousness of life."

Imagine what could happen if every spiritual soul on Earth were to realize that, at this very moment, they have the power to turn around and face God, face the shining Light of their I AM Presence, and realign themselves with the truth and the will of God within them. Imagine what could happen if these spiritual souls realized that the central lie on Earth is the belief that they are separated from the kingdom of God and that they cannot enter the kingdom on their own. Imagine if all spiritual souls suddenly, as in a blinding flash, saw the truth that the kingdom of God is within them, and therefore no force in this world can keep them out of the inner kingdom.

Imagine what could happen if the spiritual souls of Earth decided to stop looking for the pot of gold at the end of the rainbow, to stop looking for an outer savior and to stop looking for the kingdom of God outside themselves. Imagine if they suddenly decided to look within, and if they entered that inner kingdom and thereby aligned themselves with the truth of God and the will of God within them. Imagine that they separated themselves from their egos and united themselves with the will of God, out of which they sprang.

Imagine what could happen if the spiritual people of Earth accepted their true identities as sons and daughters of God, who are truly designed to be co-creators with God and who chose to descend into this world because they desired to manifest God's kingdom as an expression of God's ever-transcending will. Imagine that thousands or even millions of people suddenly decided that they would be the open doors for the manifestation of God's will on Earth.

God desires only the best for you

Oh my beloved hearts, can you feel my passion and my compassion of how I, as a representative of God's will, desire to see the will of God manifest on Earth, not out of a desire to restrict your freedom and creativity but out of a desire to see you express and unfold your true creativity and your true individuality in God, thereby co-creating God's kingdom on Earth. Oh my beloved hearts, imagine that you could step away from the Earth and look at the forest instead of the trees.

Look at how much suffering is currently manifest on Earth. Look at how people treat each other in so many inhumane ways that it is almost beyond comprehension. Look at how people treat Mother Earth, even to the point of being willing to destroy the platform that gives them physical life. How can this be? How can people be so trapped in the illusions and conflicts that from a broader viewpoint are so utterly pointless that it defies the imagination? How can people continue to battle against each other, against themselves and against God's will that only wants to set them free?

Oh my beloved hearts, can you not see that all of this suffering, all of this conflict, all of this imbalance is truly the product of the anti-will of people's egos that restricts them to a mental box, where they think other people are their enemies, that God is their enemy, that Mother Earth is their enemy? Can you not see that this anti-will is what causes people to feel threatened by anything that seems beyond their control? Therefore, this anti-will gives people an insatiable desire to control everything around them, to control other people, to control Mother Nature and to subdue everything to the will of the ego instead of allowing everything to become an expression of the will of God that is truly all light and all love.

My beloved hearts, do you sense my passion? Do you sense my compassion? Do you sense that God only wants all people to be free of this anti-will of the ego, this anti-will of the dark forces, this anti-will of the devil as the personification of evil? Can you sense that, truly, evil was never part of God and therefore evil is not the opposite of God. Evil is the opposite of your freedom to express your God-given individuality in this world. Evil is the energy veil that causes your soul to believe it is separated from God.

Oh my beloved hearts, can you not sense that God has an infinite desire to see you become free of these ego illusions, this veil of illusion that confines you to a mental box in which all of your beliefs, and even your sense of identity, spring from the duality and the separation of the ego? Can you not sense that God so loved the world that He sent His only son into the world that the world through him might be saved? And what is that only begotten Son of God? It is the Christ consciousness, the universal mind of Christ, that separates the real from the unreal and thus allows any soul to see through the dualistic illusions of the ego and the forces of this world.

Your personal savior

As beloved Jesus has explained to you, he and other beings in Heaven have given a portion of their Spirits in the form of your individual Christ self. This self is your personal savior, your personal comforter, your personal redeemer. And if you will but reach for that Christ self and continue to reach for it, then your Christ self will guide you step-by-step through the jungle of ego illusions, until you break through and see the mountain of God.

As you climb that mountain of God, you will rise above the dualistic illusions of the ego. You will even come to the point, where the devil himself – as a personification of your ego-illusions – will meet you on that high mountain. He will show you the kingdoms of this world and give you the final temptation of offering you control over the kingdoms of this world in exchange for your soul. And yet because you have bonded with your Christ self, you will be able to withstand that temptation as the Lord Jesus Christ was able to withstand it. Therefore, you can rebuke the devil and say, "What does it profit me to gain the whole world of materialistic illusions and lose my own soul in those illusions? I choose to leave behind the kingdoms of ego-illusions and enter the kingdom of God within me!"

Oh my beloved hearts, can you see that you are not trapped in a net of illusions from which there is no way out? Can you see that there truly is a way out, and it is the spiritual path demonstrated by the Lord Christ and by the Lord Gautama Buddha and by so many other spiritual teachers who have come to show you the way out of ego-illusions? Can you see that the essence of all spirituality, of all true religion, and of all personal growth is that you transcend the dualistic illusions of the ego and realign yourself with the truth of God? Can you see that the essence of the spiritual path is that you separate yourself, that your soul separates itself, from the lower will of the ego and lovingly reunites with the true will of your I AM Presence? Your Presence is an individualization of the will of God, a unique individualization that makes you the uniquely beautiful individual that you are.

My beloved hearts, do you now understand the reality of the will of God as the true will of your soul? Your soul chose to descend to planet Earth. Your soul did not choose to descend to Earth for the purpose of becoming trapped in the lower will of the ego. Your soul chose to descend to Earth because it wanted to fulfill its potential to be a co-creator with God and to bring God's kingdom into manifestation in this part of the material universe. And thus your true desire is to be a Christed Being on Earth, even to be God on Earth, and to realize the truth in the statement made by the Lord Christ that "Ye are Gods" (John 10:34). Can you now see that the true desire of your soul is to throw off the shackles of these limitations and these dualistic illusions that restrict your true will to be God in manifestation?

My gift to you

My beloved hearts, I am come to give you a gift. It is a morsel of the infinite power of the will of God. If you will accept this gift, I will place it, at this moment, in your heart center, your heart chakra. I will place it on the altar of your heart. It takes the shape of a Diamond of the Will of God, and if you will give it a little bit of attention every day you will experience that its brilliant radiance will grow in strength and clarity, until the light of the diamond will of God will dispel and replace the darkness of the anti-will of the ego and the anti-will of the forces of this world.

As the light in your heart increases, your soul will begin to ride the light beams of the diamond will of God that will take you beyond the mental box of your ego. You will then begin to feel the unlimited freedom that comes from knowing that you are one with the will of God and that the will of God is an expression of the unconditional love of God and the unconditional drive to self-transcend and become more of who you are. And it is this drive to become more that is the true definition of life, for life is something that grows and you can grow only by transcending yourself.

Life is perpetual self-transcendence, and only life will give your soul the sense of joy and peace for which it longs. After all, how can your soul be at peace when it is trapped in the consciousness of death and apart from the stream of life? True peace, true love, true joy is found only when your soul knows that it is flowing with the River of Life because it has aligned itself with the will of God within it.

My beloved hearts, I seal you now in the flame of the will of God, and I say to you, "Do not forget the diamond of the will of God that I have placed in your hearts. Let it grow and let its light dispel all darkness in your own being. And then let it grow even more and dispel all darkness on this planet, so that God's will can be manifest on Earth as the abundant life for all people."

Let there be Light on Earth and only Light! Let the Light of the Will of God be manifest on Earth and dispel the darkness of the anti-will. And there IS Light and only Light. It is finished!

If you love me, give my Rosary of God's Will

Mother Mary, February 20, 2005

I request that you spend a little time contemplating the true meaning of the events that took place almost 2,000 years ago, when my Son Jesus demonstrated the path that leads you to surrender yourself entirely to the Will of God. I ask you to contemplate that the events that led to the crucifixion and resurrection of Jesus illustrate the process that your soul can go through as it separates itself from the anti-will of the ego and is resurrected into oneness with the true will of God.

Your ego represents all of the people, all of the forces, that attacked Jesus and sought to prevent him from fulfilling his mission. Your ego represent the people who nailed Jesus to the cross, as your soul is truly nailed to the cross of ego-illusions. And thus, Jesus' final surrender on the cross, where he gave up the ghost, represents the point of total surrender, where your soul finally decides that it will no longer engage in the ego-illusions, that it will no longer seek to defend or justify them, that it will no longer seek to hide or defend its original choice to turn away from God. Instead, it will surrender that choice, and the ego-illusions that sprang from it. It will give up the ghost of this anti-will, these illusions. And thus it will allow its own ego, and the sense of identity built on the ego, to die on the cross. And in allowing the ego to die, your soul is then resurrected into the true life, the immortal life, of knowing that you are a son or daughter of God, an individualization of God, that sprang from the will of God, the desire of God to be more through you.

Thus, you attain immortal life because you are now willing to perpetually transcend yourself, to become more of who you are. You are no longer trapped by the desire to defend the mortal identity of your ego, causing you to seek to stop your growth rather than allowing that growth to take you beyond your limited sense of identity.

Learn from Abraham

Oh my beloved hearts, truly the passion and compassion expressed by the Presence of God's Will is shared by every member of the Ascended

Host. It is especially shared by the representative of God's Will for planet Earth, the beloved Master M, also known as El Morya [now Master MORE], who was the incarnation of Abraham. If you study the life of Abraham, you will see that he truly demonstrated the willingness to follow the will of God over the will of his own ego. He was willing to move out of his home country, to move out of the sense of identity in which his ego was comfortable. He was willing to wander in the desert, not knowing where he was going, but trusting that God would lead him, one step at a time, until he arrived at his final destination.

This is the journey of every soul, where the soul must decide to leave its comfort-zone, to leave its dualistic, mortal sense of identity, in which the ego believes it has everything under control. The soul must decide to take one step at a time and trust that its Christ self will lead it in the right direction.

The balance of the will of God

Many people think I am the exclusive property of the Catholic church. Some people think I express myself only through one particular apparition or that I have appeared in only one or a few places, be it Fatima, Lourdes or Medjugorje. Others think I speak through only one particular messenger or organization.

All of these beliefs are the products of ego-illusions that seek to project a dualistic image upon God and God's representatives. And as all ego-illusions, this image springs from the ego's desire for control. Yet the human ego will never control any ascended being, and thus our progressive revelation continues regardless of human expectations, as beloved Archangel Michael recently explained.

Another reason for my double appearance is to show you what it takes to be a pure messenger for an ascended being. Yes, I do speak through many people around the world, but not all of them, are pure messengers, and the reason is that they do not have balance in their beings. To be a pure messenger, you need balance between the expanding force of the Father and the contracting force of the Mother.

If you do not have this balance, you can still serve as a messenger, yet your message will be distorted by the desires in your subconscious or conscious mind. Thus, you will tend to move into one of two extremes. One extreme is to focus on the negative portents, giving dire prophecies about cataclysmic changes, seeking to awaken people through fear.

The other is to focus on the positive, giving a message that all is well and that God is ultimately in control. The first type of message often paralyzes people, making them think they can do nothing. The second type often pacifies people, making them think the don't need to do anything—specifically, you don't need to confront your ego or the forces of darkness by taking a firm stand for truth. Both reactions spring from the ego, and its attempt to control you by making you believe that you either cannot or don't need to do anything to separate yourself from it. Thus, you will see many messages on the internet that are either overly negative or overly positive.

The balanced reaction is that you do indeed need to do something about the current conditions on Earth. You need to take an active approach and separate yourself from the illusions of your ego. You need to put on the mind of Christ and take a stand for God's truth. The reason being that free will reigns supreme on Earth. As Archangel Michael explained, the Ascended Host have the power to remove all darkness from the Earth, but we do not have the authority to use our power. Human beings have the authority, but you do not have the power. Thus, the solution is that you give us the authority to release our power through you. Yet to be the open door for the release of God's power, you need to be perfectly balanced. And to be balanced, you need to rise above the illusions of the ego, so that you cannot be trapped into one of the innumerable dualistic extremes.

Therefore, I have shown you myself through the flame of Father and through the flame of Mother. If you like one of my expressions and feel reluctant about the other, consider that you might not have made peace with either God the Father or God the Mother. And if so, strive to find your inner balance. As one tool to attain balance, give the Rosary to God's Will over the next 33 days and ask me to restore balance in your being. I will help you as you are willing to give up the unbalanced illusions of your ego.

My gift to you

My beloved hearts, I too come bearing gifts today, and I come with the gift that if you will take my hand, I will add my momentum of surrender to the momentum of your Christ self. I will take you by the hand, and I will lead you back through the veils of ego-illusions that separate yourself from the original decision, when your soul first chose to turn away from God.

If you will contemplate what caused you to turn away from God while you are giving this 33-day vigil, you will find that I will truly lead you by the hand, until you see that original serpentine lie that your soul accepted and which caused you to turn away from your spiritual teacher and your I AM Presence.

If you will faithfully give this vigil, you will arrive at the point, where your soul can be resurrected into your true identity as a son or daughter of God. That is, if you are willing to fully surrender yourself to the will of God and give up the ghost of ego-illusions.

Oh my beloved, you have been programmed to believe that Jesus is above you, that he was the only son of God and therefore the only one who could be resurrected. Yet I tell you, all people are sons and daughters of God, and therefore all have the potential to follow in the footsteps of Christ. And when you allow your ego to die on the cross – without the death of your physical body – your soul can be resurrected into your true identity as a son or daughter of God. You can then follow Jesus' call to do the works that he did, and do even greater works because you build on the momentum of Jesus and all other ascended beings.

When you align yourself with the Ascended Host, you can become a focal point in the Earth for the collective attainment and momentum of the Ascended Host to be expressed through you. You can become the open door for the manifestation of the will of God on planet Earth. As more and more people dare to be that open door, you will see that things will begin to change so rapidly that all the darkness and all the seemingly insoluble problems will fade away as dewdrops fade away under the rays of the rising sun.

God is waiting for you to take a stand
My beloved hearts, the Sun of God's Will is truly rising on Earth, and if you will but separate yourself from the anti-will of the ego, and realign yourself with the true will of your soul and I AM Presence, you will enter the kingdom of God within you, even while you are still in this limited physical body. You will feel the true life of the will of God stream through your being and express itself through all your thoughts, feelings and actions. Thus, you will see that the will of God will be manifest on

Earth. It will consume all darkness until all people share the abundant life that is the will of God for this beautiful planet.

My beloved hearts, contrast the beauty of nature with the ugliness created by man in some areas. And then realize that God's will is that this planet expresses only beauty, love, peace and harmony. It is not God's will that there should be conflict, pain and suffering on Earth. And when you realize this truth, you realize that you, as the son or daughter of God, have an absolute right, given to you by God, to take a stand for truth on Earth, to take a stand for God's will, to take a stand for love, peace and harmony. And you have a right to call forth the will of God to consume the anti-will of the egos of humankind and the anti-will of the forces of darkness that think they own this planet.

You have a right to say, "No more! I will separate myself from the anti-will and from all darkness. And I will BE the will of God manifest on Earth." And thus you have a right to demand that God's will consumes the darkness, the pain and the suffering, restoring God's kingdom, God's peace, God's harmony and God's love to Mother Earth and all her children.

My beloved hearts, if you love me, give my Rosary to God's Will and set Earth free from the anti-will. Set your brothers and sisters free from the anti-will. And set your own souls free from the anti-will. Heaven is waiting for the authority to clean up this planet, yet that authority must come from you.

I am your Mother Mary, but I am also an ascended being, and as such I have the perfect balance of the expanding and contracting forces of God. And thus I am also one with the Will of the Father. And therefore, I am one with the Father who will not accept that his sons and daughters are trapped by the anti-will. And therefore, in oneness with the will of the Father within me, I say, "Let there by Light on Earth, and only Light. And there IS light. It IS finished!"

Therefore, I seal you now in the unconditional love of the Father-Mother God, anchored in my own Being and in the Being of my spiritual brother, Jesus. We seal you now in the love of the Mother of God and the in the truth of the Son of God. We seal you in the Will of the Father and we seal you in the self-transcendence of the Holy Spirit that bloweth where it listeth and thus dispels all ego-illusions that trap your souls.

It is sealed.

Wake up—NOW!

El Morya, March 25, 2005

Beware of the anti-mind

I am come to speak now on the anti-mind that is truly present in many of the students of the ascended masters. This is the most insidious mind. And it is one of the greatest dangers to a student on the spiritual path. This mind has so many disguises that it cannot be exposed in all of its facets in one discourse. Yet those of you who consider yourselves students of El Morya need to consider how the anti-mind influences your thinking, including your thinking of what it means to be a student of the will of God and a student of the ascended masters.

Truly as Jesus has said through this messenger, it is possible to take a true teaching, given through a pure and sponsored messenger of the ascended masters, and turn it into a false teaching that keeps you trapped on a certain level of the spiritual path and then, after a very short while, tricks you into actually going backward on your path instead of progressing to succeeding levels of the Mind of God.

This is not the Will of God. It is not the Will of God to see those who have found the teachings of the ascended masters start to regress. And it is especially not the will of God to see those students sit in their churches feeling holier than thou, feeling that they are better than other people on the planet, feeling they have the highest teaching on the planet, feeling that they have everything they need to make their ascension, while in reality they are regressing further and further away from the point, where they were at when they found the teachings of the ascended masters.

What have you done with our sponsorship?

Truly, no one has found the ascended masters and their teachings without being sponsored by an ascended master, who gave a portion of his attainment and his light as a gift to you to bring you in contact with the ascended masters and their teachings. Why do you think so many people in the world turn a deaf ear to our teachings and our messengers? It is because they are not ready for our teachings. And therefore, we cannot give them that final sponsorship that allows them to find the teachings with their outer minds.

So yes, indeed, each person who finds the teachings of the ascended masters has been sponsored and has been given a gift. That gift is a morsel of an ascended master's Spirit, an ascended master's light. It is truly the talent given to you from your brothers and sisters in Heaven.

And as Jesus so beautifully explained in his parable about the talents, you are indeed meant to multiply that light, multiply that gift. And we have given our outer teachings, our decrees, our rituals, as a help for you to multiply that gift. But take note of the very fact that no outer teachings and no outer ritual can guarantee that the gift of light in your heart will actually be multiplied. Because that gift can be multiplied only when you internalize it, make it part of your being, and then add your own attainment, your own individuality to it, and thereby the spark of light given to you becomes more.

Only when it becomes more has it been multiplied and has become the worthy offering, the acceptable offering, that you put on the altar of God, whereby we can then multiply what you have multiplied and give you more of ourselves. And this then becomes the figure-eight flow between Heaven and Earth, whereby God is magnified through you and God is magnified through us, and thereby the entire Earth is lifted up.

Yet for you to internalize and multiply the gifts given to you, you must be willing to step away from the outer path of mechanically following an outer teaching, mechanically giving an outer ritual, somehow thinking that at some point in the future you will automatically become the Christ, you will automatically make your ascension.

The false salvation

This is folly. This is the folly of the anti-mind, which has always been looking for a path that is easy, whereby you don't have to think, you don't have to make decisions, you don't have to run the risk of being wrong and you don't have to internalize the light. This is the dream that you buy a ticket, step on to the train and at one point the conductor comes in and announces, "The next station is Heaven." Oh my beloved hearts, if there was such a train, then all people on Earth would already have been saved.

And it would have happened eons ago, because truly this is what Lucifer attempted to do by forcing people to be saved through control. And it is precisely by forcing people to come under the control of the anti-mind that Lucifer has attempted to save people. But this can never be. This salvation is a lie.

It is the total misunderstanding of God's purpose for creating you as an individualization of itself. You are created not to be controlled by some outer authority, you are created to be a God-free being who uses your gift of free will to multiply your divine individuality and thereby become more, whereby all of creation becomes more.

Attempting to control will only cause you to become less because, through the control of the anti-mind, you shut off the flame of God that you truly are, and this then becomes a downward spiral, whereby all life contracts more and more until the self is extinguished and is no more. And yes, in a sense this is a return to the source, but it is the false return that was never God's intent and purpose.

So I am indeed come to this Earth to rekindle the spark of God's will in the hearts of all those who are willing to become more of who they are in God. And you need to become more by systemically learning to see through the insidious lies of the anti-mind, the anti-christ mind, that causes you to believe that you do not need to come up higher, that you do not need to take the next step on the path, that you do not need to transcend the level of consciousness that you have obtained.

"I have done enough"

And so you use all kinds of reasonings by the outer mind to say, "I have done enough. Look at what I have done these past 10, 20, 30 years. I have given so many decrees. I have gone to all these conferences. I have done this. I have done that."

Yet, it is entirely possible that a person can do all of these things without having multiplied the Christ flame in their heart by one iota. Yes, this will shock those who believe they have done the right thing for so many years. But there are indeed some people who have been in the ascended masters' teachings for decades but have not added one morsel to the original Christ light that they were given.

They have not multiplied their talents. They have buried those talents in the ground, and they have said, "I know that my God is an unfair and an unjust taskmaster. And so I will guard what I have been given. I will bury it in the ground because I don't need to multiply it because I have this outer teaching and this outer church to follow. And I just need to do all the right things and obey all the rules and not do any of the wrong things, and then I will please God." But you see, that will never please God. That will only please the anti-God, the anti-mind of God.

Wake up from your illusions

And so I come today with the swiftness of the Will of God and I say, "Wake up from your lies. Wake up from your illusions, your ego illusions that have been pierced by those of your brothers and sisters who have dared to give this rosary for these last 33 days." This is indeed an unprecedented turning point for planet Earth. But my purpose here is to express to all of our present and former students that this is an unprecedented turning point for you.

The principle of the Great White Brotherhood has always been that a few must lead and forge a way through the jungle, so that others might follow the trail. And I am here to tell you that there are indeed a limited number of your brothers and sisters who have dared to give this vigil of the rosary to God's will for these past days, and they have blazed a trail for you—those who are our students but are still stuck in the anti-mind and the anti-will, not willing to transcend your present level of consciousness. And they have given you an unprecedented opportunity to come up higher, if you will take it.

And if you will not take it then I say, consider the consequences. The consequences are that you will only reinforce the downward spiral in which you are trapped. Because I truly tell you, the law of God is perpetual self-transcendence. If you are not transcending yourself you are going backwards. There is no such thing as standing still.

You may think that you are standing still but the stillstand lasts only for an infinitely short moment, and then the pendulum starts to swing to the other side, and you start going into a spiral that will end in the deepest levels of hell, where there is no individuality and no life left. And therefore, there is just an explosion into nothingness.

And it is not the Will of God, that you, whom he has created as his unique sons and daughters, should descend into nothingness. It is God's will that you should use your talents given to you as your divine individuality [to the gnosis] and multiply them, so that all life becomes more and thereby God is magnified through all parts of his creation.

I am one with the will of God—are you?

I AM the Will of God. I AM one with the Will of God. And I wish you were one with the Will of God, because thereby you would know that God's will for you is to become more, and that is truly your own will. It is not separate, apart from or outside of yourself. It is the inner will of the deepest levels of your soul and I AM Presence. And if you cannot understand this, if you cannot connect to my words, even when you read them, then you need to consider the very fact that you have lost your connection to the will of God within yourself.

I am not asking you to follow anyone outside of yourself. I am not asking you to follow a particular messenger. I am not asking you to follow even what I say. I am asking you to go within yourself and reconnect to the will of God in you, so that you can be absolutely sure that you are following that will and not the will of your ego. And if you are not sure how to reconnect to the will of God within you, then use the rosary I have given as a tool for this. Because, truly, this rosary is the most powerful tool that has been released on this planet for the reconnection of the soul to the will of God since the days of Atlantis.

...

Wake up from your illusions created through the anti-mind which has become the anti-will of the ego that challenges every attempt of your soul to reconnect to the higher will of God. Wake up and realize that you have taken our teachings, given to set you free, and you have used them to create a prison around your minds that says, "I should do this. And I should not do that."

Be willing to let go of your illusions and come up higher, because I tell you, there is no more time to dilly-dally in the anti-mind. There is no more time to let the anti-will eclipse the will of your I AM Presence working through your soul. This is the time to awaken and to walk with me as I walk swiftly into new realms of Being, Being God on Earth. Because how can we bring God's kingdom to Earth unless we have those students who are willing to come up higher and dare to be God in manifestation, God in embodiment.

It is not enough that you work on making your ascension at the end of this lifetime. That was an old dispensation, and it was given because that was all the consciousness of humankind could bear at the time. Yet precisely because so many people did respond to the old dispensation, we have now come up higher, and therefore we can now bring out a new dispensation that takes you, if you are willing, to a higher level of not simply making your ascension at some undetermined time in the future, not simply balancing 51% of your karma, but balancing all of it and internalizing your Higher Being, so that you can be here below all that you are above.

Why on earth are you here on Earth?

El Morya, March 26, 2005.

I come to pour out my love

And so I come to pour out my love for you, each and every one of you. Know that the experience described by this messenger [the messenger surrendered an aspect of his ego and felt El Morya's love descend upon him as a cloud of pink, unconditional love] of experiencing the pink love of the Will of God can indeed be experienced by each and every one of you, when you surrender the will of the ego to the will of God within you. Because, after all, the will of God is not a harsh and judgmental and angry will that seeks to restrict you. The will of God springs from God's unconditional love for you that only wants the best for you.

And what is the best for you? It is that you be who you are, that you reconnect to your God Flame, that you let your light shine. Because by letting your light shine, your soul will feel its deepest fulfillment. The deepest fulfillment possible is to feel the light of your God Flame flowing through your soul, your mind, your thoughts, your emotions, your actions. And everything that human beings long for—they will never have that longing fulfilled by doing outer things. They will have it fulfilled only when the light of their God Flames is flowing through them.

And in allowing the mind of God to flow through them, they become more, and they become better and better at directing that light. And that is when there is a blending of the mind of God, the will of God, the will of the I AM Presence and the will of the soul. And you realize that the will of God is not outside of you; it is inside of you.

And the will of God is that when you overcome the ego and are anchored in your God Flame, you make decisions on your own as to how to direct that light. And thereby, you express your own God-given creativity, beyond what any other lifestream could express. And therefore you bring a unique gift that will give you that unique sense of fulfillment that comes from knowing who you are and being who you are.

So you see, God is not trying to restrict you. However, God will awaken you, when you are going beyond what is best for YOU, what is beyond the higher will of your own being. When you are allowing the outer mind and the forces of this world to make you a house divided against itself, the house that cannot stand, then God's Will will step in and discipline you and challenge you and push your ego buttons to bring out a reaction, in the hope that your ego will become so outspoken that the soul finally sees it and says, "I don't want this anymore. I don't want this limitation. I don't want to repeat these age-old patterns. I want to be free, I want something more."

Your purpose for coming to Earth
It has been my privilege to serve the Flame of the Will of God for a very long time, and I can assure you that during that time I have had the unique privilege of challenging the egos of any number of students that have come our way in various dispensations and organizations. And although many of them get riled and are not particularly grateful for having their egos challenged, I see behind the outer personality. And I see that those who are willing to be awakened find a new freedom. And at the soul level they are grateful, because they realize that it was the love of God that would not allow them to descend further and further into a downward spiral that would only cause them to lose their deepest sense of joy and fulfillment. Because when you are trapped in the ego, how can you possibly fulfill the purpose for which you came to Earth?

And so I reveal to you that many of you came to Earth specifically because you wanted to transcend and transmute and transform a particular state of consciousness. You wanted to show others that it was possible to be born into difficult circumstances, to experience various kinds of problems and limitations, and to prove that you could rise above it and thereby show other people that they too can rise above it through the power of God within them.

And so many of you may look back at your lives and see that you have made various mistakes and you have encountered various problems. And you may feel that because you have gone through these problems, you are unworthy to face God, you are unworthy to come home. But in reality those problems were never yours. It was something you volunteered to take on, in order to show others the way and in order to make a contribution to banishing that particular state of consciousness by resolving it through your own Being.

Yet through the programming of the world, where you were brought up without even understanding the concept of a spiritual mission and a divine plan, you forgot why you came. And so you have taken on the consciousness that you came to dissolve, you have begun to identify with it and you think you cannot escape it. Yet I tell you—it is time for you to awaken and realize that these limitations are not real, they are not YOU, they are not of your making. They are of the making of the lower consciousness, your personal ego and the collective consciousness. And your task, your desire, was to come down here, experience it and then separate yourself out from it.

And it is time, it is high time, to separate yourself out from this state of consciousness and show the world that no matter what you have gone through, no matter what you have experienced, no matter what mistakes you have made, there is redemption in the God within you, in your God Flame. And by connecting to that God Flame, your God Flame will consume all unlike itself, and it will consume all of your limitations, all of your past records and even the very memory of it, until you cannot even remember why you used to feel unworthy or limited.

The most important step on the spiritual path

And thus I say to you, when you connect to the Will of God within you, when you stop seeing that will as external or in opposition to your will, you have taken the most important step on the spiritual path that anyone can take. Because when you have passed that hurdle of reconnecting to the Will of God, you realize that everything that comes after is not external to your will. And therefore, you are no longer fighting yourself. You will still be fighting the consciousness of the world that seeks to prevent you from being who you are. But if you are no longer divided in yourself, oh how great a freedom that is.

What a liberation it is to overcome the division in your own being, in your own soul. And the only way to overcome that division is to realize that God's will is your will. Because if you think God's will is in opposition to your will, how could you ever make the free-will decision to enter the kingdom of God. And where is the kingdom of God? Ah, did not the Lord Christ say, "The kingdom of God is within you?" And so, how can you enter that inner kingdom if you think God's will is outside of, is in opposition to your own will?

It simply is not possible. And that is why a student on the path must first pass through the Office of the Chohan* of the Ray of God's Will. And then that student can move on to other rays and other masters.

What is true healing?

Mother Mary, March 27, 2005.

What does it mean to be healed?
And so I come today to ask you to consider what it means to be healed. What is true healing? You see, what has been explained to you over these past two days is the difference between the outer will, the human will, the will of the ego, and the Will of God. And how can you possibly understand healing, unless you have attunement with the Will of God? How can you know what should be done to bring about healing, what type of healing should occur – or if healing should occur – if you are not attuned to the will of God?

I can tell you that for many thousands of years, the karma and the darkness on Earth has been so heavy that many individual people have volunteered to take upon themselves a part of the weight of that karma. And for many of them, it has manifested in the form of mental or physical illness. And they have carried this in their bodies and in their minds, often for an entire lifetime. And it is truly the story of those who are willing to sacrifice, so that others may have an opportunity not to be so burdened by their karma and by the darkness that they could not possibly make any spiritual progress in that embodiment.

And so even though Jesus has carried a large portion of the sins of the world for these 2,000 years, there have still been many individuals who have taken upon themselves a part of the darkness to give other people an opportunity of a lifetime, where they were not so burdened in body and mind that they could not discover the spiritual side of life.

And so you must consider that for many people an illness, mental or physical, can be a labor of love. And so there is a possibility that the soul, at deeper levels, does not want to be healed of that illness or does not want to be healed just yet. And unless you are attuned to this in your own mind, how can you truly know? And thus, there is the possibility that you can seek to attain healing through unlawful means. This can be spiritually unlawful means, whereby someone else takes upon themselves the karma that you have volunteered to bear. Or it can be unlawful material means, whereby you use some form of modern medicine as a shortcut to either take away the pain or take away an illness that was meant to be borne.

And yet, there are other scenarios that come into play. For some people an illness is not caused by them carrying the karma of other people; it is caused by their own karma. So again, if they seek to pass it on to others, or if they seek to simply numb themselves to the pain, then that can be a form of dodging their responsibility.

Another common scenario that you see is that an illness is actually created by the lower mind, by the ego. And it is created to give the soul an excuse for not taking command over its own destiny, for not taking responsibility for itself. And thus the soul reasons that because I have this or that illness, I cannot rise and become the Christ, I cannot fulfill my divine plan, I cannot challenge the darkness and take a stand for Light.

And so there are some instances where the person wants to be healed, but from a deeper level, the healing should not occur. There are some instances where the soul does not want to be healed, but the healing should occur because otherwise the soul cannot grow.

So the key to knowing is to tune in to the will of God, and now we have attempted to explain to you, from different perspectives, that the most important concept that you can know about the will of God is that the will of God is not outside of yourself, is not separate from your own will—the higher will of your soul and I AM Presence. And thus you need to tune in to your own higher will and see what is God's will concerning any particular illness you have. And if you feel in your heart that the healing should occur, then you can use appropriate means.

But you also need to consider that any physical illness, any mental illness, is the expression of a particular state of consciousness. And in some cases that state of consciousness is created by your own ego, and it is your responsibility to take care of it, because truly it is something you have created from inside your own being. However, for many of you, who are open to the spiritual path, there is a different scenario that is very likely.

When you step back and look at planet Earth from a higher perspective, you see that there are many different forms and states of consciousness on this planet that are expressions of the human consciousness, aspects of the human consciousness. And each of those states of consciousness is the outpicturing in form of a particular lie that springs from the mind of anti-christ, the anti-mind.

And so you see that for each of these lies, there is a certain group of souls who have bought into that lie. They have believed that lie and absorbed it into their sense of identity. So they believe that because of this or that condition or expression, they cannot rise beyond a certain level, they cannot become the Christ in embodiment. They cannot be who they are in God here on Earth. And so these souls – once they accept this lie at the level of their identity bodies, their etheric bodies – there is no way that the soul can free itself by its own internal power.

The soul is trapped, the soul is trapped in the consciousness that Jesus called "Death." And so, how is that soul to be saved? Well, it can be saved only when God is willing to send one of his sons or daughters into the world, so that through that soul the world might be saved.

How souls can be saved

And how is the world saved? Well, it is saved when a true soul of light descends to this Earth and takes upon itself that particular state of consciousness. And then, by internalizing and expanding its connection to its Spiritual self, while it is in a body and overshadowed by the outer mind, the soul carves a trail through the jungle of ego-illusions. And it demonstrates that it is possible to take on a certain infirmity, a certain limitation, and rise above it through the mind of Christ and the mind of God.

And when another soul, who is still trapped, sees that a person from the same background, a person who had the same problems, can rise above those limitations, then that soul will often be awakened and say, "If he can do it, maybe I can do it."

And this is the principle of the great White Brotherhood, "What one has done, all can do," which really says that the only way to truly teach it to teach by example. And that is why Jesus Christ took embodiment. That is why I took embodiment as his mother in that lifetime. That is why many other Beings of Light, spiritual beings, have taken physical embodiment on Earth. They have done this to show that no matter what human condition or limitation a soul might be facing, it is possible to rise above it through the power of God within you.

You cannot give away what you do not own

Jesus, March 28, 2005.

The master key to healing
Yet how could you possible enter the kingdom of God when you feel anger against God? You do not want to come close to something that makes you feel anger or fear—you want to run away from it. So how can you enter the inner kingdom until you have resolved your anger, and how can you resolve the anger until you take ownership of that anger and see that it was something you created because you came to believe in one of the serpentine lies.

And now that you own it – now that you understand why – all of a sudden you can do something you could never do before. You can say, "This anger is mine. I take responsibility for it, and at this very moment, I own it fully."

And then you can say, "But I also realize that although I created the anger, the "I" that created the anger was the human ego, the human "I." But I am more than that human ego. I am an immortal soul, created by God in his image and likeness. And it was not my soul who created the anger, and thus I don't want the anger any more, I don't want it to be part of my being and my life experience."

And once you realize that the anger is separate from yourself – it is a thing you own and not a part of yourself – at that moment, you have the option to give it away. And instead of giving your anger, or rather trying to give away your anger, by taking it out on other people, you can give it to the one Being who will gladly take your anger. And that being is God, because God loves you and does not want to see you live a life burdened by anger or the effects of anger, such as mental and emotional and physical disease.

God wants you to be free of the anger, and God is an unlimited fire, an all-consuming fire, that can consume the anger in an instant. So God will gladly take it from you, but God gave you free will and will not take your anger until you give it to him. And you cannot give it to him until you take ownership, until you take possession, and you say, "This was created by a part of my being, and thus I accept accountability and responsibility. Yet it was created by a part of my being that is not my true self. Thus, neither my ego nor the anger created by the ego is part of my higher being. And I will no longer identify with the ego or with the anger, I will separate myself out from it. I will come apart and be a separate and chosen people, elect unto God because I have chosen to separate myself from the consciousness of death."

And when you do this, then you can take the anger and you can turn to God [the God in the kingdom within you] and say, "Oh Lord, I offer this to you, please take it from me." And if you can fully let go, it will be taken. And as the cycles turn in the material universe, even a physical condition that is the result of anger will be taken from you.

...

And so you see, there is a very subtle difference between identifying with a condition with the outer mind and stepping outside of that condition and taking ownership by realizing that, yes, you did create that condition or you did take it on, but the condition itself is the expression of a state of consciousness and that state of consciousness was not created by your soul. It was created by your ego and by the forces of this world, including the egos of other people.

Be not divided against yourself
And so, again, many souls, who volunteered to take on a condition to balance a certain amount of world karma, will get stuck in carrying that condition far beyond the point that is necessary, far beyond the point where they have actually balanced that portion of world karma and are now free to focus on the positive aspects of their divine plan, which is to bring their gifts to this world.

A soul has two purposes for taking embodiment. One is to carry the cross, one is to bring its gift. And spiritual souls often choose to take on the cross first, and once they have conquered that task, they are then free to be whole in bringing their gift. But if they are tricked into rebelling against carrying their cross, and if they are not willing to let their human ego and their attachments die on that cross, then the soul will be stuck. And this is what happened to Peter—that he recognized the Christ, but he was not willing to fully identify with me, even to the point where he was willing to be crucified next to me if that was God's plan.

And so the key to moving out of this impasse is to learn from my example, where you saw me in the Garden of Gethsemane the night before my trial and crucifixion. And again, the serpents of this world have created the false image of Jesus Christ that makes it impossible for most people to identify with me. And thus they tend to gloss over the fact that, while I was in that garden, I was deeply disturbed and deeply distraught.

I cried tears of blood. I was suffering, as so many other people are suffering, by carrying the burden that I was carrying, by carrying my cross, and by the thought of what would happen next. And I was so burdened by this that even though my soul had volunteered to come into that situation, I still asked God to take that cup away from me. And this will show you that Jesus Christ was indeed human like yourself and not some God and not some superhuman, for whom the path was easy.

The path was not easy for me. I was as frustrated and distraught that evening as any human being has ever been frustrated. And yet the inspiration you can take away from this is that I eventually came to the point, where I took ownership of my situation. I decided that I was willing to let God's will be done, and not the lower will of the outer mind. And so I surrendered myself to God and said, "Nevertheless Father, not my will but thine be done." Yet I could not have surrendered myself to God unless I had taken ownership of my situation, unless I had taken ownership to the point where, if I had had to keep the condition forever, I would have been at peace with that.

Be willing to carry your cross
And so if you have a condition in your life, be it an outer condition, be it a mental, emotional condition or be it a physical ailment, you need to come to the point of inner peace and surrender to the higher will of your own being, your own soul and I AM presence, where you are willing to say, "God, if I have to carry this for the rest of my life, I will not only be at peace with that, but I will take the situation and make the best of it because I will love that condition. And I will approach it with love, so that even if I have to carry that condition, I will not use it as a reason to turn off the flow of God's love through me. And I will let that love flow, come what may in this world."

And when you come to that point of total ownership, at that point you can surrender yourself fully to God. And at that point, you might indeed get an inner direction of how you can actually balance the karma you are carrying in a different way than through the limitation you are facing. It might be through rosaries, it might be through service, it might be through the resolution of psychology, whereby you not only resolve your own psychology but help resolve the mass consciousness, the collective unconscious of humankind, making it easier for your brothers and sisters to overcome the same condition.

And so, once you come to that point of total surrender that does not spring from fear or the desire to get away from the condition, but it springs from total acceptance of the condition that can only come from love—once you come to that point, you are setting yourself free to flow with the will of God, the higher will of your I AM Presence and soul, for your present embodiment. And at that moment, you will no longer be at an impasse.

You will be back in the flow of life, and you will feel like a burden has been lifted from your shoulders. Because even if the condition remains, you will no longer be as burdened by it, you will be free to be the loving soul that you are, to feel the fulfillment, even the fulfillment of carrying that condition because you know you are giving someone else the opportunity to rise higher and come closer to God.

Transcend time and space!

Mother Mary, May 2, 2005

Recognize those with no light of their own

Oh my beloved, so many people come to the spiritual path and come to spiritual organizations with a desire to have their egos pampered, to be praised, to be recognized, to stand out from the crowd and feel that they are somehow better than others because they are members of a particular religion or organization, because they follow a particular teaching or guru and because they do this or do that.

My beloved hearts, we have seen these ego games played over and over again for millions of years—millions of years, I tell you. We have seen millions of people awaken, for a brief moment, to the spiritual side of life, find a spiritual teaching, start to apply that teaching, and then gradually, without even noticing it, they get caught in the age-old ego games. And they use that spiritual teaching to prop up their egos, their sense of pride, their sense of being the favorite sons, the chosen people.

Oh my beloved, we have had enough of those ego games. And I know that those of you who have been willing to give these last rosary vigils have also had enough of those ego games. And therefore, it is time and high time that some people on Earth choose to set an example for all people to see that it is possible for everyone to rise above the human ego, to be free of the lies promoted by the forces of this world and to simply BE who they are as God-free beings. It is time that someone demonstrate that one can be the sun shining from within themselves, instead of seeking some kind of recognition from the world, thinking that they need something from the world in order to shine their light.

Oh my beloved, there are indeed many people on the Earth who need something from the world in order to shine light because they have no light of their own. They are empty shells. And many of the so-called high and mighty on the Earth, many of the politicians, the business people, and even many of the artists and thinkers, those who are recognized by the society as celebrities, many of these people have no light of their own. But they have learned a skill that is taught to them by the father of lies and his henchmen, and that is to be a mirror that mirrors back the light of those who follow them.

You see my beloved, there are many people on Earth who are truly the sons and daughters of God that have come into embodiment to set this planet free. And they know deep within their souls the importance of being obedient to the higher will. This is truly the higher will of God, the higher will of their own I AM Presence, the higher will of the masculine aspect of their beings, to which the soul must be obedient and aligned in order to be whole and to be nurtured and to fulfill its reason for being in this world.

Yet when the soul forgets why it is here, forgets its reason for being, its divine plan or even its knowledge that it is a spiritual being, then the soul does not know what true obedience means. It knows it needs to be obedient to something higher, but it does not know to what it needs to be obedient. And so it tends to look for some leader in this world that it can follow. And the false leaders know this, and so they set themselves up and claim to have some authority, or some skill, or some importance, and then the sons and daughters of God, who accept this person as being of importance, send that person their light. And the person then uses that light to mirror it back to the world and prop up the false image of their self-importance.

And you see this so many times, so many times over and over again by the important people, the so-called important people, of this world. And you find them everywhere, even in spiritual organizations, where they set themselves up as leaders for the glorification of their egos and not for the glorification of the I AM Presence and the God behind the I AM Presence.

Truly, God has no need to be worshipped as Jesus has explained. Yet God allows people to worship him because God is beyond the ego and will therefore not misuse the light sent in worship. And in worshipping God, people will at least not worship an idol on Earth, and so that is better than worshipping a false idol down here. And hopefully people can then transcend the need to worship anything outside themselves and come to the recognition, as Jesus told you, that the kingdom of God is within you and that you need nothing from this world in order to be whole in order to be fully nurtured.

Taking command over the four lower bodies

And yet what is the key to going through the process of coming up higher? Well it must begin with the acceptance, by taking ownership, of your situation. And when you have taken ownership, you can say, "I accept this situation as the result of my past choices. And in that acceptance I also declare that I know that when I change those choices, when I replace my past choices with enlightened choices, then my situation will change."

And then you can start focusing your attention on the process of changing your consciousness and making better choices rather than focusing on the outer situation and the unfairness of that situation, which only keeps you trapped in a lower state of consciousness, a sense of being a victim, a sense of being paralyzed and being unable to do anything about your situation.

And when you have overcome that sense of being a victim, of being paralyzed, then you can begin to realign yourself with the totality of your greater being. And the first step in that process is to realize that there is a will that is greater than the outer will of the ego and the outer will of the forces of this world, even the people around you. And that will is the will of your I AM Presence, which is the will of God individualized for you. And that was what we had you do in the vigil of the Rosary to God's Will. You realigned yourself with the higher will. And in realigning yourself with the higher will, you cleared your etheric body. And as Jesus has explained, you have four bodies and the highest of those lower bodies is the etheric body which holds your sense of identity.

And so by realigning yourself with the truth that you are a spiritual being, no matter how mortal or human you might seem, you have taken the first step on your road back to inheriting God's kingdom. For truly God's kingdom cannot come from below; it must come from Above—from a higher vibration. All good things are from Above, and as Jesus has explained, all good things must cycle through the four levels of the matter universe and that is why you start at the top. You cannot inherit God's kingdom by starting from the bottom and work your way back up. You need to start from the top and let the light of God descend because it is the light that will transform you, not the lower will, not the lower energies of this world.

And so the next step is to go within the next body, the mental body and clear that mental body of the illusions, the ego-illusions and the illusions of antichrist. And this is what you did in the Rosary of All-pervading Wisdom. And so after that comes the third step, which is to clear the emotional body, and the emotional body is the body that makes you feel nurtured or makes you feel that you are deprived, that you are caught in lack, limitations, suffering, and pain. It might make you feel that you are unjustly dealt a difficult hand by life, that you are unfairly treated by God who is withholding his abundance from you while giving it to others.

This is the Cain consciousness of being jealous of those who have more in this world, even though many of those who have the most in this world have very little in the spiritual world and thus they have nothing of real value. They have no treasure laid up in Heaven because they have chosen to have their reward on Earth.

And so you see, my beloved, the emotions are like water and you know how the water of the ocean is easily whipped into waves that are chaotic, and so is the emotional body of man. The key to realigning that emotional body with the reality of God is that it must be under the control of the mental body, specifically the mind of Christ focused in that mental body. You might see the emotional body as a child and you are the parent, and through the mental body, the higher reasoning of the Christ mind, you can make the child understand that it needs to behave in certain ways in order to be rewarded. And if that it does not behave in those ways, it will be punished, it will not receive the reward.

...

The truth about faith

And now, my beloved, I would like to speak to you on a topic that is extremely important in terms of accepting God's nurturance. You have all heard about the concept of faith as it has been promoted by so many religions, but especially the orthodox Christian religions. You have all read in the Bible that faith is the substance of things hoped for, the evidence of things not seen (Hebrews 11:1). But my beloved, what you do not always realize is that even this particular Bible quote is a distortion of the true teachings of Christ.

Jesus did not teach that faith is the substance of things hoped for. He taught that knowledge is the substance of things hoped for. And with knowledge he did not mean outer, intellectual knowledge. He meant inner knowledge, gnosis, the true inner gnosis whereby the knower becomes one with the known. Jesus did not teach that you should pray to an external God and then simply believe the answer would be forthcoming. And if your prayer is not answered, you should just keep believing indefinitely, as if those who keep believing will eventually be saved.

Jesus taught and demonstrated that you invoke God's assistance from within yourself, and you do so with the absolute inner knowing that when you ask, you WILL receive. And thus, if your prayer is not answered, you can reason that you did not have the true inner knowing. Perhaps you had faith, but not yet the full knowing that is the highest aspect of faith. So instead of simply keeping on believing, you can go to work on yourself, on resolving the blocks that prevent you from having the inner knowing – the absolute certainty – that comes through oneness with your Christ self. And so you see, many Christians have completely misunderstood Jesus' teaching on faith, and they have instead accepted the teachings of anti-christ that keep them suspended in a state of outer faith that blocks their inner knowing, their true Gnosis.

And this is a most essential key to inheriting your Father's kingdom. You see, my beloved, most religious people have also been brought up to believe in a completely false teaching concerning prayer, concerning invoking something from above, concerning invoking God's assistance in their lives. They have been taught a serpentine lie that springs from the mind of antichrist, namely that prayer is invoking a miracle. And sometimes the miracle happens, but most of the time it does not happen. And there is no way to know when it will happen and when it will not happen, because it is all a mystery that is decided by God. But you see, my beloved, this is a complete fallacy because God does not sit up in Heaven and arbitrarily decide to give one person a miracle and to withhold it from another.

It is the Father's good pleasure to give you the kingdom. It is the Father's good pleasure to give his kingdom to all of his children. But to inherit that kingdom, you must realign yourself with the reality of God. And you cannot do that through outer knowledge, through intellectual knowledge, through outer faith or through blind adherence to some ritual. You can do that only by going within. You can do it only through gnosis, whereby you transcend belief, you transcend faith, and you come to the inner knowing that when you invoke God's intercession, God's Presence, in your life, your call WILL compel the answer.

Ask and ye shall receive. Because truly it is the Father's good pleasure to give you the kingdom.

Ask, and it shall be given you; seek, and ye shall find; knock, and it shall be opened unto you: (Matthew 7:7)

But you see, my beloved, there are two things you need to know. First of all, you need to know that when you ask, your desire cannot spring from the lower desire of your ego or the desires that have been put upon you from your culture and the forces of this world. These lower desires are self-centered and they disregard the whole. And precisely because God wants ALL of his children to inherit the kingdom, he cannot answer a prayer that seeks the abundance of one person by depriving the whole. Thus, when you pray from a selfish desire, you create a counter-force that opposes the fulfillment of your desire. In a sense the entire universe will oppose the fulfillment of your desire. And if you seek to take something by force, the counter force you create will take from you what you seek to possess. As Jesus said,

For unto every one that hath shall be given, and he shall have abundance: but from him that hath not shall be taken away even that which he hath. (Matthew 25:29)

Unto everyone who has love and regard for the whole shall be given and he or she shall have abundance. Yet to him who has no love, everything shall be taken away by the very counter force he creates in seeking to fulfill his ego-centered desires. So in order to truly ask, you must realign your desires, your desire body, with the higher desires of your soul, that are part of your divine plan, and with the higher will of your I AM Presence, that is one with the will of God for your lifestream.

And when you are in that state of alignment, then the answer to any prayer will be given because the entire universe will gladly assist in fulfilling your divine plan. The reason being that your personal divine plan is in alignment with the greater plan of God, and thus what is best for you is also what is best for the whole of God's creation.

Victory Is All That Is Real

Presence of Victory, July 3, 2005

Let the Living Christ call you
Truly, study how Jesus called his disciples. Imagine yourself going about your business in your daily life, and suddenly a person comes up to you with intense, burning eyes and says, "Leave your nets and follow me!" And then he turns around and walks away without looking back.

When you are at a plateau, where you need to step up to a higher level, then – in some form or another – the teacher will come to you, be it within or without, perhaps as a person, perhaps as a book, perhaps as a voice in your head that you know is the true voice. And that teacher will say, "Leave your nets and follow me!" And that is all he will say. Not necessarily in those exact words but he will give you a clear instruction that cannot be misunderstood or misinterpreted.

And so the question is, "What are you going to do?" Are you going to follow the teacher, even though you do not know where the path leads you? Or are you going to cling to what is familiar and ask for guarantees or time to prepare. You see, the eternal motto of the Ascended Host is that when the student is ready, the teacher appears. So when that situation does happen to you, you are ready at inner levels. Your ego, of course, is not ready – and doesn't think you are ready – and will come up with a million excuses of why you are not ready and why you should not follow this person, or this teacher or this voice inside of you.

Yet I must tell you that when Jesus called his disciples, he did call more than 12 disciples. And not all of them heeded the call. But those who did heed the call did so because they instantly followed Christ. They did not think, they did not plan, they did not prepare, they did not look back. They simply dropped their nets and they followed Jesus.

There will come a point, where you will need to do this to step up to a higher level. This messenger, many years ago, had a discussion with a minister in a Lutheran church. And this very topic of how Jesus called his disciples was brought up. And the minister, who supposedly represented Christ, said, "Oh, I am sure the disciples had a long time to prepare to follow Jesus. They had at least a year to get their things in order." And this shows you the state of consciousness of orthodox Christianity today.

They have taken out the essence of the guru-chela, the master-disciple, relationship. They have put Jesus on a pedestal. And in order to do so, they have also elevated his disciples, so that they could follow Christ directly, but you cannot—because you are miserable sinner, so you need to follow the outer church instead of following the Living Christ.

You must love something more than you love the ego
And how can you make that decision, when you are so involved with your lives and the things of the world and your former consciousness? You can do so only when you love something more than what you are giving up. That is why so many people get stuck at a certain level of the spiritual path.

And I must tell you, that when I survey planet Earth today, I see millions of earnest spiritual seekers who are following this or that organization or guru or this or that teaching. They are sincere, they are earnest, they are following what is not a false teaching but is not the ultimate teaching either. Because the teaching does not directly teach that there does come a point where you must transcend, you must go beyond what you thought was enough.

This is the essence of self-transcendence. You see, my beloved hearts, when we give you any concept related to spiritual growth, or salvation, or Christhood – any concept we give you – the duality consciousness, the serpentine mind, will immediately start twisting that concept. And it will set up an idol, saying, "As long as I do this and this and this, I will be saved, I will become the Christ, I will make whatever goal has been defined."

Yet the true goal of all spiritual seekers is to continue to self-transcend. The consciousness of antichrist would prefer to have all people on Earth remain completely ignorant of the path of self-transcendence. But for those that they cannot keep in ignorance about the path, they attempt the next best thing—that is to make them follow the way that seems right unto a man, but the ends thereof are the ways of death.

And the path that seems right unto a man is simply this, "There must come a point where I am saved, where I am the Christ, where I am perfect, where I am immortal. And then I will be home free, and I can sit down and relax and I no longer need to grow and transcend."

This is the dream of the carnal mind, that some kind of plateau is reached and from then on no more growth is possible, no more self-transcendence is needed. This is what the false teachers will tell you over and over and over again. "We have the truth. Our church is the only one. As long as you are a member of this church, you will be saved, you are home free. Don't challenge your ego. Don't transcend yourself. Don't let go of the past. Just be comfortable. You are saved. You have it made."

There are millions of versions of this lie, and they all do the same thing. They seek to lull people into the state of consciousness, where they think they don't need to transcend themselves and come up higher. They don't need to take that big step forward that brings them to an entirely new level that they could hardly even envision before.

I am here to challenge the momentum of anti-victory

This is the anti-victory that has been rampant on this Earth for thousands of years, and I am here to challenge it. And I – because I love you – will start by challenging it in you.

Whatever you think is enough, I serve you notice this moment, "It is not enough!" Because what is required of you is ongoing, perpetual self-transcendence. Do you think it would be right for a river to say, "I have flowed along long enough, I am going to stop right here." Nay, because at that moment, the river would die, because the river is the ever-moving stream.

And thus, you are created as the offspring of God. You were created to be a co-creator with God and take part in the ever-flowing River of Life that is God's creation, for in God's creation nothing is stationary. All is moving and transcending and even God itself, the Creator itself, is transcending all the time. And thus if you are part of that river of life, you are transcending. You never stop. You never become attached. You never say, "I have done enough."

This, however, does not mean that you come from fear or a sense of lack or a sense that you are not good enough or that nothing you do is good enough. The entire shift in consciousness that you need to make is the shift that because life is an ongoing process of self-transcendence, there is no ultimate goal that will stop the self-transcendence. And when you fully accept this one fact, you realize that there is no point in feeling that you are not worthy because you have not reached the ultimate level that isn't there.

Allow yourself to feel the victory
Do you see my point? You can go on for eternity, feeling you are not there and you are not worthy. And you will be chasing that carrot because you will never, ever, catch up to the ultimate. So, the change is simple. Allow yourself to know that the path is an ongoing process of self-transcendence. And each time you transcend yourself, you have touched the hem of Christ's garment. You have touched the hem of the garment of the Presence of Victory that I AM.

And you should allow yourself to feel that joy of the Lord, of having come up higher. And as you begin to make this shift in consciousness, you will sense God's unconditional love. And there is no greater love than the love of a spiritual teacher, who sees the student take that very next step and leave behind the old state of consciousness. That is the greatest love you will experience. And when you begin to experience that love, there will come a point, where you suddenly look at your life, and you look at planet Earth and you say, "There is nothing in this world that compares with the love I feel for my God, for my teacher. Thus, there is nothing in this world that I would rather have than the unconditional love of God."

And thus, you become willing to give up anything in this world to experience that love. And that is when the path ceases to be a struggle, and it becomes a joyful walk. It ceases to be the Via Dolorosa that the churches have again set up as an idol, thinking they should focus on the suffering of Christ.

Suffering is not necessary
Their mistake is to think that the suffering was necessary. Yet the suffering only comes from an attachment. Something that makes you attached, so that you cannot let go of the former self and take that giant leap to the next plateau. For truly, to let go you must be willing to let your former sense of self die. And if you will look at Jesus' life without the glasses of idolatry, you will see that he faced the exact same decisions that you will face.

And even when he was hanging on the cross, he was faced with a decision. And in his mind, he had an expectation of what should happen, and suddenly he realized that that expectation would not be fulfilled, because God would not come and save him. And at that moment Jesus realized that he would have to die on the cross. And for some brief moments, even Jesus hung on to the physical life. And then, finally, he surrendered, and he gave up the ghost of his former expectation. He let his body die on the cross, as a symbol for letting a part of your ego die on the cross. And because he was willing to let the former state die, he was reborn into the resurrection, that is the eternal life.

This is the process you must follow when you realize that Jesus was the example, the wayshower, and not the idol to be worshiped. And I can assure you, that the decisions you face will be no more or no less difficult than the decisions faced by Jesus. So many think it was easy for him. But if you read the scriptures carefully, you will see that it was far from easy. And you can take some comfort in that, and realize that it is a difficult decision, but that it can be done.

And you can even take some comfort in saying, "But I can learn from Jesus' example. I can learn that if I can tune in to the love from Above, then I do not have to feel attached to the former. I can let it die without resistance, without a struggle." And the less attachment you feel, the more willing you are to come to that point of saying, "I recognize I have come to a turning point where I need to rise higher, and I need to let go of this old self."

Welcome the big decisions

When you recognize this consciously, and have the momentum of love, you can let it go without the suffering, the pain, the going back and forth, the arguing with yourself, reasoning whether you should do this or that. Instead, it just drops from you.

You keep your eye on Christ, and you follow Christ. And before you know it, you look back and you say, "But that wasn't such a big decision—why did it seem so hard at the time?" And when you have done this a number of times, you build the momentum of victory. And now you see the decision coming. You welcome it instead of resisting it. And because you are not resisting it, you do what Jesus said at Easter—you own it.

You own the condition that you need to surrender. And when you fully own it, and are no longer resisting it, then you can let it go with ease. And it drops as the scales fall from the eyes of those who are blind.

It drops away, and you see the new day. And suddenly, you are spiritually reborn into a new sense of self. And did not Jesus tell Nicodemus that unless a man is reborn, he cannot enter the kingdom of Heaven (John 3:1). And this truly is a spiritual rebirth, and not the physical rebirth that Nicodemus – as a symbol for the human consciousness – could envision.

Let it go! Let it drop. Learn to recognize when it is time to take a major leap forward on your path—and then take it with joy. Welcome it. Anticipate it. See it as the doorway to a greater freedom, the freedom of a new sense of self as a co-creator with God, basking in the Light of the God of Freedom for the Earth—Saint Germain. Basking in the radiance of the love of Jesus, who is your forerunner on the path. And basking in the warm glow of the love of Mary, who is there to congratulate you any time you take that step higher. And I, too, will greet you when you make those important decisions. And I will respectfully let Mary get there first . . . for I know that my time will come.

I call the Guardians of the Mother Light!

Saint Germain, July 4, 2005.

Where are those who are willing to let go of the ego?
And thus, when this messenger first heard me speak, in 1985, I was on the European continent. And I had to say that too many came to our activity, to the feet of the masters, to have their egos pampered. They wanted a feel-good message that they were the most important people on the planet and they were saving the planet for Saint Germain. Yet how can the human ego save the planet, when it is the human ego that has brought the planet to where it is today?

Who would be chelas of Saint Germain?
Because I come with a message that those who would apply to be chelas of Saint Germain had better first make peace with the Lord Christ and

with Jesus himself. And what is the essence of Christhood? It is that you overcome the serpentine mind, the mind of the fallen angels, which is based on pride.

There are those in the New Age community and elsewhere who claim to be spiritual leaders or gurus or messengers or channelers, and they claim to be channeling Saint Germain or other masters. Yet they have not made peace with Christ. They have not let go of the ego. They have not been willing to humble themselves. And you will see those out there who try to build themselves up because they have done or this or that important thing in this lifetime or they were this or that important person in a past lifetime.

But truly, if you will to be a chela of Saint Germain and be a torchbearer, a lightbearer a forerunner for the Age of Aquarius, then the one essential feature you must have is humility. Because I tell you, the Age of Freedom cannot come about unless people are willing to be free from their egos. And thus I tell you that the gatekeepers to the door of the City Foursquare will not tolerate the human ego. You will not enter that City Foursquare as long as you carry around the ego and seek to enter the City in order to have the ego glorified.

And therefore, I can guarantee you that if you come to me and apply to be my chela or to help me save the planet, I will say, "Go first to the Lord Christ and let him pummel you, and then – when you have gotten rid of your ego – come back and we will talk."

I am a stern master because I have seen in past ages how a Golden Age civilization can deteriorate within a few generations because the human ego is allowed to run rampant. And I am determined that in the Aquarian Age we will not have a Golden Age civilization that deteriorates in a few decades. We will have the Kingdom of God permanently anchored on Earth. And that can only happen when you, who are willing to be our hands and feet, are also willing to let go of your egos and when you don't seek to have those egos pampered so that you can feel more important than others.

We offer the path of humility

Let us live to make men free. Do you think that I am here to glorify myself? Do you think I am here to set myself up as some kind of king, as some kind of idol, who will be idolized as Jesus has been idolized by the false preachers of Christianity for 2,000 years?

Nay, I am not here to put myself up, I am not here to elevate myself above anyone. I am here to help everyone see the God within, the Christ within themselves, so they can see that there is no one that is more important than others, for God loves all. Even though people have been created to play different roles in the drama of life, it does not mean that they are more valuable. Being God's chosen people means that you are chosen for a specific mission, and as long as you fulfill that mission all is well and you are multiplying the talents given. Yet, if you – through pride – begin to think that other people should serve you, then you have lost the thread of contact to your Lord.

And then, the only way back – once you have fallen into pride – the only way back is through complete and utter humility. And that is why we prescribe for all who would be students of the Ascended Host the path of humility.

It does not matter where you came from, whether you fell from Above or whether you fell from below. The past is not important. What is important is where you are willing to go. Are you willing to be pummeled? Are you willing to humble yourselves? And thus I say to you, "In the Aquarian Age, those who are considered greatest in the eyes of God are those who have the greatest humility because they have the least ego. They have the least pride."

Do not seek to be great in the eyes of men if you would be great in the eyes of God. Seek instead the complete humility, where you realize that you are not here to glorify your individual self because you are more than that individual self. You are a part of the Body of God on Earth, and only when the entire Body of God is raised up, do you have the fulfillment for which you came. You did not come here to glorify the ego, you came here to glorify God as the All that is in all.

Form a nucleus for world change

El Morya, July 4, 2005.

Therefore, the most important concept you can take with you about the spiritual path is that you will not be given a clear vision of where you are going. If you knew the destination before you started the journey, what would you possibly learn from the journey? The important point in life is not the destination but what you learn as you walk the path, making decisions to the best of your ability, learning from all of your decisions. Whether they be considered right or wrong from an outer human perspective matters not. What matters is that you learn and that you use that decision, no matter how it turned out, to say, "Ah, but now I know how to take the next step, now I can come up higher."

And thus, no decision is truly wasted, no decision is truly a mistake—as long as you are willing to take that next step on the path. And of course, the essence of the human ego is that it will try to manipulate you, so that you do not take that next step. The essence of the false hierarchy of the fallen angels is that they will try to prevent you from taking that next step closer to God, so that you are stopped in your tracks where you are. And they have devised many cleaver schemes to create this illusion that you cannot or that you are not allowed to, or that you do not need to, take that next step and come closer to God.

Who are the seed of Abraham?

Yet I know that you will be the ones who will see through and expose these illusions in yourselves. And how do I know this? Well, first of all because I have known your lifestreams for a very long time. You are indeed the seed of Abraham. And you are indeed my own.

How can I say this in such a general statement? Well, for those of you who are here, I can say that you would not be here had you not been the seed of Abraham. And for those who are not here, I can say, as did Jesus, "Those who hear the Word of God and do it, these are my brothers and sisters—these are the seed of Abraham." Those who reach for the Will of God within their own beings and manifest that will on Earth, these are the seeds of Abraham.

I also know it because I can assure you that I paced up and down this room as you were having your ego discussions this afternoon. And I walked with a smile and a chuckle, not because I was laughing at you, but because I was laughing with joy because I cannot remember the last time I have seen a group of people so dedicated – so willing – to exposing the ego – even the ego in themselves – and then making light of it, making fun of it, and laughing that ego out the door because it simply could not stand being mocked and made a fool of.

This is indeed the key that we would like to see you use. Don't make it such a heavy thing to get rid of the ego. Make it light. Make it fun. Make it joy. Simply laugh that ego out the door. Just let it roll out that door. Stop taking it seriously. Stop taking yourself seriously.

If it isn't fun, what's the point?

The joy of letting go of the ego

This is the joy that you can have on Earth. This is the joy that you can have by coming to the point of letting go of the ego, so that you can achieve what you all achieved this afternoon, of talking about the ego without being attached to it.

My beloved hearts, we have seen many previous organizations that we have sponsored, where those who came to the organization paraded themselves as very serious and very stout and very astute chelas. And in many ways they were astute. I do give them credit for their efforts, I do honor them for their efforts. But I must tell you that when it came right down to it, many of them were completely unwilling to look in the mirror and look their own ego straight in the eye and say, "You are not part of me, and I will no longer have you in my sphere of self."

Instead, they would be reluctant to admit that they even had an ego, thinking, that when they were sitting at the feet of the Ascended Masters, receiving these elevated teachings, they surely must have been advanced students. But ah, as Saint Germain said this afternoon, that is not necessarily the case.

Those who are led to believe they are God's chosen people might indeed be given this belief as a test of humility. Will they take that into pride and continue the momentums of pride—that they have had for tens of thousands of years. Or will they finally bend the knee in humility and say, "No, I am the one who has to change. I am the one who has to admit that I have something in me that is unreal and that I need to let go of—rather than protect it and cuddle it and hide it and try to pretend like it isn't there, like it will probably go away if I ignore it long enough."

That, of course, will get you nowhere. And I have seen this so many times. You will not believe how many times I have seen people walk into an Ascended Master organization, or any other spiritual organization, and they will be confronted with one little thing that insults their ego, or otherwise goes against their expectations, and suddenly they will leave in a huff. And I have seen them also stay, and stay and stay and do all the outer things right, yet they never seem to change. And the reason they do not change is that they are not willing to admit that they have to look inside themselves. They have to take a hard look and discover the ego.

The ego is unique for each person, and that is why your own ego is the hardest one to see—for you

For truly, I must tell you, even though I commend you for exposing the different levels of the ego and the characteristics of the ego – and of course there is an almost infinite variety of them – it is one thing to know the ego on a theoretical level. It is another thing to see it in people in practical situations. And it is another thing still to see it in yourself.

This is not something that can be put into a teaching system and taught, for each person is slightly different. Each person has a slightly different way of looking at life. And thus, what is the characteristics of your personal ego will be a little bit different than the characteristics of the ego of your brother and sister. And so we cannot simply come out and give you a book that defines every characteristic of the human ego, and if you read that book you will automatically see your ego.

We can give you some general guidelines, as we will surely do. But there comes a point, where you have to take that general guideline and apply it, turn it around, somehow step outside of yourself – outside of that prison cell of the ego – and look at it from the outside and say, "Aha, now I see where you are hiding! Now I see how you have been hiding all of these years, all of these embodiments, behind this illusion that is not real at all. And now that you are exposed, I will let Michael come and take you to a place where you can be gone. For I have no more need of you! I will invoke the violet flame to clean you up and clean you out the door."

These are the ones – the people who are willing to do this – these are the ones who can be Guardians of the Mother Light. For truly, it is only the ego that has perverted the Mother Light. You may say that it is the fallen angels who have been instrumental in perverting the Mother Light on Earth. And this is partially true, but only partially, for remember the statement in Genesis, "God created man in his own image and likeness" (Genesis 1:26). And then he said, "Multiply and take dominion over the Earth" (Genesis 1:28).

Take dominion over the Earth

You see, my beloved, God did not give dominion over the Earth to the fallen angels; he gave dominion over the Earth to the sons and daughters of God. And thus, the fallen angels cannot come down here and corrupt Mother Earth and the Mother Light. They can do so only indirectly through the sons and daughters of God, whom they manage to trick into creating an ego, which then takes the Mother Light into an imperfect matrix. You see, my beloved, if the fallen angels had had the power to pervert this planet, then this planet would long ago have self-destructed and disintegrated in the fires of hell.

They must work indirectly through the sons and daughters, as we Above in the Ascended Host, must work indirectly by inspiring you to come up higher and realign yourself with the Will of God. This is the key equation that you need to understand on Earth.

The dark forces do not have the amount of power that some people ascribe to them. They have no more power than what you give to them. And therefore, when you uncover the ego and dismiss that ego, you will stop giving them power. And as their power quickly burns out and diminishes, they will be removed from the Earth. Because she will start spinning faster on her axis, and she will spin them off, for they no longer have the power to hold on.

That is the day that is not as far away as you might think. And from that moment on, you will hear almost the sound of water splashing on hot rocks and being consumed, being turned into steam and sizzling away. And that is indeed the fallen ones being spun off this planet so fast that you will not believe the changes that can happen when it finally breaks and they are starting to spin off at a faster and faster pace. Because you are raising your vibration and thereby raising the Mother Light up, until she finally reunites with the Father, with the Buddha in the crown, and outpictures that perfect lotus blossom, that perfect balance of Alpha and Omega, as Above, so below, that cannot be corrupted. And therefore, the Earth is sealed in the immaculate concept.

Hypocrites need not apply!

Jesus, July 5, 2005.

The ego has no power over you once you see it for what it is

I am here to stay with you, and what I offer is that I will be the one who will initiate anyone who is willing to let go of their egos. Anyone who is willing to have it exposed, so that they can see it for what it is, and thereby separate themselves, separate that Conscious You, out from that prison of the ego.

So many Christians think I am a soft master. Yet I am a direct master. I do not play games, and I will not play games with anyone who comes to this movement. For if you are not willing to let go of the ego, you are free to go elsewhere, where they will pamper your ego, rather than help you separate yourself from it.

Yet in saying I am a direct master, I am not saying I am an unloving master. And it is important that you contemplate the difference, because, truly, my love is the perfect love that casts out all fear. And I am fully aware that many people are afraid of having their egos exposed, fearing what will happen when they can no longer hide behind this or that cleaver argument, that was formulated in the mind of the Serpent who deceived the evolutions of this planet.

Stop tiptoeing around the ego!

So many of our former students have tiptoed around the topic of the ego, even though we have spoken about it in several previous dispensations. They have been afraid that if their ego was to be exposed, they would go through some kind of crisis, they would lose their sense of self-worth or in other ways experience an identity crisis.

Therefore, you need to simply switch your sense of identity just a little bit. You need to start asking yourself, "Knowing what I know about the spiritual path and the goal of freedom in the Christ consciousness, the goal of experiencing that greater freedom of being above and beyond the ego—knowing what I know, is there really any part of my ego that I would not be willing to give up, if I could see it?"

And I think when you meditate on this, you will see in your hearts that there is indeed nothing that you would not be willing to give up in order to come closer to the love of God, in order to be who you are and express who you are. And so my beloved, when you come to that realization, you no longer need to fear the ego or fear having the ego exposed.

You no longer need to fear making a mistake, for whether you make a mistake or not, either way it can expose part of your ego and help you overcome it. The ego has no power over you whatsoever. It only has the power that you have not seen it, or seen it for the illusion that it is, and therefore you cannot separate yourself from it. And the moment you see it, and the moment you choose to separate yourself from it, it has no power over you and you can walk right through it. And when you begin to realize that, you see that the path of overcoming the ego is not a hard path. It is not a path of fear, it is not a path of embarrassment, it is not a path of feeling like you are a failure or you were not good enough because you had this or that aspect of the ego left.

You are far more than the ego. And I will remind you over and over again that you are more, as we have done in this and previous retreats. You are so much more, and that is what we love. And when you realize how much more you are, it is no problem to let go of the ego.

Yet the essence of the ego is precisely that—that you either cannot see it or that you are not willing to let go of it. The ego is always trying to remain hidden. The ego is always trying to tell you that you cannot take that next step on the path, you cannot walk out the prison door. And then, when you realize that you can move forward on the path, the ego is trying to make you think that you don't want to or that you are not allowed to.

The ego prevents you from taking the next step
So the essence of the ego really is that the ego is what prevents you from taking the next step closer to God. Truly, the ego has many qualities. But the essence of the ego is, that it is that which prevents you from taking the next step on your path. And when you begin to realize that – and realize that the greater part of your being has an uncompromising commitment to taking that next step – then why would you fear the ego? Why would you fear to have it exposed? You would welcome having it exposed, because now you can say, "Ah, I see it. And now I can let it go."

As I said to you at Easter, the key to overcoming and walking the path is that you must give away all that is unreal. You must surrender it, you must let it go. But you cannot let it go, you cannot give it away, until you own it, until you take ownership of it. So, we can say that the ego will first of all try to prevent you from taking ownership of that part of the ego, prevent you from seeing it or prevent you from admitting, "Yes, that part of the human ego is still residing in my container of self." And then, if you do see it, it will try to prevent you from letting it go by making you think that you somehow need it.

And this is the key—to come to that realization that you are willing to let it all go because you love something more than staying in your comfort zone. And I will be here to help all of those who are willing to let go of the ego. I will give further teachings and tools on this, as the time is appropriate and as cycles unfold. But for now, I would say, "Saint Germain has declared clearly that he is no longer fooling around with anyone's ego. If you want to be a chela of Saint Germain and help him manifest the Aquarian Age, then get rid of your ego before you approach him." Well, I am the one that will help you get rid of that ego, so that you can fulfill your divine plan to co-create the Golden Age with Saint Germain.

Apply within!
Therefore, I am putting up a sign, for I am looking for those who are willing to help co-create the Golden Age. And you might have seen on businesses, there is a sign saying, "Help wanted. Apply within." [Audience laughs.] I am putting up that sign, because your help is wanted. And you must apply within, meaning within yourself, by going within and discovering that ego, and then letting it go.

Yet, I also have certain conditions. Two thousand years ago I spent a considerable amount of time and energy dealing with those who were not willing to even consider that they needed to change, that they had an ego; those who thought they were perfect, those who thought they were the wise ones, they were God's chosen people and they did not need to change themselves. It was everyone else who had a problem and everyone else who needed to change. And so my big sign says, "Help wanted. Apply within." But the small letters underneath say, "Hypocrites need not apply." [Audience laughs.]

The path that I offer is the path I offered 2,000 years ago. It is the path of total humility. And even my disciples, who had spent three years with me, had not fully understood that path. And that is why they started arguing amongst themselves, concerning who would be greatest among them when I left. At that moment I had one of these "hitting the concrete experiences," and I said to myself, "Does that mean that after three years they have not understood your message? Have you not been able to penetrate and make them see what the path is all about?"

And today I am in a much better position because there are many people who can see what the path is about. It is not the way that seemeth right unto a man, which is the glorification of the ego. Instead, it is the path of the total humility, of letting go of all of the pride of the ego, so that you can simply walk away from it and be free.

This is the path I offer. I offer it with all of my love. And I will lovingly guide you to that point of freedom. Yet I must also say that love is not always soft, for sometimes you need a firm hand to be awakened. And this relates also to how you approach other people about the spiritual path.

Know the Eternal Silence!

Gautama Buddha, July 5, 2005.

Uniting Buddha and Christ

Many of you might have wondered how you can have a spiritual teaching that unites the Buddha and the Christ. What is the connection between Buddha and Christ? Well, the Buddha and the Christ are symbols for two spiritual offices that are meant to guide the evolution of Earth to their salvation, to their enlightenment.

And the Buddha and the Christ do it in two different ways. The Buddha is the one who sits on top of the Sea of Samsara and holds the balance and the vision, holds that perfect balance for the Mother Light. The Christ is the one who descends into that Sea of Samsara, to those who are lost in ignorance and cannot ask the questions that will make them free. And he offers them a cup of cold water in Christ's name.

And this does not mean that he offers them the ultimate spiritual teaching, for truly many people are not ready for it. And thus, when Jesus says you have a right to go out and disturb those who are caught, he does not mean that you have to give them the highest spiritual teaching you can see. You need to tune in to the soul and say, "What does that soul need to take the very next step? That is the cup of cold water I will offer them." That is the function of the Christ.

So when you transfer that to the concept that there are two aspects of your God Flame, you can say, that the Alpha flame is also the Buddha flame. This is the flame that you hold as a balance for the Earth. The Omega flame is the Christ flame. This is the flame you bring to those who are lost in ignorance, so that they can be awakened. You might have heard that Christ is the Prince of Peace. Well, the Buddha is the King of Peace. The Buddha sits on the throne, holding the overall vision for the kingdom, and then he directs the prince to go out and cut free those who are stuck in the mud.

Thus, the Christ flame is the Word incarnate. And did not Jesus say – even though he was called the Prince of Peace – did he not say, "Think not that I come to bring peace to the world. I come to bring a sword" (Matthew 10:34). And what is that sword of the Christ? It is the Word, the Word incarnate that cleaves asunder the real from the unreal, so that people can see their egos and the unreality of the ego, and thereby have the free choice to separate themselves from it. That is the sword of Christ. And that is why, truly, Christ did not come to bring peace into this world. He came to disturb those who are trapped in ignorance, trapped in pride, trapped in hypocrisy, and challenge them to come up higher.

He came to set brother against brother in the sense that he would rather see people have conflict – that could bring out their egos, that could bring out the worst in them – so that they might see that aspect of the ego in themselves. He would rather see that kind of conflict – that would lead to growth – than he would see everybody remain indifferent, remain asleep, as if they were numb, walking through life as if they were sleepwalking.

So thus, the Christ does come to disturb, to stir up the pot, and to get people to move out of their indifference. And yet, the Christ is the Prince of Peace because only when you are willing to take the battle with the ego can you reach the true peace of freedom from that ego. How can there be peace if people are trapped in the ego? And so the Christ comes to bring them the sword that will allow themselves to divide the Conscious You from your ego.

I am overjoyed in the company of saints

Mother Mary, July 5, 2005.

Don't be afraid to make mistakes

You are now in the Aquarian Age, and I can tell you that throughout this gathering, you have been processing a state of mind that has burdened humankind for several decades. It is the fear that many children have before they move away from home, before they spread their wings and fly on their own. For truly, until you reach a certain state of separation from the ego, you will be afraid of freedom. It is so much easier to have someone telling you what to do. And this is indeed the key to understanding the origins of the ego—as I will give you in much more detail in the forthcoming book. [Master Keys to the Abundant Life]

Yet I will say this; when the soul realized that it had fallen and had separated itself out from the teacher, it decided that it had made such a bad mistake that it no longer wanted to make decisions. So it needed someone to make decisions for it, and that "someone" became the ego, guided by the prince of this world. And so the key to raising back up the Mother Light and reclaiming your identity is that you must be willing to make decisions.

And there will be a time, where you will have to start making decisions, even though you do not yet have the full Christ discernment to always make the right decision. But as we have said, it does not matter whether you make a right or wrong decision, as long as you are willing to learn from that decision and come up higher. Because, then, every decision, no matter what the outcome is in the physical octave, can be turned into a victory, whereby you come closer to your Christhood.

It is far better to make a mistake and know what not to do than to stand there wondering what to do. The true chelas are those, the true students are those, who are willing to TRY, who are willing to make an effort and then learn from that and then come up higher. This is truly the motto of those who are the guardians of the Mother Light. We will not, as El Morya has said, tell you in every little detail what to do because you have to express your own creativity—that is part of the bargain.

That is your end of the bargain. And as you do so, as you multiply those talents, we will then give you our multiplication factor, but you must take that first step, as you have already done. But you must keep always taking the next step, and as you go along and try different initiatives and maybe find out that they do not work as you hoped for – because the world will not respond as you hoped – then you must not allow yourself to stop. You must never allow yourself to feel discouraged and say, "Oh, it is hopeless. Nothing can be done about this planet."

Do not fall into that trap of the serpentine mind. But as we have now said several times, always be willing to take the next step. I am there whenever you take that next step. I am there to give you my full love for every step you take higher on the path.

Will you BE with us in the Golden Age Consciousness?

Mother Mary, August 7, 2005.

Beware the trap of pride
Truly, there is a sense of comeasurement that you need to have. It is the comeasurement that each and every human being has infinite value in the eyes of God. It is the comeasurement that when you do something to change the consciousness of humankind, when you take active part in the work of the Ascended Host, then your service is of infinite value.

This, of course, is not meant to be taken by the pride of the human consciousness and the ego to mean that you are more important than other people. We have no desire whatsoever to create a new movement, where the members feel that they are better or more important than others because they are members of this movement. I ask you to survey the history of religion on this planet and see how the members from almost every religion have fallen into this trap.

They begin to think that they belong to the only true religion and that the founder of their religion was the ultimate prophet sent by God.

And, suddenly, they begin to feel that they are more important than anyone else and that they are the only ones who will be saved, the only ones that are important to God. My beloved hearts, did not Jesus say, "For inasmuch as ye have done it unto the least of these my brethren, ye have done it unto me" (Matthew 25:40)?

So how can it be possible that people can begin to think that because they belong to a particular outer organization or religion, they are suddenly better than others? Ah my beloved, this is possible only because these people have used the outer organization to reinforce their egos, rather than follow the original goal of all true religions, which is to win their freedom from the ego.

My beloved hearts, do you see the importance of what I am telling you here? It is not our goal whatsoever that the Guardians of the Mother Light should become another movement that reinforces people's egos and traps them more firmly in those egos, making them feel they belong to the most important organization on the planet. We have seen this happen over and over again, even in the organizations we have sponsored in this last century.

Many people have come to an ascended master organization and have begun to feel that they now have the highest and most important teaching on the planet because they are following the Ascended Host. And thus, they begin to actually build upon the pride of the ego, until that subtle pride sneaks in and they begin to feel that because they have done so much for the Ascended Host, they are now so important and their salvation is guaranteed.

My beloved hearts, the only salvation that is guaranteed is the salvation of those who are continually willing to transcend themselves and come up higher, so that they can transcend themselves faster than their egos can manage to create another mental box in which they become trapped. Therefore, no outer organization can guarantee your salvation, and any organization that claims that it can do so has simply fallen prey to the eternal trap of the ego consciousness.

It is truly not my desire to see those of you who have been faithful in giving my rosaries, those of you who have joined the Guardians of the Mother Light, fall into this trap. I desire to see you be all that you can be by Being more than the ego.

The Golden Age consciousness

My beloved, I have found it necessary to sound this note of caution because I do observe the ego working in some of you. And I desire to see you overcome it as quickly as possible. Yet the only way you can overcome it, is by seeing it, and seeing it for what it is, so that you can consciously choose to separate yourself from it.

This, of course, is the design of all of my rosaries, namely to expose a portion of the ego, so that by giving a rosary for a time, you can begin to overcome that aspect of the ego. And thus, truly, the latest rosary, the Freedom Rosary, is another step up in terms of overcoming that ego and putting it behind you. Yet the Freedom Rosary is meant not just for your personal benefit. Truly, in the Aquarian Age, in the Age of Freedom, humankind needs to come to the realization that you cannot be truly free on Earth until your brothers and sisters are also free.

Truly, the consciousness that needs to spread among the spiritual people in the Aquarian age is precisely what I mentioned earlier, "Inasmuch as ye have done it unto the least of these my brethren, ye have done it unto me." And this, truly, is the consciousness of Christ, the Christ that is in all life. And when you connect to the universal Christ mind within you, you will begin to expand your awareness to see that the universal Christ is in all. And the Christ mind longs to set all people free to attain a higher state of awareness of God's mystery, wonder and the oneness behind all outer manifestations.

The dilemma of prophecy

The Freedom Rosary represents a step up in awareness of the Christ in all life and that the essence of freedom is to overcome the enemy within and the enemy without, the ego and the prince of this world. I want to thank those who have participated in this rosary vigil, since we released the Freedom Rosary. I want you to understand that, because of your efforts, giving prophecies on planet Earth today represents somewhat of a dilemma.

My beloved, there are many people, especially in the Christian movement, who claim that if a prophecy is not fulfilled, then that prophecy has failed, and therefore it must have been a false prophecy. Ah my beloved, this is typical for the reasoning of the ego and the dualistic mind of anti-christ. Indeed, when we of the Ascended Host give a prophecy, we give it primarily in order to give people the opportunity to raise their consciousness, so that the prophecy does not have to be fulfilled in the physical realm.

It is our goal to awaken people with the prophecy, so that they will make the necessary adjustments, whereby the things prophesied can be averted. Thus my beloved, from our perspective, a prophecy that actually comes to physical manifestation is a failed prophecy, because it failed to awaken the people and inspire them to change their ways. Do you see, my beloved, that the reasoning of the ego consciousness is often diametrically opposed to the truth of the Christ mind?

...

The comeasurement I want you to have is that when people start to use a spiritual tool as powerful as my rosaries, the Earth suddenly becomes fluid. And it becomes fluid in a way that the negative portents, set in motion by humankind's ego consciousness and karma, are suddenly liquefied, so that they are no longer inevitable. Suddenly, the future on this planet looks more fluid, and there is now no longer any guarantee that the negative portents will come to pass. Because it is indeed possible that those who have the highest spiritual awareness will use that awareness to raise the collective consciousness, whereby lessons can be learned and karma balanced without the physical manifestation of some calamity.

...

Those who do not ask with an open mind and heart will only hear the voice of their own egos or some false master, who will tell them what they want to hear – what their egos want them to hear – and not what their Christ selves, I AM Presences and spiritual teachers want them to hear.

This, of course, ties in with what I said in the beginning, namely that so many people in the spiritual and religious field come to build this new ego, which uses spiritual teachings – that were meant to set them free – as a tool to entrap them even more firmly in a mental box. And once they are in that mental box, they believe they no longer have to change, they no longer have to go beyond the framework in which they are now comfortable and feel they have everything under control—because they have the highest teachings on the planet and they are doing so much for the ascended masters. Yet who is it that has everything under control? Is is the ego – who never wants to change – or is it the Christ—who is always self-transcending?

The dilemma faced by all spiritual students
My beloved, why am I an ascended master today? Why is Jesus an ascended master? Why is Saint Germain an ascended master? Why is El Morya an ascended master? We are ascended masters today for one reason, and for one reason only—we never stopped transcending ourselves, we never stopped taking the next step. We were always willing to come up higher and go beyond our mental box, even though we sometimes had come to feel comfortable in that mental box.

Yet in the final analysis, we were always willing to transcend, and that is why we kept self-transcending, until we took that final step of transcendence that brought us permanently into the spiritual realm. Yet I can assure you that even here in the spiritual realm we have not stopped transcending ourselves, and therefore we are more today than we were yesterday or 10, 15 or 50 years ago. And this, of course, is the dilemma faced by all students of the Ascended Host.

There are those who have been students of Saint Germain for many years, some for a lifetime. Yet if their image of Saint Germain is an image based on the teachings that were given decades ago, then it is possible that the image given in those teachings has become a trap for their minds. For Saint Germain has transcended himself immensely since the teachings of former organizations were given. Yet if a student has not transcended him- or herself – and the image of the Master – then how can that student know the Master as he is today?

You can know the Master only if you are willing to transcend the image of the Master, so that you can follow the Living Master and not the dead idol, the golden calf, that has been created by your ego and which your ego claims is actually based on and justified by a true teaching given by the Ascended Host. Certainly, our past teachings were true, but your ego can turn them into a false teaching by turning them into a graven image of what the ascended masters are like, how they should speak and what they should say.

My beloved, the Saint Germain of today is so much more than the Saint Germain of 10 or 50 years ago. And if you are not willing to transcend yourself and your image of Saint Germain, then you simply cannot follow him as he moves on in the Aquarian age consciousness. You will instead be left behind to dance around the golden calf of your own making—or the making of the collective consciousness of a particular organization. And therefore, you will inevitably lose the thread of contact to the God of Freedom, the Master of the Aquarian age of freedom.

So my beloved, I ask you to go into your heart and to meditate on the Living Presence of Saint Germain. And I ask those of you who are willing to use the Golden Age rosary to take a little time, or as much time as you like, after giving a rosary to tune in to the Presence of Saint Germain, the Living Presence of Freedom, the Living Flame of Freedom that he is. And I desire you to ask the Living Presence of Saint Germain to reveal to you his vision for the Golden Age that he desires to see manifest on Earth. And if you will make this part of the rosary vigil over these next days and weeks, I think you will find that you will begin to see a potential for Earth that you had never even imagined before. Thus you will find a new sense of freedom from doom and gloom, the freedom of knowing that the future will be better than today.

If you want to BE with me, become more—as I AM

El Morya, October 22, 2005.

Do not become too comfortable

There are those who have been faithful to El Morya for decades. They have diligently decreed and called to me and to the will of God, and I am grateful for every service rendered in my name. Yet I must tell you that yesterday's level of service and yesterday's level of attainment is not sufficient for today. Thus, I ask you to consider that when I walked the Earth as Thomas More, I wore a hair shirt to avoid becoming too comfortable in the physical octave. You – who see yourselves as the chelas of El Morya – must be ever vigilant that you do not allow your egos to trick you into becoming comfortable at a certain level of service, at a certain level of understanding of the spiritual path.

The will of God is ever expanding. Thus, when we give forth a spiritual teaching through a particular organization or a particular messenger, we are giving forth a teaching that is true, that is complete, that is whole at the time it is given. Yet no teaching put into words can accurately portray and keep up with the ever-expanding will of God. Imagining that this can be so is nothing but the folly of the ego, who looks for the ultimate sense of security in the physical octave by imagining that if it belongs to the only true church or if it has the "highest teaching on the planet," then it must be ultimately safe and secure.

Truly, the ego will never be secure no matter how many illusions it conjures up to give the impression of security. And thus you – as the Conscious You that you truly are – need to be ever vigilant that you do not allow the ego to trick you into becoming comfortable in a particular teaching or in a particular understanding of the path. For truly, the teaching we gave forth through a previous organization we sponsored cannot give you a full and complete understanding of the path because the path has moved on since that teaching was given, as the path has moved on since the teachings were given by Jesus 2,000 years ago.

Thus, progressive revelation is a perpetual process that will not end until the last person on Earth has reached Christ consciousness, and therefore no longer needs progressive revelation through an outer messenger or an outer teaching, because each person has now become part of the ongoing, ever-flowing River of Life that truly is God's creation and God's kingdom.

Thus there are so many of our students in former organizations who have reached a plateau. They have said – not necessarily consciously, but subconsciously they have said – "I think I understand the spiritual path. I think I understand the teachings of the Ascended Masters. I think I know what I need to do to make my ascension and to do the work that needs to be done for raising the consciousness of the planet. I think I know El Morya and what El Morya is like. I think I know what he will say or what he will not say."

Only one way to know El Morya
Yet I tell you that unless you move on as I move on, you do not know Morya. For I will never stand still to placate the idolatrous image of a

would-be chela. My chelas are those who move on with me. And they never hesitate, they never look back. They simply leave their nets of their entanglements with their world view and their paradigms. Leaving your nets does not necessarily mean leaving a physical circumstance. It first of all means leaving the nets of your ego illusions of what the path is like, what the ascended masters are like. For truly the El Morya that you knew yesterday is not the same as the El Morya of today.

Moving higher means many things. It means that I have moved higher in oneness with the will of God. It also means that I have moved higher in being allowed to have a closer personal relationship with those who are my true chelas and are willing to move on with me. That is why I speak to you by standing in your midst, instead of standing on a platform, being separated from you. Because the need of the hour is that the chelas – the real chelas of the ascended masters – move higher with us and thereby close the gap between us and you, between our consciousness and your consciousness, so that we can close the gap between Heaven and Earth—thereby raising up Earth to the level of the Christ consciousness so that the kingdom of God can be manifest on Earth.

It is not possible to bring the kingdom of God down to the low vibrations on Earth. And therefore, the only way to bring God's kingdom to Earth is to raise up the vibration of Earth by quickening the minds of those who are willing to raise up their minds and raise their consciousness and be one with us. The need of the hour is not to be a chela of the ascended masters who sees us as separated from you, as being raised above you so far that you cannot reach us, thereby continuing the idolatrous cult that Christianity has been for 2,000 years, where it has put Jesus up on a pedestal where he is beyond the reach of anyone.

No, you need to step up from that consciousness, you need to separate yourself from the fear-based consciousness of the Piscean age and come up higher. And so you will close the gap between us and you. Because you realize that the true, ultimate goal of following the teachings of the Ascended Masters is to become one with the teaching. And then to become one with the master that brought forth that teaching, so that you realize that you are an extension of ourselves on Earth and thereby we can BE ourselves in embodiment through you. This is the need of the hour. This is the need of the new age.

Oneness is the ultimate goal of the path

Truly, we need you, those of you who are willing to become one with us. But in order to become one with us, you have to be willing to face your egos. And you have to be willing to realize the basic truth that your ego has created an idolatrous image of the ascended masters and that idolatrous image portrays us as being separated from you, as being far above you, beyond your reach. And then you need to realize why the ego has created this idolatrous image.

It is simple. As long as you believe that I am separated from you, you cannot become one with me. And therefore, your ego feels safe because it knows that it has you under control. It knows that you cannot completely separate yourself from that ego because the only way to separate yourself from the ego is to become one with the higher part of your own being.

What so many students throughout the ages have misunderstood about the spiritual path is that it is not an outer path. This is what is most obviously portrayed in the fundamentalist Christian religions who believe that by declaring Jesus Christ as their Lord and Savior, they will automatically be saved. But I must tell you that this consciousness permeates every spiritual organization on this planet, and there are many who have fallen into the trap of accepting this consciousness—which truly is the consciousness of anti-christ, the consciousness of the fallen ones!

Even in previous organizations, so many chelas have identified themselves with that consciousness and have believed that by studying the outer teaching, by giving the decrees, by doing the outer things, they would one day automatically wake up and become the Christ. This will not happen!

The Christ consciousness is the consciousness that is one with God. For many people on Earth it is difficult to become one with God. Therefore, we of the ascended masters have offered ourselves as intermediaries between the people's current level of consciousness and the consciousness of the oneness with God. Our entire purpose for doing so is to provide a bridge for you, a Bridge to Freedom – the freedom from the ego – so that when you cannot become one with God, you can become one with us. And through that oneness, you are free of the ego and can then move on to your full God consciousness.

The outer path and the inner path

Thus, when you are new to the spiritual path, you are presented with a teacher outside yourself. And for a time you need to follow that outer teacher. But there comes a point, a crucial point on the path, where you need to step up, so that you are no longer following the outer teacher, always seeing a distance between yourself and the teacher. You now step on to the true inner path, where you acknowledge that you are willing to become one with the teacher.

This is the true path, and it has always been the true path, the true path of oneness, rather than the way that seemeth right unto a man, the way that seemeth right unto the ego because it allows the ego to survive, while you still think you are making spiritual progress and moving toward the ultimate goal of the ascension or your Christhood. This is the way that seemeth right unto man because you have not separated yourself from the ego. And you have not done so because you have not truly, consciously acknowledged that you are willing to become one with the ascended master who is your personal guru.

Those who are the true chelas of El Morya are not forever following El Morya as an outer guru. You must come to a point where you are willing to merge your being with mine—that we become one. This does not mean you lose your individuality. But it does mean you lose your ego. And it is the only way you can fully lose your ego. Because, truly, you were created to be a co-creator with God, and you can only co-create with God when you are one with God's being, one with God's will, so that you co-create within the framework of God's will and never even entertain the thought that God's will could be alien to your own will.

The illusion of the automatic path

This is the need of this age. We have given you new teachings, and I must tell you that the need of the hour is your integration with us. You do not need to follow any particular example. You do not need to be a member of a particular organization—that is not my point. But if you are not consciously and lovingly striving for oneness with me, then you are not a true chela of El Morya.

If you think that doing what you have been doing for ten or twenty years or more is sufficient to be a chela of El Morya, then you are trapped in the consciousness of the fallen ones who fell because they refused to be one with God and the will of God. They separated themselves out.

And here on Earth they have created their own illusory world, where even Satan can appear as an angel of Light. Those are the wolves in sheep's clothing, who appear beautiful outward, but inwardly they are filled with dead men's bones—of their rebellion against God and their separation from the Presence of God.

It is perfectly possible to be a member of an organization sponsored by the Ascended Masters and nevertheless be following the path that seems right unto a man, the path that continues for decades to see us as separated from you because your ego wants to keep the distance so it can keep its illusions and maintain its control over you.

These are the chelas – or rather, these are the souls who claim to be the chelas of El Morya – yet when they see me coming toward them with open arms, they run and hide.

I AM MORE

It is time you recognize that I, El Morya, am infinitely more than the picture of me that you have come to accept through the teachings of any organization. So many of you have looked at the old picture of me, and what was reflected back to you from that picture was your own state of consciousness. You saw me as a stern master, and you were afraid that I would spank you. But it was the ego that had that fear. For truly, the real you has no fear—unless it identifies itself with the ego and thus takes upon itself the fear of the ego.

This very messenger has told the story of how he surrendered himself completely and instantly felt my presence, but felt my presence as the pink love that many of you associate with an ascended lady master. I desire all of you to experience the pink side of El Morya, for as has become popular in recent years, I am an ascended master who is in touch with his feminine side.

I am the fullness of the will of God. And the will of God is uncompromising and can be strict when you are in the state of consciousness that is a compromise. Yet the will of God has an Omega aspect, and it is an infinite and unconditional love for the chela who surrenders some aspect of the ego. And truly, when you surrender, you can experience that love. And truly, only when you experience the pinkness of my love can you fully overcome the fear of becoming one with me—for what sensitive soul would want to become one with a stern master who is always blasting them for any imperfection.

So to become one with me, you need to see beyond the old image. You need to recognize that it was necessary for me to be very stern and uncompromising in previous organizations. Because only by doing so could I have any chance of shaking people out of their current state of consciousness. And I would have the best chance of not causing them to fall into the consciousness of pride, the consciousness of being too comfortable—thinking that because they were members of an outer organization or had done so much in the past, they were now at a plateau from which they did not need to rise.

So I did everything I could, according to the level of consciousness and the cosmic cycles, to present myself in a certain way. But I have moved higher, and thus it is time that you see that I am more than the stern and strict master. I am truly the loving Father, the father who can look at his child playing and feel a tear well up in his eyes for the unconditional love for that child in whatever state of development it is in. And thus I have always had that love for those who are out of my own Being and those who have the potential to return home to their God by becoming one with my own Being.

And thus, I leave you to ponder the pinkness of El Morya and to consider whether you are truly one of my own or whether you are out of the Being of another ascended master. And whatever master you feel is your personal master, I ask you to consider taking that master down from the pedestal, taking that master down from the cross upon which the image of the master has been crucified by your ego and the consciousness of separation. And when you take that master down from the cross – so that he is no longer hanging up there and you are standing down below – what you realize is that you are at the same level. At that moment, you can step into the master's Presence and you can begin to merge with that master.

Mercy is setting life free

Kuan Yin, October 22, 2005.

My beloved hearts, how could I not respond to such devotion to the heart of Kuan Yin, the Goddess of Mercy? How could I not respond to the devotion of those who honor the Mother flame in the West in Mother Mary—that is one with the Mother Flame in the East? Thus is there really a difference between Mother Mary and Kuan Yin? Or are we two expressions of that same Mother Flame?

Yes, there is a difference. And yet there is also oneness. And that is truly the miracle of God's creation—that there can be differences in oneness and oneness in differences. And this is the challenge for those who are the true spiritual people on Earth—to solve this enigma, to look beyond the outer differences. To see the deeper spiritual oneness and then to honor each other's differences without allowing the ego to play its perpetual game of feeling threatened by differences—so that it goes into a flight or fight response, thinking that it needs to attack anything that is different because if it is different, it must be a threat.

Ah, this is truly the essential cause of all conflict on Earth. And one of the best antidotes is indeed the flame of mercy that I AM.

...

For what is mercy but the setting free of those for whom you feel mercy? Setting them free from the heavy burden of judgment, imposed upon so many people on Earth by the ego and by the prince of this world—who seeks to condemn anyone who dares to stand up against the powers that be and manifest any degree of Christhood.

Claim Your Freedom from Religion!

Saint Germain, October 22, 2005

Ask for proof that we exist

Some have rejected all religion, saying they no longer believe in the existence of the ascended masters. Well I must tell you, that if you do not believe in us, we still believe in you. And we are willing to work with anyone at inner levels—if they are willing to go within their hearts and truly ask for proof that we exist. If you ask honestly – and with no ulterior motives of wanting to gratify your ego because you made a master appear to you – then we will respond.

Please do not fall into the trap of asking us to appear to you in a conditional way [meaning: don't ask in a conditional way], such as saying that unless we appear at this very moment, you will never call upon us again. My beloved, that will not work, for we do not respond to the conditions that can only be created by the human ego. But if you ask with a pure heart, you will know within that we are indeed real and that the path is real.

Depending on your attainment, you might not see us physically. Depending on whether you are a visual person or a person who hears more than he sees, but you will receive an answer to an honest call. And thus we are prepared to give an extraordinary momentum to those who are willing to reach for the inner path and establish a personal, inner connection to their Christ selves and to the Ascended Host. For truly, that is the only thing that can bring forth an awakening and a different approach to religion.

Don't put the ascended masters in a box

And so I return to the different approaches taken by our students. As I said, some have taken the black-and-white approach of denying our existence. Some have taken the black-and-white approach to the opposite polarity, the opposite extreme and have put us in a box by saying, that we can appear only, and we can speak only, through one particular organization or one particular messenger. This is simply another fight and flight, black-and-white response of the ego. It is a refusal to exercise Christ discernment so that you can follow your heart's call and possibly find us in another context—if that is what is right for you. I do not say that every one of our former students should leave an older organization. But I am saying that everyone who claims to be a student of Saint Germain must follow their hearts and must be willing to heed the guru—even if he appears as an ant.

Therefore, I say to you, if you have put upon me the matrix that I can appear only through a particular messenger and I can speak only in a particular way, then you have attempted to put the God of Freedom in a box—and I do not take to boxes. I break through them as if they never existed. For truly, they never had any existence in the reality of God. And thus you might consider – if you are willing to be honest – that only the human ego could have the arrogance and the pride to think that it could put the God of Freedom in a box and stop Saint Germain from moving where he wants to move in order to raise the consciousness of this planet.

Wake up from this folly if you have been trapped in it. And listen honestly to your Christ self to see if it is time to move on as we, the ascended masters, have moved on. For we have yet much work to do on this planet, and we need those in embodiment to be here below all that you are above, so you can be ourselves in embodiment as El Morya has explained so eloquently this day.

Stop following the blind leaders

Therefore, I say to you, "Listen to your hearts. Wake up and stop following the blind leaders, the lawyers who have taken away the key of knowledge because they want to be in control." And why do they want to be in control? Because they are controlled by their egos, and through their egos they are controlled by the very mind of anti-christ.

I am the God of Freedom, and I come to set all people free from the blind leaders who are found in every religion. But I truly would like to see those who are my students be the first ones to pick up the torch of freedom and shed the snakeskin of a rigid, dogmatic approach to religion that makes you think that you can make yourself comfortable and still keep up with the ascended masters.

You will not be rewarded for blind loyalty
I must tell you that too many of you come to the altar to be pampered and to have your egos pampered, so they can feel that you who are left are the faithful and true, that you are the only ones who are loyal and that you will surely be rewarded in the hereafter for your blind loyalty. But no one will be rewarded for blind loyalty. For only those who are willing to open their minds to the Living Truth will be rewarded.

For truly, we of the Ascended Host do not reward anyone, as we do not punish anyone. The only way to be rewarded on the spiritual path is to raise your consciousness and become one with us, so that you experience the freedom and the joy that we experience because you have become one with the flame that we are.

How else can you possibly experience the joy of the Flame of Freedom—unless you are one with that freedom flame? For too many thousands of years the people of Earth have believed that blessings is something that must rain upon them from above in some sort of miraculous manifestation. Yet it has been 2,000 years since Jesus told you that the kingdom of God is within you. And yet you still hold on to the idea that by being loyal to an outer organization and blindly continuing to do the same thing over and over – without listening to the voice of your Christ self that becomes louder and louder in its attempt to reach you – by doing this rigid outer work, you think that some day you will be rewarded.

This is folly and it needs to stop, my beloved hearts. For you simply are falling so far behind that if you do not wake up quickly, then you will not be able to catch up in the time you have left on Earth. And if you are not able to catch up in this embodiment, how can you possibly ascend in this embodiment?

Freedom means perpetual surrender
And therefore, I must tell you that freedom is not something you can win once and for all. Freedom is something you must continually pursue because freedom is the freedom from the human ego. And it is the freedom that can be obtained only by perpetual vigilance, by perpetual alertness and by perpetual surrender.

Only if you are willing to continually surrender any aspect of your human self, even any aspect of the collective consciousness that enters your being, will you keep up with us. And therefore, I say to you, "Either stop calling yourself chelas of the ascended masters or look beyond the outer path and discover the true inner path!" I am not concerned whether you belong to this or that outer organization—as long as that organization does not become a trap for your mind, as long as you are still willing to flow with the flow of freedom.

But if an organization has become a trap, then be willing to acknowledge it and realize that you must either change your approach or leave that organization. Because sitting around thinking that you are loyal to the ascended masters by being loyal to the outer path and an outer organization is simply the same state of consciousness as that held by the scribes and Pharisees. And do you remember what Jesus called those who were in that state of consciousness? That is right, he called them "hypocrites," because it is hypocritical to claim that you are a truly religious person or that you are a student or chela of the ascended masters when you are not willing to move on on the inner path and rise beyond your present level of consciousness.

And thus I say to you, "Be honest. Be honest." For how can you ascend if you cling to an illusion? Do you think any ascended master ever won his or her ascension by clinging to the illusion of the ego. Have you not realized that your ego will not be allowed in Heaven, as Jesus explained when he told the parable about the wedding feast. And the man who had entered without a wedding garment was bound hand and foot and cast into outer darkness by his own ego.

Balancing 51 percent of your karma does not make you an ascended master

What is it that prevents our students from seeing that the path to the ascension is the path of becoming free of the ego and that no aspect of the human ego will be allowed to enter the spiritual realm? And thus, I must give you another teaching about the ascension, because you have come to believe that as soon as you balance 51 percent of your karma, you will automatically ascend. And the moment you ascend, you will be an ascended master. This is an illusion that I truly do not believe can be justified by the teachings given in a former organization. It came out of the popular organizational culture, and it never came from the Ascended Host.

You can ascend when you have balanced more than 51 percent of your karma, but you will not become an ascended master until you have balanced 100 percent and have completely set yourself free from the human ego. Truly, it has been said that if you balance 51 percent of your karma and do not slay the dweller on the threshold [another word for the ego], you will end up embodying that dweller. And this alone should be enough to make you realize that you cannot simply walk into the etheric realm as a full-fledged ascended master because you have balanced 51 percent of your karma but have not slain the ego and freed yourself from it.

Overcome your fear of freedom

I am fully aware, as the God of Freedom, that many people on Earth fear freedom. Truly, it can be a scary thing to have freedom, and the reason for this is that your ego has a fear of making mistakes.

The more freedom you have, the more choices you have, and thus the more mistakes you can potentially make. And therefore, the ego is always tempted to create boundaries to make it seem like as long as it stays within these boundaries it will be safe and it will never make a mistake. And truly, as Mother Mary explains in her magnificent new book, [Master Keys to the Abundant Life] there are those people who have become so afraid of making a mistake that they dare not make any decisions anymore.

And yet I must tell you that the path to Christhood is the path of making right decisions. And as I have said before, I had to make millions of decisions, millions of right decisions, to make my ascension. And I want to give you a greater understanding of what it means to make a right decision and what it means to make a wrong decision. For this is another popular myth that has been promoted in many spiritual organizations and religious organizations.

It is so easy to set up a human, dualistic scale for evaluating whether your decision is right or wrong. There are even many people who believe that if they do something that then turns out to be not what they expected or not what their peers or their society expected, then they have made a mistake. But I must tell you that the essence of life is growth. Therefore, any decision that helps you grow is a right decision. And any decision that prevents you from growing, or does not produce growth, is a wrong decision.

And that is the only true measure of right and wrong, not some of the many millions of outer characteristics that people have dreamt up in their duality consciousness. Did not Jesus deliberately heal a man on the sabbath to show people that setting up the criteria that if you do nothing on the sabbath, you cannot make a mistake was simply wrong? Because you always need to use Christ discernment. And if a person is sick, then certainly they should be healed. And if things need to be done, they should be done whether it is done on the sabbath or on any other day.

And this, then, is the true key to making right choices—to realize that the decision that leads to growth is right. And that is why it is possible to turn all of your so-called human mistakes into springboards for your victory and your growth. It does not matter that you make what seems to be a mistake. It does not even matter that you make what might be a mistake. What matters is what you do with it.

If you honestly admit your mistake and learn from it, then you have turned it into a victory because you have grown. And thus, please be not so afraid of making decisions that you enter into the realms of those who dare not exercise their Christhood but would rather follow the directions of their egos and the forces of this world.

Do you see that following the forces of anti-christ is not the safety that many people think it is? For it only leads to further bondage and takes away your freedom. My beloved, I desire to see you be free of this state of consciousness, so that you dare to have the courage to rise up. And as El Morya has already said, T-R-Y. Those who TRY have the option to learn and grow. Those who dare not TRY will remain where they are in consciousness. Yet there is no standing still, for you are either growing or you are going backwards.

The illusion that you can stand still, and that in standing still you will be safe, is an illusion that only the ego can believe in. And it believes it because it has created it, and it completely refuses to see any evidence to the contrary—until you experience such a major crises that you can no longer ignore the fact that you need to change your approach to life.

I do not desire to see you wake up that way. I desire to see you wake up the gentle way by realizing that the path is not about always making right decisions from a human perspective. The path is about learning from every decision. And before you can learn, you must indeed make decisions.

The Living Christ is ALWAYS more than you think

Jesus, October 23, 2005.

The essential aspect of the spiritual path is that you are trapped in the duality consciousness. Your mind is trapped in a mental box made up of many individual beliefs. Some might be true, some might be partially true and affected by the duality consciousness and some are entirely springing from that duality consciousness. But overall, the picture you have is either slightly dualistic or at the very least a stationary image of God's truth. And any stationary image becomes a graven image because it is not moving on. And so, as long as you cling to a graven image, your mind is trapped in the consciousness of duality.

My beloved hearts, the ascended masters are above the level of duality. We do not descend into duality. We do not communicate with people in the level of duality. We use those who have been able to raise their consciousness beyond duality to bring forth a message that is meant to show you that there is something beyond duality.

But once the teaching is in physical form, it becomes static. And if you cling to it, you turn that true teaching into a dualistic teaching, as I have explained. And that means that you lose the direct thread of contact to the ascended masters. And now, what happens is that you become vulnerable to the false hierarchy impostors who pose as ascended masters—but they are still in the realm of duality.

And it is the fact that your mind has used a true teaching to build or reinforce a dualistic image – it is this very misuse of a true teaching, this very act of turning a true teaching into a graven image – that makes you vulnerable to the false hierarchy. And therefore, I must tell you that those who are members of any of the organizations we have sponsored throughout eternity – be it the Christian religion, the Buddhist religion, Islam, Taoism, or any New Age teaching – those who are the rigid members, who cling to a specific mental image of the path, they are all vulnerable to the false hierarchy and their own egos who whisper in their ears, "You don't have to change. You don't really have to look at the beam in your own eye because you have done all these outer things, you have this wonderful outer teaching that is the highest teaching on the planet." Which by the way they all believe—that their teaching is the highest teaching on the planet.

Perpetual surrender is an absolute requirement
If you want to be in communion with the Ascended Host, you must be in a state of perpetual surrender. For only in being willing to perpetually surrender your mental images of God, of the Path, of yourself, and of the ascended masters, can you keep up with us as we expand and grow. Only in a state of perpetual surrender can you be in the River of Life that never stands still—and thus is never attached to any particular sense of identity, as has been so beautifully described in this latest rosary [the Unconditional Love Rosary].

My beloved hearts, I must tell you truly, that progressive revelation will never come to an end on this planet—until the planet is raised up to the level of the kingdom of God, where progressive revelation becomes an inner revelation. Thus, we of the Ascended Host, will not stop working with or speaking through people who are in that state of perpetual surrender.

This is an absolute statement that I make—not only for past organizations, but for the present one and future ones. I am with you always—which part of always don't you understand? Realize that it is only the ego that cannot understand "always," that cannot understand perpetual surrender—because it wants to stop the cosmic clock so it can be in control. And if you fall prey to the security needs of your ego, clinging to an outer teaching, then you will be controlled by the ego. And your ego will be the open door for the forces of the false hierarchy, as your Christ self is the open door to the Ascended Host.

Know the real Jesus
Do you see what I am saying here? If a particular group of people believe in a very limited concept of life, we cannot give them the highest possible teaching that could be given at that moment. We must give them a teaching that is not so far above their beliefs that they cannot grasp or accept it. And thus, there are many times where we give people a very limited teaching, but it is still above what they have right now. And so you might say – with the human mind – that if the Ascended Host tell different groups of people different teachings that seem contra-

dictory, then sometimes the Ascended Host must be lying. But you see, our purpose is not to give an absolute, infallible truth.

When the Living Christ comes to you, he comes to meet you at the level of consciousness you are at. And therefore, he must shake you out of your attachment to that state of consciousness. And in some cases this can be done only by giving you a statement that is so startling to your outer mind and your ego that you are literally jolted out of your comfortability—that makes you unwilling to grow by going within and reaching for a higher understanding from within yourself. You just cling to that outer teaching, thinking it can give you everything you need to know.

So my beloved, when we give a teaching, it is for your freedom. What are we to do with a group of students who use the outer teaching to actually put themselves in a mental box that is even more confining than what they had before they found that teaching? What are we to do to get these students to move on? Well, sometimes we must push their buttons by giving them a statement that is so startling that they say, "Oh, the ascended masters would never say that. Jesus would never say that."

But you see, the Jesus who would never say "that" is the Jesus that you have confined to your own mental image of what Jesus should be like. Therefore, that Jesus is the false hierarchy Jesus, not the Living Christ. For the Living Christ will literally say to you whatever is necessary to jolt you out of your current mental box and get you back to the point where you are willing to think about life and reach for the inner answers—reach for the key of knowledge.

Be willing to let me disturb you

Truly, those who are not willing to be disturbed are not my true followers. And I must tell you that this very messenger once had a discussion with a Lutheran priest who believed in sincerity that when I came to call my disciples and said, "Leave your nets, I will make you fishers of men," they did not instantly leave their nets and follow me. "Oh," the priest said, "they must have had a least a year to put their things in order and prepare to follow Christ."

But you see, my beloved, my mission was only a total of three years. There was no time for my disciples to take care of their worldly business. I must tell you that when I called my disciples, I literally walked up to them – they had never seen me before – and I looked them straight in the eye and I said, "Leave your nets and follow me," and I turned around and walked away. And those who did not follow me straight away did not become my disciples, for that was the law at that point in time.

And although the requirements have been slackened somewhat – because back then I had only three years and now we are in a more ongoing cycle – I must tell you that although you can take some time to step on to the inner path of Christhood, you cannot take forever. There must come a point where you are willing to say, "Enough is enough! I have had enough with that ego, and it is time that I step on to the true path."

When that time comes for you individually, you need to be alert, you need to be aware, because truly your Christ self, myself, or another ascended master will appear to you at inner levels. And you need to be open to hearing our voice. And if you have the attachment to an outer teaching or organization, you will reject us when we come to you.

A special dispensation

And thus, I come to you today with a special dispensation. I come to give you a teaching for how you can let go of the things that hold you back. This teaching is already given by Mother Mary in her book, but I wish to give it from a slightly different perspective in the hope that it might help those who cannot understand it even in the magnificent book that Mother Mary has given. For truly, that is why there is more than one ascended master—because our different flames can reach different people.

The abundant life is the River of Life that is ongoing. What sets you apart from the abundant life is that you hold on to something and therefore separate yourself from the ongoingness of the River of Life. This tendency to hold on to something was born the moment you turned your back to God and accepted a belief that said, "I can no longer be one with God."

My beloved, this very decision to turn your back on the guru – who was the representative of the Living Christ – caused you to enter into a spiral of separating yourself more and more from your God, from your true identity. When you find the spiritual path, you reverse that cycle and you start walking step-by-step back toward oneness.

But when you are still trapped, or at least partially trapped, by the ego, you cannot fully understand that the ultimate goal of the spiritual path is, as El Morya said, total oneness with the greater being out of which you are an individualization. Because your ego was born from the separation, and thus it can never accept oneness as the ultimate goal. And therefore, it is possible to walk the outer path and use the teachings of the ascended masters – and you can make certain progress on that path – but there comes a point where you will make no further progress until you realize and acknowledge that you need to overcome the sense of separation.

And my beloved, what stands between you and oneness is a number of beliefs and emotional wounds that give you a sense of inner pain. And you might have had a traumatic experience in the past and it created a wound in your soul. And what is the result of this wound? It is that if you think about that experience, it gives you such pain that you immediately recoil from it, saying, "I don't want to look at it. I don't want to go back into it."

But my beloved, here is the teaching I want to give you. The only way to walk the spiritual path is to be one with everything. The path is about moving away from separation, moving into oneness. So if you have a condition in your psychology that keeps you trapped in separation, then the only way to overcome that condition is to walk right into it, to no longer be afraid to look at it – to no longer be afraid to look at your fears – but to walk right into it and transform it.

This is the teaching I gave at the Easter class of saying that you cannot give away what you do not own and that you will not be able to give away your wounds until you take ownership of them. But I come to give you a higher level now. For as long as you are trapped in the wounded psychology, you will not be able to face your fears, to go right into your wounds and re-experience the situation that caused those wounds. And therefore, what you need to do is to build a momentum and a willingness to let your Christ self or your ascended master guru overshadow you as you walk right into the limiting condition.

And this is what I come to you with today. Develop that momentum. Realize that the key to growth is to move out of separation – to stop running away – and to move into oneness. And therefore, the only way to overcome a limitation is to walk right into it and transform it into something higher through the power of Christ within you, released through your Christ self.

I am here with you

And thus, what I offer you today is to be here with you in a very tangible manifestation. And I ask you, when I finish speaking, to visualize that you face your worst fears, or at least the fears you feel capable of facing. But you do not face them alone. You face them—not with me at your side, but with me overshadowing you to the point that we are one. And therefore, you do not see your fears the way you normally see them. You see the fears the way I would see those fears.

And let me assure you that I have faced every possible fear found on Earth, and I have risen above it. And thus I might say that I have somewhat of a momentum that you can trust will carry you through.

So I ask you to go into this meditation. You do not need to call aloud, but you do need to visualize. Make an inner call for your Christ self and for my Presence to descend upon you. Accept our oneness when you make that call. And then visualize the fears that keep you from moving on to the path.

Visualize that we go right into them, take a look at them and that you see with the eyes of Christ that they are completely unreal and have no actual power over you.

And then surrender them. Surrender them into the flame of Christ in your heart and let them go. Let them go, let them fall away. Truly, as Paul on the road to Damascus when the scales fell from his eyes and he saw the Living Christ, beyond the dead image of Christ as a false teacher that he accepted before.

Allow yourself to let go of what stands between you and the abundant life. I Jesus, release you from your fears. I say, "You have the permission of Christ to leave behind those fears and to accept your true identity as being a son or daughter of God who is as worthy in the eyes of God as is Christ Jesus, as is Christ Morya, as is Christ Mother Mary, as is Christ Saint Germain."

And thus, I ask you to stand as we truly blow away the old mold, giving way for the new.

I AM THE LIVING CHRIST, THE LIVING CHRIST I AM! (10x)

Thus, your hearts are sealed in my heart flame. And therefore, I now bless this communion as truly the body and blood of the Living Christ. It is done!

I release a flood tide of unconditional love

Presence of Unconditional Love, October 23, 2005.

My beloved, then consider that there are even those who have found a more open and comprehensive spiritual teaching in the many different New Age movements and teachings—and even the teachings sponsored directly by the Ascended Host. But consider that even many of them are trapped in a small box, where they have created a mental image of the spiritual path and their own potential. So even though they know they are spiritual beings, even though they are open to the path of spiritual growth, they have not truly dared to realize that the true spiritual path, the inner path behind the outer teachings and organizations, is the path to personal Christhood whereby they become the Christed beings walking the Earth.

And therefore they dare to acknowledge the truth that Jesus stated when he said, "Ye are Gods!" Truly, this is a statement that immediately arises the worst fear of the ego, because were you to recognize that you are an individualization of God and to fully accept this, then your ego would instantly lose its hold over you. And thus the ego knows that it would die.

Non-attachment is the Master Key to the Ascension

Gautama Buddha, October 23, 2005

Understanding attachments and the ego

Thus, I ask you to consider that if you have followed the spiritual path for many years, you will come to a plateau. And you can stay on that plateau almost indefinitely—if you do not come to the realization that the requirement for moving forward is to let go of any and all of your attachments. What is an attachment? It is the false belief that you need something from outside yourself, something from the earth realm, in order to be whole.

This is the lie that has been put upon humankind by the fallen ones for eons. It is the lie you believe because your egos were born of separation, and thus, the ego knows that it is not complete in itself, can never be complete in itself—and therefore believes in the lie that it needs something outside of itself in order to be saved. And if you identify with the ego, then you too will believe in that lie.

Yet the reality is that the real you, the Conscious You as Mother Mary explains in her magnificent book, is what was created by God. It was created by God in wholeness, in peace. You have lost that wholeness – or rather you have lost the sense of wholeness – by delving into the duality consciousness and developing attachments to this or that. And therefore, the only way back is to systematically cut the ties.

Why do you think God said that he is a jealous God? I know this sounds ominous and fearful, but the reality of it is that God loves you so fervently that he wants only the best for you. And he knows that the best for you is oneness with him so you know who you are a co-creator with God. So why would he allow you to remain trapped forever in a lesser sense of identity? And therefore, the true requirement for ultimate happiness, ultimate peace of mind, the ascension, salvation or whatever you want to call it, the ultimate requirement is total union with God. And that can be obtained only through complete non-attachment to anything in the material universe.

Look for your attachments

Thus, you ought to take this realization and use it to look in the mirror and consider honestly your attachments. Please take note that I am not in any way trying to put a burden of blame upon you for having attachments. On the contrary, I am come in the hope of setting you free from these attachments by helping you see that it is the attachments that keep you from walking the path and obtaining the inner peace of mind for which all people long.

How can you be at peace as long as you have an attachment? An attachment can be many things. Many attachments are subtle. Many attachments have taken on the disguise of something that is absolutely necessary. And thus, I come to reveal to you that even the spiritual path, as defined through a particular teaching or organization, can become an attachment.

Many of you have followed a specific teaching and have given specific practices for decades. I must tell you that you have all rendered a magnificent service to the Ascended Host, and we are grateful for all of your efforts. But I must also tell you that many of you have gradually developed a sense of attachment to a certain outer practice or even to a certain approach to the path, making you think you have to do all of these decrees every day or the sky will fall.

My beloved, there does come a point on the spiritual path where you have the opportunity to attain a state of consciousness in which you do not have to do all of the outer things in order to do the work that you are here to do for the Ascended Host. It has never been our intention that people should have to decree hours a day for their entire lives. There will come a point where you have the opportunity to go within and make that contact with your Christ self that enables you to radiate light in everything you do or say or think.

And thus, your entire life becomes a spiritual practice of radiating light. It is not only when you decree or pray that you are invoking light, for you are no longer at the level of consciousness where you need to invoke light from Above, thinking that the light has to come from the Ascended Host and therefore you have to call to us over and over again. There is a higher level of service, where you are the open door and the light does not have to be invoked from above because it comes from within.

Find the light within
My beloved, the kingdom of God is within you, meaning that when you reach that state of integration – of wholeness, of oneness – then the light can radiate from within. My beloved, I must tell you that there are many people who have been loyal to us by following the outer path and doing the outer practices, and they have come to that point. And some have come to that point years ago, where they would have done much more for us by stepping up to this higher level of service of simply being the light in action always.

And there are indeed a substantial number of people who are actually holding back their growth – and therefore, holding back their potential for service – precisely because they are trapped in the consciousness that they have to keep giving so many decrees for the rest of their lives. And they will not go in their own hearts and listen to the voice of their Christ self that tells them it is time to come up higher, it is time to come up to a higher level of service. And thus, can you see that even the path can become an attachment?

And I must tell that if you have passed the point where you should have moved higher, there will be a certain strain in your being. For when you were new on the path – and when it was right for you to give so many decrees – you found it easy to do so and they flowed so easily. And now that you no longer need to do so, it becomes harder. And therefore, you must strain more. You must force yourself. And if you will be willing to be honest, you will notice this strain. And I know very well that your egos can so easily give you a way – an excuse – for not changing. "Oh it must be opposition from dark forces. It must be because fewer people are decreeing, so I have to hold a greater balance and therefore it is a greater strain for me."

There are innumerable excuses. But I must tell you that the reality for many of you is that you have moved past the point, where you should have stepped up to the inner path. And this is the real cause for your strain because your soul wants you to move higher, but your outer mind will not allow it to do so. And thus, you have to keep suppressing your own soul in order to continue to do the outer practices.

Inner peace is the ultimate service
My beloved, there are some of you who think that the spiritual path should be the path of suffering, the Via Delarosa that so many Christians

believe is the only way to salvation. Let me tell you honestly where this belief comes from, because it truly comes from the ego. The ego knows that it is not worthy – in and of itself – to enter the kingdom of God. And therefore, it believes that it must buy its way into that kingdom. And it believes it is possible to buy its way into the kingdom. This is a lie, but the ego will never see that it is a lie. And therefore, the only way that you can escape the downward pull of that lie is that you realize who you are and that you are smarter than your ego and you are different – you are separate – from your ego—and therefore you can separate yourself from it.

I must tell you that at a lower level of the path it is natural – and it is indeed necessary – to be dissatisfied with your progress, to feel that you have always more to do, that you should be doing more than you are doing. Because this is the only way you can escape the downward pull of the mass consciousness, which pulls you back into becoming an ordinary human being, living the good material life instead of getting up in the morning and doing these weird spiritual exercises.

So it is necessary at a certain stage to have that sense of dissatisfaction, that sense that you should always be doing more. But the problem with this is that it makes you feel like you are always behind, you are not good enough. You are literally like the donkey who is pulling a cart, and in front of the cart is hanging a carrot from the string. And the donkey is running toward the carrot thinking it can reach it, but it will never catch up to it.

My beloved, we have no desire to see our best chelas act like a donkey for the rest of their lives, running after the carrot that they can never reach. There comes a point on your path where you need to recognize that you have done enough outer things, that you need to step up to the higher level and manifest inner peace. For the inner peace is truly the ultimate service you can give.

Imagine the power of ten thousand Christed ones on Earth. Imagine the power of just a few hundred people who have reached the Buddhic consciousness and how they can transform the planet just by being here—and being here below all that they are Above.

And so I must tell you that when you have been on the path for a number of years, there is a measure that you need to apply to yourself. And you need to take a good look at yourself and say, "Do I feel at peace with myself? Do I feel at peace with my path and my progress on the path?" And then you need to recognize that if you do not feel at peace, the way to attain peace is not to run even faster—which is what your ego tells you to do. The way to obtain peace is to step back and say, "The goal of the path is Buddhahood. And Buddhahood is total peace. Total peace comes from total non-attachment. So if I am not at peace, I must have attachments. And thus, I must let go of them – one at a time – until I too can face the demons of Mara, even when they come to me and try to make me feel guilty for not having given so and so many decrees."

Peace is the goal of the spiritual path. Be willing to let go of whatever prevents you from obtaining inner peace. For truly, we have no desire whatsoever to see our best chelas run around for decades feeling like they are never good enough, like they are never doing enough. There are so many of you who have striven for so long, and we long to give you that pat on the shoulder and say, "Well done thou good and faithful servant. Thou has been faithful over a few things. I will now make thee ruler over many things. Enter into the joy of the Lord." Allow yourselves to feel the joy that is truly shared by all in the ascended realm, a joy that can be shared by you in the unascended realm but only when you let go of the attachments that prevent you from feeling that joy in the heart—because your attention is always centered elsewhere, being so busy saving the world that you do not have time to establish the inner peace that it is the true key to saving the world.

Thus, I come to give you a portion of my peace, my Flame of Peace. If you will accept it in your heart chalice, in the secret chamber of your heart, then I will anchor it there now. And if you will spend a little time meditating on the Flame of Peace – and allowing that flame to expose to you your attachments that keep you from peace – then that flame will surely grow until it consumes your attachments and you one day sit down and say, "I will let go of all the outer things. I will enter into the peace of my Lord. I will not only be at peace, I will Be peace on Earth. And thus I will be an extension of the eternal Flame of Peace of the Buddhas of all time. And I will allow the Buddhas to expand the flame of peace on Earth through me, so that all non-peace on Earth can be swallowed up, not by what I have done, but what I am Being."

I Claim South America for the Cause of Freedom!

Saint Germain, December 21, 2005.

And I say to you, look again with the heart—instead of with the outer mind that wants to analyze and understand. Look for the peace that passes understanding, and you will find that peace in these rosaries, as you give them and let the Light of the Mother flow through you. For that is the only source of peace, namely that you become so one with the Divine Mother, who is so one with the Divine Father, that you realize that you are not simply spectators on planet Earth, that you are not here to sit by and watch while the fallen ones outplay their ego-games over and over and over again.

Overcome the sense of distance

The Living Word must be anchored by those in embodiment. I cannot do that for you. Jesus cannot do that for you. Mother Mary cannot do that for you. You must be the chalice here below for our Living Word Above, so that there is a flow and a sense of oneness. We who are in the spiritual realm have a sense of oneness with our God, we have a sense of oneness with each other and we have a sense of oneness with all life, which is why the Lord Christ declared that, "Inasmuch as ye have done it unto the least of these my brethren, ye have done it unto me.

Every ascended master feels that way about every human being on Earth. We are your brothers and sisters. We are not so far above you that you cannot reach us. And that is why I am standing in your midst, and I am speaking to you as an equal. I am not standing above you, talking down to you from some altar or some pulpit. I am standing right here, where you can reach out and touch me and know my Presence and know my Flame, for I AM here with you, as close as you want me to be.

The sense of distance that some of you feel is understandable, but it is a sense of distance that does not come from me, and it does not come from your Christ self. It comes only from the ego and from the false beliefs that have been put upon you throughout the ages by the false religions and the representatives of anti-christ. They claim to be the true representatives of Christ—but are not because they preach the doctrine of separation, the separation between man and God, the separation between God and his creation.

How can there be separation between God and his creation, when the Bible truly says that without him was not anything made that was made, and therefore God's Being is within everything? This is the lie that you can see through by going in your hearts and realizing that you were created by God and you were created out of God's own substance and Being. And therefore, when you have the teaching, given in Mother Mary's book, about the Conscious You that can identify itself as anything it conceives, then you realize that you can stop identifying yourself as a human being and immediately begin to identify yourself as the spiritual being that you truly are, even though you are here in embodiment.

And so I say to you that the key to this oneness is to hold the immaculate concept for yourself. Start with yourself! Start realizing that even though you have made mistakes, even though you have an ego, you are far more than that ego. The mistakes you made were made by you because you allowed the ego to trick you into thinking that you had to do this or that. But the ego's promptings are always illusions, and thus all of your wrong decisions are based on illusions. And therefore, they are not ultimately real, and if they are not ultimately real, they cannot have any power over you. You can step away from these decisions instantaneously and walk into Christhood, walk into the arms of your Christ self and allow it to take you up higher, step by step.

This is the key. There is nothing you could possibly have done on Earth that can prevent you from walking into the arms of your Christ self, that can prevent you from becoming the open door for the Living Word. This is what Jesus proved to all who are willing to see—that he was not born with the full Christhood, even though he had high attainment. He had to work for that Christhood, as each and every one of you do. But because he manifested his Christhood, you who are the true disciples of Christ can also manifest yours in this age.

And when you do manifest your Christhood, you see the true immaculate concept, as has already been said this evening, that everything is made from the Ma-ter light that the Ma-ter light can as easily outpicture the perfection of God and the kingdom of God as it can outpicture the current imperfections that you see on this Earth. And therefore, you realize that the fallen ones are promoting a lie, when they try to make you think that these imperfections are permanent or that they are of such magnitude that they could not be consumed by the light of God that you invoke through your rosaries and through your beings. Do you see that this is the lie they have put upon humankind for ages?

...

Even if one person in embodiment could save the Earth – which simply is not possible – but even if it was possible, we do not want to see that happen. Because we want to raise humankind to the level of understanding that God is within every person and that only when you come together in unity will you become the MORE, will you manifest the MORE on Earth, will you manifest God's kingdom on Earth. So we have no desire to see our students pursue the path of egotism and selfishness, of seeking to elevate themselves above others. We desire to see you realize the truth of the oneness of all life, so that you seek to raise up all life.

Did not Christ say, "He who would be greatest among you, let him be the servant of all." And the truth behind that statement is that when you are truly great, and have great vision, you see that you are not a separate individual but that you are part of the Body of God on Earth, and so is every human being. And thus you realize that the only true way to elevate yourself is to elevate the All, the entire Body of God.

This is what Jesus had seen and what he had embodied. This is what every ascended master has seen and embodied. Because until you see the reality of oneness behind the outer differences, you cannot ascend to Heaven. You cannot leave behind the ego based on the consciousness of separation and come into the oneness with your higher self, with your God and with all life—that is the only thing that will get you to Heaven. Oneness is the only key that will allow you to enter that strait and narrow gate – that is so narrow that it is a singularity – and only when you are one in your being can you enter that gate. As long as you are divided and have any aspect of the ego in your being, you cannot enter the straight and narrow gate of total oneness.

...

This is the pattern that we need to see for the Golden Age, where you are not told by some external authority what to do, but you go within your hearts and you know from within what is the right thing to do. Therefore, you circumvent the entire ego that we have seen outplay itself in previous dispensations and organizations, where some of the students would listen to what we said in dictations through our messengers and would then determine to take outer action. But the outer action was motivated in large part by the ego and their desire to show off to the leaders of our former organizations and even to us.

My beloved hearts, trying to impress the Ascended Host based on a motivation that springs from the ego is not likely to succeed. We have seen all the games played by the human ego, and we are determined that our true students shall not be burdened by this in the Aquarian Age, nor shall our sponsored organizations be dragged down by those who are not willing to let go of their egos.

We cannot and we will not sponsor individuals or organizations who allow the ego to play its games of superiority, of showing off, of feeling better than others and of thinking that it can impress the Ascended Host by some outer service that does not spring from love. We want our students to step up to the pure motivation that everything you do is done out of love for God Above, and out of love for God below, as you see God in every form of life and even in planet Earth herself.

This is true service. This is the requirement for the Aquarian Age.

See the Living Christ in yourself—and let the Living Word flow through you

Jesus, December 23, 2005

The one purpose of all spiritual teachings
Truly, every spiritual teaching can be said to be about one thing—the reawakening of people to their true identity as sons and daughters of God. And it is only through the consciousness of the Christ that they can know and accept that they are sons and daughters of God. For truly, as I said 2,000 years ago, no man knoweth the father save the son or to whomsoever the son might reveal him (Matthew 11:27). Thus you can know God only through the Christ consciousness, and thus you can accept yourself as a son or daughter of God only when you have some measure of the Christ consciousness.

And that Christ consciousness must come from the universal Christ mind, but most people on Earth cannot make contact with that universal Christ mind. And thus they need the Word made flesh, the Living Christ in embodiment, or the Living Christ speaking through someone in embodiment, to make contact with that Christ consciousness, and therefore have the reawakening of who they are, their true sense of identity, so they can accept themselves for who they truly are.

I know that you will look at this with some trepidation and some fear, for it is natural that at the beginning stages of the path, you do have fear. And it is a fear that springs from many levels of your being, including the ego, but even your soul, even the Conscious You, can have some fear of what will happen if you accept the Living Christ in your being and accept that you are a son or daughter of God. Because truly, when you fully accept that, your life will change—it will never be the same.

So there is always a fear of letting go of that which you know, that with which you are familiar, that which gives you a sense of comfort and stability in a world that is always changing. But my beloved, we can help you overcome that fear if you are willing to let it go. But we cannot take it from you unless you are willing to give it to us. And thus, it must be you who makes the decision that you are willing to face your fear, so that you can see that it limits you, that it is unreal. And so that you can decide that you no longer want it, and thereby let it go.

The Master Key to the Success of Spiritual Movements

Archangel Michael, December 24, 2005

What has been missing in spiritual communities is the willingness to expose the ego

These forces will work in any way they can to do what the dark forces have always done to those who work for the light, and that is, "Divide and Conquer." They will do anything they can to divide you, by projecting doubt and fear into your own minds and by projecting conflicts or disagreements into your relationships. Do not fear these forces, but do be alert and know that they can be subtle. But when you are willing to expose your own ego, then they have very little power over you.

My beloved hearts, this truly is the ingredient that has been missing in almost every past religious or spiritual organization on this planet: The willingness to freely look in the mirror and expose your own ego. And then the realization that in order to overcome the ego you need to come into oneness, oneness with your Christ self, oneness with the ascended masters, oneness with God and oneness with each other.

Because, truly, it is not God's will that one person saves planet Earth. That is why it is such a travesty that Jesus has been raised up as the only savior of humankind, for he never came to set himself apart from anyone. You must understand that God wants many, many people to be part of the raising of the consciousness of Earth but that you will have the maximum impact only when you come together in oneness, in harmony, in unison. And thus you must guard your oneness against the division of the mind of anti-christ, whether it be working in the ego, whether it be working through dark forces or whether it be working through other people.

It is time to understand my true message of oneness

Jesus, December 25, 2005.

Will you enter in?
You might recall that I talked about the key of knowledge (Luke 11:52) and that the lawyers had not been willing to enter in, and that they were seeking to stop others from entering in. Well my beloved, the key of knowledge is the realization that the true goal of the spiritual path – and the only key to salvation – is to come into oneness with God and oneness with all life. Oneness with God as the God Above and oneness with all life as the God in manifestation here below.

The lawyers have not understood or have not been willing to recognize the key of knowledge, so they have not been willing to enter into oneness. And therefore, they are using their spiritual teaching to raise up themselves in comparison to others. And in so doing they are, in subtle and often unrecognized ways, seeking to prevent other people from entering into oneness. Because they do not want other people to exceed their own level of spiritual growth, for if that were to happen, then they could no longer maintain their illusion that they were more spiritual, more advanced than others.

So you see, my beloved, when you walk the spiritual path from a self-centered perspective, there will come a point where you cannot grow further. Your growth will come to a halt. Most people do not recognize this with their outer minds, but at deeper levels of their being they know they are stuck, they are not growing. Yet they do not realize that the reason they are not growing is that they have not let go of the illusion of separateness, of trying to raise themselves up above others.

So because they are not willing to let go of this illusion, they are attached to the feeling that they are more advanced than others. So you see, my beloved, the mechanism that comes into play here, when the person subconsciously knows that it cannot grow beyond its present level, and when that person is attached to feeling better than others, then the only way to maintain the illusion of being better than others is to prevent others from growing!

Because if others were to continue on the true path of growth, they would quickly exceed the lawyers who have stopped their own growth. Do you see, my beloved, this mechanism? You need to learn to recognize this mechanism. It is good if you can see it in others because truly there are some who have taken this to the extreme, and you will see them in every spiritual organization where they go around with an aura of superiority, even if it be subtle. So it is good if you can recognize it in those who are so extreme that it is obvious.

But I tell you, you must also learn to recognize it in yourself because this very tendency, that I am talking about, is the essence of the ego. And the ego of every human being is caught in this trap of not wanting to grow, not wanting to elevate all life and therefore wanting to hold back others. And my beloved, when you seek to hold back others, you truly hold back yourself as well. It is inevitable.

As I have stated before through this messenger, the real message behind my saying to "do unto others as you would have them do unto you" is that whatever you do to others, you are inevitably doing to yourself at a deeper level of your being. So if you seek to hold back others from growing and coming into oneness with God, it is because you have allowed your ego to stop your own growth at a certain level.

My beloved, it is most important that you uncover the subtle ways in which the ego is trying to stop your growth or trying to stop the growth of others. For if you do not, you will become stuck on the left-handed path.

Raising your motivation

So what is the key to overcoming this problem? Well, it is to realize that if you want to grow beyond a certain point, you must raise your motivation for following the path. You must learn to recognize that your ego is self-centered and that your ego is very good at using a spiritual teaching in order to make it seem like it is such an advanced student. You must learn to unmask this in yourself and then, instead of feeling guilty, instead of coming down on yourself, you simply realize, "Oh but this is just the ego playing its games, and I am more than the ego, and I want to come up higher. I want to really take my spiritual growth to the higher level that Jesus demonstrated."

And in order to take your growth to that higher level, you must enter into the sense of oneness with all life here below and realize that you need to use what you have internalized in order to help others. Only when you give out what you have received in the time you have followed the spiritual path, will you take your growth to the next level. Because it is only then that you multiply your talents.

Do you see, my beloved, that my parable about the talents is so fruitful and vast and has so many meanings and interpretations. And one of them is that when you are following the spiritual path based on the self-centered motivation, seeking to raise up yourself only, there will come a point where your growth stops and you have now buried your talents in the ground. And so only when you raise yourself above that point, will you multiply your talents. And only then can God multiply your own light, your own growth, and take you to that higher level.

Simplicity is not so simple

This is the most essential teaching that you could possibly internalize about the spiritual path. My beloved hearts, I see so many people who find the teachings I have given through the messengers that we have set before you. They find the websites, they find a book, they start reading here and there. And the people I am talking about whose growth has come to a halt, almost all of them have the same reaction, "Oh but I already know all of this. And I have found even more advanced teachings, that give me a far more advanced intellectual understanding of the path and the spiritual reality. This is too simple for me."

And so they move on. Yet I must tell you that the teaching I have just given you here, and the teaching that we have given through this messenger, is the most profound teaching given on this planet in recorded history, because no other teaching has exposed the very core of the spiritual path with such directness and such simplicity.

And what is the effect of the simplicity? Ah my beloved, simplicity is not nearly as simple as you might think. For truly, that which appears simple, appears simple only to the ego, to the intellect, to the outer mind. And it appears simple because the ego and the intellect cannot do what they always seek to do, which is to interpret a teaching in such a way that it makes them seem so advanced because they can understand this teaching.

Do you see, my beloved, that there is a danger for those who have followed the spiritual path for a long time but have not truly entered into the inner path of oneness? They seek, inevitably, a higher and higher teaching just as an addict seeks a greater and greater fix. And they think that in order to find the higher teaching, it has to be something that is difficult to understand, because the ego and the intellect reasons that the more difficult it is to understand, the more advanced it must be. And so they become almost addicted to seeking spiritual teachings, and they overlook the very pearls that are so simple that the ego cannot manipulate and misinterpret it because there is no room for misinterpretation—if you are willing to look at the teaching and truly listen to what it says.

My beloved hearts, be not as the lawyers. And if you have been caught in the pattern of being a lawyer, then be willing to look in the mirror and say, "This is not why I have striven for these many years. I have not put forth so much effort on the spiritual path in order to end up as the lawyers who rejected the Living Christ. I must change my motivation, I must raise my motivation, I must come up higher. I must look beyond the ego itself, the self-centeredness, for I will have no part of it anymore. I am disgusted with that selfishness, that self-centeredness, I am disgusted with the ego's incessant attempts to elevate itself above others. I want to find the true path that Jesus and the Buddha and all other teachers have demonstrated. I want to look at Mother Teresa who lived an entire life of selflessness, I want to look at Jesus, Mahatma Gandhi, the Buddha and other great examples of people who lived a life of selfless service. This is what I want and I am willing to be reborn and to rethink every aspect of my approach to the spiritual path in order to really come up to that level of selflessness and service to all life."

Why the first shall be last

My beloved, if you look at spiritual organizations, you will see that there are many people who have put forth a great effort. They have taken up leadership positions in those organizations. And many of them have been responsible for putting forth the effort that has helped those organizations grow to where they are today. Yet too many of these leaders have become stuck in the consciousness that I am talking about here, of seeking to elevate themselves and their organization, building the subtle sense of superiority that they belong to the most important spiritual organization on the planet—because their organization has the highest teachings on the planet or is sponsored by the Ascended Masters or whatever outer characteristic they use to build a sense of superiority that truly can spring only from the ego.

And so you see those who have taken up leadership positions and consider themselves worthy to hold a leadership position in a spiritual organization. Yet I must tell you frankly that nobody who has not stepped onto the path of selfless service is worthy to hold any position of authority or leadership in any spiritual organization whatsoever. That is why I said to my disciples, "He who would be greatest among you, let him be the servant of all" (Matthew 20:27).

But you see, my beloved, what I am asking you to do today is to realize that what I said to my disciples 2,000 years ago was a reflection of humankind's consciousness at the time. It is now 2,000 years later. We are now on the brink of entering the Aquarian age, and if you want to be a true spiritual seeker in the Aquarian age, you need to raise your consciousness beyond what it was in the past. And you need to raise your consciousness beyond the entire level of consciousness that compares itself to others.

Do you see, my beloved, that my disciples, even though they had followed me for three years and had the opportunity to internalize my teachings through my example, by being in my Presence, they had not truly internalized my message. They were fighting amongst themselves about who would be the leader among them when I passed from the screen of life. Can you see that in so doing they were stuck in the duality consciousness of comparing, of thinking that one person was more important than others, that one position in a spiritual movement is more important than others. And thus, by attaining this position, you have elevated yourself above others and now your ego can feel safe that it must be saved when you hold such a high position. Can you see that this is simply the consciousness of duality?

Why the Ascended Masters Sponsor Organizations

El Morya, December 29, 2005.

The test of humility
In a sense this is the only test that we of the Ascended Host have ever given to our students. Will you receive the teaching with pride or will you receive it with humility? Will you take a spiritual teaching and use it to elevate your ego and reinforce the ego's sense that it is more important than other egos? Or will you use the teaching to separate yourself from the ego and come into alignment with the higher will of your own being.

My beloved hearts there truly is no other test. If you could understand this one teaching, you could use it to win your ascension and win your Christhood, so that you could be here below all that you are above and thus become the instrument for manifesting God's kingdom on Earth.
...

You see my beloved, we have two ways of teaching. And this is what most of our students in previous organizations have not understood. Our first approach is to give you a teaching in order to inspire you from within, so that you can come up higher by internalizing that teaching. If that does not work, then we take a different approach. Our first approach is to tell you and to help you see from within what you need to overcome in order to see your ego and how you must separate yourself from it.

Now, if you cannot see the ego through a teaching, then our second approach is to actually reinforce your ego, thereby causing it to act out in such ways that hopefully it will become so obvious that you cannot ignore it and that you suddenly see that this just is not right.

And thus, you see, there are two ways you can learn. You can learn through the inner teaching or through observing the outer unfoldment of events—the outplaying of the ego. And even those who are still stuck in the organization have an opportunity to learn. Even the leaders have an opportunity to come to the point, where they have acted out their need of control—and reach a point where they suddenly tire of it and say, "I have had enough of this. This isn't the true way. I must find a better way. I must find a way based on love."

Reach for the One Vision—the Vision of Oneness

Elohim Cyclopea, December 31, 2005

Thus, I say to you, "Remain true to the vision of the Ascended Host, the vision of oneness, for without it you will not achieve your highest goals, neither individually nor together." Do you see, my beloved, the ego thinks that by going its own way, doing things its own way, it can achieve more than by waiting for those other people who give it such trouble because they will not agree with its wisdom and logic?

But my beloved, I tell you this is nothing but an illusion because truly God is one. And God desires to see his kingdom manifest on Earth. And that kingdom can manifest only when people come together, sharing a common vision that supersedes their individual visions, especially the visions of the ego.

We look to establish the true Sangha of the Buddha

Gautama Buddha, January 1, 2006

You must make two decisions in order to be healed

My beloved, only the power of the I AM Presence, the power of the Father, the power of the Buddha can truly set the Mother light free from an imperfect matrix and therefore heal you from the wounds in your psychology. Yet in order for that power to be brought down into your lower being, you must be willing to surrender your attachment to your wounds, to your hurt, to your pain. This, therefore, becomes a twofold action and it requires you to make two decisions. You must decide that you are willing to align yourself with the will of the Father. This is what Mother Mary demonstrated when she said to the angel "Not my will but thine be done." This is what Jesus said when he asked the Father to take the cup away from him and still said "Not my will but thine be done."

But you must understand that this is your own higher will and not a will that is alien to you or that seeks to restrict or limit you. On the contrary, your own higher will only seeks to set you free to be all that you are. And thus, in order to submit, to surrender, yourself to your own higher will, you must be willing to dispense of the lie of the fallen angels that God's will is contrary to your own, that it restricts your free will or takes away that free will. This is a lie they have put upon the evolutions of Earth for eons, and truly it is a lie that in this day and age you must challenge, you must grow beyond.

For when you do surrender to the higher will of your own being, then the light can be released and descend into your form. But the healing is not complete by the light descending, for you must also be willing to let go of your attachment to your pain, to your hurt, to your sense of anger or non-forgiveness toward those who have hurt you, even your non-forgiveness towards God or yourself.

This then can best be done when you understand the ego and understand that it wants to keep you trapped in this little box, where you are so focused on yourself, your own pain, your own needs that you have no thoughts for other parts of life. And that is why, truly, the best way to heal yourself is to seek to heal others, to give to others.

My beloved hearts, when you realign yourself with the will of the Father, draw down his light and then – at the same time – you are willing to serve others, then you will establish the figure-eight flow. And as that flow continues, it will literally pull out of you all imperfect conditions and energies so that you are healed gradually. And as you are healed, the intensity of the light will increase. You can hold more light, and as you give out more light, God will multiply what you give, will multiply your talents. And thus, to him that hath more shall be added until all life is raised up.

How to move to the next level of the path

Yet I come tonight to give you a special teaching to people who have been in any spiritual organization for some time, and they have either left that organization in disappointment or they have felt a certain emptiness or a certain unrest as if it was time to move on. This is because when you have been on the spiritual path for some time – and have focused on your own personal healing and growth – you will reach that critical point – which both Jesus and Mother Mary have explained on the website and in Mother Mary's new book – where you simply cannot grow any further by focusing on your personal growth.

The only way for you to grow beyond that point is to redirect your focus and seek to help others. My beloved, for many sincere spiritual students this can be a very difficult challenge, because they have been focused on their own growth for a very long time. Many of them have been focused on a specific approach to saving the planet or serving the ascended masters. And when you have been focused on one approach for a long time, it is virtually inevitable that your ego manages to raise up certain walls around your mind that cause a certain rigidity. You become comfortable with your approach, and now it becomes difficult to let go of that sense that you have achieved a certain maturity on the path, that you know your way around, that you have a sense of comfortability, perhaps even a sense of security.

This is something you see in every religious or spiritual organization found on this planet. You see, my beloved, that many people have served tirelessly and with great zeal for a long time, and they have attained a position of leadership. And now – suddenly – a certain comfortability or rigidity steps in, and suddenly the ego manages to convince people that it is more important to maintain their present position in the outer organization than to recommit themselves to taking the next step on the spiritual path, so that they can rise to an entirely new level.

The dangers of becoming comfortable on the path
This, my beloved, is indeed why Jesus said that the first shall be last and the last shall be first. For my beloved, what happens when those who are the most experienced, those who have attained positions of leadership, become rigid in their approach to the path or in their approach to a particular teaching or organization? Well, I will tell you what happens. Their growth comes to a halt.

Yet there are those who have not been in the organization for as long, and they have not become rigid and they are still committed to growth. So they use the teaching or the organization to grow, and there comes the inevitable point where they start growing beyond the level of spiritual attainment of those who are in leadership positions. And so, my beloved, what will inevitably happen is that those in leadership positions suddenly feel threatened by those that they had considered as being below them in the hierarchy that they had established in their minds.

Suddenly they realize that these newcomers, these upstarts, want more than just passively following the leaders. And in some cases it is true that those who are less experienced want to fulfill their ego desires, or maybe they lust after the power of those in positions of leadership. And thus, truly, they are not worthy of those positions.

Yet I must tell you that in virtually every organization of any merit there is a certain group of people who are beginning to grow out of the ego and manifest their Christhood, and thus they have an inevitable and unstoppable longing to express that Christhood. And so they truly are the ones who are worthy to hold positions of leadership or in other ways express their Christhood within the framework of the organization. And if those who have positions of leadership were equally committed to manifesting and expressing their Christhood there would be no conflict. For truly, all would then find their place and be able to express their Christ attainment and their God flames. But what inevitably happens is that the leaders who have lost their commitment to growth feel threatened, and so they seek to hold back the ones that are growing in Christhood.

The greatest problem in spiritual organizations

My beloved, this is the greatest tragedy of any spiritual organization—when this process comes to a head and the inevitable confrontation occurs. My beloved hearts, so many scenarios have outplayed themselves throughout the ages that if I were to tell you about them, you would literally feel nauseated. You would feel like throwing up in disgust by seeing how the ego – again and again – has managed to cause sincere spiritual seekers to enter into the dualistic game of trying to prove who is right and whose ego is better than whose.

My beloved hearts, this has been going on for so long that we of the Ascended Host have simply had enough. We have said, "Enough is enough. It is time for us to establish an organization, a movement on this planet, where these ego games can no longer destroy the organization and destroy those who are sincerely following the path."

My beloved hearts, I speak sternly now for I do indeed come as the force of the Father, the force of the Buddha, to bring you into alignment with the higher will of your own being and make you see that you too have tired of these ego games. You have in many past lifetimes been involved with spiritual movements. You have put forth sincere efforts, only in the end to see your efforts dashed and your pearls cast before swine, where they were devoured by those who were so caught up in the ego games that they would not let them go.

You too have come to the point, where you have said, "Enough is enough" and that is why you are where you are today in consciousness. Yet I know that there are some of you that are not yet open to the teachings we are giving because you have been too hurt, you have been too put down. And you have allowed yourself to take those hurts personally, to become attached to them, so that you are not willing to let them go. You are not willing to realign yourself with the higher will of the Father which says, "My child it is time to come home. It is time to stop playing in the sand. It is time to stop hiding your head in the sand, but to rise up, stand firm and be who you are. Come up higher! Let go of these old hurts, let go of these old wounds and realize that you were hurt by others because they were trapped by the ego and you allowed yourself to feel hurt because you were trapped by the ego."

And so the only solution is that someone has to step outside of that ego game. And my beloved hearts, I am calling you to be that one who will step outside of the ego game and recommit yourself to the true path, the path of Oneness.

Chapter 4:
Ego Teachings, 2006

Always look for the practical solution—not the ideal solution

Saint Germain, January 3, 2006

Yet you need to do two things to have the maximum impact on your nation. You need to first establish the connection to the God power that you have within you, within your I AM Presence and within the Ascended Host. You need to establish that sense of oneness with us, so that you no longer fall for the lie that you are simply human beings, walking around here on Earth, and that you have no more power than any other human being. My beloved, you are not human beings. You are SPIRITUAL beings walking the Earth in a human body. And the power that you have is only limited by your ability and willingness to let the power of God stream through you.

And then, the second thing you need to accomplish is to come together in a true spiritual oneness, the true sense of oneness here below, where you are not seeing each other as being competitors, as being in opposition to each other. You realize that when you have differences of opinion, as you naturally will have, the only way to resolve such differences in a harmonious way is to always look for the higher vision, the higher purpose, that can supersede the lower differences, quite frankly, many of which spring from the ego.

How to resolve differences of opinion

Yet, of course, not all differences of opinion spring from the ego. In many cases it is simply that your God Flames are different, and thus you tend to focus on different solutions to the same problem. In many cases, both solutions can be valid. So which one will you act upon? Well, perhaps you can sometimes act on more than one. But in many cases, what you need to do is to raise your consciousness and tune in to us, so that we can tell you which solution is the most practical one in this particular situation.

As I said, we are not looking for the ideal solution because in many cases the ideal solution cannot yet be manifest because we are not close enough to the Golden Age. So we are looking for the most practical solution in this particular situation. And that is why you must understand that when you have attunement, you will often see a solution that seems ideal to you because it seems ideal based on your God Flame. And that is why many times we see our devoted chelas be in opposition to each other, where each person is arguing for the solution that is best—seen from the perspective of his or her God Flame.

My beloved, it is sad for us to see two people who are in disagreement, when they are both right in the sense that from the perspective of their God Flame, the solution they see is the ideal one. So what I ask you to consider is that even if you can see the ideal solution to a problem or situation, it may not be possible to manifest that solution because it simply isn't practical—given the outer conditions and the consciousness of the people. And that is why I ask you to tune in to El Morya's flame of Practical Realism, to my flame of Diplomacy, so that you can avoid these confrontations and look for the most practical solution and unite behind that practical situation.

This, my beloved, will bring you such a great sense of oneness of purpose, such a great sense of harmony and peace among each other, that you can truly form that platform that will bring the divine solution down from the Ascended Host.

There is only one test of chelaship—will you pass it?

El Morya, January 4, 2006

If the messenger be a person whom you perceive as an ant, will you heed the message anyway? Or will you fail the essential test of chelaship and thus lose the thread of contact to the heart of El Morya?

It is not a matter of what I say, how I say it or through whom I say it. It is a matter of your ability to read the vibration of the voice, to read the inner message in the words and thus recognize the Master Morya beyond outer appearances. This, my beloved, has always been the true test of chelaship. Can you recognize the master regardless of the disguise that he may be using at the moment?

My beloved, those of you who are familiar with the Master Morya – as I have presented myself in several previous organizations – will know that at my retreat in Darjeerling I have a gruff gate keeper. Why is that so? Many people in the world think that we of the Ascended Host are interested in attracting the greatest possible number of chelas, but it is not so. Our primary concern is to present every person that comes in contact with our teachings with the essential test of chelaship.

And that test is whether you can look beyond outer appearances and catch the inner message that is deliberately disguised, so that the outer mind finds it difficult to recognize the master behind it. Thus, you might say that the gatekeeper at my retreat has the function of acting as a filter for those who are not willing to let go of their preconceived opinions about how they should be greeted at the retreat of the Ascended Master Morya.

The essential quality of the ego

You see, my beloved, the essential quality of the human ego is that it cannot – it will not – see reality. It has created a mental image, a graven image, an idol and it seeks to project it upon what it calls reality. Thus, when a person who is trapped in the ego consciousness comes across the outer teachings that we have released in any of the organizations we have sponsored throughout the last century, that person already has a mental image of what a true spiritual teaching should be like, of what a true spiritual master should be like, and the person seeks to project that image upon our teachings, upon our messengers and upon ourselves.

Obviously, once we give an outer teaching that is released in the physical, whether it be in books, or on a website, we cannot control who finds that teaching because we have no desire to control free will. Yet what we can control is how we use the outer teaching to present students with the essential test of chelaship which, as I have said, is the test of humility.

You see, my beloved, the ego is not a chela of the Ascended Masters. The ego is a chela of the false hierarchy and the false gurus who have come to this Earth for a very long time, peddling their theories that spring from the mind of anti-Christ. This goes all the way back to the Serpent in the Garden of Eden, and now that you have heard Maitreya's landmark discourse, you will know that there is much more to understand about the story of the Garden of Eden and every mystery school following it, even the outer religions of this planet—that do not deserve to be called Mystery Schools even though they have plenty of mystery.

The test has always been whether a person is willing to look beyond his or her ego, thus being willing to question and look beyond the mental image, the graven image, created by the ego and inspired by those who have long ago rebelled against God and have decided to seek to lead everyone else astray, falling for the ultimate temptation of pride, of thinking that if they can get everyone to worship them and agree with their beliefs about God, then they must somehow be right.

What amazes me the most about would-be chelas

Ah my beloved, if you could see the depth of the pride of the fallen angels, most of you would be shocked to the core of your beings, for their pride is almost absolute. And by that I mean that there is almost no opportunity whatsoever to turn a soul around who has descended to that level of pride, thinking that it knows better than God and certainly better than any of the representatives of God sent to this planet by the Ascended Host.

Thus, my beloved, when I, Morya, look back at the organizations that I have sponsored throughout the last century, I must tell you that what amazes me the most is that someone can come in contact with an outer teaching and an outer organization sponsored by the Ascended

Masters. The person starts studying the teachings. The person starts applying the teachings, at least the outer aspects of the teachings, such as giving decrees and prayers. After a certain time, and for some it only takes weeks, and for others it takes decades, these people begin to feel that they are now worthy to be chelas of El Morya or another Ascended Master.

They think that because they have studied the teachings and can repeat the teachings, the outer word, because they have practiced and given so and so many decrees or even because they have passed certain outer initiations that they have been exposed to, suddenly they begin to think that they have reached a level of mastery. And now, my beloved, their egos whisper in their ears – or even the false hierarchy impostors whisper in their ears – that they have become such advanced chelas that they no longer need to be tested in the essential test of chelaship. Because they are so advanced, because they have done so much, they do not need to be tested in humility.

Yet my beloved, it is precisely the chela who has done all of the outer things right for a number of years who more than anyone else needs the test of humility. For the more you have done on the outer, the more you have done on the outer path, the more you need the test of humility so that you can transcend the outer path and realize there is an entirely different level of chelaship to which you have the potential to ascend—if you are willing to look beyond the outer teaching and even your preconceived opinion about how the "real" chela should follow that outer teaching and the outer path. This, my beloved, then is the essential dividing line between those who call themselves chelas and those who are chelas of El Morya.

Are you willing to become one with El Morya?

My beloved, we welcome many lifestreams to our outer teachings. We have set up certain barriers of entry that turn back some, but those who are willing to pass those outer hurdles are welcomed. Yet being a member of an outer organization, doing outer practices – even for decades – does not mean that you automatically become a true chela of El Morya who has discovered and has been willing to follow the inner path of discipleship.

This my beloved, is something that I wish the majority of the members of every past organization we have sponsored would wake up and understand. For if they were to understand this, they could very quickly accelerate their spiritual attainment to the point that we could start working with them in an entirely different way, and therefore their service to this planet could be multiplied manifold.

Yet those who are not willing to look beyond that outer image, created by their egos, cannot make that leap of faith, giving up their preconceived opinions, their sense of superiority, their sense of comfortability on the outer path in order to once again bend the knee in humility and say "El Morya I am willing to be God-taught. I am willing to be taught the higher way of true chelaship, the inner way of becoming one with you El Morya, with your God flame, thus becoming in essence the twin flame in the physical octave of the Ascended Master El Morya."

Yes my beloved, in previous organizations we have given teachings on twin flames, but those teachings were adapted to the level of consciousness that humankind had at the time. They were very linear, but there is always a higher understanding, a higher teaching. Our previous teachings are not invalid – there are twin flames at the soul level – but there is indeed a higher teaching where there is a vertical relationship of twin flames between your being here below and the higher Being out of which you are an individualization.

Thus, my beloved, I the Ascended Master El Morya have many twin flames that are embodied on Earth at this hour. It is my desire that all of those should be awakened and recognize who they are. For were that to happen then I, Morya, could be myself, my spiritual being, in embodiment through my chelas below. Do you see, my beloved, this is the path of oneness.

It is time to purify the heart

Mother Mary, Easter Sunday, April 16, 2006

You need my compassion more than I need yours

My beloved, every Easter, there are indeed many people who think back to how I must have felt when I met Jesus on his road to Golgotha and later stood at the foot of his cross watching him die. Every Easter I feel the outpouring of love and compassion that so many feel when they reenact or contemplate this scenario. Many of those who are mothers think about how they would have felt if their own son had been treated like this. And thus, they send me a wave of compassion. And while I appreciate their loving hearts, I must tell you that I feel much greater compassion for each one of you, who are still in embodiment and who are still trapped in the duality consciousness.

I even feel a special compassion for the many Christians who contemplate Jesus' death and my own affliction. Yet they do not understand that these events happened a very long time ago and both Jesus and I are now ascended beings who are free from the pain of the duality consciousness and the human ego. Thus, we have won our immortal freedom and we no longer need compassion or sympathy from human beings. On the contrary, it is human beings who need our compassion, for you are still trapped—trapped in the duality of the human consciousness because you have not conquered the last enemy called death. This is truly the spiritual death caused by the ego, the illusion of separation from God that leads people to walk the false path, the way that seemeth right unto a man but the ends thereof are the ways of death.

Thus, my beloved, I must tell you that there are so many people on this planet who are walking this false path of death. And truly, this is cause for compassion from all of us in the ascended realm. My beloved, I must tell you that the way that seemeth right unto a man is the way that Jesus called the broad way, the wide gate that leads to destruction. What is that broad way? My beloved, there are many Christians who believe that the broad way is any religion besides their own, even besides their own particular branch of Christianity.

But I must tell you that it is not so. The broad way that leads to destruction is not followed simply by people who are not religious or by people who do not belong to Christianity or even any other particular religion. The broad way that leads to destruction is indeed followed by many people who consider themselves to be highly religious and who faithfully attend their church services in whatever church they profess to be the only true church and the only road to salvation. You see, my beloved, the unfortunate truth about religion on this planet is that religion has been so heavily influenced by the duality of the human ego and the subtle illusions of the mind of anti-christ that almost every religion on this planet has become the broad way that leads to destruction.

This broad way is the path that makes people believe that they can be saved, that they can enter the kingdom of God, that they can attain eternal life without overcoming the very condition that caused them to be separated from that eternal life, to be separated from God's kingdom, in the first place. That condition is, of course, the human ego which is born out of your separation from God.

Our God does not require blood sacrifices

Thus, it is a sad fact that most religions on this planet – at least in their mainstream versions – present the broad way that leads to destruction. They promise you that if you follow their directions, you can be saved without giving up the ego, without looking for and pulling the beam from your own eye. Ah, my beloved, this is such a subtle illusion, and it is so easy for people's egos to make them believe in this illusion.

Even many of those who claim to be followers of the Ascended Masters, and who have studied the teachings we have given through various messengers over the past century, are actually following this broad way. They think that by studying an outer teaching or practicing certain rituals for invoking light, they can actually be saved without overcoming their egos, without separating themselves from their egos and putting on the mind of Christ. My beloved, my heart goes out to all those who are trapped in this illusion and who walk what they think is the path to salvation, but it truly is the way that ends up in the death of the soul, the spiritual death of the soul.

I especially feel compassion for the many Christians who are, at this Easter time, thinking they are saved through the blood that Jesus spilled on the cross. My beloved, it is time and high time, that Christians everywhere realize that our God is a God of unconditional love, and a God of love does not require blood sacrifice as atonement for sins. The entire idea of a blood sacrifice as atonement for sins was a primitive concept that from the very beginning was not understood correctly by the people who received it. Thus, the human ego has, from the very beginning, perverted the concept of a sacrifice. And in every religion where sacrifices have been performed, this perversion has quickly been taken into extremes, and none more so than in the religions that required human sacrifice.

Thus, the idea that Jesus' death on the cross was the ultimate sacrifice, and the ultimate payment for humankind's sins, is such a primitive idea that it sometimes truly boggles the mind that anyone in this modern age can believe in it. How can people fail to see that no loving God could possibly require his sons – any of his sons or daughters – to be treated this way as a payment for people's sins?

The reality is that certain passages in the Scriptures were given in order to help the Jews make the transition from the Old Testament practices of blood sacrifice in the very Temple of God to the new teachings that Jesus came to give—namely that no blood sacrifice was necessary when you reach for the mind of Christ that is the ultimate atonement for sins.

Thus, the practice of Holy Communion is not a celebration whereby you eat the blood and flesh of Jesus. It is meant to be a celebration whereby you partake of the wisdom and the love of the Christ mind so that you allow that Christ light to enter your being, where it becomes the leaven that raises the whole loaf of your consciousness. Thereby, you too, attain that mind of Christ and through that Christ mind obtain ultimate freedom from your sins.

My beloved hearts, how can it be that so many Christians believe in this illusion, even to the point where they are not willing to consider any other teaching than the idea that Jesus' blood on the cross has washed away their sins? My beloved, it can be only because their hearts have become closed to the higher truth of God, the Living Truth of Christ that is truly raining upon the just and the unjust every moment of every day.

Overcome your fears

My beloved hearts, as a final note, let me ask you – all of you – to recognize that in order to take full advantage of my new rosary and the teachings on the chakras, it is absolutely essential that you purify your beings of all fear. You will not be able to establish the figure-eight flow between the upper and lower chakras if you have fear in your beings. That fear will block the figure-eight flow and drive the light down in the lower chakras from which it cannot rise as long as fear reigns in your being. And thus you need to become consciously aware of your fears and make a special effort to overcome them by simply letting them go.

My beloved, I am aware that a number of our students have for many years been concerned about world conditions. There are indeed many students for whom this concern has been the driving force in their efforts to give decrees, prayers and rosaries. Yet I must tell you that if you are to take advantage of this new dispensation and teaching, you must not let your concern for the world be manifest as fear.

Truly, if you look for problems, you can easily conclude that the world is in a terrible state and that immense calamities could happen at any moment. But my beloved, you could have done the same at any time in the past. For if you are willing to look for the negatives, they have been there since the Fall of Man.

Yet despite the fact that there has always been darkness and negativity on this planet, in every generation some people have managed to rise above it all and win their eternal freedom in the Light. They have done this by transcending their fears, by letting go of their fears.

My beloved, I know that fear can be a strong driving force at a certain level of the path. And there are indeed many people who need to have a certain fear for a time, so that they can put forth the effort to overcome their egos. Yet I must tell you that fear can become a trap. And it is indeed sad for me to see that so many people have been students of the Ascended Masters for decades, but they have not overcome their fears.

My beloved, no Ascended Master in Heaven has any fear in his or her being. You cannot ascend as long as you have fear. And thus, even though fear can serve as a driving force at the lower levels of the spiritual path, fear cannot take you to the top of the path. You cannot ascend by using fear as a motivation. You can ascend only when you overcome all fear. And you overcome fear only when you realize that it springs from the ego and it must be let go. You then realize that the power of God can overcome all conditions on the Earth, no matter how dire they might seem to a certain level of consciousness.

Thus, my beloved, it truly is time for you to step up to a higher level of focusing on the immaculate concept instead of focusing on all of the manifest or potential problems on this planet. My beloved, I see many of you who indulge yourselves in dire prophecies, in conspiracy theories or in watching the political process for any potential problem that might come up. I see many of you who have literally worried yourselves sick by contemplating all the problems and all the things that could potentially go wrong on this planet. This, my beloved, is indeed a negative habit, and it is time that you conquer it!

My beloved, I am being stern and direct, for I am indeed the fierce Mother who is here to defend her children against the onslaught of what in many cases are malicious demons who pound at your subconscious and conscious minds 24 hours a day in order to focus your attention on the negative portents. My beloved, I must tell you that there are people who are controlled by dark forces and who are thus used as tools to create websites or emails that focus on the many things that could go wrong, even though most of them are completely unrealistic and made up. My beloved I ask you to very sincerely consider using utmost Christ discernment to simply refuse to indulge your minds in some of the sources of negativity that you have partaken of for many years or decades.

It is not necessary to focus your attention on every negative email, website, article or book that comes along. It is not necessary to watch every TV program that spells out problems or dangers. I have need of those who will dedicate their lives to holding the immaculate concept of this planet for the transition into the Golden Age. These people cannot do this while they have fear in their beings.

In order to overcome that fear, it can be necessary for many of you to go through a period where you deliberately ignore all negative portents. I know very well that Jesus told you to be wise as serpents and harmless as doves, and part of being wise as serpents means that you must know what is happening on the planet so you can make calls for it in your rosaries. Nevertheless, there are many of you who have forgotten the other part of his admonishment, namely to be harmless as doves. Doves are harmless because they have no fear, because it is fear that causes you to show aggression and do harm to yourself or others.

Thus, my beloved, by focusing on the negatives without the love, the perfect love that casts out fear, you only become more pulled into

Thus, they have allowed their egos to create the idol of Jesus Christ as the only son of God who is the savior who will come and wash away their sins with his blood and raise them to Heaven or bring God's kingdom to Earth. This is the sense of spiritual paralysis, where you think that you cannot do anything on your own. And thus, you need an external savior to bring you into the kingdom of the external God.

The most primitive concept about salvation
Now my beloved, while this is a primitive concept, it is indeed not the most primitive concept about salvation found on this planet. For it is indeed better to believe in an external savior than to believe that your ego is the savior. For at least – when you believe in the external savior – you recognize that there is an authority that is higher than your own ego. But when you are trapped in the illusion that your ego is your savior, that your ego knows everything and that the path outlined by your ego – whatever form that path takes – will take you to Heaven, then you are so trapped that it is virtually impossible for a spiritual teacher to reach you.

And thus, as has it been explained to you, you cannot pull yourself up by the bootstraps of the ego. My beloved, it cannot be done!

There are any number of religious, spiritual and New Age teachings and gurus, who will tell you that it can be done and that they can help you do it, or that they can do it for you, whereby you can be saved without letting go of the ego. I must tell you: they are lying to you!

They know – in most cases – that they are lying. But they lie anyway because they truly realize the old saying that there is a sucker born every minute. There are people who are so trapped by the ego that they are not willing to look at the beam in their own eye. And thus, these false gurus create a system, a philosophy, that says you can be saved, you can enter the kingdom of God, without pulling the beam from your own eye, without even seeing that beam. Thus, you can live your own life feeling that you are now saved, that you are now better than others because you belong to this spiritual philosophy or organization or you are following this ultimate guru.

And thus, you can look at the beam in the eyes of all other people, looking down upon them with spiritual pride and feeling that you do not have to recognize that you have the same beam – because you too have an ego – and that you need to pull it if you want to be saved. Instead, you can continue to believe that you can walk your path toward salvation without confronting your ego, without taking responsibility for your path, without making the absolute, the completely firm, one-pointed choice that you are willing to abandon the ego and walk into the greater light of your Christ Self and your I AM Presence.

The false path of the false gurus

My beloved, there is indeed a very large segment of spiritual seekers today who are on the right track, in the sense that they have opened their minds and hearts to something beyond traditional doctrines. Yet they have fallen into the trap – set by the false gurus of the New Age movement – that you can grow spiritually, that you can reach a higher state of consciousness, that you can make your ascension, without letting go of the ego, without making an absolute, firm, one-pointed choice that overcomes the division in your being and says, "I am willing to let my ego die! I am willing to overcome it. I am willing to leave it behind. I am willing to choose the life of the Christ consciousness over the death of the duality consciousness."

My beloved, this is a firm choice. This is not a choice that you can waiver about. I am not saying that everyone on this planet is ready at this moment to make that choice. Which is why, when I walked the Earth 2,000 years ago, I did not call everyone to be my personal disciples. But I must tell you that those I did call to be my personal disciples, they had one chance and they had one second to make their choice.

I literally walked up to them, during whatever they were doing, and I said, "Leave your nets. I will make you fishers of men." And I turned around and walked away. And if they did not leave their nets and walk with me and made that absolute choice to commit themselves to being disciples of Christ, then I had to leave them behind. There was no two ways about it. There was no thinking about it for two weeks and then coming back later. It simply is not the way the spiritual path works.

You can take a long time to think about it. But there will come a point, where you are ready to make a firm commitment to step up to a higher level of the path. And if you are not willing to make that firm choice and never look back, then you cannot rise.

Your ego might manage to trick you into thinking that you can rise or that you have risen, because after all you now follow this outer guru, you belong to this organization, you do all these outer things, you understand all these teachings with the intellect. And therefore you must be an advanced student, you must be better off than you were a year or ten years ago, you must be better off than all these other people you compare yourself to. But I tell you, it is all an illusion created by the ego.

Because as long as you compare yourself to anyone in this world, you are not truly on the path to Christhood, which is the path to discovering your unique individuality that is anchored in your I AM Presence, and it is different from the individuality of any other person on this planet.

Overcome value judgments and find true self-esteem
Thus, one of the sure signs that you are still trapped by the ego is when you have these value judgments and comparisons, comparing one teaching to another, comparing yourself to others and thinking that there is only one truth or there is one higher truth. This is nothing but the comparisons of the ego, the spirit of vain competition. Because there is no competition on the path to Christhood. You are an uniquely beautiful, wonderful individual, created by God. Your job on Earth is to unite with the higher Being that you are, the true individuality in your I AM Presence, and then express that uniqueness. And when you realize that you are unique and that God loves you with the same unconditional love he has for everything, the spirit of vain competition melts away and is as nothing.

Thus, you realize that you can find an entirely new approach to self-esteem. For I understand that many of the people who follow the false gurus follow them because they have been put down for many lifetimes. Many of the most spiritual people, the most kind and loving people on Earth, do indeed have low self-esteem because they have been put down by the forces of this world, by the prince of this world, who have told them that they are wrong for being spiritual, that they are no good, that they shouldn't act this way, that they should live like everyone else.

And so, many spiritual people have low self-esteem, and they fall for the trap of the ego to compensate for that low self-esteem by seeking to follow an outer path that gives them the impression that because they have now learned all these things and understand them intellectually – they have taken all these classes, they have done all these prayers or decrees or invoked all of this light and done all this meditation – now they must suddenly be somebody from an outer perspective and thus they should have self-esteem. But you see, you will never have true self esteem until you allow it to come to you directly from your I AM Presence, which is God in your Being and therefore is the internal God and the internal savior and the only source of true self-esteem. Because it is the only way to connect to the unique individuality that is your cause for self-esteem.

So my beloved, ponder the teachings that you have received today, for they indeed contain the key that very few other spiritual teachings on this Earth contain at this point. Some of them have elements, but very, very few, if any, can give you the teachings in one complete package about the ego and the false path. And if you will contemplate these teachings and be willing to look beyond the subtle pride of the ego – the temptation to set yourself up – and you will reach for the true self-esteem that is the nurturance of the Mother through the divine matrix, the divine blueprint, of the Father, then you will be able to overcome all of these needs to follow this false path of the ego and to seek to compensate by outer knowledge or outer accomplishments for the lack of wholeness that you feel deep within your being. And thus, you will be able to truly accept your true identity as a son or daughter of God who is complete and whole in your divine individuality—and thus has no need to feel unwhole, has no need to feel that you are in competition with others. And thus has no need to compare yourself to others.

As I said to more than one of my disciples when they were squabbling about these outer things – even debating who was going to be the leader among them after I left – I said, "What is that to thee, follow thou me." Follow the inner Christ and let all of these outer concerns fade away from you. Let the Sun of your I AM Presence shine in your being and let the sun melt these ego desires, ego concerns, the entire false path and its dualistic beliefs, whereby you compare because you think you are not good enough the way you are, the way God created you. And the reason you think this is because you have not connected to who you are, to the beautiful being that God created.

Therefore, use the tools that we have given to reconnect. As I said, seek first the kingdom of God – which is the direct inner contact to your I AM Presence – and then everything else you desire – including self-esteem and inner and outer wholeness, including communication with your higher Being and the Ascended Masters, including the abundant life – all these things will be added unto you when you reach for your I

AM Presence instead of reaching for the false path and the false gurus set up by the ego.

But realize that you will – at some point on your personal path – have to make a choice. Do you want to continue in the consciousness of the ego, the consciousness of death, or will you abandon that consciousness and let the dead, meaning the ego, bury their dead – of all the attachments and all the unfulfilled things and all the competition in this world – and you walk with me, the Living Christ, into the Light of the Sun of your Being. Therefore, the challenge is always, "Choose life or continue to choose death?"

You must choose one or the other, for if you have not chosen life, you have subconsciously chosen death and you are not spiritually alive. You have no life in you until you allow the Christ consciousness to enter your container of self, your lower being. There is no two ways about it. You cannot cheat. God is not mocked. You cannot cheat God's law even though the ego will continue forever to believe that it can and come up with shortcuts and various schemes, and it tries to make you think that you can avoid confronting and overcoming the ego.

Let go of this impossible dream, I say, and you will experience a spiritual growth beyond what you have even imagined up until this point on your path. And I say this to anyone who might hear or read this statement, because I tell you that there is not one human being on this Earth who cannot come to a higher level of his or her spiritual path. It does not matter how long you have been on the path – how many times you have meditated, how many decrees or prayers you have given – it does not matter. You can always come up higher!

And indeed, up until the moment you ascend, you can go into a blind alley of becoming comfortable, where you are falling prey to the ego's subtle temptation that you do not need to go higher. This, my beloved, is the illusion of the ego. And I tell you, there are many of you who have long ago come to the point, where the only thing you need to do in order to come up to a higher level is to make that decision to let the ego die, to choose life. And then make the firm commitment that you are willing to rise above the ego, to see through any of its limitations and then accept who you really are in Christ.

I AM the Way, the Truth and the Life. No one comes to the Father but by me. The "me" is not the outer person of Jesus Christ, the "me" is the Christ consciousness. You will not enter the kingdom of God through the ego. You will enter the kingdom of God through the Christ. Therefore, choose the life of the Christ over the death of the ego and let the ego die!

I need those who will walk the Path of Peace

Elohim of Peace, May 4, 2006.

Why is Jesus the Prince of Peace?

My beloved, some of you will be aware that Jesus was called the Prince of Peace, and it is indeed because he served on the sixth ray of Peace and ministering service. He did indeed study under the Elohim of Peace that I AM. I taught him many things. As he, at inner levels, attended the retreat of the Elohim of Peace, located in the etheric realm over the island chain of Hawaii.

Why did Jesus study under the Elohim of Peace? Because he came to inaugurate the age of Pisces, which is the sixth age in a series of seven that are meant to take humankind and the Earth to a higher level where, indeed, the Golden Age and the kingdom of God can be physically manifest on this planet. Thus my beloved, Jesus came to inaugurate what is designed to be the Age of Peace—meaning that in this past 2,000-year cycle, humankind was designed to overcome all war.

Yes my beloved, I understand that when you look at the world today, you will see that there is much war and rumors of war going on on this planet. Indeed, one might say that the tension is building and that there is a potential for war here, there and everywhere. Yet my beloved, if you could see deeper, if you could see to the level where I see, you would realize that these are simply the death throes of the forces of war that have been ruling this planet for thousands of years. Yet their opportunity is fast coming to an end.

And thus it is time – it will shortly be time – for them to either surrender their warring ways and start the Path of Peace or to be taken from this planet, so that the Earth can continue to grow without being pulled down by the weight of these lifestreams—who have, for thousands of years, dedicated their entire beings to making war, mastering the art of war, always engaging in the dualistic struggle to destroy what they have defined as the enemy. Yet in reality these lifestreams are warring against themselves because they are trying to deflect attention from the conflict in their own beings by creating conflicts between themselves and others. Thereby, they have an excuse for defeating the enemy without instead of finally facing, conquering, and defeating the enemy within that is their own egos.

The illusion behind war

My beloved, study some of Jesus' teachings. Why do you think he told you to turn the other cheek? Is the saying not a magnificent teaching on how to overcome war? No matter what anyone does to you, you do not respond with violence. You respond by turning the other cheek. And when you do so, you become an open door for the God Flame of Peace to shine through your being. And thus, that God Flame of Peace will consume the warring in other people. Yet, if instead you respond to violence with violence, you close your being to the Flame of Peace. You close your solar plexus chakra to the Flame of Peace. And instead you engage in – and thereby inevitably reinforce – the downward spiral of violence and conflict on this planet.

My beloved, look at history and see how – for thousands of years – human beings have created such downward spirals in any number of places on this planet. Look how individuals who are loving and kind – individuals with the best of intentions – are time and time again drawn into such a downward spiral of conflict that never ends. My beloved, how can such a downward spiral possibly come to an end? There are those who are so blinded by the warring in their own members, by their own egos, that they think the only way to stop a spiral of violence is to take it to the extreme of destroying those whom they have defined as the enemy that is the cause of the violence.

Yet this is nothing but an illusion. And Jesus gave any number of teachings to attempt to shake people out of that illusion and make them realize that you cannot combat violence through violence. There is only one way to stop a spiral of violence and conflict, and that is that someone must decide to respond to violence with non-violence. Someone must decide to turn the other cheek instead of perpetuating the spiral of violence that can otherwise go on indefinitely, eventually becoming a self-reinforcing spiral that pulls people into it as a black hole pulls everything into its nothingness.

My beloved hearts, ponder these facts. Study the teachings of Jesus, the life of Gandhi and other people who have truly embodied the principle of turning the other cheek, refusing to respond with violence. There is no other way for war to be banished from the Earth than by having the top ten percent of the people on Earth fully embody the principle of non-violence. Yet my beloved, in order to embody that principle, you must overcome the warring in your own members. You must follow Jesus' teaching and be willing to look for the beam in your own eye instead of focusing all of your attention on the mote in the eye of another.

…

My beloved, this is the essential key. The Living Christ never, ever has any desire to put down, limit or destroy any other part of life. The Living Christ has only one desire and that is to raise up every other part of life because it knows that only by doing so does it raise up itself. My beloved hearts, Jesus himself said it, "Inasmuch as you have done it unto the least of these my little ones, you have done it unto me." The reason is that Jesus knew the oneness of all life. He saw that all other people are part of the Body of God, and therefore when you hurt any part of that body, you are hurting the whole—and therefore you are hurting yourself.

Only when you come to this realization can you fully love others. And only when you fully love others, can you fully be a focus for the Flame of Peace. Because only when you seek to raise up others, instead of seeking to punish them, can you radiate the Flame of Peace that will consume their propensity for anger or violence.

My beloved, darkness can be removed only by bringing light. Therefore, conflict and war can be removed only by bringing the Light of Peace. And in order to remove conflict among the people of Earth, someone must bring the Light of Peace by loving everyone as God loves everyone. This, my beloved, is the key to peace on a planetary scale. But then what is the key to peace on the individual scale? What is the key whereby you personally can become the open door for the Flame of Peace?

Overcoming false expectations

Ah, my beloved, what is it that robs you of your personal peace, your inner peace? Well, it is true that everything begins in the heart. And the key to attaining inner peace is to purify the heart, a work which you have begun with this latest rosary. Thus, it is indeed the work done by this rosary that has magnetized my flame and opened the door for the bringing forth of this teaching. Thus, you might consider this a work well done.

But I come to take this to another level. For I see that so many people, who are sincere spiritual seekers, are pulled away from peace because their attention is pulled away from the heart. Truly, if you could center your attention in the heart, and through that contact your own personal God Flame, you would never lose your peace.

But too often your attention is drawn away from the heart, and in many cases it truly is drawn into the solar plexus chakra that is right below the heart. This is the chakra that is the center for your emotions. And it is so easy for the forces of anti-peace to stir up this chakra, so that your attention is immediately brought down to the solar plexus and thereby pulled out of the center of the heart.

Thus, my beloved, what is the key to avoiding having your attention drawn into the feeling body, into the wild emotions that are like waves on the ocean, whereby you too become a wave on the ocean of the collective emotional body that is driven by the wind and tossed? Well, my beloved, the primary factor that robs you of your peace is that you have an expectation of how life should be. And when life does not live up to your expectation, then you go into a negative emotional reaction that immediately pulls you out of peace.

But you see, my beloved, the problem is that during your upbringing in this lifetime – and over many lifetimes – you have allowed your ego to build an expectation that is completely unrealistic and completely out of touch with your original purpose for coming to Earth.

You see, my beloved, in the core of your being you have a memory of the spiritual realm. You have a memory of a realm in which there is peace and in which the kingdom of God is manifest. You also know that this is the way things are meant to become here on Earth. And thus, you know that you descended to Earth in order to bring your God Flame and make a personal contribution to bringing God's kingdom to Earth.

Yet what you do not realize is that even though this is a true expectation, your ego has used it – has turned it slightly, has perverted it – so that now it has become a false expectation. You see, my beloved, your ego has created the expectation that this Earth should be – already – like the kingdom of Heaven. And when you encounter conditions that are not the way that you know they should be, the ego makes you believe that it is necessary or acceptable or unavoidable for you to go into a negative emotional reaction.

The ego has come up with any number of false beliefs that seek to justify why it is acceptable for you to go into a negative emotional reaction when the ego's expectations are not met. But my beloved, you did not descend to Earth with the expectation that the Earth should already be the kingdom of God. You descended to Earth knowing that the Earth was far below the level of the kingdom of God and that you were here to help bring the Earth higher.

Do you see the difference? There is an essential difference between expecting that you come to some perfect place that is supposed to live up to the standard found in Heaven, or between expecting that you come to an imperfect place and that it will require work, effort and patience to bring the Earth to the level of the spiritual realm.

If you descend expecting Earth to be perfect, you are easily trapped into responding negatively when you encounter the fact that the Earth is not perfect. Yet if you expect that the Earth is not perfect and that you are here to work, then you are not as easily pulled into that negative reaction.

My beloved, do you see what I am trying to tell you? When you allow yourself to think that the conditions you encounter in life should live up to a certain outer standard of perfection, then you make yourself vulnerable and you open yourself up to disappointment. And this disappointment will immediately pull you away from the centeredness of peace.

Yet why do you become disappointed? So many people allow their egos to make them believe that they have nothing to do with, that they did not cause, the sense of disappointment. Why, certainly it was these other people or these imperfect conditions on Earth that caused these disappointments. But my beloved, a true spiritual seeker needs to realize that your disappointment was not caused by anything outside yourself.

It was caused by an inner condition, namely that you have an unrealistic expectation of what life should be like here on Earth.

You see, my beloved, you came here to bring your personal God Flame and to let that light shine. My beloved, you came here to let the light shine during any conditions you might encounter on Earth, so that the perfection of your God Flame could consume the imperfections that you encounter on this planet.

What has happened instead is that you have allowed your ego to create a very subtle expectation that you should not allow your light to shine until certain outer conditions are met. My beloved, do you see the subtlety here? You are here to consume imperfections, and the only way to do this is to let your God Flame shine through you in the face of all imperfections. Instead, you have allowed your ego to trick you into thinking that when you encounter imperfections, you should stop your light from shining. Instead, you should look for certain outer conditions to be present before you can let your light shine.

My beloved, think back to Jesus' words. He told his disciples that those who wanted to be known to the world as his true disciples should love one another. He also told you that it was not enough to love those who loved you, that you had to love even your enemies. Do you see how this connects to what I just told you? Do you see that Jesus was saying that you should love all people no matter what they do?

Instead, the ego has tricked people into thinking that you should love other people only when they live up to certain outer requirements. Only when they supposedly deserve your love should you give them your love. But you see, my beloved, this is the lie. For truly, there is no such thing in God's mind as deserving or not deserving. Jesus told you that God lets the sun rise upon the [evil and the good] and the rain descends upon the just and the unjust.

So you see, my beloved, God does not create conditions. He lets his light shine upon all because he knows that letting the light shine is the only way to raise up a person. And it does not matter how much that person is trapped in darkness, for only by letting the light shine will the person be free of the darkness. So you see, my beloved, if you are to love other people as Christ loves you, then your only concern about other people must be to help them overcome whatever darkness is temporarily clouding their minds. You are here to set them free by loving them, by shining your light upon them. You are not here to judge them according to a human standard and judge who is worthy of your light and not worthy of your light.

I am not thereby saying that you need to treat all people the same, or that you need to indiscriminately let other people abuse you. For the light of God is highly intelligent, and it will give to each person what that person needs in order to be free. But in order for you to be the open instrument of this light, you must overcome the expectations, even the expectation for what other people should be like. You may look at a person and you may say, "That person is trapped in darkness and needs to be set free," but you have no need to make that judgment.

You simply remain centered in the heart, centered in your God Flame, and then you allow your God Flame to give to that person what that person needs. And for some it may be unconditional love. For others it may be tough love that challenges their illusions and calls them to come up higher by demanding that they see that there is a better way.

Become a prince or princess of peace

Ah, my beloved, if you would give the greatest service for eradicating conflict and war from this planet, then commit yourself to walking the inner Path of Peace, so that you can learn from Jesus, so that you can learn from the Prince of Peace, until you too can become a prince or princess of peace. You can inherit your Father's kingdom and then give it to all.

My beloved, the sixth ray is the ray of Peace. And the seventh ray is the ray of Freedom. The Earth is destined to move from the Age of Peace into the Age of Freedom. Yet my beloved, how can there possibly be freedom until there is peace? For if you do not have peace in your own being, how can you possibly be free? You will be enslaved by the emotional thralldom that pulls you away from peace at the slightest provocation. As soon as some condition on Earth does not live up to your expectation of perfection, then you are pulled out of peace. And since hardly anything on this Earth can live up to the expectation of perfection, you are constantly in a state of non-peace.

Likewise, how can the Golden Age of Saint Germain be manifest on Earth as long as the dark clouds of war are hanging as a constant threat over this planet? How can nations truly build the Golden Age if everything they build could be destroyed in a matter of minutes through a nuclear holocaust or even through a conventional war? Look at the nation of Iraq today. How can you build a nation, how can you build a future, when at any moment a bomb can be exploded and destroy what people have built?

This, my beloved, shows you that the key to freedom is peace. And I have now given you the key to peace. Will you apply it, or will you allow the ego to continue to trick you into believing that only when certain outer conditions are met can you be at peace?

You see my beloved, the ego wants you to think that only when certain conditions are met in your personal life, can you be at peace about your own life. And only when certain conditions are met in the world, can you be at peace about the future of this planet. Yet I tell you, it is a lie. For the outer conditions are nothing but the reflection of your inner conditions. And thus, you will never have conditions of peace in your own life or on your planet until you make the decision to be at peace inside yourself—regardless of the outer conditions.

You see, my beloved, the essential expectation that the ego has built is that your inner peace depends on peace in the outer world. This is the illusion of the ages, for your inner peace depends on nothing outside yourself. Your inner peace depends only on one thing—your inner contact with, your centeredness in, the God Flame of Peace. And there is nothing that can stand between you and that inner contact with the Flame of Peace because, as Jesus also told you, the kingdom of God is within you. Meaning that no outer conditions in your own psychology or being, or on the planet on which you live, can come between you and your oneness with God, your oneness with the Flame of Peace.

Thus, my beloved, stop looking for peace outside yourself. Start looking for peace the only place it can be found—in the kingdom of peace that is within you in the Flame of Peace that I AM, and that I am willing to share with all those who will dedicate themselves to being at peace regardless of outer conditions.

Thus, peace be still and know that I AM God. Peace be still and know that the I AM Presence within you is God. My peace I leave with you. Multiply it and radiate it to all life so that this planet can be at peace.

The true alchemy of the heart

Saint Germain, May 25, 2006.

There is power and there is Power

Yes, my beloved, I know that some will say that nothing could be more powerful than the violet flame decrees, but it is not so. For the power is not just an outer power. The power is not something that you just invoke. The power must, as everything else, come from within. And it comes from within only when you reach integration and Oneness with your own higher Being, so that you are here below, all that you are Above.

And through that Oneness, a power can be released that is beyond the comprehension of most people, even beyond the comprehension of many Ascended Master students who have given the decrees and techniques released in previous organizations. For the rosaries are designed not just to invoke the light, but to provide the platform for the integration of your lower being with your higher Being. And thus, through that Oneness, your higher Being can act in an entirely different manner, that is at such a higher level that there is no comparison. It is truly, like Jesus said, "My Father worketh hitherto, and I work."

This is the power that comes only through Oneness. It cannot be faked. It cannot be forced. It is not a matter of belonging to a particular organization or giving a certain amount of decrees over so many years. There is no mechanical means that will provide that integration and Oneness because there is no substitute. There is no way of cheating. There is no way of putting on an appearance of being one with your higher Being, as many spiritual people in many different organizations and religions have been good at putting on an appearance of being spiritual and religious because they lived up to the outer rules and practices in their particular religion. Which is something we have seen our fair share of in Ascended Master organizations.

Stop playing the ego games!

And thus, we have now reached the point, where we can release the teaching that this must stop and that our students need to come to a higher level of not playing games. Not playing the ego game of pretending to be a good person. It is time, at the end of the Piscean Age, to realize that Jesus himself said this over and over again 2,000 years ago, when he chastised those who were the hypocrites, the scribes and the Pharisees, who pretended, who honored God with their mouth, but their heart was far from him.

There is no way to fake the purity of heart, the openness of heart, the oneness of heart. It can only be achieved through complete surrender to the higher Being that you are. Whereby you become one, because you now realize that the will of your Higher Being, or the Will of God, is not alien to your own will. It is your own greater will, it is your reason for coming into embodiment, for coming to this planet in the first place.

And thus, you are not working against your own purpose. You are not divided, you are not trying to serve two masters. Where the one master is your divine plan that you agreed to before coming into embodiment, when you were in a state of Oneness with your Higher Being and your spiritual teachers. Yet after coming into embodiment, and growing up and being faced with the trials of life, you built an outer personality, outer expectations. And now that outer personality is warring against the higher Being and your divine plan, thinking you have to do this or that here on Earth. You have to accomplish these or those goals, that were programmed into your mind by society or by your parents. And then you think – after you have attained these goals – you can finally be spiritual.

This is not the way things work, as Jesus clearly said, "Seek ye first the kingdom of God, and all these things shall be added unto you." If you think it can be done the other way around, you are putting the cart before the horse. It will not work! Millions of people in all kinds of spiritual organizations have attempted to make it work. And I must tell you that not one has ever been successful and no one ever will be.

So give up the dream. Give up the illusion that what the Ascended Masters want or what God wants is an outer appearance of pretending. We don't want you to pretend to be someone else according to some man-made standard created by some religion. We want you to BE who you are. But the Being we want you to be is, of course, not the ego, the outer personality created by this world. We want you to BE your own higher Being, your own I AM Presence, your true Being in Heaven. And even BE the greater spiritual Being out of which you are an individualization.

And thus, some of you are indeed individualizations of the same greater Being out of which I came. And thus you might attain a greater Oneness, first with me as a representative, but then even with that greater Being out of which we came so many eons ago. And some of you are one with the Beings of other Ascended Masters. And we are not here to stand between you and the higher Being out of which we all came. We are only here to show you who you are by showing you an example that we have united with our own higher Being.

The essential principle of alchemy

Thus, I ask you to contemplate the essential principle of alchemy, a principle that has been misunderstood by so many people, even so many spiritual people, even Ascended Master students who have read my teachings on alchemy given so many years ago. The principle of alchemy is that you take what is imperfect and you transform it into something perfect—not by making it conform to an outer appearance but by transcending the outer appearance and making it conform to the immaculate concept, held in the mind of God, in your own Higher Being.

Note the essential difference. People will look at conditions on this Earth and they will say, "This is not right." The reason why you know it is not right is because in the deeper part of your being, you have the immaculate concept for how the kingdom of God should be here on Earth and how your own divine plan should be unfurled. But what happens in the world is that you build a worldly expectation of how things should be. And that worldly expectation obscures your own inner knowing, your divine plan and the reality of the kingdom of God.

So when you find the spiritual path and become more aware of the need to raise your consciousness and raise the planet, you impose, you superimpose, the image of your worldly expectation upon yourself and upon the world. And you think that alchemy means that you take what is imperfect and transform it into the worldly image of "perfection" that has been created in this world through the mind of anti-christ, through your own ego, or even through people who are well-meaning but simply are not attuned to the reality of Christ.

And so, all of your life, you can run after this false goal that is not the true goal. And thus, you are simply going from one extreme to the other. You are trying to get away from worldly imperfection [which is only an appearance] by creating the outer appearance of worldly perfection.

My beloved, listen carefully. You can make progress by doing this. Realizing that your own life, your own consciousness, is not where it needs to be, setting a higher goal and striving for that goal can lead to progress. But it will only lead to a certain level of progress, and then you will stop—unless you understand the true principle of alchemy, namely that you completely surrender all of your worldly expectations.

You do as Jesus said, you lose your worldly life for the sake of becoming one with Christ truth, becoming reborn according to the immaculate concept for your own Being. And in that total surrender of the lower expectations and of the ego, then you can obtain Oneness with your higher Being. And that Oneness is the philosopher's stone, the golden means, the cup of Christ, the X-factor, that both alchemists and many other people have been searching for throughout the ages. Thinking that if they found something in this world that had magical properties, then that something would transform them into perfect human beings, or transform lead into gold or transform the Earth into the kingdom of God, without them going through the process of obtaining Oneness through the death of the ego.

Dare to let your light shine!

Mother Mary, May 26, 2006.

Stop hiding your light!
Yet I must also tell you that those of you who are on the spiritual path have descended to this world for a specific purpose, and that is to bear witness to the truth that there is something beyond the death consciousness, and that by allowing God within you – as your own higher Being, not as the external deity – to work through you, you can take dominion over the Earth. Meaning that you can take dominion over the Ma-ter Light and realign it with the immaculate concept, held in the mind of Christ.

And this, my beloved, is indeed why you came. And I must tell you that there are some of you who have fallen for the subtle lie perpetuated by the prince of this world that says that when you are in this world, you should adapt to this world, rather than using – or rather letting loose – the power of God within you, so that that power can take dominion and make the Ma-ter Light adapt to the immaculate concept held in the mind of God.

Thus, you are not here to please people on this planet. You are not here to adapt to their death consciousness and the culture that springs from the death consciousness, so that you do not dare to be who you are. You do not dare to let your light shine for fear that it might disturb somebody, and that they might get angry or blame you or put other negative images upon you, that are designed to stop you from shining your light.

You are not here to hide your light under a bushel. And there are some of you who have been hiding your light for a long time. I am in no way blaming you for this. As I said, it is very understandable, given the current conditions on Earth, that you can feel hesitant to express your light.

I am simply here, as the representative of the Divine Mother, to give you a little tough talking to, a little tough motherly love, and say, "There comes a time when you have to make the decision that you will stop hiding your light. For until you do so, you will not move beyond the point where you are at, where you are not fulfilling your divine plan – you are not fulfilling your role as a co-creator – of having dominion. You are letting the Mother Light – in its current imperfect form – have dominion over you."

And that, my beloved, is denying God within yourself, denying Christ within yourself. For Christ, as Jesus demonstrated, will never adapt to the consciousness of death but will challenge it wherever it is encountered, will challenge those who are the false hierarchy of death, the false teachers of death who promote their lies in all manner of subtle manifestations. Including what I expounded upon earlier today in the environmentalist movement that has attracted so many wonderful and loving people who simply have not understood what I said. That the Mother's love must work within the framework of the Father's greater love that leads to self-transcendence and growth, which is the only way that planet Earth can transcend itself and come back to its original purity.

Thus I say to you: "Stop hiding your light." You are not ready to let your light shine. But you – meaning the lower sense of identity created by the ego – you are not the doer! God within you is the doer. So allow God to BE through you. Be not afraid to let your light shine, even if it might offend someone. This, my beloved, is an essential test of Christhood.

And I have told you before that even Jesus hesitated when he was at that moment, at the wedding in Cana, of having to turn the water into wine. And I had to give him a certain sternness in my gaze, where I looked him straight in the eye, penetrating to the very core of his soul. And I must tell you that he was somewhat shocked, because he had rarely seen me in that capacity. Yet he was awakened instantly and was willing to then take up his mantle, take up his role, and start his mission—take that final step from which there was no turning back.

For my beloved, who is it that wants a way out? Who is it that wants a way to turn back from the path to Christhood? Do you think it is your Christ Self? Or your I AM Presence? Or do you think it might be the ego? [Audience: "The ego."]

You are right! Only the ego can set up conditions in order to try to maintain some form of control. For it knows that if you follow that path to Christhood, it will lose all control over you.

Why difficulties can be blessings in disguise

Hercules, May 26, 2006.

Why many spiritual people experience difficulties in life

And thus, you realize that when you give up the separate will of the ego, you do not lose your will, your ability to make choices, as the ego and the prince of this world would have you believe. The Will of God is not a straightjacket, where you can only do what some outside will imposes upon you. No, my beloved, for the Will of God is indeed the will of your own higher Being. And when you recognize that as the reality of your life, then you recognize that the Will of God is not an external will.

And that is when you can follow the greater outline, the greater vision, of your divine plan out of pure love. Because you realize that it is not some external deity, some angry being in the sky, who is imposing that will upon you. It is indeed your own choices made when you were not involved with the situation you are facing in this physical body.

And thus, I must tell you, my beloved, that many of the challenges you face in life as spiritual seekers are not necessarily caused by your karma or even by world karma. They are caused by the fact that before you came into this lifetime, you made the choice that you wanted to come into Oneness with the greater Being that you are while still in embodiment. You wanted to make that your divine plan, and you wanted to fulfill that divine plan. And thus, my beloved, you looked down upon the Earth and you made a realistic assessment of how easy it is – once you are in a physical body – to be overwhelmed by the many pressures of this world, so that you forget your divine plan, the greater vow you took before you came here.

And thus, you said to your spiritual teachers, "Do not allow me to remain asleep. Do whatever it takes to wake me up. So when I go in the wrong direction, put a barrier in front of me that obstructs that path, so I can no longer go in that direction. And then if I start going in another direction, put a barrier in front of me again, until I finally come back to the center of Being and give up that lesser will that springs from the ego and even is imposed upon me as I grow up in a world that is so far from the will of God.

When I go down the wrong path, stop me! Do whatever it takes. The harder I insist on going down that path, the harder I want you to block me so that I do not continue to go down that path, but eventually wake up and realize that I am here for a greater purpose, that I chose before I came into the dense conditions I face in this dense physical body and in the situations I face with the people that I came to help."

Do you see my beloved? So many things in your lives are conditions that you have wanted as a way to prevent you from going down the wrong path. And when you see it that way, you can stop focusing on that condition. You can stop seeing it as something that is imposed upon you, either by karma, by some unjust coincidence, by fate or by an angry God. You can see it as something that is actually meant to liberate your soul, your Being, to fulfill your reason for Being.

And thus, you can change your outlook on difficulties, and you can realize that they are a potential for stepping back, for re-evaluating your life. As was so beautifully described a few minutes ago, that a severe illness can be a wake-up call, where you realize, "I am going down the wrong path. I need to step back and re-think my life and reconnect to my own higher Being and that greater Will of my own Being."

Re-evaluate your life and forgive all

So my beloved, with this in mind, you should be able to look at your life and the difficulties you have faced and come to that sense of inner peace that allows you to let go of the hurt, the wounds, the sense of injustice, any anger or resentment for having gone through these difficult experiences. And you stop focusing on the past, you stop focusing on the problems.

Instead, you reach up and reconnect with your own higher Being and say, "Ah! The obstacle was only to prevent me from going down the wrong path. And now I see the right path, and I have no more time to worry about past obstacles for I have such a love for fulfilling my right path that I have no attention left for anything else." And that is when you reconnect to the peace and joy that we desire you to have.

Surely, we do not desire you to have an awakening by going through a crisis or facing a terminal illness. We would rather have you, as was also described, come to that realization during your daily life because you finally decided to think outside the box, to use the conscious self's ability to project itself outside of its current mental prison. And thereby, you saw your life with the same greater perspective you had before you came into embodiment. And now you can reconnect to why you came into embodiment in particular conditions and situations and why you are here, what is your divine plan.

When you stop wanting to do it the human way, that is when you can discover your divine plan—and do it, not God's way in the sense of the external God but God's way in the sense of God the I AM THAT I AM within you, that is your own higher Being, that is YOU. This is the illusion you need to overcome—that you are separated from God, that you are different from God, that you could not possibly be a son or daughter of God. Because of all these conditions on Earth that you have been brought up to think are real, unavoidable, permanent or maybe even the Will of God—as some indeed believe that God created them as sinners, or God created them as homosexuals, or as any other limiting condition that people have come to see as permanent.

Yet nothing in the material universe is permanent! For it is the Will of God that everything should transcend itself in an infinite spiral that has no limits, except the limits that you might impose upon it by thinking, "I could not possibly be that." But did not Jesus say, "With men this is impossible, but with God all things are possible?" And so when you realize that you are One with God, that God is within you, that the Kingdom of God is within you, you realize there is no limitation, there is nothing that is impossible, when you are willing to be a co-creator with your God.

My beloved, rejoice in the accomplishment of reaching this state of realization of what the spiritual path is about. Take it, run with it, integrate it, do not allow yourself to forget it. Do whatever you can to internalize it, to reach up for that divine plan. Look at all the things that prevent you from surrendering to the greater Being that you are. And when you see them, then follow them, go after them. Make them visible so you can see how unreal they are and how they are not your real choices. They are only the choices of the lower will of the ego.

My beloved, I love the Will of God. And I love to see those on Earth who come to realize that the Will of God is their own higher will. Thus, be sealed in my love for the Will of God. Invite me to help you keep true to that love, which you also have in your own higher Being. Ask me to help you overcome all resistance and all lies, all wrong concepts of the Will of God and your relationship to God. Ask me to help you overcome all the graven images. Ask me to help you give up the ghosts of your limited, mortal separate sense of identity and will.

I will send you to bear witness to Christ truth in this age

Jesus, May 26, 2006.

Learning from your ego or from your spiritual teacher

Only when you have a certain purity of heart, can you see God. Only when you have a certain purity of heart, can you see God within yourself. And only when you see God – at least a glimpse of God – within yourself, can you let the ego die. For you know that if God is within you, how could you possibly die when the ego dies. And thus, blessed are the pure in heart, for they shall see God. Blessed are the meek, for they shall inherit the Earth.

And the meek are those who will no longer play the ego games but are willing to let them go—to be as a little child, who is willing to learn, to grow, to open your mind to ever new concepts in the infinite growth that is the mind of God. Oh my beloved, the joy of seeing so many of you, all of you here, being willing to partake in this discussion earlier today on the topic of death is indeed very dear to my heart.

So many people on Earth are so afraid of death, that they dare not look at it and see that they have been brought up with a false image of death—as they have been brought up with a false image of life. And thus, they cannot free themselves from the illusion that keeps them trapped in the consciousness of death. They think that if they give up that illusion, they will give up their very life. Yet did I not say, "He who seeks to save his life shall lose it, but he who is willing to lose his life shall find it." Shall find the true life that is the God Flame, out of which you are an individualization.

And as I said 2,000 years ago, I came into this world to bear witness to the truth. And this is done partly through the spoken word, but it is done also by letting your light shine before men, that they may sense that God Flame that you are and know that there is something beyond the duality consciousness, the death consciousness. For my beloved, is it not true that when you share teachings and concepts and ideas that are expressed in words, then the ego can always find a way to argue with what you are saying.

And thus, people can always, if they are trapped by their egos, feel justified in rejecting what you are saying or interpreting it in such a way that it seems like they really don't have to change themselves. They don't have to pull that beam – that ego – from their own eyes. And thus, they can remain on the false path to salvation – the broad way that leads to destruction. Because it is not the way of giving up the ego, but affirming the ego as your true identity and as the "real savior" of your soul.

The ego as a substitute teacher

Yes my beloved, when your conscious self first decided to turn its back to the spiritual teacher – the representative of God that you had in whatever higher realm you found yourself in when you decided to experiment with the duality consciousness – when that first happened, you made a decision, and it caused you to lose contact with the teacher. And thus, you felt alone. And you could not bear that sense of aloneness, and therefore you created the ego as a substitute teacher, as a replacement for the real teacher, whether it be Lord Maitreya in the Garden of Eden or other ascended beings in other realms and systems of worlds. For truly, many people on Earth come from far-away places in this universe and beyond.

And thus, my beloved, it is indeed true that many people believe that the ego and the prince of this world are their true teachers. There are even those who believe that the devil himself is the true liberator of humankind because as they say "Until we rebelled against the will of God, we did not truly have freedom and free will." There are those who seriously believe that it was in the act of rebelling against God that human beings attained free will. But my beloved, if you did not already have free will, how could you have the option to rebel against God? And if God really was out to control you, why would he allow you to rebel against his law and separate yourself from him?

My beloved, I know that the ego and the false teachers of this world have an array of sophisticated arguments against this simple logic. But when you look at it with the innocent mind of a child, you realize that all the sophistication is just camouflage, and it makes no sense. And thus, you can avoid following the subtle logic of the false teachers of this world who have only one goal in mind. And that is to keep the Conscious You thinking it is separated from your own higher being and from your God—and that you cannot come back to oneness with God on your own, that you need a savior from outside yourself.

Bear witness to the truth of Christ
Which is why, indeed, the false teachers in this world – assisted by the egos of those who were in powerful positions in the early church – managed to turn Christianity upside down – to turn my true teachings upside down – and thus present an entirely false image of Christ. So that it is a sad truth that the mainstream Christian churches today are teaching a doctrine that is entirely anti-christ, and indeed springs from the mind of anti-christ that seeks to create the impression of salvation through control rather than salvation through surrender. Whereby you surrender the ego's control and accept God control because, as Hercules said, you realize that the Will of God is not alien to your own because God is not outside yourself.

Dare to disturb people

Vajrasattva with Shiva, May 27, 2006.

Dare to disturb others
I ask you to contemplate the very fact that the key to awakening humankind is to show them the Will to Be, the Will to Be More, the Will to go beyond. For I must tell you that this planet is in such a state of darkness and heaviness that most people cannot pull themselves out. And therefore you cannot be a spiritual teacher, you cannot be an example, unless

you are willing to shake them out of their burdens, out of their blindness, out of their darkness.

My beloved, it cannot be done by passively talking to them and trying to appeal to them and trying to appeal to their intellects. Because what is needed to shake them out of the burdens they are weighted down by is an acceleration of consciousness. And you must be willing to be the open door whereby the light from above, the light of the Holy Spirit, can flow through you and you become that open door for the acceleration of someone else's consciousness.

And therefore, you cannot be shy, you cannot be hesitant, but on the other hand you cannot will it with the ego either. And thus, it is a delicate balance that requires the love of the heart and the absolute surrender to the will of God, to the Being of your own higher will. Therefore, you can become the instrument but you must be willing to let the spirit flow and disturb other people, even if they first become angry or react in other negative ways. Thus, my beloved, be willing to be that acceleration and to be the open door for the Holy Spirit to flow and wake up another soul, who for lifetimes has been asleep and cannot penetrate the darkness of the emotional wounds or the sophistication and the doubt of the intellect and the serpentine mind.

And thus, they need that quickening that cuts through all the density and shows them that there is something more, and that they have always been longing for it. And now suddenly they can see the truth that they could not see before, because surely you have all been in situations where you have explained your truth to people but they cannot see it, they cannot connect to it. And why can they not? Because they are not connected to their own inner Being, because it has been overshadowed by the darkness in their auras and their forcefields.

And thus, unless you give them both the understanding and the acceleration of the spirit, you cannot awaken them. They cannot be awakened because both are needed. Both are needed – the Omega action of you giving them understanding that you have internalized—but you need to add the Alpha action of the Holy Spirit, flowing through you and delivering that thrust that propels them out of their paralysis, their sense of being stuck, their state of non-being, and their state of their unwillingness to be. This is the non-will of the ego, even the non-will of the physical body, the non-will of the emotions, the non-will of the intellect.

Thus, my beloved, ponder this. Allow yourself to connect to the higher Being that you are. Do not seek to force it, but be willing to allow the power of the Will of God, the Will to Be, to flow through you when it is needed to awaken another soul.

Find centeredness in the heart

El Morya, May 27, 2006.

Bridging the gap
Now my beloved, I am fully aware that some of you either do not know what your God Flame is, or you might understand it intellectually but you have still not established that heart connection to it. My beloved, I ask you to consider that the central challenge on the spiritual path is very simple. The path implies that you are at a particular step and you need to move up to the next step. In other words, there is a gap between where you are now and where you need to go. So the central challenge on the spiritual path is how to close that gap. And for many people it can seem insurmountable.

My Beloved, one of the major tactics employed by the dark forces and the ego, is to create the illusion that it is impossible for you to bridge the gap. They have used Jesus as a primary example in the West, but in every religion there has been created this monster of idolatry concerning the leader or leaders of that religion. Jesus was so special, was so far above everyone else that how can you possibly close the gap between your present level of consciousness and the superior level of consciousness that Jesus demonstrated. The same thing with many leaders of many organizations.

There are indeed many gurus and teachers in this world today who are not necessarily false gurus—they are well-meaning individuals, they have attained a certain spiritual attainment, perhaps even certain abilities. Yet if they do not understand the dynamics of the path, they often teach essentially by saying, "Look how advanced I am. Come up to my level!" But they do not provide a step-by-step path between where people are at in consciousness and where they are at themselves.

And thus, you see my beloved, if these individuals are not aware of this, and are yet too focused on themselves – that they have not truly let go of the self-centeredness but they have a little bit of ego left – then even though they have genuine spiritual attainment, and they actually have the ability to help people grow spiritually, they have not yet bridged the gap between their own attainment and the attainment of those they teach. And thus, even though they might give a genuine teaching, it is actually a false teaching in the sense that it discourages those who accept the teaching because they think they cannot bridge the gap between their consciousness and the consciousness of the teacher. Because they see no logical step-by-step path between their level and the level demonstrated by the teacher.

A fundamental problem for spiritual teachers

And this then brings you to another understanding of the spiritual path, an essential dynamic of the path that even we of the Ascended Host cannot circumvent as long as people are trapped in the ego. For you see, how can we make anyone motivated to follow the spiritual path unless we demonstrate to them that there is an advantage to following that path. And so we do that by giving people examples who demonstrate a higher level of consciousness, perhaps certain abilities that are beyond the ordinary. And yet, the ego can then use this to create that aura of idolatry, or infallibility, around the leaders, which makes it seem impossible for others to bridge the gap and attain the same consciousness as the leader.

Yet my beloved, for many years we have said, "What one human being has done, all can do, all can attain." And thus, I ask you to seriously ponder whether you have – in your own being – some element that makes you look at the Ascended Masters, or anybody in embodiment that you consider to be more spiritually advanced than yourself, and think, "Oh, I couldn't possibly do that, I couldn't possibly attain that." And then I ask you to recognize that if you see this, it can only come from the ego. It cannot come from a realistic assessment from the Christ Mind because the Christ knows, as Jesus said, "With men this is impossible, but with God, all things are possible." And thus you see, you of your own self could not bridge the gap but God within you can indeed bridge that gap.

So my beloved, we of the Ascended Host are constantly attempting to come up with ways and means to help people bridge the gap.

…

Yet I ask you again, as we have said before, to keep in mind that every tool we give you can become a trap, if you become too attached to it and think that you should be able to get all your answers in a specific way. And thus, I desire you to recognize that every tool we give you as a means to an end must not become an end in itself, for in that case it is no longer helping you to grow but only helping to keep you trapped.

Getting more accurate answers

Thus, my beloved, I ask you to recognize that many of you have a certain ability to get answers. Some of you might even feel very sure that the answers you get are accurate, absolute, infallible. But I ask you to consider that this is only a phase on the spiritual path, and it is a necessary phase where you begin to come out of the tendency to blindly follow the blind leaders.

You begin to come into your own, you begin to trust that you can know on your own the difference between truth and error. But there is a subtle temptation, where the ego will use this to make you think that you are always right, that you always know in an absolute manner, what is truth and error. As we have attempted to show you very gently, there is always a higher level of understanding of any concept on the spiritual path.

This is a principle I would like you to anchor in your minds. For as long as you are on Earth, you are not beyond learning something more, discovering a deeper layer of understanding. And yet if you allow your ego to trap you in the sense that, "I have the perfect discernment, and I know the truth," then you are not open to discovering a higher truth than the one you know. And take note that I am not saying that the truth you know might not be correct. In many cases, many of you do know the truth. But truth is not something that can be captured in words or even concepts on this Earth. Which is why Jesus said, "God is a spirit, and they that worship him must worship him in Spirit and in Truth."

So God's Spirit is the River of Life, which is constantly transcending itself. Which is why we have given you rosaries and teachings to help you reconnect to the River of Life. For when you lock your mind on the sense that you have now discovered some ultimate guru or belief system and now you have everything you need to make your ascension, then you set yourself apart from the River of Life. For you essentially say to God, "I have everything I need, leave me alone."

And that is truly what you say to your spiritual teacher, to your Christ Self and to the Ascended Host. And I must tell you that a substantial number of the people who used to have a certain connection to me – and therefore could rightfully call themselves chelas of El Morya – have lost that connection for the simple reason that they have not been willing to move on with the River of Life. Even though they were prompted by me and by their Christ Selves to move on.

I am not even talking about moving on to another organization or other messengers or another teaching. I am simply talking about moving to a higher understanding and realizing that even though they have a good understanding of the path, that there are still layers and levels to be discovered. And it will not end as long as you are here on Earth. For that matter, it will not end even in Heaven until you have attained full God consciousness, which I can assure you is still a ways away for all of you.

Beware of the temptation

And if I possibly could, I would love to see all of you make that switch, make that turn of the dial of consciousness, whereby you realize that you can – at this moment – come into Oneness with the WIll of God—if you are willing to give up every aspect of the lower will of the ego.

Thus, I will give you another tool. Whenever you sense you are dealing with a particular concept or problem in your psychology or an outside situation or force, keep in mind that you are being tempted by the prince of this world, as Jesus was tempted after his stay in the wilderness. See that the prince of this world and your ego are standing right next to you, whispering in your ear something that takes you away from that sense of inner Oneness. And then create for yourself, depending on the situation you are dealing with, an affirmation that counteracts what is coming to you from the ego and the forces of deception.

Create an affirmation or a habit of centering in the heart so that you turn their own strategy against them. So that their very attempts to take you away from the centeredness in the heart becomes an encouragement for you to make an extra effort to center yourself in the heart, in the oneness with the Will of God. If it helps you, visualize my presence with you in your heart as the Presence of the Will of God, the Master of the Will of God. Then by all means I will be happy to be there, and so will any other Master on the Seven Rays, or whomever Master you are currently working with.

But fix in your mind the idea that when your ego and the forces of this world are trying to get you away from Oneness, then use their own tactic to come closer to Oneness, to center in Oneness, to BE in Oneness. And then you will see that the devil will flee from you, as he fled from Jesus when he realized that Jesus was not going to be tempted.

Don't take the devil too seriously

This my beloved, is indeed an important key. And when you use their own tactics to center in Oneness, you can overcome the tendency to take yourself, and the devil, and the ego, too seriously. And then you can employ what I have said in my past lives, when I said as Thomas More, "The devil, the proud spirit, cannot endure to be mocked." And then you can laugh at the devil, and he will flee, for he cannot stand the sound of laughter, especially when you are laughing at him.

But even when you are happy and laughing out of the pure joy of being alive on Earth, the devil flees. For he cannot stand those who are happy, are centered and at peace. They disturb him! And that is why some of you will notice in your lives that you have met people who are angry with you, or blaming you for seemingly no outer reason. But it was your light, your inner light, your peace, your happiness, essentially your God Flame, that disturbed them. And thus they were agitated because they saw that if you could be More, then they could be More too. But because they were not willing to change, they did not want to be around you. So they wanted to drag you down into their own misery so that they had an excuse for not changing themselves.

My beloved, do not take these people so seriously; they have no power over you. And thus, I say to you, find a way to center in the Oneness in the Heart. Find a way to laugh at the conditions that seem so dire. And do not allow yourself to enter into the vibration of thinking that the world is going to hell in a hand basket, for I assure you that it is not.

Become the open door for the Living Christ

Jesus, May 28, 2006.

Raise up a chalice for the Living Christ
Thus, my beloved, I call your attention to the necessity of contemplating the concept of being Right on each of the seven rays. Being Right means being balanced. For, as has already been said, the eight-fold path of the Buddha is to be Right by being on the middle way.

And thus, my beloved if, you think back to the delivery earlier, [Kim Michaels had given a lecture about Jesus' mission] you will see that there was an expression of God Power. But there was not the misuse of God Power that you indeed see in some Christian preachers who go on with their hellfire and brimstone preaching, and therefore become unbalanced and indeed qualify power as the power of the ego.

And I must tell you that it is unfortunately possible that some of these people can have a certain momentum of God Power from past lives. And thus, they may seem to give a very powerful speech, and indeed there may be some flow of the Holy Spirit through them, but it is perverted by their egos who are blinded by their pride or by their desire for control. So that they will not express the God Power that is in alignment with the Will of God, and therefore seeks to awaken people without in any way forcing or manipulating them against the law of free will.

Thus, my beloved, each and every one of you – if you are willing – have the potential to become the open door. That means following the path, healing your psychology, overcoming the ego, but it also means raising up a chalice so that the Living Christ can flow into a vessel, and not be the pearl that is cast before the swine of the human consciousness of the world. And thus, raising up a chalice means that you study a topic that is dear to your heart. You study it until you have the concepts in your mind, to the point where the Living Christ has something to work with and can therefore express itself through you.

So what you saw earlier was that when Kim got up to give that lecture, he had no idea what was going to be said, except that it was going to be about the three years of my mission. Yet, because he has studied and read and written about the topic of my life, and knows the scriptures to some degree, he had the vessel prepared that could be the chalice for the Living Christ to flow through him—even though his outer mind had no preparation.

And the same can be true of each and every one of you, when you prepare yourself. So that, at any moment, when you encounter a situation where the Living Christ desires to express itself through you, you are not taken aback and you do not fall into the trap that all of you sometimes fall into—of saying, "Oh no, I couldn't be the Living Christ in this situation. I am not ready. I am not worthy. I do not know enough. I am too tired. Perhaps tomorrow, but not now."

And yet, did I not say, "You know not when the lord of the household cometh?" You know not when the Living Christ needs to use you, because you are the only person who can give that cup of cold water to a particular person who is trapped in some outer situation, or in the blindness of the ego. And thus they need that cold water to be splashed in their face, so that they can be awakened and realize there is a better way to live, there is more to life.

And so, my beloved, contemplate the concept of the brides who made themselves ready by keeping their lamps trimmed, so that when the bridegroom came, they were ready. Whereas the foolish virgins, who had not trimmed their lamps, first had to go out and buy oil, and thus, the bridegroom had already entered the bridal chamber when they came back.

Did Jesus die on the cross?

My beloved hearts, I will now give you a teaching about the fourth stage of my mission and life—namely my death on the cross and my resurrection.

There are books in this world that claim that Jesus Christ did not die on the cross—that he had learned some kind of technique taught in the mystery schools of the ancient world of how to withdraw the breath from the body for a time, so that it seemed like the body was dead but it could be reawakened through specific methods. It is claimed that giving me the vinegar while I was hanging on the cross was a means to allow myself to put my body into a coma and withdraw the soul.

So my beloved, what is the reality? Well, the reality is that I had studied in the mystery schools of the ancient world. The reality is that I had indeed learned the technique of withdrawing the breath, thereby putting the body into a state where it would be declared dead in any hospital in the modern world. It was indeed my plan, along with a few of my supporters, to go through the crucifixion and use this technique to give the impression of dying on the cross and then being reawakened.

This was my intent. But it did not come to pass. For as I was hanging on the cross, I realized that this was not God's will. It was indeed God's will that I, Jesus Christ, went through the experience of physical death, having faith that whether I was resurrected or not would be according to God's will. And so you see, my beloved, even the consciousness of wanting to cheat death was in a certain sense a lack of faith on my part, thinking that I somehow had to give God a little bit of help. And thus, I had created a ghost—a ghostly image of how my ascension, how my crucifixion, should take place. And it was indeed that ghostly image that I had to give up while I was hanging on the cross.

For I experienced that – as I started going through the process of withdrawing the breath – God's Presence withdrew itself from me. And thus, I knew that it was not the will of God to continue. And thus I cried out in affliction, not knowing what was next. And then I surrendered myself, surrendered the ghost, and let my body die.

And it was indeed this act of total surrender – of being willing to die on the cross – that was the key to my resurrection. Thus, my beloved, why would I build, why would I create, this ghost that it was necessary for me to remain physically alive instead of leaving it up to God? Well it was, my beloved, partly because my entire mission in Palestine was indeed very much adapted to the beliefs of the Jews. I did and said many things that were aimed at fulfilling the prophecies in the Old Testament, so that the Jews might accept me as their Messiah and therefore raise their religion out of the Old Testament law and prophets that was now obsolete.

Therefore, knowing how close-minded the leaders of the Jewish religion and many of its followers were, it was necessary to do and say many things that were specifically adapted to fulfilling the prophecies given forth about the coming of the Messiah. And while in that consciousness, I built that ghost of thinking I could go through this process of being crucified without having the physical body die. And thereby, my intent was to continue my mission elsewhere.

Perpetual surrender
So my beloved, I tell you this that you may have an understanding of how subtle the ego can be. And how to the very end of your spiritual path, and your spiritual mission on this Earth, the ego can manage to trick you into creating a ghost about your mission on this Earth. And I ask you to contemplate this and learn, once again, from my example, thus not being permanently trapped by such a ghostly image imposed by your ego or imposed by other people. For as has been discussed, the world might recognize the presence of the Christ, but the world will want to impose its dualistic images upon how the Christ expresses itself in this world.

And it is very easy for all of us, when we are in a physical body, to adapt in subtle ways to the ways of the world, rather than always being completely open—giving God a clean slate on which to write. Thus, I ask you to contemplate that for as long as you are in embodiment, you need to maintain some awareness of the need to give up the ghost continually. And therefore, I ask you to contemplate the concept of perpetual surrender, whereby you never allow your ego to trick you into thinking that you have now passed some turning point on the path, and now you are beyond the ego or the need to surrender.

My beloved, if you are always willing to surrender, and if you are always alert for what you need to surrender, you cannot be permanently trapped in the consciousness of death. For I tell you, the consciousness of life is indeed the state of perpetual surrender, and thus we who are ascended, and reside in the spiritual realm, are in that state of perpetual surrender.

And I know that many of you, through the Christian dispensation, through previous organizations sponsored by the Ascended Host, have come to see an Ascended Master as being somehow perfect. And therefore, how could that Ascended Master need to surrender anything? But you see, my beloved, an Ascended Master does not need to surrender the ego. But an Ascended Master, at any given time, still has a sense of identity.

And yet in order to maintain its place in the River of Life, even an Ascended Master has to – at certain intervals – surrender its current sense of identity and accept a greater sense of identity, thus becoming more in the process. This process will not end until you have manifested the full God Consciousness exemplified by your creator. And, my beloved, even then it will not end, as we will surely describe in the book by Maitreya that will be forthcoming in due time. [Master Keys to Spiritual Freedom]

The Key to establishing the Mystery School on Earth

Lord Maitreya, May 28, 2006.

The essential truth about the Mystery School

So you see, my beloved, when there is no fixed doctrine in the Mystery School, then you do not have the ego games of judging whether any new idea that is presented is right or wrong in comparison to the infallible doctrine. And what you have indeed seen here amongst yourselves, is that there is more than one valid way to express truth. And what you have seen is that there is no point in arguing over particular words or interpretations of particular Bible verses. For when you argue at the level of duality – the intellectual level – the spirit of truth runs away from you—you cannot grasp it.

So the reality is that when two students have different viewpoints or different ways of expressing a truth, it is not a matter of playing the old ego game of who is right—thinking that one must be right and the other must be wrong. No, it is a matter of using the differences to honestly and openly reach for a higher understanding.

For my beloved, here is the essential concept: Maitreya's Mystery School teaches the Path of Oneness. If two students on that path are not in a state of Oneness with each other – because they have different views or different expressions – then the true goal is NOT to establish whose viewpoint is right. The true goal is to transcend the outer viewpoints and reach for the Spirit of truth that brings you into a Oneness that goes beyond the outer words and beliefs.

My beloved, do you see how profound this one truth is? And do you see, when you look back at history, how few people on the Earth have grasped this one concept—which could revolutionize religion on this planet, which could revolutionize every aspect of society. If people would realize that when there is conflict and disagreement it is a sign that both sides need to reach beyond the outer conditions and reach for the spirit of truth, the spirit of love, and thereby honestly, openly and sincerely – with pure hearts and pure intentions – strive for Oneness.

Who created the soul

Thus, I have many more teachings to give you along the way. Surely I will teach about the soul for as you have discussed here, the soul was not created by God. It was created by the Conscious Self after it separated itself from the spiritual teacher and the I AM Presence. And so, I will give you a glimpse of the teachings on the soul that can be brought forth in the future. For you see, my beloved, when the Conscious You has awareness of its I AM Presence and that it is part of a greater Being, then there is a sense of continuity. Yet, when the Conscious You loses that connection, where shall its continuity – the continuity of its sense of identity – come from, when it now has to re-embody on Earth, and the slate of memory is wiped clean when it comes into its next embodiment.

How can a co-creator with God learn and grow if it does not remember anything from its past life, and therefore has to reinvent the wheel all over again in each embodiment? Thus, when the Conscious You loses contact with the I AM Presence and its treasure laid up in Heaven, there must be a vehicle for maintaining – even at the subconscious level – the memories of the co-creator's experiences in this world. So that there can be a continuity and the co-creator does not have to start from zero every time.

And this vehicle, then, is what most spiritual teachings call the soul. And yet, the word soul has been used in so many different ways that it has been degraded to the point where Mother Mary chose not to use it [in the book Master Keys to the Abundant Life]. Yet, we will give you a more sophisticated teaching and definition of the soul.

So indeed, the soul is what you create. It is what you fill into the container of self. And yet, the container of self might also contain the ego, which is apart from the soul. Because whereas the soul has substance, the ego, as we have said, is not a substance. It is a ghost because it is basically a collection of decisions, and therefore you cannot pinpoint the ego as having substance. You must look beyond and discover the decisions that make up the ego, until you reach that one decision that caused you to turn your back on the Path of Oneness.

Anchoring the Mother Light in the base chakra of America

Mother Mary, June 21, 2006

The base chakra is the basis for manifestation

Instead of accepting that it is the Father's good pleasure to give them the kingdom, people seek to take that kingdom by force by perverting the Mother Light. My beloved hearts, the base chakra of your individual being, and the base chakra of a nation, is truly the "space" where material abundance is brought into manifestation. It is through the base chakra that you manifest an abundant material life.

Yet in order to manifest God's abundant life, the base chakra must be in alignment with the heart. It must be under the guidance of the heart because only the heart is the open door between your lower being and your higher Being. And only when you are centered in the heart, and allow your higher being to direct your life through the heart, will you have God's abundant life.

My beloved, what happens when the heart is closed off because of hardness of heart? Well, what happens is that you are still co-creating through the base chakra. But now you cannot co-create in alignment with God's greater plan nor with your own divine plan. And thus, what happens is one of two things.

One is that the base chakra itself becomes polluted by self-centered short-term desires, whereby the person enters the endless quest for pleasure, seeking physical pleasure, whether through sexual activity or any other means. This becomes a downward spiral because when there is no connection to the heart, there can be no true enjoyment of the pleasures or the possessions of this world.

True joy, true fulfillment, comes only when you manifest things and experiences in the material realm that are in alignment with God's purpose and with your own divine plan. When you are out of alignment with this higher vision, anything you do will give you a sense of emptiness, of never being quite fulfilled. Thus, ego-desires can never give you true happiness, as ultimate fulfillment comes only from knowing you are raising up both yourself and all life.

And thus, no matter how much sex or how many possessions people have, they are never satisfied, they are never filled—they are still empty. This leads people to try to misuse the Mother Light instead of allowing the clarity, the vision, of the heart to manifest the abundant life that God desires to give all of his co-creators. They now seek to take it by force by doing it according to what their egos think they need—right now, right here. Thus, there is no concern for long-term consequences, there is only what feels good right now. And thus comes the whole concept of, "If it feels good, do it!"

"Eat, drink and be merry, for tomorrow we die," as they say. And truly, so many people in this area live this way. They might go out and work throughout the week, but come the week-end, they go out to eat, drink and be merry, not caring whether they live the next morning.

The other thing that happens when the heart is closed off is that if the base chakra is not ruled by the endless quest for pleasure, it will be ruled by the head, by the analytical mind, and its quest for whatever it seeks, which is often power and superiority. Thus, you see in this area an enormous amount of corruption and an enormous striving for, even an entire culture of, making easy money with no regard for how it affects other parts of life.

You also see the perversion of the intellect, the perversion of the crown chakra, which is seeking superiority over other people, rather than seeking the connection to the God within that gives you the knowledge that you are one with God and all life is one with God, and thus what is the point of seeking superiority over others. The true fulfillment comes from seeking to raise up all life rather than creating the state of inequality that gives the impression to some people that they are better than others because they have more power or more possessions.

Those who start wars cannot stop war

Mother Mary, September 8, 2006.

My beloved hearts, I am your Mother Mary, and I come to congratulate all of you who have participated in this latest vigil of the Invocation for Loving Yourself. My beloved, if you could see the beautiful light that has spread throughout the Earth as a result of so many people giving this rosary, then you would surely rejoice with me. For I can tell you that this glow – that is of the softest pink, like the petals of a rose in the morning sun – has spread around the Earth. It has indeed formed a band of energy that has consumed a very substantial cloud of negative energy that had been hanging around this planet for a very long time.

Oh my beloved, it has been a burden on this planet that the false humility, created by dark forces and prideful people, have prevented so many of the truly spiritual people on this planet from loving themselves, loving their spiritual selves, loving themselves as spiritual beings, as sons and daughters of God. For truly, my beloved, consider how – ever since your childhood – you have been indoctrinated with the belief that it is wrong to love yourself, it is wrong to appreciate the self that you are. Yet my beloved, I hope you can now see that the real you, the Conscious You, is the self that was created by God. And therefore, it is worthy of love. God loves that self, and therefore why should you not love the self that you are?

Surely, you do not love the human ego and the outer personality that is not created by God. But there is nothing wrong with loving the self that is created by God and recognizing that it is created by God. And thus, those of you who have given this rosary, whether every day or just a few times, will surely have felt an increase in love in your being. And I can assure you that on a planetary scale, you have begun an upward spiral that will make it easier for all people to love themselves, to love their spiritual selves and to see beyond the tendency in this world to always focus on the negative.

Oh my beloved, consider how many people have made it almost a lifestyle to always criticize and point out the negative. And my beloved, when you realize the creative power of the human mind, what do you think these people are creating when they always focus on the negative, rather than focus on the positive?

I am not saying you need to be like an ostrich and stick your head in the sand and refuse to recognize that there are problems on this planet. For surely, that will not lead anywhere near the Golden Age. Yet what I am saying is that while recognizing that there are problems on this planet, you choose to see them as temporary manifestations that are not ultimately real. And then you look beyond those outer appearances to the reality of God, the reality of the Ma-ter Light that is behind all appearances.

Therefore, you do not – as Jesus said – judge according to appearances. You judge by reaching for the vision of the Christ mind that helps you see God's reality behind all temporary appearances. Yet my beloved, how can you do this in the world around you unless you have first done it in your own being, by seeing beyond the ego and the outer personality and realizing that the Conscious You is a son or daughter of God, is a co-creator with God, and is fully worthy of God's love. For only when you love yourself can you love others as yourself.

This my beloved, is a most profound truth that Jesus gave 2,000 years ago. But oh how few people have understood that truth. Look how many Christians have been brought up, have been programmed, have been brainwashed into seeing themselves as miserable sinners and thinking they should feel guilty for simply being alive. Oh my beloved, what is the insanity that indoctrinates the innocent mind of a child with this heavy burden of sin and guilt? Yes my beloved, this must indeed come to an end, and your rosaries have dealt a very severe blow to this consciousness of self-hatred that has permeated this planet for far too long.

The need to invoke peace

Thus my beloved, I come to congratulate you with a work well done. And as we of the Ascended Host have said for many years, the reward for service is more service. And thus, I ask you to build on the foundation that you have laid through this rosary for loving yourself and now give a vigil of these next two rosaries for peace, that we are releasing.

For my beloved, there is indeed a great need for invoking the Flame of Peace that can consume the conditions that lead to war. Yet why have we waited with these rosaries for peace until you have given the rosary for loving yourself? Because my beloved, if you do not love yourself, how can you be at peace within yourself? And if you are not at peace within yourself, how can you be a force for peace in this world?

You see, my beloved, life is really not that complicated. If you love yourself, you will love other people. And thus, you will not commit acts of violence against them nor will you respond with violence even if others are violent toward you. For you will know, through the clarity of your love, that they are more than the outer personality and the ego that commits acts of violence. And thus, instead of seeking to punish them, you will seek to raise them up out of their illusions and set them free from the energies, even the dark spirits – even the demons – of war.

Yes my beloved, there is indeed a need to invoke peace in this world. For as is clearly stated in our rosary, there can be no freedom without peace. And as you well know, Jesus was called the Prince of Peace precisely because he came to inaugurate the Age of Pisces, which was meant to be an age of peace. Thus my beloved, it was indeed the Divine design that at the end of this two-thousand-year period humankind would leave war behind them.

Obviously, as is plain for everyone to see, this goal has not been fulfilled —yet. But my beloved, this goal is far closer than you might think when you look at world events. For has not this two-thousand-year period seen an unprecedented amount of wars. And has not this past century seen an unprecedented amount of wars on a very large scale. And thus, I can assure you that there is indeed a growing realization among humankind that war MUST come to an end. And the only thing that is lacking for this to actually manifest is that people come to a recognition of the true cause of war.

The true cause of war has a personal and a planetary aspect. The personal aspect is, of course, the warring in the members of individuals, which is caused by the human ego. And the planetary aspect is the presence of a small elite of lifestreams, the power elite, who are absolutely committed to power or to proving God wrong. And thus, they will do anything to stir up conflict as a means to either control the people for their own gain or simply destroy this planet in order to thwart God's plan for the Earth.

Who can stop war?

Thus my beloved, what needs to happen is truly that people are awakened and come to see the consciousness of war for what it is. This awakening must, of course, start among the top ten percent of the most spiritually aware people on this planet. For they are truly the ones who can turn the tide away from war and toward peace. Yet the unfortunate fact is, as Jesus has pointed out in his discourse on the human ego, that many of the most spiritual people on Earth have been trapped in gray thinking. They have come to think that all that is necessary is that they love everyone and ignore every problem. For if a problem is ignored, it will surely go away by itself—or so they think.

Yet my beloved, the reality is – and history proves this for anyone who is willing to take a closer look – that no problem will go away by itself. As has been said, for evil to triumph, it only takes that good people do nothing. Thus, I must tell you that the most spiritual people, the top ten percent of the people on this planet, are the only ones who can remove the consciousness of war from the Earth. Yet they must do so by beginning to remove the warring in their own members, namely the human ego.

And this, my beloved, is precisely the problem with gray thinking, namely that it gives the ego a protected status as an untouchable part of people's psychology. For in thinking that all that is necessary is for them to be loving and kind, they are also being loving and kind to their own egos. And my beloved, you do not overcome the ego by being tolerant of the ego. You overcome the ego only when the Conscious You awakens to the existence of the ego and becomes completely intolerant of the ego, so that you will no longer allow it to run your life or to have any presence in your being.

Thus my beloved, there is indeed such a thing as the perfect hatred, which is not a hatred in the human, dualistic sense, but is the Flame of Love that burns with such brightness that it will no longer tolerate anything other than love. It will simply not tolerate anything that springs from anti-love, and thus it consumes anything based on anti-love—instantly.

This my beloved, is indeed what must happen if war is to be banished from this planet. The top ten percent of the most spiritual people on Earth must wake up and realize that they have allowed the ego to remain in their own consciousness, and thus they have allowed the consciousness of war to remain in their own subconscious minds. And as long as they allow this to happen, then God simply does not have the authority to remove the consciousness of war from this planet or remove the beings who are absolutely committed to war and thus embody the consciousness of war.

And thus my beloved, I must tell you that even though it is the bottom ten percent, the power elite, who create every war on this planet, it is actually the top ten percent, the spiritual elite, who are responsible for allowing the consciousness of war to remain on Earth. My beloved, do you see the equation?

The power elite are so trapped in the consciousness of duality that they are not likely to change their minds in the foreseeable future. It is not likely that they will be converted to the cause of peace and non-violence and suddenly destroy all their weapons and refuse to exercise power over the population. Thus, what MUST happen is that the top ten percent of the people on Earth wake up and decide that they will no longer tolerate war on this planet. They must realize that they are the ones who have the potential to bring forth God's judgment so that war can be removed from this planet.

And how do you bring forth God's judgment? Well, my beloved, you can judge the consciousness of war only when you have removed the consciousness of war from your own being, when you have removed the warring in your own members by removing the human ego.

True tolerance and false tolerance

Thus my beloved, it is indeed necessary – for planet Earth to rise above war – that there is greater tolerance among people. Yet as with everything else, the ego can pervert every positive quality, even the quality of love, forgiveness and tolerance. For the false tolerance is that anything goes, that anything should be allowed. The false tolerance makes people believe that they should not take a stand against war but that they should simply focus on being loving and kind, thinking that then war will go away by itself.

But my beloved, do you not see that if the good people do nothing, then they give free reign to those people who are committed to war? And thus, they will inevitably drag nations into war as has indeed happened over these last five years since the terrorist attacks in New York on September 11, 2001.

My beloved, do you not see that the United States has been dragged into war and conflict by those who are using terrorism as an excuse for increasing military spending and using their military superiority to supposedly bring democracy and freedom, but in reality further the cause of the power elite? Thus my beloved, even though there is a substantial number of very spiritual people in the United States, you can clearly see that these spiritual people have not been able to provide enough of a counter-weight, a counter-balance, to prevent the United States from being dragged into war by the power elite.

And this alone should show you that the spiritual people in the United States have not done their job of removing the warring in their own members. They have not been willing to face their egos and overcome those egos, so that they could have the moral authority to call forth the judgment of God upon the power elite in the United States, who are dragging this nation into war and who surely have plans to drag it into further wars around the globe.

Yes my beloved, I am being the stern mother, for it is indeed time that the most spiritual people on this planet wake up and realize that the future of this planet hangs in the balance, and they are the only ones who can tip the balance in the favor of peace. Thus, as Jesus said, "If you love me, keep my commandments." If you are a spiritual person and you claim to love God and love the spiritual realm, then keep the commandment to remove the beam from your own eye.

Stop thinking that it is other people who are responsible for the fact that there is war and violence on this planet. Yes, these people are the ones who commit violence and start wars and they make the decision to do so. But as I have tried to point out, they are simply acting on a certain state of consciousness that is dragging them into actions over which they really have no control. And so the problem is not the people, but the consciousness of war that hangs over this planet as a black cloud.

And why is this consciousness still hanging over this planet? Well, it is because God has not been given sufficient authority to remove that consciousness. Archangel Michael and his legions of Blue-flame Angels, have not been given the marching orders to consume that consciousness and remove all beings who refuse to let go of that consciousness. And why have they not been given that authority? Well, they have not been given that authority because the top ten percent of the most spiritual people on this planet have refused to overcome the warring in their own members by becoming completely intolerant toward their own egos.

Yet if those top ten percent were to awaken and make a firm commitment to overcome the ego, then in removing the beam from your own eyes, you would indeed give God the authority to remove the consciousness of war from this entire planet. And when the dark cloud of that consciousness is removed, I can assure you that even those who are now committed to war would suddenly wake up and be able to see the insanity of their actions. They cannot presently see that insanity because of what we might call the fog of war that blinds people to the existence of a nonviolent solution to their problems.

Only true emissaries of peace can stop war

Why is the public blinded by the consciousness of war? Well, it is simply because, as Jesus has explained, the eighty percent of the general population will either follow the lowest ten percent, namely the power elite, or the top ten percent, namely the spiritual elite. And precisely because the top ten percent have been so blinded by the gray thinking of the ego, they have not been willing to overcome the consciousness of warring in their own members. And thus they have not been able to act as the forerunners who could bring forth the new vision of how to actually solve the problem of world terrorism through peaceful means.

So my beloved, once again, the balance of this planet, the future of this planet, is indeed in the hearts and minds of the top ten percent of the most spiritual people. Will they choose to walk the Path of Peace, or will they choose to continue to walk the path of false peace, which makes them think that they can be emissaries of peace without overcoming their egos.

You see, my beloved, you cannot be an emissary of peace unless you first declare all-out war on your own ego. For only when you have removed that beam from your own eye, can you see clearly how to remove the mote in the eye of another. And only then can you become a true emissary of true peace. For truly, peace cannot come about through the false tolerance which says that anything goes. Peace can only come about through the true tolerance of the Christ mind, the tolerance that is based on a clear discernment of what is of God and what is not of God.

And thus, a Christed being can see that when people commit acts of violence, it is not because their real selves are evil or bad or violent. It is because the conscious self has withdrawn into a cave and has allowed the ego to act out through the consciousness of duality that always operates with two opposites. And it is this consciousness that causes people to think that they must fight the enemy, and therefore violence is necessary or unavoidable.

Thus my beloved, only when people have Christ discernment can they see the difference between the person and that person's actions. Only when they have Christ discernment can they see that the actions are caused by a state of consciousness that springs from the mind of duality, the mind of anti-christ. But behind the actions and the outer personality is the conscious self of the person, and that conscious self was created by God. And thus, all people are truly brethren and part of the One Body of God on Earth.

Only when you see beyond the outer actions, will you be able to turn the other cheek and respond to violence with love. And in that love, you will potentially set your brothers and sisters free from the consciousness of war. For by turning the other cheek, you will indeed awaken them. And those who will not be awakened, those who hold on to the consciousness of war, will then be judged and they will be removed from the planet. But even this is actually an act of mercy, for these lifestreams will then be sent to another realm, where they can receive further opportunities for overcoming the consciousness of war, opportunities that are not available to them on Earth as long as the Earth is in its present condition.

Rise above all fear of war

So my beloved, it is in no way my intention to cause any kind of fear or panic in your being. I am not asking you to start acting in an unbalanced or fearful manner. I am asking you to stay in the flame of loving yourself that you have invoked during the past rosary vigil. I am asking you to let nothing disturb that state of love and that state of inner peace. And then I am asking you – based on that inner peace – to give these two rosaries with the absolute knowledge and determination that when you ask for peace, you shall indeed receive it. When you call forth the Flame of Peace, then that flame will indeed consume the consciousness of war. [Invocation for Invoking the Flame of Peace and Invocation for World Peace]

And thus my beloved, I am asking you to overcome all fear. And if indeed you sense elements of fear concerning war in your own being, then go after them. Use these two rosaries to specifically call for all fear of war to be consumed in your own being. For it is truly only the ego that can give rise to such fear, and your ego will be hiding behind that fear, seeking to divert your attention to becoming so concerned about conditions in the world that you do not look at the ego, expose it and overcome it.

Thus my beloved, realize that whenever there is fear, the ego is hiding behind it. And thus, instead of focusing on the object of fear – as the ego would have you do – look beyond the fear itself and expose the ego. And then ask for it to be consumed by the Flame of Peace, the Flame of Ecstatic Peace, coming from the Elohim of Peace. For truly, that Flame of Ecstatic Peace is able to consume all fear. For how can there be fear when your entire being is infused with the ecstatic peace that knows nothing but peace.

So I ask you to open your heart and your chakras, to open your entire being to that Flame of Ecstatic Peace. I ask you in this coming time, as you give these rosaries, to immerse yourself in the Flame of Ecstatic Peace, to allow that flame to enter your being and consume all unlike itself.

Be spiritual regardless of outer conditions

Mother Mary, September 30, 2006.

My beloved hearts, I am Mary the Mother of all life. For I have become one with the flame of the Divine Mother that truly encompasses all life in the material world and all life in the spiritual realm. I come with a message of peace, of love and of gratitude. For truly, we, the Ascended Host, are grateful that you have come to be here with us.

My beloved, it might seem as if we meet in strange places—in this place in Sweden. But think about the conditions that Jesus and his disciples endured many years ago, when they walked the dusty roads of ancient Palestine. Many Christians have grown up with a vastly distorted image of Jesus and his life, thinking there was great glory, fame and fortune and that Jesus was treated as the celebrities you have today.

But my beloved, the reality was far different. For Jesus did not stay long enough on Earth to become a celebrity as you understand it today. He was not known beyond the borders of Palestine. And even within Palestine he was not known by many people, nor was he revered as he is revered by Christians today. After all, he was born in a manger. And why was this so? It was to show human beings the all-important truth that it is not the way things appear to the outer senses or the outer mind that is important. What is important is what is not seen with the senses but what can be felt and experienced in the heart.

This, my beloved, is what counts. This is all that counts. And thus, we have always attempted to help the spiritual people see that it is not the outer appearances that are ultimately real, that the outer appearances are not permanent and that they truly have no power over your mind—unless you allow your minds to become identified with the outer conditions, even with the ego itself.

The call for spiritual people
So you see, the call for the spiritual people has always been to be spiritual regardless of the outer conditions they face in their personal lives or on the planet as a whole. The spiritual path, the true spiritual path, is

not a matter of attaining outer fame or fortune or the status of a celebrity as some church leaders and some preachers have indeed attained. We do not desire our true servants to be looked upon as celebrities or to be idolized. We do not desire our true servants to set themselves up as being above others. For what is the purpose?

The purpose, the true purpose, of all of our servants is to show people that there is more to life than the outer appearances and that they do not need to be limited or held back by the material conditions they face, or even by the psychological conditions they face in their own minds—but that you can transcend these outer conditions no matter what they are. And you can become more because the real you, what I have called the Conscious You, is more than any outer conditions, more than the ego, more than the outer personality.

You are not a human being. You are not a piece of living meat. You are a spark of the flame of God. An individual spirit spark who has the potential to become one with the All of God's Being. And yet you are in a physical body on Earth. And so you face the challenge of balancing the knowledge that you are a spiritual being with the practical everyday reality that you all face on this planet. And this, my beloved, is a challenge that all of us who have descended to Earth have faced. Jesus and I faced it. And we sometimes had as much difficulty as you have in balancing the daily reality with our spiritual vision and goals.

My beloved, this is natural. And I do not desire to see you become frustrated and think that you should be more spiritual, that you should be doing this or doing that, so that you frustrate yourselves and get down on yourselves for not doing enough. For truly we have done so ourselves. We have seen many other spiritual people do so. But in this age, the Age of Freedom, we desire to see many people rise above that, rise above that sense that it is not enough, that you are not doing enough.

Nothing you can do will make a difference

But I tell you, that if you are Being who you are, then that is enough. For in Being here below what you are Above, even when you go about your daily activities, you can radiate the Light. And it is truly the Light that will make the greatest difference. I am not saying that you should do nothing to expose the imperfections and the false beliefs on this planet. I am not saying that you should do nothing about bringing peace. Nevertheless, it is a wise student who realizes that there is nothing that you can do that will make the ultimate difference.

Because what will make the ultimate difference is Being. Allowing the Light of God to flow through your lower being in all aspects of life. This is what will make the critical difference on Earth. And so we do not desire you to become frustrated and to come from this sense that, "I need to be doing more," so that you get yourself in the frame of mind where you feel like you are always running behind the train, and the train is driving away from the station and you can never quite catch up. And then some people, toward the end of life, feel like now the platform they are running on is beginning to run out, and they still have not caught up to the train. And they become even more frustrated and they try to run even faster.

My beloved, if I could, I would set you free from that mindset which is another subtle plot of the ego. The ego does not want you to discover the spiritual path. But when it cannot stop you from doing so, it will try to turn your spiritual path into a big frustration, where you feel like you are always behind and it is never enough. So my beloved, allow yourself to know, to realize, that Being is enough. And then focus on establishing that inner contact of Being, contact with your Higher Self, contact with the Ascended Host, whomever is closest to your heart.

And then let your doing flow from your centeredness in Being—and that way, your doing will be balanced. And thereby, it will not be you who is doing the work; it will be the Father within you, the God Flame within you, who is doing the work. And thus, you will know the truth, that with men it is impossible to create peace in the world. But with God, with your God Flame, all things are indeed possible. And this is the key.

God government versus human government

El Morya, September 30, 2006.

The origin of the power elite
My beloved, this denial of the spiritual reality goes back a very long time on this planet and beyond. It goes all the way back to the fall of those beings in spiritual realms who decided that they would not move higher when the realm in which they lived moved higher. Instead, they would deny God, deny God's will, deny God's will that all life becomes more. They would choose the path of becoming less, and they would drag as many as they could with them on that path.

And as you know from Mother Mary's book, when a certain sphere ascends to a higher vibration and becomes part of the spiritual realm, then those lifestreams who are not willing to move on must then descend into a lower sphere, into a lower vibration. And yet because they have descended from a higher sphere, they not only have a sense of superiority, pride and arrogance, but they also have a certain knowledge, a certain attainment, that allows them to be very clever, very intelligent in an intellectual, logical, rational way that is far beyond many of the lifestreams who start in that lower sphere in order to work their way up.

And that is why you have the formation of a power elite who believe they are better than the people and have a right to rule the people and that the people should be their literal slaves. This, my beloved, goes back a very long time to civilizations that are not currently known. But even in your own known history, you can see the pattern and you see it few places more clearly than here in Europe, where throughout the middle ages you had the feudal lords who owned everything, even owned the people who lived on their land.

This, my beloved, certainly was not God government, nor was it the will of God. It was a totally perverted system. And it should show you that there is nothing that can be given that cannot be perverted by the human ego—as long as most of the people are blinded by the duality of the ego. For it is true that there is a potential that a king can be an enlightened ruler. And if the king is in a higher state of consciousness, he can give birth to an heir that is also in a higher state of consciousness. So the higher form of rule, the higher God government, can indeed be passed on through inheritance. But this system is not fail-proof, as is no system on Earth in the current level of vibration of this planet. And therefore, it too became perverted. And you saw throughout the Middle Ages how one insane king would have insane children that would lead on and on and on, until the God government that was meant to be, had deteriorated to the point where it was human government.

...

Do you not see, my beloved, that when you take Jesus' discourses on the ego and transfer them to the field of government, you see that what the ego wants is to create a society that is static and that can maintain the power and privilege of the elite while keeping the population in such a state that they are not dissatisfied enough to risk their lives in a revolt against the power elite. What the ego basically wants is to create a human society that functions much like an ant hill, where the population serves to provide the privileges for the elite. And then the ego wants to maintain that society for as long as possible.

But you see, my beloved, it is not God's Will to create a static society that will remain the same for ever and ever. It is God's Will to create a society that is constantly transcending itself, so that the members of that society will be urged to constantly transcend themselves, to learn more, to come up higher, to develop their thinking, to develop culture so that everything is in a state of growth. This is the River of Life. This is how God government is.

And that is why you see so many civilizations in the past that have collapsed. And why have they collapsed? Because they became taken over by a ruling elite who, once they had power, became concerned about only one thing—maintaining their power and their privilege instead of continuing the upward growth, the self-transcendence, of society. This is the mindset of those fallen angels who rebelled against God's plan when their higher sphere, in which they lived, transcended itself and they could no longer remain.

Do you now see that this is the pattern of stopping growth, of creating a privileged position for themselves and then maintaining it indefinitely? This is the pattern that has been going on for eons on this planet.

And it is time that the spiritual people realized this, that they come out of what Jesus has so brilliantly called gray thinking. And realize that it is not enough to be spiritual, to love everyone indiscriminately without Christ discernment. That you need to come to that higher state of knowing true love, the love of God, the love that is so one with the Will of God, that it loves the Will of God and that there is no greater love than the Will of God, which is self-transcendence.

Let the people of Europe choose the Living Christ!

Jesus, October 1, 2006.

Thus, the eternal question, presented by the Living Christ is, "Will you choose life or will you choose death? Will you continue to choose death or will you leave behind the consciousness of death and be reborn into the consciousness of life, that the Living Christ bestows upon all, as his body and blood that is broken for all who are willing to take it?"

Thus, the question to ask yourself is, "Am I alive in a spiritual sense? Or am I still weighted down by some aspect of the death consciousness that then makes me feel burdened, overwhelmed, focused on myself or whatever it may be?" I ask you who are here and all who might hear or read this, to take a minute to center in your heart and ask yourself that question. "Am I really alive right now? Am I fully alive?" Or is there an entirely new level of life that I perhaps have glimpsed but have not yet internalized and become? So my beloved, ask yourself this question honestly, "Am I fully alive?"

Stop sleepwalking through life

Now then, I am not in any way trying to make you feel burdened or guilty for not being alive. I am trying to help you see that almost everyone is still, to some degree, burdened by the death consciousness. For it is indeed a black cloud hanging over the planet. Yet what I hope I can help you see is that there is something beyond that death consciousness and that it is possible for you to step up and glimpse that consciousness of life. And then internalize and embody it, until it becomes your everyday reality and you are in that consciousness 24 hours a day and radiating that consciousness, sharing it with all people.

And my beloved, this is truly the goal of the path of Christhood — to be fully awake, fully alive all of the time and to not sink into that death consciousness that makes you just sleepwalk through life. Yes, my beloved, your ego is shaking in its boots as you are hearing these words because it knows that when you are fully awake, there will be no room for the ego.

And thus, it has come up with thousands of cleaver schemes to prevent you from being fully awake, to prevent you from letting that light shine. And it has found an inroad into almost everyone's consciousness, that causes you to think that you should not be awake, you should not let your light shine, or that you should not be awake in certain situations. This, my beloved, is the trap. And it is very subtle because – through the force of habit – you become so accustomed to it that you barely realize that you have slipped away from the consciousness of life into the consciousness of death.

Do you not see, my beloved, that all true spiritual teachers, that have come to this planet throughout the ages, have had the same message and the same goal. And that is to awaken people to the reality that there is an entirely higher level of life that they are not even aware of? We want you to be free as we are free. We want you to be all you can be and more. For the potential is always more, for God himself is more, is self-transcendence. For God is the Living God. And the Living Christ is the only begotten Son of the Living God.

And the Living Christ can never, ever be put into a man-made doctrine of philosophy or church or organization or system of any kind. For there is no man-made system that can hold the Living Christ, for he will break whatever chains people put upon him. There are no chains that can hold the Living Christ, and thus there should be no chains that can hold you. There should be no prison that can hold you for an entire lifetime — if you are willing to exercise the potential you have been given by God, the potential to become the Living Christ on Earth.

...

Think about how far we have come in being able to communicate, so that people all over the world can find a higher teaching. The outer teaching that is all they need in order to trigger what they already know in their hearts. For truly, God has written his law in your inward parts. And all you need is an outer stimulus that can help you reconnect to that inner law and that inner truth, and then you can become a spiritually self-sufficient person who has the Christ discernment to know what is real and unreal in your own psyche and in your own world.

Indeed, it will take a period of what I call magnificent confusion before you will have worked your way through the temptations of the worldly consciousness that are many and subtle. Nevertheless, by being willing to enter that state of confusion, to experiment, by being willing to make mistakes and recognizing those mistakes and learning from them, you can shorten the time it takes before you come to that inner wholeness that is sufficient for you to take the firm stand, whereby you can fully and finally rebuke the devil so that he must withdraw from you. Because even the devil realizes that when you take that firm stand on the rock of Christ, if he keeps tempting you, he will judge himself. And since he does not want to hasten his own judgment, he must run away from you.

Come into the consciousness of life

This, my beloved, is the difference between life and death. And I desire all of you to come into the consciousness of life as quickly as possible. I recognize that you cannot all do this in a split second, that you have healing to go through. But nevertheless, spend a little bit of time and attention now and then to ponder the difference between the consciousness of life and the consciousness of death. Reread these words. Listen to them again, when you feel you need to reconnect. Make it a part of your consciousness that you know the goal is to rise above the consciousness of death and enter into the consciousness of life.

If you will make this part of your path, you will make much swifter progress. You will shorten the time until you come to that point of making that ultimate decision to choose life, the final decision that frees you from the fear and doubt that you could fall back down. My beloved, it is indeed possible to be in embodiment on Earth and be beyond the risk of falling back down into the blindness of the ego and the duality consciousness. It is possible to come to a point, where you know you have been spiritually reborn and it simply would not be possible for you to forget that higher state of consciousness that you know is ultimate reality.

Certainly, it is always theoretically possible, but in all actuality – having worked your way up through the consciousness of death – you would not again fall for the temptation that caused you to fall so many lifetimes ago, when you first left off from your spiritual teacher. And my beloved, this does not mean that you know everything, that you are the perfect human being.

But it does mean that you know that you would never again fall back into living a completely unconscious life. And that gives you a sense of peace of mind, which is what you see exemplified in many spiritual people throughout the ages who have come to that sense of inner peace, of knowing who they are and daring to be who they are, even if they are not perfect or still make mistakes and certainly don't know everything and still need to sleep and take a shower and do these other mundane things that people do to take care of the physical body.

Encourage each other

My beloved, this is the inner peace that I desire to see you have. For I am the Prince of Peace. I came to demonstrate that it is possible to be on Earth and be at peace. And I want all of you to have that peace. And if you are willing to look at the elements of the death consciousness that pulls you away from that inner peace, and do whatever is necessary – use whatever tools that are available in the world or that we have given you in order to work through those elements of death – then indeed you can make progress.

And I think you will recognize, when you who have faithfully given the rosaries, studied these teachings, when you come together for a conference with people you saw at the last conference only a few months ago and you see that they have changed. And suddenly, you can then look in the mirror and see that you too have changed but it was just so gradual that you didn't notice in your busy daily lives.

And I strongly encourage you to help each other see how much you have changed. Not in a prideful way, as we have seen in all our past organizations, where those who claimed to be students of the ascended masters entered into this subtle spiritual pride of thinking that they were the most advanced spiritual seekers on the planet. My beloved, that is not what I am talking about. I am talking about you acknowledging the growth you see in each other and helping each other realize how much you have grown in just a matter of a few months. Because it encourages you and helps you realize that you can continue to grow and continue to come closer and closer to that state of inner peace, where the world cannot touch you, cannot touch your relationship to God. Because you have discovered the truth that the kingdom of God really is within you and that no human power, not even the power of your own ego, can prevent you from entering that kingdom—when you are willing to leave behind all those elements that pull you back into the outer world.

Nothing can stop you, except your own attachments to the things of this world. And when you realize that, even that is a sense of peace. For you know that if you keep looking at one attachment at a time, as you are able, and letting go of one attachment at a time, you are moving forward step by step toward that breakthrough point, where you can finally let go of the very sense of attachment itself. That gives you that inner knowing, that inner peace, that allows you to say, "I and my Father are one. And there is nothing that can take away that oneness."

The Alpha and Omega of the Living Christ

So my beloved, I too can be gentle. And it is indeed in order that some people see the gentleness of Jesus. Yet if these people do not recognize that the gentle and loving and kind and compassionate Jesus is the Omega aspect of my God Flame and that I also have an Alpha aspect, then their image of Christ is not complete. For my beloved, the Omega aspect of the Living Christ does indeed comfort people, love them, raise them up. It is the Omega aspect of Christ that gives people a cup of cold water in Christ's name. For truly, if people are suffering with a specific problem, then you need to help them overcome that specific problem instead of giving them a sermon about the higher purpose of life which they are not capable of receiving in their present state of consciousness.

And thus, you did indeed see that when I walked the Earth, I healed the sick, I comforted people in whatever state of consciousness they were in, so that they could overcome their afflictions—and by overcoming their immediate affliction, then have the opportunity to move higher. Yet how can they move higher unless they also recognize the Alpha aspect of the Living Christ that calls them to come up higher and to never get comfortable, to never stand still.

The Living Christ is a whole being that embodies all aspects of God and thus has the potential to reach all people and help them take the next step on their path. For it is by taking the next step and continuing to take the next step that you will make it all the way home. You see, my beloved, there are many false teachers that will promise you that there is a shortcut, so that you can skip a number of steps and jump from your present state of consciousness to the state of enlightenment or being saved or whatever they use to entice people.

But there is no shortcut, for if there was a shortcut, surely all life would already have been saved. You cannot skip steps, and therefore be alert for those who claim that you can be saved or make your ascension without dealing with the ego. For my beloved, we of the Ascended Host are very well attuned to where humankind is at in consciousness. And we know that in this day and age humankind is ready for the teachings on the ego. They are ready to recognize that the ego is the main factor that prevents them from manifesting their Christhood. And thus, I must tell you that any teacher who claims to be teaching about Christhood but is not teaching about the human ego, well that teacher, my beloved, cannot be connected to the Ascended Host.

This does not necessarily make them false teachers, for they might still have valid teachings for people at a certain level of consciousness. But if you claim to be teaching about Christhood without teaching about the ego, then you are not in tune with what we of the Ascended Host are bringing out in this age. And thus, you see my beloved, you must choose which teacher you will follow. And that is why all of you who are here and those who are following my website know that the teachings on the ego are essential. You know it is essential for yourself, but I think you also sense that they are essential for humankind.

It is time for humankind to recognize the ego

If humankind does not recognize the existence and nature of the ego, then civilization cannot make that leap of mastering the initiations of the consciousness of Pisces and moving into the consciousness of Aquarius. It simply is not possible. And that is why we are using a variety of people to bring forth teachings on the ego, whether it be psychologists or self-help gurus. I can assure you that anyone who teaches openly, sincerely and honestly about the human ego is attuned to the Ascended Host at some level. They may not be officially sponsored as messengers but they are certainly sponsored at some level and inspired to bring out these teachings.

For there are at present very few people who teach about the ego while still being completely blinded by the consciousness of death. And thus, although not all who teach about the ego have the full understanding of the ego, they are very much working for the goal of the Ascended Host in this age. And thus, I do recommend that you study teachings from a variety of sources about the ego. Because the more you understand about the ego, the better chance you have that one day the specific words you read will click in your consciousness and release that understanding that helps you see an aspect of your ego that has so far remained hidden.

My beloved, even though I try on my website to give teachings on the ego that are suitable for people at many levels of consciousness, the website is not meant to reach every level of consciousness. And I cannot explain every aspect of the ego in so many different ways that I can reach everyone. Thus, there could be another teacher out there who has brought forth a certain teaching, a certain wording, that could help you, that could unlock that understanding. And so again, do not limit yourself. I have no desire to see my website or this movement become like the movements in the Piscean Age that claimed that they had the only truth or that you should only look at their teachings.

Study the ego from many different angles. Study the spiritual path from different angles. And then use your discernment. For even if you read something that is not sponsored by the Ascended Host, that might even contain errors, it is an opportunity for you to increase your discernment. And if you are not willing to study even that which is inaccurate, how can you truly increase your ability to discern between reality and unreality? And how can you then increase your ability to help others.

Do you see, my beloved, there is no reason to have regrets over the fact that in the past you have studied a teaching that you might not consider to be the highest possible today. For you increased your own discernment by doing so, and you also increased your ability to help those who are still stuck at that level of consciousness. Now that you have come up higher, you can help others come up higher. But had you not known how they think, what questions they have, how could you help them.

Open your hearts to the unconditional love of Christ

Now, my beloved, I desire to give you an opportunity to center in your hearts and to open your heart to experiencing the true unconditional love of Christ, the true love for your being that the Living Christ has for you. So I give you this opportunity to meditate on my Presence in silence.

Take the time you like, until you feel you have had enough. But open your heart to feel the love that I have for each one of you. For that love is all-consuming, is unconditional. It is an ecstatic love that will not accept the mundane, the human love. It will not be held back, it will not be restricted. It wants to flow and it will forever flow, just like you cannot dam up a mighty river. So focus on that love and allow yourself to accept that you are fully worthy to receive the love of Christ.

Allow yourself to enjoy the journey

Mother Mary, October 1, 2006

My beloved, one of the things that can cause people to become stressed on the spiritual path is when they hear a master talk about a high vision and high goal. And you look at yourself and say, "But I am so far from being there, where I should be in consciousness." And then in recognizing the gap, you almost become discouraged and feel so overwhelmed that you sense there is no point in even trying. This, of course, is exactly what your ego wants you to feel. For then you do not even try. And if you do not try, you cannot transcend yourself and so you will remain stuck. So now you feel even worse about your situation than before you found the spiritual path and did not know that there was a possibility of attaining a higher state of consciousness.

So I understand that some people sometimes look at the people in the world who are living a normal life and say, or perhaps just sense unconsciously, that it was so much easier when you didn't know about the path. It was so much easier when you could just live life like everyone else and feel like you were normal, you were okay.

But you see, my beloved, the reality is that there is never any reason for you to feel that you are inadequate—as long as you are willing to take one small doable and believable step at a time. This is all that is required. It is a trick of the ego to get you to focus on this high goal and say, "I should be the Christ right now. And since I am not, I must be a bad person. There must be something wrong with me. I must not be doing something right."

And then you go into the trap of doing more, of being frantic or running faster. And you can do this for ten or twenty years. Yet there is still the gap between where you are now and where you think you ought to be. It is like the donkey running to catch up with the carrot that is dangling in front of its nose. But the more it runs, the more it pushes the carrot in front of it. And so many people have done this with the spiritual path.

Find your balance on the path

That is why, as El Morya said, you sometimes need to step back and recognize that there is a higher approach. And this is the approach that we have been talking about throughout this conference, of Being instead of doing. I will not expound upon it in detail for it already has been done and more will be said as time is appropriate. But I do want you to contemplate the concept that as long as you are transcending yourself and taking one step at a time – and continuing to take one step at a time without stopping – then you are moving forward. And that is really what God wants you to do. And if you keep moving forward, taking one step at a time, you will eventually reach your goal.

And so, on the one hand there is the extreme of thinking that you need to attain this high goal and thinking that if you do all the outer things, you must be on the way to that goal and you must be a good chela. On the other hand there is the extreme of thinking that you could not possibly reach that goal, and therefore you are no good and therefore there is no point in trying. But again, there is the middle way, my beloved. And that is what we desire you to find, for that is the key to peace of mind.

You see, my beloved, when you ascend, you look back at your time on Earth and you see that all of your embodiments were a journey. And then you look forward and you see that even though you are now an ascended being, way up there is the Creator and the God Consciousness.

And there is a long road from where you are to the God Consciousness. And so you realize that life is a very long journey. And then you see that there is no point in thinking that only when you reach the end goal will you be able to relax, to feel at peace and to enjoy what you have attained. You realize that each time you take a step forward, you have the potential to feel that sense of victory and joy. And you see that it really was pointless that when you were in embodiment you tortured yourself by feeling inadequate. And that is what I want to impart to you today.

You see, my beloved, it is so easy to think that you could not possibly attain what you see others attaining, be it this or that spiritual master. But the reality is that you can attain it—if you keep moving forward. And the reality is that although there is an end goal on the journey called life, there is an almost infinite number of steps. And thus, the journey will not become enjoyable until you decide to enjoy rising from one step to the next. And my beloved, you can decide that at any level of the journey, be it in the ascended realm or here in the material universe. And I would love nothing more than seeing all of you reach that level of inner peace, of allowing yourself to enjoy the journey, allowing yourself to feel that sense of victory when you have taken one step forward.

All I want is constantly growing chelas

El Morya, October 1, 2006.

My beloved, El Morya I AM, and many of you have known me for a long time. Many of you have studied the teachings I have given through previous messengers and organizations. And you have come to formulate a certain image of me as being the stern and strict disciplinarian, the blue-ray master of the first ray who is no-nonsense and who demands rapt attention, who demands that you make an extraordinary effort, that you are constant in your application of the spiritual path and the tools that we give you.

But I would give you a higher understanding of the concept of being constant. You see, my beloved, to the outer mind, to the analytical mind and to the human ego, the concept of being constant can mean only one thing. That is that you keep doing the same thing over and over and that you do not let anything distract you or take you away from doing what you have determined is needed in order for you to rise to a higher level of the spiritual path.

And my beloved, there is indeed a point on the spiritual path where you must be constant in order to break through the mass consciousness, your own past momentums and karma and your own psychology that threatens to pull you back into repeating the old patterns over and over and over again. So because you are trapped in such a pattern, you need to create a force, a momentum, that can break that pattern. And you cannot build a momentum without constant repetition because the bad habit was built through repetition and it must be counteracted through repetition by building a positive momentum.

Be not insane

So this is indeed in order at a certain level of the path. But there does come a point on the spiritual path where you need to rise to a new understanding of the concept of constancy, an understanding that is not dualistic but is beyond dualism. And that understanding is that constancy does not mean that you forever keep doing the same thing. For as Albert Einstein said, based on inspiration he received from Above, "If you keep doing the same thing and expect different results, you are insane."

And you see, my beloved, there comes a point where mindlessly repeating the same rituals or habits becomes insanity. There comes a point where you have to be willing to say, that what I have done so far has indeed brought me to the point on my path where I am right now, but can I reach the higher stages of the path if I keep doing the same thing? And indeed, there will for every chela, for every student, come certain points on your path where you need to rise to an entirely higher level. And you cannot rise to that level if you keep approaching the path the same way you have done in the cycle that took you to your current point.

So therefore, there are times when the wise student will step back and say, "What do I need to change? How do I need to change my perspective on the path?" And indeed, the sensitive student will know exactly as Arcturus said, that when you realize that following the path has become a source of stress, has become a burden, has become something that takes you away from peace, from the sense of inner freedom, then you know you have stayed too long in the old patterns. And now you are no longer progressing but you are spinning your wheels. You are treading water and you are getting nowhere, even though you are running faster and faster and faster and doing more and more and more, thinking that if you just do more and more or run faster and faster, you will eventually break through.

Well my beloved, it cannot be done that way and that is explained clearly in the old story that Saint Germain has told many times of Kuthumi and I going to the mountain to get a message. Where I was the one who with my blue-flame momentum ran straight up the mountain and straight down, and yet I did not retain the message. Whereas Kuthumi took time to listen to the birds and smell the roses and he indeed, although he took longer, retained the message in the end. This is also the story of the Buddha who realized that the extreme of the worldly consciousness and the other extreme of asceticism was not the true path but that you needed to find that middle way of a different approach.

It is an absolute truth that there is not a single human being who can find a specific spiritual teaching or technique and keep doing that for ten, twenty or thirty years or even a lifetime and then automatically make their ascension or attain Christhood. It is not a mechanical path. It is a path that requires you to think, to internalize, and that must happen because you are not fixing your mind on doing certain outer things or believing certain beliefs or studying certain teachings. You are willing to step back and look at the bigger picture, look for inner direction and then follow that inner direction rather than following the outer direction of an outer teacher, organization or even your own outer mind or ego.

A delicate problem for the Ascended Host

Do you see, my beloved, we of the Ascended Host are facing many delicate problems. And one of the delicate problems that we have always been facing is that there are two types of chelas. Some are driven by a lot of ego and a lot of ambition. And they are often the ones who are the first to want to do something in a spiritual organization. And they want to take charge and they want to take control because they feel that they are right and they know how things should be done.

And thus, they show initiative. And sometimes we need to work with these people in order to get things done, in order to cut through and get an organization rolling. But in the end, if an organization is led by this kind of chela, there will often be a tremendous clash of egos that will then cause the organization to stall or go into a downward spiral that basically breaks it apart from within and often results in the splitting up of an organization, as soon as the connection to the Ascended Host is broken or even before.

So the other kind of chelas are the humble and meek chelas. Those are the ones who have the purity of heart, the humbleness. And this is good. But often the pure and the humble do not have initiative, are afraid to take a stand, are reluctant to come out and say, "You know I think it would be better to do it this way." And when they meet up with the more aggressive, more self-confident chelas, they often fold. They often refuse to speak their truth, thinking that perhaps they are not right after all.

And you see the challenge. If we have only the meek and humble then an organization simply will not get off the ground. Yet if we have only the more aggressive chelas then an organization will get off the ground but it will also collapse under its own weight. And so what is the solution to creating a viable, spiritual organization in the Aquarian Age? Well, it is indeed that we have chelas who are balanced, who have a balance of Alpha and Omega, the balance of the expanding force of the Father that makes them willing to take an initiative, to take a stand. But yet also the balance of Omega that makes them humble, that makes them sensitive, caring and loving towards others.

The spiritual path should make you more free, not less free

Elohim Arcturus, October 1, 2006.

My beloved, it is indeed good to have a goal but it is not good if that goal becomes a cause for stress, if you feel so burdened by not having attained your goal that you cannot enjoy the journey towards the goal, or if you feel that you must work harder to obtain that goal and thereby do not have the inner peace that is the key to attaining the true goal of spiritual enlightenment. Jesus said it well, "What shall it profit a man if he attains the whole world but loses his soul." What shall it profit you if you do this or do that on the spiritual path yet lose your inner peace, your inner freedom?

We have seen this in several organizations we have sponsored directly and in many other churches or spiritual organizations. Where people become so focused on the outer path of doing this or doing that, that instead of gradually becoming more and more free, they actually become more and more imprisoned because they turn the spiritual path into a race against the clock or against dark forces or against this or against that. Or they turn it into a race of comparing themselves to other people, feeling that if they are doing this or that outer thing, then they must be more spiritual than others.

Yet in the process of doing all these outer things, they become so stressed out and burdened that they can barely bear the strain. And so comes the temptation of the ego to judge based on appearances and say that, "If other people are not doing for the ascended masters as I am doing, if they are not as burdened or are suffering as much as I am suffering, then they are not truly making progress on the path. They are not truly helping the ascended masters. They are not truly as spiritual as I am.

Keeping your peace while letting your light shine

Gautama Buddha, October 1, 2006.

The true definition of the eightfold path
You see, my beloved, when you rise above duality, you clearly see that there is something that is unreal. But that which is unreal is not in opposition to that which is real, as that which is humanly wrong is in opposition to that which is humanly right.

That which is unreal is simply unreal. It is outside reality, separate from reality. But it is not and cannot be in opposition to reality. For that which is real can have no opposition.

Thus, the first step on the spiritual path is to reach for something beyond duality. And that is what Jesus expressed so beautifully when he said, "Seek ye first the kingdom of God and his right-eousness." Seek ye first the higher "right" of God. This is also what I expressed in the definition of the eightfold path. So many Buddhists have misinterpreted the eightfold path and believe that it can be defined in human terms. What is right livelihood. What is right action. What is right thought. What is right association and so on.

But you see, the true definition of the eightfold path is that you reach for the "right" of God that is beyond duality. But how can you reach for that right, that higher right? Well, you can do so only when you realize the noble truth that everything that springs from duality causes suffering, and that the cause of suffering is wrong desire that is based on an attachment to the things of this world – be it the sensual pleasures or the desire to be right in a human sense – and feel that you are better than those whom you define as wrong because they are different from you or hold opposite views from you.

Oh my beloved, there are so many people on this planet who spend their entire lives seeking to establish this sense of superiority of being better than others. They always see themselves as being in competition with others and this goes from the so-called ordinary people, who are, as the saying goes, seeking to keep up with the Joneses, in having better houses, bigger cars and more material goods. And it goes all the way up to the people in the power elite who are seeking to have more power than those other people in those other power elite groups with whom they are comparing themselves.

My beloved, you can spend lifetimes on this senseless quest of seeking to be thought right among men. Or you can reach up for the reality of being right with God. Yet in order to be right with God, you must be willing to consciously and willfully choose to let go of your attachments to the things in the material realm. For as long as you are attached to being right with other people, to being popular or not to be seen as an outcast or ridiculed for your beliefs, or your lifestyle or your actions, as long as you are attached to anything, any appearance in this world, to your standing among human beings, then you will not be free to grasp the higher right of God or to express that right.

So my beloved, I taught 2,500 years ago, that non-attachment is the key to peace of mind. And that teaching is true. It is timeless. It is eternal. Yet as Jesus has pointed out, there is no teaching expressed in words that the human ego cannot pervert. For anything expressed in words can be taken by the dualistic mind and interpreted according to this extreme or that extreme or even the false concept of the Middle Way as something that is right between the two dualistic extremes.

So you see my beloved, even the concept of the Middle Way can be misinterpreted. For truly, I never told people to come to the midpoint between the two dualistic extremes. I taught them to transcend the entire scale of duality, the entire consciousness of duality. And this is the essence of Buddhahood. Yet to transcend duality you must be willing to let go of the desires, the beliefs, the attachments that spring from duality. And thus you must come to the point where you love the right of God more than the right of man.

And this must in the end be a conscious decision you make. Truly, not everyone is ready to make that decision. But certainly those who are the spiritual people are ready or can quickly become ready. And if you will contemplate these concepts, you will come to a point where you feel a spontaneous, inner surge of love for the higher reality of God that suddenly makes it easy to let go of some attachment. And once you realize how easy it is to let go of one attachment, you can build a momentum of letting go of the attachments as quickly as you see them.

Knowing what is right

Now my beloved, as you discussed this afternoon, it is not necessarily easy to always know what is right with God. And the reason for this is that there is no outer rule that can be given in this world for what is right according to God's absolute reality. For each situation, each person, is different. And so in one situation it might be right to do one thing. But in another situation, that might seem similar based on outer appearances, it may be right to do what seems to be the opposite. And thus, you cannot know this by setting up rules with the analytical mind that loves to create labels and say that, "Under these circumstances you should always do this. And under those circumstances you should always do that."

Well, my beloved, this will not work. For then you have pulled yourself into the realm of the intellect which can only operate in the field of duality. Yet you can attain much by consciously working on non-attachment. For truly, when you are non-attached to the outer appearances, you will not be tempted to respond according to a human standard for what should be right in this or that situation. You will then be able to reach up for the higher reality of God, so you will spontaneously do what is right.

Yet in order to do what is right with God, you must realize that non-attachment is not the same as indifference. My beloved, if you will study my life as the Buddha incarnate, you will notice that I walked a path of attaining complete non-attachment to the things of this world. And then, after having attained that non-attachment which is commonly in Buddhist terms called Enlightenment, I still faced an initiation that many Buddhists do not understand or even look upon. For I faced the temptation that the forces of this world said, "Oh, but what you have seen, what you have attained, is far too advanced or complicated for the people on Earth. You will not be able to explain it to them. They will not be able to understand it. None will understand you, so don't bother to go out in the world and bear witness to your truth. Just stay in Nirvana and leave the world to the forces of duality. Do not attempt to enlighten the people, for they will not understand."

Well, my beloved, I passed that initiation only by connecting to the I AM THAT I AM within me, to Brahman himself. And through that connection I got the clear impulse, "Some will understand." And I went out and started preaching my truth and some did indeed understand. Thus, you will face the same initiation. First you face the initiation of attaining non-attachment to other people's reactions, so that when they reject your light, your God Flame, your truth, you are non-attached to their reactions. And you do not allow their rejection to become an excuse that the ego can use to trick you into turning off your light or being quiet about challenging the unreality on Earth.

Yet in attaining and working on that non-attachment, you will then come to the temptation of thinking, "What is the point of seeking to enlighten people when they are so far down into the consciousness of duality and seemingly are so uninterested in anything spiritual?" And my beloved, it is a delicate balance to remain non-attached but at the same time not to become indifferent, not to give up, not to become a pacifist who just sits there and lets the world do what it will do without challenging what is unreal. And each of you must find your own balance, for I tell you, there is an idolatry in the world which thinks that it was easy for me to walk the path and pass my initiations and then find my balance and go out and preach my truth.

Likewise, they say it was easy for Jesus to pass his initiations and then go out and witness to his truth. But I tell you that it was fully as difficult for Jesus and myself as it is for you. You see, my beloved, we all have certain elements of the human condition that we must surrender and overcome before we manifest a higher state of consciousness. And the human conditions that each of us have are precisely those conditions that are the hardest for us to see. So Jesus was not born in the fullness of his Christhood. And I was not born in the fullness of Buddhahood, as is clearly seen in our lives.

Therefore, we too had to overcome our own points of blindness that we could not see. And precisely that which we could not see was as difficult for us to overcome as it is for each of you to overcome that which you cannot see. Do you see, my beloved, it is such an illusion to think that Jesus and I and other spiritual masters were above you and that it was so much easier for us. For indeed it was not easy at all. But the fact that we made it should be an encouragement that you too can make it. For as has been the motto of the Ascended Host for a long time, "What one has done, all can do." And in this age we might say, "What one is Being, all can Be!" For truly it is not doing that is the key but Being.

How to bear witness to your truth

Thus, my beloved, let me give you at least one hint of how to go out and bear witness to the truth, how to let your light so shine before men that by seeing your good works they see that it is not the outer person that is the doer, but the light of God within you that is the true doer. In order to do this, you must be non-attached without being indifferent. So let me give you the key that if you will strive to remain at peace, even when you are challenging other people, then you will always be in the higher right of God.

So examine yourself. Are you reluctant to challenge others? Do you feel fearful, guilty or have other negative feelings when you do challenge others? In that case you might consider that you still have some attachment to an outer appearance that is preventing you from challenging others with the true inner peace of the Christ and the Buddha who have obtained complete non-attachment. And then you just look at that. You work on it. You go to the core of it and you let it go.

My beloved, do you seriously believe that Jesus and I did not have any remnants of the human ego when we were born? I know very well that there are many people in Buddhism and Christianity who believe in this idolatry. But it was not so. For we had indeed elements of the ego, attachments and spiritual blindness that we needed to overcome. And how did we overcome it? My beloved, it did not happen in one glorious moment of breakthrough into nirvana as some teachers portray it. It happened one little step at a time. Much of this has never been recorded because it was an inner path. And at the time that we both gave forth our respective teachings, humankind was not ready to understand the idiosyncrasies of the human psyche that people in many areas of the world are capable of understanding today.

Thus, we could not even teach it at the time. And we had to give forth a simpler teaching that was adapted to the consciousness that people had back then in those far darker times. Yet I tell you that in today's age you have the teachings and the tools to systemically overcome every attachment. And when you lock in to your own higher being and to your own God Flame – and know that you are that flame, and not the outer personality, or the ego or the body or the person that other people have created in their minds – then you will be able to come to a point, where you are willing to let go of any attachment as soon as you see it.

And you know that no matter what might come up, you will be willing to let go of it. And this is the true hallmark of a true spiritual seeker who has begun to find that which so many still seek without knowing what they are even seeking. And thus, even though you are not necessarily completely free of attachments, you can still obtain the inner peace that passes understanding because it is not based on any outer security in the form of having bigger bombs or bigger cannons than these other nations. Or even the false intellectual security of thinking that because you belong to this or that religion, or this or that scientific world view and understand all of its concepts intellectually you are sure to be saved.

No my beloved, it is a peace that is beyond all outer appearances that does not depend upon any conditions in the material realm and therefore cannot be taken away by any conditions in the material realm no matter what happens. This is the inner peace that I desire to see all of you have. And this is the inner peace I had attained before I started my mission. Yet I must tell you that you will make faster progress if you are willing to bear witness to the truth that you see even though you may not yet see the highest truth.

For my beloved, Jesus and I had to set forth certain examples. And so we withdrew from the world until we had attained a consciousness that would allow us to fulfill our missions. But precisely because we were meant to set up examples, we also faced a tremendous opposition to those missions that you do not face individually because in this day and age it is the priority that many people walk the path together instead of just one person being the forerunner. So each of you individually is not facing the same opposition that we faced, which is why you can start bearing witness to the truth even before you have obtained complete non-attachment and peace of mind.

And indeed, by doing so you will make greater progress than if you withdrew from society until you had attained a higher state of consciousness. So be willing to bear witness to your truth even if you are not perfect, even if you are still disturbed by other people rejecting you. For if you have that courage, that willingness, you will surely make much faster progress, especially if you are willing to look at yourself and say, "Ah, but why was I disturbed by other people's reaction? Is there not an element of the ego hiding behind that disturbance? And so if I look at it, can I not expose my ego and then surrender it?"

Indeed, my beloved, you who are here and who went through this exercise of giving the rosary the way you gave it can look at yourselves and say, "Was I fully comfortable and at peace by standing up and reciting a part of the rosary? Was I fully expressing my God Flame or was I still concerned about other people's reactions or getting the words expressed right?"

My beloved, if you discover such concerns, look at them and say, "Why did I feel disturbed? Why could I not be at peace, for after all, if I am expressing my God Flame then why should I feel disturbed about any appearance?" You see, my beloved, the peace you need to strive for is that you can bear witness to your truth and let your light shine no matter the outer conditions or the reactions you get from other people. You are not disturbed. They do not take away your peace. You do not feel rejected because you have no attachment to how they should respond. You simply allow their free will to work itself out and leave it up to them whether they will accept or reject the higher truth that they have now seen in you.

And when you can have that non-attachment, nothing will disturb you. Nothing will take away your peace. And my beloved, I do not want you to think that you are so far away from Buddhahood that it would take you the rest of your life or even years or decades to obtain that inner peace, for it is not so for most of you. You can attain that inner peace in a relatively short period of time if you will make use of the teachings and the tools that you have.

This, my beloved, is a realistic goal—that you as a worldwide community, can obtain if you will openly put your minds to it. And so as my final message I hurl that challenge at you. Take the tools you have been given, the rosaries, the ego discourses, but also be willing to talk about this openly and ask questions. And help each other. Inspire each other. And be willing to be open and honest with each other and say, "I think you still have an attachment and that is why you are disturbed about this. Let us see if we together can discover the cause of that attachment so that it can be surrendered into the Flame of Ecstatic Peace."

The master key to growth is integration between your Higher and lower Being

Mother Mary, October 20, 2006.

Why spiritual people have often failed to attain their highest potential

Well, my beloved, we of the Ascended Host have sponsored many gatherings of people throughout the last hundred years and more. We have often had great gatherings and great success. But I must tell you that in the vast majority of cases, we failed to establish the complete figure-eight flow between the people below and us Above. And why did we fail to achieve this ultimate goal? Well, it was because the people below were not able to come into oneness with us Above. And why were they not able to come into this oneness? Because they did not have the sufficient teachings on the human ego, and they did not have the vision of how necessary it is to overcome that ego and come into oneness with your own Higher Being, so that you can be the open door here below for your own Higher Being which is one with the Ascended Host above.

My beloved, this is not necessarily because the people were deficient in any way, but because times were not ready for that higher teaching to be brought into physical manifestation, where anyone could find it, either through a book, or now through the internet. Yet times are now ready and that is why we have indeed – through my book [Master Keys to the Abundant Life] and through Jesus' teachings on the ego [Unmasking the Ego] and the forthcoming book by Maitreya [Master Keys to Spiritual Freedom] – we have determined to bring out the teachings that can once and for all raise the spiritual people on Earth to the full clarity of what is going on in the religious life, the spiritual life, on this planet. So that they can finally see why so many spiritual and religious movements, even though they have had great progress and great teachings and great hearts, have so often failed to reach their highest potential and make the essential difference in the world.

The basic burden of the heart

Thus, my beloved, other masters will surely give other teachings on the heart. But I will give you the basic teaching that you need to know and need to understand in order to clear the heart and be that figure-eight flow between your Higher and lower being.

There are many things that burden the heart. There are many things that can cloud the heart. But the essence of all of these things is simply this—selfishness, self-centeredness, a focus on the lower self, not just the ego, but even beyond the ego. Your lower self can become so focused on itself that it does not have any attention left over to direct toward the Higher Self Above or direct out to see how it can help people in the world and how it can help bring about the vision of God for this world.

And when there is not that vision to tune in both Above and below, to look beyond the self both Above and below, then how can there be a figure-eight flow in your being? Because you will shut off most of the light and the divine direction that comes to you from above. You will not want the light to disturb you, to disturb your ego and it's sense of comfortability that comes from having you under its control. Neither will you want to follow the divine direction because it might require you to do something different than what you have imagined you should be doing with your life.

And thus, my beloved, you will not even hear the divine direction that flows to you all the time. You will color it by the outer mind, by your expectations. And those expectations, if you will analyze them, are all centered around the ego and the sense of identity as being a separate being in the material world.

The quintessential serpentine lie

Now, my beloved, if you will analyze what caused the fall of most human beings on Earth, you will realize that it was that they all came to believe in the quintessential serpentine lie. And that lie is that God's will is in opposition to your will, that God is a tyrant who is seeking to impose his will and his law upon you and in so doing wants to take away your free will and restrict your creativity.

This is the lie that in a disguised form was presented to Eve in the Garden of Eden. For had not Maitreya told her that if she ate of the forbidden fruit – which represents the consciousness of duality – that she would surely die. And did not the Serpent say that she would not surely die. But in fact, there was more than what was recorded in the Bible because the Serpent made Eve believe that not only would she not die, but that she would find the real form of life, the life that God did not want her to have, the life that could only be found by rebelling against God's Law and God's Will. For the Serpent would have you believe that you can only have truly free will by going against God's Will. And this impression has, of course, been reinforced by the main religions in the Western world who are all so focused on the masculine aspect of God and deliberately deny the feminine aspect of God.

And so, what has come down to the West, including through Christianity, is the whole idea that women were responsible for the fall of humankind. But the symbol behind that outer statement is that the feminine aspect of creation and the feminine aspect of your own being is responsible for your fall and for the fall of humankind. My beloved, there is some truth to this. For the masculine aspect of your being is the spiritual self, your I AM Presence. And the feminine aspect is what I in my book have called the "Conscious You" or the conscious self.

The conscious self is what descends into the material world. It is the conscious self who is the co-creator with God, who is charged with multiplying its creative abilities and taking dominion over the Earth. And it does so by building a sense of identity through which it expresses itself. And therefore, the identity, the etheric, body is the highest of your four lower bodies, and everything that follows in your lower bodies is colored by, is springing from, is the result of the sense of identity that you have built.

And so it was the Conscious You who made the decision to believe in the serpentine lie, to leave off of your oneness with God's Will. Yet the reality is that it is also the feminine aspect of your being, your conscious self, who must make the decision – the only decision – that can bring you back into oneness, which is what Christian's call salvation.

For my beloved, it is another serpentine lie that after you have separated yourself from your own Higher Being, there will be some outer savior, some outer religion, that will save you, who will do the work for you. And it is a lie that you cannot save yourself. This is the lie that Jesus challenged when he said, "The kingdom of God is within you."

The serpentine plot

And thus, my beloved, the lie that has been perpetrated now through the Western religions for thousands of years is that the feminine aspect of your being is responsible for the Fall, is bad, can only make wrong choices and therefore must be disciplined and suppressed by—what? My beloved, this is what religions do not tell you. They do not tell you that the feminine aspect of your being must be brought into alignment with the higher part of your being, the masculine part of your being. No, they say that the feminine aspect of your being must be controlled and disciplined and restricted by some external deity, an angry being in the sky. And thus, my beloved, do you see the subtlety of the serpentine plot?

First, they get you to leave off from your oneness with your Higher Being by making it seem like your Higher Being is an external deity, who is a tyrant that is trying to impose his will upon you. And therefore, you should run away from that and exercise your free will in opposition to God's "restrictive" laws. And then they create a set of religions in the Western world who say that the only way to be saved is to submit yourself to the will of this external deity, which they first told you was a tyrant that was trying to take away your freedom.

And so, you see my beloved, they first get you to run away from the external God in the sky. And then they try to tell you that the only way to be saved is to submit yourself completely to that external being in the sky. So do you see that what has happened here is that they have attempted to create what we call a spiritual catch-22, where you are running away from something at the same time as another part of your being is feeling that it has to force itself to run towards that something?

And because you do not want to run toward the angry being in the sky, you do not want to submit yourself to the angry being in the sky and his external will, you are forever a house divided against itself. And thus, you cannot stand in the presence of the Living Christ. And thus, you cannot sense the presence of the Living Christ because you do not sense the burning in your heart, because the burning in your heart is so overshadowed by all the turmoil created by the divisions in your psyche. For that original division has mushroomed into many other divisions that take all kinds of shapes, in the form of all kinds of psychological problems or in the form of desires for the things of this world or the belief that following an outer religion and doing all its outer rituals and practices will save you.

And because of all these different things that are pulling you in so many different directions, you do not have the attention and the time to center in your heart. And that is why so many people in the world today cannot focus on the spiritual path, even though they have more free time than ever before. Yet their free time – which is Saint Germain's gift to them so they can pursue the spiritual path – their free time is being eaten up by all these outer things, all these compulsions that they cannot let go of, simply because they are so divided that they do not realize they are being pulled in different directions.

And they can never see beyond all the surface divisions to see the central division that is behind it all – and that their egos and the prince of this world do not want them to see – because once you see that central division, you can then look beyond the outer divisions and go to the core, you can take the axe and cut the tree at the root instead of dealing with the branches. And once the tree comes tumbling down, the tree of anti-life, then there will be a clearing in your mind, and you will now see the Tree of Life, which is the tree of oneness rather than the tree of anti-life which is the tree of division.

Knowing your own higher will

So my beloved, as we have pointed out before in the Will of God rosary and in the introduction to that rosary, the key insight is to realize that God's Will is not an external will—because God is not an external being. The being in the sky, the angry being in the sky that is seeking to impose his will upon you, is not real. That god, which is worshipped by the main Western religions, Islam, Judaism and Christianity, does not exist. It is a product of the human mind, the mind that has fallen into duality and thus has created this false image of an angry being in the sky who is opposing the will of human beings.

In reality, this false god is only opposing the anti-will created by the mind of duality, the consciousness of anti-christ. And thus, the consciousness of anti-christ has created both the angry being in the sky and his opposite, the devil. And it has set up a conflict between them that is meant as a smokescreen to pull you into aligning yourself with the false god instead of realizing that the real God can never be an external deity.

Because the real God is an internal God which is what Jesus told you when he said that the kingdom of God is within you.

Well, my beloved, if the kingdom of God is within you, where is God? Is he not in his kingdom? So if the kingdom of God is within you and God is in his kingdom, then God must be within you. And that is why Jesus could attain the consciousness of saying, "I and my Father are one." And that is why you too can attain that state of consciousness by letting the mind of Christ be in you, as it was in Jesus.

And this, of course, is the last thing that the prince of this world and the forces of this world want you to know. And that, my beloved, is why they have set up a false path. For my beloved, the strategy of the prince of this world is to first create a problem and then set up the only solution to that problem. Only, that solution can never solve the problem because that solution will not deal with the cause of the problem, which is separation.

And so, you now have not only the traditional Western religions, but even many newer religions and even many New Age movements, who are reinforcing this image of the external God and reinforcing the image that the only way to salvation is to follow an external path. And I am not here simply talking about being a member of an outer church and blindly following its doctrines and rituals. For that is only the lowest aspect of their strategy.

The more sophisticated aspect of their strategy is to catch the most spiritual people by causing them to follow a false path, a path that still reinforces the image that God is outside yourself and still reinforces the image that the real problem in your being is the feminine aspect of your being. And the feminine aspect caused the fall, and therefore the feminine aspect must be suppressed, disciplined, restricted, by that external deity and his law, stated through this or that religion and doctrine or even this or that New Age teaching.

The higher truth about discipline

Now, my beloved, as I said earlier, it has not in times past been possible to bring out the fullness of this teaching, for humankind was not ready for it. And even those who were conscious chelas of the Ascended Masters were not ready for it in the form that we are bringing it out now. And that is why, in previous organizations, we have even had to present an outer path. And part of that path has been teachings on the ego or the dweller on the threshold and the whole idea that you had to discipline yourself.

And my beloved, please be sophisticated enough to realize that there is a necessity for spiritual people to discipline themselves. Because when you first find the spiritual path, your inner being, your inner space, can be in such turmoil by the divisions created by the ego that you simply do not have the attention to tune in to your heart or even read between the lines of an outer spiritual teaching. And therefore, you do need to go through a period of discipline, of training, of purification, where you still the mind until there is enough silence, there is enough open space, that a higher direction can enter your lower being. And this cannot happen except through discipline, where you are strong, where you are determined and where you follow a disciplined outer path.

So my beloved, I am not saying that all organizations or teachings that present a disciplined path are wrong. What I am saying is that following the path of outer discipline cannot lead you to the ultimate goal of spiritual growth. It can only lead you to a certain stage of the path. And the question then becomes, "Will you become stuck at that level or will you be able to transcend it and move beyond?"

Attaining integration

You see, my beloved, for you to go through this integration between the masculine and feminine aspects of your being, the first thing you need to overcome is the serpentine lie of the external God. You need to realize that the true God is within you and that you are open to knowing the true God, who is your own Higher Being, your spiritual Self, your I AM Presence. And therefore, it does not make any sense whatsoever to say that God's will could be in opposition to your own will. For when God is not an external deity, then his will is not an external will. It is the will of your self, of your own Higher Being.

And how can the will of yourself be in opposition to yourself? Well, it can be in opposition not in reality but only in the mind, because the lower part of your being, the conscious self, has come to identify itself as being separated from God, separated from your Higher Being. And therefore, you think there can be two wills in your being. But my beloved, in reality there cannot be two wills in your real being. The only will that can be in opposition to your higher will is the will of the ego. And so, it is only when the Conscious You identifies itself with the ego that you can believe there is any opposition, that there is any division, any contradiction between your will and God's will.

The will of the ego will forever be in opposition to God's will. And so only as long as the Conscious You identifies itself with the ego, will you believe there is an opposition. Once the Conscious You awakens and realizes – and this can happen in a flash, my beloved, as I described in my book – that you are one with your Higher Being, then the Conscious You will see that its will – your will – is the same as the will of your I AM Presence.

You did not come here to rebel against that will; you came here to express that will. And that was the reason you chose to come here in the first place. It was only when you met the opposition in this world – when those in this world, those in the duality consciousness, did not want to receive your light – it was only then that you started thinking that maybe there was something wrong with expressing the light of your Higher Being. And maybe you should turn off that light or turn it down and not let your light so shine before men and not bear witness to your truth.

And that was when you started believing in the serpentine lie that you should adapt to the way conditions are now in the material universe, rather than multiplying your creative talents so that you can take dominion over those conditions and transform them and their present imperfections into the kingdom of God. And this, my beloved, is what has happened to the top ten percent of the spiritual people on this planet. And that is why those top ten percent are not being the force that they were meant to be, the force that they wanted to be before they came here.

And I must tell you that the top ten percent of the most spiritual people all chose to come here not for self-centered reasons but because they wanted to raise up this planet and help bring in the Golden Age of Saint Germain. And you who are beginning to awaken from the illusions, you need to start seeing yourself as the emissaries of the Ascended Host who have the potential to bear witness to this truth that you are now beginning to see. So that you can go out and awaken all those in the top ten percent to who they are and why they are here, so that all of these people can begin to fulfill their reason for being.

But my beloved, we are not asking you to convert everyone to one particular religion or belief system. We are asking you to see the universal teaching that transcends all outer religions, all outer organizations.

Do you see, my beloved, the teaching on the ego, that we have brought forth now, is universal. It cannot be confined to this or that church, or this or that New Age organization, or this or that guru. No one in the physical octave can have a patent on the teachings of the Ascended Masters. They are our gift to humankind.

And in the Aquarian Age I can assure you that the old idea that there is one religion, or one church that has the ultimate teaching or the only true teaching, will fade away as it has already started fading away for the old religions in the West, where more and more people see beyond this black-and-white approach and realize that it is not true. And so, my beloved, can you see that the last thing we would want is an Aquarian Age organization which becomes trapped in that old mindset.

But this will require that the leaders and the members of such an organization are willing to overcome the ego, which has an eternal desire to feel better than others. And it will use any excuse for building the sense that, "Oh, we are surely better than others because we have the sophisticated teaching. We understand something that these other people don't understand. So God must love us more. Surely El Morya must love us more because we are his chelas."

But you see, my beloved, El Morya loves everyone more—when they are willing to become more by transcending themselves. And when people are not willing to transcend themselves, they cannot receive the love that all of us have for all of the people on Earth. We love everyone on Earth, and we desire to see everyone transcend their current level of consciousness and come up higher.

We do not give special favors to anyone because unconditional love cannot be expressed in a conditional way. And that is why you will see that in past organizations we have been careful not to elevate people, unless it was done specifically for a testing of their souls, of whether they would use that seeming elevation to build the value judgment that they were better than others or whether they would remain humble of heart or become humble.

Are you awake?

Gautama Buddha, October 20, 2006.

The Buddha I AM. Gautama was my name when I walked the Earth. And though I still answer to that name, I have a higher name that I shall one day reveal to you, when you are ready to receive it because you have attained a higher integration with your own inner name, your own Higher Being that you are.

My beloved, after I had entered Nirvana and had returned to the material universe to preach, I encountered three men who were struck by my peaceful radiance. They were struck by my God Flame radiating its light through my outer form. And so they asked me several questions about what I was. Was I a God, an angel and other questions. My beloved, who among you know the answer I gave them. What did I say to them when they asked, "What are you?" [Audience answers, "I am awake!"]

That is right. I simply said, "I AM awake!" So my beloved, what do we of the Ascended Host want to see for our chelas in embodiment? [Audience answers, "For us to be awake!"]

That is right. We want you to be awake as we have become awake. Whether we attained that sense of awareness after we ascended or while we were still in physical embodiment, you have the potential to become awake while you are still on Earth. And therefore, you can become free of the state of illusion, the state of sleepwalking through life, whereby you feel that life is a treadmill, where you go around and around and you never seem to get anywhere. And life seems to have no purpose or deeper meaning or direction.

My beloved, look at humankind and ask yourself the question, "How many people on this planet are even somewhat awake, to the point where they are consciously aware that as they go through their daily lives they are more than that?" And thus, because of that awareness they have a deeper appreciation for life.

My beloved, when you are awake, the essential realization is that you are more than these outer manifestations. You are more than your outer situation. You are more than your physical body. You are more than your lower mind, your outer personality that has been shaped by this world. You are more than this. And what happens when you know that you are more? Well, you are not fully identified with this world, with your lower being and the outer personality, even the ego. And when you are not fully identified with it, your mind is not trapped in the mental box created by the ego. And thus, at least once in awhile, you can step outside that mental box and look at life from a broader perspective. You can look at the big picture. You can see the forest instead of pounding your head against one tree trunk.

The key to freedom in not the ascension
And this, of course, is the key to freedom. The key to freedom is not that you leave behind this physical body for good in the process of the ascension.

My beloved, are you awake? Did you hear what I said? The key to freedom is not that you leave the material universe behind in the process of the ascension. It would seem I am contradicting earlier teachings, given through other dispensations, in which we of the Ascended Host did focus on the ascension as the goal of life. So why do I now say that the ascension is not the key to freedom? Because, my beloved, you cannot ascend unless you are awake.

And becoming awake is not a mechanical process that can be obtained by following certain outer rules or doctrines or rituals. It is a creative process that can be attained only through awareness that becomes internalized and therefore results in the ultimate LIFE decision. A decision that is not produced by you, that is not willed into being, but a decision that comes spontaneously from within because one day you decide that you are willing to be awake. You are willing to go beyond the state of consciousness that you have been in so far. You are willing to rise to that higher state of awareness, where part of your attention, part of your being, part of your sense of self is always outside your current situation, is always looking at the big picture, looking from a broader perspective. And therefore never looking at life fully from inside the mental box of the ego.

My beloved this is not an awareness that will come spontaneously. It is not a matter of meditating X hours a day for X number of years. It is not a matter of doing any other ritual. It is an awareness that must come ultimately from within. But it is an awareness that can be cultivated by your willingness to always look beyond the immediate situation, to always look beyond the current box of the ego, so that you do not identify fully with that box and become trapped in it.

My beloved, this awareness of being fully awake is what we desire to see for all of you. And the reason for this is that we have become awake, we have become free, and thus we want all of you to attain that same freedom, that same joy, that same state of bliss. This is the peace that passeth understanding, the bliss that is beyond any outer conditions. For it does not depend on any conditions in this world, for you realize that the key to bliss is to connect to the source of bliss. And the source of bliss is not found in the material world. It is found in your own Higher Being, from which the source of life itself comes for you.

Nirvana is not annihilation
My beloved, you were not created with no purpose. Life is not a treadmill. I am fully aware that some of my followers – or those who claim to be followers of the Buddha – have created a world view that they claim is based on my teachings, a world view that states that life is just a process of being created, of rising to the level of the Buddha consciousness and then merging back into, disappearing back into, Nirvana where you are obliterated. Well, my beloved, it is a fiction of the human imagination, for Nirvana is not annihilation. It is a higher state of life that most people on Earth cannot fathom. And therefore, to them it might seem that when you enter Nirvana, you disappear. But you only disappear from the sight of those who are not awake, who have not risen above duality.

You see, my beloved, the teachings given by Mother Mary and Jesus on the ego and the duality consciousness are indeed the quintessential teachings for the Aquarian Age. For humankind is ready to recognize the existence of the ego. And they are ready – with some serious coaching – to understand the concept of duality and how it influences your thinking, how it blinds you to reality, how it binds you to this treadmill of always fighting some opposing force, never being able to reach your goal, never being able to break through and get where you want to be in life.

And the reason is that you have been fooled by the ego and the prince of this world to believe that your bliss is in this world. And thus, you have been told to follow your bliss and seek it in this world. For in order to attain it – they say – you have to overcome this opposing force. And so you get locked into this battle of fighting against the opposite duality. And my beloved, this is a battle that can go on indefinitely—until you run out of time.

For when you are engaged in this battle, you are indeed creating your own opposition. You are polarized to one of the dualistic extremes, you are unbalanced, you are off the middle way. And in that imbalance, you create the opposition to your every effort because you project an unbalanced view into the cosmic mirror. And the mirror has no choice but to project an unbalanced material circumstance back to you as a result.

So being awake truly means that you realize the mechanics of the dualistic struggle, and that you decide that you will raise your awareness so that you become aware of the dualistic forces in your own being, the forces that divide you against yourself, that divide your lower being against your own Higher Being. And thus, in this division, you create those circumstances that oppose your goals.

And in a sense, this is a grace, for it is a safety mechanism built into the material universe. It is simply designed to make sure that when you go off of balance, when you go off the middle way, your imbalance creates an opposing force that seeks to pull you back to balance. So the further you go into one extreme – the harder you push to get to that goal that you have set for yourself – the more you create the opposition that opposes your effort and seeks to pull you back to center.

The double illusion

But, of course, you do not see it that way. You do not see that the material universe is providing a service to you by seeking to counteract your imbalance. Nay, you allow your ego to tell you that the universe is opposing what is your right—your right to be free and do whatever you want, regardless of the material universe, the law of balance. And so not only do you create an imbalance that creates an opposition, nay you then rebel against the opposition that you created, projecting that it was not created by you but by some external force, be it the devil or by other people.

And so, now you are fighting two battles. And out of two battles will spring a third battle, and out of the three battles will spring a fourth. And pretty soon you are so enveloped in all these dualistic battles that you have no attention left over to step back and say, "Might there be a better way? Might there be a middle way? Might it be possible to step off the treadmill of fighting dualistic battles and find a way to go beyond this struggle?"

And so, my beloved, this is the message of my life, where I first – growing up – lived a material, worldly life, then jumped to the opposite extreme of living in a forest, torturing myself and my physical body because I thought my physical body was the enemy and that I had to discipline and control it. And so the true reality that most Buddhists have not yet understood is that I truly realized that my body and the material world was not the enemy of my spiritual growth. I saw the enemy, and it was me, my lower being, my ego, my attachments, my expectations that life should be a certain way.

So what we truly desire to see for our chelas in this age is that you come into this awareness and rise above the dualistic struggle in your own being. But we desire to see this not simply for your own sake, not simply for your liberation or for your own bliss—we desire to see it because in this age we have a need for those who are willing to demonstrate the spiritual path for others.

Well, my beloved, how do you demonstrate the spiritual path for others? The ultimate way is not to lecture or preach by giving them an outer intellectual teaching. No, the ultimate way is to be who you are, to be awake so that you can radiate the light that you are. This does not mean that you need to be silent, for, truly, I also gave teachings. I did not simply say "I AM awake" and let that be it. But when I gave those teachings, I did not give them the way they appear today, twenty-five hundred years later, where they have been written down and translated and retranslated and transcribed and retranscribed, and thus been somewhat diluted, as any teaching that passes through the minds of many unenlightened human beings.

Deliver the Living Word

No, what I gave was the Living Word that was endowed with my God flame, with my Inner Being. And my beloved, we desire all of you to be able to deliver that Living Word. And I do not mean that you have to stand here in front of a group of people and give a dictation from us. I mean that as you speak to people, whether in a lecture situation or one-on-one, you are speaking freely from your Inner Being. You are letting your light flow so that the words are not the essence, the words are simply chalices for the light.

The words carry the Light, and they enter the other persons' energy fields and uplift them and transform them. And they are suddenly awakened to the realization that there is an alternative to the state of consciousness of sleepwalking through life, because they see in you something more. They see you are awake, you are excited, you are enthusiastic, you are being who you are, you are at peace. They sense your bliss, and they say, "I want that!" And then you can tell them, "You can have it. And if you want a suggestion, here is the path I have followed. Your path will be different, but at least you have a starting point."

All of you who are willing to study and internalize these teachings have the potential to reach that state of radiating your inner light of being the example of the spiritual path, the path of self-transcendence, the path of becoming more.

So you see, my beloved, truly we of the Ascended Host are able to raise the vibration of a forcefield. And this is one of the reasons we give dictations that are an expression of the Living Word. But you too can do this. You too can be the open door for raising the vibration, for quickening other people, raising their consciousness so they realize that there really is more to life. And if he can find it, if she can find it, maybe I can too.

For as we have said before, Jesus, Gautama, Krishna, Maitreya, Mother Mary, Saint Germain, El Morya, we are not the best examples for people, because they have already put us on a pedestal and think we are beyond the scope of normal human beings. And thus, they don't think that they can follow our examples. And that is why we need you to demonstrate the path so that they can identify with you, be awakened, be inspired, be uplifted by your mere presence. For it is the presence, the I AM Presence, that uplifts, that raises up, that accelerates, that multiplies so that your talents are multiplied and you become more.

So my beloved, we of the Ascended Host have need of you to be our counterparts in the material realm, to be our spiritual twin flames that you can be the open door here below, that our greater light can shine through and uplift those who have not yet seen that there is an alternative to sleepwalking through life, through living for three-score and ten without ever experiencing a moment of awareness, of being awake and truly appreciating what life is.

Overcome the focus on self

Yet as Mother Mary said, for you to reach that state, you must overcome the focus on self, on the little self, the narrow self, the self in the box. You must cultivate a greater love. You must find your greatest love, the love for which you came here originally—the gift that you wanted to bring to Earth. The gift that you simply desired to express, and your desire is so strong – your love for that gift is so strong – that you were willing to come here to express that gift.

And so you must, if you are willing to be awake, reconnect to that greater love and let that love grow so that it will become a magnet that simply pulls you out of that normal state of drudgery, of sleepwalking. And you are awake because you love to be awake, you love to feel that light flowing through you. You love to see it uplift other people. You love to feel that you are a part of the Ascended Host and our endeavor to raise the consciousness of humankind.

And so, my beloved, there are of course many traps that the ego has devised for preventing you from reconnecting to your greater love. And one of the more subtle ones is to set up an unrealistic expectation for what the spiritual path should be like, and thereby cause you to pursue spiritual growth in an unbalanced manner, whereby, as I said, you create your own opposition. And so your spiritual path, instead of becoming a process of greater and greater liberation, becomes an ongoing struggle that becomes harder and harder, until you finally break under the strain and give up and say, "I never want to have anything to do with that again."

And my beloved, if you will be honest, you will see that many of those, who used to call themselves chelas of the ascended masters, have gone through this process—have broken under the strain and have given up on the spiritual path. Or they have decided that this is the level where I am comfortable and this is the level where I am willing to serve, but I am not willing to go beyond it.

How to become awake

My beloved, becoming awake is not a matter of finding the philosopher's stone or some secret formula. It is a process, and the essence of that process is self-observation, the willingness to look at yourself, to look at the beam in your own eye, instead of focusing on the mote, the splinter, in the eye of another. For when you are willing to observe yourself without attachments, without seeking to see only what your ego wants you to see, then you have already started separating yourself from the ego and its illusions.

And this separation is the key to a greater awareness, a greater self-awareness, whereby you realize that you are more than that little self that lives in this small box and is so focused on itself and thinks the rest of the universe should be here to serve it. Instead, you see beyond it and you start seeing glimpses of the Higher Self that you are. And that will reconnect you to the higher love that you are and for which you came to Earth.

And suddenly you will start realizing that although life can have its ups and downs, behind these outer appearances is a deeper reality. And in that deeper reality life on Earth is an incredible opportunity, an incredible gift. An incredible opportunity to express yourself, your creativity, your inner being and to uplift others, to re-polarize an entire planet to the highest vision of God.

My beloved, take some time once in awhile out of your busy daily schedule and contemplate what a wondrous opportunity you have by being in a physical body in this material universe. Look beyond your daily situation. Look beyond your challenges. I know that they sometimes are severe, or at least seem to have a certain reality. But once in awhile look beyond them and see that behind every challenge is an opportunity for self-transcendence. And when you look for that self-transcendence, then you will not think that you are the doer who has to solve all of these problems, that you know you cannot solve with your outer mind. Instead, you will immerse yourself in the flow, whereby the light of your I AM Presence will flow through you, and that light will then dissolve those problems that seem like insurmountable obstacles to the outer mind.

And thus, when you take time to appreciate life, then life will become easier to appreciate. And then your life will no longer be the drudgery of the dualistic battle against forces that oppose you at every turn. Your life will become what we all desire to see for you, an upward spiral leading to greater and greater freedom, until you finally break through and achieve that complete non-attachment that is the true key to peace and bliss.

Let your vision be MORE

El Morya, October 21, 2006.

Living vision or dead vision?
For my beloved, nothing that is of God stands still. Nothing that is of God stands still! God is self-transcendence! For this is how the Creator creates—by transcending his former state and becoming MORE. So my beloved, you may have a spiritual teaching, a religious doctrine, and you may think it gives you all you need to know about God's reality. But if your vision stands still – does not grow, does not become MORE – then your vision has become a graven image. And my beloved, no graven image can ever convey the reality of the Living God.

Look upon the world, look upon the religious people, for in them truly all spiritual people can see that even though they have a vision and claim that their doctrines can explain all there is to know about life, you can surely see that their vision is a graven image. Their doctrines are graven images, and they go to church every Sunday worshipping before those idols that have no resemblance whatsoever to the Living God. For how can any image ever depict the Living God? Thus, my beloved, you see so many Christians who hold on to an image of God that is completely out of touch with reality. For God is not an angry being in the sky. He is the Living, Loving God. God has no desire to punish anyone. God does not even desire to punish the devil, or Satan or Lucifer or whatever Christians name the adversary.

For my beloved, God only desires to see all life transcend itself. And this is the one thing I would like you to understand from this discourse. My beloved, God has no desire to punish anyone. For punishment as it is seen by human beings, often means that you restrict someone from growing. And God would never restrict anyone from growing, from transcending themselves. God only wants all life to be free, to become MORE—as God is constantly becoming MORE.

So you see, my beloved, the image of an angry and punishing God is indeed a false image, a graven image that springs from the duality consciousness. And it is created because human beings in embodiment are projecting onto God the qualities of their own egos. For you see, my beloved, the ego feels threatened, feels constantly threatened. And thus, the ego has a desire to control. And when someone else will not submit to the ego's control, then the ego wants to punish that someone else. And so you see, my beloved, the desire to punish, the desire for revenge, springs from the sense of being threatened. And the sense of being threatened can come only from unreality.

For my beloved, how could anything real be threatened by anything? Do you think that God sits up in Heaven and feels threatened by the devil? Do you think that God sits up in Heaven and feels threatened by anything human beings do or could possibly do on Earth? So my beloved, God is not threatened by anything, and thus God has no need to control. Nor does he have a need to punish those who will not submit to control.

So you see, my beloved, so many people have a vision that there is a God. But they have the wrong vision of what God is like. And thus, one might wonder, would it be better for these people that they had no vision of the spiritual side of life whatsoever? For in many cases, I must tell you, that those who have no vision, who are stuck in the material, are often more open to learning something new than the people who call themselves the most devout religious people, whether they be in this religion or that.

Being open to a new understanding

And so, my beloved, as a spiritual teacher – which all of us in the Ascended Host are – we often find that there is the least opening among the people who claim to be the most religious or the most spiritual. And so, now that I have given you an example that I trust you can see, I would ask you to look in the mirror and look at yourselves and your own vision.

My beloved, there is not a single person on Earth who has the full and complete vision of the reality of God. Let me say it again, "There is not a single person on Earth who has the full and complete vision of the reality of God!" There never has been such a person, and there never will be.

For while you are in physical embodiment, it is not physically possible to have the full vision of God because the human brain, the human nervous system, is too limited to bring that vision to your conscious awareness. And my point for stating this obvious truth is to make you realize that all of you can benefit from expanding your vision, from raising your vision.

My beloved, there is no one who is an exception to this. Have I made myself clear here? [Yes] So then, you should be willing to look at yourselves – not in a condemning, not in a controlling, not in a punishing way – but you should be willing to look at yourself and say, "Are there any elements in my being, in my consciousness, that resist an expansion of my vision?" And if you sense such a resistance, then you know that the ego is hiding behind it. And it has an intention, which is to restrict you so that it can keep you under control. And that is why it does not want you to expand your vision, because when you do, what will happen? Well, you will find the truth that will make you free from the ego's control.

Now, my beloved, I will now speak, not only to you here, but I will speak into the collective consciousness of not only those who have found a spiritual teaching that was directly sponsored by the ascended masters, but I will speak to all those who have gone beyond the black-and-white stage of being religious and have risen to the stage of being more open to a spiritual teaching, a higher spiritual understanding. This includes all those in the New Age community. So again, as we did in Europe, I speak into the collective consciousness and this time it is the collective consciousness of the entire planet.

My beloved, the biggest problem that we face as spiritual teachers is that too many people will find a spiritual teaching that will expand their understanding of the spiritual side of life. And then, after a while, they will begin to listen to the subtle voice of the ego and the false teachers of this world—who tell them that now they know all they need to know. And thus, they just need to keep doing what they are doing now, believing what they are believing now, and they will make it to whatever version of salvation that they have been given in their teaching.

My beloved, I must tell you that the only realistic hope for the raising up of planet Earth into the Golden Age is that the top ten percent of the most spiritual people continue to raise their consciousness, until they attain either the full Christ consciousness or a high degree of Christhood. And knowing this full well, the false teachers of this world are working overtime, trying to get these spiritual people to go into this blind alley of feeling that now they have reached a sufficient level of spiritual vision. And they have the vision that is needed.

So, as I have said, this is an illusion! There is no one who can fulfill their spiritual mission without continuing to raise their vision as long as they have breath in the material realm. My beloved, I must tell you that there is a substantial number of people in the New Age movement and in ascended master organizations, who have grown for a time and then reached a plateau that is below the fulfillment of their divine plan and their highest potential. And they have then gotten comfortable or perhaps even discouraged, and so they have stopped their growth.

No fixed or final vision

And this, my beloved, will not cut it—neither for you personally nor for the planet as a whole. For you see, my beloved, what does it mean that the Earth is raised into a Golden Age? Is there a fixed vision for the Golden Age?

My beloved, you sometimes see organizations who conduct a fundraising campaign. And they create a big sign and they draw a thermometer, and at the top they have the sum that they are trying to raise. And then they show by lines and coloring how high they have come, how close they have come to the goal. And so, when the goal is reached and they have collected the sum of money that was their goal, then that particular mission was fulfilled.

And so, my beloved, what many of you have come to think – because this is the way the ego and the linear, analytical mind thinks – is that bringing in the Golden Age is similar to this, that it is some kind of spiritual fundraising campaign where we have a top goal. And when enough prayers or decrees or rosaries or enough good vibrations have been released, then we have reached the top and the Golden Age is suddenly there.

But you see, my beloved, the Golden Age is not a fixed quantity—it cannot be quantified. The Golden Age does not mean that society has reached some kind of perfection, and now it will no longer change or grow. For you see, my beloved, the essence of a Golden Age is that society is not in a static state of perfection but is in a continual state of self-transcendence. This is the Golden Age. And in past ages, when civilizations had reached the Golden Age, what caused those civilizations to decline was that they stopped transcending themselves. And so the Golden Age came to a halt and the society went into a downward spiral.

And thus, my beloved, it is not a matter of you having the vision that if you do a certain amount of outer things or understand a certain truth, then you are doing what you need to do to bring about the Golden Age of Saint Germain. No, my beloved, what you need to do to bring about the Golden Age of Saint Germain is to enter into and remain in the River of Life that is continually flowing and transcending itself. For only then will you give the highest possible contribution to bringing about the Golden Age of Saint Germain and your own ascension and Christhood.

Stopping just before the goal is reached
You see, my beloved, when you look at the pyramid, the Great Pyramid at Giza, you will see that the King's Chamber is two-thirds of the height of the pyramid from the base. And the two-thirds mark is the level where the Christ is meant to appear. And so what I am trying to explain to you here is that a substantial number of former or present ascended master students and people in the New Age movement have come very close to that two-thirds mark.

Yet instead of pushing harder and going above it, where the Christ starts appearing in their being, they have somehow come to believe in a fallacy of the ego, in an illusion of the ego. And they have stood still, they have stagnated. And they are standing there and they are spinning their wheels. And some of them are moving hard and working hard, but they are getting nowhere for they are not willing to raise their vision to see what will it take to come over that hump and enter into the light of Christ. And the reason they have not done this is that there is some illusion of the ego that they are still attached to, that they are not willing to question, that they are not willing to look in the mirror and see, "Oh, I have this problem. I am the one that needs to overcome it."

Judgment is the hallmark of the fallen consciousness
My beloved, my point for this long discourse is to bring you to the realization that when people are stuck in one of these dualistic states of consciousness, it is inevitable that they begin to become very critical and judgmental toward those who are not stuck in their states of consciousness.

And that is why my point here is that if you look at people, perhaps even dare to look at yourself, and say, "Do I feel a need to criticize others? Do I feel a need to judge others? Do I feel a need to evaluate others?

Can I identify that in the back of my mind there is always a voice, there is always a process, of criticizing, of judging, of evaluating everything, of comparing to some standard that I am not even consciously aware of? Can I recognize in myself that there is a tendency, sometimes, to blame—to blame myself, to blame others, to criticize, to condemn, to judge, to look for imperfections, instead of looking at the immaculate concept."

My beloved, my point here is to show you that too many of those who formerly were ascended master students, or who still call themselves ascended master students, have not been willing to step up to the level of Christhood. They have instead become stuck in one of the states of consciousness that were originally created and reinforced by the fallen angels. And therefore, they have become judgmental and critical of anything that is different from that state of consciousness and its characteristics.

They are constantly judging and evaluating anything that comes to them. Because it is as if they have a mental box, and any idea that comes to them must somehow fit into that box and be put into a little drawer with a label on it, so they feel that they have the idea under control and so that their egos will not feel threatened by the idea. And so that the people themselves, the conscious selves, will not feel an urge to go beyond the mental box, to think outside the box.

You see, my beloved, what I want you to see from this discourse is that even if you have a very sophisticated vision of the spiritual side of life and have a sophisticated outer understanding of the teachings of the ascended masters, it is still possible that you can be stuck in a state of consciousness that is not the ascended master consciousness but is the consciousness of the fallen angels. And so, my beloved, whether you actually fell from above, or whether you descended on a rescue mission, or whether you evolved from the Earth, it does not really matter.

What matters is that as long as you are in a state of consciousness that has the characteristics of the fallen consciousness – the judgmentalness, the judging after appearances as Jesus said – as long as you are in that state of consciousness, you are not expressing your Christhood. And therefore, you are truly not an ascended master student. You are not truly a chela of El Morya because you are refusing to become MORE.

And instead of you becoming MORE, and constantly transcending yourself, you have accepted an upper limit. And now you are spending your attention on judging others whom you think do not live up to your standard, the standard that you have used to box yourself in—and your ego is now using to try to control everybody else and box them in, so that they will not disturb your vision by demonstrating that there is something beyond the box.

When your forgiveness is unconditional, your joy will be full

Mother Mary, November 26, 2006

My beloved hearts, if your telephone rings, would you not pick it up? And when you pick up the phone, do you not listen long enough to at least find out whether the person on the other end has an important message for you or is simply trying to sell you something. And thus, my beloved, if you do realize that the person at the other end has a message for you, would you not do your utmost to listen to that message and understand what it says?

Surely, my beloved, you will treat your telephone and the person calling with a certain measure of respect. Thus, my question to you is, "Why would you not treat life itself with the same measure of respect?"

Ah my beloved, you will say that you surely have respect for life. But I would beg to question whether that is really so. For you see, my beloved, life itself can be compared to a telephone. Every situation you encounter can be seen as a telephone call from life itself. And yet, my beloved, there are so many situations in life where you do not pick up the phone and listen to see if that situation has an important message for you, a message that can help you transcend yourself – or some limitation – so that you can be free and be more in the River of Life.

Why you encounter the same problems again and again

You see, my beloved, most people go through life with blinders on. They are only half awake, only half aware of what is happening. And thus, they do not realize that life is a continuous string of situations—with each situation having a message that can help them rise higher and overcome some erroneous belief, some misconception that limits them and the expression of life itself through them.

My beloved, so many of you have these situations happen over and over again in your life. And you often cry out, "Why does this keep happening to me? Why is God doing this to me? Why are other people doing this to me? Why is destiny or fate or luck doing this to me?" But my beloved, you do not take time to stand back and say, "Why am I doing this to myself?"

You see, my beloved, every situation in life can be viewed as a telephone call, and there is a message in that call. But so often you do not bother to pick up the phone and listen to the message. And even those people who pick up the phone – who do consider that they might need to learn something from certain situations – well my beloved, they so often do not truly listen for the message behind the phone call. They do not truly listen with the inner ear, trying to understand the message, trying to understand that which they cannot see with the outer mind.

And so they listen to the message, they evaluate, with the outer mind. And therefore, they do not see the message, they do not hear the message, for the outer mind cannot fathom that message. For my beloved, if your outer mind had already understood the message that life is trying to give you, then why would life bother to call you on the telephone by having you experience the same situation over and over again?

Life does not punish you

You see, my beloved, it is a complete misconception of the human consciousness and the human ego that life is trying to punish you. And I can assure you, my beloved, that life itself – and life is created by God, so even God itself – has no desire to punish you whatsoever. Thus, it is an absolute law that once you have learned the lesson you need to learn from a specific situation, then you will not encounter that situation again.

And therefore, my beloved, when you encounter the same situation over and over again, it is because you have not learned the lesson. And that is why life keeps calling you and presenting you with the same situation over and over again, so that you have another opportunity – and another and another – to learn the lesson.

So my beloved, instead of grumbling, instead of complaining that the same thing keeps happening to you over and over again, I have a very simple suggestion to you. Simply pick up the phone and listen for the message that life is trying to give. Then learn that lesson. Resolve the belief that you need to resolve in order to move up higher. And I can guarantee you that – as if by magic – you will not encounter that same situation again.

My beloved, life is not very complicated. Life is really very, very simple. And the underlying message behind every situation you encounter in life is simply this: "The material universe is a mirror!"

The Ma-ter light will take on the forms that correspond to the contents of your consciousness. It is your state of consciousness that projects an image onto the Ma-ter light. And the Ma-ter light can do nothing else but to reflect that image back to you—both the image in your conscious mind and the image in the subconscious layers of your mind, your emotional, mental and identity bodies.

My beloved, life is very simple. Life itself is the principle of growth—of becoming more, of self-transcendence. So the message that life is always trying to give you is that you can become more. And by seeing your limitation, by seeing the limiting belief that you have – about yourself, about the world and about God – you can transcend that limitation and come up higher and be more in God's ever-flowing River of Life.

You see, my beloved, so many people have wondered about the meaning of life, the purpose of life, the secret of life. So many people have searched for the philosopher's stone, the magic wand, some kind of shortcut that will allow them to suddenly be in a state of bliss, or a state of having what they think they need in order to be happy. Yet my beloved, the secret of life is very simple—it is self-transcendence.

And my beloved, this does not mean that you need to attain some remote state of perfection that might seem beyond your reach. It simply means that every time you transcend yourself, you are in the flow of the River of Life. And thus you have the potential to experience the joy, the bliss, that truly is that River of Life.

And so the message that life is trying to give you in every situation is that when you encounter a limitation, if you are willing to look inside yourself and acknowledge the belief that causes you to experience that situation as a limitation and then let go of that belief, well then my beloved, you will rise above the sense of limitation and instead be in the bliss of the River of Life.

There is an alternative to suffering

So my beloved the law of God is simple. You have free will to do whatever you want. You are a co-creator with God. And you are here to learn how to use your co-creative abilities to create situations for yourself that you can live with, that you can grow with. And thus you learn in two ways. One is by listening to direction from within, from your Higher Self, from your I AM Presence, from your spiritual teachers. But if you will not listen for that direction, or if you will not use even your reasoning mind to find direction on your own, well then you must learn in the other way, which is the school of hard knocks—by seeing the Ma-ter light reflect back to you physical circumstances that outpicture the circumstances in your mind.

And thus, my beloved, the law of God is this. You have a right to create any mental image you want. You have a right to project that mental image outside your own mind. But when you do so, you will inevitably experience the physical situations that outpicture your mental image. You will experience what you project upon life. You will experience what you co-create through the power of your mind by projecting a mental image onto the Ma-ter light.

And thus, my beloved, God and myself and all spiritual teachers, firmly uphold your right to co-create any circumstance you want. Yet my beloved, we would like you to understand that if you co-create circumstances that cause you suffering, then you have an alternative to continuing to create the same circumstances. Yet the only way to stop the repetitive cycle that leads to suffering is to change the cause of the outer circumstances.

And my beloved, I know full well that throughout history people have come up with all kinds of excuses that make it seem like they are not in control of the outer circumstances, that they did not create them, that somehow God, fate, luck or other people created those circumstances. But my beloved, the stark reality is that you have co-created your own circumstances because you have formed mental images and you have projected those images onto the Ma-ter light.

And thus, the only way – the absolute only way – that those outer circumstances can be changed is that you change the cause of the outer circumstances. For my beloved, would you not agree that if you want to change an effect, you have to change the cause that creates that effect? And what I am telling you is that the effect is your outer circumstances. And the cause of that effect is the mental images you hold in your mind. And thus, the only way to change your outer circumstances is to change those mental images.

My beloved, how can you change the mental images in your mind? Well, there is no other way but to do so consciously by seeing the mental images – seeing that they are based on the duality consciousness, on the illusions of the mind of anti-christ – and then consciously letting them go, replacing the illusions with the truth of Christ.

My beloved, please take note of what I am saying. It is not a matter of somehow justifying the beliefs you have accepted in the past. Oh my beloved, if you will look at this honestly, you will see that when so many people are confronted with a possibility that they might have an imperfect belief, they go into a defensive reaction. My beloved, this defensive reaction is the reaction of the ego – the default reaction of the ego – which simply will not acknowledge that it could be wrong. And thus it goes into a reaction of trying to defend or justify its beliefs.

Yet my beloved, what I hope you can see is that if you keep trying to justify a past belief, you will simply build on to that belief. And thus, you will keep sending mental images into the cosmic mirror that are based on that original belief. And so, of course, what can the cosmic mirror do but send back to you the same kind of circumstances that you have created all along?

So my beloved, will you please realize that if you keep doing the same thing and expect different results, then you are trapped in the basic insanity of the human ego. And therefore, you must step away from the old patterns and simply be willing to openly acknowledge that certain beliefs from your past are limiting yourself. And thus, it is not in your own best interest to uphold those beliefs. On the contrary, it is in your own best interest to simply let them go.

You are more than your past

My beloved, the key realization here is the teaching I have given in my book, and that we have given over and over again on our websites, including in Jesus' discourses on the ego. That teaching simply says that the core of your identity is the conscious self, the Conscious You.

The Conscious You is a spark of God's own being. And thus, it is infinitely more than your past, than any circumstance or any belief from your past. And thus, your conscious self has the God-given right and the God-given ability to step outside of its identification with your past. And my beloved, you can do so at any moment, including right now.

Thus, I ask you to acknowledge that there is a force in this world that is very determined to keep you trapped in your identification with the past, so that you do not think you can let go of the past. And so that you might even fear that if you let go of the past, you lose your very identity. My beloved, this force is comprised of your personal ego, the egos of other people and the entire dark force, the force of anti-christ, what Jesus called the prince of this world. And thus, the prince of this world will constantly come to you, and he will come to see if he can make you attached to the past, so that you are not willing to simply let it go, to let the imperfect beliefs go by acknowledging that you are more than any imperfect beliefs.

My beloved, do you truly hear what I am saying here? You have the God-given right and the ability to let go of any imperfect belief from the past. How can you do this? By being willing to look at the belief, acknowledge that it is unreal, that it springs from the mind of anti-christ. And then you can acknowledge that you are more than the belief. And thus, the belief is simply like an old worn-out coat that you took on sometime in the past. But you can take that coat off at any time and throw it onto the fire and let it be burned so that it is consumed and is no more.

And thus, you can take off the old sense of identity, based on that belief, and throw it into the spiritual fires of the violet flame and the flame of forgiveness, and you can simply let it go. For my beloved, the flame of forgiveness, what we have called the violet flame or the flame of mercy, is simply the cosmic eraser that allows you to take the old worn-out sense of identity that you have built and throw it into the fire. For my beloved, your God is truly a consuming fire that can consume all imperfect sense of self that you might have built in any past lifetime.

And so my beloved you have an alternative to repeating these old patterns. And that alternative is to take off the overcoat of your imperfect sense of identity and throw it onto the bonfire of God, where it will be consumed and you will then be free as if that identity had never existed.

The master key to letting go

But my beloved, what is the master key to doing this? What is the master key to letting go of an imperfect sense of identity? Well my beloved, it is the willingness to forgive. In order to be free of your past, you must forgive and you must forgive unconditionally.

Do you see, my beloved, that your ego has tricked you into thinking that in order for you to forgive, certain conditions must be fulfilled? For example, many people believe that in order to forgive someone who has hurt them, then that person must somehow be punished first. And only when the person has been sufficiently punished, can you forgive that person. Or some people might believe that only if the other person has truly changed, can you forgive that person.

This, of course, is a belief that will be like a double-edged sword, where one edge of the sword is pointing to yourself and therefore able to give yourself a nasty wound. For beloved, what you do unto others is what you have already done to yourself. This is the reason why Jesus told you to do unto others as you want them to do to yourself. But the deeper meaning is that you can only do unto others what you have already done to yourself, both good and bad.

So if you think that other people must live up to certain conditions before they can be forgiven, then you also think that you must live up to certain conditions before you can be forgiven. And my beloved, your ego is very clever at defining such conditions and defining them in such a way that no one can live up to them, including yourself. And that is how your ego keeps you trapped in the cycle of never wanting to forgive others and never wanting to forgive yourself. My beloved, your ego essentially makes you believe that because you have made certain mistakes in the past, you are unforgivable, you are unredeemable, you can never rise above that past and be free of it.

Do you see, my beloved, that the last thing your ego wants you to realize is that you have the God-given right and the power to simply walk away from the imperfections of your past? Your ego does not want you to realize that you can do this. And it does not want you to realize that you can do this by openly acknowledging the imperfect beliefs that caused you to encounter those physical situations that gave you so much pain.

Thus, my beloved, will you not please realize that the master key to rising above your past is to forgive—but not to forgive in a human way that is based on outer conditions. No, my beloved, the master key to rising above your past is to forgive unconditionally.

Do you see, my beloved, when you have not forgiven another person, you are in reality holding on to the old situation. And that means you are holding on – whether you are aware of this or not – to the pain created in that situation when the other person hurt you. And that pain pulls on your conscious attention and pulls you into remembering that situation. And whenever you think about that situation, you reinforce the original hurt, the original pain and the original anger against the other person. And thereby, you tie yourself to your past and you actually reinforce the past.

And thus, you see, my beloved, by not forgiving the other person, you are harming yourself because you are holding on to the imperfect images and feelings, and you are projecting them onto the Ma-ter light. And thus the Ma-ter light must reason that you want to experience situations where other people hurt you. And thus, what is the Ma-ter light going to give you? Well, my beloved, it has no other option than to give you future situations where other people hurt you. Because it truly believes that that is what you want to experience, based on the fact that you are projecting a mental and emotional image into the cosmic mirror of other people hurting you.

Non-forgiveness hurts yourself

So my beloved, can you finally see here that when you do not forgive other people, you are in reality hurting yourself? And what is the excuse you use for not forgiving others? Well, it is that they do not live up to the outer conditions that your ego has defined. And therefore, it seems as if – as long as other people do not live up to those outer conditions – you cannot let go of the situation, you cannot forgive and rise above it.

But my beloved, do you not see that this is the very same psychology that caused you to be hurt in the original situation? Because what happened in the original situation was that somebody else did something to you. But my beloved, it was not what they did to you that caused you to be hurt. It was the imperfect beliefs that you hold about yourself and life that caused you to respond to that situation in a way that hurt yourself.

And so, do you see that what really caused the hurt in that original situation was that you had a belief that turned you into a passive victim? You thought that when other people did certain things to you, you could only respond with negative feelings that cause you to be hurt. And thus, it was this belief that turned you into a victim in the original situation.

And my beloved, can you not please see here that even today you are holding on to the belief that you are a victim by thinking that only when the other person lives up to certain conditions can you forgive that person and let go of the situation. So can you not see that by not forgiving, you are actually perpetuating the original situation—projecting the beliefs and the feelings from that situation into the cosmic mirror, thereby inevitably setting yourself up to reap what you have sown. Which is that you have projected an imperfect mental image into the mirror, and thereby inevitably set in motion a chain reaction that will eventually return to you physical situations that reflect your mental image.

Thus, my beloved what can break this situation? Well, there is only one thing that can break it. And that is that you pick up the telephone and listen long enough to realize that what life is trying to teach you is that it is your own beliefs that cause you to be hurt. And only by changing your own beliefs, can you break the cycle of experiencing physical situations that put you in a situation – in your own mind – where you think that your only potential response is to respond as a victim and feel hurt.

Take back your power to choose how you respond

And thus, my beloved, can you not please realize here that the only thing that can change the equation is that you change the way you look at the equation, the way you look at life, the way you look at yourself. My beloved, you must take back your power to respond to situations based on a choice you make today – now – instead of a choice you made in the past.

For in the past you chose to accept an imperfect belief about yourself. And as long as you allow that belief to remain in your subconscious mind, well my beloved you cannot make a choice as to how you will respond to the situations you will experience in the present. For that choice was already made in the past, and you can only repeat the same old pattern over and over again.

So what can break the situation is that you become aware of what is happening, and therefore you decide to go back and look at the original belief and dismiss it as being unreal. And when you have dismissed the belief, then, my beloved, the next time you experience a similar situation, you will not have that baggage weighing you down. And thus, your mind will be able to say, "But you know, I don't have to respond to this situation by feeling hurt, by feeling afraid, by feeling ashamed, by coming down on myself and thinking I am a bad person because someone else treats me as if I was a bad person."

Instead, you can realize that what the other person does to you is a reflection of that person's state of consciousness. It is not because the other person has an imperfect image of you, although this might seem to be so based on the person's outer mind and actions. In reality, the person has an imperfect image of him or herself, and the person is projecting that image upon you. But you do not have to accept the other person's image of you. For you have a God-given right to live your life based on the images in your own mind. And thus, you can choose to respond to the other person freely—when you do not accept the other person's images or any other limiting beliefs from your own past.

And so what is the key, my beloved, to letting go of these imperfect images that you accepted in the past or that other people have accepted? What is the key to not being affected by the imperfect beliefs of other people or the imperfect beliefs of your own past self? Well, it is, my beloved, to forgive—to forgive by being completely non-attached to what is projected at you from other people or from your own mind. It is to accept the absolute power to unconditionally forgive yourself or other people and to simply let go of all sense of hurt, all sense of pain.

Chapter 5: Ego Teachings, 2007

Let 2007 be the year of unconditional peace

Gautama Buddha, January 1, 2007

My beloved, take one look at history and see the fallacy of the human logic – the dualistic logic, the logic of anti-christ – which has made so many people believe that they must create peace through force, through revenge, through destroying their enemies. What is indeed the incredible fallacy that makes people believe in this logic?

Well it is, my beloved, very simply that there is something they are not willing to give up in themselves. There is something to which they are attached. And that something is not just an outer thing, be it a piece of property or anything else in this world. No my beloved, that to which people are attached is indeed something that is in themselves. It is a part of their egos, and they are not willing to let go of the belief that makes them feel that they have some kind of superiority, some kind of right to do what they want to do here on Earth.

Thus, my beloved, all of the outer reasons and justifications that people come up with for engaging in conflict and warfare are lies, are facades. They are nothing but pretensions and hypocrisy. For the true reality is that people wage war because they are trying to defend their egos. There is a part of the ego that people are not willing to give up. And I am not here just talking about individuals but groups of people, even entire nations or civilizations.

The superiority complex in the Middle East

Now my beloved, every coin has two sides and so has every conflict. Is there indeed not a similar mechanism in the Middle East, in the Arab and Muslim world, whereby they also wage war because there is something in themselves, a part of their own egos, that they are not willing to give up. And so what is, indeed, that something?

Well, my beloved, it is in fact the same mechanism, although with a slightly different disguise. Nevertheless, it is also the need for superiority, the need to feel that somehow one is favored by God because one is a member of the Muslim religion which is the highest religion on Earth, or so they think.

And so you see, my beloved, that this insane drive for ultimate superiority is indeed the most extreme outcome of the human ego that has been allowed to run rampant without any checks from people's true beings, their conscious selves. Thus one might wonder how long this insanity will go on on this planet.

And I will tell you how long it will go on. It will continue until the top ten percent of the most spiritually aware people decide that they have had enough of it. Thus, they will start by pulling the beam from their own eyes, for indeed there are many people on this planet who are truly spiritual and have engaged in spiritual activities, yet they have allowed their egos to fool them into feeling a subtle sense of superiority because they have done this or that spiritual activity. They have meditated for so long, they have given so many prayers or rosaries or decrees or what have you.

Thus, my beloved, this must indeed stop at the top by the most spiritually mature people being willing to look in the mirror and say, "We have to overcome this. We have to let go of this subtle spiritual pride and intellectual pride because we can understand spiritual concepts. We have to overcome this. We have to come together in true humility, and then we have to make the calls so that God will remove this planetary beast of superiority, so that other people can be set free from the gravitational pull of this beast that seeks to pull the entire planet into a black hole."

You cannot stop conflict by destroying your enemies

And thus, my beloved, what I desire you to visualize for the year 2007 is that humankind finally wakes up and realizes the essential truth that the only way to attain peace is through unconditional forgiveness. My beloved, it is the insanity of the ego to believe that one needs to compensate for the violence of the past before peace can manifest in the present. It is the insanity of the ego to believe that one can compensate for the errors of the past, that one can ever fix what was broken in the past, that one can ever put Humpty Dumpty together again after his fall from the great wall of time.

For my beloved, if you will think about this with the rationality of the Christ Mind, you will see that for thousands of years people have attempted to destroy their enemies, to seek revenge, to somehow make up for the violence and the mistakes of the past. Yet despite all of the fighting, all of the violence, all of the warfare, the errors of the past have not been erased. And the reason is simple.

Violence creates an action that generates an opposite reaction from the universal mirror. And thus, when you take action from the dualistic state of mind, you will create an opposition to your action that traps you in a dualistic struggle with an enemy. And this dualistic struggle will continue for as long as you stay in the dualistic mind.

And thus, what can break the spiral? Well, only one thing—that you stop acting from the consciousness of duality and rise to the consciousness of Christ, so that you do not seek revenge, but you forgive seventy times seven. You do not resist evil, but you turn the other cheek. You become as the Buddha, sitting under the Bo Tree, and you are unmoved by the demons of Mara who attempt to draw you into their dualistic struggle.

Thus, you realize that the dualistic struggle can go on forever and can consume your entire existence—past, present and future. And thus, you must come to realize that there is something more, something you want more, namely the peace of Christ, the peace of Buddha. And so you must say what Jesus said to his disciples, "What is that to thee, follow thou me." What are these dualistic struggles on Earth compared to following the Christ and the Buddha into the eternal peace of the Mind of God?

And so you must decide what you want. Do you want to continue the dualistic struggle, or do you want to attain eternal peace? And if you want peace, then how can you do so? Well my beloved, you cannot attain peace by winning the dualistic struggle, for there are no winners in that struggle. You cannot attain peace by solving a problem created by the duality consciousness, for such a problem cannot be solved. You cannot attain peace by somehow compensating for creating the errors of the past, for the mistakes made through the duality consciousness cannot be corrected. My beloved, you cannot fix the duality consciousness. You can only leave it behind!

The lesson of the fact that, after thousands of years of struggle, humankind have not manifested peace is indeed that you cannot manifest peace through duality. You can only manifest peace by rising above – by transcending, by surrendering, by letting go of, by becoming non-attached to – duality and all of its appearances.

Thus, you must give up the ghost of the past. You must reach for the non-attachment of the Buddha, the unconditional mercy of Kuan Yin, so that you can let go of the past. And instead of trying to fix it, you simply forgive. You forgive unconditionally. You forgive indefinitely.

And you even enter the state of perpetual forgiveness, where you are forgiving past, present and future. So that you know that whatever may be done to you in the future will be forgiven even before it is done. And in this way you can lock in to the immaculate concept of Mother Mary, where you can hold the immaculate concept – for yourself, for other people, indeed for the entire planet – that no matter what happens in the physical, it will not perpetuate the dualistic struggle. It will not draw you or other people back into or further into that dualistic struggle. But instead, people will overcome, they will rise above it, they will leave it behind. They will decide to suddenly forgive, where they have never forgiven before and to simply turn the other cheek and let the Law of God repay the wrongs committed by others.

The key to peace

This my beloved, is the essential key to peace. You cannot bring about peace through any amount of action done from the dualistic state of mind. You can only bring about peace by rising above duality. And in order to do that, you must let go of all of the appearances of duality. You must become non-attached to them so that you know that the peace of Christ, the peace of Buddha, the peace of the Divine Mother, indeed the peace of the Divine Father, is far more important than these dualistic appearances that are nothing but mirages in the desert.

And then, my beloved, when you have let go of the past, when you have let go of duality, when you have become non-attached, well at that point you might indeed take certain actions to bring about peace. But these actions will not be dualistic, they will be taken with the single-eyed vision of the Christ Mind, which is also the vision of the Divine Mother that holds the immaculate concept for all life. And thus your actions will be balanced, and they will not create a reaction, an opposite reaction from the universe, not even from other people.

Leave the eternal struggle and find freedom in the Eternal NOW

Mother Mary, February 18, 2007

My beloved, when it comes right down to it, the past and the future are nothing but illusions, mirages created by the sense of separation from the allness of life that I love to call the River of Life. My beloved, there are those who believe that heaven is a place of eternal rest, where angels sit around on pink clouds, playing harps. There are those who believe heaven is the Buddhic Nirvana, which they – in contrast to the Buddha's true teachings – have come to see as a place where nothing changes, where there is no growth, no individuality, no differentiation.

Yet my beloved, what must die so that you – the Conscious You – can be resurrected into eternal life, is not your individuality, your sense of self. Nay, my beloved, what must die is the separate sense of self, the self that is based on separation from the River of Life. This is the self that is born out of your refusal to take up the responsibility to become the Christ, to become one with all life through oneness with the guru.

My beloved, there is no more important relationship for people on Earth than their relationship to a spiritual teacher, or as such a teacher is often called in the East, a guru. Oh yes, my beloved, the word "guru" has indeed received a bad name in the West, in large part due to the many false and fake gurus who have come out of the East and have attempted to take advantage of the spiritual awakening that has been going on in the West now for several decades.

Yet I must tell you that there is a reality in the fact that you need someone who is not trapped in the duality consciousness in order to escape your own dualistic illusions. For as Jesus has so lovingly explained in his ego discourses, the main characteristic of the ego is that it blinds you to reality. This is what the Buddha called the veil of Maya, the veil of illusion, that makes you vulnerable to the forces of duality, which the Buddha called the demons of Mara.

Discover the parallels between the teachings of Christ and Buddha

Yes, my beloved, there are indeed many parallels between the teachings of the Buddha and the teachings of Christ. And that is why you will see that this new Invocation of the Eternal NOW, for the first time ever, blends the teachings of the Christ and the teachings of the Buddha. This, my beloved, is an extremely powerful ritual, not only for you personally, but also for the world at large.

For I must tell you that the main strategy used by the forces of duality is indeed the strategy of divide and conquer. And how could it be otherwise? For how could the forces of duality do anything but divide others, as they are divided in themselves through their entrapment in the consciousness of duality, the consciousness of anti-christ and anti-buddha. For my beloved, as you should realize by now, the true teachings of Christ are the teachings of inner oneness, oneness with your own higher being through oneness with a teacher, or master or guru outside yourself.

For did not Jesus himself outpicture that Path of Oneness with his disciples? Did he not attempt to raise his disciples from the state of consciousness in which they were trapped when he found them and then take them into oneness with himself? And was is not so that few of the disciples were able to enter into that oneness. Specifically, Peter was the one who outpictured the difficulty that many among humankind have in understanding the true message of Christ. Namely, that you not simply follow Christ and elevate Christ to an idol that will do the work for you, but that you come into oneness with Christ, the oneness that can be attained only by following the inner path, the straight and narrow way, the Middle Way.

For you see, my beloved, both the Christ and the Buddha, in their true inner teachings, taught the inner path, the Path of Oneness. How can you be a true follower of Christ unless you come into oneness with Christ, unless you let that mind be in you which was also in Christ Jesus, so that you can do the works that Jesus did, and greater works. And how can you be a true follower of the Buddha unless you come into oneness with the Buddha?

For is it not so, my beloved, that the essence of the teachings of the Buddha is that everything is the Buddha nature. And so, when you see that everything is the Buddha nature, how can you fail to come into oneness with the Buddha that has embodied the Buddha nature? And likewise, did not Jesus talk about the Word and does not the Gospel of John say that in the beginning was the Word and without him was not made any thing made that was made. So when you see the essence of the teachings of Christ, you see that everything is made out of the Word, out of the universal Christ Mind. And thus, when you see this, how can you fail to see the universal Christ in yourself and thereby come into oneness with the universal Christ Mind and all who have previously come into oneness with that Mind, namely Jesus, Gautama, myself and all the true saints and sages of the ages, those who are found in every religion.

For my beloved, did not Jesus clearly spell out for Christians that unless their righteousness exceeds the righteousness of the scribes and Pharisees, they should in no wise enter the kingdom. And was not the righteousness of the scribes and Pharisees an outer righteousness, where they took pride in following the outer letter of the law, the outer scripture, in minute detail, thereby thinking they could guarantee their way into heaven. And did not Jesus say that the kingdom of heaven comes not with observation, for the kingdom of God is within you? So it is not clear, my beloved – is it not obvious for those who have ears to hear and eyes to see – that Jesus called all to come into oneness with him, which is why he said, "I am the way the truth and the life. No man comes to the Father but by me," meaning the universal Christ consciousness with which I am one in the eternal now.

What keeps people in the eternal struggle?

So my beloved hearts, what is indeed the blindness that blinds people to these evident truths, these truths that should be self-evident, or would be self-evident if people were not blinded so that they cannot see the obvious. Oh my beloved, so many people think that they are religious or spiritual, but they are as blind as the people who thought the Earth was flat, for they see not that which should be obvious if they would only open their minds and hearts.

And yet, my beloved, what is it that prevents people from seeing the reality and the truth of Christ and Buddha? Well, my beloved, it is that they are not mindful, that they are not awake. And why are they not awake? It is because they have allowed themselves, without realizing what happened, to be pulled into the eternal human struggle. And this is the struggle that is set up between two dualistic extremes. And these extremes take many different forms, my beloved. But there are always two extremes. And they pull you to go into one of the extremes, thinking that if only you can cross some line, you will win the ultimate victory. Yet I tell you the absolute truth that there is no victory possible in the realm of duality.

There are always those who promise you that if you shun the one dualistic extreme and come into the other dualistic extreme, you are guaranteed to be saved. And this, my beloved, is the promise of every false religion that has ever been seen on this planet. And unfortunately, the majority of humankind are still believing in this false promise of a false salvation, an outer salvation through belonging to this particular outer religion or belief system, following its leaders or practices.

Oh my beloved, it is this eternal human struggle that causes all of the suffering on Earth. And we have no other desire than to see you awaken to the reality that this struggle is unreality, and that by shunning that unreality – attaining the Christ discernment that allows you to see through it and see the reality of God behind it – you can overcome that struggle. You can pull yourself out. You can raise yourself above the eternal human struggle.

For my beloved, the Buddha truly said – as one of the four noble truths – that life is suffering. But life is only suffering when you are trapped in the consciousness of duality that binds you to this eternal struggle of seeking to avoid the one dualistic extreme, that is portrayed as bad, and coming into the other dualistic extreme, that is portrayed as good. Yet even though some people are very sincere and strive for an entire lifetime, perhaps even many lifetimes, to escape the bad dualistic extreme and come into the good dualistic extreme, they never quite make it.

And my beloved, why is this so? Well it is so, my beloved, because the duality consciousness sets up a goal that is unreachable, that is unattainable. You see, my beloved, no one has ever fully escaped the dualistic extreme that many call evil and reached the dualistic extreme that many call good. And why is this so? Because when you are trapped in duality, you have entered a realm where you are being pulled on by two opposing forces. And my beloved, the closer you get to one dualistic extreme, the more you will be pulled back toward the other extreme. And why is this so? Because as you move away from the centeredness of the Middle Way of Christ and Buddha, you are the one creating the force that pulls you back.

You see, my beloved, there are so many people who believe that when they are pulled away from what they define as good, it is because they are being pulled away by the forces of darkness, the forces of evil. And my beloved, while this is true, I must tell you that the reason why you are being pulled by the force of evil – the reason why the force of evil, the prince of this world, has anything in you on which it can pull – is that you are trapped in the realm of duality.

Being humanly good prevents you from entering heaven

You see, my beloved, if you were not being pulled away from good, what would happen was that you would go into a state in which you thought you were perfectly good, and you would stay there indefinitely. Yet my beloved, as Jesus said – when he said, that the righteousness of the scribes and Pharisees would not get them to heaven – was precisely that being humanly good is not sufficient to get you to heaven. For being humanly good is still in the realm of duality.

So you see, my beloved, if it was indeed possible for you to escape human evil and go into the extreme of human good, you would still be trapped in duality—yet you would believe that you would be saved. And therefore, you would not strive to go beyond that state. And if you did not strive to go beyond, you would never attain salvation. You will not be saved by becoming a good human being, for this is still a sense of identity that is separated from the spiritual identity in which you know you are an individualization of God's own Being.

So you see, my beloved, the force that human beings call evil is indeed evil, but it is evil in a dualistic sense. And as long as people are trapped in duality, it actually has the function of preventing them from going into the opposite extreme of human good, of relative good, and staying there indefinitely.

Now my beloved, this is a subtle point, and I do not want you to misunderstand or misinterpret what I say. I am not saying that evil is good. I am not saying that evil is part of God's plan. I am not saying that God wants evil to remain on this planet. I am only saying that as long as people insist on expressing their creative powers through the mind of duality – as long as they insist on trying to preserve the separate sense of self, the identity of the human ego – then they will be subject to the force of evil.

For people do indeed create both the relative good and the relative evil that blinds them to God's reality beyond duality. And therefore, you can never fully attain goodness or peace on Earth. This is what the Buddha knew, and that is why he said that life is suffering. For he knew that as long as you are trapped behind this veil of illusion, this veil of Maya, you cannot escape suffering. Jesus knew this as well and expressed the same truth, only in slightly different words.

Overcoming the planetary momentum of death

Mother Mary, April 05, 2007.

Time and death are illusions

You see, my beloved, time truly is one of the greatest illusions in the material universe. Time causes so many people to lose sight of what is important in the eternal life because they become so enveloped in the daily life, and they forget that they are not here simply to live a daily life of struggle, of running around from here to there, never really getting anywhere.

So you see, my beloved, time must be conquered before the last enemy can be conquered. And what is that last enemy? Well, as the Bible says, the last enemy is death. But my beloved, throughout this conference we will give you a new view of death. For you will understand that there is a worldly image of death and there is the spiritual reality, where death can be seen in a different light – not as the enemy, not as something to be feared – for death truly is not the end but it is a release from limitation, a release from struggle, a release from unreality.

For you see, my beloved, as I have explained in my book and as Maitreya has explained in his, there is a core of your being that is beyond time, beyond space and therefore beyond life and death—as people see it in this realm. You may call it the Conscious You or anything else you like. But there is a reality of your being that allows you to be aware that you exist, that you are conscious. And this is the reality that can be set free from limitation, from the limitations of time and space.

And thus, how can that real self, how can that conscious self, be set free? Well, it can be set free only by overcoming unreality, by overcoming illusion. And so how can you overcome illusion? Well, my beloved, you can overcome illusion only through a total release from that illusion. And that release can happen only when the illusion itself – and the self that you have built from that illusion – is allowed to die.

Your attention endows your illusions with life

For you see, my beloved, the Conscious You is an extension of God's very own Being. And it is through the Conscious You – through the nexus of the Conscious You – that the light streams from the upper part of the figure-eight flow, from the figure eight of your own Higher Self to the lower part of your being, your sphere of self that is conscious in this world.

And so, whatever the Conscious You places its attention upon, it will endow with light—and thus it will endow it with life. You see, my beloved, everything in this world can be said to be a mirage—an illusion that has been temporarily endowed with life through the attention of the conscious beings who have co-created or created this world.

And so you see, my beloved, when you create – or come to believe – an illusion that you think is real and that you think is the real you, you endow that illusion with life through your attention and through the light that streams through it. This does not make the illusion real, it does not make it eternal, it does not give it eternal life. But it does give it a temporary life in time and space

The fear of death
And so, my beloved, how can the Conscious You be free of what it has created unless it is released from it? And in order to be released from it, it must allow the unreality that it has created to die. And yes, my beloved, what you are feeling – what you are dealing with in this day and age – is nothing less than a cosmic process. For you see, my beloved, ever since humanity started descending into the duality consciousness – started creating millions and billions of these illusions that envelop this planet – well, ever since then they have feared death.

What is it that fears death? Well, my beloved, it cannot be the real self. But the ego fears death, because it fears losing whatever life it has. And so you see, my beloved, humankind as a whole is enveloped in, is captured in, this illusion that death is to be feared. And therefore, they hold on to the form of life that is the highest form of life they can see right now. And they think that if that limitation – if that unreality – goes, they will have nothing left.

And so you see, my beloved, what the spiritual people in this age are up against is the planetary momentum of the fear of death. And whether you are in this teaching or that organization matters not, for all truly spiritual people around this planet are engaged in the same process of helping humankind rise above and see through the illusion that death means loss, that death is the end.

And that is why some of you will feel a certain fear and trepidation when you contemplate death, or when you contemplate the death of some illusion, some part of the mortal self. But my beloved, you are doing this not for your own sakes alone, but for the planet and for humanity as a whole.

The Living Word and love
So my beloved, why have we called you to a conference where we will talk about the restoration of the Word and Love? Because they go hand in hand as the Alpha and the Omega. As you will hear more about throughout this conference, the Living Word can indeed be shocking because it cuts through the illusion and makes it much more difficult for people to deny that they need to change. And at a certain level of the spiritual path, this can be difficult to bear. Because you are still somewhat identified with the outer self, with the ego, and thus you go into

this fear mode of fearing that if the ego is exposed, then you will suffer a loss and you will not know who you are.

So that is why you need the Omega balance of Love, of understanding what Love is – of tuning into it in your hearts – so that you can allow the process of the Living Word exposing the unreality without going into a state of shock or trauma or denial because you do not have enough Love. And so, only those who truly love can let go of the illusion. Only those who love unconditionally, as Jesus loved unconditionally on the cross, can give up the ghost and let that ghost die—even if it means that a part of what they thought was themselves dies in the process.

Why you will be justified or condemned by the WORD

Jesus, April 6, 2007.

Becoming one with the WORD

And what will it take to become one with the Living Word? Well, it will take what Mother Mary talked about yesterday, the willingness to see in yourself those elements that are not real, that are not in alignment with the WORD , that are based on a dualistic illusion. And then the willingness to see that these elements are not really you, even though your ego might believe that they are, even though you might have been brought up to think that they are. Because as you grow up in this world   where there is so much duality – how could you not come to identify yourself with certain dualistic illusions?

My beloved, this is natural. None of us condemn you for this. We all know what it is like to be in physical embodiment and how difficult it is. And my beloved, many of you have taken on these illusions voluntarily. And why have you taken them on? Because you wanted to demonstrate to others that it is possible to be totally enveloped in an illusion, yet still rise above it. So get on with rising above it and do what you came here for. Realize that you are more than these illusions. Be willing to look at them. Be willing to reach for the Living Word.

My beloved, we give you the Living Word in an outer sense, in our releases, in our books, through many different sources. And you can study these teachings, but the outer word will only change you if you allow it to become the Living Word in your heart, where you integrate it and where you receive, through your Christ self, the inner equivalent of the outer word. The inner equivalent that is adapted to your particular consciousness, your particular beliefs.

Each one of you hearing this will have a slightly different perspective, a slightly different understanding of the words that I speak. This is natural. And so what you need to allow is that the outer word that you hear stirs a process in your heart, whereby you receive the particular words that will help you resolve your particular illusions.

My beloved, there are many people who have a very similar illusion, such as for example in the Christian churches, where they think that by being a good Christian in an outer sense, their entry into Heaven will be guaranteed. But even though there may be a million people who believe in the same outer illusion, each person has a slightly different way of understanding it. And therefore, they have to find their own words that will help them resolve the illusion, help them see that it is an illusion and finally have that light bulb go off inside their heads and say, "Aah, now I understand, now I see it!"

My beloved, the Living Word, the outer Living Word, will help you only by stimulating that inner "Aha" experience, where you suddenly see from within what you could not see before, and what you cannot see with the outer mind. Truly, it is valuable to have an intellectual understanding of the spiritual path, and of human psychology and of the ego. But you can have a very sophisticated intellectual understanding, yet it still has not clicked, you still have not seen it.

Why people do not see the beam in their own eye

Or you can, as the scribes and Pharisees, have a very sophisticated intellectual understanding that allows you to judge when other people are not getting it, when they are not understanding, when they are not changing as they should be changing. So you are very good at seeing that splinter, that mote, in the eye of another, but it still has not clicked that you have the same thing. For my beloved, if you see something in the eye of another, there is only one reason why you can see it—because you have it in your own consciousness. Do you understand this, my beloved? Ponder this point.

If you meet a person who says, "The sky is green!" and you realize that he really believes the sky is green because he is looking through yellow glasses, then you know that – because he is seeing through a filter – that is why he sees the sky as being green. And so, the same thing for you if you see a particular flaw in another person. If you look honestly at yourself – and see that there is something that always annoys you with other people, something you always take note of with other people, perhaps something you criticize with others, or perhaps something you see as being wrong in the world – my beloved, why do you see this? Well, my beloved, it is because you are looking at the world through a particular filter. And you have the exact same characteristic in your own mind. And because you are looking through that characteristic, that filter, you are projecting it onto the world.

Now, my beloved, I am not saying that other people don't have faults. All people have faults. But what I am saying is that if you will be honest with yourself, you will realize that the reason why you see certain faults in others is that you see through the filter, because you have a lens in front of your vision and it colors what you see according to the characteristic of that lens. And that lens is not something that you have mechanically put in front of your eye, it is a belief that you have, that things should be a certain way, or they should not be a certain way.

And that belief is then what forms a filter, and you look at the world through that belief, and you evaluate everything based on that belief. And you have had that belief for so long, and you probably think it is either natural, or necessary or beneficial or maybe the only right way to look at the world. And therefore, you do not see the filter, you do not see that you have a filter, and so you focus on other people, what they do, what they say.

And my beloved, they might very well be doing something that is not right, something that needs to be changed. But you see, my beloved, YOUR entry into the kingdom of Heaven, your personal entry into the kingdom, will not be determined by what other people do or don't do. Their actions, their words, have an impact only on their entry into the kingdom. So what YOU should be concerned about, first of all, is your own entry. And that will depend exclusively on what you do, what you say. And that depends on the words that you have in your mind, what kind of filter you have—that you see the world through but you do not see the filter.

Look for your own filter
And so, my beloved, the key to entering the kingdom of Heaven is to step back and become aware of the filter through which you are looking at the world. For when you become aware of the filter, you can begin to examine it, and you can see that the filter is made up of certain beliefs. And when you examine those beliefs, you see that they are not completely in alignment with the reality of the Living Word.

When you are willing to see your filter, to discover it, and when you are willing to ask for the Living Word, you will get these "Aha" experiences, you will get these insights that come to you—sometimes at the strangest moments when you are in the middle of some activity, or even when you wake up in the middle of the night and suddenly understand something that you had never seen before. And suddenly, you will see that your beliefs that you had held for a long time – the beliefs that you thought were absolutely true and necessary – they are unreal, they are out of alignment with the reality of the WORD, the Living Word, because you now experience that WORD in your heart. And you know that your outer beliefs do not fit, they are not the right key, they will not unlock the door to the Christ consciousness because you are, as I said, judging on appearances rather than judging righteous judgment.

You see, my beloved, that is why I said that I came not to judge the world but that the world might be saved, because I came to reconnect everyone to the Living Word within them, which is what I called the Comforter—which I said I would have the Father send in my name, and he would bring all things to your attention that I have taught you. And the Comforter is the Living Word in your own heart, your Christ self, which will give you that inner Word that unlocks the understanding for you, the understanding that is beyond any outer words.

My beloved, it is a reality that I could be talking unceasingly for the next ten years and you could be sitting here listening to me for the entire time, yet you might be no closer to having that inner realization. You might have a very sophisticated intellectual understanding of my teachings, but until you see it in yourself, "Aah, I am the one who needs to change, I need to pull that beam from my own eye and then I will see clearly," until that happens you have not really started the path that I came to offer the world—the straight and narrow way that leads to eternal life.

The WORD wants to set everyone free

And so you see, my beloved, the key is to become one with that Living Word, so that you do not need to judge yourself or judge the world through the outer mind, through the dualistic filter. In fact, you do not go around judging anybody, but on the other hand you do not go into the other extreme of thinking that everything is just wonderful. You have the true Christ discernment of knowing what is real and what is unreal. And you simply have no judgment, no negativity, no criticism toward what is unreal. You just realize it is unreal and then you allow yourself to be the open door, whereby God might speak through you and allow you to bring forth some aspect of the Living Word that might unlock the understanding for another person.

But I tell you that there are many times when you will see other people and see something unreal but you will not feel an inner prompting to address it. And there can be many reasons for this, but when you get inner attunement, then you will know when to speak and when not to speak. You will not sit there – and this is a pattern that many of you notice in yourselves – you will not sit there and evaluate with the outer mind, "Oh I should say this, I should tell this person what he is doing wrong."

When you are in that mode of consciousness, when you are in that mode of judging based on the outer mind, the intellectual mind, then you will know you are not one with the WORD. Because the Living Word is not like that. The Living Word is not the hellfire and brimstone of the Christian preachers who are trying to scare people into submission. The Living Word does not seek to condemn or criticize anyone. The Living Word has only one desire and that is to set everyone free.

And so, human beings are so quick to judge, they are so quick to create a hierarchy, a false hierarchy, saying that this person is better than that person, and this person is really, really bad. My beloved, this is what I encountered in ancient Israel, where the Jews were so sure they were God's chosen people, that they looked down upon everyone else that lived in their society or around them – the publicans, the sinners, the

Samaritans, the Romans, the tax collectors, what have you – all of them were considered by the Jews to be subhuman.

And you see many people in today's world who have set up their own classifications, "Oh these persons are really, really bad, they don't deserve to live, they should be killed, or they should be imprisoned for the rest of their lives." But you see, my beloved, why do these people think this way? It is because they see the world, they see other people, through a filter

Why you judge yourself

And my beloved, if you look at the world through yellow glasses, what happens when you stand in front of a mirror? Well, my beloved, you will look at yourself, you will look at your mirror image, and you will look through yellow glasses. So by the same standard that you judge others, you will also judge yourself.

For you see, my beloved, when the Conscious You has entered into the prison created by the ego, it will see everything through the filter created by the ego—and therefore it will see itself through that filter. And that is precisely why, the words, the beliefs that you have in your mind, will justify or condemn you—because you are justifying or condemning yourself. Judge not that ye be not judged. For you are the one judging yourself. You are the one who looks upon yourself and says, subconsciously, "I am separated from God, I am a sinner, I am not worthy to enter the kingdom." Or perhaps you say, "I know better than God, I know better than the Living Christ, surely I will enter the kingdom." And surely, you are not open to the possibility that perhaps you will not.

And so you see, you are the one who keeps yourself outside the kingdom by the way you look at the world, because that is the way you look at yourself. And as Mother Mary has explained so beautifully in her book, the Conscious You is who it thinks it is in the realm of time and space. And if you think you are separated from God, then you ARE separated from God—in your own mind. And thus, you can never enter the kingdom of God, and that is when you become susceptible to the illusion, the master illusion of the ego, which wants to maintain its own existence and therefore does not want you to find the straight and narrow path of self transcendence, of inner transformation.

So as an alternative, it has to create the false path, the outer path that makes it seem like you can enter the kingdom of God by doing all these outer things. And then, at some future time when certain outer conditions are fulfilled, you will automatically enter. But you see, my beloved, that future time will never come. For when can you enter the kingdom of God? Can you enter yesterday? Can you enter tomorrow? No. You can enter only in the Eternal NOW.

And when you contemplate the words of this Invocation of the Eternal NOW, when you really let them sink into your consciousness, you see how profound they are and how they too, how this rosary in its entirety, is designed to give you precisely these "Aha" experiences of seeing what stands in your way—what keeps you out of alignment with the Eternal NOW, with the Living Word, what keeps you outside that state of consciousness that is the kingdom of Heaven.

The WORD is beyond manipulation by the ego

So my beloved, ponder these words. Ponder what I have said here, and what I will say again in different ways. The Living Word is what gives you the opportunity to see beyond the filter of duality to realign yourself with the reality of God, the reality of the universal Christ mind, which is the only reality there is, the only reality that is beyond manipulation by the ego.

For you see my beloved, the Living Word can never be manipulated by the ego. There are many people in the world, who think they have the Living Word, but they have imposed an overlay, because they are looking at it through a filter. They have not yet become one with it, but when you become one with the Word, because you are open and you say to yourself, "Listen, I have been on the spiritual path long enough, tiptoeing around my ego, now I want to see it, I want to see what I can't see, I want to overcome it, I want to see that beam in my own eye because I have had enough of being hindered by this, I have had enough of carrying this cross. I am ready to give up that ghost and let it go, as I saw Jesus do when he was hanging on the cross and finally let it go."

This is your potential for this conference. You may be able to do this on Easter Sunday, but even if you do not, Easter Sunday is not just one day. For the kingdom of God is at hand, meaning it is always there. So do not panic if you do not have a breakthrough at a certain time, but contemplate these things, contemplate your willingness to let go of these illusions and realize that before you can let them go, you must see them. And the only way to see them is to connect to the Living Word, which allows you to see the reality of the dead word, the dualistic word, that might contain an element of truth but is twisted just so slightly that it brings you off the straight and narrow path. And now you do not have the right key to open the door to the inner kingdom.

My beloved, I thank you for your attention. For I must tell you that it is a great joy for me to be able to bring out this teaching—that I could not bring out 2,000 years ago for humankind was not ready. The outer knowledge was not there nor was the inner willingness to come up higher in consciousness. Oh how I wish I could have brought out these teachings 2,000 years ago and that people could have understood them and have used them, for these 2,000 years, to grow. But you see my beloved, cycles are cycles and when you become one with the WORD you become a practical realist, for you realize that people can only come up so many steps at a time before they start losing their bearings, losing their moorings, losing their sense of continuity, their sense of identity.

Are you serving a dead god or the Living God?

Nada, April 6, 2007.

Pursuing your original Love
And so, my beloved, how can you connect to that Allness? Well, my beloved, you must pursue Love. You must seek to understand Love. You must seek to reconnect to the original Love in your being. For I tell you, it does not matter where you are today, for you started out as a pure being in the immaculate concept. You descended into the world of form because you – the greater you that you truly are – had a true desire to serve all life, to raise up the sphere into which you originally descended, whether it be this sphere or another one. You came here out of a true desire.

You might have fallen into a different state of consciousness and have forgotten that love and that desire to serve all life. But you can reconnect to it because it is still at the core of your being. And if you will to grow beyond a certain point, then you MUST reconnect to it, for there is no other way.

You see, my beloved, the lie of the fallen beings – from Lucifer and all of the other ones who have pride – is that they actually believe that they can raise themselves up to such a point where they will become equal with God, or more important than God. But this, my beloved, can never be done as long as you are trapped in the illusion of separation. You can grow to become a God in your own right, as Maitreya explains, but you can do so only when you realize that God is the All that is in all—and you seek to serve the All, to raise up the All. You become one with God's desire to raise up this sphere until it becomes, indeed, the kingdom of God in manifestation, and all is Light and there is no longer room for any shadows or lies or illusions.

Once you connect to that oneness of the All, then you can become equal with God. But you see, my beloved, you become equal with God by becoming one with God. You can never be equal by being separate from God—for there is no such thing, for God is the All. And so, my beloved, since God is the ultimate reality, how could you become equal with the ultimate reality as long as you think you are separate from ultimate reality? There is only one ultimate reality, so you see, the logic of those beings who have fallen into the duality consciousness is fundamentally flawed. They cannot see this, your ego cannot see this, your intellect cannot see this. But – aah – the heart can see this.

When the heart is purified and opened, the heart can know the oneness of all life. And that truly is the first part of the spiritual path—to come to know in the heart the oneness of all life. And then to carry out that oneness in all your actions and words, so that you serve the One in the All. This, my beloved, is how I won my ascension so many thousands of years ago—by serving others, by serving those who were closest to me in that last incarnation, by serving without thought of self. For truly, when you come to sense the oneness, you realize, "It is not about me," me meaning the separate self. It is about the real me, meaning the All.

Thus, my beloved, I am grateful for your providing the platform that allowed me to release this teaching, which is more than the words I have spoken but truly a complete release of the vibration and the thoughtforms of the sixth ray of service—selfless, unconditional service.

Why you are not forgiven for rejecting the INNER WORD

Jesus, April 6, 2007.

Wherefore I say unto you, all manner of sin and blasphemy shall be forgiven unto men: but the blasphemy against the Holy Ghost shall not be forgiven unto men. And whosoever speaketh a word against the Son of man, it shall be forgiven him: but whosoever speaketh against the Holy Ghost, it shall not be forgiven him, neither in this world, neither in the world to come. (Mt 12:31-32)

So, my beloved, I, Jesus, am indeed also on the sixth ray of service. So I wanted to put in my two cents worth, as they say. For you see, my beloved, what is true service to life? It is when you serve ALL life. And what does it mean to serve all life? Well, there is only one way to serve all life, and that is to flow with the Holy Spirit, which is precisely that force of God, that aspect of God, that is designed to accelerate all life so that all life becomes MORE.

And so you see, my beloved, even though my words were ominous, given 2,000 years ago, they were designed that way because of the consciousness at the time. Where people were still so stuck in precisely what Nada identified as the false desire to serve the remote God, thinking it was the angry, judgmental being in the sky that they were serving through their religious activity. And so, my beloved, here you have the scribes and the Pharisees strutting around like peacocks – feeling that they were holier than everybody else in Israel – serving God. Yet, in reality they were serving the false God. And that is precisely why I said that unless your righteousness exceeds the righteousness of the scribes and Pharisees, ye shall in no wise enter the kingdom (Matthew 5:20).

And why is this so? It is so because the scribes and Pharisees were trapped in the duality consciousness, and they saw themselves as separated from God. Because when you see God as the remote God, you obviously see God as being outside yourself and you as being outside of God. And so how can you possibly enter the kingdom of God, which is where?... [audience answers: "Within you."] Within you. We will eventually get you to understand this, so that if I woke you up at four o'clock in the morning and said, "Where is the kingdom of God?" you would say "Within me." [Laughter]

The illusion of serving the remote God

My beloved, joking aside, this is the most serious matter you could possibly have to contemplate. For you see, ninety percent or more of the religious people on this planet are trapped in the illusion that what they are doing is serving God. But they are serving the remote God, they are trying to please the remote God, they are thinking that if they do outer things, in an outer religious activity, then the outer God will let them into the outer kingdom. And it is truly the broad way that leads to destruction — it simply cannot be done.

So my beloved, when you are trapped in that duality consciousness, you are trapped in the ego's belief that if it does all the outer things right, then God will have to let it into the kingdom. This is such an integral illusion that the ego will never be able to see it as a fallacy. This is precisely why we have given you the teaching that there is a part of you, the Conscious You that is more than the ego and that can separate itself from the ego.

For you see, my beloved, as long as you identify with the ego, you will not be willing to come up higher, to become MORE. Because you want to cling to the illusion that as long as you stay in this outer church – and do these activities that you have decided will get you to heaven – then God will have to accept you. And the ego will not let go of this illusion, because it knows that if you were to see through this illusion, then you would no longer need the ego and the ego would die. So the ego believes that it is a matter of life and death to make you cling to this illusion. And as long as you identify with the ego, you too think it is a matter of life and death or a matter of salvation or damnation — the difference between going to heaven or going to hell.

And so you see, my beloved, I am not saying that the scribes and the Pharisees were evil people. I did not call them evil; I called them hypocrites because they thought they were serving God, and they were not willing to recognize the reality that they were not serving God — or rather they were not serving the Living God who is in all.

This is the reality that I came to demonstrate to them through words and deeds and even by my Presence. They would have none of it, for they were not willing to let go of their egos. They were not willing to let that mortal self die on the cross, so they could be reborn. That is why Nicodemus could not understand me when I said that unless a man be born of water and of spirit, he cannot enter the kingdom (John 3:3).

Why you are forgiven for rejecting the outer Word

My beloved, when you are stuck in this illusion of the remote God, you will reject the Living Word. You will find ways to counteract the Living Word. What the scribes and Pharisees did was only the most primitive version of this rejection, and there are far more subtle ones that I will talk about in the coming discourses. Yet what they did was to reject the person who had come to bring them the Living Word because that person – myself – had become one with the Living Word, which is the only way to truly bring the Living Word—although you can for a time be in a state where you are the open door for the Living Word but have not fully become one with it.

And so, when I came to them representing the Living Word, they rejected the Word. And you see, my beloved, that is why I said that those who speak blasphemy against the Son of man, it shall be forgiven them. Because you see, my beloved, even though I represented the Living Word, the scribes and the Pharisees inevitably saw me as being outside themselves. So I represented the Living Word that was the external Word—and so do I now when I speak through this messenger, whom you identify as being different or separate from yourself.

This is the nature of the physical octave, of being in a body, because you know that the body is separate from other bodies. You know that there is a part of your mind that is separate from other minds. So you see, you have this duality that is inherent in the physical octave at this point—which is not quite the same duality as what I normally call the duality consciousness of the ego.

For truly, your senses are not evil, they are simply doing what they were designed to do, which is to detect the vibrations that make up the physical universe. And in the physical universe, the vibrations are separate and have created separate, distinct forms. But what really happens is that the ego takes this sensory perception of separateness and builds onto it, and then builds the duality consciousness which says that you are separate because you are nothing more than the body, and the senses, and the outer mind or even more than the soul which is also separate from other souls. Do you see that this is subtle and difficult to grasp?

But, my beloved, even though you are in a physical body, even though you see the world through the physical senses, you – meaning the Conscious You – have the ability to know that you are more than the body, more than the senses, and that there is more to know about the universe than what you can see through the senses. And this is indeed what you all know because that is why you are spiritual people. Otherwise, you would not be on the path, unless you knew from within that there is more than the outer world and the senses.

For what you need to do is realize how the ego has used the senses to build this illusion of separation. And then you can separate yourself from the identification with the separateness. This is what the scribes and Pharisees were not willing to do. This is what even my own disciples were not all able or willing to do. For you see, my beloved, when the Living Christ appears upon Earth, he does not come to say, "Here I am, I am the Christ, I am the only Son of God, I am so much better than any other human being on this planet."

No, the Living Christ comes to say, "Look, I have discovered God within myself, and so can you discover the God within yourself. And when you discover the God in you, you will know that it is the same God that I have discovered in me. And therefore, you will know that you and I are one at a deeper level that goes beyond the separateness of our physical bodies and even our separate minds."

So you see, my beloved, this is a deeper oneness that the Living Christ comes to exemplify to people, to awaken them to that oneness. And so what did they do with my teachings and my example? They said, "We will have none of it, we want to cling to our ego's illusion of the external God and the external path to salvation." And so they killed the Living Christ. They killed the Son of man when he stood before them in the flesh.

Why you are NOT forgiven for rejecting the INNER Word

And as I said, those who speak a word against the Son of man – including killing him, killing his body – it shall be forgiven them. But then, my beloved, what happened after my death on the cross, my resurrection? What did I say I would do? I said I shall pray the Father that he shall send you another Comforter (John 14:16). And that Comforter is the Holy Spirit. And that Holy Spirit is an aspect of the Living Christ, but it is an aspect of the Living Christ that does not come to you from without—it comes to you from within.

So you see, my beloved, as I talked about earlier, there comes that point where you need to see something from inside yourself instead of hearing it from the outside. And it is precisely the function of the Holy Ghost, the Holy Spirit, to give you that "Aha" experience, that inner realization, that helps you see the dualistic illusion and snap out of it instantly, when you see it as an illusion.

And so, my beloved, here is the subtlety expressed in my quote. If you speak a word against the Son of man – who is clearly external to you, at least in a physical sense – then you are forgiven that, because this is an outer action. But the sin against the Holy Ghost, the speaking a word against the Holy Ghost, is when you deny the Living Christ that comes to you inside yourself, when you refuse to listen to that inner Christ, the Holy Spirit, when you refuse to change your consciousness.

And why is it that that sin – that speaking the word against the Holy Ghost – shall not be forgiven? Well, it is because the rejection of the Holy Spirit within you happens at a deeper level of your consciousness than your outer actions. You see, my beloved, it is quite possible to have a difference, a separation, between your outer actions and your inner thoughts.

And you all know this from your daily experience, that sometimes you are not able to do what you really knew was the right thing. And this is because there is a gulf between your outer actions and your inner consciousness. And so it is possible that somebody can be so trapped in an outer consciousness that they can actually condemn and persecute the Living Christ, the Son of man, while actually in their inner being having a pure heart.

And this is what you saw exemplified in Paul, who persecuted the Christians until he had an encounter with the Living Christ so intense that it shattered his illusions and shook him out of the illusion that caused him to reject me in the form of Jesus and reject my disciples.

But you see, my beloved, Paul went through that experience on the road to Damascus because he was willing to listen to the Holy Spirit that came to him from within (Acts 22:6). For contrary to what many people think, I did not appear to him as the external Christ standing beside him. I appeared within as the internal Christ, as the Holy Spirit. And though he had rejected the external Christ, he did not reject the internal Christ, and therefore he was converted and he was healed. And therefore he became one of my foremost apostles.

You see, my beloved, it was the inner man of Paul that was ready to represent the Christ, even though at some point the outer man was not ready. And that is why he sinned against the Son of man, he spoke a word against the Son of man. But when it came down to the critical moment, he did not speak a word against the Holy Spirit, he did not reject the Spirit, he accepted the Spirit, converted, changed his life dramatically and followed that Spirit for the rest of his embodiment.

So, my beloved, at the deeper level of your being, you can reject the Spirit—and what is the deeper level of your being? Well, my beloved, is it not the heart? For as I said earlier, the heart is the center of your being. What you speak with your mouth it is simply what is in your heart that overflows. So you see, the deeper part of your being is the very core of your sense of identity. And until you let go of a false sense of identity, you will continue to reject the Holy Ghost. And as long as you reject the Holy Ghost, you cannot overcome your illusions, you cannot come up higher, you cannot overcome separation.

And that is why – as long as you reject the Holy Spirit within yourself – you will remain outside the kingdom of God. For you cannot enter the kingdom of God within you except you accept the one Spirit, the Holy Spirit, and become one with it. Do you see, my beloved, the subtlety here that could not be explained 2,000 years ago—and that even today cannot be understood with the reasoning mind, even though the collective reasoning mind is much more sophisticated today than it was back then.

The master key to overcoming sin

And so, there is another quote in the Bible which says that the sin against the Holy Ghost shall not be forgiven. But the reality is, that it shall not be forgiven until it is forsaken. And you see, my beloved, when you forsake the sin, the rejection of the Holy Ghost, then you immediately become one with the Holy Spirit. And then your sin is forgiven because you are no more the same person that sinned. You have become MORE. And you see, this is the reality that we have been trying to tell you in many round-about ways.

You are who you think you are—until you think you are MORE. And when you realize and accept that you are MORE, the old self – the limited self – has died. And you have been reborn of the Spirit—when you accept the Spirit, which comes to you to set you free from that limited sense of identity. And so you see, those who speak against the Holy Spirit, those who speak against the WORD, do so because they are not willing to change their consciousness. And it is their consciousness, as I explained earlier, that keeps them outside the kingdom.

And so, what does it mean that the sin against the Holy Spirit shall not be forgiven? Well, my beloved, the traditional image of the Christian churches – of the remote being in the sky – makes it seem like it is God or Christ or the Holy Spirit who has to forgive your sin. But it is not so. It is YOU who have to forgive your sin by forsaking it, by changing your state of consciousness.

And the moment you change that state of consciousness, you are free of the old consciousness. And it was the old consciousness that was the real sin, not the outer actions—not even the outer actions of persecuting the Living Christ or killing him or his followers. All these things can be forgiven the moment you are willing to change yourself, to change your perspective, to let go of the false spirits – the multitude of spirits, the legion of spirits of duality – that pull you hither and yon into identification with the things of this world. The moment you are willing to let them go and come into oneness with the One Spirit, well then you are free of the former self. You are no more that being.

My beloved, there is a saying that no fallen angel has ever been redeemed. And it is true. Because as long as you see yourself as a fallen angel, you cannot redeem yourself, you cannot enter the kingdom of God. So therefore, you must let the identity of a fallen being – or a sinner – you must let it die, so that you – the Conscious You – is reborn into a new identity. Do you see the reality here?

Reconnecting to the love that brought you to this world

Mother Mary, April 7, 2007.

My beloved hearts, you have earned my Presence with you, for you have given this rosary [The participants had given the Rosary for Loving Yourself before the dictation] with such love that I desire to share with you the Presence of the Divine Mother, the Presence of the nurturing love that truly all of you have need of. For you have – for a long time – embodied in a world that is not only devoid of love but is filled with anti-love.

And so it is impossible to be in this world without being wounded, without being hurt, by those who are so trapped in anti-love that they actually feel threatened by anyone who expresses love. And so, when they are exposed to those who express love, they feel they have to somehow silence them, beat them down, stop the flow of love through them, so that they can overcome the sense of panic that literally makes them believe they will die if they receive true love.

Recognize that Earth is a planet with much anti-love

And so, my beloved, the view I would give you is a view that has been expressed in my own book and in Maitreya's book. But I would express it in a slightly clearer way. You should look upon this planet not the way you were brought up to look at it—whatever that might be. You should look upon it as a world that is designed specifically to give certain beings an opportunity to live in a world where they can deny God's presence for as long as they like—or almost as long as they like.

And so, you who are the spiritual people should realize that you have come here as a sacrifice. You came here because you desired to descend into this world, where so many beings had become trapped in anti-love and you wanted to bring the sunlight of love, to give them an opportunity to experience that there is something beyond anti-love. And so, when you look at this, you can realize that you volunteered to come into a situation that you knew would be very difficult. You knew that your love would be rejected, you knew that you would be hurt and bruised.

And, my beloved, I am not saying this to justify the hurt, to justify the abuse. I am saying it because when you accept the reality of this planet, you can overcome the very dysfunctional and non-productive attitude of feeling that you should not have been treated this way, that something is wrong, perhaps even feeling, as has been mentioned before, that "God should not have allowed this to happen to me."

And you see, my beloved, when you go into that frame of mind – of feeling that some injustice has been done to you on Earth, possibly even that God has been unjust toward you – then you inevitably become a victim of the consciousness of anti-love that you came here to eradicate. And then you cut off the flow of God's love through your being. And now you feel that God has abandoned you, for you no longer experience that love. But, my beloved, it is not that God has abandoned you. It is, as is said in this wonderful rosary, that when you do not feel God's love flowing through you, you do not feel God's love for you.

For love is not a static force, it cannot be captured, it cannot be controlled, it cannot be put in a mental box. It can be experienced only when you allow it to flow. And so when you allow yourself to become trapped in the consciousness of anti-love, then you shut off the flow and now you no longer experience unconditional love. So then what is left?

Well, only conditional love is left—the worldly form of love, that even those who are trapped in anti-love need. For surely there is not one being who can live without love. But the problem is that so many beings cannot receive the true unconditional love, and so they are on an impossible quest, a never-ending quest, to fill the desire for love. But they are seeking to fill it with conditional love, thinking that the love they receive should live up to certain conditions and that they should seek to possess the love or the persons through whom that love is being expressed.

You came here to bring love

You see, my beloved, this becomes a Catch 22. And so, as Saint Germain so eloquently put it last night, we who are your spiritual teachers face the dilemma of how to awaken you without shattering your self-esteem, or even your sense of identity. And truly, the only way to escape the duality consciousness is by reconnecting to the love that is still there in the core of your being.

For my beloved, I realize you are in this world and you look at life and the universe from inside the mental box of this world. But I tell you that you did not come here, you did not decide to descend here, with the limited perspective you have now. And so even though you may have been bruised and hurt and have shut off the flow of God's love and feel abandoned by God, I can assure you that you came here out of love.

I realize that there are some of you who have come here from higher realms and who feel that you have been unjustly sent here by God. But nevertheless, you did not start in that higher realm. You started in an even higher realm. There was a point where your lifestream decided to first descend into the world of form, into the latest sphere in the world of form. And that decision was based on love, the desire to express your true God quality, your true divine individuality, and bring that gift to the world, to light up a world.

And so, it is possible for you to go beyond the outer facade and reconnect to the core of that love in your being. And when you do so, you will realize that you love something more than what you are experiencing right now. And I tell you, my beloved, it is only when you recognize that you have a love for something more than what you have right now that you can overcome your current limitations. For you can overcome your current limitations only in one way, namely, as we have explained many times, by letting the old sense of identity die. And in order to be willing to let the old die, you must have a love for something more. Which then makes you realize that letting the old die does not mean a loss, for you will be reborn into a higher state of identity.

You see, my beloved, when you have the negative awakening that Saint Germain talked about – where you realize that you are a terrible person and you need to change, you are a miserable sinner – then your sense of self-esteem is shattered and you feel like in order to overcome the bad aspects of yourself, you have to destroy your sense of self. Because you think there is no sense of self beyond the ego.

You cannot overcome selfishness by destroying the self
So my beloved, there are indeed people in this world, both in traditional religions and even in new spiritual movements, who believe that the way to spiritual growth is to destroy all sense of self, all sense of a

separate self. But you see, my beloved, this is coming from a negative. This is coming from wanting to eliminate a negative by creating another negative or by destroying the first negative which is another negative action. And so as two wrongs do not make a right, you cannot correct an imperfection by acting out another imperfection.

So there is no way to destroy something, for deep within you, you have a basic survival instinct that is even beyond the survival instinct of the body and the survival instinct of the ego. Because your true divine individuality wants to survive and wants to grow and wants to express itself in this world—it wants to fulfill its original reason for being, its reason for coming here. And so, if you try to destroy all sense of self, you end up working against yourself, seeking to destroy not only the false sense of self of the ego but also the true sense of self of your divine individuality.

And this simply cannot be done. You may actually be able to destroy much of your sense of self but you will eventually come to a point, where the inner conflict becomes so intense, so illogical, so contradictory that you simply cannot stand it anymore. And so this is not the way. The way to salvation is not through self-denial or self-destruction. It is through self-transcendence.

You are not seeking to destroy the old self. You are simply seeking to transcend it and be reborn into a new self, a higher self, that replaces the old. Yet, the trick, my beloved, is – as Jesus demonstrated on the cross – you cannot be reborn into the new until you allow the old to die.

And so, here is where the scary part comes in. For there will be a cosmic interval between the death of the old and the resurrection of the Conscious You into a higher sense of identity. And so, when you let the old die, you will literally feel like you are plunging yourself into a vacuum.

I say you will feel like it, because in reality you will not. Your conscious self will not lose consciousness. It will remain conscious. But as you are at the moment of having to give up the old self, you will feel like there will be nothing after that old self. And that is what Jesus experienced on the cross when he cried out, "My God, my God, why hast thou forsaken me?"

What was it that pulled Jesus beyond that state of fear and paralysis, that state of panic? Well, it was that he had integrated into his being the higher love that brought him into this world. He had uncovered that love, and so he knew in his conscious mind why he originally came here. And therefore, he did not feel like a victim of life. He did not feel that God had unjustly sent him into this world. For even though he had his trials and tribulations, deep within him he knew that he had volunteered to come here and he knew what could happen to him.

So because he had the conscious awareness of the deeper, innermost love of his being, he realized that he simply needed to give up the ghost of the last vestiges of the separate self. And in his love for God he was willing to do that. And so what I am saying to you is that the essential key to everything is to reconnect to the deeper love of your being, the innermost love of your being, that originally caused you to volunteer to descend into the denser sphere to bring your light and your love. And so this is a topic you might meditate upon as you go from here.

Reconnect to your original love

This is something you can take with you, the idea of seeking to reconnect to the original love of your being. And, my beloved, my entire book [Master Keys to the Abundant Life] is designed to help you reconnect to that inner love. And I assure you that that book was designed to help a broad range of people, even those who for a very long time have been trapped in the consciousness of anti-love. And so no matter how far you might have descended into anti-love, if you will keep reading and re-reading and studying and absorbing my book while you give the rosaries, then you will eventually break through.

For I assure you that I am a capable spiritual teacher. And I am capable of taking a child by the hand, even if it is an unruly child, and bringing that child to my heart—even if the child comes kicking and screaming. For my beloved, I have dealt with my share of unruly children, one of which bore the name of Jesus, who was by no means an easy child, as he well knows. [Laughter] And as we have often sat together and chuckled about some of his naughtiness, some of his stubbornness, some of his extreme sense that he was right. [Laughter]

So you see, my beloved, when you are in a human body, you have certain human imperfections. But so what? They are all unreal, they can all be transcended, they can all be left behind. There is not one of you who cannot transcend your imperfections. But you can only transcend them by letting them go. And you can only let them go when you know that there is going to be something to take their place, something that is more than the imperfection.

And you can only know that through love. Because when you reconnect to the original love, you also reconnect to the source of that love. And therefore, you know that you came from that source. And therefore, you know that you are infinitely more than your present sense of identity.

My beloved, think back to the meditation of yesterday of seeing the images of distant galaxies and the vastness of this physical universe, and see how it gives you a different perspective. And you realize how small the Earth is compared to the vastness of the physical universe. Well, when you reconnect to your original love, you take that broader perspective to an even higher level. You magnify it a billion, billion times. For God's love is infinitely greater than the vastness of the material universe, and so you have an entirely different perspective.

And it is through that perspective that you can see how ridiculously insignificant are these things that you have held on to on this planet, and that other people hold on to. And that is when you can let them go. And that is when you can reconnect to your original purpose, so that when the angel of God appears to you within your heart – in the form of your Christ Self – to remind you that it is time to start some aspect of your own divine plan then – instead of rejecting it, instead of explaining it away, instead of finding some clever reasoning why you cannot possibly do this now—perhaps in 10,000 lifetimes but not today – then instead of this reaction you can simply come to that point of surrender and say, "Oh Lord, be it unto me according to thy will."

For you realize that the Lord is not the remote being in the sky who is seeking to force his will upon you. The Lord truly is your own higher being. And you are only being reminded of the higher choices you made when you had the broader perspective that has been lost as you entered the denseness of this world.

Passing through the screen door to heaven

Jesus, April 7, 2007.

Then the Pharisees and scribes asked him, Why walk not thy disciples according to the tradition of the elders, but eat bread with unwashen hands? He answered and said unto them, Well hath Esaias prophesied of you hypocrites, as it is written, This people honoureth me with their lips, but their heart is far from me. Howbeit in vain do they worship me, teaching for doctrines the commandments of men. For laying aside the commandment of God, ye hold the tradition of men, as the washing of pots and cups: and many other such like things ye do.

And he said unto them, Full well ye reject the commandment of God, that ye may keep your own tradition. For Moses said, Honour thy father and thy mother; and, Whoso curseth father or mother, let him die the death: But ye say, If a man shall say to his father or mother, It is Corban, that is to say, a gift, by whatsoever thou mightest be profited by me; he shall be free. And ye suffer him no more to do ought for his father or his mother; Making the word of God of none effect through your tradition, which ye have delivered: and many such like things do ye.

And when he had called all the people unto him, he said unto them, Hearken unto me every one of you, and understand: There is nothing from without a man, that entering into him can defile him: but the things which come out of him, those are they that defile the man. If any man have ears to hear, let him hear.

And when he was entered into the house from the people, his disciples asked him concerning the parable. And he saith unto them, Are ye so without understanding also? Do ye not perceive, that whatsoever thing from without entereth into the man, it cannot defile him; Because it entereth not into his heart, but into the belly, and goeth out into the draught, purging all meats? And he said, That which cometh out of the man, that defileth the man. For from within, out of the heart of men, proceed evil thoughts, adulteries, fornications, murders, Thefts, covetousness, wickedness, deceit, lasciviousness, an evil eye, blasphemy, pride, foolishness: All these evil things come from within, and defile the man. (Mr 7:5-23)

By now you are beginning to see the pattern of how the scribes and Pharisees were always objecting to the Living Word, brought forth by me as the Living Christ. This, my beloved, is a pattern that by no means is limited to the scribes and Pharisees, for you see it in every religion, in every civilization, in every spiritual tradition, in every worldly tradition.

And my beloved, what is the essence of this pattern? Well, it is precisely that the ego is trying to build up the outer appearance that it is acceptable in the eyes of God because it is living up to all these outer conditions. And so, my beloved, when people are blinded by the ego, they identify with the ego, they are attached to the outer tradition they have created—the outer tradition that says they are saved because of the outer things they do.

Many are ready to go beyond the outer path

You see, my beloved, I am not bringing this up to necessarily find fault with those who are attached to outer tradition. For, as a realistic spiritual teacher, I know that there are people on this planet who are still very much like children and who need to still be in an outer organization, an outer church, where they can believe that by belonging to that church and following a few simple rules, they will be saved. There are literally people, a certain portion of the population on Earth, who have that legitimate need. And as a spiritual teacher I do not expect them to rise out of that need in one lifetime.

Yet, I can also tell you that there is a large group of people on this planet – in this day and age – who are ready to leave that entire mindset behind—but who have not yet done so, partly because they have never been taught. But why have they never been taught? Because they have not so far been open to the teaching. And that is why the eternal spiritual law cannot take effect for them. For is not the law very clear? When the student is ready, the teacher appears. Or should I say, my beloved, when the student is willing, the teacher appears? For until the student is willing to hear the Living Word of the teacher, what is the point of the teacher appearing?

Well, there is indeed a point, and that is why I came to Earth. And the point is that the teacher can awaken people from their sleep and shake them out of their comfortability. And you see, my beloved, there comes that point, as I talked about yesterday, where there is a gap between the outer person, the outer personality, the outer mind, and the inner being of the person. And so you have a large percentage of people on this planet who at inner levels are ready to step up to truly understand what the spiritual path is about, but their outer minds are not ready. For their outer minds are still too controlled by their egos. And the people do not understand the ego, and thus do not understand the need to separate themselves from it.

And so, what is a teacher to do? Is he going to sit around passively and wait until the people wake up by themselves? Or is he going to say, "But at inner levels they are ready, so I will go down in a form they can see, in a form they cannot ignore, in a form they cannot deny, and I will do my best to awaken them to the inner reality for which they are ready." And so, my beloved, this is the true motivation behind all true spiritual teachers who have ever come to this planet—to awaken those who are ready, so that they can snap out of the outer mind and truly be awakened to the inner reality of who they are.

Is there any absolute truth?

And so, my beloved, I desire you to understand more of the nature of the Living Word. And truly I will speak more about this. But I want to leave you with one thought to contemplate and that is: There is a dream in religious tradition of finding some absolute, some infallible scripture or teaching that is absolutely true at all times and for all conditions. And so many people look for that absolute truth and think there has to be such a thing as absolute truth.

But what I desire you to contemplate is my words spoken 2,000 years ago, "God is a Spirit, and they that worship him must worship him in Spirit and in Truth" (John 4:24). Take note that I did not tell people to worship God through the scriptures. And so how can it be that so many people in the Christian world think that they can only know God and contemplate God through the scriptures—and that any idea about God must conform to scripture or it is false?

You see, my beloved, the Living Word is what allows you to rise above duality, but only when you internalize it and make it come alive in your heart. So as I speak these words into the physical octave – where you can hear these words – if you only listen to my words with the intellect, then these words are not the Living Word. They are the dead word in your mind, even though I speak them from the spiritual realm, and I, as the Living Christ, truly am expressing the Living Word in the material universe. The Living Word does not come alive in you unless you allow it to come alive, allow it to transform you, allow it to show you something that you have not so far seen and that your ego is not willing to see and does not want you to see.

So you see, my beloved, there is no way to express an absolute truth in the physical universe. Because anything that is expressed becomes subject to interpretation. And so, people impose their filters upon it and, depending on their willingness to see through their own filter, they can kill the Living Word in an instant, in the instant it enters their being.

You have heard the saying that what someone says to you goes in one ear and out the other. Well, I can tell you that there are many people who listen to the Living Word, and the Living Word goes in one ear but then the dead word comes out the other ear. And so it has no effect on them, for these people have made the Word of God of no effect in their tradition, in the tradition that is between their ears, namely in the brain and the analytical mind. For they are not listening to the Word with their heart but only with their mind. And that is indeed why I could say that these people honoureth God with their mouth but their heart is far from him (Matthew 15:8).

Going beyond a dualistic view of God's Will

El Morya, April 8, 2007.

True freedom of choice

And so, how can people escape duality? Well, they can do so only by reaching for something outside their current mental box. And indeed, in the beginning it is necessary for people to have some kind of hard-and-fast rule which says essentially, "If you do this, you will go to hell. If you do that, you will go to heaven." For this allows people an absolute guideline that their own egos cannot manipulate. And if they will follow that guideline, even as many people do in a traditional Christian churches – where they are very black-and-white in terms of following outer rules – well then they can at least gradually grow out of the total domination of the ego, the total inability to determine what is right and wrong in a higher sense, for everything seems gray to them. Or everything seems dualistic.

Yet as we have explained, there comes that point where you have to step up and not simply follow the outer rules, but go within and get your direction from within instead of blindly following an outer rule, or an outer doctrine, or an outer leader. And this is indeed when you have to attain the deeper understanding of the Will of God that I am talking about. And that understanding could not be given in previous dispensations, which is why many of the students of those dispensations still hold on to the black-and-white view of the Will of God—as something they have to follow without questioning, almost as if they were robots following a leader.

And yet, my beloved, when you come to the realization that there is more to it than the black-and-white and gray thinking, you suddenly realize that you cannot take the Will of God and draw it down and create some rule that applies to all situations. This is the ego again, with its incessant dream of an automatic salvation where it says, "Give me a rule that I do not eat with unwashen hands, so that I can believe that as long as I follow that outer rule I am guaranteed to go to heaven."

A Buddhic perspective on how America can represent Christ in the world

Gautama Buddha, April 8, 2007.

I Gautama come to greet you. And surely, some in the West will wonder what the Buddha is doing interfering with their celebration of the resurrection of Christ. Yet my beloved, in heaven there is only oneness. So how could there ever be any separation between Christ and Buddha? And so, I do indeed come to give you the Buddhic perspective on being the Christ in action.

For you see, my beloved, there is a difference in degree – not a difference in kind – between the missions of Christ and Buddha. They are in a sense like the Alpha and the Omega. The mission of the Living Christ in embodiment, the Word incarnate, is to go out and actively seek out people who are trapped in some mental box or other, or as we call it in Buddhism, who are trapped behind the veil of Maya, the veil of illusion created by Mara, the demons of this world, the prince of this world.

The role of the Living Christ is to go out and challenge these people's illusions, in order to awaken them to the reality that there is something beyond the illusion, there is a different way to live. And so, the Christ must be outgoing, must be active, must be challenging. And therefore, the Christ also incurs the wrath of those who will not be challenged, who will not change, who will not look in the mirror and pull that beam from their own eye.

And once people have been awakened and have followed the path of Christhood for a time, they will then be open to the path of the Buddha, which is the path of non-attachment. And so, where the two paths converge and become parallel tracks is for those students who are more mature and can see beyond the outer religions of Christianity and Buddhism. And can see that Christ and Buddha came to Earth teaching the same universal teaching, the same universal path, only teaching it in different cultural contexts and with slightly different words.

When students become unbalanced
Yet there is still nuances that must be known by the advanced students. And here is the one that I would discourse on today. For you see my beloved, it is indeed possible that a person can become awakened to the path of Christhood and gain some grasp on that path, start the path, start the form of service of realizing that there are many things in this world that need to be changed, there are many illusions that need to be challenged. And the person might indeed start challenging these illusions but then there is always the risk that the person can be trapped in a blind alley by becoming imbalanced.

You see my beloved, there are many spiritual and religious people who have been awakened to the need to do something, to bring about better times, a higher form of society, a more spiritual society, or even a golden age. They have gone through an awakening or a conversion experience, have become all on-fire for working for God – however they see it – or working for the ascended masters. And they have thrown themselves at it with great enthusiasm, with great eagerness.

And in one sense, we of the Ascended Host love to see people in this phase, for they are certainly far more alive and far more entertaining to watch than the people who still sit there in front of their television sets, thinking the goal of life is to eat popcorn [Laughter] and flip through the channels until their brains are so pacified that they can hardly think an individual thought, being so overpowered by the mass consciousness that comes through the television set that they are like the dead, the spiritually dead.

Yet my beloved, as gratified as we are in seeing people becoming awakened, I must tell you that we very often see these same people going into the blind alley of taking an unbalanced approach to what they see as their work for God, perhaps even what they see as their divine plans. We have seen this in all religions and we have seen it in previous organizations sponsored by the ascended masters – that a certain percentage of students will become almost over-anxious in creating world change. And they are so "fired up," as they say, about this that they lose all perspective and all balance.

And what is the cause of this, my beloved? Well, it is that they do not have the Buddhic perspective on what it means to be the Christ in action. For you see, my beloved, as the Living Christ in action, you cannot be completely non-attached to the point of saying that nothing really matters. You cannot buy into the gray thinking that everything will turn out okay in the end because somehow Jesus or a UFO will come and save this planet.

And thus, as the Living Christ in action, you expose yourself to people's ridicule and condemnation. You often go up against their egos, and you do so because you truly care. You care enough that you are willing to let them reject you and persecute you, even as Jesus cared enough to let them nail him to a cross so that they received an opportunity to see their own duality outpictured.

And so as the Living Christ you do have a caring. And this is why you go out and you are willing to disturb people. Yet maintaining that caring is a very delicate balance. For it is very easy to become overanxious, to step over the line and become attached to a particular result of your actions, to become attached to getting a particular reaction from other people.

And this, my beloved, is a very fine line. It is the line between remaining on the straight and narrow way of Christ or stepping on to the broad way of anti-Christ. For you see, even though you are caring about other people, wanting to awaken them, you must never forget that God has given them free will. And so you must simply give them the example, the knowledge, the insight, the wisdom, the Living Word, that gives them a free choice to abandon the duality consciousness. But you must not become attached to a particular result.

The outer expression of such attachments is those who play the game of numbers. How many members does their church have? How many members in their religion? Look at how many Christians pride themselves on the fact that Christianity is the biggest religion in the world. But then when it comes right down to it, Christianity is so diversified that you can hardly call it a coherent religion.

Yet my larger point here is this: those who play the numbers game, those who are comparing their religion to others – having a need to feel that their religion is better – obviously demonstrate that they are attached. They may still serve out of a – to some degree – pure motive, but there is an attachment that perverts that motive and even opens them up to the serpentine lie that the end can justify the means.

You are not here to change the world

So my beloved, how can you walk the tightrope of being the Living Christ in action without going too far into any of the dualistic extremes? Well, you see my beloved, you must first of all keep one truth in mind: As the Living Christ, you are not here to produce a specific outer change on Earth!

You are not here to raise up America to recognize the ascended masters. You are not here to produce world peace. You are not here to expose the power elite and their manipulation of the economy. You are not here to overthrow the international banking system. You are not here to overturn Roe vs. Wade.

Take note that I am not saying that some of these things are not worthy goals that need to be obtained, that need to happen. But you are not here to make it happen. For my beloved, what is to happen on this Earth must happen through the free will of the people. And thus, you see my beloved, how the American form of government – how the Constitution, the Declaration of Independence – how they incorporate the concept of "we the people."

What you can do as the Living Christ is to awaken the people, so that they can make the best possible choices. But the Living Christ is not a dictator who comes in and takes power, and takes power away from the other dictator who is identified as the real bad guy, as the real villain in the play.

For you see, my beloved, when you fall into the trap of thinking that you are here to produce a specific result – when you are here to overthrow the rule of this or that other group of people or these or that dark forces – what have you then done? Well, you have done what Jesus described when he described the world as a stage and life as a play with separate roles.

Do you see, my beloved, there are many roles defined in this world based on the consciousness of duality. And there is a role created by the serpentine mind to specifically trap those who have been awakened to the path of Christhood but who have not yet attained balance. And so, they go into that role of thinking that as representatives of Christ, they have to fight and destroy the representatives of anti-Christ, and produce a specific result by overthrowing this or that action taken by those they identify as the representatives of anti-Christ.

Do you see, my beloved, how subtle this trap can be? How easy it is for a person who has become awakened to the spiritual path – who is all on fire to serve God, to serve the cause of Christ – to step into that role without noticing what has happened. And then people can go off on a tangent, sometimes for decades, thinking they are working for God, they are working for the Ascended Masters, yet in reality they are simply outplaying another dualistic role that does virtually nothing to further the true cause of the Ascended Host, which is to raise the people above the consciousness of duality.

Do you see, my beloved, what I am saying? We are not primarily concerned with creating world peace, getting America out of Iraq, overturning Roe vs. Wade, overthrowing the monetary elite. Our primary concern is to awaken the people from the blindness caused by the duality consciousness, because when the people are awakened from duality, they will make the right choices. And thus, once duality has been conquered, all other things will fall into place. Do you see? As the Christ said, "Seek ye first the kingdom of God and his righteousness, and all these things shall be added unto you."

Non-attachment to specific results

We have seen over millennia how those who have followed a true religion, a true spiritual teaching – be it all the way from the teachings of Abraham, the teachings of Moses, my teachings as the Buddha and Jesus' teachings, to the Ascended Masters' teachings released over the past century – well, we have seen how people have started following these teachings, but in their over-anxiousness they have become attached to producing outer results. And so, they have gone into the blind alley of seeking first certain things in this world instead of reaching up for the real goal of truly embodying the teaching that they are following—to the point where they become the teaching, they become one with the teaching, they become one with the teacher.

And if you first seek that goal of oneness and the right use of your creative faculties – which means the balanced use of your creative faculties – then the outer results may or may not be added unto you. For again, it is God's will that people have free will and that they are allowed to outplay that free will on Earth. Certainly, we of the Ascended Host want to see certain outer results. Ultimately, we want to see the kingdom of God and the Golden Age of Saint Germain physically manifest on

Earth. But do you see, my beloved, that it cannot come about by going about it the wrong way. For as Jesus put it, "With men this is impossible, but not with God, for with God all things are possible."

So what is the second thing you must ponder in order to find the balance? Well, it is precisely what I taught as the Buddha, namely non-attachment. Non-attachment is not the same as non-caring, as indifference. For truly, when I had attained Buddhahood, I was not non-attached to the point of being indifferent. Which is indeed why I did not simply stay in Nirvana and experience that state of bliss that we have talked about earlier.

I volunteered to come back to Earth and teach, thereby exposing myself to the forces on Earth. Not that these forces could touch me, but nevertheless I still had to walk in the world of duality and deal with students who came to me in various stages of the duality consciousness. And although there is very little record of this, I can assure you that some of the students that came to me personally were very much trapped in the duality consciousness and did much the same to me that some of Jesus' disciples did to him—as he has talked about exemplified in Peter who wanted to impose his mental box upon the Living Christ, forcing the Living Christ to conform to that mental box. So there were students who wanted to force the Living Buddha to fit into their mental boxes rather than allowing the Buddha to take them beyond those boxes.

So my beloved, non-attachment is the key to Buddhahood. And non-attachment is the key to Christhood. And that non-attachment comes from understanding what I have explained. The true goal of the Ascended Host for this Earth is the goal of raising up the consciousness of the people beyond duality, so they can fully reach up and discover the Living Word within themselves, thereby spontaneously making right decisions. Because they have what some of my later followers have called the "beginner's mind" and what Jesus described when he said, that unless you become as a little child, you shall in nowise enter the kingdom.

Why the beginner's mind is key

And why is that? Because you have that pure mind – that non-attached mind, that non-biased mind – that does not seek to force the world to fit into your mental box, that does not seek to force God and the Living Word to fit into your mental box. But you are willing to flow with the Living Word, to be the open door and allow the Living Word to express itself through you, whereby you are in the River of Live, flowing with that river. And thereby, the light of that river can flow through you and awaken others.

For my beloved, you do not seriously believe that Jesus and I awaken people through intellectual arguments, do you? You do not seriously believe that we were so sophisticated that we could override the intellects of those who challenged us. Surely, you see in the Bible that Jesus confounded the intellects of the scribes and Pharisees, but nevertheless as soon as he was gone, they went right back to their scriptures and found some quote in that scripture that made it possible for them to justify overriding or ignoring what he had said, thereby rejecting him as the Living Christ.

Find bliss beyond your expectations

Ascended Master Patrick, May 18, 2007

The test of overcoming all expectations
You see, my Beloved, there is a teaching I would give you that relates to what I started talking about, of my feeling somewhat depressed over the lack of response. And I must tell you that this came from my own conditions, from my own expectations, where my spiritual vision of going to Ireland had been used in subtle ways by my ego to create the expectation of certain outer results, of seeing a physical manifestation of many people converted. Even a subtle sense that I could see the results from my labor, not that I had a desire to be elevated, but I had a desire to see that my labor had borne fruit, that I had made a difference.

And so this, my Beloved, is something that all Saints and spiritual people have struggled with and must struggle with. For the spiritual path, as we have said, is not an outer path, so in a sense why would you expect outer results? Yet I realize full well – for I have gone through it myself – that there is a point on the path where you need to see some result of your action in order to keep going. And therefore, at the lower levels of the path, you do need to see that you are making a difference, by seeing outer differences, outer results.

But I tell you, as you walk the path – especially when you come closer to Christhood – that there will come an essential initiation, where you will need to let go of all your expectations, all of your conditions of wanting to see a certain outer result. For if you do not, you cannot manifest your Christhood.

For the Christ is completely non-attached to what response he gets from the people on Earth, for his is not here to awaken them. He is here to let his light so shine before men that they have the opportunity to see that there is an alternative to the serpentine, human state of consciousness. But the Christ knows that he is not here to chose for them, but to give them the opportunity to choose, which they did not have when they had only seen people who talked religion based on the serpentine mind.

And so my Beloved, if you think back to your own experience of walking that mountain yesterday, you will see that you might have a certain vision, a certain expectation, of what might happen at the top. Certain things you would like to see, certainly a little ray of sunshine and a lot less rain, or perhaps other expectations. But I must tell you that those who are the true overcomers on the spiritual path – those who win their ascension, those who fulfill their divine plans – are those who are willing to take a look at such expectations and say, "I am not here to fulfill these outer expectations and conditions. For I am only here to let my light shine."

You see, my Beloved, when you have expectations, especially when you have expectations of how other people should respond to you speaking the Word, well then you set yourself up in a dualistic situation, where your inner fulfillment and peace depends on something outside yourself, depends on other people who have free will. And it is predictable, is it not, that there will be some people to whom you preach the Living Word, who will use their free will to refuse to rise above the serpentine consciousness. And thus, they will refuse to go along with you and, my beloved, when they reject the opportunity to come up higher, what must they do? Well, their egos must justify this rejection, and how do they do this? By criticizing you, by putting you down, by putting your teaching down, by finding slick serpentine ways to cast doubt on the validity on your teaching, the purity of your motive or any other thing they can think of.

So you need to recognize, my Beloved, as you have talked about today, that some of you realize that you are reluctant to stand up and let your light shine. And surely, we who have ascended all understand this, because we have gone through it. But I tell you, we went through it precisely because we came to the point where we recognized that we were not here to please or even awaken other people. We were here to let our light shine. And that was our job. That was our job number one, as they say. And it was the only job.

So you see, when you make that shift – and it is a fundamental shift in consciousness – your inner fulfillment does not depend on anything outside yourself. And it is only then that the prince of this world will have nothing in you, whereby he can discourage or scare you into not sharing your light at all. Or whereby he can play on your pride and get you to feel that surely you must be pleasing to God because you have preached to all these people and done this or that to promote this or that teaching.

Do you see my Beloved, there is always the two dualistic polarities of fear and pride, the inferiority/superiority complex. For one cannot exist without the other, but YOU can exist without both of them—when the Conscious Self recognizes that it is more than this dualistic personality and identity. And thus, you are willing to let it die, as Mother Mary said. You realize that surrendering this dualistic personality is not a loss but a gain.

And my Beloved, this is what happened to me that day, when I sat at that creek. I finally saw the folly of my attachment to outer results. For my Beloved, why did I start my mission in Ireland? Because I had a divine vision, an inner spiritual vision. And so what was the folly of thinking that I could only continue following that vision if I have certain outer manifestations. No, I needed to be true to the inner vision, to be non-attached to the outer. And when I had that non-attachment, I can assure you that I had further visions, and I felt a much greater inner fulfillment than I could ever have felt, even if the entire country of Ireland and been converted by me personally.

Find the true bliss beyond dualistic expectations
Do you see my Beloved, as Jesus talked about at the last retreat, there are these dualistic roles in the play that you can play. But as long as you go into a dualistic role, surely you can experience joy, but it is the joy

that is in a polarity with sorrow. But beyond it is the bliss of God. And that is what you can experience when you let go of those expectations.

So my Beloved, if you truly want to be the saints of the Aquarian Age, the forerunners of the Aquarian Age, look at your expectations, look at your attachments, be willing to let go of them and say, "I am not following the spiritual path, I am not promoting a spiritual teaching, I am not speaking the Word in order to see a particular outer result. I am simply speaking the Word because it gives me the unconditional Joy of God to feel that Word flowing through me. What else could I possibly need than that? Why do I need some human beings pampering my ego, telling me I am special, I am doing a wonderful job, when I know from within that I am being who I was created to be, and I feel the infinite joy of the flow of the River of Life through me."

You see, my Beloved, when you are in the darkness, a little flashlight can seem like a great comfort. But when the sun is high in the sky, do you sit there staring at the flashlight, or do you look up at the sun? For truly, my Beloved, there are many people on Earth who do follow the lesser light of the moon, even when the sun has risen. But those who are the saints, those who are the overcomers, those who have ascended, are those who look for the sun within themselves, who see that Sun of the I AM Presence, and who follow it, never again looking back to the moon. You might have needed the moon at some point, but when you connect to who you really are, you no longer need it, and you can let it drop away from you and never again have expectations or desires that human beings should treat you a certain way.

What does it matter to you, my Beloved? Why would those who have the Spirit of God ever need approval of those who are in the serpentine consciousness? Be they among the people, be they in Church leadership, be they in the governments, be they in the media, be they among the rich or the powerful and the high and the mighty, why do you need it? Why do you think Christ stood in the hills and preached to the common people? Why do you think that I did the same most of the time? It was indeed because we realized that that is where you find those who are open-minded, those who are the meek who shall inherit the Earth.

And my Beloved, when you look back at history, look at those who are the high and the powerful. Look at the empires they have built of various kinds. Well my Beloved, have they not all crumbled? And so can you not look at the empires that you have today and say, "They too will crumble, for the ever-moving flow of the River of Life will wear them away, will smoothen them out, for the high shall be made low by the passage of time."

And so, the meek shall inherit the Earth, the meek being those who are willing to go beyond the dualistic games of playing either Lord or follower, Master or slave. But indeed, being the independent ones who say, "I do not need to control other people, nor do I need someone to control me and tell me what to do. For I am willing to take responsibility for my own path, and make my own choices."

This is the difference between those who have overcome and those who are still in the dualistic state, where they suffer and have joy and suffer and have joy, and suffer and have joy in an endless cycle—that will not end until you make the decision that "Enough is enough!" and you will no longer play the game.

Unconditional acceptance leads to unconditional surrender of all conditions

Mother Mary, May 18, 2007.

My beloved hearts, there truly is no greater joy for your spiritual mother than to experience her children sharing their heart flames in an environment where everyone is accepted for their uniqueness. For my beloved, if there was one message that I would want to get across to all humankind, it is precisely this: In heaven everyone is unconditionally accepted for who they are. For in heaven we see only the uniqueness of your individuality in God, the individuality for which you were created, and the individuality that you yourself have co-created in oneness with the Christ flame in your heart.

My beloved, this unconditional acceptance, could literally solve all of the world's problems and remove all of the world's conflicts—if, of course, it could be accepted unconditionally by the people of the world.

And here precisely is the problem. For so many people in the world have been conditioned to think that there must always be conditions.

Your conditions keep you outside the kingdom of God

Do you see, my beloved, it is precisely the conditions that prevent you from experiencing the kingdom that is within you. For you think that you are separated from that inner kingdom. And what is separating you, my beloved? Well, you might very well think that it is some outer condition such as your sins, your karma or your psychology. But these outer conditions are nothing but symbols, symbols for the fact that in your own mind, in your own being, you have come to accept conditions. And so you have come to believe in the lie, the serpentine lie, that in order to come back to God you have to fulfill certain conditions.

But my beloved, what was it that separated you from God in the first place? It was conditions! You began to believe that you needed to fulfill certain conditions in this world in order to be worthy to enter the kingdom of God, which you had now come to see as being outside of, separate from, yourself.

So my beloved, there is a mountain in Ireland that primarily is climbed by Catholics who do this as a penance because they have come to accept the basic belief that in order to be saved they have to fulfill certain conditions in this world. And the more painful those conditions are, the more they think they are paying back their sins. But my beloved, why did Jesus say that unless you become as little children ye shall in no wise enter the kingdom? Do little children have conditions? No! They love unconditionally. And they accept love unconditionally. They do not have the adult sophistication of the mind and the intellect to even come up with these conditions. But they learn quickly by observing their adults around them, from their parents, to their teachers, to their ministers in church, where they quickly learn that in order to receive love or whatever else they need, they need to live up to certain conditions.

And so, that makes them susceptible to believing in a religion that says that if you put yourself through pain by walking up a very steep mountain with lose rocks, perhaps even doing it barefoot, then somehow through that pain of yours, the God in heaven is satisfied and will now forgive you your sins and let you into his kingdom. And yet, my beloved, the reality is that God will let you into his kingdom any time you let go of the conditions that you think keep you outside that kingdom.

And so you see, that the more pain they put themselves through, the more distance they create in their minds between themselves and the kingdom of God. For they will not truly contemplate and accept the momentous statement made by Jesus that the kingdom of God is within you. Did he not say, "The kingdom of God comes not with observation?" And is walking barefoot up a mountain not observing some outer rule, some outer concept, of what it takes to enter the kingdom of God?

God accepts you for who you are

You see, my beloved, your Creator, your God, accepts you right now unconditionally for who you are. And there are two meanings to this statement. For my beloved, it should be obvious, given the knowledge that you have—and, certainly, I realize that most of the world do not have these teachings or do not accept them, but you who accept these teachings can understand that you were created out of a greater spiritual being who came out of an even greater spiritual being and that chain of being reaches all the way back to the Creator. Perhaps you do not fully internalize and accept this teaching. But you can understand it – at least intellectually – and therefore you can understand that when you were created out of the Creator's own Being, surely God the Creator accepts himself. And certainly God the Creator accepts that part of its own Being that is imparted to you. And so you should be able to understand and accept that God can have unconditional acceptance for that part of your Being that truly is an individualization of the Creator.

Yet my beloved, I desire to give you an even deeper teaching, which I know will require you to stretch the mind and the heart and to watch your emotions and see the inner reaction. And so I ask you, as I am speaking these words, to watch your reaction, your thoughts, your feelings—the conditions that come up in you. For my beloved, I must tell you that many of you might look at yourselves today and say, "I can understand that God accepts my God Flame, my I AM Presence, my divine individuality, but surely I have fallen into a lower state of consciousness. I have created an ego. I have accepted conditions. I may have psychological issues. I may have done certain things in my life. And surely how could God accept this? So how could God accept the outer personality, the outer sense of identity that I have created in this world?"

But you see, my beloved, the reality is that God accepts you for who you are right this moment. And God's acceptance of you is unconditional. Watch your reactions. Watch how your ego will struggle with this statement and come up with reasons for why this cannot be so. "For if God accepts me for who I am right now, then why do I have to go through this arduous path of penance and forgiveness of sin and being saved by some external savior?"

And my beloved, the truth is, the path that you have to go through is the path that you have created through the conditions that you have accepted. And so depending on what kind and how many conditions you have accepted, there is a path for each one of you to follow. But here my beloved, is the essential key that so few people have understood. The path that you have to follow to qualify for your freedom is NOT fulfilling the outer conditions that you have come to accept. The path is to let go of those conditions!!! To come to see that they are unreal, that they are illusions, that they are dualistic illusions created by the serpentine mind, by the fallen state of consciousness, by the consciousness of separation and duality.

So you see, my beloved, many of you have already realized this because you have experienced this in your own lives, that you had to go through a period of searching or depression or outer difficulties, only to come to a point where you surrendered, you let go, where you said, "I don't need this belief anymore. I don't need this vicarious atonement. I don't need to feel like a sinner."

And do you see, my beloved, the essential difference between thinking that in order to be saved you have to fulfill an outer condition, and so you strive all of your lives to be a good Catholic or a good Muslim or a good Hindu or a good New Age person or whatever you think is the outer path. And yet the alternative is to realize that the real path, the inner path, is to let go of the conditions that are inside of you instead of trying to fulfill outer conditions, that only take your attention away from the kingdom of God that is within you, making you think that you have to enter some external kingdom, that you need an external savior or an external church or to fulfill some external conditions.

Do whatever it takes to let go of your conditions

So you see my beloved, sometimes it is indeed necessary for you to ascend a physical mountain, to realize that you did not need to ascend the mountain because you can find it all inside yourself. Yet there is nothing wrong with ascending the mountain in order to come to that realization.

Yet there is nothing wrong with going halfway or not going at all. You see, whatever you have to do on the outer to be able to surrender the outer, it is fully acceptable.

But I wish to impart to you – and that I could inspire you to impart to the world – that the essence of the spiritual path, the essence of salvation, is precisely to overcome the inner condition that makes you think you have to fulfill an outer condition. And when you realize that – when you fully realize it – then you can let go of the outer conditions. You can be reborn of the Spirit.

For my beloved, did not Jesus say to Nicodemus (John 3:5), that in order to enter the kingdom a man must be born of water and he must be born of Spirit. Well my beloved, following an outer path is the process of being born of water. But when you come to the point of realizing what I have just explained – that it is not the outer conditions, but it is letting go of the inner conditions – well then you can experience the total surrender – the unconditional surrender – that brings about the rebirth of the Spirit, whereby you can suddenly accept who you are. And my beloved, when you accept who you are right now, then you can let go of what is unreal instead of holding on to it.

For my beloved, do you understand the very subtle psychological mechanism that comes into play here? When you accept the serpentine lie that in order to enter God's kingdom you have to be acceptable to God – and what determines whether you are acceptable to God is whether you fulfill certain outer conditions defined in this world by some institution or teacher or even by your own ego – you see my beloved, when you believe that in order to be saved, you have to fulfill these outer conditions, well the psychological mechanism that comes into play is that you cannot fully accept that you have these conditions [that you do not fulfill those conditions]. You cannot, as Jesus has said, take ownership of them.

And when you cannot take ownership of them, you cannot surrender them. For you cannot look at them squarely and say, "But this is unreal. And I no longer need to carry this with me. I no longer need to accept this condition or to accept the belief that caused me to accept whatever illusion I have carried around for a long time."

So when you think the path is about fulfilling outer conditions it becomes impossible for you to look at your own imperfections, to look at your human condition and say, "This is unreal, this has to go." Instead, you do what so many people in the world do. They ignore the beam in their own eye. And either they focus all attention on the splinter in the eye of another or they focus on the outer path, saying that if only I give so many Hail Marys, and light so many candles, or walk up a mountain barefoot, and put myself through this or that pain, then God will have to accept me even though I have not let go of the conditions that keep me – in my own mind – outside the inner kingdom.

So you see, my beloved, when you come to that realization – that God accepts you for who you are right now – then you can say, "Well if God can accept me even though I might look at myself as being an imperfect human being, well then certainly I can accept myself." And the reason why you should be able to accept yourself is precisely this, my beloved, that God has given you free will. And what that means is that God has given you the right to enter this world and to create a certain world view based on whatever conditions you have chosen to accept. And God has set up the universe as a mirror, to mirror that view back to you, so that you can create for yourself any experience you desire.

You must choose to let go of your conditions

Do you see, my beloved, that God gave you free will. God has given you the right to create the experience that you are having right now — because you have free will. And God accepts that you have a right to create your present experience. But my beloved, when you realize what the path is all about, you realize that you can let go of the experience you have right now at any moment. When you realize that: number one, that it is unreal; and number two: I have had enough of that experience. I don't want it anymore. I don't need it anymore.

And you see, my beloved, when you come to that realization, your path will take on a new meaning. Your life will change, as some of you have expressed here because you suddenly realize that all of the outer conditions are unreal and they cannot keep you outside the kingdom unless you allow them to do so by continuing to accept them.

And this, my beloved, is precisely what the world wants you to do. The world wants you to continue to accept these conditions that you have come to believe and that the world still believes: your family, your friends, your society, the world at large, your priests. They want you to accept the conditions that they accept. For if you do not, you disturb them in their belief that they could not change themselves, that they don't have to take responsibility for their own lives and their own salvation for they can just wait for Jesus to appear in the sky or wait for some miraculous apparition by Mother Mary or wait for Saint Patrick to come back in some chariot of fire to lift up the people.

Do you see, my beloved, that this is why there has always been idolatry of the saints and the sages who have stood out from the crowd? For by elevating us, it gives people's egos an excuse for saying, "They were special so I cannot do what they did." But my beloved, if you will honestly look at my life as Mother Mary, what was so spectacular that I did in that lifetime? My beloved, I gave birth to a child. But have not many women done so? Surely, he was at times a difficult child, but certainly other children have been a challenge to their parents. Some of you would probably admit that you challenged your parents in many ways. And some of you feel that your children have been a great challenge. So why was I so different?

So you see, my beloved, if there was one thing that I would want the world to learn from my lifetime as Mary, it was that what was special about me was my willingness to surrender—to surrender everything. To flow with the inner prompting that came from my higher Being. Ah, you say, but did I not have an angel appear to me and tell me what to do? And yes, but how do you know how that apparition took place? For I can assure you that it was not the version that Hollywood has come up with in their ever-accelerating quest to do better than the latest movie and to have more special effects or more violence.

You see, my beloved, this is again the idolatry of the world that wants to create these conditions. For you see, my beloved, your ego is born of conditions. Your ego seriously and truly believes that it could not survive without conditions. Which is true because the moment you let go of your conditions, your ego will have no hold over you. Neither your ego nor the prince of the world will have anything in you. So your ego does not want you to surrender because the more conditions you have, the more your ego has control over you and the more comfortable your ego feels.

So there are many people in the world who have become so identified with their egos that they are so comfortable in having created this very neat little box for themselves, where they feel they have everything under control and their lives are so ritualized, and every morning they get up and they do the exact same thing. And they go to work and they come home and they watch the same shows on TV and everything is ritualized and regimented. And yet if they were thrown into a new situation, an unexpected situation, they would disintegrate. They would not be able to handle it.

And so my beloved, you see in your own lives that you have been willing to come away from your comfortability, even to come to a retreat like this, or find the spiritual path in whatever form, and allow it to change your life. And my beloved, the only true difference between those of us who have ascended and those who have not ascended is that we were willing to surrender – gradually – all of our conditions. We were willing to die daily (1Co 15:31), as Paul said, to have some of our conditions die every day. And we kept doing this over and over and over again until there suddenly was nothing more to surrender because we truly had been willing to lose our lives for the sake of following Christ.

The essence of the spiritual path is surrender

And you see, my beloved, certainly it was a big surrender for me to break off my very comfortable and regimented monastic lifestyle to suddenly go back into the world and have a child. It was again, a big adjustment to realize that we had to take that child out of Israel and flee to Egypt. There were many other adjustments as Jesus grew up and as he gained a clearer vision of his mission, and I gained a clearer vision.

Joseph's death was a big adjustment for me, left with many children. When Jesus left home at an early age to go on his spiritual pilgrimage—when he came back. Certainly my beloved, when I stood in front of the cross watching him struggle and finally watching him give up the ghost of him giving up the last of his conditions, which inspired me to give up the conditions I had about how my son's life and mission should unfold

For as Jesus has explained, he had certain illusions until the very end on the cross. And I too had certain illusions about how his spiritual mission should unfold. I even had certain illusions that I held on to after that, until the end of my embodiment when I finally let go of them all.

And so, I simply tell you this: you have already surrendered much to be where you are right now, whether you are at this conference or elsewhere. You have surrendered much, my beloved. So is it so difficult to accept that the path is about one thing—surrender, letting go of conditions? For my beloved, once you accept this, it becomes so much easier to surrender the conditions. For you realize that the more you surrender, the more free you feel inside. And so you build a momentum, and once you get beyond a certain point, you realize that surrender is not loss, surrender is not sacrifice, surrender is not the Via Dolorosa. Surrender is joy. Surrender is freedom. And the more you let go of, the more free you are.

And so, my beloved, this is my gift to you this morning, the gift of surrender. Should you need help surrendering or gaining a clear vision of what to surrender – seeing the illusion so you can let it go – then apply to my heart. Give a rosary if you feel you need to. Or simply ask me and then listen for my answer. Listen both within and without. For I will find a way to give you the answer you seek. If you cannot hear me in your heart, I will send you a book or a person who will tell you.

Let us rise above the fighting over land!

Saint Germain, May 20, 2007

How can people claim ownership of land?
What is your land? Well, is it a physical manifestation, is it a physical place around which you can draw a border, or is it more than that? For my beloved, what I desire you to look at this night is the very fact that one of the major causes of war on this continent – and indeed throughout the world – has indeed been the fact that so many people have allowed themselves to feel ownership of a piece of land. And in order to protect that land – or to expand it by moving a line on a map a few kilometers this way or that – they have been willing to kill untold numbers of their fellow men.

My beloved, what folly is this that human beings develop ownership of a piece of land and call it theirs? My beloved, does not the entire planet belong to the Earth Mother? For is not the entire planet an outpicturing in form of the Earth Mother herself? And so who can draw a line on a map and say, "This is now our land. We own it, and if someone wants to move here, we will kill them before they kill us."

So my beloved, why does this sense of ownership develop? Well, there are two reasons, as there are two reasons for everything. One is the personal reason of the ego of each person that needs the sense of security and being in control. And so when you feel that you own a piece of land that is yours, personally yours, and you can draw a border around that land, then you begin to think that no one can take it away from you, and so the ego feels secure and in control. And on a larger scale a group of people will develop a national identity, draw a border around a piece of land, and then again, their collective ego will feel a sense of security and control.

But my beloved, there is the greater issue behind the human level. Namely, as Jesus talked about when he talked about conspiracies, that in the higher realms – the mental, emotional and etheric – there are fallen beings who are plotting to control this world, and control the people thereon. And my beloved, how do they control the people on Earth?

Well, they do it primarily through the divide-and-conquer method, the divide and conquer philosophy, the divide and conquer strategy. You see, my beloved, in Heaven we are all one because we know individually that we are one with the Creator—and thus we know that everything came out of the Creator and therefore we are one with each other.

Truly, the people on Earth are meant to manifest the Body of God on Earth, to see themselves as part of the one body of God. And when they do so, well there will be no room for darkness and duality on this planet. For how can there be warfare when all people see themselves as one? Who can be foolish enough to see their right arm as an enemy, and cut off that right arm when they truly realize the arm is part of their body and without it the body will suffer, potentially die.

And so, you can only kill another human being when you do not see yourself as part of the Body of God and therefore cannot see other people as part of that same body. And so, in their strategy to prevent the emergence of the consciousness of Oneness on this planet, the fallen Beings have plotted to divide humankind.

And certainly, there are many ways they can do this, but I would bring to your attention that one of the primary ways is precisely to divide them up in groups that live on a particular, well-defined piece of land with borders around it. And then make them believe that they have some kind of obligation to defend that land, or to expand it by killing other people when necessary.

…

For my beloved, have you not come together here from many different nations? Did any of you come marching in here wearing your national colors, separating your chairs from those from other nations with whom you have had a difficult relationship, perhaps because they always beat you in a soccer game or some other rather silly human competition? [Laughter]

No, my beloved, you walked in here forgetting about any national identity, instead embracing and reaching for a higher identity, namely that of Sons and Daughters of God who are spiritual beings who are so beyond the human divisions. And as you have discussed earlier, my beloved, you have indeed come together in oneness. And thus I must tell you that you have set a pattern, you have started a new momentum — a new seed has started sprouting in the collective consciousness of Europe.

And as this is maintained, and hopefully reinforced in the future through other conferences, you can indeed see how the flower can begin to unfold. And suddenly, there is another type of awakening in Europe — that if we are more than sinners, if we are more than highly evolved animals, if we truly are spiritual beings, well then we can no longer define ourselves first and foremost by our national identities. We must now define ourselves as spiritual beings who are part of the Body of God.

And thus, the national identity suddenly takes on lesser importance, and comes in its rightful place as being of lower authority than the spiritual identity. And this is what can then start a new current in the collective consciousness, where suddenly the rigidity around national identity and specific borders begins to soften and fade. Until, my beloved, people begin to question, "Why should we continue these old patterns of having a fixed opinion about other people, just because they live in a particular nation that we have traditionally seen through a specific filter, which we now realize is dualistic in nature and is but an illusion?"

The key to understanding among nations
And so my beloved, this is indeed one of the greatest problems that causes conflicts among nations. It is the human ego's tendency to generalize, to look at the members of another nation, not as individual human beings but as a sort of non-humans that all fit into the same label. Which

is then what makes people reason that all citizens of the neighboring country are bad or evil people who are out to get them, and therefore we must defend ourselves by killing them all.

And once you enter into that state of consciousness, how can there be understanding or even communication among different nations? For you will not be able to communicate or attain understanding with other people unless you see them as unique individuals instead of judging them all based on some illusory national identity that you have created in your own mind—and that might be completely out of touch with the reality of who these people are.

And so my beloved, I look to the spiritual people to realize that you are, of course, all unique individuals. Which means that there are unique individuals in every nation. And thus it makes no sense to say that all Englishmen are like this, or all Frenchmen are like that, or all Germans are like that. For truly, within a nation of millions of people, there are people of every type of individuality. They are all individuals—they are good people, they are not so good people, they are selfish people, they are altruistic people.

They are found everywhere, for my beloved, when you realize you are more than the physical body – more than an animal, more than a sinner – you realize that you do not belong on this Earth. You did not come forth out of the Earth, whether it be out of the dust of the Earth, whether it be out of the animal evolutionary chain. No, my beloved, you came from the spiritual realm, so you are truly beyond all these outer human divisions. And therefore, you see yourself without seeing yourself through the filter of human divisions, and thus you can see other people without seeing them through that filter.

And when this begins to happen in greater measure – as it has already started to happen in Europe – well then a momentum will be built and a shift will begin to occur. And that is then when people will begin to realize that those of the neighboring country are people much like themselves. They are different in some ways but they are not different in fundamental ways. Because at the deeper level of your being, well your neighbors are Sons and Daughters of God as you are. Surely, they have their ego-based state of consciousness, but when you are willing to recognize that your nation also has an ego-based state of consciousness, then you see that you cannot allow yourself to fall prey to the illusion that your ego is not as bad as the ego of the next nation—and therefore it is justified that you assert your ego by killing the others.

Hypocrisy at the national level
Do you see, my beloved, it is like two little boys sitting in the sandbox and they start arguing. And in order to trump his case, one boy says to the other, "My dad is stronger than your dad!" and the other says, "No my dad is stronger than your dad!" And they keep arguing like this, and I must tell you that many of the arguments among human beings are really born of a situation where one person says, "My ego is better than your ego!" and the other says, "No, my ego is justified. Your ego is bad but my ego is Okay!"

And that is what happens even on the national level, where a people are so blinded by their ego-based national state of consciousness that one nation believes it is perfectly justified in taking the stand that this other nation is bad and therefore they should go out and kill them or conquer them and suppress them or control them. For by suppressing them through force and violence, they would actually be doing God's work and they would be improving the planet.

The key to the ultimate victory is ultimate surrender

Elohim Victoria, May 20, 2007

Dare to leave the dualistic struggle behind
For you see, my beloved, it is not a matter of fighting some gigantic, epic battle against the forces of darkness, defeating them in a giant explosion. No, the true revolution that will change the Earth is an inner revolution, where you dare to be who you are and rise above the dualistic struggle, thus refusing to feed it.

This is the true victory we are looking for—those who will overcome and be who they are in God. You have dared to start that process.

And you can surely continue it. Yes, my beloved, I sense how some of you have your doubts. But I am not asking you to attain the Christ consciousness in the next five seconds. I am asking you to continue to do what we have talked about, namely put one foot in front of the other. Take one step at a time and simply determine in your mind that come what may, you will – for the rest of your lifetime – continue to take one small step at a time, always looking for the next step. Never allowing yourself to be held up by the sense of comfortability, or the sense of fear or the sense of hopelessness.

My beloved, all I am asking is this: Always look for the next step you can take. Look for how your ego is trying to come up with an excuse for why you should not take that step. And then realize that it is nothing but an illusion and determine to not let it hold you back but to take that next step anyway. That is what I am asking, my beloved. For that is what will win your victory.

Understanding non-dual Victory

Thus, my beloved, you see that as with everything, there is dualistic perspective and there is a higher supra-dualistic perspective. And when you reach for that higher perspective, you see that there is a different approach. Even an approach where you do not need to be forceful or powerful in order to win. For my beloved, I have earlier spoken with greater power through this messenger, but I choose to tone down the power in order to impart to you a different aspect of the Flame of Victory, a more quiet aspect of that flame that is based on an inner knowing that there is only victory.

For my beloved, when you read Maitreya's book, [Master Keys to Spiritual Freedom] you can read between the lines that there has never been a sphere that has not ascended that there never will be a sphere that will not ascend. For there is no question that God's vision and design for this world of form will be manifest. It is only a matter of how long it will take before the beings who have used their free will to separate themselves from God will either realize the folly of their ways or run out of opportunity, so that the sphere in which they have lived will ascend without them.

Thus, my beloved, the force that drives the spheres to ascend is simply this: constant self-transcendence. And my beloved, you are never in a situation that you cannot transcend—IF you are willing to transcend yourself. For have we not said over and over again that your outer situation is a manifestation of your state of consciousness? And so, even though you might feel right now that you have no power over your outer situation, I must tell you that you do have power to change your state of consciousness one small step at a time, one illusion at a time.

And thus, the sense that you are paralyzed and can do nothing has no reality to it. For my beloved, you can always surrender. And it is precisely in unconditional surrender that you win the victory. For as has been explained by Maitreya in his book and by Jesus and Mother Mary before, you cannot perfect the human consciousness. You can only rise above it. And in order to do that, you must surrender it. You must let it go.

And so my beloved, do you see it has been said that it is better to conquer yourself than to conquer a city? And indeed, conquering yourself is not a matter of fighting a battle. It is not even a matter of fighting your ego or the different divisions of your ego that cause a warring in your members. It is only a matter of surrendering them, leaving them behind—realizing that you are more than this. And therefore, accepting that you can rise above any condition—when you are willing to look at it, to understand why it is unreal and then simply let it go.

Thus in the softness of the Flame of Victory, I seal your hearts and I express my gratitude as well. For you have set forth another movement, another momentum, in the consciousness of Europe, namely that of VICTORY THROUGH SURRENDER.

A special dispensation to help Europeans rise above the past

Gautama Buddha, May 20, 2007.

So when you cannot fix the past – when you cannot change it – how can you be free of it? Well, you can be free in only one way—by letting it go! You can be free of the past, not by holding on to the anger and hatred against another group of people, not by seeking to compensate for the wrong that was done to your people in the past by committing a greater wrong by destroying those who have wronged you before.

Understanding true forgiveness

You can be free of the past only through forgiveness, but only through the special type of forgiveness that is unconditional forgiveness. For my beloved, even though the world has a hard time understanding unconditional forgiveness, if you will think about this, you will realize that there is no other form of forgiveness but unconditional forgiveness. For as long as there are conditions, you have not truly forgiven, have you my beloved? Nay, you have not.

You have in fact created a very subtle sense of logic, which gives your ego an excuse for not forgiving other people. For you have in your mind set up conditions that say that only if they live up to those conditions are they worthy of your forgiveness. And so your forgiveness is now no longer determined by you making the choice to forgive, it will be determined by the choices they make.

And so, what have you done with this subtle reasoning? Well, you have given away your own power over your own destiny. And you have put your destiny in the hands of other people. And who are the people in whose hands you have put your destiny? Are they not the very people that you see as having wronged you in the past? And so what sense does it make that you would allow them to control your future by letting your forgiveness be conditioned upon their response or non-response?

Do you see, this makes no sense whatsoever? For my beloved, if someone has wronged you, why would you want to in any way be dependent upon them? Would you not want to be free of those who have wronged you, so they can no longer control you. So how can you be free from other people? Well my beloved, you can only be free through total and unconditional forgiveness.

When you forgive other people, you are not setting them free; you are setting yourself free. And if they are not willing to come up higher and forgive you, then they will be left in their old state of consciousness but you will transcend that dualistic state of consciousness and rise higher. And as we have said, the universe is a mirror. So it will inevitably reflect back to you conditions that reflect your higher state of consciousness. Whereas those who were your enemies and not willing to forgive will receive back conditions that reflect their state of consciousness, so they will still have an enemy but it will not be you. For you are now free to rise above the dualistic struggle.

And so, my beloved, when you look at this continent, you will see that there are places where entire groups of people are so focused on the past that it is literally consuming their present and overpowering their vision of the future. Even to the point where they do not have the ability or even the courage to envision a better future, a golden future.

And so, my beloved, how shall there ever be a better future as long as people are so focused on the past that the past becomes prologue and sets the pattern for continuing the dualistic struggle that has been going on for centuries? Thus, you see that for things to change, there must be some who will come to the realization that they want to be free and that they cannot be free by seeking to change the past, by seeking to right the wrongs of the past. They can be free only by forgiving the wrongs of the past, by leaving them behind and rising above the old state of consciousness, the old view of other people, the old view of themselves, and the old feelings of anger, hatred, fear or the sense of being threatened.

My beloved, it is the sense of struggle that creates the struggle. For it is your consciousness that sets the stage for what you experience in the physical. And thus, if you seek to change outer conditions before you change your consciousness, you are, as the old saying goes, putting the cart before the horse. And you will get nowhere.

An opportunity to let go of non-forgiveness
And my beloved, in this regard, do not forget to look in the mirror and practice unconditional forgiveness toward yourself. For truly, many of you find it easier to forgive others than to forgive yourself. But my be-

loved, unconditional forgiveness is unconditional. Meaning that it is not dependent upon any conditions on Earth. And so to forgive your neighbor unconditionally, you must be willing to look beyond his or her imperfections. And so you must do with yourself.

My beloved, if forgiveness is unconditional, what conditions could you possibly have to fulfill in order to be worthy of that unconditional forgiveness? Do you not see the logic of this, my beloved? You do not need to be worthy of unconditional forgiveness. You are worthy of it right now.

And thus, as the sealing of this release, I offer you the opportunity to take all non-forgiveness of yourself – all sense of being imperfect, of not being good enough, of having made this or that mistake – I give you the opportunity [that I will] take all of it.

Envision how you gather these imperfections from all corners of your forcefield, all corners of your aura. You draw them together, and you might envision them as black threads that are interwoven with the fabric of your being, but you see, my beloved, how you pull them out of your being as so many black threads.

And you pull them together and you pull them tighter and tighter towards your heart. And in the light of your heart, you begin to see them. And you pull them together in a ball. And now you see how you cram together that ball, making it tighter and tighter, as if it was a roll of yarn or string that at first is somewhat unruly, but as you keep pulling it together, it becomes more and more compact until it is so small that you can hold it in both of your hands.

And now, my beloved, I invite you to envision that you hold that ball of yarn of non-forgiveness in your hands, and you throw it into the burning furnace of my heart chakra—that burns with a light so bright that it will instantly consume any imperfection on Earth. My beloved, be not concerned about my ability to be able to consume and transmute this substance. For am I not the Lord of the World? So truly, there is nothing you can have that could be so bad, that I could not consume it. So take it now and throw it into my heart chakra and see how it is consumed instantly upon touching the fire of my fiery love for you.

And now, my beloved, accept that you are free of this non-forgiveness. Accept that you are worthy of the unconditional forgiveness. Accept that I, Gautama Buddha, the Lord of the World, have forgiven you unconditionally and completely. And thus, as Jesus said, "Thy sins be forgiven thee. Now go and sin no more." Do not go back into the old momentums and recreate the non-forgiveness of yourself—even if you continue to make certain mistakes. When you make the mistake, seek honestly to learn from it but then forgive yourself rather than holding on to it.

For my beloved, the very fact that you are open to these teachings – the new teachings of the Christ and Buddha for the Aquarian Age – demonstrates that you have the potential to be one of the forerunners for the Golden Age. But how can you fulfill that mission if you hold on to non-forgiveness of yourself? How can you demonstrate forgiveness to others if you do not practice it towards yourself?

So forgive yourself, and let go of the conditions that your ego and the forces of this world are using in order to trick you into thinking that you are not worthy of forgiveness. Or even trick you into believing the age-old lie of the serpentine mind that once you have made a certain mistake, you are doomed forever and can never be redeemed.

I tell you, the reality is that God has no other desire than to see you rise above all imperfections on Earth and become the God-free being you were created to be. And you can rise only when you accept unconditional forgiveness. For what I have said applies on a continental scale, it applies on an individual scale. You cannot right the wrongs of the past. You can only learn from them and then let them go by unconditionally forgiving yourself.

Thus, my beloved, I have said my peace, and I seal you in the Flame of Unconditional Forgiveness. And I seal this conference, my beloved. For I want you to know that you have earned this dispensation. You have earned it for Europe as a whole. And this shows you how a few people can indeed be the forerunners for raising up the many.

So allow yourselves to flow with the music that will be played. Allow yourself to feel the Presence of the Buddha where you are. For when everything is the Buddha nature, then you are the Buddha nature. Meaning that you are already the Buddha—if you could only accept it, and accept it unconditionally.

For when you are already the Buddha, how could there be conditions that you have to fulfill before you become the Buddha? And thus, ponder the eternal truth that the ego and the intellect can never fathom— that you cannot become the Buddha. You can only BE the Buddha.

Be MORE than normal!

Saint Germain (4), July 14, 2007

Do not allow the norm to prevent you from expressing your light

And thus, again, question the norm, question the unquestionable, think the unthinkable, accept the unacceptable. Be what you are not supposed to be—dare to be here below, my beloved, all that you already are Above. Accept a new norm, which is that you are a spiritual being and that it is normal and right for you to express your spiritual reality in whatever form comes to you from within. And accept that there is no norm in this world that is going to stop you from expressing your spiritual reality, even if it means creating a website or writing books that cause some people to think that you are crazy or insane.

Even if it means speaking out in ways that will challenge other people and therefore cause them to go into the default reaction of the ego—of saying that there must be something wrong with you. Which then gives them an excuse for ignoring you, so that they do not have to change. Thereby, they can ignore the fact that if you can be different, they can be different as well, and so they can continue staying where they are comfortable and where they do not need to take responsibility for themselves.

For do you not see, my beloved, that being normal in your society takes away your need to take responsibility for yourself, to discover who you are and to dare to express who you are? For you just need to be normal and flow along with the mass consciousness. And this is a very easy and comfortable way to live, for you do not really need to think—for the norm has done all the thinking for you.

I challenge you to rethink the concept of ownership

Saint Germain (6), July 15, 2007

The world is designed to give you abundance

For you see, my beloved, you have been sent into a world that is very well designed for giving you the abundant life. In fact, God has designed this world to give you anything and everything you want. However, if you seek to own something, you will limit your possessions to that which you can currently conceive instead of flowing with the River of Life.

Do you see, my beloved, that you have been given free will by God? And you have been given the ability to impose images upon the Ma-ter Light, causing the light to take on form, whereby it will temporarily stagnate in a certain form. As I said, you have the right to do this, to create any form you desire. Yet what God desires to see for you is that you do not settle for the forms that you can currently conceive, but that you are part of the ongoing movement of the River of Life. So that, instead of holding on to one limited form, you are constantly transcending yourself, constantly transcending your former mental images so they do not become graven images. And therefore, you are not seeking to hold on to one particular form, for you are willing to transcend that form, allowing that form to become more.

And do you see, my beloved, this is what the human ego and those who are trapped in the fallen consciousness cannot fathom? For they believe that if a particular form is changed, they will lose that form. And you see, my beloved, in a sense this is true. For if you have ten dollars in the bank and they accrue interest and now you have twelve dollars, well in a sense you have lost the ten dollars, at least the sense of having ten dollars in the bank. But is it really a loss, or have you received something more?

There IS MORE to Life!

El Morya as Master MORE, October 26, 2007

Christhood depends on nothing outside yourself

Therefore, let go of the sense of hopelessness! Let go of the sense that your Christhood depends on other people or institutions in society. For, my beloved, the reality demonstrated by Jesus is that individual Christhood depends on nothing outside the individual.

Look at Jesus. At one point or another almost everyone around him questioned the sanity of what he was doing—even his mother, who had a very high vision that he had a special mission to fulfill. So did his brothers, so did his disciples from time to time, almost all of them failing to see the greater vision. Yet Jesus withstood the onslaught of all of them – the people, the Scribes and the Pharisees, the high and the mighty as well as the low who pulled upon him to be their king and throw out the Roman occupiers – he withstood all of them and manifested his Christhood anyway.

Of course, this cannot happen, my beloved, unless you are willing to look at the ego and overcome that ego. Because otherwise it will be inevitable that your ego will pull you into a false "Christhood," an imitation of Christhood, that makes some people think that they are the saviors, that they are the wise ones who know best how things should be done, and thus they are the saviors of the people. This is what you saw in Peter, where he would argue with Jesus and tell him how he should conduct his mission. This is indeed the consciousness, my beloved, that started with Peter, was institutionalized by the Catholic Church and was directly responsible for the emergence of the period called "the Dark Ages" in Europe.

Understanding the Dark Ages in Europe

For what happened in the Dark Ages was that people's individual creativity was squashed, to the point where few people dared to stand out and bring forth an individual contribution and new ideas in art, literature, philosophy, religion or inventions of a practical nature. And, my beloved, see how this very consciousness created the idea that people can be divided into two separate categories—some who are above the population, who form an elite.

Jesus might be at the top but was there not always a church hierarchy of the false preachers, the wolves in sheep's clothing that Jesus warned his followers about but that they did not heed? And therefore, those wolves took over the Christian church and turned it into an institution that suppresses the people and makes them the blind followers of the elite—who are themselves the blind followers of their egos and the non-material forces beyond who are ruling their egos.

And so throughout the dark ages this consciousness spread throughout Europe. And I can tell you that if you look at how the plague, the Black Death, spread throughout Europe, I can assure you that at higher levels there was a similar spreading of the black cloud of this consciousness that the people are inadequate—that they do not have a divine spark and a Christ potential. That they cannot rule themselves and bring forth something unique from within themselves, but that they must always look for someone else to do it for them. This is, then, what gave rise to a monarchy based on the incredible illusion that it was appointed by God to rule the people, to rule its own people, and that the people were actually given to the monarchy by God as its slaves, as its subjects, and that the monarchy could do whatever it wanted.

For you see, my beloved, the Catholic Church had already given up the willingness to tune in to the higher Will of God, thereby institutionalizing the dualistic will of man, the dualistic will of the ego, as the ultimate authority in society. And so, it was just a matter of time before the monarchy fell into the same trap of thinking that it was the ultimate authority in society. And then you saw the ultimate power struggle between the monarchy and the church. And this is what Saint Germain has already described previously in our series about restoring the Word— that the church and the church hierarchy formed the established power elite, and the monarchy and noble class who owned the land formed the aspiring power elite. And the power struggle between them went on for some time, but then finally had the "resolution" that the British monarch now declared himself the head of the Church of England, thus bringing all three into a certain unified state, where now the perverted trinity of Father, Mother, Son was complete.

The missing link in history

For what is it that the elite has done to suppress the people? Yes, you will look back at history and say that the king had some real physical power and he used it ruthlessly. Nevertheless, let me tell you that there never has been a regime on this planet – be it the British monarchy, or the Communist Party in the Soviet Union, or the emperors of Rome – there never has been a regime that had enough physical power to suppress the people with physical power alone. For had the people come together at a critical mass and stood up against that physical power, then the powers would have fallen. And this you have seen in a number of nations around the world.

So therefore, physical power is not enough to suppress the people. And that is indeed the missing link in history, where historians tend to look back, and they look only at the material circumstances, thinking that the cause of everything that happened in the world must be found in the material realm. But I tell you that the cause of everything that happened in the material realm is found in the consciousness of the people, the collective consciousness. And thus, my beloved, I tell you – truly – what they have used to suppress the people is the Word, the perversion of the Word of God.

The Word of God is the consciousness of Christ that allows you – as I started out this discourse talking about – that allows you to discern between what is real and what is unreal. And so, in order to suppress the people, they must take away that key of knowledge. They must create this false reality, where they have now created two dualistic polarities that seem to be inseparably linked in a dualistic struggle for supremacy. Yet both of them are lies.

And so this, my beloved, is one realization that needs to be brought out at this time in Britain and elsewhere, for it is the essential realization that must be spread before a Golden Age can dawn—namely the whole nature of duality. And this, my beloved, is of course why we of the Ascended Host have brought forth the new book, The Art of Non-War, which is written in a way that is more universal than any other book we have brought forth through any dispensation whatsoever. Thus, it has a potential to reach the people and awaken them to the basic dynamic of the duality consciousness and how it prevents them from discerning what is real and what is unreal. So every action they take, every idea they believe in, does not really lead to change because it merely perpetuates the dualistic struggle which is the very root of their suffering and their limitations.

But that dualistic struggle starts in the consciousness, for the elite themselves could not perpetuate the dualistic struggle unless the people responded. And that is why you see the unholy alliance between those in the power elite who want power, and those among the people who do not want power but want to give away their power and have other people make decisions for them. So that they do not have to face the potential of making wrong choices, but can criticize those who make choices no matter what choices they make. And yet even this can shift almost as in the blinking of an eye. And it will shift when enough of the top 10 percent process that state of consciousness in their own beings and overcome it once and for all.

Overcoming possesion
And so, my beloved, what is the key to overcoming this consciousness in your own being? Well, my beloved, there are some of you here that are aware of the potential that people can be possessed by a force that is outside themselves. This might be something you call a demon, an entity, a discarnate soul or whatever you want to call it, my beloved. The essence of such possession is that something enters your container of self, your four lower bodies, and once inside it starts to rule the roost and cause the Conscious You to withdraw and say: "I can no longer be in command of myself," or perhaps it doesn"t even say that, but without realizing it, it gives away its power.

And so, my beloved, what is the key to overcoming this? For I am sure you can see that in a sense, everyone who grows up on Earth is possessed by something from outside themselves. For have I not said – and do not many of you know – that you have taken on elements of the mass consciousness. And the mass consciousness is also an alien energy that enters your energy field and now begins to pull on your thoughts and emotions and your sense of self.

So, my beloved, we have given you the image of the figure eight flow. And the upper figure of the figure eight represents the spiritual realm, and the lower figure, the material realm. So, my beloved, what is in the upper figure of the figure eight of your own being? [Audience answers: "Your I AM Presence"]

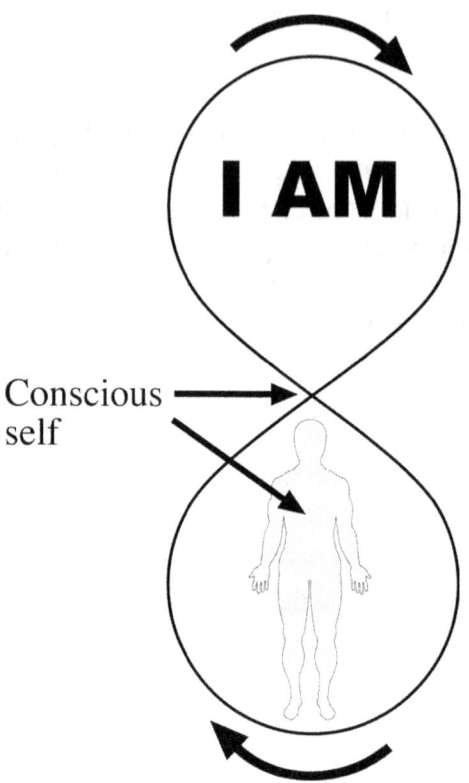

Your I AM Presence is in the upper figure, and in the lower figure is your four lower bodies, your container of self, your soul, whatever you want to call it. But, my beloved, what is supposed to be in the center, in the nexus of the figure eight? Your conscious self, as we have called it. It can be called other names for it truly does not matter. But what I want to point out to you is this. For any outside force to enter your lower being, there must be room for that force to enter. There must be a division in your being. For if there was no division, nothing could enter.

Do you see, my beloved, your I AM Presence is one, is one with its source, your Creator. So nothing from the Earth can enter your I AM Presence because it is undivided. There is no space, no opening, for any lower vibration to enter. Yet in your lower being – once you have become a house divided against itself by believing in the dualistic lies – then there is room for outside forces, ideas and energies to enter.

But you see, my beloved, there is only room because your conscious self has not taken responsibility for itself, for your lower being. It has not taken the responsibility to be the Christ in your being, and therefore be the mediator between your I AM Presence and your lower being. For when your conscious self occupies that position in the centre, in the nexus, then you will be as above so below. You can be here below all that you are above. And thus there will be no division below, as there is no division above.—and nothing alien can enter.

Well, what is the key, then, to overcoming the division? You see, my beloved, you have been divided because you came to believe in a dualistic lie. And there are innumerable dualistic lies—so many that we could not possibly expose them all. But they all spring from the one lie, which is the essential lie, that there can be a division in infinity; that the Infinite can be divided into parts, where one part is separated from the whole and therefore one part is separated from another part.

And this lie comes in as soon as your conscious self descends below the nexus of the figure eight. You see, my beloved, at any point below the nexus, there is distance. Now, distance does not necessarily mean division, for it is indeed possible that the Father and the Mother can be united in a true polarity of Alpha and Omega, Yin and Yang.

It is only when the two become opposites through the dualistic mind that you have division. So it is quite possible to have the distance that you see in this realm of time and space without there being division, for there is still Oneness. But where must the Oneness come from? It must come from your conscious self occupying its rightful position in the nexus. Not by being down here [points to lower half of the figure eight] and identifying itself with any lower self-concept, any divided concept of self.

And, my beloved, the idea I wish you to ponder is this. In mathematics you have the concept – well you have two important concepts – one is the symbol for infinity which is the figure eight, but you also have the concept of a single point, or a singularity as it is called. Well, my beloved, the singularity is a point that has no extension in space. What does that mean, my beloved? It means it is beyond space, for space implies extension, which means that there is more than one point—there is distance. And this is when you can have two points which are now separated by a distance.

But you see, my beloved, your conscious self is what gives you self-awareness, but listen carefully now. Your conscious self is an extension of the Being of the Creator. But here comes the mystery for you to ponder. Your conscious self is pure awareness. It does not have a sense of identity as being this or that. It simply IS, my beloved.

You see, you have had – for many years – the concept of the I AM and the I AM Presence. And listen carefully—this is a perfectly valid concept that we have given you for a reason. For we know that once you have descended into duality – and have accepted a sense of identity as being separated from your source – well, you cannot in one jump overcome that sense of separation. So we have given you the concept that you have a spiritual identity that is anchored in the spiritual realm—and thus cannot be destroyed or distorted by any false identity you have taken on in the lower part of your being in the material realm. And this is indeed to take the awareness of the conscious self and redirect it from feeling that it is centered down here [in the lower part of the figure eight] and gradually bringing itself closer and closer to this nexus point.

But you see, my beloved, when your conscious self ascends to the nexus, it does not disappear. But the sense that it is separated from the Allness of the Creator, from the Infinite, that sense of separation disappears. For that separate sense of self is what dies and what Jesus talked about when he said: "He who seeks to save his life shall lose it. But he who is willing to lose his life for my sake shall find it."

And so, even the concept of the I AM is a concept that – although valid at a certain level of consciousness – needs to be transcended in order for you to go beyond a certain point on the spiritual path. For do you see, my beloved, that there is the "I" and there is the "AM." And do you see that right there, there is a distance, which is what implies the potential for a division. For you see the "I" that is the mediator between your higher and lower being, can come to say: "I AM not this up here, expressing itself through this below—no, I AM something down here, defined as being separate from what is above."

And this is where division creeps into your being. So the only solution to this, my beloved, is that your conscious self, which is the "I," comes to realize that the "AM" is only a tool that it is temporarily using to express itself in the material world. But the "I" begins to realize that rather than being that lower identity, it is MORE than that lower identity.

For do you see, my beloved, the letter "I" is a single line, and again in mathematics, a line has no extension in width. So you see now that there is no division, no horizontal division, in a line. So when your conscious self realizes that it is not this or that, it stops saying "I AM this' or "I AM that" in the world, but it actually comes to say "I."

You see, my beloved, the concept of an I AM Presence is useful, but if you begin to think that you are the I AM Presence, well, even that is a slightly dualistic concept because you might see a division between the "I" and the "I AM Presence." But what you need to come to is the point where you are just the "I" and you know that that "I" is One with the All, with the infinity of God. For the "I" is not a finite being. My beloved, the "AM" here below is a finite being but the "I" is not.

Now listen carefully. Even the I AM Presence is a finite being, not in the material realm, but in the spiritual realm which is also part of the world of form. And, my beloved, how is the world of form created? Well, it is created out of the Creator's Being. But it is created because the One Creator, the infinite Being of the Creator, expressed itself as the two polarities of Alpha and Omega.

For you see, my beloved, the world of form has form, does it not? And you see on planet Earth many forms that are separate from other forms because they are defined by their differences. If there were no differences, there would be no expressed forms. All would still be the unexpressed Oneness of the Creator. So the Creator must divide itself into the two polarities. And yet those polarities are ultimately – although they are expressions of the Creator's Being – they are finite. For they have extension, differences.

Again, differences and distance does not mean division, for nothing in the spiritual realm is divided. But it still has extension in what we might call spiritual space—not to be confused with physical space. And so, my beloved, people are so conditioned to thinking in terms of the world of form and differences. And in order to raise them up to a higher state of consciousness, they had to be given certain concepts that they could understand with their minds—as they were in a very divided state when, for example, Genesis was released on this planet.

Understanding the name of God

So now you have the concept of Moses going to the mount and communing with God, or rather with a representative of God. And Moses knows that the people will not accept him unless he gives them something concrete that they can use to picture this God that he met on the mountain. So he asks God to give him a name. And God uses the name I AM or I AM THAT I AM, but you see – as we have said before – this is not really a name. It is a riddle, a Zen koan, my beloved, that you can contemplate. And you see that even the concept of I AM THAT I AM is a concept that is adapted to the consciousness of the people in a dualistic state.

What is really being said here? I AM THAT I AM is implying that at any moment I AM Being whatever I want to Be. And thus, when you understand the reality here, you understand that God is really saying: "I am not a static God. I am not a dead God. I am not a graven image. And no matter what graven image you create on Earth, you cannot fit me into that mental box. For your mental box must be finite, but I AM infinite."

And so, what God was really saying is that at any moment in time, I will be what I AM. And you all know that the more correct translation of the original text is: I WILL BE WHO I WILL BE. Yet the consciousness of I AM THAT I AM is valid, because we have given you the model of the upper and the lower and that the lower being needs to come into alignment with the upper. And how do you do that?

You do that by realizing that up here [in the higher part of the figure eight] is the I AM THAT I AM, and down here [in the lower part] is your sense of identity, your sense of I AM—I AM this, I AM that. And what you need to do is to come to a point where you can say: "I am THAT I am, up there."

That, however, is not the end of your spiritual growth. It is, rather, the beginning of the true spiritual path, where you realize that there is more to your identity than can be defined in the material realm. And so, you need to reach beyond the material realm. And indeed, you have something to reach for, you have something to unite with, where your sense of identity down here can become One or identified with the Being up here, so you know "I AM here below all that I AM above, for I am THAT I AM."

Yet there is a higher level. For as I said earlier, your conscious self is not the I AM down here [the lower part of the figure-eight], but neither is your conscious self the I AM up here [the upper part]. Your conscious self is a state of pure awareness that can never be identified with anything in the finite world. And even your I AM Presence is in the finite world.

So when you truly attain enlightenment, Christhood, Buddhahood, Oneness with God, whatever you want to call it, well then the "I" of your conscious self stops identifying itself as this or this. Well, what does it identify itself as?

Well, my beloved, it identifies itself as the All. And this is when you have the symbol of the "s" around the "I", which symbolizes the figure eight, where your "I" is in the center, but it really is no longer in the center, for it realizes that the mathematical symbol of infinity drawn as a figure eight—yes it has a single point in the centre, but the entire periphery of the figure eight is made up of single points.

And really, my beloved, when you realize that a single point has no extension in space, then you can realize that a single point is not really a point. For if there is no extension in finite space, how can you say that here is a single point that is separated from the Infinite? For if it was separate, it had to be in the realm of the finite world and thus it had to have extension in space.

And so you realize that the single "I" is everything at once. And that is when you will know what Jesus said: "And the king shall say, inasmuch as ye have done it to the least of these my brethren, ye have done it unto me." [You will also know what Jesus meant when he said that when your "eye" or your "I" is single, your whole body is full of light.]

Loving God with ALL your heart, mind and soul

That is when you can fulfill the requirement that Jesus gave as the absolute requirement for Christhood. For when he was asked by the Scribes and Pharisees about the greatest points of the law he said: "To love god with all your heart, soul and mind." Because, my beloved, how can you love God with all your heart, soul and mind? Well, you can only do it when you realize that you ARE God, that there is no longer separation. For if you see a separation between yourself and God, you simply cannot love God with ALL your heart, mind and soul. It is not possible.

So then you have fulfilled the Alpha aspect of the equation of Christhood. But the Omega aspect is to love your neighbor as yourself. But how can you do that, my beloved? Only when you see your neighbor AS yourself, as your greater Self. For if you see a distance between yourself and your neighbor, you are not truly loving your neighbor AS yourself.

And you are not truly loving yourself if you are seeing a distance between yourself and the Creator. For only in Oneness with your Creator, will you experience the fullness of God's love, which is an infinite, unconditional love.

And so, there is always a higher teaching that can be released. And what you will see, my beloved, is that there are always those who will cling to the old, for they have taken the old teaching and put it in a mental box, and now they are comfortable. Well, who is comfortable, my beloved? Only the ego can be comfortable with any mental box in the finite world. For the "I" can never be fully comfortable until it is one with infinity.

And so, you always see that those who want to stay with the old, who want to stay where they are comfortable, are still blinded by their egos no matter what they might think. No matter what clever, intellectual arguments they might come up with, they are still blinded by their egos, for they have not truly been willing to look for the beam in their own eye, even though they have a teaching that talks about the ego and the need to look for it.

It is entirely possible to understand that teaching only with the outer intellectual, analytical mind, and therefore take the teaching and turn it into a mental box that gives the ego that sense of security because it feels it has even the spiritual path under control—even Christhood, it has under control. And that is precisely what you saw Peter attempting to do with Jesus.

Peter recognized that Jesus was beyond a normal person but he was not willing to follow Jesus and attain Oneness with the Living Christ. He wanted – until the very end – to put the Living Christ in his own mental box. And even though he let the Living Christ expand his mental box that little bit, he would not take that final step of throwing away the mental box by letting the mortal self die and being spiritually reborn—being born of water and of Spirit.

What does it mean to be reborn of water and of Spirit? Well, several things. But one certainly is that being born of water is that you come the understanding with the mind that you actually need to surrender the lower self. For in coming to that understanding the "I" of the conscious self can then separate itself from the mortal self because it realizes that if the mortal self dies, the "I" will not die. It will be reborn into its true identity as One with the All.

And when, my beloved, you give up that finite identity and merge into the infinite identity, then you are not an "I" located in the nexus, thinking "I am this, and I must express that down here." Because there is no distance. You are everywhere, above and below. And so, you are just letting the I AM Presence flow through your nexus into the four lower bodies and express itself through those four lower bodies without the "I," the conscious self, having to think about this or even feel that something from outside of me up there is flowing through me here and expressing itself down there. Because it has stopped thinking that "I AM here and only here." It knows it is everywhere in the consciousness of God. And that is when the "I" becomes the "Is" for now the energies, the ideas, the reality from the spiritual realm can flow through you into the material realm.

But not only flow through you, but also be expressed by you because you are now fully conscious of everything you do. And in every situation you are not thinking: "Oh, I don"t want to be in this situation, I wish it was over." You are simply there with the Allness of who you are, expressing that, and thereby transcending and transforming the situation so that other people are raised up. And so that the you have mastery over the material realm. And so, the matter light is raised up, is freed from the imperfect matrices that have been put upon it through the duality consciousness. It can be instantly set free, whereby the water is turned into wine, the dead are raised, the sick are healed.

This is what you saw in Jesus. Jesus had united, he had become the IS and that is why God could manifest these so-called miracles through him—that are not miracles, they are simply the natural state of the Mater light expressing the reality of the Father, rather than the unreality of the duality consciousness. And as I said with the mass consciousness that can be pulled here and there, the matter light has volunteered to express any form that God's co-creators impose upon it.

But this does not mean, my beloved, that the matter light has no consciousness. It does not mean that the matter light enjoys taking on the negative forms that you saw in the movie of violence, and images that are not in harmony with the higher principles. The mother light would at any moment gladly shake this off and instead instantly manifest the higher reality of God.

Change is always possible

So again, nothing is hopeless. Change is possible. That, my beloved, is what the power elite do not want you to believe, and they especially do not want the people to believe it. They want them to believe that status quo cannot be changed, or certainly cannot be changed beyond certain boundaries. And this, my beloved, is the lie that Jesus challenged and that we need those in physical embodiment who are also willing to challenge.

And this implies many things. You do not always have to come out strongly and give a teaching like I have given today, which surely, as they say, will blow many people away, as I know some of you are holding onto your seats here. [Audience laughs]

Nevertheless, there are many more gentle ways to awaken people to the fact that change is always possible. Look at history, my beloved. Look at how much society has changed in a thousand years. Think back—go to one of the museums you have in Britain and elsewhere, and see how people lived in the Stone Age. And then see how you live today, only a few thousand years later. And then see how much has happened just within the last century, just within your lifetime. How computer technology has transformed society.

For, my beloved, should not a realistic assessment make you see that change is indeed possible? And that change can have many levels? And is it not possible to help people see that the reason why society is at a higher level today than in the Stone Age is that there has been an expansion in consciousness, and that it is the expansion in consciousness that drives all progress?

And then, my beloved, it is not that difficult to make people see that because the expansion of consciousness has become one-sided in the West, where people have forgotten spirituality – partly because of the perversions of Christianity that took Jesus' true teachings away from the people, and then because of the consciousness of materialism – well then, people have become unbalanced and that is why you have a one-sided progress. Where you have technological progress and the technological progress itself creates problems, which people cannot solve because they do not have the corresponding expansion in their spiritual awareness. My beloved, this is not, as they say, rocket science. It is possible to make many, many people understand these concepts, when you make them your own and express them in your own words.

The Living Christ is the true King of Britain

Jesus, October 28, 2007

Why there is no absolute system

And so, my beloved, why did I come to this Earth? Well, I came first and foremost to give people that key of knowledge that allows them to connect to truth within themselves—not by intellectually understanding an outer teaching, but by experiencing the Spirit of truth within themselves. For this is the only factor that can help humankind rise above the dualistic struggle.

And my beloved, yesterday was raised a very important question of how the living word can be restored as the ultimate authority in society. And the answer was given that it cannot be institutionalized, and this my beloved is the key that you need to ponder until you fully internalize this truth.

For my beloved, when you look at humankind, can you not see that there has always been a quest to come up with the ultimate system? This might be a religion coming up with the absolute truth—an absolute, infallible religion. It might be a political system—communism, capitalism, what have you. It might be an economic system. But the dream is that we can come up with some ultimate system, and once we have established that system, we will have the perfect society.

But you see, my beloved, this is not how a truly Golden Age is brought forth. For there is no system that will work indefinitely. And why is this so my beloved? Well go back and listen to or read the wonderful discourses given by Saint Germain in California, about how past Golden Ages deteriorated. And you will see that any system you create becomes a closed system, and therefore immediately becomes subject to the second law of thermodynamics, which is, in a sense, the force of the Holy Spirit that compels everything to grow and transcend.

So what I need the most spiritual people to realize is that bringing forth the Golden Age is not a matter of coming up with some ultimate system or philosophy that will answer all of your questions. You need to let go of this dream, for my beloved, it is a dream that springs from the ego and has been espoused by the Power Elite for eons, by those fallen beings who left off the oneness with God. And therefore, in their separation, attempted to achieve through control what God would have given them freely if they had been willing to stay in the River of Life.

For you see, my beloved, the ultimate system, so to speak, is the flow of the River of Life. And that flow cannot be encapsulated, cannot be imprisoned, in a system on Earth. It must remain the flow that changes society as the need arises, for surely, my beloved, even the ego will pervert the concept of a Golden Age and think that a Golden Age is a static society. But it is not—it is a society that is constantly growing and therefore going through different phrases.

You will not have a Golden Age society that remains the same for a thousand years, even though some Christians interpret the Bible to mean that I thought that there would be a Kingdom of God that would remain steady and the same for a thousand years. No, my beloved, the Kingdom of God – manifest on Earth as a Golden Age society – is a society that is constantly growing towards greater and greater abundance.

And what does that mean, my beloved? It means that the society is going through distinct phases, just like the growth of a human child that grows from infancy to childhood to adulthood. Only, a Golden Age society will keep transcending itself, and therefore will never go into the stage of old age and death that human beings experience.

And so what does that mean? It means – to use a crude analogy – it is perfectly natural for a baby to wear diapers, but it is not natural for a ten-year old child, is it? And so, a society needs certain ideas, certain rules, at one level of its growth, but when it transcends that stage, it no longer needs the same rules and ideas.

And that is why you cannot have a system, my beloved, that can be applied to a society for the indefinite future. For if the system or the philosophy or the idea is based on truth, then it will cause the society to transcend itself, and that means that the system must also transcend itself. And then it really is no longer a system as envisioned by most people.

And that is why what is needed is not the emergence of some kind of system, but the emergence of a critical mass of people who are willing to acknowledge their Christ potential and express that. So that at any given moment, they can bring forth through their higher selves –

they can bring forth from the River of Life – the exact answers that are needed in order to bring society forward. But more than that, they can also bring forth a constant recognition that society needs to be aligned with timeless principles in order to be sustainable, in order to avoid disintegrating from within.

For only through transcendence is there sustainability. Only through death is there survival, meaning the death of the limited, separate self. Only by being willing to lose ones life for Christ's sake, will one find eternal life, and that applies to an entire society as well. For only when you are letting the old die, can you be reborn into a new identity, a new being, a new nation in Christ.

So my beloved, give up the false dream of an ultimate system, an ultimate philosophy. You can keep chasing it forever, but why not recognize that this is the dream of the fallen beings, this is the dream of those trapped in the ego.

And you know better. You are spiritual people, so you do not need the ultimate system or the ultimate religion. You need a living system, a living philosophy, a living church that is based on the living Christ, and therefore the River of Life is flowing through that system, through that church, through that government, through those educational institutions, through business. And my beloved, certainly you can see that of all the institutions of society, the business world is probably the one that understands best the need to adapt to changing circumstances, the need to transcend one's former way of thinking. But this must be transferred to all areas of society.

Preach the universal Word

So my beloved, this is what I encourage in you—become universal! And in order to help you overcome your fear of speaking out, I would remind you of what we have said before: It is not your job to convince or convert other people. You see, my beloved, so many religious and spiritual people go out to evangelize, to preach, but they think they have to preach a certain system, a religious system because they have to get other people into the fold. For they think only those who are in the fold will be saved.

Well, my beloved, do you not see what I have been saying in this discourse? Any system on Earth is a closed system, and so no matter which closed system you are in, you will not be saved, for the true key to salvation is to be in the River of Life. Now, you can be in a system on Earth and still be in the River of Life, but only if you have that inner recognition that there is a higher truth, and that you are willing to flow with it.

So you see, it is not your job to go out and convince other people of a certain truth. It is your job to present them with a choice between the myriad of dualistic ideas and an idea that comes from the higher truth of Christ, the higher principles.

And so, my beloved, you will see in today's world that many people already sense at inner levels that there is a higher truth. And that is why you will see that many spiritual people resent any attempt to convert them to a particular church or a particular system. But those same people will not resent you if you simply share a universal truth with them, and just allow them the freedom to do whatever they do with it.

So my beloved, consider this. Many of the people who go out and preach a religious or spiritual truth do so because they still have an ego-based need for acceptance. They are actually hoping that other people will accept what they say, so that they can feel accepted in themselves. For they do not have the love for themselves that Mother Mary spoke about.

Yet my beloved, you as spiritual people need to strive for that love, and when you have that love for yourself, when you know you are in that flow of the River of Life, you will not go out and preach your truth from the point of deficit, from the point of you needing something – whether it be acceptance or recognition or something else – from other people. You will be in the flow of the River of Life, as Saint Germain was talking about, where he said that you come from a state of being full, so you can give to all without needing to receive anything in return.

And when you do that, you have that unconditional love, where you freely share who you are, you share the truth that you have internalized, and you leave other people completely free, for it makes no difference to you whether other people accept or reject what you say.

My beloved, listen to what I am saying. When you are in the flow of the River of Life, you know that your purpose, your fulfillment, is to let your light shine. You are like the Sun, my beloved, who is just shining its light upon Earth, and the Sun is not in the least bit affected by what human beings do with the sunshine that reaches Earth. For the Sun continues to give, and when you have set yourself free from all sense of not being worthy, all sense of not loving yourself, you can have that freedom to just shine your light with other people. And you know that when you have expressed your truth, you have done your job, and surely by expressing that truth, you have multiplied your talents. And you know that you don't need to receive anything back from the people, for in you multiplying your talents, surely God will multiply what you have given to others and give you more.

And so you see, my beloved, you have escaped the consciousness of lack that springs from the fallen consciousness, where you think that you have to take something from Earth. Instead, you realize that God is the source of all good and perfect things, so why do you need something from other people when you can receive directly from the source. This, my beloved, is true spiritual freedom. And it is what Maitreya spoke about in the last chapters of his book. [Master Keys to Spiritual Freedom] It is what will change the religious debate on this planet. And it is indeed true that if you could change the religious debate, all others areas of society would begin to change as well.

Project a new vision of the world upon the Ma-ter light

Gautama Buddha, October 28, 2007

The revolution in consciousness
My beloved, the revolution is always a revolution in consciousness, for there can be no other way to change the physical. I know that in today's age this will sound strange to many people. But that is because your world view – which is based on scientific materialism and the perverted religions of the past – is so primitive that you actually believe that matter is separated from spirit, that mind is separated from matter. Despite the fact that your quantum mechanics has told you differently, Western civilization – because, primarily, of the influence of materialism, but also because of a subtle influence from orthodox Christianity – has not

been willing to take the philosophical consequences and realize that if the mind of a scientist creates the outcome of an experiment, then everything must be influenced by consciousness, which truly means that everything is consciousness.

Thus, everything is an outpicturing in matter of what is going on in consciousness. And thus, my beloved, I will give you a concept that will be difficult to grasp for the linear mind but there is value in stating it and throwing it into the mass consciousness, and into the minds of those who are receptive.

You see, my beloved, we have in other books given the concept of a movie projector, where the light from the light bulb flows through the film strip and is projected as images on the movie screen. We have said before, my beloved, that if you want to change the images on the movie screen, it is not efficient to work at the level of the screen. It is far more efficient to go to the projection room and change the images on the film strip. And this illustrates that if you want to change the physical conditions on Earth, it is not the ultimate to work by physical means, but it is far more effective to go to the cause and change the images in the collective consciousness that are simply being projected onto the matter light.

Yet, what I want to give you here is the further concept that when you think about how a movie works, my beloved, you realize that it is not really a moving picture. For the film strip has individual images, each one being only fractionally different from the previous one. And if you saw the pictures separately as still pictures, you could easily see the difference. But because they are projected in such rapid succession, your eyes cannot see the individual pictures and they blend together as one continual movement.

Well, my beloved, that is also what happens to your senses when you look at the matter world. You think that the matter world is a continuous presence and has a continuous existence. Yet my beloved, what your scientists used to believe in classical physics was that light was a continuous stream. But what was discovered in the precursor to the theory of relativity and quantum physics is that light is not a continuous flow, but is indeed quantized as tiny separate particles, called photons.

And so you see, my beloved, the image I want to give you is that the Earth really has no continuous existence. For at very rapid intervals, the physical Earth is like a movie that is projected onto the Ma-ter light. And your senses see it as something solid and something that changes very slowly. But in reality that image is changing in very small intervals that are simply projected so rapidly that you do not see the individual movements, but are fooled into thinking that the Earth has a continual existence and therefore is beyond your power to change.

But my beloved, do you not see that the pictures on the filmstrip are changing all the time? And as soon as the picture changes, the image on the movie screen will change instantly. So if instead of having a very small change between one picture and another – if instead you had a very big change – well then the image on the movie screen would instantly change, my beloved.

And so, it is that the current state of the Earth, the current state of limitation and suffering, is an image that is simply projected through the filmstrip of the collective consciousness. The light is provided by we of the Ascended Host who have vowed to serve the evolutions of Earth – and to have our light support their experimentation with free will – so they can have a continuous opportunity to outplay that free will by reaping the physical consequences of it.

And so you see, we are simply providing the driving force, but the actual physical conditions that you see on Earth are the projections of the images held in the collective consciousness. And that is why, my beloved, it is potentially possible to instantly remove all limitations, all suffering on Earth—if you could change the collective consciousness. And that is why, my beloved, there is always hope for the changing of any physical circumstance—if only the consciousness will change. And what you have indeed seen in the course of known history is a continual change in humankind's consciousness, a continual expansion.

Overcoming the lowest common denominator

I admit that at times this has been a very slow and gradual change, so that the individual images hardly varied. But you will see, my beloved, that in the last century the change has sped up and become much more rapid. And there is indeed a potential that this can continue or even accelerate beyond what most people can envision. And indeed beyond what some people can handle, for they cannot handle the change [especially the power elite who want to maintain their privileges and power].

But my beloved, is it right that the Earth should accommodate the lowest common denominator? Is it right that the Earth should continue to be held at an artificially low level in order to allow the lowest 10 percent of the lifestreams to remain in embodiment? Is it not time that we instead see the top 10 percent rise up to claim their rightful inheritance, realize that they are the meek who shall inherit the Earth—but in order to inherit it they must claim it, so that the Earth can spin faster and spin off those who will not adapt to change.

Well my beloved, it is indeed possible, as other masters have said, that the collective consciousness can go through a revolutionary shift, almost instantly at least as measured with historical time. And my beloved, we of the Ascended Host are of course ever hopeful that many more people, certainly many among the top 10 percent, will come to a recognition of our existence and of the teachings we have given, as you have done. But from a realistic viewpoint, it would be far too optimistic to hope that a large percentage of the population within the near future would come to accept the highly advanced world view that you have adopted. So we are not asking you to go out and seek to convert the entire population to that world view. Which is why we have talked about giving people universal principles, and so, naturally, we are always seeking to give you the tools that will help you in this quest.

And in this context let me say that this forthcoming book The Art of Non-War is indeed our latest effort in this ongoing process of making spiritual teachings and concepts more universal, more easy to understand for a wider audience. And so, I can assure you that we have great hopes that this book can indeed reach a wide audience and become somewhat the talk of the town that will contribute to a shift in the collective consciousness, where people begin to understand the nature of the dualistic mind and the ego. Thus coming to see that all of the things they don't like about their society, all of the things they don't like about history, can be traced back to one cause—namely the existence of the human ego and how it turns every idea into a dualistic idea that will inevitably create tension and conflict that so often leads to war.

And so, my beloved, if people in great numbers can come to realize and acknowledge these simple ideas – yet very profound ideas – put forth in this book, well I can assure you that we can greatly accelerate the movement away from war and the rumors of war and the potential for war. And indeed have a true state of peace that is not a forced peace, not based on the fear of what would happen if nuclear weapons were unleashed, but indeed is a peace that although based on understanding, it passes understanding. For people have gone beyond understanding but have actually come to experience what we in the book call "the Infinite" within themselves.

So, my beloved, take this book as an inspiration of how you can learn to express spiritual principles in a universal way that is very difficult for people to argue against with the dualistic mind, although, of course, the dualistic mind can argue against any idea expressed in words.

Yet it is possible to find a way to baffle the dualistic mind, as has been done in Zen Buddhism through the koans, as was done by Jesus in many of his koan-like statements. But you will see that it is possible to do this even in a contemporary language, where you can simply state a truth in such a way that the linear, analytical, dualistic mind is baffled, is shocked and therefore it does not know immediately how to respond. And therefore, there is a moment of silence, an interval of silence, in people's minds and that gives their Christ selves an opportunity to come in and help them actually feel in their hearts that there is a truth here that goes beyond what they have been taught and what they have believed so far.

And this then forms the basis for a new world view, a shift in perception. And as that world view grows and spreads, my beloved, the sky is literally the limit for how Western civilization can shift away from duality—away from using force to get everything, but shift into the abundance consciousness of realizing that nature is not our enemy, other people do not represent an enemy, and God is not the enemy. For indeed they could realize the truth in Jesus' words, "Fear not little flock, for it is the Father's good pleasure to give you the kingdom."

And why is this so? Because the Father has unconditional love for his offspring. And so, when you realize this, you realize that there are no conditions that can prevent you from having the abundant life that God wants you to have—unless those conditions are set up in your own individual mind or in the collective mind. Whereby you project these images of lack and suffering and limitation, instead of projecting the images of abundance that then immediately would be outpictured by the ma-ter light and be your new reality.

So this, my beloved, is how the Earth could shift into a different dimension. Not by some heavenly force doing it all for you, but by humankind providing better images through which the light from above can flow, thereby impressing itself and those higher images upon the ma-ter light.

Reconnect to your highest love and fulfill your divine plan

Saint Germain (2), December 15, 2007

Decide to be all you can be

So you see, my beloved, greater love has no man or woman than to lay down his life for a greater cause. So greater love have none of you than to lay down your comfortable lifestyles for the greater cause of bringing the Golden Age into embodiment.

So you see, my beloved, the reality is that poverty can be defined in different ways. I have talked about those who are trapped in extreme poverty, and all of you can truly see this—that there are millions of people on Earth who live in such poor physical conditions that they are trapped in both material and spiritual poverty. But everything starts in the mind, and so I would remind you that there are many more people who are trapped in a form of spiritual poverty, where they have at least some material abundance, but they think that is all there is to life.

And then I would go even further and say, "Well, who are the most poor people on this planet?" Well, those are the people that I partly talked about earlier today, where I said that there are many people who are partially awakened to the need for change—for they have been trapped in some intellectual pursuit of change through man-made ideologies or belief systems, not realizing that true change can only be brought through the oneness of Spirit and matter, the oneness of Father and Mother so that we close the figure-eight flow between above and below.

And so those that are the most poor are those who have the inner potential to be More, and to bring about a Golden Age, but who are trapped in some illusion of the outer mind that prevents them from expressing that potential. And thus, you who are the spiritual people might look in the mirror and say, "Am I also poor because I am not living up to my highest potential, being all that I can be?"

My beloved, listen to what I say – for I speak with a greater love than you will ever encounter on Earth – I am not coming to you to make you feel bad about yourself and your service and your life up until this point. I love you. I am coming to you precisely because I love you. And I want you to stop, to step back and to say, "Is my life truly in alignment with my divine plan? Am I fulfilling my highest potential, or is there More?"

And if you realize that there is more – and I can tell you that for each one of you there is More, it is only a matter of whether you are willing to separate yourself enough from the ego to acknowledge that there is More – well, my beloved, be willing to lay down your comfortable sense of life and change your life, shift your consciousness, shift your outer life to bring it into alignment with a highest vision you can see right now.

My beloved, you must understand that there is hardly any person who has ever come to this Earth with a full awareness of their divine plan. Not even Jesus had this full awareness, even though the idolatry of many Christians and even the idolatry of many New Age people – even some ascended master students – would make it seem as if he knew even from early childhood who he was and what his full mission was, having this or that ability to do supernatural things even as a child.

My beloved, hardly anyone has had a clear recognition of the fullness of their divine plan. For part of your divine plan is to demonstrate the path of becoming more, and the path of becoming more is precisely that you start where you are and you do something with what you have. You take what you have and you make it more. And then, as you have made it more, you will gain a higher vision of how to take what you now have and make that more. And that is how life progresses, my beloved.

Poverty is hatred of the Mother

Saint Germain, December 20, 2007

Understanding the fourth ray

Thus, my beloved, we now come to the fourth ray of purity, and it is represented by the white light. And you know what happens when you send a ray of white light into a glass prism, my beloved: you split it into all the colors of the rainbow. So you see, my beloved, the fourth ray is in the middle, with three rays before it and three rays after it. And thus, what happens to a new lifestream that descends into the matter sphere is that it must first be tested on the first ray and learn to express God Power. When it has some proficiency in God Power it will begin to be tested on the second ray and express Wisdom. And then it moves on to Love.

But you see, my beloved, the first three rays are, so to speak, the beginning of the path of initiation. And we know well that as a lifestream begins those first three rays, it has not yet attained Christhood, or even a certain degree of mastery. Therefore, my beloved, there is – in an ideal situation – a great deal of guidance that is offered to such a lifestream.

If the lifestream takes advantage of this guidance, then it will integrate the lessons of the first three rays and be well prepared for the initiations of the fourth ray, where it must begin to stand on its own. And thus, on the fourth ray of Purity, a lifestream cannot be tutored in every little detail, for it must of necessity show that it has integrated what it has learned as a result of its tutorship on the first three rays.

Thus, my beloved, you see that on the first three rays – when the lifestream experiments with expressing Power, Wisdom and Love – there is a great deal of forgiveness. So that, when a lifestream makes a mistake, well it is instantly forgiven and helped by the teacher to see its mistake, so that it can rise above it. That is, of course, a lifestream can be helped by the teacher – the true spiritual teacher – only according to its free-will choices and its willingness to learn from the mentorship of the teacher.

own choices is precisely how you learn, and therefore it is an opportunity, my beloved.

When you receive a return current from the cosmic mirror that is not pure according to your highest vision, then that is an opportunity for you to realize that what you sent into the cosmic mirror was not a pure impulse—and that is why the mirror reflects back an impure material manifestation. So you now have the opportunity to rise up, my beloved, and purify your co-creative efforts.

That is, of course, if you are willing to allow what comes back from the cosmic mirror to awaken you to the need to look in the personal mirror and do what Jesus said, namely look for the beam in your own eye — of where you have allowed impurities to gather in your eye – in your vision, in your mind – thus causing those impurities to form a colored film that inevitably colors your mind. And thereby colors everything you send into that cosmic mirror, making it inevitable that the mirror can only reflect back to you an impure manifestation.

Taking full responsibility on the fourth ray

So you see, my beloved, the fourth ray is the ray of God Purity and the ray of the white light of the Mother. And so what happens when a lifestream has built this momentum of misusing power, wisdom and love, and when the lifestream – when faced with the fourth ray initiations – refuses to look in the personal mirror, when the lifestream refuses to purify itself? Well my beloved, if the lifestream will not purify itself, there can be only one reason. And that is that that lifestream is not willing to take full responsibility for itself and its use of its creative power.

So my beloved, if you are not willing to take full responsibility and recognize the fact of life that what comes back to you in the material universe – in the world of matter, in the world of Mother – is a reflection of what you have sent out—well then, my beloved, if you will not take that responsibility what must you do? Very simple, my beloved, for if what comes back to you from the cosmic mirror is not your fault – because you are not willing to recognize that you could have sent out an impure impulse – well then, my beloved, it must be someone else's fault, must it not?

For you see, my beloved, this is one of the core issues of the ego. When something is not to living up to the ego's expectations of how the material world should be, then there must be something wrong and therefore it must be someone's fault. And if you are not willing to consider that it might be your fault – in the sense that you have used your co-creative abilities in an unbalanced manner – well then you must place blame outside yourself—on someone else.

And my beloved, who is that someone else? Well, it is quite simple. For you see, my beloved, it is precisely the white light of the Mother that forces you, so to speak, to face the initiations on the fourth ray. The initiation of whether you will raise your co-creative abilities to a higher level and use them to raise up the All, raise up all life, or whether you will use them to gather more to the separate self. Will you seek to gather more of the things of this world to the separate self? Or will you rise to the higher level of seeking to make everything in this world MORE – meaning More of God's Light, more of God's abundance, my beloved – and thereby raising up all life, even raising up the material sphere to the perfection of the Kingdom of God, as Maitreya explains in his book.

So, my beloved, it is precisely the white light that forces you to face the necessity to look at how you have used your co-creative abilities in expressing Power, Wisdom and Love. And it is the white light that gives you a sense of comeasurement. For, my beloved, is it not so that in most cultures on this planet white is associated with purity? When you do your laundry, do you not want it to be white, rather than gray or dirtied by other colors.

How hatred of the Mother begins

So you see, my beloved, when you rise to the initiations of the fourth ray, what will happen is that your spiritual teachers and your I AM Presence will release a greater amount of the white light of purity into your energy field. And this, my beloved, is much like shining a bright light into a dark room. Do you see, my beloved, that when the room – when your energy field – was still in the shadows – when it was not brightly lit – well it was more difficult to see what was pure and what was impure in your energy field?

It was more difficult to see where you had expressed power, wisdom and love in an impure manner and where you had expressed it in purity. And so this allowed your ego to hide in the shadows, so to speak, and find excuses for saying that an imbalanced expression was not really that bad, and therefore you did not have to face it and change it right now.

But when that white light of purity descends, my beloved, well you can no longer hide in the shadows. You are forced to take stock of yourself and see what is pure and what is impure. For you now have the white light as a sense of comeasurement for what true purity means, even what true power, what true wisdom, and what true love means. For as the white light shines into your energy field, it will naturally brighten the colors that are there, my beloved. For you know well that as the sun rises in the morning, well at first everything looks gray, but as the light intensifies, you now begin to see all of the colors of the flowers and the sky.

And so, my beloved, naturally the white light will make it easier for you to see where you have an impure manifestation of the blue color of God Power, an impure manifestation of the golden color of God Wisdom, and an impure manifestation of the pink ray of God Love. And thus, your ego cannot so easily deny the need for change.

But, of course, my beloved, if you are not willing to look in the mirror, then the ego always can present you with an easy way out. And that easy way out is to place blame on the white light itself, the white light of the Mother, my beloved. And thus, the reasoning from the mind of antichrist, which the ego believes and seeks to make you believe, is that it is not YOU who has imposed an impure image on the Ma-ter light. It is the light itself that has manifested an imperfect manifestation that now burdens you, or does not give you what you want. It is the Mother who is against you, and who is refusing to give you what you want.

And so, the reasoning is that the Mother is wrong, that there is something wrong with the Mother and that you should seek to use your creative abilities to control, even punish, the Mother. Rather than immersing yourself in the pure white light of the Mother, so that you can purify your energy field and have the clear colors of the first three rays shining through the brightness of the fourth ray, thereby expressing your co-creative abilities with a higher degree of selflessness.

So you see, my beloved, when you are not willing to look in the mirror and pass the initiation on the fourth ray, well then the inevitable outcome, my beloved, is what we call hatred of the Mother. For you see, my beloved, when you believe in the lie that the Mother is not merely reflecting back to you what you send out – but that the Mother is deliberately forcing you to encounter an imperfect manifestation – when you believe in that lie, well you will almost inevitably turn your fear into hatred of the Mother.

How Lucifer fell

For in hating the Mother, you can avoid looking in the mirror—seeing your own impurity. Instead of recognizing that the impurity is inside your own mind and energy field, you do what the ego does best—you project the impurity outside yourself, projecting it onto the Mother light, saying, "Oh this planet Earth is such a low place. There is such a lack of resources. There is such an imbalance in nature. Our bodies are so limited and manifest disease so easily. There is not enough money for everyone. There is not enough resources. There is not enough oil. Everything is so limited and restricted. And this is the Mother's fault, this is the fault of Mother Earth because she will not give us the abundant life."

And so you see, my beloved, you have an entire class of lifestreams that fell on the initiations of the fourth ray. Most of them fell in higher spheres, but it was the same basic initiation. And thus, you may know that Lucifer himself fell on the fourth ray, and he fell because of the pride of not being willing to look at his own impurities and therefore projecting those impurities on the Mother light, building up hatred of the Mother.

And you see, my beloved, this is where you need to understand how ingenious God's universe is designed, and how ingeniously the law of free will actually works. You see, my beloved, when a lifestream refuses to voluntarily look at the beam in its own eye, well then that lifestream has put itself beyond the reach of the true spiritual teachers of humankind.

We cannot reach that lifestream, for we work exclusively within the framework of the law of free will. And thus, my beloved, you realize that there is no point in that lifestream remaining in the mystery school. And that is why the lifestream then falls or descends into a lower sphere, or outside of the mystery school. And what happens to that lifestream is that it descends precisely into a sphere that corresponds to its level of consciousness.

So you see, my beloved, when a lifestream has hatred of the Mother, it will descend into the most dense level of the world of form, which is currently the material universe, where it encounters the lowest vibration of the Mother light—and therefore has an opportunity to learn by encountering precisely that which it has come to believe is responsible for all of its problems. And so you see, that by being forced, so to speak, to face that which it was not willing to face in the mystery school, the lifestream has the only remaining opportunity left open to it to pass its initiations—and overcome the false beliefs that caused it to fall in the first place.

The question, of course, is whether the lifestream will actually do so or whether it will continue to build upon the momentum of denial, thereby building up more and more hatred of the Mother—until its time runs out and there is no opportunity left for that lifestream to become MORE, making it necessary for the lifestream – the separate lifestream – to be dissolved in the final act of dissolution in the Court of Sacred Fire. Where the intensity of the white light of purity burns away all impurities that have been built up over what would be corresponding to millions of lifetimes on Earth.

Freedom means surrender into oneness

Saint Germain, December 29, 2007

For I AM the God of Freedom, my beloved, and I will not be slowed down by anyone. And thus, I move on—simply leaving those behind who are not willing to move on with me. This does not mean that I do not care for those I leave behind, my beloved. But it does mean that I care more for the greater cause of freedom, of building the Golden Age, which is a cause that is far greater than any organization or any individual, my beloved.

This is what you will see also when I was the Wonderman of Europe traveling around, seeking to work with the crowned heads of Europe who thought – each one of them – that they were the most important king on Earth, and wanted me to treat them according to that self-assessment, which of course sprang entirely from the ego. And thus, in some cases there were kings that would not work with me because I would not treat them as if they were the most important king. For I saw the bigger picture and the need for a unification of Europe—that surely went beyond what any single king could grasp at the time.

And so, my beloved, you who claim to be ascended master students should be smarter than this. You should be able to see beyond your own ego and its need to feel that you are more important than any other spiritual people on this planet. For, my beloved, we need to move beyond the relative dualistic game of comparison, of thinking that one teaching, one organization, one guru, one messenger is more important than anyone else. What IS most important on Earth is all of the people who have some attunement to the Ascended Host.

Receive a higher teaching on freedom

Well, my beloved, what is the essence of poverty? Well, it is that you are separated from God's abundance, my beloved. So the essence of poverty is separation.

Well, my beloved, what is the essence of anti-freedom? Well it is that you are separated from God, you are separated from oneness with God. And out of that illusion of separation spring countless other illusions that keep you trapped in a mental box, where you define borders around yourselves and say, "I am inside this mental box. All other people are outside that mental box. And God is somewhere way beyond that mental box." This, my beloved, is anti-freedom.

I know that in previous dispensations I and other masters have spoken about freedom, and the Flame of Freedom. But what we could give at that time was what the people were ready for. And so I come now to give you a higher teaching on freedom. For, my beloved, as I gave a higher teaching on service and saying that most of you had a limited view of service, well I can assure you that most of you also have a limited view of freedom.

What exactly does it mean to be free, my beloved? Well, the separate mind, the ego, defines freedom as the ability to do whatever it wants, to have whatever it wants, to have all of its needs fulfilled. And thus, you see, indeed, in human society, even in spiritual and religious movements, a certain attitude that if we can do whatever we want, then we are free. Meaning, to some degree, that if we can escape the consequences of our actions, then we are free.

And so, you see many spiritual people, my beloved, who have attempted to walk the spiritual path for the purpose of learning some magical formula, of finding some philosopher's stone, that will allow them to do whatever they want and escape the return current of the consequences of their actions. And they believe this is freedom.

But I tell you, my beloved, this is a completely perverted concept of freedom that springs from the consciousness of those who have fallen into duality and thus have left off from oneness with God. For it is freedom only for the separate self, my beloved. But that is not true freedom. For the separate self has no reality, no existence in God—and thus, how could it ever be free?

You see, one separate self can gain freedom only by taking freedom from one or more other separate selves. Which is why you saw – during the feudal societies – that one landlord had great freedom, materially speaking, but he had taken freedom from thousands of peasants who lived on his land and whom he treated as property. And this, of course, cannot be true freedom. For when you look at this – even with the logical, linear mind – you realize that you could not possibly have all people on Earth be landlords or emperors. For who is going to be the slaves that keep the emperors in power and in comfort?

This, of course, is not logically possible. So therefore, you need to rethink what it means to be free. And you need to realize that true freedom does not mean to escape the consequences of your actions. It means to actually acknowledge the reality that the physical universe is the cosmic mirror that sends back to you what you send out.

The separate self can never be free

So, my beloved, if you free your mind from the illusion of separation and the entire consciousness of seeking to gain something for the ego, for the separate self – if you free your mind from those illusions that spring from the consciousness of separation and lack – then you will begin to project into the cosmic mirror images and ideas that do not seek to raise up the separate self—but seek to raise up other people, to do something for humankind.

As was said earlier, you develop a global awareness, where you seek to raise the all, rather than the separate self. And when you do this, my beloved, the cosmic mirror will gladly and lovingly – as cycles go through the four levels of the material universe – reflect back to you exactly what you are sending out.

And thus, you will escape the limitations that are created by the separate self and its belief that, in order to gain for itself, it must take from others. For there is not enough wealth and abundance in the material world to go around for everyone. Thus, my beloved, if you will begin to shift your thinking and take a look at this – even with the outer logical mind – you can begin to see that what takes away your freedom is the illusion that it is possible to gain something by taking it through force. Instead of seeking to do what Jesus meant when he said, "Seek ye first the Kingdom of God and his righteousness, and all these things will be added unto you."

The Kingdom of God is within you, so you seek first that inner oneness with your own higher being. And when you attain that oneness with your own higher being, you begin to see that as you are connected to God, so are all other beings connected to God through their higher selves. And so you see that if you work to set other people free, then God will give you the multiplication of your efforts—which is beyond anything you could possibly attain by taking it through force in the material realm.

Literally, my beloved, the message that Jesus brought was the message that God is ready to give you infinite abundance—if you are willing to share that abundance with everyone else, instead of seeking to hoard it for the pleasure, or the sense of security, or power of the ego, the separate self.

You see, my beloved, what you realize when you begin to contemplate these concepts is precisely that there can be no true freedom in separation, my beloved. And why is this so? Where is freedom meant to be found? Well, freedom can be found in only one place and that is in oneness—oneness with your higher being, oneness with your fellow beings, oneness with your source, oneness with the Infinite as we call it in the new book [The Art of Non-War].

For only when you are one with the Infinite can you have infinite freedom. And only when freedom is infinite can it be truly free. For you see, my beloved, the concept of freedom that most people have on Earth is a dualistic concept, where freedom is always seen as being in opposition to bondage, or anti-freedom. And there are many people on Earth who are not able to even grasp the concept of infinite, non-dualistic freedom, freedom that has no opposite, my beloved, for it needs no opposite.

Understanding infinite freedom
In fact, I can tell you that some of you – and many spiritual people around the planet – have had glimpses of experiencing true non-dualistic freedom. But you have not been able to fully acknowledge or understand it with your outer minds, my beloved. Because your minds are still so focused on the dualistic polarity, where you think that in order to be truly happy, you have to know what it means to be truly unhappy. And thus, you can experience freedom only when you have experienced bondage, because you need the contrast in order to know what it really means to be free or happy.

But I tell you, my beloved, beyond this dualistic interplay of light and darkness, there is the reality of God, which we have often called bliss because once you start putting words on it you limit it. Because people immediately start projecting their dualistic concepts and images on it. Yet, my beloved, true freedom is true bliss that has no opposite.

And when you first experience it, you might not know what to do with that experience. And it literally takes some adjustment, especially of overcoming the linear thinking of the outer mind, before you realize that this is a state of freedom that is truly free because it can never have an opposite. So you can never be anti-free when you are in that state of Being, that state of flowing with the River of Life, what we call the flow of the IS.

You see, my beloved, what we desire all of you to have – all of you who are ascended master students, all of those who are in the top ten percent among humanity – we desire you to have that awareness, that experience, of the reality of God that is beyond the dualistic extremes. So that you no longer look at the world through the filter of duality, my beloved.

Save the world by saving yourself
My beloved, what we desire you to see is that there comes a point where focusing on the problems and the negatives actually becomes an excuse that the ego will use to get ascended master students to focus so much on changing world conditions that you simply say, whether subconsciously

or consciously, "I do not have time to work on my personal psychology, for I have to save the world for Saint Germain."

But you see, my beloved, how do you save the world for Saint Germain? You do so precisely by starting with yourself, by overcoming your own ego, so that you come into that oneness with your own higher being. So that instead of running around doing, doing, doing, you are instead centered in the peace, the higher bliss, of Being.

And therefore, you are the open door which no human can shut, because you have decided not to allow your ego to shut that door that is your connection to your higher self. And therefore, the light of that higher self, the Being of that higher self, can radiate through your lower form and anchor its light, its vibration, here in the physical octave. And this, my beloved, has a far greater impact than anything else you can do, including any amount of violet flame decrees or rosaries.

This is not to say that you do not need to take outer actions. But what we desire to bring you to, is the point where your outer actions do not spring from the outer mind, and the outer will, and the outer determination. They spring from the inner reality of who you are, so your outer actions are based on Being. You are Being as you are doing. That will have the maximum impact on this planet!

Integrating the teachings on the Eighth Ray

Saint Germain, December 30, 2007

Saint Germain I AM, and I come to discourse with you on what it means to gain mastery on the seven rays—and thereby qualify to move on to the eighth ray.

My beloved, in previous dispensations we have given the concept of the secret rays. And we have spoken about them in vague terms. You might wonder, my beloved, if these rays are secret and cannot be spoken about, why mention them at all, why not simply leave it unspoken?

Well, my beloved, there is a test built into this. For we of the Ascended Host are skilled teachers, and we have observed humankind for a very long time—thus knowing what it takes to give people the tests that are appropriate at different levels of the path. And so you see, my beloved, by talking about something that is secret, something that is reserved only for special initiates – as we have done in a number of different religions and organizations – well then we give people the test of pride—whether they will seek that which is secret with an inordinate desire to elevate themselves in comparison to others. Because they now have some knowledge that most people do not have, and thus these initiates can feel special, my beloved.

Real students and false students

And thus you see, my beloved, the purpose behind doing this is the simple fact that there are two types of people who come to the spiritual path and who come to spiritual teachers. There are those who are the genuine students, who are seeking to grow, who are seeking to overcome the ego by internalizing the lessons of the teacher.

But then there are those students, my beloved, who do not have a serious intention of letting go of the ego or the separate self. In fact, they come to the teacher – be it a true or a false teacher – in order to elevate that separate self, in order to reinforce the belief that the separate self can be saved, can somehow be perfected or justified, so that it can gain entry into heaven.

And so you see, my beloved, you might have had a somewhat one-sided or naïve view of the spiritual path or of the Ascended Host and how we teach. You might have thought that all people who come to the spiritual path must be genuine students. But we of the Ascended Host can see through all of the smokescreens that people's egos have built over many lifetimes.

And thus, we see the inner condition, the condition of the heart—of whether that person has actually genuinely locked in to what the spiritual path is all about. Or whether that person has not yet understood the essence of the path, namely that it is to rise above the separate self— rather than somehow perfecting that separate self.

Now, my beloved, we of the Ascended Host do not judge people according to human judgments. We welcome virtually anyone who has a potential to change. And thus, we often allow students to come into our organizations—and in some organizations we have allowed those students to attain high positions in the organization, even though we see that they have not yet truly committed to the true path of overcoming the ego. And we see very well that they are using our outer teachings and the outer organization in order to seek to create for themselves a position that makes the ego feel important, feel special, feel elevated above others. Because they have been in the teachings for so long, they have studied so much, they have decreed so much, they have had contact with the messenger or they have this or that outer position, my beloved.

A movement in which no person is more important than another

And so, I know that some of you have come into contact with ascended master organizations and been somewhat shocked by the fact that you find these ego-centered people who are often abusing their power or treating others unkindly, which you did not expect to find in an organization that has the profound teachings of the Ascended Host.

But you see, my beloved, as Jesus has explained, our previous dispensations were designed to help people master the initiations of the Piscean age. And one of the initiations of the Piscean age, my beloved, is precisely that you need to overcome the illusion, as I have already mentioned—that one person can be more important than another.

This, my beloved, is why you see that in an Aquarian organization we do not set up a hierarchy that allows some people to climb to a position, where they can feel they are important for outer reasons. We seek to go beyond the Piscean initiation – and the Piscean focus on the outer hierarchy – and establish a new movement that sets a pattern, my beloved, where no one is more important than others and where the ego does not have room to hide behind outer rituals and outer positions.

For it is a movement that recognizes the subtle games of the ego, and where people are not afraid to speak out and expose those games. Rather than the pattern we have seen throughout the Piscean age of those who are of lower rank always bending the knee and refusing to speak out against those who are of higher rank, thereby creating a situation where – once ego-centered people have attained leadership positions in an organization – it is virtually impossible to remove them from those positions. And therefore, the organization starts going into a downward spiral that either leads to it being split into multiple factions, or to it gradually dying out by losing its members as it has lost the sponsorship of the Ascended Host.

Now, my beloved, you must understand that we allow people of all kinds to come into our teachings and movements, even this one. For we give people an opportunity. And people deserve an opportunity for many reasons that often go back many lifetimes, my beloved. And thus, you might look at a person's outer personality and say that this person has some rough edges, but nevertheless when you see behind the outer personality, you see that that person still deserves an opportunity to be in contact with an ascended master teaching.

So, my beloved, do not judge based on human judgment. But on the other hand, do not be passive and let someone abuse you. Find that middle way, where you do not judge, but you are – on the other hand – non-attached to other people's reactions, and therefore have no compunctions about speaking out and bringing to someone's attention that they are playing an ego game.

Why some fail the test of pride

So, my beloved, you must understand that my purpose for bringing this to your attention is to show you that throughout the history of ascended master organizations, there has been a certain percentage of the students who came into contact with the organization and who failed the test of pride. The test of overcoming pride by seeing it as pride, and thereby surrendering themselves into the humility that really is the oneness with God, the oneness with all life.

For, my beloved, when you surrender your separate self into the oneness with your infinite self, well then you see that it is meaningless to create value judgments based on the beliefs of the separate self. And thus it is meaningless to talk about one person being better or more important than another. For truly all are of equal value in the eyes of God.

So what I desire you to understand from this is precisely that until you have overcome the subtle test of pride, you cannot even begin to grasp the concept of the secret rays, the concept of the rays that are beyond the seven rays that have been known to humankind for a long time. For you see, my beloved, it is actually possible to walk the path of mastery of the seven rays while still having some ego left, having some pride left, even using some of the things you learn on each of the seven rays to build up the ego and the sense of superiority.

It is even possible, my beloved, to attain some mastery on the seven rays and thereby attain a certain mastery over the matter realm – over the Ma-ter Light – being able to manifest certain outer, visible phenomena, such as psychic phenomena, psychic abilities, the opening of the third eye, or even an ability to, in certain ways, manipulate matter.

And you see that there is a certain small percentage of students throughout the world who have attained some mastery in this respect. And thus, they can produce a phenomenon that might impress the uninitiated, the unawakened, for they look only for the outer phenomenon but do not look beyond to the quality of the heart. And thus they do not see the selfishness, the self-centeredness of the person who is seeking to build him- or herself up by claiming or demonstrating some ability beyond the normal.

See the inner mastery beyond outer mastery
So what I desire you to see here, my beloved, is that as you walk the path of attaining mastery over the seven rays, it is essential for you to realize that walking the path of mastery does not simply mean that you attain an outer mastery of the seven rays. It means that you also attain an inner mastery, whereby you actually come to see that the seven rays are not separate—that you actually cannot even view the seven rays as a linear phenomenon.

I know, my beloved, that when we gave the concept of the seven rays, it was unavoidable that the analytical mind would look at this as a linear phenomenon. There is the first ray, the second ray, the third ray and so on. But you see, my beloved, the spiritual world is not linear—it is spherical, it is One.

It cannot be separated into neat little categories that the analytical mind can then label and categorize and organize into a system. For you see, my beloved, what we are attempting to help you realize in this latest invocation [Creative Freedom of Will] and in the forthcoming invocations is precisely the need to go beyond a mechanized view of the seven rays and lock in to the fact that the seven rays are creative qualities, not mechanical qualities.

Beyond a linear view of the rays
And thus, my beloved, the reality here is that when you start the path of initiation on the seven rays, you might start out on the first ray of will.

But when you have passed that initiation of will, you do not simply leave the first ray behind and then move on to the second ray as a completely separate initiation.

My beloved, I know – again – that the linear mind creates certain images, and so many of you have come to believe that when you are studying on the first ray, well then you are studying under the master MORE, or El Morya as he used to be named. And thus, you go to the retreat of Master MORE. And then, when you move on to the second ray, you study under that master, and go to that master's retreat, and so on through the seven rays.

But you see, my beloved, these are images that we have given you because humankind was still so trapped in the linear mind. But the reason I am giving you this teaching is that so many of you who have been willing to study the teachings we have given on the AskRealJesus website, and who have been willing to give the rosaries, and thus you have been prepared. Perhaps you knew this, perhaps you were not aware of it, but you have been prepared to step beyond the linear mind and reach for a more spherical understanding of the spiritual reality and the spiritual path.

And thus, my beloved, we need you to step up and realize that although there are seven rays that have certain qualities, the rays are not separate. They are not isolated from one another, they are all intertwined. So you see, my beloved – again because of the limitations of words – let us just say that a student begins studying on the first ray. But you see, my beloved, on the first ray you find embodied all of the other six rays.

So you are not simply studying will or willpower, you are studying willpower with the shade of will, willpower with the shade of wisdom, willpower with the shade of love, purity, vision, service and freedom. So in order to pass the initiations on the first ray, you have to have some concept of and mastery over the other rays as well.

And then, my beloved, when you do pass these initiations that are focused on the first ray and move on to the second ray, it does not mean that you leave the first ray behind. It means that you take with you what you have learned on the first ray and incorporate those lessons on the second ray, where you now begin studying wisdom with the shade of will, wisdom with the shade of wisdom, wisdom with the shade of love, and so on.

Chapter 6:
Ego Teachings, 2008

Let 2008 be a year of positive change

Mother Mary, January 1, 2008

And so, my beloved, before the year 2012, it is necessary that humankind comes to a recognition of the Divine Mother and the importance of unifying the Divine Mother and the Divine Father. And this must begin in the year 2008 with a serious recognition that the big monotheistic religions have become completely unbalanced by ignoring the Divine Mother, by putting women down, and even making women responsible for the fall. Which is, as we have explained before, not a reality but really – to be quite honest with you, my beloved – an extreme outcome of the male ego's refusal of responsibility, thus projecting guilt and responsibility for the fall upon women, instead of acknowledging that it is part of the nature of every human being – male or female – that is responsible for the fall into duality.

And thus, my beloved, you see the deplorable situation that those who are trapped in the mindset of the monotheistic religions, especially the male members of those religions, are not willing or able to look at the beam in their own eyes and cast out that beam. And precisely because they will not look at that beam, they go into a state of male pride, my beloved, where they feel that the only way out of a particular situation is to attack and destroy those that they now project as being enemies. Instead of recognizing that the enemy is, as the popular saying goes: "We have seen the enemy, and it is us." For it is the ego that is the real enemy, not other human beings.

And so, my beloved, we look forward to, in 2008, a growing awareness that there is a serious flaw in the monotheistic religions. And that it must be corrected in this age by a new awareness of the feminine aspect of God, as a counter-balance to the misuse of power in the name of control that you have seen outplayed in all three of the major monotheistic religions—that has resulted in so many wars, such as the crusades and many other atrocities, including modern-day terrorism.

So, my beloved, hold the matrix that there will be an awakening, a growing awareness, of the Divine Feminine and the importance of incorporating the Divine Feminine into all aspects of one's religious and spiritual life, my beloved. Which of course includes giving men and women completely equal status in any true religion, so that women can hold any position and perform any task in that religion and its hierarchy. For you see, my beloved, men cannot by themselves get out of the trap of a male-dominated religion. They need women to help as a balance, to literally save them from themselves and their focus on the masculine aspect of God, which inevitably leads to an abuse of power even in the name of God or in the name of some greater good.

And this, my beloved, is, of course, the lie that has been the justification for so many atrocities. And you will see – if you take an honest look at history, my beloved – that men are more prone to falling prey to this lie that the ends can justify the means. Whereas women are more sensitive to life and therefore often will not accept that it is acceptable to kill human beings in order to bring about some supposedly greater good. For they see that the killing is always wrong and thus cannot be justified by any cause, no matter how just it might appear to the male ego.

...

You need to hold the matrix, my beloved, that women in the Islamic world will finally wake up and begin to make their voices heard. For again, the changes that need to happen in the Islamic world are so dramatic that they will not come from the men who are blinded by the male ego—of thinking that their monotheistic religion is the only true religion, and that their approach to that religion is the only true approach. So it is only the women – and a small percentage of the men who have attained balance – who have the potential to speak out and bring about balance, a more balanced approach.

This, my beloved, is of course an issue that will require major prayer support from those outside the Islamic world. For my beloved, what was it precisely you saw in the recent assassination in Pakistan? It was not so much an assassination of a particular politician, but an attempt to assassinate the influence of women in politics and religion in the Islamic world. It was an attempt to stop the moderating, balancing influence of the female element in the Islamic world. And to continue the several thousand year old cycle of systematically suppressing not just women in a physical sense, but actually suppressing the Divine Feminine. And thereby creating imbalance after imbalance, conflict after conflict, where there seems to be no purpose, there seems to be no end in sight—but it is simply the male ego having become a closed system, and therefore creating one self-destructive situation after another, not being able to stop it.

The kingdom of God is at hand— through the union of the Divine Father and the Divine Mother

Jesus, March 23, 2008

Greetings, my beloved, on this Easter Morning—meant to symbolize my resurrection from the grave, from the tomb. But yet I, Jesus, did not come to this Earth to symbolize this for myself, I came to symbolize the potential – for all human beings – to let the human self, the mortal self, die. And thereby be resurrected – not into a new physical life or spiritual life in some higher realm – but to be resurrected, my beloved, into a new sense of identity, where you no longer deny the reality that you are a co-creator with God.

Thus, you acknowledge that the kingdom of God is within you, that you are one with your father, that your father has worked hitherto, and that you are willing to work by being the co-creator that you were sent here to be. So that you can play a part in bringing the kingdom of God to Earth. This is the purpose for which I came, this is the purpose for which I went through the physical events of the crucifixion, my death on the cross—in order to symbolize what is possible for all human beings spiritually, my beloved.

Christ unifies the Divine Father and the Divine Mother

For you see, 2000 years ago, it was indeed necessary to give people physical, visible, outer manifestations, or they would have not been able to lock into the potential for overcoming death, the consciousness of death. But of course, in giving those outer manifestations, it was foreseeable and inevitable that many people would focus on the outer manifestations, failing to see the hidden symbolism behind them, and thereby failing to see the universal aspects of my mission and message, thinking that it only applied to the Jews, thinking that certain things only applied to me, or that certain things only applied to Christians.

For truly, my beloved, the Christ consciousness is universal. The entire idea of the Christ Consciousness, my beloved, is that it unifies the material and the spiritual. It unifies what you might call the Divine Father, and the Divine Mother, so that there is no separation between the Creator and its creation. For of course, as it is stated in the Gospel of John, without him was not anything made that was made.

And that is precisely why the kingdom of God is within you, because God – God's being, and God's Presence – is embedded within everything, my beloved. And it is only a religion that is based on separation that could have turned Christianity into a monotheistic religion, thereby raising up the graven image of the external God. The angry, remote being in the sky, looking down upon you, ready to judge you for any transgression and send you to a hell for all eternity.

My beloved, it is time that the Christian people, those who call themselves Christians today, wake up to the reality of my true message—that I did not come to create another religion that denies their Christ potential, as the Jewish religion did at the time (and still does, for that matter). I came to awaken all people to the potential to find the kingdom of God within you, and thereby become an extension of that kingdom on Earth, the co-creator who co-creates that kingdom and brings it into manifestation. Thereby giving the abundant life to all people, both the abundant material life and the abundant spiritual life.

God sees no difference between spiritual and material

For you see, my beloved, in God's mind, in God's vision, there is no difference between the material and the spiritual. This is an illusion created from the duality consciousness, the consciousness of separation that was brought to this planet by the fallen beings from higher spheres, but that has also been espoused by many people on this Earth. And you see, my beloved, only the duality consciousness makes it possible for the ego to exist. And the duality consciousness also gives the ego the potential for creating the illusion that the ego has attained what it craves the most, namely some kind of superior status, compared to other people on Earth.

And that, my beloved, is precisely why so many people in so many different areas of the world – and in so many cultures and religions – will not let go of the duality consciousness. This even applies to those who call themselves Christians. They will not let go of the duality consciousness, for if they were to let go of it, they would have to realize and recognize that the salvation I brought to this Earth is not exclusive to themselves, to the members of their own particular little church—that they have defined for themselves, thinking that they can thereby exclude all others from being saved.

So my beloved, what does it then take to overcome that duality consciousness? Well my beloved, it takes a recognition, a realization that God the Father was never separated from God the Mother. For you see, what has happened in the duality consciousness is that you have created these gender roles, and you have created these images – dualistic images that makes it almost impossible for us to communicate the reality, the spiritual reality. For when we say a word, you immediately start – you meaning the people on Earth – to impose your dualistic images upon them.

So when I say "God the Father," immediately people project an image based on the gender roles that have been defined in human society. And when I say "God the Mother," they project another image based on their image of women. But those images are both dualistic, are both unbalanced, and thus they cannot lead you to the correct understanding of what it actually takes to be saved as the Christians call it. Which truly means that you enter the kingdom of God, which as I said is within you, as the symbol for the fact that the kingdom of God is not a physical state, is not a spiritual state—it is a state of consciousness.

It is not that you have to travel somewhere physically in order to enter the kingdom of Heaven. It is not even that you have to shed the body and ascend to some spiritual realm in order to enter the kingdom of Heaven. The message I came to bring to Earth was embodied in the saying I preached in my early days, where I said, "The Kingdom of God is at hand." Meaning you can experience it right now by entering the state of consciousness that is the Kingdom of God.

And what is that state of consciousness? It is the state where you have overcome the illusion of this world, the illusion created by the prince of this world, so that you overcome the illusion that God in the Father aspect, in the Alpha aspect, could ever be separated from God in the Mother, Omega aspect. For you see my beloved, it is true that there are two aspects of God. There is the one Creator which is the Infinite, which is in-divided, in-divisible. But yet that infinite Creator has expressed itself in the world of form, but in so doing has expressed itself as form, has embedded its own Being in form, has created everything out of its own Being. And therefore, even though there is still an aspect of God that is the undivided Creator, nevertheless God has also divided itself into the world of form, the Ma-ter light that has taken on form.

The role of Christ is to unify Spirit and matter

So you see that God the Father is not separated or distinct from God the Mother in the way you think of it, based on gender roles on Earth. God the Mother is another expression of God the Father, and your role as self-aware beings in the matter realm is to awaken to the reality that you are extensions of God the Creator. And thus, you can be the open doors for God the Creator to bring its kingdom into manifestation on Earth. But you can be those open doors only when you overcome the sense of separation from your source, from your Creator, so that you finally say, "I and my Creator are One." And you recognize that you were never separated in reality.

For my beloved, if God is infinite, it must mean that the Creator is everywhere, so how could you ever be separated from the Creator, separated from your source? It cannot happen, except as an illusion created in the mind that is based in separation.

...

So you see, my beloved, that is why I said that the Kingdom of God is within you. For as long as you picture God as the remote being in the sky, you will never obtain union with that God. You will only obtain that union when you find the God that has expressed itself as You – as form – and you acknowledge your union with that God. Then you overcome the sense of separation.

Then the masculine and feminine come together in perfect union, in perfect harmony. Then the inner has become the outer, and the outer has become the inner, as is quoted in the book of Thomas—and then you overcome that separation. Now you know who you are, now you know why you are here. And at that moment, you are reborn, my beloved, as I attempted to explain to Nicodemus—who could not understand it because he could not separate himself from the linear, analytical mind based on duality and separation.

But what did I say, my beloved? "No man can ascend back to heaven save he that descended from heaven." Only the conscious self can ascend back to heaven. And it can only ascend back to heaven when it realizes that it was never separated from heaven, it was never separated from its source, for it is an extension of the Creator's own Being.

That is when you are reborn into realizing who you always were, who you always have been. But this does not mean that you then disappear, for it now means that you can take the individuality you have created in the world of form and raise it up and resurrect it so that it becomes one with the divine individuality anchored in your I AM presence. But in order for that to happen, you must let the unreal individuality – the individuality that is based on separation and duality, the mortal human self, the ego – you must let that identity die on the cross by giving up the ghost—the ghost that is some sense that you are separated from God.

And when you finally give up that ghost, then the human self will die. Then you can be reborn into knowing who you are, and then the Divine Mother and the Divine Father will come into perfect union in your being, and you will be as Above so below. You will be here below all that you are Above.

Overcome your grand illusions to find a higher level of service

Mother Mary, June 27, 2008.

See the cosmic perspective
So you see, my beloved, we who are one with the Divine Mother, we who recognize ourselves as expressions of the unexpressed God – as God in form, as God in mater-realization – we, my beloved, see the cosmic perspective. So we see that when a person on a small planet called Earth represents the Divine Mother, then the purpose of that person being in embodiment is not to be the leader of a particular religion, but to serve the greater cause of raising the awareness of the self-aware co-creators. Even those who have forgotten who they are and therefore are not strictly speaking self-aware. But who nevertheless have the potential at any moment to switch back into self-awareness, the awareness of the self as a spiritual being, as an extension of God.

And thus, our purpose is always to facilitate that growth in consciousness that is the ultimate purpose of the world of form. The growth that we fully realize can only – only – happen through free will. For it cannot be forced, my beloved. Self-awareness, the expansion of self-awareness cannot be forced from outside the self. It must come from within the self.

And thus we recognize that after beings lost their way, then they started outpicturing all kinds of manifestations on Earth that were not in alignment with their highest potential—the immaculate concept that we hold. Yet, in our infinite and unconditional love, this did not cause us to go into a negative feeling of anger, frustration, or even wanting to blame or punish. We simply accepted what was. For we always accept what is - as an outplaying of free will.

And thus, our concern is then how we can help a lifestream that has started descending the spiral staircase come to the turning point and again start ascending. And as such, we must meet people wherever they have chosen to descend in consciousness. And we do so with no judgment, with no fear, anger, blame—all the negative human emotions.

And my beloved, why do we not have such emotions? Because as was said earlier – which you surely recognize was an inspiration from me – we do not have any "shoulds" or "should-nots." The word "should" is not in our vocabulary.

Do you need to always have opinions?

For you see, my beloved, when you truly, fully, unconditionally accept free will, you do not even have an opinion about what people should or should not do with their free will. You set them free to experiment and we, as the representatives of the Divine Mother, allow self-conscious beings to outpicture whatever they want to outpicture, allowing our light to take on the form that they think they need for some reason or another.

Often, my beloved, it is because they are blinded by the ego, which only sees itself and cannot possibly see the cosmic perspective that we see. And thus, the ego is focused on itself—and our focus is on helping the conscious self of that person see that the ego is trapped in dualistic lies and illusions, and that the Conscious Self truly does not need the ego.

But yet, what does it take for the conscious self to come to that realization? Well, sometimes it takes that a lifestream outpictures certain manifestations that from a human perspective might seem negative or selfish. But they are nevertheless necessary for the lifestream to realize that this is not truly what it needs. This is not fulfilling its true needs, its true longing for something more to life, the longing that the ego can never share and cannot understand but can recognize is there.

And thus, the ego seeks to compensate for it by forcing the conscious self to believe that it needs something in this world. And thus, the person then seeks to attain that something, whatever it may be, and only – in many cases – when that something has been attained, will the conscious self awaken and realize, "No, this did not complete me, this is not what I was seeking, there must be something more to life."

And then – often – it happens that the ego manages to convince the conscious self that although what it previously told it that it needed was not the real thing, then surely this other thing in the matter world will satisfy the conscious self's longing. And sometimes it takes many lifetimes before the conscious self awakens and says, "Maybe what I am truly longing for is something that I cannot find in this world? Maybe I can never attain a sense of completeness from anything in this world, maybe there is something beyond that world. And maybe I should start looking for it?"

And that, my beloved, is when the lifestream comes to the turning point. It has reached the lowest level on the spiral staircase to which it needs to descend. And now it can pause, it can start shifting its gaze from the self-centeredness of the ego to a broader perspective. It can start looking up the spiral staircase and realize that perhaps it can find what it is seeking by ascending the staircase—since it now is beginning to realize that it might never find it by descending the staircase.

You no longer remember what it was like to be blind

And so you see, my beloved, many of you who are spiritual people and have reached that turning point many, many lifetimes ago – or perhaps some of you did not even have to descend to a low point – so many of you can no longer remember how it was to be so trapped in the ego's illusions that you were always looking for completion or security or belonging in the material world.

And thus it is difficult for you to understand and show patience for those around you that you see outpicturing conditions that you can clearly see will only limit themselves and can never lead to any kind of fulfillment. And you are of course right, but you are not right when you cross the subtle line of thinking that because you can see it, others should also be able to see it.

For you must realize, my beloved, that the reason why you can see something is because you have come to an inner realization. Yet these other people have not yet come to that inner realization, and your inner realization has no effect on someone else. And thus, what unfortunately happens to many sincere lifestreams – even many who descended to Earth for the purpose of seeking to raise the consciousness of humankind – is that they get lost in the illusions, they get seduced by the illusions of duality, the original illusions of the original fallen angels who started believing that it would be better if they could override free will and force people to be saved.

And thus, you start believing, my beloved, that other people should start living their lives according to your inner realization. And thus, you become caught up in the game that you see in most mainstream religions, of seeking to want to change people's outer behavior, or outer beliefs, instead of following what has always been the true path of the

Ascended Host—namely seeking to help people attain the inner realization that is the only key to their progress and growth.

Do you see, my beloved, the fundamental difference between the approach taken by the Ascended Host and the approach taken by the fallen beings who are seeking to control? And my beloved, many of them actually believe they are doing this for a greater cause. They are doing it because it is right, it is in the best interest of all the people. It is even in the best interest of the unfoldment of God's plan. For God simply cannot understand his own plan and his own creation. For surely these fallen beings understand it better than the Creator itself.

Beware of the ego's subtleties

And this is then the ultimate blindness of the ego. Yet I must tell you that this consciousness – which is essentially the consciousness that the ends can justify the means – is very subtle, very persuasive. And it is very pervasive in religious and spiritual movements, even in Ascended Master organizations, my beloved.

If you study the organizations that we have sponsored in the last century alone, you will see a very clear tendency for the members to believe that they belong to some superior teaching. And therefore, it was only in the best interest of the people, and of God's plan, and of the plan of the Ascended Host, if others were gently forced to see the validity of their teaching, even holding the vision that everyone on Earth was converted to their teaching.

Yet failing to see that this was simply their egos, playing the ultimate trick of wanting to convert every human being on Earth to its own belief system, thereby thinking it could prove that this was the one true, absolute, infallible belief system on Earth. A fallacy, of course, which the conscious self can never be fully satisfied with. Nevertheless, the conscious self can be seduced into pursuing this cause for a very long time before it starts realizing that this is not actually what it is seeking. For it starts realizing that there must be more to God than what can be captured in any belief system on Earth, my beloved.

And thus, we look to you who are part of this new initiative, to be wiser. And I do not say this in order to encourage a sense of superiority, but I do say it as a test as to whether you will use it to build a sense of superiority. But we do look to you, who have been given a more advanced teaching, to be wiser than previous students in not building the sense of superiority, the sense that you have a superior teaching and that all others should – by force if necessary – be converted to that teaching.

Knowing the Way of the Cosmic Christ

For we look to you to see, my beloved, that when Jesus made the statement "I am the way, the truth, and the life. No man cometh unto the Father, but by me," then, my beloved, this too was a test to see if those who followed Christ would build that sense of superiority, would allow the ego and the false teachers to turn the movement of Christianity into one more religion based on the concept that this is the only true one.

And so you see, we look for you to acknowledge that when Jesus made such statements, and others that are not recorded in the Bible, my beloved, that he was speaking as a representative of the Cosmic Christ, the universal Christ mind. And thus, when he said, "I am the way, the truth and the life," it was the Cosmic Christ speaking through him. And thus the universal Christ mind is the way, the truth, and the life, my beloved.

You who have been given a teaching, should not fall prey to the trap of thinking that you should turn this teaching into a system, and that system is now the only true way. For what is the true way? Well, it is the consciousness of Christ, the spiritual consciousness, the consciousness of the Divine Mother, of the Divine Father, and of the Holy Spirit, my beloved.

And so, you recognize, I trust, that this is the consciousness that is the Way. And it is the potential in every lifestream to shift its sense of identity, to tune in to that universal consciousness, realize that it is an extension of the One Being, of the Creator, and thus overcome separation and duality.

That, my beloved, is the Way. And that way cannot be followed if you think that you have now found or defined some ultimate belief system on Earth, and thus all you need is to follow the prescripts of that belief system until you are somehow magically saved at some future time.

And thus, my beloved, the true way is the Path of Oneness. Oneness with your higher being, with your Creator, with your spiritual lineage Above. And oneness here below, between people in embodiment, who no longer see themselves as human beings, but as the spiritual beings that you truly are.

...

And every time a Being ascends from Earth, that Being adds its own momentum to that collectiveness of the Holy Spirit, that flow of the Holy Spirit. Jesus did so, Krishna did so, the Buddha did so. All beings who have ascended have added their momentum to it, increasing it every time, making it easier for people to tune in to that Holy Spirit, my beloved. And therefore receive a portion of the Spirit that allows you to know truth from within and allows you to go out and speak that truth with the power that has the power to awaken people from their blindness, to shake them out of their blindness and thus give them an impetus for that inner realization.

You see, my beloved, that this does not force people to have that inner realization. But it gives them the foundation for having it if they are open and willing to have it. And thus, the power of the Holy Spirit can cut through the density of the collective consciousness, the density of a person's own past momentums, so that the person is shaken and therefore is, so to speak, in an interval in time—put on pause. The person's mind is put on pause, and now the person has a moment to tune in within and ask if there is more to understand about life, more to experience about life, than the person's ego-based, fear-based dualistic belief system.

...

How to have discernment

And so you need to have discernment, my beloved, so that you know what is the Holy Spirit and a false spirit. And of course, many things can be used to gradually build your discernment, including considering whether a spirit seeks to make you feel superior to others. For then you know that it cannot be the one Holy Spirit, but only a dualistic spirit.

But you also need, my beloved, to make a critical assessment of yourself, to look in the mirror, to look for the beam in your own eye. For I tell you, my beloved, what makes you susceptible to the lower spirits is your attachment to one of your ego's desires, which then makes you vulnerable to hearing what you and your ego want to hear in order to fulfill that desire.

And thus, many of you have certain false concepts about the spiritual path, about your role on Earth, such as I expounded upon earlier, about you thinking it is okay to force people into the one true religion for their own good. If you have such desires, my beloved, or even a desire to be seen as a savior of the people, perhaps even THE savior of the people, well then you cannot hear the Holy Spirit, my beloved.

For what will the Holy Spirit tell you? It will tell you how to overcome duality and enter into oneness. For the Holy Spirit is an extension of those who have walked that Path of Oneness. And thus, it will expose all illusions in your being. Not all at once, but as you can handle it, and as you are willing.

And thus, my beloved, if you have those self-centered desires of wanting to raise up yourself or do some ultimate service for God – thinking that God will reward you and make you an important person, either on Earth or in Heaven – well then you will not hear the Holy Spirit when it whispers to you as the still small voice within. You will hear the loud voice of a spirit who will tell you that this is how you can achieve your desire, this is how you can fulfill God's cause—by doing this or that outer thing, my beloved, achieving some kind of glory or recognition from the world.

Be not deceived by your own desires

And so you see, you are deceived by your desires, your attachments, that center around raising up the separate self, rather than letting the separate self die, seeking only to raise the All. But you see, my beloved, the All is also in you, so there is a certain validity to raising up God in yourself—for how can you help raise up God in all life if you have not first done it in yourself. But you see that when you raise up the All in yourself, it is fundamentally different than seeking to raise up the separate self.

And so, my beloved, I must tell you that the key to attaining this discernment is to strive for balance in all things. And this is where some of you could make great progress on your path, by striving for balance, by being willing to acknowledge where you have been out of balance, where you have attained unbalanced desires of seeking to raise up the separate self, for some grand scheme or another.

Perhaps even thinking that you are destined to be a messenger or a representative of the Ascended Host, my beloved. And thus listening to the false spirits who tell you that there is a shortcut to attaining this status, where you do not need to expose the beam in your own eye, even though all other representatives of the Ascended Host have had to do so. No, you are special, so you do not need to follow that path of discipline that Jesus demonstrated. For perhaps, maybe you are even more important than Jesus, you are higher than Jesus, you are more spiritually evolved. Or whatever the ego and the false teachers will whisper in your ear, my beloved.

And if you have an unbalanced desire, you might begin to believe this and entertain grand visions of what should happen – what SHOULD happen – my beloved. So the question is, when do you then come to the point of giving up this idea of what should happen, so that you are willing to step into the River of Life and flow with that river. Which will raise you up but only to the extent that you are working to raise up the All. The All in yourself, the All in all others.

You are close to a higher level of service

And so, my beloved, I ask you to ponder that some of you do have a certain attainment that has brought you to a point, where you are close to being able to serve the Ascended Host in a more direct capacity than you are doing right now. Perhaps as you see our messengers doing, although your way of service might be different.

But nevertheless, the image I want you to hold is that you might be close to stepping up to that more direct form of service. But there may still be an imbalance somewhere in your being, that is deceiving you and thus making you susceptible to the lower spirits that whisper in your ear and thus prevent you – with their constant unceasing chatter – from hearing the still small voice of the Holy Spirit who never seeks to force but only seeks to awaken and inspire.

And thus, if you would take an honest assessment, study our teachings on the ego – study the new Course in Christhood [Master Keys to Personal Christhood] that Jesus has so lovingly prepared for you – well then you might realize that if you are willing to let go of a few illusions – perhaps just one grand illusion – then you can actually step up to that service, where you can be more of an open door and start fulfilling that part of your divine plan.

But I ask you to recognize, my beloved, that until you are willing to give up the unbalanced desires, you will not be able to serve as an open door for the Ascended Host. You will only become an instrument of the false teachers, who will whisper some grand scheme in your ear, rather than the true reality of oneness—the oneness of all life.

NOW is the time to embrace the Golden Age consciousness!!!

Jesus and Saint Germain, June 28, 2008.

Jesus:
So then, let Christ be raised in all, for that is why I came to this Earth. Do you see my beloved, it is complete insanity – and I say deliberately "insanity" – to think that there can be only one Son of God, only one Christed Being on Earth. My beloved, this is the lie that must be exposed. It must be exposed for what it is, no matter how painful it might be for those who have made themselves the blind followers of the blind leaders and would prefer to continue in their illusion, my beloved. That if they stay loyal members of an outer Christian church, declare me as their Lord and savior, then they will automatically be saved—whereas all others will go to hell.

You see, my beloved, if you understand the reality of why I came to this Earth, you will see that I came to give LIFE, the abundant life to ALL people—not to a select, small group, my beloved. Do you understand that I descended in the Middle East precisely because there is hardly a place on Earth where you find a greater concentration of the very consciousness that is the antithesis to Christhood, namely that some people belong to a special group, the chosen people, who are fundamentally above and beyond anyone else?

Do you see, my beloved, that I came to challenge the Jews to overcome that consciousness – that they had built for thousands of years – of being this little tribe that somehow was favored by God. So that God was only concerned about saving the Jews and was willing to condemn all others to hell for eternity. This is the very consciousness of the fallen beings, my beloved, who in denying God in themselves must therefore deny God in all others.

And therefore, when one person is raised up – and demonstrates an extraordinary consciousness – and they cannot kill that person and they cannot kill the movement he started, well then they will kill the example by raising that person up to some unique status so that no one else can follow, my beloved.

This is the fallacy of current Christianity. It must be exposed, my beloved. And who can expose it but those who are in touch with the Divine Feminine? For you see, my beloved, it is the feminine aspect of men and women that has the ability to feel oneness with all life here below. And it is only through the feeling of that oneness that you can overcome the illusion that only some people are meant to be saved. And so that you can tune in to the reality that God wants to raise up and save everyone, my beloved.

This is the Mother – the Mother Flame, the Mother aspect – who wants to raise up all of her children, not just a few, and who then can come to see all people as children of the Mother, my beloved. Thus realizing that the false image of the male judgmental God – the selective God, the monotheistic God up there in the sky – is truly a false image that has nothing to do with the reality of the Father-Mother God. Who truly, my beloved, when the Father aspect of God, the unexpressed God, has expressed Itself as all self-conscious beings, then what sense will it make, my beloved, that God does not want to raise up every aspect, every expression of itself? But would want to condemn certain people to hell based on some criteria defined by a particular religion, the religion of a small, little tribe on this small, little planet, called Earth—which is like a speck of dust in the vastness of the universe my beloved.

Do you see that thinking that you belong to the chosen people is the ultimate expression of ego, is the ultimate spiritual blindness? The ultimate insanity of thinking that out of the vastness of the universe only these few people who belong to this particular tribe – or this particular Christian fundamentalist church – will be saved whereas all others will be tossed aside as dry grass that you throw into the fire, for it is worth nothing.

How could God possibly think that an extension of itself is worth nothing? It is only the ego who can divide people up based on worth, saying that some people have a superior worth and some people have no worth at all, my beloved. Thus, again, I yield to Saint Germain.

Saint Germain:

So then, once we have the illusions of Christianity taken care of, my beloved, we can then begin to look forward to the Age of Aquarius. For truly – although we must deal with the problems of Pisces and the illusions of humankind – we of the Ascended Host have no desire whatsoever to spend an infinite amount of time dealing with the problems on Earth, focusing on the negative, focusing on what must be overcome, my beloved. For we are, of course, God-free beings. And what does it mean that we are God-free beings? It means that we love expressing our God quality, our God flames, our individuality—that is the individuality that God gave us as the ultimate gift. Thus, my beloved, I have no desire to continue for an indefinite period of time giving dictations on what is wrong with planet Earth and what needs to be corrected—although I certainly will again point out certain problems.

Nevertheless, my beloved, I desire to get on with the work of bringing forth the vision of Aquarius and what can become of that Golden Age. And thus, I too wish to congratulate you for the fact that – collectively – the spiritual people on Earth have indeed raised their consciousness to a level, where it is now possible for us to look beyond the limitations of the Piscean consciousness and start bringing forth that vision of Aquarius—which I shall surely do in teachings forthcoming.

For certainly, this cannot be done in just one release, for my vision is vast, complex and it indeed requires a gradual build-up for people to truly lock in to and understand the vision of Aquarius. But what I will give you now is the sense of what freedom actually means, my beloved. For if you look at the understanding you have of the true inner teachings of Christ, you will see that what Christ is all about is freedom—setting you free from the prison of the ego, the duality consciousness, the consciousness of anti-christ. This, my beloved, is the cross that you are all crucified on by the ego and the ego's momentums—by that mortal identity.

And thus, the true goal of Christ is to set people free from having all of their energy tied up in the ego games, my beloved, so that there is no room to be creative. And this is indeed the joy of Christ: to see people rise up and be free to express their God-given creativity. For, my beloved, do you not see that the Christian churches have been used not only as a way to control the population in an outer sense – by making them conform to certain outer standards of behavior – but they have also been used to control people in an inner sense by causing them to shut off their God-given creativity, not daring to express any of that creativity, my beloved. And this is indeed the real travesty of the false Christianity—that it has not allowed humankind to be raised up to the level, where people are ready to embrace the freedom of Aquarius and express their creativity in bringing forth the manifestation of the potential for the Aquarian age.

Remembering your own sins no more— by being MORE

Master MORE, June 29, 2008.

So my beloved, why does an ascended master who for a century has been known by the name El Morya get the crazy idea to change his name to Master MORE? Well my beloved, who AM I as an ascended master? AM I not indeed a spiritual teacher, seeking to raise up those who are yet unascended to overcome the limitations that keep them from the ascended consciousness, from the Christ consciousness—that is the only key to enter into the Kingdom of the Infinite?

And thus, in teaching this, I Am well aware of the pitfalls of the path, the trickery of the human ego. Of how it is constantly seeking to trick the best students into falling into the rut of taking a teaching given and turning it into a closed mental box that now keeps them trapped, my beloved, rather than raising them higher.

Thus, if you take an honest look at virtually every religion on this planet – and even at the organizations that we, the Ascended Host, have sponsored over this past century – you will see the same pattern, my beloved. After a time, the students start forming a mental image of what it means to be a student of the ascended masters, of what it means to be a Chela of El Morya or Serapis Bey or Saint Germain or Jesus or another Master.

And thus my beloved, as that mental image becomes more and more pronounced, and as it starts spreading through the mass consciousness of the organization, then it begins to gain a strength that eventually overpowers those who are not strong enough to see through it. And thus my beloved, you should realize that any movement, any group of people that starts meeting on a regular basis, will form a mass consciousness, a group consciousness. And it will eventually – if the members are not aware, if they are not alert – it will begin to form a force that will seek to overpower the individual and get the individual to follow the mass consciousness – rather than following the teaching released through the organization from our level and following the inner direction that you get within your own heart.

Beware of the ego's trap

And thus my beloved, what you have seen in previous organizations is truly the formation of a certain image of what it means to be a Chela of El Morya. And I must tell you honestly that only a very small percentage of the members of any previous organization have managed to avoid this trap. Whereas the majority of them have fallen right into it, allowing their egos to make them feel special because in their organization, they have the right definition of what it means to be a Chela of El Morya. And therefore, of course, they are better chelas than anyone else.

And so, they now focus all of their attention on being the best possible chela that they can be – and my beloved, please note that I am not condemning anyone for this – I am simply exposing the reality of what is happening in the duality consciousness of the ego. I am in no way passing any judgment upon this. This is what happens, and I know this full well.

Yet I am trying to point it out to those who have ears to hear, that they may see the trap before it springs and catches them. For you see my beloved, it is often so that the most eager students – the ones who are actually in some ways ready to step up to a higher service – are the ones who have the greatest desire, the greatest drive to be a good Chela of El Morya. Yet if they are not alert, and if they are not balanced, my beloved, then their desire to do well becomes a trap.

My beloved, do you fully understand that you live in the material universe that is still dominated by the duality consciousness? Which means that the ego, the prince of this world, the false teachers can use anything – and I mean anything – to create a trap?

Yet the flip side of the coin, my beloved, is that it is also possible to take any teaching – no matter how distorted, no matter how false – and still transcend the teaching and attain Christhood. As you indeed see a few people who have taken the distorted teachings of orthodox Christianity and still managed to rise above it, to go within.

Overcome your graven image of El Morya and know MORE

Thus what I am endeavoring to have you understand is that we of the Ascended Hosts cannot bring forth a teaching expressed in words that the ego and the false teachers cannot pervert and use to create a trap. Yet on the other hand, the false teachers of humankind cannot create a false teaching that is so distorted, so far from the truth, that people cannot transcend that teaching and still manifest Christhood. Do you see my beloved, there cannot be any guarantees in the material realm? Partly because of the duality consciousness, partly because of free will.

And so my beloved what I am pointing out to you is that if you will take an honest look at yourself and see that you have – whether it be from a previous organization or whether it be for other reasons – but that you have built an image of who El Morya is and what it means to be a Chela of El Morya, well then, I must tell you that you are no longer my chela—you are a chela of a graven image!

For you see my beloved, I am MORE than any image you could possibly create of me. And, thus you see that the entire drive to create a graven image, whether it be of God or an ascended being, can only come from the ego and its desire, its compulsive need, for control, my beloved.

And thus, the ego is constantly seeking to create the ultimate mental box and put God in it, put me in it, put Jesus in it. But the first person who is put in the mental box created by your ego is yourself. And the last person to leave that mental box is yourself. For you see my beloved, the beauty of Jesus' teaching to do unto others, is that what you do unto others, you have already done to yourself. For after all, who is yourself? Is it not the All?

And so my beloved, I came to a point where I recognized that despite my efforts in previous organizations – to give forth teachings that could not be turned into a closed mental box – well, I had not attained the goal that I desired to attain. And that is why I decided to take the step to change the name to Master MORE. To more directly signal that I am MORE, forever MORE.

And thus my beloved, you may look on the Internet and elsewhere, and see that there are organizations who claim to be sponsored by the ascended masters and they have brought forth new images of El Morya that are different from the ones of previous organizations. And they might claim that these new images reflect my Being as I am today as compared to the old. Yet I tell you truly my beloved, I, Master MORE, I, El Morya, have not sponsored any image of me for a long time now.

For I desire to have no image, for the reality is, my beloved, that I AM one with the MORE of the River of Life, the process of constant, never-ending, ever-expanding, self transcendence. And thus my beloved, if I were to commission an artist to paint a picture of me, well then before the paint was dry, I would have transcended myself a million times. And thus, how could the picture possibly reflect who I AM. And thus, how could any picture be more than a graven image? Which is why, in a previous conference, Saint Germain kept jumping off the wall, my beloved. [Laughter]

And I have felt like doing the same thing many times, when I see those who could potentially be my best chelas hold on to a graven image; whether it be a physical picture or mental picture in their own minds. And I want to say to them, "Come with me on this grand adventure of being MORE—instead of sitting there feeling content with the less that you were given at a previous time."

The real cause of the murder of the Divine Mother

And so my beloved, what am I leading up to with this? It is to give you an understanding, my beloved. An understanding based on your own experience in this lifetime and in today's age of what was the real cause of the murder of the Divine Mother on Lemuria. For it was this very process, my beloved, of the tendency of the ego and the false teachers to create graven images of God.

And what is the purpose of the Divine Mother, when there was a representative of the Divine Mother in embodiment? Well, it is the same purpose as Lord Krishna, as the Buddha, as Jesus, as every true spiritual representative or teacher. It is to shatter and challenge the mental boxes, the graven images, that people have created, for this is the essence of the path.

And thus my beloved, those who murdered the Divine Mother entered into the consciousness of wanting to walk the mechanical path, wanting to worship a graven image—which then gave them control, not only over the image, but over the path, and gave them the illusion of control over their material circumstances. And thus my beloved they were not willing to transcend the graven image and come up higher. And so, when someone challenged their graven image, they would do almost anything to silence that challenge. And in some cases going to the extreme of killing that person, either by slitting their throat in a temple or by nailing them to a cross, my beloved.

So you see, what I am trying to point out to you here is that there may be some of you who have a sense that you were on Lemuria, and you were there when the murder of the representative of the Divine Mother took place. Yet my beloved, what I am trying to give you is a different perspective, where you realize that all human beings on Earth have been and are stuck in the consciousness that caused the murder of the Divine Mother.

Do you see, my beloved? The unwillingness to transcend is the very consciousness that caused the murder of the Divine Mother on Lemuria, elsewhere, and the murder of the representatives of God throughout the ages. For this has not only happened with Jesus and the Divine Mother on Lemuria, it has happened countless times, my beloved, and is still happening today. Even in the form of psychic murder, where you silence those who could have spoken out and brought society forward.

So you see, what I am calling you to realize is that what needs to be overcome is that consciousness, the unwillingness to transcend, to self-transcend. And I am also calling you to realize here that I am not saying this to give you any sense of guilt. I am, in fact, saying it to perhaps push your buttons a little bit, so that you can see if you feel guilty over this. For then there is something you need to look at, my beloved.

For have we not explained so beautifully how the Divine Mother feels about the murder of her representative? That there is no judgment, there is no anger, there is no negative feelings—there is only unconditional love. And in unconditional love there is not even the need for forgiveness, my beloved.

How hatred of the Mother begins

Do you see that whatever you have done in this or past lives, it is of no consequence, my beloved, in the grand scheme of things? For everything is created out of Ma-ter light, which is like the sand in the sand boxes you all used to play in as children. Whatever you do with the sand, whatever kind of castle you build, you cannot hurt the sand, my beloved. But neither can you create anything permanent, for when you leave it and the sun comes out and dries the sand in your castle, then it begins to crumble.

Do you see, my beloved? God is not the angry, judgmental God who has put you into a world where the slightest mistake you make will qualify you for hell for all eternity. God is the loving God who has put you into a sand box and said, "Build anything you want, for you cannot hurt the sand. You can only hurt yourself."

But you truly hurt yourself only in your own perception, my beloved. Thus, do you see, whatever mistake you have made has no consequence in the grand scheme of things? But it has a consequence in your own world, in that it can make you feel guilty, unworthy, fearful, even angry. And so the subtle, psychological mechanism, my beloved, is that when you allow yourself to feel condemnation, self-condemnation, for the fact that you have made a mistake—well then you enter into a state of pain that can easily become so intense that you refuse to look at the decisions, the consciousness, that caused you to commit the outer actions, my beloved. And if you refuse to look at the consciousness, well how can you resolve it and move on. And this then is what becomes the Catch 22 – for some people even a Catch 33 or a Catch 99 – for they have built so many layers of this guilt, anger and fear.

And so you see, my beloved, this is the essence of what caused the murder of the Divine Mother. For the unwillingness to transcend comes from the unwillingness to look at something from the past – and learn from it – because it is too painful. And thus, the ego will always trick you into lessening the sense of guilt so that you can live with it. And how does the ego do this? It does so by causing you to project outside yourself that it was not really your fault. It was something else that made you do it.

And in many cases, my beloved, what happens is:

You descend into embodiment in the material realm, where everything is created out of the Ma-ter light.

You make a mistake, which we do not see as a mistake, but you see it as a mistake.

It causes pain.

You will not look at the pain. So you project that it was not your fault. It was some condition in the material realm that made you do it.

And now what have you done? You have projected onto the Mother that it is the Mother's fault. And how can this not lead to hatred of the Mother, which then – when you are challenged to realize that no, it was not the Mother who made you do it, it was you who made the choice to do it – well then you want to silence that voice.

For you are not willing to look at the pain, to go into the pain and realize that although running away can diminish the intensity of the pain, you will still never be able to run away from it. Instead, you will have the lesser intensity of the pain as the constant companion. But if, instead, you would turn around – walk right into the pain – then you would for a short time feel the intensity of the pain, my beloved, but you would walk through it and realize that you are more than the pain. And that there is peace, release, surrender, freedom on the other side.

The cause of self-hatred

But as long as you run away, you cannot do that. So what must you do? You must justify running away by again projecting layers of images and illusions onto the Mother. Which then causes you to feel more and more resentful, coming to the point of having hatred of the Mother, my beloved. Which is truly a hatred of self; but who are you? You are an expression of the Father, but you are in the Mother of God. For all in the world of form is the Mother. And so, you are also the Mother. So when you hate the Mother, you are hating yourself.

But you see my beloved, what is it you are hating? You are hating something that is an illusion. And what is the grand illusion? Well, it is the illusion caused by the fact that the lowering of the collective consciousness on a planet like Earth has given matter a certain density, where it seems like your actions have physical consequences that you cannot escape and that will follow you for a long time. And thus it seems like the Mother really is punishing you for your mistakes by some physical consequence.

Yet my beloved, the reality is that the Mother is not punishing you. The Mother is at any moment reflecting back to you the images that you hold in your consciousness. And thus, what you are hating are these images that are not the Mother—that are not you. They are created out of the duality consciousness which is unreal. So what you hate is unreal.

And the only way out of it is to look at it from a realistic perspective and recognize that it is not real. Admit that it is not real. Admit that you chose to believe in an illusion. But that neither God the Father nor God the Mother will hold you to that choice and will say that once you have made that choice you should be bound by it forever. It is only the devil who will seek to make you believe in this lie.

The Father and the Mother have given you the free will to change your mind at any time, to undo an imperfect decision by making a right choice—a LIFE decision to replace the death decision. My beloved, what I endeavor to give you here is a greater understanding of how you hold yourself back.

The difference between memory and Akasha

Now my beloved, I will speak to you of the difference between memory, human memory, and what you have come to know as the akashic records. For you see my beloved, in previous teachings we have given the image that there is something called the akashic records, which is truly a certain energy frequency that records everything that has ever happened in the material universe. So that you can, so to speak, rewind the tape in the VCR and replay an event that happened 10,000 years ago or 50,000 years ago.

And there is something called the akashic records. But you see, when you hear of the concept of the akashic records, you project the state of your own consciousness upon it. And so you think that what is recorded in the akashic records is what you saw in that situation when it happened 10 or 10,000 years ago.

So you think that if I was to take you to my retreat and show you a big screen on the wall – for I can tell you that I have ultimate flat screen TV [Laughter] – then you think that what you would see on that screen is the same that you saw when you were in that situation many years ago. But it is not so, my beloved.

For you see, what is recorded in the akashic records is what happened the way God saw it. And God looks at this, the Ascended Host look at this, the Divine Mother looks at this with no human emotions, as we have stated—none of the human emotions that you have, that might cause you to look at things with a negative overlay, my beloved.

Think about the fact that you all know; that you might have a traffic accident and you call in 5 witnesses and ask them to describe what they saw, and they saw 5 different versions of what happened. Well my beloved, imagine that you were in a situation many thousands of years ago when the murder of the Divine Mother on Lemuria happened. Imagine how all of the people who participated in that event—how they each have an individual vision of the event.

But none of them saw the event the way the Ascended Host see it. For each person saw it through the filter of their own consciousness, my beloved. And because of that filter, each person built a personal image that includes a mental picture but also a set of intense emotions about the event. And the emotions give to each person a personal pain. And the pain is so intense that the mechanism I just described kicks in, so that they will not look at the pain and thus must project the cause of the event outside themselves. And this very running away from looking at the event is what prevents you from rising above and being free of the event. My beloved, do you see this? Audience: "YES!"

This is the very key to overcoming the ego. If you truly see and experience what I am describing here, my beloved, the key is to determine within yourself – to look at what takes away your peace – and realize that what takes away your peace may be the pain; but behind the pain is an event from the past where you did something that caused you to accept a completely unrealistic self-image. A self-image based on the lies and illusions of duality.

Be willing to see what really happened

And if you will then determine that you are willing to walk through the pain, then you can come to the point where you can say, "I am willing to look at the event," but I ask you beloved Christ Self, beloved Jesus, beloved Mother Mary, beloved Master MORE – whichever Master is close to your heart – ask that Master to show you an inner vision of the event directly out of the akashic records, my beloved. So that you are not bound to look at the event only through the filter of the duality consciousness, which then will forever prevent you from seeing the illusion, seeing that you are more than the illusion and thus letting the illusion go.

So ask to be given that vision. What really happened? Not what your ego tells you happened. For I tell you that the ego and the false teachers will make you believe in a false image that makes you think that it is God the Father or God the Mother who is condemning you. And thus, you cannot lock in to the unconditional love that is the key to consuming the event.

And thus, what I wish to give you here is the understanding that when you created that mental image of the event, you created – in the separate part of your mind – an image that is removed from the reality of what is recorded in the akashic records. A graven image, and that image is stored in your personal memory—the memory of the separate self, the mortal self you have built.

So you have, so to speak, a personal version of the akashic records. Only, what is recorded there is not what really happened, but what you think happened, seeing through the filter of the ego. And do you see my beloved, that as long as you do not challenge that mental image, that graven image, you will be bound by it because you will be condemning yourself to staying in the mental box formed by the image.

And you can never escape it; you can only keep running away from it. And in so doing, perhaps building layer upon layer that makes it harder and harder to either face the pain or to get to the bottom of what really happened because your attention is taken off on all these tangents. And thus, you can never come to that center, that point of stillness my beloved, where you can ask, "God, show me what really happened. I am willing to know?"

And I tell you, when you see what really happened – and I say this regardless of what mistake you could possibly have made – when you see what really happened, you will see that it is no more important than a child building a sand castle and deciding it didn't look the way he wanted it, so he erases it and starts building a new one.

Give yourself the benefit of the doubt

Do you see what we said about the Ma-ter light? It will out-picture any image you project upon it, for it has no judgment. So at any moment, the Ma-ter light sets you free to let go of the old image and project a better one. You do not need to feel guilty about having projected an imperfect image, for God gave you free will. And God wants you to learn. And if you learn, was it really a mistake? What was the big deal, as they say?

Sometimes my beloved, you just have to give yourself the benefit of the doubt. Instead of feeling so absolutely convinced that you are a bad person. Be willing to question that image – projected into your mind – and say, "Maybe, I am just a child of God who built a sand castle that I really don't like anymore. And so I don't need to be bound by it; I can erase it and build another one. And my Divine Mother and my Divine

Father will rejoice when I build a better castle. They will not make me feel guilty or unworthy or afraid or anything."

Can you see, can you sense, can you feel my desire to see you be free of these old patterns? Can you sense that I am a representative of God, both as Father and Mother, my beloved? For as an ascended being, I have the perfect balance of masculine and feminine. For if I did not, how could I have ascended?

…

So be not afraid to strive for such a close relationship with an ascended being, yet be aware that it can be attained only to the degree you are willing to let the separate self die. For we can, I trust you can see, never compromise our office by entering into union with your ego.

You cannot overcome the past without looking at the past

Master MORE, October 31, 2008.

Acknowledging your real worth is not pride

I ask you to seriously ponder that although you have been brought up to believe that acknowledging your worth should not be done – because it can lead to pride – I ask you to acknowledge that this is an illusion. This is a plot perpetrated by the false teachers and the ego.

I am not here talking about a pride – a human pride – that makes you think you are better than others. But you see, my beloved, the sense of separation that I am talking about as the cause of conflict in Europe cannot be overcome on an individual level unless you overcome both the ego's pride of feeling superior to others and the ego's non-pride of feeling inferior or thinking you cannot recognize your own self-worth.

My beloved, you need to find the middle way, the balance between these extremes as you have been well taught by us, for there is always a middle way that is beyond the dualistic extremes. And in this case, in or-

Dare to appreciate yourself

And so, what I am leading up to here is the recognition that we have no desire to see anyone on Earth become less, or make themselves less. We desire to see all people become MORE. We of the Ascended Host do not look at any people as bad, as evil, as beyond being raised up to a higher level. We hold the immaculate concept. We see the potential for all to be raised up, and therefore we have no desire to punish. We have no desire to shame. We have no desire to belittle any nation, any people. For we always see beyond the outer characteristics. So do you see that you cannot rise above the sense of superiority or the sense of separateness by making yourself less?

There are some who think, my beloved, that in order to avoid pride they have to make themselves so humble. But you see, pride is one extreme. Humility in a human way is the other extreme, the other polarity. You do not escape duality by jumping from one polarity to the other. You escape duality by finding the middle way.

And so, I ask you each one individually, as I already instructed this messenger to say to one person earlier today, to take some time in your busy schedule and to sit down; not give any rituals, not give any rosaries, not read any teachings, not think, not analyze. But to take some time and just sit down and appreciate—appreciate who you are, appreciate God, appreciate the Ascended Host, appreciate nature, appreciate other people, appreciate something that opens your heart. And when you have then opened your heart, then allow yourself to appreciate yourself. Not your ego, not your separate self, but appreciate your real Self as an individual expression of God, as an absolutely unique expression of God. And therefore, allow yourself to recognize that you are MORE than the separate self.

The secret to overcoming the ego

My beloved, you have all heard the expression, "Nature abhors a vacuum." Well, you cannot overcome the separate self, the ego, by destroying that separate self. For you cannot live without a sense of self. That is the price you pay for being an individual, self-aware expression of God.

You have to have a sense of self, and so those who attempt to destroy the self cannot ever make spiritual progress. Even though some of them may think they have done so—they cannot. You cannot make spiritual progress by making yourself a vacuum. You can only make spiritual progress by transcending the duality and recognizing that you are MORE, because you are out of a greater spiritual being in the spiritual level right above the material universe. And that spiritual being is out of an even greater spiritual being, and this Hierarchy of Light goes all the way to the Creator.

This is how you can overcome the separate sense of self by Being MORE. And thus, do you see that this works on an individual level, where you cannot overcome your own separateness, but even more so it works on a national, and even a planetary level, where you cannot grow spiritually if you find yourself in a vacuum. As you indeed see many people in Europe, who have given up on traditional religion – and for good reason – but have then not found anything to put in its stead. And therefore, they can easily be swayed into various forms of extreme expressions that give them a sense of identity.

For do you not see that what Nazism and Hitler offered certain people was a very clearly defined sense of identity, which then allowed them an easy way – seemingly an easy way – out of the state of being in a vacuum, of having no clear identity, no clear sense of who they are? This has been the lure of all totalitarian ideologies—Marxism, Nazism, all others that you have seen.

It has been the lure of materialism, the sense that material things is your god and is your purpose for living. It has been the lure of power and those who seek power. And so, you see that it is only by finding something that is beyond the Earth – where you begin to acknowledge that you are MORE than this material identity – it is only then that you can escape that sense of material identity.

And yet, in order to do this, you must overcome the programming from both church and secular materialistic philosophies that you are not a spiritual being – or at least not a unique spiritual being – and certainly not a son or daughter of God. And in order to do this, you have to be willing to take some time to look in the mirror – I speak not physically, but metaphorically – to look in the mirror of your soul, and recognize that your true Being is MORE than these outer things.

How can Europe be free when the minds of the people are imprisoned by illusions?

Saint Germain, November 1, 2008

Is your country truly free?
And thus, be honest then and look over here in Europe as well – to the countries that claim to be free societies – and then consider whether they can truly live up to that high label, my beloved. Are you really free in the western part of Europe? You may have democracy, you may have human rights, you may have freedom to move around, but are you truly free if you have been brought up in a culture that is so infused with duality, that they cannot even give you a clear, concise image of who you are and why you are here?

How can there be freedom when a society is trapped in a dualistic struggle between the traditional, orthodox, mainstream religions that have been used for centuries – nay for millennia – to control the minds of the people and make them believe that they are not sons and daughters of God, that they are not anything more than sinners, that they do not have a Christ potential? And on the other hand of the battle field is the materialists – the aspiring power elite, seeking to overthrow the established power elite of religion – promoting their idolatrous image that you are nothing more than a sophisticated animal and that life has no purpose beyond the material realm.

Ah, how can this be freedom? How can people be truly free when they do not even know who they are and cannot answer the questions, "Why am I here? Where did I come from? Where am I going? Is there a God? Is there something beyond the mental box created by the ego?" But they cannot even ask that last question, because they are brought up without any awareness of the ego, of the duality consciousness, of the illusion of separation. Being brought up to believe that what they see in this world is real—has some ultimate reality. And because it has this ultimate, objective reality, then it exists independently of their own consciousness—meaning that they have no power over material conditions.

The ego has no reality
And thus, I might say that some of you, in your discussion and understanding of the ego, have come to a somewhat unrealistic image, where you think the ego has some actual substance, some actual reality, so to speak. As you think that the physical matter that surrounds you or that makes up your bodies has some actual reality.

It does not. It has no more reality than you assign to it in your minds. Nevertheless, you confuse the ego with the substance that is misqualified through the ego. That substance partly makes up your soul, your four lower bodies, especially your physical, emotional and mental bodies. But it is not the ego. Your ego has no substance, because your ego is a conglomerate of beliefs, of illusions.

You see, my beloved, when you go to a movie theatre and watch a movie unfolding on the screen, you are seeing images. But those images started as ideas in the minds of a writer or a producer or a director. And then those images were turned into something that has substance and can be displayed on a screen. But what you see is not the ideas, the images in the mind of the creator of the movie. Those images remain there as nothing but ideas. They were given substance, but the substance is not the same as the idea.

Thus, do not fall into the trap of thinking that your ego has actual substance. Your ego is nothing but ideas, beliefs, illusions—based on the greater illusion of separation. For you see, my beloved, when you fall prey to the illusion that your ego has some actual existence, you also fall prey to the illusion that evil, that evil forces, have some actual existence. And thus, you think they have power over you.

Matter has no reality
You also fall prey to the illusion that matter has some actual existence, and thus you fall prey to the greater illusion that matter has power to limit your Spirit. And that, of course, is the very essence of anti-freedom in the material octave, where you think that matter is so real. But in reality it has no true existence, for it can exist only as an image projected by a conscious mind onto the movie screen of the Ma-ter Light. And it can continue to exist only as long as there is actual light flowing through that projection mechanism that is the mind.

But the moment you change the image in the mind – truly change it – then the Ma-ter Light will change what it out-pictures. How do you think, my beloved, that as the Wonderman of Europe I could take a diamond – the hardest substance known on Earth – a diamond with a flaw inside of it, and I could remove that flaw, without cutting the diamond open, which would have destroyed it? Well, it could be done only because I did not accept that matter was ultimately real.

And that was the message I was attempting to get across to the stubborn, thick-skulled kings of Europe, who thought they knew better than everyone else, even better than God. And certainly better than this eccentric character, who claimed to be some special being with special insights about how they should run their kingdoms.

The stage is set for a breakthrough

My beloved, there is probably no more ungrateful occupation on Earth than trying to get a king or an emperor to change the way he is running his kingdom. It is not a career path that I could commend to any of you. But I do recommend the career path of recognizing that while you may not be able to change the minds of the kings, the blind leaders of the blind, you can indeed change the minds of a great portion of the people.

For in this day and age, the stage is indeed set for a major breakthrough, where people can suddenly be awakened and understand and grasp a higher vision of freedom than they have ever seen before. And so again, as Kuan Yin spoke until your cups were running over, I have done the same. I have gone around the circle. I have gone up the staircase of your chakras, but I have gone around the circle of European nations. And indeed, I have infused the oxygen atoms themselves with my Flame of Freedom.

Choose ye this day the parallel universe in which you want to abide

Jesus, November 2, 2008.

"Lord God on High, omnipotent reigneth," thus are the words of the song you have heard, taken from the scriptures. But I, Jesus, did not come to awaken humankind to the Lord God on High who is omnipotent. I came to awaken them to the God within—who is the respecter of his own law of free will and thus does not seek to control you. But seeks to help you unfold all that you are, all that you were created to be—even being more than you were created to be. For your God loves to be surprised by the creativity of the extensions of itself, my beloved.

He is not the tyrant up in Heaven who wants you to conform to a certain belief system, a certain ritual of outer behavior or ritualistic coming together in worship or prayer. The Lord God on High – meaning the Lord God that is in a higher vibration than the material universe – that Lord, that God, wants to be expressed through you in a spontaneous, creative flow of new ways of manifesting the abundant life on Earth.

Christ is beyond any authority on Earth

It is not God who wants to control your thoughts and your behavior. It is those who have attempted to set themselves up as gods on Earth—or as the only representatives of Gods on Earth. Inserting themselves as the High Priests of the temple – as the alpha perversion of the power elite – and the money changers in the temple—as the perversion of the ego, the perversion of the feminine, the omega polarity.

So my beloved, you will see that there have always been two main groupings in the power elite, in the false teachers. Those who pervert the expanding force of the Father, those who pervert the contracting force of the Mother. And in many cases they have formed an unholy alliance, my beloved, and this can be seen out-pictured here in Europe, going back many centuries.

For go back to the song you have just heard, "King of Kings and Lord of Lords." Well my beloved, that original statement was meant to signify that Christ is beyond any ideas and graven images created by the consciousness of anti-christ. And therefore, Christ is beyond any authority on Earth – whether it be the king, or the emperor, or the Lord, or the Pope, or the priest, or the cardinal or the bishop. It matters not, for Christ is beyond all of them.

For Christ cannot be corrupted by the dualistic consciousness, Christ cannot be forced into a mental box created by the consciousness of anti-christ—which is – as we have said many times – based on the illusion of separation, whereas Christ is based on the reality of oneness, the oneness of all life.

In oneness, no one is Lord or King over another

So you see; when life is one, no one is in control. No one is lord over another; no one is king over another. And do you then see that when the ancient Israelites demanded a king, well then they only reinforced the illusion of separation—and it was not truly the people who demanded a king.

It was the aspiring power elite at the time; those who lusted after the power held by the high priests and wanted their own share of that power—out of their perversion of the omega aspect of wanting to control the people's daily lives, whereas the high priests wanted to control their minds. And do you then see that here in Europe the concept that Christ is King of Kings was perverted to the point where the kings started claiming that they were representatives of Christ—that they were standing between the people and Christ, and that they had the ordination of Christ for their kingship and for the fact that the son of the previous king, the oldest son, would always become the next king.

Well my beloved, if you go back to ancient times, they had kings but the kings were not simply appointed in succession. You were appointed through some agency of the spiritual realm, be it an oracle or in other manners whereby the Spirit could appoint the king. Often raising up a person who was born and raised as a commoner to be the next king, so that that king knew what it was like to live among the people and had not been born in a royal castle, far removed from the ordinary people, growing up in this closed environment, and therefore naturally becoming halfway insane, so to speak, being brought up to be insane in the sense that he was insensitive to the plight of the people. This, then, is indeed one of the great problems; perhaps one might say the great problem on Earth, especially here in Europe.

Find the Living Christ in the kingdom within

You see, my beloved, Europe is in many ways intended to be what it to some degree has been, the cradle of new ideas, of new inventions, of new philosophies and ideologies that can bring progress and freedom to the people. And precisely because this is the divine intention for this land, those of the power elites – the two power elites – have congregated here and have attempted to divide the people amongst each other and divide the people from their God within.

This, then, is the pattern that you will see on this continent, over and over again, successfully completed by the Catholic Church who used my inner teachings about the inner kingdom to set themselves up as the spiritual representatives of Christ on Earth. Claiming that you could only be saved and reach Christ through the hierarchy of the church.

Now my beloved, it is true that you can only reach Christ through a certain hierarchy—you will see that we have often talked about you seeing yourselves as part of a certain hierarchy of Light. But you see, as I came to demonstrate 2000 years ago, you do not need a hierarchy on Earth in order to claim your oneness with the hierarchy of light.

For the kingdom of God is within, and you have the key of knowledge, you have the ability to know truth in your own heart. And therefore, you do not need an outer authority to define dogma and doctrine for you, based on some literal interpretation of a scripture that was outdated before it was even written down, my beloved.

Any scripture is outdated before it can be written down

For do you not see that whereas Master MORE has said that if you were to paint a portrait of him, he would have transcended himself before the paint was dry? Well, I can assure you that I, Jesus, transcended myself many times before the early gospel writers decided to put pen to paper and write down the story of my life.

And so, you will see that from the very beginning, the Catholic Church was based on this falsified concept that you can make Christ conform to worldly ideas, beliefs, mental boxes, graven images, my beloved. And they have attempted to turn the living Christ into a graven image. And they have been successful in swaying many people to worship this image. Many souls have worshipped this image over and over again over the past 2,000 years, coming from one embodiment into the next, being born into a Christian culture where they were then, again, exposed to this rigid view, this rigid image of Christ.

How many lifetimes does a soul need to spend sitting in a Christian church – looking up at the crucified Christ at the head of the church – before that soul begins to feel that there must be more to the inner message of Christ? Ah my beloved, that is a question that I wish I could answer. But I look upon humankind and I scratch my head and I say, "How come they have not yet had enough?

How can they still be sitting there every Sunday, singing these same old hymns, listening to the same old sermons, given by the same old priest—who has seen this as a lifetime calling to basically give the same sermon over and over again every Sunday?" He might think there is a variation, but it is the same sermon for it reinforces the graven image of the external Christ who will one day come back and save you. Whereas I wanted to be seen as the internal Christ who will help you transcend yourself, so that you might indeed experience the kingdom of God right where you are.

Quantum physics: the interplay of consciousness and the Cosmic Mirror

My beloved, what is the essence of the message I preached 2,000 years ago? Well, let me make a leap in consciousness to the present age and explain to you how the message of Christ can be understood through the discoveries of quantum mechanics, quantum physics.

For you see, my beloved, quantum physics has discovered and proven that when you interact with the material universe, that interaction is not physical—it is not bodily, for the universe is made of tiny subatomic particles that are actually simply energy waves. And your consciousness can interact with them, meaning that your consciousness can interact with the most fundamental level of matter. Well, right there, there is proof of what I attempted to explain 2,000 years ago in my statement, "Do unto others as you want them to do unto you."

For do you see, that what you do unto others is an expression of your consciousness? And your consciousness interacts with the most fundamental level of matter itself, which is what we have called the Cosmic Mirror. And what quantum physics has discovered is that before a scientist makes an observation, there is no manifest matter particle, there is no manifest electron.

You cannot determine the exact position and momentum of the electron, for it does not exist as an exact quantity before the observation is made. It exists only as a potential, my beloved. And then, there are even a number of potentials, and scientists have discovered that there is a fundamental uncertainty built into the universe, which is in stark contrast to the world view that has been promoted by both materialistic science and traditional Christianity. And before that, even by traditional religions, such as the Jewish religion that I came to renew.

Or, the view that has been promoted is that you have no influence over the matter realm. That God created the world the way it is, and therefore so many people have been lured into the illusion, my beloved, that they look at the conditions of the world as unchangeable.

In the middle ages they looked at the suffering, and their souls cried out, "Why did God create a world with such suffering?" But the only answer they got from the Church was, "It's a mystery, we cannot know. It must be the will of God that we suffer, so we should be content in our suffering and not try to do what Christ exemplified—turn the water into wine, raise the dead, heal the sick, walk on the water of the human consciousness and raise our consciousness to the wine of the Christ Consciousness."

Do you see the insanity of this? And then see that what science has proven is exactly the fact that God has given human beings dominion over the Earth, he has given them free will, and he has given them a mind that can interact with the Cosmic Mirror itself. So that what they project upon that very fundamental level of matter is what will be outpictured in the physical circumstances in which you live.

The mind is a radio receiver

For you see, what physicists have discovered is that before they make an observation of an electron, the electron does not exist as an actual particle but as a potential to manifest in a certain location. They can calculate the probability that the electron will manifest in a certain location, but they cannot know for certain until they make the observation. And why is this, my beloved?

It is because it is only when your consciousness interacts with the deeper level of reality that God has created—it is only then that things become manifest in the level of vibration where your consciousness is currently identifying itself. As we have said before, your mind is like a radio receiver that has the ability to tune in to different stations, but most people on Earth have been conditioned to tune their minds to the vibrational spectrum of the material universe – to that radio station of the material universe – and to think that that is the only level of reality that they can experience and that there is nothing beyond it.

Or, that though there is something beyond, they cannot contact it themselves within their hearts, for only the priest or the Pope has the bigger radio that can tune in to Heaven. Well, I tell you, my beloved— there is no super radio station in the Vatican or anywhere else. For there is only one radio – one kind of radio on Earth – and that is the one each of you have in your own hearts.

That, my beloved, is the only way to tune in to heaven. And those who claim otherwise are simply representatives of the power elites, that in their separation from God are seeking to control humankind. And they know that they can only ultimately control you through the mind by making you believe that there is nothing outside the prison in which you are currently abiding.

Experiencing circumstances according to your state of consciousness

So my beloved, back to quantum physics. There is a theory in quantum physics that when an observation is made, one particular event or particle becomes a physical manifestation in this universe. The question then arose, "Well what about all the other potentialities that could have come to pass, what happened to them? Do they simply disappear as the waveform collapses, or is it possible that each of them is actually manifested in a parallel universe?"

This is the so-called "Many-worlds interpretation," stating that there are an infinite number of universes. And each time you make a choice, well there is an exact copy of yourself who makes another choice that you might have made. If you choose A, your double will choose B and live in a parallel universe to experience the consequences of that choice.

Well, my beloved, this is not reality, for you are one Being. And I can assure you that even God saw that it would be a little too much to expect that there could be an infinite number of copies and you could still maintain some kind of integrity. So, you are one Being but of course there are levels of your Being.

So there is a certain reality here, that if you make one particular choice here in the physical realm, then you do not experience the consequences of that choice only with your conscious mind—for your greater mind extends into the emotional, the mental, and the etheric realms of planet Earth. And you will experience the consequences of your choice at those levels, depending on your state of consciousness and where you fit in. For as Maitreya has explained in his book there is only one level of the material universe, but there are many levels of the emotional and the mental especially, and even some divisions in the etheric.

You are one Being, existing in multiple dimensions

So, it is possible that you can live here on Earth in a physical body, but you have a low state of consciousness that attunes your emotional body to one of the lower levels in the emotional realm. And thus, it is entirely possible that you can experience a particular physical event, yet in your mind your experience becomes very negative, very dominated by fear. Whereas another person may have a higher state of consciousness that is attuned to one of the higher levels of the emotional realm, and therefore can experience the exact same physical situation but have a vastly different experience—a much less fearful experience, my beloved.

So what I aim to give you here is this concept that you are one Being but you exist in multiple dimensions. And one might indeed consider the physical, emotional, mental, and etheric levels of the material universe as parallel universes, as parallel worlds. And so, what you see is that here in the physical, your body might take a certain action, but what determines your life experience is not the outer action but actually how you perceive the action or its consequences, how you experience your circumstances.

And so, what I am endeavoring to explain is that there is a reality here—that if you look at humankind, you will see that there are many groupings of people, where you can put them on a scale according to their level of consciousness. And each of these levels are, so to speak, living in a parallel universe, for even though they all have a physical body, they are in their consciousness attuned to various levels of the emotional and mental realm. And the level to which they are attuned, will determine how they look at the material world, and how they experience life—it will determine their life-experience.

Consciousness on a scale of higher or lower frequencies

This, then, very much ties in with the teaching I have been giving for some time, where you can divide the population into the top 10% – or the most spiritually aware people – the bottom 10% of the most self-centered, ego-centered people, and the 80% of the general population who are somewhere in between those two. So, what I desire you to understand here is that it is the level of consciousness that determines where people fit into this scale—it is not their outer power.

Obviously, the most powerful people on Earth are not necessarily – and in fact are rarely – in the top 10%. The top 10% are not somehow superior to others, for in order to enter the top 10% you must overcome duality and the need to feel better than others. You must not go into the false humility that is the opposite, but the realism that we have talked about in previous dictations at this conference, of simply realizing who you are, as a co-creator with God. That is what determines your entry into the top 10%, so we are not here giving a teaching that the ego should be allowed to turn into a teaching of superiority giving rise to pride, for then you have not understood the teaching.

It is indeed a reality that there are those who have attuned their consciousness to higher frequencies, to the higher radio stations that are broadcasting the truth from the Ascended Master's octave. And they, then, have raised their consciousness to the point, where they can attune to a different radio station than the general population, and certainly the lowest 10% who are often attuning to the radio station that has traditionally been called hell.

For you see, hell exists in the emotional realm, where those beings who have become completely self-centered – have become so eaten up by the their own anger against God, and their anger against themselves – that they have formed the realm where the anger has become so intense, so hot, that it will be experienced as a hell with flames that burn you in eternal torment. For these beings that are trapped there, are in eternal torment, even though they do not always see this, because they are so focused on their anger against God that their anger is consuming their awareness to the point, that they cannot even realize that this is uncomfortable to them and that they wish they could get out of it.

Consciousness as a gravitational force

So you see, when you look at the scale of the bottom 10%, the top 10% and the 80% in the middle, you see that there are many different levels on that scale. And you can then can go to the people who are in embodiment and who are part of the lowest 10%, and you will see that there are people at the very lowest level who embody a certain state of consciousness, and they are forming a gravitational force that seeks to pull the minds of everyone else down to their level of consciousness.

They do this not only through their minds, they do it through their actions, where they have attempted to embroil people into war, so that when people are trapped in war, trapped in battle, some people will rise in honor, whereas others will descend to the very animalistic tendencies of killing anyone who seems to come in their way—or conquering a village and raping the women, or otherwise displaying complete disrespect for life. And thereby they pull them down to that level of being an animal. And they pull those down who look at these atrocities and become angry and seeking revenge, and so they create this downward spiral, where people are pulled down more and more and more.

And so, you see that there are those in the lowest 10% who are living in a particular universe that you who are spiritual people can scarcely imagine. And I do not in fact encourage you to try to imagine how these people experience life. For I myself descended into hell – meaning I descended into their level of consciousness to seek to raise them up – but I did not do this until I was resurrected, and therefore had shed the body and the human consciousness. And certainly, I do not encourage you to descend to that level while you are still in a physical body.

This will only be reserved for a very few people, and so you strive to raise your consciousness rather than lowering it. Unless, of course, you need to go down and look at something in your psychology from past lives and undo a decision that you made at a lower level of consciousness. But you do not attune to the consciousness of others, for you do not need to undo the decisions made by others—as only they can do that.

The top 10% must bring positive change

Now, my beloved, the message I want to get across here is that God gave human beings dominion over the Earth. You have people in the lowest 10% who are the blind—they are the blind seeking to lead the blind of the general population. They are aggressive, they are completely self-centered and focused on themselves. My beloved, you cannot expect these people to suddenly awaken and start raising their own consciousness and that of the 80% of the people.

I am not saying that people from the lowest 10% have not been awakened; it does happen but only a small percentage. So what I am saying is that you cannot expect positive change on this planet to come from the lowest 10%. So where must positive change come from? Well, if you look at the 80%, they tend to be followers; they do not have a strong enough sense of self to go against the grain, to refuse to fit into the mold defined by society. And so, who must then bring positive change? Well, it can only be the top 10%, my beloved, and this is what you need to realize.

As an example of this, look at Europe during the Second World War. It was a conflict that killed millions and millions of people on this continent. Millions of people lost loved ones, millions of people saw their homes destroyed, their cities destroyed—even a nation destroyed. Yet if you go to other parts of the European continent, you can find people who lived almost normal lives during the five years of the Second World War. And why is that, my beloved? Because they were at a different level of consciousness than the people who were directly involved in the war!

My beloved, do not believe that things just happen to happen a certain way. Everything is a manifestation of consciousness. There is a reason why certain people had congregated and embodied in the same areas, the geographical areas, where they became embroiled in the direct war. There is a reason why other people had embodied in other parts of Europe where they were not so directly involved. There is a reason for this, and it is their level of consciousness. So what I am endeavoring to explain is that even in a conflict as serious as the Second World War, you will see that people at different levels of consciousness had very different experiences of the physical events.

Parallel universes in consciousness

And what I endeavor to explain is that you too, today – as the spiritual people – you are, so to speak, living in a parallel universe compared to the greater population and those in the lower 10%. Consider the very fact that you are sitting in a room here, in a monastery of a particular

Christian order that has existed for a very long time, and has a very set, rigid organized tradition. Consider that you are sitting here listening to a person who claims to give voice to the real Jesus Christ, whereas right below you are the monks of this order who are sitting doing their Sunday service, claiming that they are worshipping the real Jesus Christ and would be shocked to really understand what is happening here. Do you see that even though you are in such physical proximity, you are living in parallel universes in the mind?

So the idea from quantum physics of parallel universes is not wrong, only they are not physically parallel universes – they are not parallel universes in the material vibrational spectrum – they are parallel universes in consciousness. And this is the magic of planet Earth in the material realm—that it allows people to exist – as Maitreya explains in greater detail in his book – in the same physical location yet be in parallel universes in consciousness.

Christhood shifts the entire spectrum of consciousness

Now, what that means is that there is a correspondence between the parallel universe that you live in as the spiritual people, and the parallel universe of the lowest 10%. For you see, my beloved, it is a law of God that before a certain manifestation of duality – a certain manifestation of darkness, of evil, can be removed from the Earth – before that can happen, there must be those in the top 10% who have raised their consciousness to a certain level, where they have freed themselves from those aspects of the ego that are being out-pictured as that manifestation of darkness.

They must free themselves, but they must also then take a stand and say, "This manifestation of evil is no longer acceptable in my world!" And only when you stand on the Rock of Christ – because you have been willing to remove the beam in your eye, that aspect of the ego which is being out-pictured as that manifestation – only then, when you stand on that Rock of Christ, will you have the authority – or we might say, you will give God the authority – to remove that manifestation of evil from this planet and remove those who will not voluntarily raise their consciousness beyond it.

Do you see that this is how progress occurs on this planet? There must be some in the top 10% who have reached the level of Christhood that corresponds to the perversion of that level among the bottom 10%.

And only when we have those – a critical mass of people at that level of Christhood – can the perversion of that level be removed. And that way the entire spectrum of consciousness is shifted upwards.

If you look at the spectrum of human consciousness that you find on this Earth, then you will see that the way progress happens is that the entire spectrum is shifted upwards. It is now possible to go one step higher for the top 10%, but those in the bottom 10% cannot go below a certain level or they will be removed from the Earth.

This is the only way that progress can happen; it cannot happen in any other way, my beloved. It cannot happen through force. It cannot happen by one totalitarian nation conquering the world and establishing the kingdom of God through force. It cannot happen through one religion conquering the world. It cannot happen in any other way but a shift in consciousness, whereby those who have the potential must rise, claim their Christhood, purify their own minds of a certain manifestation of the duality consciousness; and then declare with one voice, with one mind, with one heart, that this must stop, for enough is enough!

Can any man-made system bring the Promised Land to Earth?

Lanello, November 2, 2008

There is only one conflict on Earth

For when you dare to actually look at what has been going on – when you dare to look at why it has been going on – you see that even though there is a seemingly endless stream of conflicts on this planet and this continent, you see, my beloved, that there really is only one conflict that has simply been repeating itself over and over again in different physical circumstances.

And that conflict is, of course, the conflict between what we have called the power elite and the people of God. It is the conflict between those who have fallen, as Maitreya explains in his ground-breaking and magnificent book—that I dare say, I wish it had been possible to bring that forth while I was still a messenger in embodiment, for it would have explained so many things; so many questions that were left hanging to the teachings that could be brought forth at the time.

Nevertheless, reality is reality, the now is the now, and so when you see that these fallen beings fell because they honestly, seriously, sincerely – or should I just say naively – believed that they were smarter than God and knew better than God how to run an entire universe. And so they fell into the duality consciousness, ended up on Earth, have embodied here over and over again ever since. And they have repeated the same old pattern of seeking to attain ultimate control over the people in the mistaken belief – the absolutely naïve belief – that that could prove God wrong and prove them right.

As if, my beloved – when you consider what you know today in the modern world about the vastness of the material universe – as if what happens on one little planet such as Earth would actually prove God wrong—the God that strung the Pleiades, that strung the galaxies. How could what happens on this little planet ever be significant in the grand scheme of things? But such is the intense blindness of the human ego—that it actually believes that it has the power to change the fate of the universe. What folly, what folly, I might say.

God cannot be mocked

This is what must be seen by the people—that it is completely, utterly naïve to believe that God can be mocked by human beings. And only when you have that realistic sense of reality of the Law of God – the actual, absolute immovability of the Law of God – only then will you see that you need to escape that illusion.

And you need to stop following the blind leaders, those who are trapped in that illusion. For if you do not stop following them, then you are like a ship without a rudder that is being carried by the current down the Rhine and will be wrecked on the Lorelei Cliff, as a representative for the rock of Christ. For do you not see that the very force that is at work in the second law of thermodynamics is the Rock of Christ that breaks down all closed mental boxes. It breaks down all closed systems and reduces them to the lowest possible energy state, for without the constant infusion of the life of Christ nothing is sustainable.

And thus, those who in some higher sphere chose to cut themselves off from the eternal stream that is the life of Christ, well then they have only a certain time. Their days are numbered, my beloved, and there does indeed come a point where they are ready to be taken because they have had enough opportunity to be expressed.

The need for Christed ones
But then there is – as we have spoken about – that condition that someone must be raised up to the level of Christhood out-pictured as a perversion by these self-centered, egotistical beings. And unless there is someone who dares to step forward and accept that they are the Christ – accept that they are a son or daughter of God – unless that happens, well then they cannot be taken.

And I can tell you, that there are right now a number of these beings, who have had their lawful opportunity, and they are simply being sustained on this planet by the fact that nobody has dared to claim their Christhood. Which, of course, is the very plot that they have engineered from the very beginning—even while Jesus still walked on the Earth. And they attempted to set the stage, thinking that they could kill him physically. And then, of course, when that did not work, going to Plan B and killing his teaching and example—that no one dare to step forward.

Dare to communicate from the heart

Master MORE, December 31, 2008.

There are those on Earth who deny that they have free will. But it is not the Spirit who denies this, but can only be the ego that denies it. For the ego does not want the conscious self – the Spirit – to make choices. It wants to maintain control, and thus it will not allow the conscious self to make the choice to acknowledge that it has choices. [The ego will not allow the self] to acknowledge, for example, that it has the choice to go beyond the limitations of the body, or even the identification with the body in which so many people are trapped—believing they are nothing more than matter.

So, this is the difference between those who are still asleep and those who are beginning to awaken. How do you awaken? You awaken by recognizing that you have a choice—instead of falling into the pattern that you hear so many people express: "I had no choice," or "I had no other choice than doing what I did."

My beloved, when you hear a person make this statement, you know that this person has not been willing to take responsibility for his or her life, for his or her situation. For when you do take that responsibility, you recognize the very fact that no matter what the outer circumstances might be, you always have a choice to adjust your state of mind and choose a different reaction to those circumstances than what might be the standard reaction among 99% of the people living on this planet—and what might indeed be the standard reaction that has been programmed into your mind since childhood.

There are those, my beloved, who have perverted the teachings of Christ to the point, where they do not recognize that the essence of Jesus' teachings was that you have choices. For did Christ not say, "Resist not evil. Turn the other cheek."

Well, is it not so that most people on this planet have been programmed to resist evil and to give back in kind—to respond in kind? So do you not see that the essence of the teachings of Christ is that you have the potential, the ability, to choose to turn the other cheek—even when someone strikes you on one cheek?

Understanding self-awareness

But then, how do you avoid judging, how do you avoid criticizing, how do you avoid blaming, how do you avoid comparing that person to some standard that you have in your mind of what you think is best for that person? Well, my beloved, consider that the first ray is the first ray of the Will of God and the Power of God. So then, when you come to contemplate the will of God, you recognize that the ultimate will of God is to create self-aware extensions of itself. But what is self-awareness? Well, as was said in a hidden sentence in this latest rosary [Invocation for Consuming World Fear], you actually, my beloved, cannot have self-awareness without having free will.

For if the self does not have the ability to choose, it is not a self—it has no identity, it cannot choose what it will be. For you will notice that when Moses on the mountain asked God to give him a name, God said "Yod He Wav He—I will Be who I will Be." Not the "I AM that I AM," as is so often translated. But the reality is that God did not give Moses a name because God is the ever self-transcending Being. And thus, God said, "I reserve the right to be who I will be at any moment."

This, then, is the essence of free will—that you choose who you will be at any moment. And so, this is where you must begin to communicate from the heart—by choosing who you will be in relation to the person or persons with whom you are communicating. Will you choose to be trapped in the illusion of the separate self—that you are separate from them, that you might be in opposition to them, that they might hurt you, that they might threaten you? Or that you need to control them for their own good, for you know best?

You see, when you choose to be the separate self, you cannot respect the free will of other people. And if you do not respect free will – and when I say "respect" I mean complete, unconditional acceptance – well then you cannot actually experience oneness with others.

For you see, oneness cannot be forced. Oneness cannot come about as the result of force or control. Oneness must be based on a complete, unconditional acceptance of the Creator's decision to create extensions of itself, give them individuality and give them free will. Whereby they have the potential to choose—to be more, to be less, to be this, to be that.

Your highest potential

This is the sublime – the supreme – decision of your Creator. When you understand and accept this fully and totally, then you can be in oneness with the Creator—the Creator's intent, the Creator's purpose of not forcing or programming people to be raised up to a certain standard. But instead allowing beings the free will and the space to choose to Be MORE, to choose to come into oneness with each other, to choose to come into oneness with their source.

This is the plan of salvation of your Living God, your living Creator. What has happened is, of course, that certain beings in an unascended sphere, that has since ascended, chose to rebel against that plan and that decision. They chose to use their free will to rebel against it. And so, they entered into the consciousness of separation that is a potential when you have free will. They have since taken over the collective mind of the beings who embody on this planet and certain other planets throughout the galaxies—but your concern should be primarily this one, as you are stuck here until you learn the lessons and decide to take back your free will.

And in order to take back your own free will and truly make free choices, you must come to a respect of the Creator's decision, the Creator's choice, to give you and all other self-aware beings free will. For only when you respect the free will of others, can you truly accept your own free will and your own right to choose to Be MORE, even though yesterday you might have chosen to be less.

For you see, as was also mentioned in this latest rosary, the ultimate lie of the false teachers is that once you have chosen a lesser identity, you cannot simply let go of it, you cannot abandon it, you cannot rise above it. But when you understand free will, you understand – you accept, you experience – that you have the right to say with your God, "I will Be who I will Be." And therefore, you can choose to let go of that old identity, to let it die, to let it vanish, to let it go into the flame that you are—as you were guided in this meditation during your giving of the rosary.

This is your highest potential, my beloved—to choose to be MORE than you were a second ago. This is the only way to overcome the blocks to communication, the way that is based on oneness and seeks to raise all life instead of seeking to tear down.

Respecting the free will of others is the key to your own freedom

For you see, my beloved, when you truly accept free will and the wisdom of the Creator's choice, you recognize that God gave each individual being the right to choose what they will be. And thus, when you meet another with whom you might have had conflicts in the past, when you accept free will, you accept that that person has an absolute God-given right to be in the state of consciousness in which that person in currently abiding. This is their right, my beloved. God has given them that right.

And unless you have fallen prey to the illusion of the fallen beings – that you know better than God – you should accept that God has given them that right. And thus, you accept that whatever consciousness they are in, they are exercising their God-given right of free will, which gives them the right to choose to be anything they want to be. Yet God has also set up a material universe that will then, so to speak, make sure that they actually experience the state of consciousness in which they are choosing to be, even the physical manifestations of that state of consciousness, as everything is the manifestation of consciousness.

And so, when you understand and accept this, you do not need to judge them. You do not need to have a standard in your head for how you think they should be. You can set them free to be who they will be at that moment.

How can you set them free? Well, by giving equal acceptance to your own free will that you give to theirs. For when you accept that they have a right to be in that particular state of consciousness, you also accept that you have a right to be in any state of consciousness that you choose. And you have complete freedom to choose your state of consciousness independently of the choices made by any other human being, even independently of the collective choice made by every human being on Earth.

This is what Jesus demonstrated—that despite the fact that all of the people he met during that embodiment had chosen not to be in the Christ consciousness, he still had the right to choose to be in the Christ consciousness, to be the Christ and to demonstrate it.

And when you understand that you do not need to let other people's choices influence your choices, then you will have the blending of the Alpha and Omega, where you can set others free and set yourself free at the same time. Which means that when you interact with another, then you know that regardless of their state of consciousness, you can choose your own state of consciousness. And you can communicate with that person based on your free-will choice of a certain state of consciousness—without feeling that their state of consciousness, their words, are forcing you to respond in a certain way.

A common cause of conflict

For do you not see, my beloved, that much of the conflict between human beings is precisely due to the fact that so many people believe that when they encounter another person – who does not behave or speak to them the way they think they should be spoken to – well then their only option is to go into a negative frame of mind—be it fear, be it anger or any other negative emotion? And so, the Spirit immediately feels trapped by having to go into that negative reaction. But if it does not fully accept free will or take responsibility for itself, then it will blame the other person for forcing it to go into a negative state of mind—instead of acknowledging the reality that it is making the choice to enter that negative frame of mind. And also acknowledging that it could just as easily choose a different reaction, a higher reaction, a reaction based on love rather than fear and one of the many shades of fear. For truly, all negative reactions and emotions spring from the fear that comes from separation.

And thus, you see that the key to overcoming all of these negative emotions – the key to avoiding the trap of going into these emotions – is indeed to step back and say to yourself, "I can choose oneness even if that person has chosen separation! The fact that another person has chosen to see him- or herself separated from me – to see me as an enemy, as an opponent, as a threat – does not mean that I have to make the same choice. I can choose oneness! And I can first of all choose oneness with my own inner being, whereby I go within, in my inner sanctuary."

Your inner sanctuary

And this inner sanctuary, my beloved, you should all be aware of. For the pearl of great price can be seen as the secret chamber of your heart, which is the very core of your heart. For certainly, when we say "heart," you realize we are not speaking about the physical organ that pumps blood, but about the heart chakra and the very core behind it—that point that is so infinitely small that it could never be found by any amount of material digging and even the best microscopes constructed by science.

And so, you realize that there is that point within you, that point that is the meeting ground between the material and the spiritual realm. And that is the core of your being, where you can always retreat and re-establish your oneness with your own Higher Being. And you should not only see it as a point, but work on making it a sphere that you expand and expand and expand—until it extends way beyond your physical body and your energy field. So that you are always enveloped in that sphere and nothing can actually come in and touch your outer mind, even the analytical mind.

And so, once you retreat into that inner sanctum, connect to the oneness with your own Higher Being and realize who you are, then you can choose a different reaction than a standard, programmed response that you have grown up, perhaps over many lifetimes, to give in certain situations.

You are not a robot

My beloved, think back to what I said in the beginning about the people who deny that they have free will. Well, what is the implication of this? If you do not have free will, you are an automaton, you are a robot, you are a machine, my beloved. For what is the essence of a machine? Well, if you push a certain button, you are guaranteed to get a certain reaction from the machine. If you do not get that reaction, the machine is not working correctly—there is something wrong, something that needs to be fixed.

Well, you see, my beloved, you are a creative being. The fact that someone pushes your buttons does not mean that you have to respond in a negative way—for you can choose not to be a computer. You can choose to be a co-creator, and you can co-create a better response by reconnecting to your own Higher Being and realizing that – certainly – your I AM Presence – who is beyond anything in the material world – cannot be affected by somebody else being in a bad mood. And thus, it would never respond in a negative way to other people—no matter what they do to you.

And so, when you establish that oneness, then you have a foundation for co-creating with your higher self a positive response, an uplifting response, a response that seeks to uplift the other person rather than defend yourself or attack back and seek to tear the other person down, silence them or whatever responses you see repeated over and over and over again

To be MORE, or not to be MORE
So the question really is – in any situation you encounter, no matter what other people do or say – the question is: Do you want to be MORE in that situation? Or do you want to be less—meaning that you allow the other person or your own ego or the mass consciousness to control you and force you to be less than you truly are, as the infinitely creative co-creator that you are created to be. This is the choice—choose ye this day whom you will serve. Will you serve the lesser? Will you serve the MORE?

If you serve the MORE, then respect that God has given you that free will to choose to be MORE in any situation. And do you not see, my beloved, that when most people choose to be less, they do indeed form that self-reinforcing downward spiral that can cause humankind to go into the great depression, as it was called in the 1930s.

But even consider, my beloved, that psychologically – emotionally, spiritually – humankind have been engaged in something we might call the great depression from a spiritual level. And they have been engaged in it for a very long time—thinking that they are powerless, that there are certain limitations they cannot go beyond. Because they do not recognize the very reality that all is an expression of consciousness and that all elements of consciousness are the result of choices that you make—whether to accept this or that as part of your consciousness, as part of your identity. Whether to accept that this is who I will be today, thereby implying that you are not being more than the identity that feels trapped in the material universe.

The high and the low potential
So, where am I going with all this rambling? Well, my beloved, I am seeking to get you to the point where you realize that [this book, and the process of reading it,] has a high and a low potential. It can be just another spiritual book, where you feel good and you end up feeling lighter and you say, "Oh, that was great." And then you go right back to your old momentums and your old habit patterns. Or you can choose to make it an absolutely life-changing experience, whereby you come

up to a higher level, from which there is no way back—because you have so firmly planted your feet on the rock of Christ within you that you know you cannot – you will not – go back to these old patterns and momentums.

This is the choice you have every time you read a spiritual book. But I tell you that at this particular time it is more important than at any time in the past to consider that choice, to consider that potential. Now I, of course, am an ascended being. I am in no way, shape or form threatened by the choices you make—nor do I have any desire whatsoever to control you. My beloved, we of the Ascended Host – as opposed to many of the beings who channel through various channellers – need nothing from you. We don't need your money, we don't need your attention, we don't need your energy, we don't need your obedience, we don't need you to worship us. I am a God-free Being, my beloved, and in so being, I can set you free to be whatever you choose to be. Thus, I have no desire to influence your choice, but I do indeed have a right – a God-given right – to make you more aware that you have the potential to make a different choice.

Chapter 7: Ego Teachings, 2009

Wisdom is more than intellectual knowledge

Elohim Apollo, January 1, 2009

Be wiser than the ego

So you see, my beloved, you need to be wiser. You need to use that wisdom of the second ray and say, "I will be MORE than the people who defend their illusions. I will indeed enter into the heart. I will not go into the analytical mind and seek to defend my illusion when someone comes to tell me something from the heart."

You see, my beloved, sometimes there will be people who are trying to tell you something about yourself and they will not be entirely centered in the heart. They may have a certain vibration of frustration or anger because after having put up with you for some time, they have finally gotten fed up and now they are speaking out. This, then, is one of the most common reasons why people find an excuse for not listening to others. But I tell you that if you are the wise ones, then you will say that whenever someone says something to you, you will look beyond the imperfections of the other person. You will look beyond the vibration. You will look beyond the words. And you will go within your heart and say, "Is there something here that is real, that I need to see? Does this person have a point? Has this person seen, even if imperfectly, something in me that needs to be corrected?"

You must, of course, also be wise to another entrapment of the ego, namely the tendency to use the analytical mind to argue for or against your beliefs, to argue for and against what the other person is saying. You must become wise and use the teachings we have given on the duality consciousness and realize that the duality consciousness can prove any point. For the duality consciousness is based on the analytical faculty of the mind, the intellect.

Know the limitations of the intellect

Now, my beloved, it is not my intention to say here that the intellect is a bad thing and is something you should avoid. You see, my beloved, the intellect is simply a necessary part of the mind. But it is a part of the mind that is specifically designed to help you deal with the world of form. And as we have explained – most profoundly by Mother Mary and Maitreya in their books – the world of form is characterized by differences, which is what makes one form stand out compared to another. And the analytical mind is simply designed to help you deal with these differences, analyzing and categorizing the various characteristics that separate one form from another. It even allows you to make some judgments about what is constructive and what is non-constructive, what actually expands yourself and all life, or what restricts yourself and restricts all life.

This can, to some degree, be done by the intellect, especially when the intellect is under the tutelage of the heart. But, of course, as with any other faculty, the intellect can become an end in itself. And thus, you see those who are never connected to the heart and who believe that the intellect is superior and, thus, has no need to be under the tutelage of the heart, for it is perfectly capable of knowing truth on its own. But you see, my beloved, as I said, the intellect is designed to help you distinguish between what is in the world of form. The intellect cannot discover ultimate truth, ultimate reality. It cannot even deal with these concepts.

And thus, you see many people who have been trapped by the intellect who will argue for hours for a particular world view or idea, although they actually realize that on a deeper level they do not believe there is any ultimate truth or any ultimate argument. For after all, they see that any argument with the intellect can always be counteracted with another argument. And so, they have come to believe that there is no ultimate truth.

Knowing ultimate truth

How, then, will you connect to ultimate truth? Well, only through the heart, my beloved. Only the heart, as Master MORE has said, can connect to the ultimate reality that all life is one. This realization is, of course, the ultimate expression of wisdom. For you will see that there is intellectual knowledge, which is very good at coming up with all the details but is not very good at seeing the big picture—for only the heart can see the big picture. So naturally, the intellect – being focused on differences, being designed to analyze and categorize differences – cannot reveal, cannot fathom, the underlying reality of the oneness of all life.

And so, those who are trapped in the intellect are trapped in seeing themselves separated from others, separated from God. And thus – suddenly – the existence of God and the nature of God becomes a topic for intellectual argumentation. Rather than being seen as being a challenge to connect to that God, to experience God directly in the heart, rather than arguing which image of the remote, external God is the ultimate one. And this is what many intellectual theologians have done over the ages, of course, without ever coming one step closer to the direct experience of the oneness of God's Being.

Your ego

You will see, my beloved, that many times people trapped in the lower mind can come up with what they think are unassailable arguments for this or that or the next thing. This is what you will see, for example, outpictured in the scribes and the Pharisees who challenged Christ and in the Brahmins who challenged the Buddha. Yet, the one who has gone into the heart and connected to the oneness of all life can come up with a statement or a saying that confounds all of the best intellects on this planet, that jolts the mind. And therefore, it opens the heart to a direct experience that is beyond anything that can be analyzed and categorized by the intellect.

For certainly, it is helpful when you are in physical embodiment to have a certain ego where everything is categorized, so that you can quickly respond to certain situations. But you see, when that ego becomes an end in itself – and you think it contains all the wisdom you need – you do not step back and say, "Can I now compare my responses to the wisdom of my higher self and therefore gradually ascend to a higher response, one that is based on oneness, the oneness of all life and the desire of life itself to raise up all life, to raise the All?" This is the true wisdom of the ages.

And, as the Buddha said, you are very close to manifesting that kind of wisdom, many of you already having it in glimpses as was expressed this afternoon. But all of you could stand to focus on locking in to it and truly opening your minds and hearts to that higher wisdom. And also allowing that higher wisdom – and allowing each other – to show you where you are still holding on to certain dualistic arguments and illusions that cause you to make subtle judgments about other people or about life on Earth—what it should or should not be.

For you see, my beloved, when you judge what life should be or should not be, you will also be judging yourself. And when you are judging what you should be or should not be, well then, you cannot BE. For in analyzing something, you have separated yourself from it, and therefore you are not being. You cannot, as Master MORE said, be who you will be at any given moment, for you are now judging based on the idea that there is some predefined response to every situation.

Stop killing your creativity

But then where is creativity, if everything is predefined? For again, my beloved, nothing is static in the reality of God. There are many spiritual teachings on this planet that cater to the subtle belief that there are certain invariable laws of God, and once you understand those laws and make use of them, then your salvation is guaranteed. But again – as we have said now in many different contexts and disguises – salvation is a creative process, not a mechanical one.

And thus, you might think about God Wisdom and think that up here in the spiritual realm we have a great book, and in that book is written all the wisdom of the world and it can never change. But you see, my beloved, wisdom is a creative force, and creativity is not predefined. It is indeed spontaneous.

And so, there are many expressions of wisdom that we, who are the guardians of the second ray of God wisdom, do not know because no one in the lower spheres has as yet chosen to express them—and thus surprise us to where we can say, "Well done thou good and faithful servant. Thou hast been faithful over a few things. I will make thee ruler over many things by giving you greater wisdom, for you have been willing to express that wisdom in new, creative, and surprising ways."

The "untouchable" within you

Thus again, be willing to let others tell you what you cannot see, and you will find that you will make much greater progress. My beloved, it is a common reaction that you have a need to defend some aspect of your lower being as being untouchable, as being beyond criticism, as being beyond questioning.

Yet you will see, my beloved, that there are some people who have gone beyond that point. They have gone beyond that fear of looking at something, where they are willing to look at anything and everything, even expose it in public. For when you are not seeking to protect the lower self, then why do you need to fear the exposure of it—if that exposure of some element of your lower self could inspire and help another? Well, is that not why you are here—ultimately?

And so, consider and observe that there are some among you who are free to speak about themselves and their own imperfections. There are others who never say anything. And there are others who are somewhere in between. But consider that you all have the potential to be inspired by each other, to come to that point, where there is nothing you need to defend, nothing you need to hide. For if there is some element of duality in your consciousness, well then, your attitude is, "Let it be brought out in the open so I can see it, for I know I AM MORE than this. And thus, I want to see it, so that I can rise above it and be freer than I was before."

Do you not see that those who have no fear are free? For even though they may still have certain manifestations of unreality they are dealing with, they are not so identified with it that they seek to protect or hide it. And this is freedom. It is not yet the total freedom from duality, but it is the freedom of not being fully identified with duality and thus, knowing you are MORE.

Do not try to understand love—let it flow!

Elohim Heros and Amora, January 2, 2009.

We come in Oneness, known as Heros and Amora, Elohim of the third ray, to give you some understanding and – if you are willing – some direct experience of how love relates to communication from the heart.

Why, my beloved, did we have you give the Rosary for Overcoming the Past before this dictation on love? Well, my beloved, consider how you were asked during this rosary to affirm radical forgiveness, unconditional forgiveness, of everything from the past—from yourself to other people, to God, to the Ma-ter light. You see, when you are anchored in unconditional love, your past does not disappear but it ceases to have power over your present—and thus it also has no power over your future. Why is this, my beloved? Because when you are One with that flame, with that River of Life of unconditional love, well then you know that you are MORE, infinitely more than any manifestation from your past in this limited sphere here on Earth.

My beloved, you might have walked outside and seen a sunbeam reflected from a puddle on the road. But you see, my beloved, that sunbeam does not identify itself with the puddle. It knows it is a sunbeam. And thus, you see that even though a sunbeam can be seen through a dirty window and be somewhat colored by that window, it is in your eyes that the sunbeam is colored, whereas the sunbeam knows it is an extension of the Sun. And thus, you too are, of course, an extension of the Sun of your I AM Presence, even the Sun of your Creator.

And when you allow yourself to reconnect to that reality, then you will feel the unconditional love of your Creator flowing through you. And then, how can you identify yourself with any of the situations and conditions and events that have taken place in your past on this Earth? You will know you are infinitely MORE. You will even know that other people are more than the manifestations of the past that you have experienced. And thus, then you will be able to overcome the most common tendency that causes conflicts on Earth, namely the tendency to hold on to a past image of oneself and of others, even a past image of the world and of God.

Your past becomes your ego

For you see, my beloved – building on the discourse from yesterday about wisdom and about the intellect and how the intellect is designed to work with the world of form to detect differences, to categorize differences, to analyze causes in the world of form – you see that what happens to many people, in fact what happens to all people, is that they create a ego in their subconscious minds. Most people are not even aware of this, but some, like some of you, are beginning to peel back that veil to be aware of how they have created these images in the past. And now, when that ego is created, any new event is then instantly compared to the ego. You meet another person, and instantly and subconsciously your mind seeks to label that person in order to know in which category, in which drawer from your past, you can place that person, so that you will also know how you are supposed to respond to that person based on how you have responded to other people from that category in the past.

And so you see, my beloved, in many cases you have people who meet each other for the first time – at least in this lifetime – and so, one would think that when you meet another person that you have never met before, you would meet that person on a blank slate, you would give that person an opportunity to be himself or herself. But most people cannot do this. They are instantly and subconsciously seeking to put that person in a neat, little category in the subconscious ego. And thus, as soon as they have enough input from the person that their subconscious minds feels they can now label that person, well then they are no longer responding to that person as a unique individual. They are responding the way they would have responded – and, indeed, the way they did respond – to similar people in the past.

The basis for conflict

This, of course, is how you see, in its extreme form, the conflict between various groups of people, such as based on skin color, race, or even the conflict between men and women. For you meet a person and instantly you evaluate, "Is it a man or a woman?" Well, then I need to behave such and such. "Is that person black or white?" Well, then I need to behave such and such. "Is that person a Jew or any other race that I am familiar with?" Well then my behavior must be adjusted accordingly.

For surely, if that person belongs to one of the millions of black people or the billions of women on this planet, well then that person must behave the way all the other people in that category do—or so the intellect reasons. For it cannot connect, as was said yesterday, to the infinity, to the unconditionality of the River of Life, but can only relate to the limited world of form where everything is categorized by something. And what is that something?

Study the intellectuals with wisdom

Well, my beloved, here is where you need to use wisdom to study the intellectual people on this planet – those who think they know best – whether they are found in the field of science, in the field of government, or in the field of religion. Study them a little bit, and then go a little bit deeper. You see, my beloved, you will find that there are intellectual people – very intelligent people, my beloved, and often well-meaning – who are absolutely convinced, based on their intellectual reasoning, that science is the only true way to know reality, that there is nothing beyond the material universe, and that all religion is simply an unreality conjured up by the mind. Likewise, you will find people who are absolutely convinced, based on intellectual reasoning, that their political ideology or their political system is the only true one, and it will bring God's kingdom or some other edenic state to Earth. Of course, in the field of religion you find theologians who are absolutely convinced that their religion is the only true one, that all others are false, that science is false, that science has no validity, and so forth and so on.

And so, what you realize when you look at this is that every person has a certain coloring, a certain world view that sets the tone for that person's personal ego. In other words, people are often very convinced that their ego is not subjective, that their ego is the only real way to look at life. And therefore, they never question that basic paradigm, that basic world view that is the very foundation for their ego and thus colors everything in it.

Going into anti-love

And thus, what happens when people accept such a limited view is that they inevitably, my beloved, go into a vibration of anti-love. For when you accept one particular limited view and elevate it to the status of infallibility – the only right one – well, then of course you cannot escape the fact that there are other views on Earth. And therefore, you go into the dualistic struggle of having to defend your view against the opposing views or the competing views, sometimes even thinking you have to destroy those competing views, even destroy or kill the people who embody them or who have chosen to believe them.

And so, you see, this sense of being threatened by other viewpoints – by other limited beliefs, by other world views – well this is a sign, my beloved, of anti-love. It is a sign that you have been ensnared by the false teachers of anti-love, that you have absorbed the consciousness of anti-love, and that you have allowed that consciousness to influence – perhaps completely make up the very foundation for – your personal ego. It has colored the very core of your world view, how you see the world, how you see God, how you see other people. And it colors how you see yourself, and how you relate to the world, other people and God, even how you relate to yourself, how you view yourself.

And so, what I endeavor to explain here is that when you are in this state of mind, you cannot communicate from the heart. For as we have said before, the heart is based on oneness—the core of your being is one with all life. And thus, in order to connect to that oneness – to accept that oneness, in order to let it flow through you and find expression through you – well you must be willing then to question your ego, to question your world view, and to consider, "Is it based on love or is it based on anti-love?" And you see, my beloved, true love, real love, living love, is unconditional.

What you do to others

For of course, my beloved, as Christ said, "Do unto others what you want them to do to you." The underlying meaning being that what you do onto others shows what you have already done to yourself—subconsciously. For when you create a ego and use it to judge other people, is it not obvious that the first person to be put in the ego is yourself?

For you, naturally, must already have judged yourself before you start projecting that judgment outside yourself towards others. And so, when you judge others, well then you put yourself in a mental box that prevents you from experiencing that you are loved unconditionally by your Source. And therefore, of course, you cannot experience unconditional love but are bound to repeat the endless cycle of seeking to justify your version of conditional love.

So what can break the stalemate? What can break the catch-22? Well, it certainly helps to use the understanding of the mind – not the intellectual, but the higher understanding – to recognize what we are talking about, to recognize the need to simply go beyond that ego and to step back from the filters. Until you are so far back that you can see beyond the filters, and you can begin to get a glimpse of the world that is beyond the filter, the real world. Then you can see the Sun as it really is, so that you can see your Higher Being as it really is and thus experience the unconditional love that your Higher Being has for you.

You can then come to the absolute, stunning awakening, where you recognize that your I AM Presence does not see the world through the filter you have created in your lower mind. This, my beloved, is not something that a person can do instantly, even if confronted with this teaching. It can take many years, even many lifetimes, for a person to gradually separate itself from the ego to the critical level, where the person's conscious self begins to recognize that the ego is not always right.

Your ego has no influence over reality

Look at some of the people in the world who are totally caught up in a particular conflict. These are the people where their conscious selves completely identify with their egos and their egos' view of the world. And so, for them it is a matter of life and death to defend their religion or their political ideology, even by killing other people in order to do so.

You have, of course, as spiritual people, begun that separation from the ego, where you see that the ego is not always right. But it is wise to consider that there are subtleties to this and that it is necessary for all spiritual people to actually come to that absolute, undeniable moment of truth where you recognize – you experience – the limitations of the ego.

Think, my beloved, back to when people during the Middle Ages believed the universe was very small and that the Earth was the center of the universe. Then think how you today have grown up realizing that this Earth is like an infinitely small speck of dust in a very, very large universe with billions of galaxies. And then look at the fact that there are billions of people on this planet who are still caught up in the belief that by praying to God or performing certain rituals, they can actually control God and get him to do something for them.

This is the recognition you need to come to—that your ego has absolutely no power over reality. No matter how convinced your ego is that its view of the world is reality, it is still a complete illusion. And outside of the ego's own little parallel universe, there is the real world that is in no way, shape or form affected by this—as the Sun is not affected by anything that takes place on Earth. Do you think the Sun is affected at all by the fact that it is a cloudy day right now? Surely, you realize that there may be a few clouds over your own place here but that there are vast stretches of the Earth where there are no clouds.

Unconditional love knows no conditionality

So you see – again – when you are caught in looking at the world from a certain perspective – where you are trapped in thinking that your little ego and your little ego is the center of the universe – well then you cannot experience unconditional love, that unconditional love is unconditional—which means it is given to all people on Earth 24 hours a day, my beloved.

You cannot actually place yourself in any sphere – be it in the material universe or another realm – where you are cut off from the unconditional love of God. It is not possible. For how can you shut out something that is unconditional? It penetrates all conditions! You may think you are cut off from it, but you are only cut off from it because you are seeing the world through that ego that says, "Love is such and such, and it is not this or that."

And so, when you communicate with other people, you are, of course, communicating with another person through your personal ego. And the other person is communicating with you through his or her personal ego. And that is why you will see that people with vastly different egos often clash. And that is why you will see that people tend to congregate together with people who have similar egos, so they can avoid the worst of the conflicts. But you see, my beloved, coming together with people who have similar illusions as yourself is not helping you rise above those limitations. On the contrary, by reinforcing the validity of each others illusions, many of the spiritual and religious people around the world are actually helping each other hold back their progress—for they convince each other that their view of reality is the only true one.

Your real self is still pure

Elohim Purity and Astrea, January 2, 2009

Seeing all impurities

For you see, my beloved, I wish you to look beyond any image you may have of the representatives of the fourth ray, such as the idea that we are disciplinarians or that we judge people. We do not judge anyone. But we do see impurities and purities—we see the difference very clearly. And no human being, no serpentine mind, can fool us into mistaking an impurity for a purity. It is simply not possible, for we are above the duality consciousness.

So what we are here to help you achieve is a sense of co-measurement. For have we not explained the importance of the ego that you have in your minds and how the analytical faculty of the mind will use such a ego? And thus, can you not see that your view of the world is colored by the ego, and thus, of course, your view of purity and impurity is colored by the ego? As I have explained, some people indeed have come to believe that holding negative feelings or negative images of others is part of the work of their god and therefore in some sense must be pure.

And thus, the reality is, my beloved, that you cannot discern between purity and impurity by using the human intellect. Even if you were to study all of the spiritual teachings in the world and fill your subconscious ego with their statements about what is pure and impure, you still would not be able to fully know – to fully experience – the difference between purity and impurity.

How, then, can you come to know the difference? By encountering our Presence, our Purity in the Light, in the presence of which no impurity can hide, no impurity can disguise itself as purity. So you see, we are not here to judge you in any way, for you might think that we only see your impurities. But this, of course, is not true, for we certainly also see the pure elements of your being. And I can tell you that there is not anyone who is serious about the spiritual path who does not have many purities in their beings, many pure images and views and understandings of the world, many pure feelings. This was so eloquently expressed today in your discussion by people who had experienced some unconditionality, such as feeling happy, feeling gratitude, but a gratitude and a happiness that was not opposed by the dualistic opposite of ingratitude or unhappiness.

How purity is perverted

For do you see, my beloved, what the false teachers have attempted to use in order to trap the more spiritual people – those who have started to wake up – is that they have taken the pure qualities of God and they have attempted to turn them into dualistic qualities by defining what they think is an opposite. But, of course, the purity of God is unconditional – is infinite – and thus cannot have an opposite.

Only in separation from Oneness can there be opposites. And thus, only the duality consciousness can create opposites, meaning that when the forces of darkness create an imperfection – a perversion of a God quality – they are actually not creating an opposition or a perversion of the God quality—they are creating two qualities at once. They are creating the dualistic form of love and the dualistic form of anti-love. And those are the two qualities that oppose each other.

But when people do not see this – do not see that even human love is impure – well, then they are trapped in the eternal human struggle of seeking to cause human good – relative good, dualistic good – to win over dualistic evil. And it cannot be done, my beloved.

For even if you think your intentions are pure and you are working for the cause of good or the cause of God – but you are seeking to fight other people who are evil – well then by the law of action and reaction, you create the opposite to your unbalanced action. And thus, you can never win that battle. There can never be peace on Earth by killing other people. There can never be peace on Earth by continuing conflict and holding impure feelings and impure images of other people.

Our offer to help you

And so, you who are the spiritual people have begun to realize this, but many of you have so far only begun to understand it at a certain intellectual level and with some intuitive insights. So what we offer you from the fourth ray is that we will manifest our Presence with you – as you are willing – and we will form that mirror of purity that will allow you to see both the purity and the impurity in your beings.

Now, some of you may have apprehension about this—being concerned that you might see so many impurities that you will be overwhelmed or ashamed or afraid that you will not be acceptable in the eyes of God. But then you need to study the teachings given earlier on the first three rays, and you will recognize that God does not condemn you. God only wants you to be free from the impurities. But God has complete respect for the Law of Free Will.

Those impurities have entered your being as a result of choices you made. Those choices were often not free choices because you were manipulated by the false teachers or by the state of affairs on planet Earth, where there is so much conflict. Nevertheless, you made the choice. And the impurities can only leave your being when you make the choice to let them go, my beloved.

You can invoke the Violet Flame 24 hours a day for the rest of your lifetime – you can give rosaries, prayers, you can fast, you can do anything you can think of, my beloved – but an impurity cannot be taken from you until you release it. And you cannot release it until you see the original decision that caused you to allow it entry—and then undo that decision by replacing it with a pure choice, a choice based on the recognition of purity.

Understanding the catch-22

You see, my beloved, the goal of the false teachers is always to put you in a catch-22 from which you cannot move on, you cannot progress. Shame, guilt, fear, are the very powerful tools that they use to create such a catch-22, where they fool you into absorbing certain impure beliefs and generating impure feelings. And then, they give you the further impure belief that what you have done is wrong and therefore God will condemn you for it—unless you seek to hide it. And that, then, prevents you from going through the process I have just explained of sensing the Presence of Purity, seeing freely the impurities, and freely letting them go.

There are other clever, subtle ways in which the false teachers have caused you to feel that you cannot let go or that you should not let go of these impurities, including, of course, the entire concept of the automatic outer path, where you do not need to look at the beam in your own eye. You only need to declare Jesus Christ your Lord and Savior or get down on your knees five times a day and face Mecca, and then – "poof"

– one day you will be saved. And this, then, is why people feel that they cannot – or they should not, or they will not, or they do not need to – take an objective look at themselves and experience the difference between purity and impurity.

And so, knowing that you are ready to take that step of taking an objective look at yourselves, I will then offer our assistance. I will offer to manifest my Presence with you, as does my consort Purity, as does Serapis Bey and all other representatives of the fourth ray—including Mother Mary who as the Mother of God is truly on all rays. For she is beyond any ray, beyond the level of a chohan, beyond the level of an archangel, but has merged into the universal purity of that Mother of God.

So choose the master whom you want to manifest his or her Presence with you, that you may have a sense of co-measurement of what impurity is holding you back from breaking through and having that turning point that Master MORE explained this book can be for you. We will offer to give you this as you sleep during the night, if you will ask to go to the retreat of Serapis Bey at Luxor. Where you will meet the master of your choice, who will show you the impurity that blocks your breakthrough but will also show you a pure aspect of your being that is the anti-thesis to that impurity, to that block—and thus enables you, empowers you, to overcome that block and rise above it.

For you know you are MORE than that impurity and that no matter what might have happened in the past, nothing can stick to your immortal being, nothing can stick to your conscious self, for you have the right "to be who you will be" and to decide at any moment to be MORE than those impurities and to step out of the identification with them. Let them go, I say, for I think you have had enough of them and you realize it is time to move beyond. This, then, is our gift, my beloved.

Communicate that life is MORE

Mother Mary, January 3, 2009.

Truth will not fit in your database

You see, my beloved, as Pontius asked when he was faced with the Living Christ in embodiment: "What is truth?" Well then, when you look at the Earth, you will see that so many people, so many groups of people, have their individual databases. And as has been explained, the very foundation for such a database is that you have a certain world view and belief system, you have certain paradigms that you consider to be absolutely true—and thus they are beyond questioning.

And you see, that, then, means that when each of these groupings of people consider the question "What is truth," well the question, the topic, has already been colored by their basic world view. For certainly, they are not open to any expression of truth that might upset the apple cart of them feeling that they have managed to force truth to fit in a nice file folder in their database—and therefore, they have their lives under some form of control.

So then, my beloved, the reality, of course, is that you are God-free spiritual beings, individual extensions of your Creator, co-creators with that Creator. Do you see, my beloved, that this is the essence of the problem with the database—that it imposes an image, a graven image, upon your identity? And when the conscious self accepts such an image, well then it also accepts the corresponding limitations to its self-expression on Earth, thinking that its self-expression must fit into the mold and therefore there are certain expressions that are acceptable and some that are not acceptable. Meaning that suddenly the conscious self is no longer a co-creator, who is allowing God's force of constant self-transcendence to flow through it. It has now become something less than the fully creative being it was designed to be by the Creator itself.

The force of liberation

And thus, my beloved, what happens when you hold on to those images in the database and will not question them? Well then, there is a built-in force in the Ma-ter light that we have talked about as the second law of thermodynamics – as the force of Kali – that breaks down all imperfections. Even what the Hindus call Shiva, the God of destruction, the destroyer of all that which has become, so to speak, set in stone and has taken on the form of a graven image, meaning any image that does not change.

You see, that force itself will break down those towers of Babel that people have built – and that they think can reach into the heavens and that are not changeable or that could never fall apart – those institutions in finance that they think could never fail or should not be allowed to fail. So that they think that when the institutions are in danger of failing, the government should step in. And I tell you, when the government does step in to prop up those institutions and prevent them from failing, well then there is a real possibility that the government will have to fail in order to set the people free from the illusion behind it.

You see, my beloved, there will always be that force of the Mother light – out of the unconditional love of God – that will not allow God's co-creators to be trapped forever in a limited sense of identity. And thus, it will come in and it will indeed overturn the moneychangers and their tables, overturn the illusions. It will upset the apple cart, my beloved, until the souls are free—free to bask in the light of creativity that is the very force of life itself. For what God – you might ask logically – would allow his own co-creators to be forever trapped in that lesser sense of identity, when he knows that they are so much more?

The immense power of surrender

Do you see, my beloved, that I am not seeking to give you some outer rule for how you should communicate with others? For when you rise above the initiations of the fourth ray, you rise above the level of consciousness where you need rules, outer rules, that you follow. You rise to the point where you need to begin to open yourself to the flow from your own Higher Being, so that you are not acting based on some rule in your database. You are allowing the creative force of life itself to either bypass the database or you have purified the database of the imperfections – the matrices, perhaps even the valid matrices – of how the creative force should flow. And thus, you are allowing it to flow freely.

My beloved, I have served for some time on the fifth ray of truth, and one of the concepts I have attempted to communicate to the world is the need to surrender, the power of surrender—the immense power of surrender. You may think that surrender is a passive activity, but it is not, my beloved. It can indeed be an immense power. For you see, when you surrender the finite, you become empty, empty of finite matrices. And in that emptiness, you become the open door for the infinite to find expression through you—without being hampered by those finite images in your database.

And thus, when you are truly empty through surrender, the greater power can flow through you, and it is greater than any power that can be attained through any of the forceful means that people have come up with. Which is indeed why you saw that Moses had greater power than the black magicians in the Court of Pharaoh, that Jesus had greater power than the scribes and the Pharisees and the temple priests, or the demons who came to challenge him. For it was not his power, it was a greater power of the flow of life itself that could flow through him because he had become empty. And in being empty of the finite, then being filled with the Infinite.

This does not mean that you become as nothing, but it means that your individuality becomes empty of finite restrictions, and thus your true individuality can be expressed. For there are those who think that Jesus was not an individual. But of course, it is not true. Jesus expressed Christhood through the prism of his individuality. And another might express Christhood in an entirely different way, as many people have indeed done without being recognized as such—partly because of the Christian illusion that there is one Christed being who could ever walk the Earth. And thus, people fail to allow Jesus the victory that he expressed when he said "Those that believe on me shall do the works that I did and even greater works," my beloved. For surely, that is the desire of Jesus as a true teacher—to see his students surpass him in their expression of creativity.

Serve fully by being at peace

Jesus, January 4, 2009.

Question the unquestionable

For let me tell you that one of the greatest plots of the false teachers is to create an environment where none dare to speak out about the underlying paradigms and assumptions that they have elevated to the status of infallibility. Think about what other masters have said about the database in the subconscious mind and how it is founded upon a particular world view. Well, the false teachers have attempted to pull everyone into accepting one of the dualistic belief systems as the foundation for their personal database. And therefore, they attempt to create an environment where no one dares to speak out and challenge those dualistic illusions.

And thereby – can you see, my beloved – that as long as those dualistic illusions are not challenged, well then the people look at every aspect of life through the filter of those illusions, having built their personal databases entirely on those illusions. And thus, how can they ever come to see the living truth? How can they come to experience the Spirit of Truth which cannot – certainly, you can see – be fit into any database based on duality? And this is, then, the catch-22, where the false teachers, the blind leaders, seek to hold people indefinitely, thinking that if they can hold people trapped, they can maintain control over this planet—not being able to realize that the very force of the Mother Kali will break down all of their prison walls.

For you see, my beloved, as my Mother explained, you cannot be satisfied, fully satisfied, by anything in this world. So even if you have a beautiful theological foundation that describes God and the Heaven world and the road to salvation, then you still cannot be fully satisfied with it, my beloved. Do you see that even the teachings we have given in this day and age, teachings that are way beyond the old dogmas and doctrines, teachings that I have put on my website and that are available elsewhere, those teachings by themselves cannot satisfy you fully? For you desire to go beyond an outer teaching expressed in words and experience the Living God, the Spirit of Truth within you.

Is objectivity possible?

And this is, indeed, the desire that is the hope for the awakening of humankind, when you dare to witness that you had that desire, that you were willing to follow it, and that you have indeed experienced the Living God—as this messenger expressed in his video, where he talks about the only proof of the existence of God is the direct experience. Look through the comments on that video, my beloved, and see how those trapped in the duality consciousness seek to deny or ridicule every aspect of it, seeking to come up with a very "clever" belief, my beloved, (and "clever" of course being in quotation marks), that everything is just a matter of subjective experience, that there is no objective experience, no objective reality.

Yet, my beloved, understand the subtle difference. You are an individualization of the Creator's Being. The Creator is omnipresent. Your sense of self is focused at a particular localized point. The Creator sees everything from the omnipresent perspective; you see the world from your localized perspective. Do you see that, certainly, you do not have the omnipresent perspective of the Creator? But does that mean you cannot have an objective experience?

Well, that depends on how you define "objective," my beloved. For you see, if the materialists are right that you cannot have an objective experience, then they have nullified their own philosophy and argument. Because then it follows logically that materialism and their belief in materialism – and their belief in the superiority of materialism over any form of faith – is also their subjective experience. And thus, they cannot be any more right than any religion. And they are in fact arguing that, "My subjective experience is superior to your subjective experience." And this of course – if they were honest – nullifies their entire argument.

And thus, we come to the realization that we need a slightly deeper understanding of the concept of objectivity, my beloved. And it is very simple. As we have said, any human being on this planet is at this very moment looking at the world through his or her personal database that forms a filter for how you look at everything, how you categorize any experience by relating it to your previous experiences and beliefs in the database. Seeing the world through the filter of your database is a subjective experience. Whether you are a religious person who believes in God – but has never experienced the Presence of God – or whether you are a materialist who denies the existence of God, you are seeing the world through your subjective filter.

But you see, my beloved, it is indeed possible for human beings to come to see one or a few steps beyond their present filter, to expand their database, or even to go beyond the database and experience a new understanding, a higher understanding.

Science and objectivity

My beloved, for centuries science has precisely empowered people to see beyond some of the hypocrisy and superstition created by the rigid Christianity of the Middle Ages. And do you not see, then, that science itself claims that it is possible to have an objective experience? What scientists are currently denying is that one can have such an experience through consciousness.

But as quantum physics has proven, you can never have an experience that is not coming through your consciousness. So the question of how objective your experience is depends on how dense the filter of your personal database is. Which means that when you go through a conscious effort of questioning and challenging the assumptions and beliefs in your database – replacing them with a higher understanding, or perhaps discarding them altogether – then you can gradually work towards a state of consciousness where even though you still see the world from a localized perspective, you are not seeing the world through the filter of a database filled with dualistic beliefs. And this, my beloved, is the true definition of objectivity.

This does not mean that there is some ultimate standard of objectivity that you can attain while still in embodiment. For the only ultimate standard of objectivity is the omnipresent awareness of the Creator. But nevertheless, it means that those who are willing to see beyond duality – those who are willing to consider how their view of the world is colored by their database – well they can work towards a state of mind where they are clear from the dualistic beliefs. Instead of seeing through a glass darkly, as Paul expressed it, they can now "see him for who he is." They can see Christ reality. They can see themselves as spiritual beings, extensions of the Creator's Infinite Being, focused in a particular point in the finite world, but with an infinite potential to go beyond it and embrace infinity.

Let the Holy Spirit speak through you

Saint Germain, January 4, 2009.

Your drama takes away your freedom

Thus, my beloved, what then is the key to being free? Well, it is, of course, to realize the reality that what prevents you from being free is that you have created a drama, a personal story, that you think you have to keep outplaying indefinitely. For you somehow have become trapped in it, identified with it. And thus, you think that the drama gives you something that you need, something you cannot live without.

And that something is – as has been expressed by other masters – something from the material world that you think you need, that you think will complete you. But my beloved, as has been said before – and as we will say again until you finally get it – you can never be fulfilled by anything in the material world. You can only be fulfilled by something from the spiritual realm, namely one of the flames of God. And you can only experience something from the spiritual realm by being the open door for it to stream forth in the material realm and thus raise up all life.

Now, my beloved, you know that I was embodied as the person who gave birth to a substantial portion of the Shakespearian plays, thus you should realize that I enjoy drama as much as anyone. [Laughter] And certainly, I could not help but sit back with a chuckle as I watched the drama that you so lovingly and willingly outplayed last night.

Do not for a moment believe, my beloved, that there was only one or a couple of people who were playing in that drama, for you were all out-picturing certain roles in your own minds, depending on how you saw the drama, how you looked at it, how you looked at the persons who were on the forefront of it. For that way of looking at the drama, that way of experiencing it, will – if you are honest and willing – show you your own drama.

Were you embarrassed by certain things? Then you are outplaying a certain drama. Were you afraid that certain things would be said? Then that is your drama, giving you that fear, that desire to limit what can be said in a conversation. And do you see, my beloved, that when you have a drama that gives you a need to limit what can be said, then you obviously are not free to let communication flow from the heart, for you seek to restrict that flow.

Free communication has no standard

Now, you see, my beloved, sometimes you may think that communication from the heart has to live up to a certain standard for what you believe is "heartfelt" or "spiritual" or "loving" communication. But as has been explained earlier, sometimes the heart can take on a certain coloring, depending on the person's basic world view. Yet, if the person is still willing to speak that in the open then they have an opportunity – by bringing it out in the open in front of other people – to see it in a different light than they have seen it before. And therefore, they move closer to that breakthrough point, where they finally clearly see it for what it is. See that it is only something their conscious selves have taken on, see that they are so much more, and thus they can finally make that decision: "I no longer need this drama in order to get what I need, for I know I can get it from inside myself."

You see, my beloved, your personal drama is like a maze. And you are trapped in the maze and you cannot find your way out. And you have come to believe – because you have come to identify yourself with the drama – that you are trapped there by external forces or other people and that you cannot escape. But you see, my beloved, you will never escape the drama – the maze, the labyrinth – until you realize that the drama was not created by God, by other people, by fate, by chance. It was created by you!

And thus, you are the only one who can find your way out of the maze, for you are the only one who can decide that you will no longer see yourself as the person who is trapped in the maze. You will shift your focus and realize that you are more than that person, more than the maze, more than the subconscious ego that prevents you from getting out.

...

And so, what you can then do in order to accelerate your own growth is that you can look at yourself, and you can see what kind of reaction you typically have when you speak out to other people and they respond in a way that causes you to react to their response. How do you react? Then trace that back—what is the feeling? Get in touch with the feeling. But then see beyond the feeling—what is the thought behind the feeling? Analyze, categorize, intuit about the thought and what it actually says about your view of yourself, other people and life.

Then go beyond the thought and get in touch with what is the underlying pattern, that basic assumption that forms the foundation for your ego, and what that says about your sense of identity—how you see yourself, how you see yourself in relation to the world and how you see yourself in relation to God. Notice whether you see yourself relating to the external God or you are beginning to be more in tune with the internal God. This is an essential key to your freedom.

A cost-benefit analysis of pain

My beloved, every ascended master who has ascended from Earth has done precisely this: self-observation—objective, non-emotional, non-judgmental, non-blaming, self-revelation. This means being willing to have that revelation of what is pure and impure, what is not quite there, what keeps you trapped in certain reactionary patterns. Every ascended master has done this until the moment they ascended. Every person who has reached spiritual maturity is doing this constantly. Those who are not doing this constantly are those who are so trapped in their dramas that they are not able to do this, because they think that if they see something in themselves that is not according to a certain standard, then it will cause them pain or self-condemnation.

So then, what do you do if you honestly realize that this is the case for you—that you are still so wounded that you find it difficult to look at yourself without going into fear or self-condemnation? What do you do, my beloved? Well, there is not necessarily only one answer, but the more intense the pain, the more you might consider that there can come a point where you simply have to make a very hard, objective calculation—kind of a cost-benefit analysis, as they say in the business world. And you may have to say to yourself, "Do I want to live the rest of this embodiment experiencing the pain and discomfort I am experiencing right now?" If the answer is "Yes" then by all means pursue that, for you have the total freedom of the Law of Free Will to do this. I have no judgment whatsoever of you. I simply state that then I, as the God of Freedom, cannot help you.

But if you come to the conclusion that you do not want to live the rest of your life in this pain, then you need to realize that the pain comes from a wound. Looking at the wound will cause you more intense pain than you have right now. For the fact is that the personal drama that you are outplaying has allowed you to cope with the pain to a certain degree, where it has become familiar, tolerable, perhaps even giving you a sense of contentment that this is just the way life has to be. And so, you can deal with the daily pain in many cases, even though it is there constantly.

And therefore, looking at the wound and the mechanism behind it will cause you a more intense pain. But nevertheless, if you work through the wound and heal it, then not only will the intense pain disappear but the constant numbing pain will also disappear. And it is, my beloved, absolutely the only way that anyone has ever found any healing whatsoever.

There is no shortcut

My beloved, as an ascended being I can assure you there is no shortcut! You will not enter the kingdom of God without looking at the beam in your own eye. Christ said it 2,000 years ago. It is a timeless, eternal truth, also expressed by the Buddha. It will not change, because the Law of Free Will will not change. And what you have created for yourself as a self-image that keeps you trapped in a painful state can only be changed by your own choices.

It is almost like some of the choices that doctors can face, for example in a war, where a wounded soldier is brought in and they have the choice that either they cut off a leg or the person will die. What do you do in that situation? Well, you have to do what is best for the person's survival. Likewise, for yourself: Will you keep living with the pain that you have, or will you go in and do whatever is necessary—including seeking professional help in the psychological field, which this messenger has done, which many people who have made progress on the path have done. Will you do that, and then take a giant leap forward?

For my beloved, I can assure you that no matter what your pain might tell you, there is no wound that cannot be healed. It is absolutely impossible to enter any kind of prison from which you cannot escape. You can always be free. The fact of the matter is that your freedom from any condition is just a few choices away. In fact, if you could make one choice, you could instantly escape from your present condition. If you are willing to go through the extreme process of finally giving up defending your drama and being willing to go through the sense of spiritual death of not knowing who you are, and then in realizing that you are not the human – you are not the wounds, you are not the drama – opening yourself up to that direct inner experience that you are MORE.

The choice, then, is yours. You are not a victim of anyone or anything but your own past choices. Any past choice can be transcended by making a better choice in the present. Not in the future, my beloved, for the future never arrives—the moment to make choices is always now. The question is, which "now" in the string of "nows" in your life, will you make the now where you finally make that decision to do something about the wounds and the pain, rather than trying to live with them and actually defend your pain, defend your drama?

Helping others escape the drama

This, then, brings us back to communication, my beloved. Imagine the doctor faced with a wounded soldier. He has absolutely no desire whatsoever to cut off the person's leg, or to do some other procedure that causes pain, but nevertheless he is there to save the person's life, if at all possible. Imagine that you are meeting a person or that you are dealing with a person – and many of you do not even have to imagine it, for you are dealing with such persons on a daily basis – who is totally trapped in their drama, in great pain, perhaps even suicidal or in other ways schizophrenic or out of balance. You are faced with a similar choice, my beloved. What do you do, then, to help the person escape the trap of their personal drama?

You see, when a person is identified with their drama and is acting out the drama, that person is constantly seeking to pull all other people into their drama. For the drama does not only involve that person. The person has created a drama that might contain the entire world, and the person has then assigned – as the scriptwriter assigns roles – has assigned various roles to all the people that it encounters, including you. And the person simply wants to get all people to live up to their predefined roles, so that they reaffirm the reality of the drama.

For why is the person caught in a drama? As we have said, because you assign ultimate reality to the dualistic beliefs in your ego. And so, if you really want to help that person be free, you cannot play the role they want you to play, for that only reaffirms their prison, their sense of being trapped in the drama, the sense of the reality of the drama. So you must refuse to play that role. So, my beloved, what will happen to the person, what will they feel when you refuse to play the role? They might feel angry, they might feel hurt, they might feel afraid. My point is that when you refuse to play the role they have assigned to you, you will cause them more pain—you will intensify their pain, just like a doctor might have to cause physical pain in order to save a patient.

So the question is, my beloved, "Are you willing to do this?" Are you willing to serve in that capacity? Can you actually be so free in yourself that you can refuse to enter another person's drama, and thereby let that drama be intensified in your presence until the person becomes so agitated that he or she finally comes to that breaking point of saying, "I can't do this anymore. I give up."

A non-linear view of karma

Master MORE, April 17, 2009

The Alpha and the Omega of healing
So you see, there is an Alpha aspect of the will of God, which has given you complete freedom of choice. And there is an Omega aspect of the will of God, which desires you to use your freedom of choice to become MORE, not less. And so, what is the lesson, then, in terms of true healing? Well what is true healing? It is self-healing!

For what is the purpose of life? It is the growth of the self, the growth of your self-awareness, my beloved. Which is the entire purpose for the world of form. Where you might start out with a very localized sense of identity – being identified with some material form, such as your physical body – but yet, no matter how limited that identity might be, you have the potential to grow in self-awareness until you reach the consciousness of the Being out of which Being you are. Yet this growth is self-growth. It is not forced upon you by God. For self-growth cannot be forced.

And thus, the beginning of true healing is indeed when you recognize that you have chosen to separate from Oneness. Thus, the reason why your physical body or your mind needs healing is that you have made choices that limited yourself, rather than expanding your sense of self. You became trapped in the illusion, whereby you have come to see yourself – not as a spiritual being who has temporarily taken on a particular role and costume in the drama of the material universe – you instead think that you are trapped in this universe, trapped in a particular role. This then, is giving away your power to heal yourself.

How can you exercise that power? Well, my beloved, when you truly understand free will, you recognize that it is free, completely free, my beloved. God has given you a will that is completely free. Which means that as you can choose to take on a particular costume – no matter what that costume may be like – you do, at any moment, have the complete freedom to separate yourself from the costume—to just take it off, to let it drop from you, to let the old man die and to be reborn in a new sense of self. This is recognizing the power that God has given you. And thus, you recognize that it is the ego and the false teachers, those in the serpentine consciousness, who are seeking to take away your power by making you believe that you either are that costume, that role, or that you cannot simply just take it off.

Opening up to a new view of karma

For you see, my beloved, when you look at humankind there is indeed a dividing line that you might observe: that many are still completely identified with the physical body and their growing up in a particular circumstance of family, culture, nationality, religion, ethnicity, race or whatever division you have. Yet the more spiritual people have started to awaken from that illusion and realize they are more than these outer identities and labels and divisions. But still, when you begin to awaken and realize you are more, well then you are faced with the lie that you cannot simply walk away from your old identity. For you have made mistakes, you have sinned. And somehow your sins must be repaid, your karma must be balanced.

But you see, my beloved, may I ask you to partake of a little thought experiment here. Let us take the old teaching given in the East – even a teaching that we have found it necessary to give in previous dispensations of the Ascended Host – namely, the teaching that karma is some external force. You have committed errors in a past life and you owe some kind of debt to life and the scales must be balanced. The energy you have misqualified needs to be rebalanced, my beloved.

Now, this is not necessarily incorrect. You have free will to do anything you want. But what is it that allows you to do anything in the material world? Well, it is that you are receiving a portion of spiritual light from your own I AM Presence, which you then express through your four lower bodies. And you are, of course, responsible for what you do with that energy. For you cannot permanently leave the Earth behind until you have at least raised up all energy that you have qualified with the vibration of non-love, thus limiting all life.

You must come to a point where at least your presence on this Earth is a balance—you do not pull life down. Of course, you did not come here to pull life down, nor did you come here to struggle for hundreds of embodiments only to come back to a balanced point and then leave. You came here to bring a positive gift, to shine your light in the darkness of the material universe and to ultimately raise up this sphere, as Maitreya explains, to where it can ascend and out-picture the kingdom of God.

Yet, let us then consider that you are a co-creator who has experimented with free will over many lifetimes. You have taken on a certain role, identified yourself as a separate being, and you have used the energy given to you by your I AM Presence to seek to own and possess things for that separate self. Perhaps seeking to raise it up in comparison to others, thereby attaining some prominent position in society that enabled you to put other people down, so that you would seem more important.

There are, of course, many ways to make such karma, as we call it. But now look at this realistically, my beloved, and recognize that there is nothing that can be said with words that cannot be twisted and turned by the serpentine consciousness and the serpentine logic. For this is the essence of the serpentine logic—that when you eat of the fruit, you become "wise as God," you become as God, "knowing good and evil," which means that you enter into the duality consciousness, my beloved. Where you now think – your ego thinks – that it has the right to define good and evil in an ultimate sense.

Which is why you see that there are religions on this Earth that define themselves as being the only true religion, thereby defining the absolute belief that all non-members will burn forever in hell. There are those who have espoused a particular political philosophy as superior to any other, therefore giving rise to the belief that it is justified that they seek to suppress any other philosophy, imposing their own system upon the rest of the world.

And so, you see now how the serpentine consciousness entraps you in this belief—that the forms you see in the material world have some ultimate reality. And thus, you cannot simply walk away from them. You are crucified, by the form, by the image, by the consciousness. And so, as was out-pictured by Jesus, you enter into the drama of life, and they may indeed "crucify" you. And it seems like there was, even for Jesus, nothing he could do but play that role.

Look at the stations of the cross out-pictured here in this place through the Catholic tradition. Jesus is condemned to death. Jesus accepts his cross. However, even that is a passive act of accepting what others want to put upon him. Jesus falls, someone helps Jesus carry the cross, someone wipes his tears, someone attempts to tell him not to go through with this. He is nailed to the cross, he dies, he is taken down, he is put in the tomb. All passive things, my beloved.

And so, what is missing from the steps of the cross, the stations of the cross? Well many things, but for one, my beloved, the reality that Jesus chose to enter into Jerusalem, knowing full well what might happen. And most importantly, while hanging on the cross, he chose to give up the ghost, thereby in an instant putting off that sense of the separate self, my beloved, showing the potential that all of you have to instantly let the old being, the old self die. And thereby not cease to exist, as the false teachers and the ego would have you believe, but indeed being reborn into a greater sense of self, the self that you still are in the eyes of God.

A revolutionary view of karma

Now, my beloved, there is a deeper reality. And so, returning to the concept of karma, what is the illusion superimposed upon the concept by the serpentine mind? Understand that the serpentine mind is based on separation, and when you are separated from your source, what must you believe about the power of God?

You must believe that it can only come from outside yourself. For when you see yourself as a separate being, you cannot accept that the power of God can come from inside yourself. And thus, you are susceptible to the belief, my beloved, that in one extreme you need an external savior. In the other extreme that you need to do something down here, on Earth, as a separate self, in order to be redeemed of your sin or to balance your karma.

Now, my beloved, beware of what I am telling you. Be alert now, and perhaps even step back and see how your own outer, analytical mind will seek to play tricks on you, so that you either do not hear my words or do not hear the true meaning. What was said earlier? That you have come to accept that there is something wrong with you, something particular, some particular problem that blocks you from entering the kingdom of God. But you see, my beloved, what is truly wrong with you is the concept that there is something wrong.

And where does that concept come from? From the illusion of separation, from the creation of the separate self! There is indeed, one might say, something wrong with the separate self if one wants to think in dualistic terms. But there is nothing wrong with you, the being that you truly are.

From a greater perspective there is not even anything wrong with the separate self, for God does not think in terms of right or wrong. God only thinks in terms of what is real and what is unreal. And only that which is created in oneness, as an expression of oneness, only that is real. Whereas anything created out of the consciousness of separation is not real and thus cannot affect that part of you which is real—cannot limit it, cannot encage it in a particular role, or costume, or form or sense of self.

Do you, then, begin to see, my beloved, what karma truly is? You have been so accustomed, so conditioned by the dualistic mind, that you have come to believe that there really are two opposites—and that one of those opposites is God, and the other opposite is that which is anti-God. This, my beloved, is the arrogance of the fallen beings, who in their spiritual pride believe that by rebelling against God they actually had an affect on God and the spiritual Beings who have not separated from oneness. But you see, my beloved, God is not in the opposite polarity of separation. God is One, undivided, indivisible, unconditional. How can any condition oppose that which is unconditional?

Do you see that in oneness there can be no conditions? So how do you separate from oneness? By creating conditions! But how can you create conditions? You must create two conditions, at least two, that oppose each other. For if there is not the opposition, then you still have oneness, and so you have no separation.

My beloved, I AM the master of the Will of God. I have my beloved friends on the other six rays. Am I in opposition to Saint Germain because I am on the first and he is on the seventh, thus on opposite ends of the linear scale? How could this be possible? How could the Will of God oppose the Freedom of God, when it is the will of God that all beings be free—and that you become free by being one with the will of God that raises all life?

So do you see, my beloved, that you may think that in a past life you created bad karma and that in order to ascend, you must balance that karma by creating good karma. But good and bad are dualistic conditions. You cannot neutralize, balance or negate one dualistic condition by going into the opposite. You cannot overcome a problem with the same state of consciousness that created the problem.

So what is karma? It is that you use your creative power through the filter of a separate, dualistic self. My beloved, anything you do through that filter creates karma that separates you from oneness. Do you see that it was because you came to see yourself as a separate being that you became focused on the self, and therefore might have done something that was egotistical or selfish according to the standard definition—thus creating what most people see as negative karma? It was the illusion that you are a separate being that caused this.

Well, then, how can you counteract that by doing something else through the separate self? Do you see that the very concept that you have created negative karma as a separate self and that you have to balance it as a separate self is illogical, contradictory? For as long as you are striving to balance the karma that you see as being made by the separate self, you are reinforcing the illusion that you are a separate self.

When balancing karma hinders your ascension

My beloved, you may think I am saying the same thing over and over—and I am. But I am saying it with slightly different angles, for I am giving you a geometric thought-form. And if you do not see it from one perspective, perhaps you will see it from a slightly different one. So, the idea is this: Consider how the concept that you have to balance your karma reinforces the sense that you are a separate being. For does it not imply that you cannot ascend – meaning, in its essence, come back to oneness – until you have balanced the karma?

Which means that in your mind you are saying, "I am a separate being, and I must remain a separate being until, at some future time, I have balanced the karma made as a separate being and – "poof"– I will one day ascend without fully understanding how this is happening." Thus, some of you have indeed, in previous Ascended Master dispensations, been given an image – or we might say you have accepted an image – that even the ascension is a somewhat passive process, where you balance your karma and then the rest just happens automatically, my beloved.

This is not so! How do you ascend, my beloved? By taking back the power of your will! Do you think, my beloved, that I, Master MORE, am standing up here in heaven seeking to force people to ascend? For what would be accomplished by that? They would enter heaven with the same state of consciousness they have right now. And we do not want any long faces in heaven, nor do we want any other of the theatrical faces that you see on Earth. For we want you, as you are, in oneness.

We are not thereby saying that you return to heaven the same as you came out. For you learn by being in these denser realms, you expand your sense of self beyond what it was created as. But as you come back into oneness, you recognize that you and we are not different. You are extensions of our very own Beings, my beloved.

And thus, my proposition to you is simple. Consider that you, as a separate being, come to the conclusion that you are – after all – a spiritual being, that you came from heaven and that you want to return, but in order to return you have to balance your karma. And so you set about this with the same consciousness of separation.

Now, my beloved, some progress can be made this way. You can balance energy. You see, we have the Alpha of your state of consciousness that you superimpose upon the energy, the Ma-ter light. We have the Omega of the Ma-ter light taking on a lower vibration as a result of the images you superimpose upon it. And so, you can actually, to some degree, fulfill that balancing act, for certainly a selfless act will balance karma, as you call it. But I must tell you that you cannot complete this process while you still see yourself as a separate self. It is not possible.

Why is it not possible? Because of what I have explained—you can only enter the kingdom of heaven by becoming one with the power of

God within you. And you can only become one with that by overcoming the separate self.

You must choose to ascend, my beloved—as this messenger realized many years ago when he considered the outer requirements given in a previous dispensation and saw that there had to be something missing. For it could not be a matter of fulfilling outer requirements and then, "poof," you are in the ascended realm. It had to be a decision, a choice.

A faster way to rise above karma

So while you can make some progress from the consciousness of the separate self, consider another route. Consider that instead of focusing on balancing karma, as some external force, you instead listen to the words of Christ, my beloved. For did he not say, "Seek ye first the kingdom of God and his righteousness and all these things shall be added unto you."

What is the kingdom of God? It is indeed the Christ consciousness based on oneness, where you have the righteousness – the right use – of your creative power—that you use it to raise up the All instead of the separate self. And so, consider that instead of focusing on an outer, somewhat mechanical, act of balancing karma, you focus on switching your sense of identity, switching your self-image, switching your perspective. Going through that seismic shift in identity, where you no longer see separation, but see oneness.

What will happen in the process, my beloved? What will happen is that you take back your own power, you reconnect to the Higher Being you are and now you can say with Jesus, "I and my father are one. My father worketh hitherto and I work."

And so, my beloved, when you come into that state of oneness – at least some degree of oneness although not yet the full Christhood, but still some degree of oneness – and you see that you still have some karma left, my beloved, how hard do you think it is to balance that karma when you have the power of God flowing through you to do it?

Do you see, it is much easier to walk the path by first seeking oneness than by seeking to fulfill an outer requirement of balancing karma, and then thinking that oneness will come automatically? Thereby limiting yourself – perhaps for the rest of this embodiment – to only exercising the power that comes through your separate self, instead of the power of the greater being that you are.

Illusions, my beloved—illusions! How subtle is the logic of the serpentine mind? How subtle it is, when you look at it from inside the separate self. How obvious it is when you reach for the Christ mind and gain that unconditional perspective, where you do not see truth as expressed in a particular word or teaching, but you have followed the call of Christ: "God is a Spirit, and they that worship him must worship him in Spirit and in truth."

And when you know this Spirit of Truth, you know the vibration of truth, and you have the ultimate co-measurement, the ultimate guiding rod, the staff of Moses, my beloved, that will part the waters of the dead sea—as a representation of the duality consciousness. So that you may walk across safely and yet, when the hordes of death come behind you, the waters of their own dualistic consciousness close upon them. And they are swept up in the turmoil, while you walk to the other side, to the land of Israel, that which Is Real.

A non-linear view of reincarnation

So, my beloved, as a parting thought, consider that you have heard that El Morya was embodied as Thomas More, as Thomas Beckett, as this or that Master, or this or that historical figure, and finally, if you go way back, embodied as Abraham. But you see, my beloved, Thomas More is dead. Abraham is dead. For although you may think that I was embodied as Abraham, I tell you it is not so. For before Abraham was, I AM.

Am I thereby denying that there was a previous embodiment as Abraham? Am I denying the teaching given? No, I am not. I am asking you to step up higher and realize that as an Ascended Being, I have become one with a greater Being out of which the being came that embodied as Abraham. And thus, the sense of self that embodied as Abraham and as these other figures is no more. I AM MORE. I have risen beyond any earthly sense of self. I have taken off the costumes. I have stood naked before the pool of healing waters, and I walked through it to the other side. I AM reborn, as you can indeed be reborn, my beloved.

As this messenger was inspired to say to someone yesterday, "Follow your bliss!" Consider what gives you the greatest joy. For you will find that what gives you the greatest joy is the sense of oneness with your inner Being, with your God Flame, with the greater spiritual Being out of which you have come. Use that as the measuring rod for whether to do this or to do that, here on this stage of life. What gives you the nect to the fount of wisdom? Well, of course, in the heart. Which is why before we could give a conference on the restoration of true healing, we had to give one on restoring the flow from the heart, the communication from the heart. For it all goes together, yet we must take one step at a time. You cannot, my beloved, intellectually understand what it takes to transcend the separate self.

Even this messenger has for a long time been thinking that if only we, of the Ascended Host, would give some kind of teaching through him, then that would awaken the people who are struggling, who are so willing to change but cannot see what it is that is standing in their way. And it is in compassion for these people that he has been asking us in his heart, "Isn't there some way to help them see, to help them understand?" But only recently has he come to see that it is not possible to give an outer teaching that is a magic formula that will mechanically unlock the understanding of anyone who reads it. Not even if they study it in a more profound way than with the intellect alone.

Why do you seek a guru?

You see, my beloved, as my Brother MORE was explaining to you last night, once you have taken on a role and identify yourself with that role, you believe that you cannot simply step out of it, you cannot simply walk away from it. And thus, my beloved, do you see – building on what my brother explained – that as long as you think you are missing some crucial piece of information, you are subconsciously affirming the image that you are separated from Christhood, from the kingdom of God, from enlightenment or whatever it may be.

What is the crucial piece of information that you have not yet found? It is the realization that what is wrong with you is the sense that there is something you do not know – something that you do not have access to within yourselves – and thus must find from an outer source. Again, this is subtle. For, my beloved, as MORE was also explaining, you do need something from an outer source in the sense that you need something from outside the closed circle of your separate sense of identity. Which is why we, of the Ascended Host, have established a long tradition of the guru-chela, the teacher-student/disciple relationship, my beloved. For while you are trapped and identified with a particular role, you need the teacher, the guru, to come and simply demonstrate to you that there is a state of consciousness beyond your current state of consciousness.

And thus, what you see, my beloved, is that so many spiritual students seek a guru or a teacher because they believe that the guru or teacher can give them the information they are lacking. And in some cases people are lacking a certain understanding. For as you grow in understanding, you can begin to detach yourself from the illusions. But yet, there comes a point where you now have sufficient understanding, and it is no longer a matter of receiving that crucial piece of information, that secret formula, that philosopher's stone, that final initiation that you receive on the 33rd step or whatever secret initiatic process you think you have to go through.

No, my beloved, it is a matter of recognizing that after that point, you cannot progress by only listening to the outer teaching given by or through the teacher. You must go beyond the teaching and absorb the vibration that is coming through a true teacher. And this, my beloved, is precisely why it is essential to practice your discernment and not follow the false teachers of this world. And what do I mean with the false teachers?

For you see, here is another subtlety. You may go into the world and see the many teachers out there, and you may look at the teaching they are giving forth and you may say, "That is true. That is very profound. This person must be a true teacher."

But, my beloved, listen to what I just said. It is not the outer teaching alone, for there are many teachers in the world, and even in the mental realm, who have attained great knowledge. Just as you have the libraries of the world and the academics who have attained great material knowledge, or even great theological knowledge. But the crucial distinction is—have these teachers truly gone beyond the outer wisdom and recognized the underlying, superior, undivided, unconditional wisdom which boils down to one realization, namely that all life is one!

And thus, there is absolutely no point in seeking to become a teacher in order to be thought wise among men and raise up the separate self. There is only one true way to be a teacher, and that is to constantly strive for oneness and greater degrees of oneness, until the separate self melts away and you are not now concerned by anything. You are not seeking to raise yourself up, you are not feeling rejected, you are not concerned about other people's reactions. You are willing to be an open door for the fount of wisdom to flow through you.

Even though that fount is expressed in outer teachings, there is the underlying vibration that comes from the River of Life, which is truly the oneness of all those who have overcome the illusion of separation, the consciousness of duality. That is the flow of the Holy Spirit, where we have all added our Being to that wind of the Holy Spirit that seeks to enlighten the people on Earth.

You see, this is the key, my beloved. A false teacher may have great knowledge, may have great teachings, but is nevertheless seeking some advantage for the separate self, whatever that might be. Some have great knowledge but seek to attract female students for sexual exploitation. Some seek money. Some seek pride and a sense of superiority. Some need to be constantly admired. And so, regardless of whatever truth may be in their teachings – truth, when you evaluate it based on the intellect and the linear mind – well they are not true teachers if they have not connected to the underlying oneness and therefore are simply seeing themselves as an open door.

They are not the ones who have the wisdom, the wisdom that is flowing like a living fount, like the living word that is not just a teaching that you can study with the intellect, but the sound. The words are cups of light that contain that vibration that is the final step that people must take in and accept in order to rise up beyond the separate self.

I have no secret formula to offer you. For there is none.
Not so long ago, Gautama, himself – the Lord of the World – gave the image of a dark lord that was supposedly residing in a castle guarded by all these lower ranks of those who serve the dark lord out of fear. And yet, if you walked through the fear and actually walked into the castle, you saw that there was no dark lord. Now look at how many people in the world – in spiritual and New Age organizations, in traditional religions, in science and academic circles – have a similar image. That somewhere there must be the ultimate temple of wisdom, and when you walk in there, you see the secret formula that will enable you to know all things and master all things.

Well, I tell you that if you could go to this imaginary temple, penetrate to the very core, there would be no secret formula whatsoever. For you see, my beloved, God hides his face from the profane. God hides the secret of life from those who are approaching it from the consciousness of separation. You only discover the secret of life by becoming one with something that is more than the separate self. Only that something must, of course, be part of the River of Life.

How can you fully receive the wisdom that I, Lanto, represent? By looking beyond outer words and teachings. By tuning in to my vibration and accepting that you are worthy to receive that unconditional love with a tint of the unconditional, infinite wisdom of God. For, my beloved, the true wisdom that I AM – with which I have become one – cannot be reduced to words that can be spoken in the material world. They cannot be reduced to formulas or rituals or teachings. They are alive, they defy any structure whatsoever, my beloved.

Going beyond your own mind structure

Understand this—certainly you need structure in the material universe. We are not trying to break down structure. We are seeking to raise up structure to out-picture the kingdom of God and the Golden Age of Saint Germain.

Yet, for you, personally, there must come a point where you are willing to go beyond the structure that you have built so far. For that structure still serves to maintain the ego's sense of security and control. And therefore, as long as you cling to the structure, cling to the sense of what you know, of what you think you know, you cannot receive the unconditional wisdom. It is only by absorbing that wisdom that you will fully transcend the sense of separation and come to see that which you cannot see right now.

There is no way, my beloved, to outsmart the intellect and the dualistic mind by using the intellect and the dualistic mind. You see, my beloved, for every dualistic argument there is a counter-argument that will negate it. Which means that any form of dualistic wisdom is relative. It only exists within the dualistic framework; it must have an opposite. Thus, how can it be absolute wisdom, how can it be unconditional wisdom? It simply is not possible.

Thus, in order to be the wise ones, there comes a point where you have to say, "I have attempted to understand now – for a long time – but now I see that it is not by seeking an outer, structured wisdom that I will go further. I will not overcome the catch-22 I am in by attaining some understanding. For I am in a catch-22 because I see myself as not having wisdom. And thus, how do I overcome the catch-22? Only by being willing to let go of all I think I know, to be like a little child, to have the childlike mind that is not asking but that simply observes."

Why did I have you enter the meditation of walking out of the closed library into the spring, the miracle of life? Because this is what you need to do. You need to walk away from all that the ego thinks it knows about the spiritual path, and find some way to simply absorb your own Higher Being, a particular master, or even something from nature. Where, my beloved, your mind switches its focus and you now experience oneness with something beyond the separate self. Only in that oneness, in that experience of oneness, will you be whole. Only in that oneness will you be healed, my beloved.

You are always worthy of love

Archangel Charity with Paul the Venetian, April 18, 2009

"And though I speak with the voice of men and of angels and have not charity, I am nothing." Words to meditate upon, my beloved. As you have heard a piece of music that even in a less than stellar performance nevertheless conveys the grandeur of the vibration of the archangels.

Charity, I AM. And I come to give you a sense of what charity really is, my beloved. For indeed, charity is not the entirely right word, but given the limitations of language, there was no word that could adequately convey the vibration behind it. You, in your language and understanding, might come up with a better word and indeed, it is, "unconditionality." For that is the vibration that is conveyed through the third ray—that you normally call the third ray of love.

But love, as so many other words, has received such a dualistic overlay over time that it is almost a useless word, my beloved. Unconditional love, therefore, is, of course, a much better concept. But why not simply unconditionality?

For what is the River of Life? It is the unconditional expression of any God quality. There is no way to progress beyond a certain point of the spiritual path without truly tuning in to the vibration of unconditionality—as you heard from Lanto, tuning in to the vibration of wisdom.

There are, then, so many people in spiritual and religious movements who have come to understand the need to rise above selfishness, self-centeredness and the lower expressions. And yet, what they are seeking is to attune themselves with the vibration of love, but it is the dualistic love that is opposed to fear, anger, hatred. Yet, love in the divine sense can, of course, have no opposite or it would not be divine.

For again, as Master MORE has said, it is the grand illusion of the fallen beings that they actually oppose God. Yet, of course, you can only oppose that which is in the realm of duality. So what you oppose is a graven image of God. Thus, so many people are not opposing anything but they are seeking to come into love. But if you seek to come into attunement with a graven image, how can you ever reach true love? It is, as Lanto explained, impossible.

Consider unconditionality

Thus, the need to consider unconditionality. Unconditionality. Which is, indeed, why we have given you the concept that at a certain point of the path, it is necessary to stop trying to change yourself. And the only way to switch out of that last illusion of the separate self is to accept yourself – unconditionally – for who you are.

And so, you have heard of the need to make that shift from the first two rays. And I, along with Paul the Venetian, come to give it to you from the perspective of the third ray.

For you see, my beloved, how can you progress to the fourth ray of purity unless you tune in to unconditionality? For is it not the conditions that manifest impurities in your minds and bodies—even in the physical body of the Earth, seen as so many natural imbalances and disasters. Again, there is no sacred or secret formula that will work automatically. For you see, the concept that you are not able or worthy of expressing a higher love, well that concept, that conception, is the problem.

Love is an unconditional force that wants to be expressed. You do not have to do anything in order to be an open door for the expression of unconditionality. What condition could you possibly have to fulfill in order to express that which is unconditional—and thus flows and flows and transcends and grows and expresses, regardless of any conditions?

Do you see, again, the impossibility of this? How illogical it is, and how only the separate self can believe this. You are more than the separate self. But, my beloved, as long as you hold on to the concept that you need to move to a certain state of perfection – before you are able or worthy to have the love of God flowing through you – well then, as long as you see yourself separated from the flow of love, the love cannot flow. For it will not accept any conditions.

You have the right to accept conditions for yourself. But do not fall into the trap of the subtle consciousness of the beings who are completely identified with duality—and therefore in their arrogance believe that they can form an opposite polarity to God. You cannot limit God, you cannot limit love. You cannot limit the expression of love.

You either let it flow, or it flows around you. There is nothing in between. You may think there is something in between because human beings have for so long created the dualistic, relative image of love, as an opposition to hatred, anger, fear etc. And so, some people have become very good at putting on a facade of being loving and kind.

...

Overcome your fear of rejection
Love does not seek to own. When it does not seek to own, it follows that it needs nothing in return. You have discussed, my beloved, the fear of expressing love out of fear of rejection. But when there is fear of rejection, you have not yet tuned in to the vibration of unconditionality. For when love is expressed unconditionally, how could there be fear of rejection? How can unconditional love be rejected? Unconditional love is self-contained. It finds its joy simply in being expressed, in expressing itself, in flowing.

When you think that you have to express love only for one particular person – and that you want that love to be received by that person – perhaps even be received in a certain way, well then, my beloved, you are not in the flow of unconditional love. You have tuned in to the lower vibration of conditional love. You may still have love for a person, you may still desire to express that love, but you have not yet reached the highest potential, and so you fear rejection or you seek to own or posses or have something in return.

But you see, my beloved, when you think that you need something from any human being or from any source in the material universe, you have a sense of lack. You have a deficit consciousness—that you are missing something and that someone else must come in and fill it, fill that hole, so that you can be complete. But you see, my beloved, this is all an illusion.

Even the concept of twin flames as it was perceived by earlier dispensations – that there was one human being who was your twin flame and therefore that twin flame was the perfect love who would complete you – even that is not the highest understanding. For your real spiritual twin flame is your higher self, your I AM Presence. And only by coming into oneness with that will you be complete, will you be whole, my beloved.

Unconditionality and healing

And so, what then does this mean for the entire concept of healing, that is the topic of this conference? It means, my beloved, that you cannot heal yourself from the consciousness that you need healing. You cannot become whole from the consciousness that sees itself as unwhole.

Thus, the only way out of the catch-22 is to transcend the illusion that you are not whole. This, of course, sounds like another catch-22. For how can you transcend the illusion that you are unwhole while you are feeling unwhole?

But the reality is that you can—when you recognize the fact of who you are. You are a self-conscious being, and as Master MORE explained, you have been given complete free will. And therefore, you have the freedom to create any experience that you desire to experience. And how do you create an experience? By stepping into a costume, a role, and then thinking this is who I AM. But as we have said, no matter how much you have identified yourself with that separate sense of identity, you still are who you are.

And therefore, you have the potential to recognize and acknowledge who you are. And you have the potential to say, "It was not some external force – be it a serpent or some other external force, even the external God who wanted to punish me – that caused me to descend into the sense of unwholeness. It was choices I made."

And when you recognize that you made the choices to descend into the sense of unwholeness, it follows logically that you also have the power to change those choices, to replace them with choices that bring you into wholeness—or rather, that bring you out of the illusion that you are separated from wholeness. For how can you indeed be separated from anything that is unconditional?

"Unconditional" means that it is everywhere present. You cannot find a place where the unconditional love of God is not present, my beloved. It is impossible. You are like a fish denying that it is wet. And I know that fish have not been generally seen as having a high intelligence, but nevertheless, you can see that for a fish, that is pretty stupid. [Laughter]

And so, you recognize, of course, that your ego is not all that smart—even though it thinks it is. Even though other people may think it is. Even though you can, indeed, as some have done, manipulate yourself into a position, where most of the world thinks your ego is pretty smart or superior in some other way. Yet, when you can begin to laugh at the ego, then you have already started to separate yourself from it.

My love is always there

I am pausing to take in the return current of your consciousness—of your fears and your doubts about what we are saying to you in this and the previous releases. I am absorbing the consciousness. For you see, my beloved, the fact that you doubt my words, that you are afraid to implement them, does not mean that I do not love you. I love you regardless of how you respond or do not respond to my words and my vibration. My love is unconditional, it is timeless. If you cannot accept it now, be not dismayed. You do not need to beat yourself up over the fact that you cannot instantly accept what you are hearing.

I want you to know that I am always there. My love is always there. If you cannot accept it now, then, at whatever time you can, do not fall prey to the illusion that because you could not accept me that time in the past, you cannot accept me now either, for you are not worthy. Do not build layers and layers of illusions. But remember my words—my love is unconditional. You do not have to fulfill a condition in order to be worthy of it. You have only two options—you can accept or you can reject. But my love is unconditional, so if you reject my love, I am not affected by that rejection.

And thus, I still love you unconditionally. Which means that no matter how violently you might reject it at this present moment, at any moment in the future when you desire to throw off that costume, my love is there for you to accept. Your ego may want you to think that this cannot be so. Yet it is so. It has always been so. It will always be so.

This is the truth about love. This is true love. If you desire to feel separated from my love, if you desire to reject it, I love you for rejecting me. Whatever you feel, whatever you think, I love you.

Feelings and thoughts are fleeting images that pass through the mind. But turn off the film projector, and you will see that the screen of life is still white, no matter what images were projected upon it. Your core being, your conscious self, is a blank screen, in the sense that although you were created with individuality, you were not created with conditionality. You were not created with any dualistic conditions, my beloved.

You were created with unconditional individual characteristics. And I know full well that your linear mind cannot comprehend this concept. But there must be some expression of words that you can ponder, until you come to the point of switching your perception—and you recognize the reality of unconditionality and the unreality of the conditions set up to obscure the white screen by making you focus on the fleeting images that can never satisfy your true being, your true longing for love.

How can any love coming from this material realm satisfy your built-in longing for love? For your built-in longing for love is the longing for oneness with who you are, your own Higher Being. Your longing to be in the flow of the River of Life by fulfilling the role for which you were created by your Higher Being—to be a co-creator and to bring the kingdom of God into manifestation in the material universe.

My words are coming to you through a person in embodiment who, as is inevitable when you are in embodiment, has a limited capacity for love. For certainly, one cannot be in embodiment and at the same time be in the fullness of the ascended consciousness—which is in the fullness of unconditionality. Yet, do not focus on the outer messenger. Go beyond the outer form, go beyond the sound of the voice, go beyond the words.

Follow the words, follow them as a stream of consciousness that reaches to the very being that I AM. One with the hierarchy of God Love, of unconditional love and with all of the beings who are expressions of that unconditionality.

Follow, then, that stream of consciousness and recognize that my capacity for love is indeed unlimited. And thus, I can take in and consume any condition that you desire to surrender to me. And I give you, thus, as the conclusion of this release, an opportunity to release into the stream of my consciousness any condition that you desire to let go of. For you have said, with Master MORE, "Enough is enough."

Acceleration is the key to wholeness

Serapis Bey, April 18, 2009

You can accelerate beyond any earthly condition
And so, you have heard from the master of the first ray how it is necessary to use your will power to consciously take back your power. You have heard from the second ray of how it is necessary to go beyond outer wisdom and study and to come into gnosis with the Spirit of Wisdom. You have heard from the third ray of how it is necessary to come into oneness with the flowing fount of love, the River of Life. Yet I tell you, that once you have passed the initiations on these three rays, it is necessary to take another step—that many of you have not actually understood, even though you may have studied the teachings of the Ascended Masters for a long time.

My beloved, in order to be able to receive this release from my heart, this messenger had to pass a test himself. For it has been a long several days for his physical body and even his emotional and mental body—especially feeling the energies in this place, where his natural tendency for compassion wants to see all of the people here healed, yet knowing that, of course, it cannot take place. And so, before he took this dictation, he went to his room, feeling his energies were low and thus, as is natural, thinking, "I need to rest for a few minutes." And so he laid down to rest, and suddenly he was open to receiving the thought from my heart, "You do not need to rest, you need to accelerate your being."

You see, my beloved, this is the essence of the initiation of the fourth ray of purity. For you may walk through the initiations on the first three rays. You may have a sense of accomplishment. You may even feel so enveloped in love that you think you do not need to go beyond it. But I tell you, it is necessary to go beyond in order to reach the fullness of wholeness. And in order to go beyond that level of the third ray, you need, indeed, to accelerate, to step up.

And so you see, this is one of the major blocks to healing, my beloved. For what do people naturally feel when their physical body breaks down? They are tired, they are in pain, they feel drained of energy. Well, certainly, they feel, do they not, that "I cannot possibly accelerate. I am too tired, too sick, feeling too bad." But you see, this is unreality.

You are not tired, sick, or feeling bad unless you choose to step into one of the roles that the other masters have talked about and identify yourself with that role. Identifying yourself as feeling bad, feeling tired, feeling drained, feeling sick, therefore by the very focus of your mind on that image making it a manifest reality, albeit a temporary one, in your physical temple.

Transmuting or removing energy

And so, you see, as the other masters have attempted to explain to you, there is the illusion created by the ego and the dualistic mind and the entire mass consciousness on Earth, my beloved, that because of this or that condition you are experiencing, you cannot accelerate. You need rest, you need restoration.

But I tell you, there is no such thing as rest. You will not become whole by resting. This is not to say that you do not need rest. But I am saying that there comes a point where you need to recognize that it is not rest that you need at this particular stage in the healing process—it is acceleration.

Now, you can, of course, not say to an ill person, "Get out of your bed and accelerate." For that person needs to be taken through the steps of the first three rays. First realizing what Master MORE explained so carefully, that you need to take back your power to make decisions. Then having the wisdom to know what is real and unreal and that all these conditions and mental images are ultimately unreal. And then locking in to the flow of love, of knowing that no matter what mistakes you have made in the past, you can just walk away from it.

But let us go beyond that expression of walking away from something, for in reality, of course, you cannot walk away from anything. You cannot, as other masters have attempted to explain, rise above the duality consciousness by using the duality consciousness. And thus, my beloved, let us look again at the concept of purity and the need for purification. It is very easy with the linear, analytical mind to step into the image that you have a container – your aura, your physical body – that has taken in impurities from the world, and therefore it needs to be cleansed. It needs to be purified by removing those impurities, by taking them out and putting them somewhere else.

This is logical to the linear mind. And I understand that some of you will even use previous teachings to say, "But have we not talked about this very process, is that not the idea of the violet flame to transmute the misqualified energy?" But you see, there is, again, a subtlety that the more mature students need to contemplate. The act of transmuting energy is not the same as removing energy.

You see, as has been explained, you receive spiritual light from your Higher Being. You choose how to focus your consciousness, your awareness. You color the light with a higher or a lower vibration. The light that is colored with the lower vibration will eventually work its way down through the four levels of the material universe, until it reaches the level of your physical body. And when it accumulates to a certain concentration, it will begin to burden the cells so they cannot function properly, and thus disease will manifest.

What is it that has caused the coloring of the light, my beloved? It is the illusion of a separate self, the focus on you being separate from other people. And thus, the belief that you have a right to do what is best for you, even if it harms other forms of life—or other such beliefs that justify self-centered, egotistical behavior. And so, now you recognize that you are ill, your body is ill, and it may kill you. And your first instinctive response is: Get rid of the disease. Which means getting rid of the impure energies. But you see, my beloved, even though you sometimes take on energies from the world, you cannot take anything into your system unless there is already the state of consciousness that corresponds to the energies you are taking in.

And thus, you see, again, that if you simply say, "I want to take this energy that is making my body ill, remove it from my body, and dump it on the world," then you have not truly come to a higher spiritual understanding. And thus, you are naturally seeking to overcome a problem from the same state of consciousness that created the problem—namely the illusion of separation. And so, you see, indeed, that many people when they become ill become very self-focused, very self-centered. And they just want to be healed, no matter what. And this, of course, cannot lead to true healing. It may lead to a suppression of the symptoms of the physical body but that, of course, is not the same as true healing.

Accelerating imperfect energy

So what will it take to be truly healed? It will take that you use your insights that you have gained on the first three rays—that you take responsibility for the energy that is truly a reflection of your consciousness. And you say, "I will stop the process of coloring light with a lower vibration. I will first look at the beam in my own eye, I will consider whether it is imperfect beliefs – illusions – in my own consciousness that has added to the accumulation of misqualified energy in my four lower bodies and in the four lower bodies of Mother Earth."

"Then, I will change that consciousness, so I can stop misqualifying light. I will look at the message in the disease manifest in my physical body, look at the consciousness and come to see and surrender that consciousness. But when I have then stopped the continued process of misqualification, I will take the next step and say, 'But I also want to purify the energy that I have already misqualified, so that I do not burden other forms of life.'"

For in making that decision, you are switching out of the separate self, you are switching out of the self-centered perspective, my beloved. But now is where you, then, need to reach the ultimate clarity of recognizing that the only way that you can purify the energy is not by somehow destroying that energy, or removing it to some remote location, some cosmic garbage dump somewhere. The only way is to accelerate it, so that it shakes off the imperfect vibration and is again raised to the level of love, the level of purity.

But what is purity? Well, my beloved, it is, of course, unconditionality. Again, there is a dualistic concept of purity, as the opposite of impurity. And thus, when you are in the dualistic mind, you think, of course, that in order to attain purity, you have to again overcome, destroy, or seek to run away from and cover over the impurities. And so, you do not want to look at the impurities. And you go into the state of mind that you do not want God to see your impurities, you do not want other people to see them, you do not want your spiritual master to see them. And thus, you seek to hide.

And in seeking to hide them from your God, and your master, and other people, you of course first of all hide it from yourself. For you cannot then look at it yourself. And yet, if you cannot look at the impurities, you cannot do the one thing that is needed to overcome them, namely to accelerate them out of the impurity, to raise the vibration.

Again, you see, the catch-22 created by the mind, the dualistic mind. What is purity? It is not the absence of impurity. It is a particular vibration, a frequency, a living stream of consciousness. I am one with that stream, and I am radiating it through the words that you hear. So you have an opportunity, when you hear or read this release, to tune in to and absorb that purity, so that at the end of this release, you will not simply feel that I have given you theoretical concepts, but that I have given you more, a sense of co-measurement and oneness with the vibration of purity.

The extreme realism of purity

For you see, the linear mind will seek to tell you that before you can become pure, you must get rid of the impurities. And then, when you have emptied yourself of impurities, then you might be worthy to receive some grant of light from above. But you see, again, the illusion and the lie of the duality consciousness.

My beloved, consider who I am. I represent the fourth ray of purity. What are we assigned to accomplish by God? We are assigned to help all life attain purity. Is it logical, my beloved, that I would stand here saying, "You are impure, and when you raise yourself to a level of purity, then I will work with you." How would I ever accomplish my job and my assignment from God if that was my approach? Do you see, it is not logical? Yet, the dualistic mind and the false teachers want you to believe in this so-called logic.

...

Become like a rocket

You, as the spiritual being, can raise that vibration. You can accelerate it. You see, my beloved, you are like a rocket that is sitting on the launch-pad. The engines have been started, they have been revved up. They have smoke and flames coming out. Yet, you do not quite dare to push the button that lifts you off from the Earth. For many of you, that is the only thing holding you back—that you have not come to that point, where you are willing to recognize your full potential and to truly accelerate yourself out of the problems, out of the wounds, out of the setbacks, out of the diseases, out of any condition that you think is holding you back. And your ego desperately wants you to keep thinking that it can hold you back.

A rocket, if it had self-awareness, would see itself as a rocket and would know that when it is put on the launch-pad, when it is fueled, it is just a matter of pushing the button and then it will accelerate out of the force of gravity, until it escapes the gravity of Earth and goes into orbit. This is simply a matter of the laws of physics. But of course, when you are talking about self-aware beings, it is not just a matter of laws. For you have, when you have passed the initiations of the first three rays, followed the laws to where you are ready, you are on the launch-pad. But we still have, of course – as is the case any time you deal with self-aware beings, – a decision that must be made.

A decision to push the start button, so that the full force of the rocket can be released. A rocket that has not left the ground is not a rocket. It is a pile of scrap metal. Yet, it has the potential to take flight and move beyond the gravitational pull of the Earth.

You are like rockets, sitting on the launch-pad. And you are still waiting for someone to come and push the start button. But I tell you, that "someone" will never come, for the someone that must push your start button – instead of pushing your ego buttons – is you.

You are the only one who can make the decision to accelerate, to take off, to not let anything stop you, my beloved, to not let anything hold you back. And this, again, is an essential ingredient in true healing. For what is it that the mass consciousness, the consciousness of duality, wants you to believe when your body gets ill? It is that you cannot simply accelerate away from the illness. You cannot escape it—it is permanent, it is unavoidable and this and that and the next thing. It wants you to believe that the disease is ultimately real and thus has power over you.

But, of course, it is unreal—but how do you escape it? Only by looking at the reality that no matter how you feel, no matter how burdened you feel, you are more than these burdens. And thus, you have the potential to decide, to unleash the full power of the rocket of your I AM Presence and accelerate your being, accelerate your cells, accelerate your very atoms, my beloved, and rise above the vibration—even raising the vibration of the burdened cells and atoms.

Overcoming perfectionism

Yet, what is perfection, my beloved? For when you rise to the fourth ray and go through the initiations, I can assure you that one of the greatest tests for the students that come to my retreat is to overcome perfectionism. Perfectionism is a curse put upon humankind, my beloved. It is a concept that has been perverted by the duality consciousness. And thus, so many people believe that perfection means that you live up to certain conditions. But my beloved, any condition can exist only in the mind of duality. Any condition in the mind of duality has an opposite polarity, or it would not exist.

Love is in opposition to hatred or fear. And if love has an opposite, it cannot be perfect love. For perfection cannot have an opposite — even though you may talk of imperfection. When you realize the reality, you realize that imperfection is not the opposite of true perfection. For perfection is simply beyond imperfection.

And thus, what has been done by the mind of duality is to create a dualistic concept of perfection that can, indeed, be in opposition to imperfection. And thus, you think that what makes you imperfect is a certain condition, and in order to become perfect, you have to take on another condition. But do you see that whether it is an "imperfect" condition or a "perfect" condition, any condition that you take on only affirms the reality of the separate self.

For it is your ego that makes you feel unworthy. And it is the ego that struts of spiritual pride — feeling better than others by having taken on the condition that it has defined as perfect. And so either way – whether you are conditionally imperfect or conditionally perfect – you are trapped in the conditions of the separate self. And how do you, then, overcome it? You overcome it by seeing the illogical nature of this concept and realizing that you cannot set up any condition that defines perfection. In fact, if you were to truly look at the worldly concepts of perfection, you will see that they are in all cases not clearly defined.

For when you start to define what perfection is, you immediately run into a dualistic argument — is it this or is it the opposite? For maybe one could argue that the opposite of that particular condition also has some merit. And maybe that should really be part of perfection, or should it be another one, or a third one, or a fourth one? And before you know it, you are so confused that you do not know what is up and down, and so how can you reach perfection?

And so, you need to come to the point where you recognize that it is not possible to define perfection by setting up any condition whatsoever. Perfection means unconditionality.

Unconditionality does not mean the loss of individuality. You do not become nothing by becoming unconditional. You become no thing, meaning, no condition in the dualistic realm, no thing in this universe. You become free of being tied to anything – any "thing" – any sense of identity in the dualistic realm.

The initiations of the fourth ray

Thus, you see, indeed, that the pyramid at Giza was originally designed for spiritual initiates on the fourth ray of purity. The king's chamber – or so it is called – was meant to represent that state of the death of the conditioned self.

Those who had been prepared – through a very long, gradual and difficult process of initiation – would be led into that chamber, would be put in the sarcophagus and would then be left alone, my beloved, for 24, 36, or 48 hours—being left in complete darkness, complete silence, complete sensory deprivation. Which, as you will know from those who have been exposed to this as a form of torture is, indeed, the extreme fear of the separate self. For it does not know what it is when it has no sensory input. And so, if you were to be exposed to this initiation before you were prepared for it, there is a high likelihood that people would go insane immediately upon experiencing that sensory deprivation.

Yet, an initiate that is prepared can use it to simply accelerate its sense of self out of the body and go to a higher realm, as you all do at night, my beloved—perhaps without being consciously aware of it. And so, this, then, is the process that you are all going through, that you have been going through in a more difficult way than the initiates who came to a mystery school and isolated themselves from the world, my beloved. For you are going through it while still being immersed in an active life in the world. But the process is much the same, although more gradual. You are coming closer and closer to the point, where you can let the separate self die and surrender to unconditionality, the unconditionality of your higher self, your true identity.

And so, the fear, of course, is, "But if I give up the ego and the separate self, what will I have left?" Do you think, my beloved, that this sense of fear is alien to me? How do you think I qualified for my ascension, unless I experienced that fear myself, faced it, and overcame it? How do you overcome that fear? By knowing you are MORE than the separate self, and then making the decision that you will not simply let the separate self die and be nothing—but that you will be reborn in the process by accelerating your entire being.

The Alpha and Omega of transcendence

You may think, my beloved, that all that happened to Jesus on the cross was that he hung there, going through the sense of separation of being left by God and then gave up the ghost, as we have talked about earlier. But the deeper reality is that giving up the ghost was the Omega side of the equation. The Alpha side was that at the same time as he gave up the ghost of the separate self, he deliberately and willfully accelerated his sense of self to that higher vibration of the purity of who he really is—as that spiritual being that was never confined to the lower sense of self.

The giving up is the Omega, the acceleration is the Alpha. And there is a point where you have given up enough that you are capable of making that final push away from the gravitational pull of whatever separate self is left—and even the gravitational pull of the mass consciousness. And at that point, there is only one thing that is necessary. And that is the Alpha thrust of accelerating your sense of self, whereby you accept that you have shifted your identity.

My beloved, you may say, "But I cannot, in one step, accept that I am the full Christed being." This is not what I am asking you to do. I am asking you to acknowledge that you have followed the spiritual path, that you have gone through the necessary steps and that you have indeed reached a point of attainment, whereby you are able to accelerate your service. For you have gone through enough in your own being that you are now ready to bear witness and help other people. You are able to step up, my beloved. You are able to step up your service and your sense of self. Many of you have reached that level of attainment.

The only thing that is left is the acceptance of this fact. But the acceptance of this fact is not a passive thing. Acceptance might seem passive—that you accept something given to you from without. But acceptance also has an active quality of deliberately and consciously making the decision to choose to accelerate your sense of self. And in accelerating it, experiencing it. And in experiencing it, accepting it even more fully. And thus, this is the key to healing.

Closing the gap on the spiritual path

Mother Mary, April 19, 2009

The only way to be free is to stop running away

My beloved, what have the masters that have spoken before me been saying? They have been saying, my beloved, that when you accept the illusion of separation, out of that illusion springs an image that is projected upon the Ma-ter light and that will eventually manifest as some kind of condition in your physical body. But the illusion of separation is an act of running away, running away from God. And so, trying to run away from the condition in your body or the consciousness behind it will not set you free. The only way to be free is to stop running away, my beloved.

It is, as has been said before by us, that if you keep doing the same thing and expect different results, well, you are not likely to get different results, are you now. So there comes a point of truth, a point of realism, where one must ask oneself, "If I keep doing what I have always done, is it likely that my life will change?" And so, as I have inspired this messenger to say to several people, but I desire to bring it out for a general audience, ask yourself, ask yourself, "Am I happy in my present state of consciousness and in my present circumstances?"

My beloved, listen carefully—many of you will instinctively say, "No I am not happy." But I ask you to step back and ask this question at a deeper level. For what we have explained in the previous releases in this series of discourses is that you have free will—that everything that you are facing in your life is a result of choices you made. And because of that, you have the potential to take back your power and change the choices of the past by making choices that are not based on separation and duality but choices based on oneness. And you can, indeed, have, the power, the wisdom, the love—and the acceleration of the three of them coming together in that intensity of the white light that propels you beyond your present state of consciousness, any state of consciousness.

So you, who are the spiritual people, must come to that point, where you say to yourself, "Am I happy in my present state of mind?" Meaning, if I have not taken back my power to change my present state of mind, is it because I actually enjoy torturing or putting myself down? Is there something in this experience of seeing myself unworthy or feeling alone that I have not had enough of? And if you honestly recognize that you have not had enough of that experience, then know that I, nor any other being in heaven, will not condemn you for it. For we respect free will absolutely and unconditionally.

You have a right to any experience you desire for as long as you desire it—within certain boundaries of time and space, of course. For nothing in time and space can be permanent or last forever. But within very wide boundaries, you have the right to any experience you desire. And so if you honestly recognize that you desire to continue with the experience that you have through your present state of consciousness, then embrace it, my beloved. Embrace your misery, your sense of unworthiness, your sense of aloneness, your fear. Embrace it and enjoy it, for this is what you have chosen to manifest right now.

The gap between where you are and where you want to be in consciousness

And then, if you find, with your self-examination, that "I am not happy in my present state of mind," then you have another consideration to make. You see, my beloved, it is possible – because you have not been given the correct understanding of who you are and of free will – it is possible to be in a twilight zone, in a no-man's land, and this is what other masters have attempted to explain before me.

This is the catch-22, where there is a part of you that wants to change, but yet you cannot change. There is something holding you back, something that prevents you from fully changing. And you might look at spiritual movements and see so many people who have been walking a spiritual path for many years, my beloved. They have studied teachings, they have practiced techniques, they have sought healing. They have attempted in many different ways to change their life experience, their state of consciousness.

Yet you will see so many people who have gone through the first three rays, to some degree taking back their power, for you cannot be in a spiritual movement or on the spiritual path without realizing that you have to do something. They have also spent countless hours studying spiritual teachings, and thereby they have increased their understanding. They have even had so-called peak experiences of experiencing a higher state of consciousness, perhaps even unconditional love in glimpses. They might even have put the three together and accelerated themselves beyond the level of consciousness they had 1, 10, 20 or 30 years ago.

Yet, there is still a gap between where they are and where they want to be. They are not happy, they are not at peace in their present state of consciousness. They are not, as the saying goes, walking their talk. They can talk a good game of spiritual theory, but when it comes to applying it in their practical, everyday life, there is a gap. And so you see, what I endeavor to start with this release is then the Omega aspect of this crash course in the restoration of true healing.

Knowing about the figure-eight flow

And so, I ask you to visualize that on the wall behind this messenger is drawn a figure-eight and you are looking straight at it. So what I give you is seen from your perspective, not from the perspective of the messenger facing the other way.

So now visualize this figure-eight in front of you and realize that the lower figure represents the material world, whereas the upper figure represents the spiritual. In personal terms the upper figure is your I AM Presence and Higher Being. Even the Higher Beings out of which you came, reaching all the way to the Creator, which we might represent as a point at the very top of the figure-eight. Although, of course, the Creator needs no real representation, for by creating a representation, we might cause some to reinforce the image of the external creator. Nevertheless, for the purpose of this linear illustration, let us simply make it so.

And then look at the opposite point at the very bottom of the figure-eight. That is where you are in consciousness when you awaken and begin your spiritual path. This may not have happened in this lifetime, or it may have happened by you having an experience in this lifetime, where you felt that your life had turned around and you realized that you had to change something in your life. For some it may come as a hit-rock-bottom experience, where they feel they cannot possibly go any lower, they cannot possibly continue doing what they have been doing.

But for many of you, you have already had that experience in past lives, and you came into this lifetime knowing that there was something you had to find. And you were looking and searching for what it was, and there then came a point where you became consciously aware of the spiritual side of life and the potential to actively raise your consciousness by your own efforts, so to speak, of being willing to go through the initiations of the first four rays, as described previously.

And so, now visualize that you start at that very bottom point, of the lower point of the figure-eight flow. That is the point where you consciously start walking the path. And at that point, you start with the initiations of the first ray because it is not enough to realize that you can take a step—you have to summon the will to take a step. So, you have already summoned some of that will, or you would not be where you are today, where you can even find and receive this message. So then, you go through the initiations of the first ray of power and will, and you climb up the left side of the figure-eight, the lower figure of the figure-eight, going in a clockwise direction, as if the lower figure was a circle.

And so, you come to a certain point of having passed enough of the initiations of the first ray that you can move on and begin to internalize more knowledge, more understanding, more wisdom. And you study, and you study, and you study. And after you have internalized and climbed to a higher point on that circle, well then you come to the third ray of love and you receive some experience of something beyond your normal state of consciousness. It may not be the full unconditional love of God – although it is certainly possible to have that experience – but there is some love. And then you have climbed to the point, where you are now approaching the nexus of the figure-eight.

And the nexus, of course, is the point of the Christ, my beloved. And what is, for the purpose of this discussion of personal healing, what is that point of Christhood? It is the point that Serapis spoke about, where you decide that you can take what you have gained through the first three rays, put the blue, the yellow and the pink together – having attained some measure of that balance of what has been called the threefold flame of the heart – and blend the three together to the intensity and the purity of the white light, and then use that white light to consciously and deliberately accelerate your state of consciousness to a certain level.

...

Why can't people close the gap?

And so, my beloved, why is it that so many people in spiritual and religious movements can have the will to change – can have the wisdom of spiritual concepts and may even see how they need to change, can have had an experience of unconditional love, of a higher state of consciousness that is possible, can even have gone through the acceleration of raising their consciousness – yet there is still a gap? There is still a gap that they cannot close—they cannot come to that sense of inner peace, for they cannot embrace whatever situation they face and stop running away, stop seeing that gap, and fully be in the moment, whatever the moment might bring. Why is that, my beloved?

Well, it is because after you pass the initiations of the first four rays, you have entered that point of the nexus of the figure-eight, and now you face an entirely new kind of initiation, my beloved, that very few people have understood. So listen, attentively.

Look at the mindset, when you realize you are at the bottom of the figure-eight and you want to rise higher. You gradually expand your vision that there is a spiritual realm beyond the material. And you build your desire to come into oneness with that Spirit, to reach up. And because you have had the images of the external God in the sky, you might build the subtle sense that you have to raise your consciousness into the spiritual realm.

You might take on the subtle lie that the material world is an enemy of your spiritual growth, and that you need to escape the material world and ascend into the spiritual realm. And so, you might think that as you climb that lower figure of the figure-eight and reach the nexus, that is the point where you are free. Now you can go into the upper figure of the figure-eight and continue the initiations there.

And then, so many people think that what they have done on the spiritual path, on the first four rays, they simply need to continue that mindset and that thrust, and that will carry them on to the fifth, the sixth and the seventh ray and beyond. And so they think they have to continue in that direction, to continue to do what they have been doing.

And this, my beloved, is a fundamental error, a fundamental misunderstanding. I use strong words because I want to shock you into realizing that if you truly want to close the gap between where you are and where you want to be, you need to change your mindset, for it is the mindset that sustains the gap, irregardless of the fact that you have made much progress on the path so far.

You cannot go beyond the fourth ray by using the mindset that helped you climb the lower figure of the figure-eight to the nexus point. This is what Jesus describes in his book on personal Christhood. But I desire to give you a different perspective as well. For you see, what will it take to experience true healing, my beloved? You cannot become whole, you cannot become healed, by will power alone, by wisdom alone, by love alone, or by purity alone.

Surrender is the only way

Why not? Because as you climb that lower figure of the figure-eight, you are carrying with you the separate self. And as some of you have come to realize and see clearly out-pictured in your own minds, it is inevitable that as you increase your understanding of spiritual concepts, your ego will not simply die. It will morph itself into a form that for a time will make you believe that the ego can actually be perfected and become acceptable to God.

In other words, the belief says that it is possible to use a spiritual teaching and spiritual practices to perfect the separate self, so that it lives up to some condition that will make it acceptable in the eyes of God and therefore gain it entry into the kingdom. This is what Jesus illustrated in his parable about the wedding feast, where all are invited, but if you come in without a wedding garment, then you cannot stay.

You will not actually be cast into outer darkness by any external force, but the reality is that there is still a remnant of the separate self, and it will pull you out of the wedding feast—and that is what creates the gap that you seemingly cannot cross. You are trying to fit the square peg of the separate self into the round hole that leads to heaven. You are trying to carry that luggage with you through the narrow door into the train that simply will not fit. And so you have to decide that if you want to get on the train, you have to leave your luggage behind and give up the ghost.

How do you, then, give up the ghost? This is the question you need to ponder. You cannot give up the ghost by seeking to perfect the ghost. Thus, the only way is the path of surrender. Surrender, my beloved, may sound like a strange concept, for you have grown up in a culture on this planet that is infused with the consciousness of competition and war. What does the word surrender mean in war? Well, it means that you give up and you are defeated. What does surrender mean in competition? That you give up winning and therefore you lose.

But do you see, my beloved, that the concept of win or lose is dualistic, indeed? One must lose in order for another to win. Where is the true victory in that? And so, surrender in a spiritual sense is not, my beloved, a passive act of giving up. It is an active process of giving up the ghost. Giving UP, not giving up. You give UP the ghost to a higher vision, for you are willing to give UP the separate self in order to become more whole.

You are willing to give UP a part of that separate self in order to experience more wholeness. You are willing to give up one dollar to receive a million in return. And thus, there is no loss in true surrender. There is only freedom. This is what many of you have not fully locked in to in your minds.

You are not responsible for other people

And so many of you on the spiritual path feel a sense of responsibility towards others. And what happens when you feel that false sense of responsibility, my beloved? Well, what happens is precisely that you cannot have full mastery of your own state of mind, for subconsciously you believe that because you are responsible for other people, you should allow your state of mind to be dependent on their state of mind, thereby thinking you have to allow your state of mind, your life experience, to be dependent on the choices made by other people.

You will never close the gap, my beloved, as long as you hold on to this false sense of responsibility. For you will never be in a situation where all other people on this planet will be in total agreement with you. They are individuals, they are different. And so what you are essentially thinking – at a subconscious level; not consciously – is that you can only attain happiness and inner peace when all of the people behave in such a way that they do not pull you out of the centeredness of happiness and inner peace. And thereby, you see that for this to happen, all of the people must become like you. For if they are different, then how could they not disturb your sense of peace? This, of course, is the ego who has this feeling.

But as long as you have not seen that this is an aspect of ego, you can identify yourself with it. And so, you must ponder this until it clicks, so to speak, and you literally experience the reality of free will. And you literally experience that surrender of the false responsibility—that your state of mind depends on other people's state of mind, that your state of mind depends on material conditions in this universe.

...

Completing the circle of initiation

Do you see that when one starts at the bottom of the figure-eight, one clearly sees that there is a gap between where I am, and where the kingdom of God is, so you have to create a thrust, my beloved, in order to rise above the gravitational pull of the mass consciousness, as Serapis illustrated with his analogy of the rocket. There has to be momentum, you have to create a force, and you have to do it partly with the state of consciousness you are in at the time. Which means that your separate self, your ego, will be involved.

And therefore, the ego will color your efforts to some degree by its desire for self-elevation and for feeling important. And that is why you respond to spiritual teachings that tell you that you have an important mission to save the world for Saint Germain and bring the Golden Age, and do all of these outer things. And so you think that you actively have to be part of this, you have to create some kind of force or thrust that makes it manifest. And this is correct, through the initiations of the first four rays. But you will not get beyond that point until you realize that what has carried you to this point, my beloved, will not carry you further, it will weigh you down.

Look at a rocket again that has several stages. First it has a very large booster that is meant only to accelerate it to a certain point, and then the fuel in that booster is burned out. And it must now be separated from the rocket and it falls away and the rocket starts another engine that takes it beyond to orbit. Do you see, my beloved, that if you insist on holding on to the mindset that boosted you through the first four rays, you cannot progress, you are stuck in a no-man's land? You are feeling that you want to change, that you have to change, you see a glimpse of what has to change, but you cannot internalize it, you cannot bring it into your consciousness.

And thus, the illustration that I want to give you here is that when you come to the nexus point of the figure-eight, you have the potential to attain a new perspective, the perspective of the Christ mind, the mind of oneness rather than the mind of separation. And when you attain that perspective of the Christ mind, you see clearly that the path forward does not go into the upper figure of the figure-eight. No, it goes out from the nexus point and down on the right side of the figure-eight, where you now begin to descend again.

And why does it seem like – in order to rise higher on the spiritual path – you have to start descending? Well, it is because what you have done so far is to take a part of your consciousness and thrust it beyond the mass consciousness, but there is still a part of you left, and that is why you feel a gap, that is why you are not quite there, you are not quite together, you are not quite whole.

And so, you must use the higher thrust and insight and perspective you have gained with a part of your mind, to go down again and rescue, so to speak, all other parts of your being, all other fragments of your soul, if you want to call them that. But even beyond that, you must come to recognize that you are one cell in the Body of God and that your job is not just to resurrect that one cell that you are, but to resurrect the entire body.

And so, in order to rise higher personally, you must begin to share and give out what you have gained, by then seeking to go out into the marketplace and reach other people, as Jesus demonstrated, by going into the marketplace of life, giving people what they needed, whether it was a higher spiritual teaching, whether it was healing, whether it was a cup of cold water in Christ's name, a listening ear. You all have qualities that you are aware of, or can quickly become aware of, that can help other people. Some of you have expressed it, all of you have it. All of you have already used those qualities, but you need to come to the point where you are willing to use them more consciously. Not for your own personal growth, but for the selfless service of raising other parts of life. For it is in that service that you are healed.

...

For my beloved, you have heard us talk about the closed circle. What is the closed circle, what is the closed system? It is the mindset of the ego and the separate self. What is – if you strip away all of the outer camouflage of the separate self – what is the one question asked by the ego and the separate self, my beloved—the constant question that the ego is projecting out from itself.

It is this: "Validate me. Tell me I am real. Tell me the illusion I have created, the image I have created of what life is, what God is, what I am, tell me it is real. Affirm it. Affirm me. Affirm me. Affirm me."

How can you help people who are so trapped in this consciousness that they are not willing to rethink it, to reconsider it, to consider that it might be wrong? Do you help them by affirming their illusion? Of course not! So how can you help them? By demonstrating that you are not trapped in that illusion, by standing there firm and letting them attack you, letting them ridicule you, letting them ask questions—but you remain who you are. And thus, you demonstrate that whatever they throw at you, they cannot pull you into their state of consciousness.

And thus, you are not affirming the reality of their state of consciousness—you are demonstrating the non-reality of it. And that is why you need to work on your attachment to the reactions of other people, for you cannot stand firm in who you are if you have a sense of responsibility for others, if you are attached to their reactions, or if you are still so identified with your separate self that you want validation from others.

You are a spiritual being, my beloved. You are here to help those who are trapped in duality. Do not expect that you can open your mouth and they are instantly going to say, "Oh, he is right." They cannot see it. Do you not see that?

And therefore, do you not understand that for you to help a person, you must demonstrate repeatedly that you will not affirm the person's state of mind. And therefore, you must sometimes – as some of you have experienced, with your friends or even family – you must let them question or attack or seemingly reject you many times. But if you can stay centered and non-attached, my beloved, one of two things will happen. Either the person will have a breakthrough and see that they can follow your example and reach a higher state of consciousness—and thus, they will come with you up. Or they will come to the point where the Law of Free Will mandates that they have had enough opportunity, and therefore they reach what we have called the judgment. And that does not necessarily mean that they are condemned to hell, but it means that they have had enough opportunities from you, and therefore, you can now move on and seek to help others. And thus, you do not need to encounter that person or even that state of consciousness anymore.

But you see, you need to come to that point where you are non-attached to whatever state of consciousness you encounter. This, of course, is difficult, I understand. Do you know why I understand? Because I see that the consciousness that you will encounter, my beloved, the consciousness you will encounter in other people is exactly the consciousness that you have not yet raised in yourself.

Whatever wounds you have left, whatever unresolved substance you have in your own being, that is what you will encounter from others, because the unresolved stuff in your own being will act as a magnet that magnetizes these other people to you. And therefore, it is, of course, the most difficult for you to depersonalize your relationship with these people and remain non-attached. For the very unresolved substance in your own mind, the beam in your own eye, holds you into an attachment and a dualistic reaction.

The unconditional joy of true service

Lady Master Nada, April 19, 2009

You came here to bring light
And so, indeed, you see, as was explained, that when people come into a spiritual movement, their ego morphs into a so-called spiritual ego or spiritual persona that takes on the characteristics that it thinks it needs to take on. And in many cases that means that people accept that you should behave a certain way. There are certain things you should not say, certain things you should not express. As this messenger himself realized during the conversation at lunch time, that he grew up in an environment where everyone suppressed their emotions, and he had overcome to the point of feeling comfortable expressing positive emotions, but not feeling equally comfortable expressing so-called negative emotions.

And many of you will recognize the same pattern. You realize that in a spiritual movement, certain things are appropriate and certain things are not. But you see, my beloved, why do you have four lower bodies? Because, the material universe is at such a low vibration that you cannot express light here from the etheric level directly. You then needed lower bodies corresponding, gradually stepping down the light, eventually reaching that level of the material universe with its density.

And so, you have four lower bodies that are designed to be vessels for transferring the light. Which means that if you are to express your light in the material universe, you must express it by letting it flow from your Higher Being into your identity body, into your mental body, into your emotional body, and then into the physical where you express it in different ways, but one example is certainly through speaking the word—but also by a smile, by a look, by expressing that emotion that is genuine and sincere, thus uplifting another person.

Suppressed emotions block the flow of light

But what I want to bring to your attention here, my beloved, is that what stops the light is the decision to suppress something. And so, when things are suppressed, they cannot flow. And when they cannot flow, well they must accumulate. And so, now you have so many people who accept a certain sense of identity that sets limitations, and so they accept mental limitations of what is proper to think or believe. And then they accept other limitations for what emotions are proper. And so, you see the suppression in the emotional body. And thus, the suppressed emotions will naturally begin to accumulate. And as the emotional body fills up, there is no longer the flow of light that can penetrate through the suppressed emotions.

And thus, the light cannot reach your physical body and renew the cells. And so the cells begin to out-picture that they cannot flow, that they cannot bring forth new life and so they bring forth lower manifestations. And so, as a spiritual person, can you see that when you realize you need some kind of healing in the physical body, your spiritual imagery, your spiritual persona, your spiritual culture can be a direct block to that healing? Because you are not willing to acknowledge that in order for you to be healed, you have to re-establish the flow of light through the emotional body. And the only way to do this, my beloved, is to go into the emotions that have accumulated and get them flowing again.

And in many cases this means that you must stop suppressing the negative emotions and give expression to them for a time, my beloved—no matter how wrong or shallow they might seem. As you just heard one person explain to you that she went through several years of journaling, expressing whatever came to her. And had she not expressed it, she would not have re-established that flow and thus could have continued for the rest of her life, being stuck at a certain level of consciousness. Do you see, my beloved, how you think with the outer ego that has taken on this aura of spirituality, you think that in order to reinforce the image that you are a spiritual person, you cannot express any negative emotions? For you may indeed get a negative reaction and have others think negatively of you.

And so, you want to continue to suppress these emotions. But in suppressing them, what are you doing? You are continuing to block the flow. And so, you cannot break through – in your conscious awareness – to your conscious acceptance of who you really are. And therefore, you remain trapped in a lower sense of identity. Do you see, my beloved, certainly the negative emotions are not pleasant. And certainly they should not necessarily be expressed in a group setting. But you, individually, need to express the emotions so that you can work through them and not only theoretically understand, but directly experience that you are more than the emotions.

For what will happen is that as you give expression to them, and as you look at them, you will see—at some point, you will have that Aha-experience of realizing, "But this is not who I am. I am more than this. This is just energy that has taken on a certain vibration, a certain condition. But this is not the fullness of who I am. I am feeling this way, but that does not mean that I am this way." And so, you see that unless you look at the emotions, you cannot come to see that you are MORE. And thus, when you run away – do not want to acknowledge that you even have negative emotions, and do not want to give them expression – well then, you are continuing to reinforce the gap, as Mother Mary spoke about, between where you are and where you want to be.

And you cannot cross that gap, as we have given the illustration earlier, that you cannot move from point A to point B by first moving to the halfway point, and then to the halfway point of the remaining distance, and continuing to break the distance into smaller and smaller segments. But you can continue this indefinitely because there will always be a gap.

The flow must be re-established, my beloved. And when a river has frozen over in winter, the flow can be re-established only by the ice becoming liquid again. But before it can become liquid, heat must be applied to it. And the heat is applied to your pent-up emotions by your conscious awareness, by your willingness to look at them. And also, my beloved, to acknowledge that you had those negative emotions at some point.

I am not thereby saying that you need to acknowledge or accept the emotions as real or permanent. But what you need to come to is the point where you can accept yourself for having those emotions, or for having had them in the past. And then you can look at yourself and realize that you had or have certain emotions because you are in a certain state of consciousness. And then you come to realize – as has been said previously, most clearly by Mother Mary – that God loves you unconditionally regardless of the state of consciousness you are in. And if God loves you unconditionally, then can you not then accept yourself unconditionally? Well, you can, if you are willing to simply shift your awareness, my beloved.

You can instantly change your self-image

For this is what I desire you to see—that you can instantly make a choice, away from non-acceptance and into acceptance. You see, why did you begin to suppress your light? Because you did not feel that your light was acceptable to others. And thus, you began to think that the light was not acceptable in a general sense. And how can you re-establish the flow? By coming to the point where you recognize and truly decide that your light is acceptable because it is acceptable to God, it is an expression of God. And therefore, it is acceptable that you express that light in this world, regardless of how it is received or rejected by those who are in a state of consciousness where they too feel unworthy to receive that light—and therefore want not to be disturbed by the light.

...

The initiations of the sixth ray

And this, my beloved, is why – after you have passed the initiations of the five first rays – you come to the sixth ray of Service. For as Mother Mary explained, you are not beginning to bring spirituality into the material realm until you go full circle, back to the point where you started—and now have integrated spirituality instead of having it as a theoretical concept. Instead of having it as a goal "out there," you have come full circle to where you can accept who you are—accept yourself as the spiritual being who is expressing its being in the material realm. But in order to get to that full acceptance, you must practice. And how do you practice? You practice by serving other forms of life, my beloved.

And what is true service? Well, it is that you come to the realization that service is not something you do out of your own needs, out of your ego's need to feel validated, to feel useful, to feel secure, to feel superior, to feel good. Your ego can create this spiritual persona that attempts to get you to serve in order to reinforce the ego's needs.

But true service is when you say, "This person has a particular need, and I can not let my own idiosyncrasies stand in the way of my being the open door for that need to be fulfilled." Or you can reach the other way and say, "The Ascended Masters have a need for something to be expressed, and I cannot let my outer personality stand in the way of this happening." As this messenger said to himself when he realized that Jesus wanted to use him as an open door for bringing forth a new awareness of his true teachings. And he had to say to his own sense of insecurity, "I cannot let that stand in Jesus' way—I need to step outside of it."

My beloved, it is when you begin to serve a higher cause or serve other people that you truly begin the process of separating yourself from the needs of the separate self. For you may think that you have given service to life, and many of you truly have given service to life. But I want to bring to your attention that some of you – and many people in the world – have done outer acts of service that many will deem as being service, but they have done it in order to fulfill a need of the separate self. And therefore, in giving that service, my beloved, they reinforced the reality of the separate self.

Take an honest look at many people in religious movements who have dedicated their lives to serving God in a particular church, perhaps by doing a humanitarian mission. But they have done it with a subtle overlay of wanting to demonstrate the superiority of their Christian faith or their particular church—as even Mother Theresa was tainted by her uncritical acceptance of the Catholic Church. And so, you see that even though these people perform outer acts that are good, the more good acts they perform, the more they reinforce the illusion of the ego—that it is good. And that by continuing to perform good acts, it will eventually reach a state of ultimate goodness, where it will be acceptable in the eyes of God.

This will never happen, as Mother Mary explained with the parable of the wedding feast. You can fool the entire world, but you cannot fool

God. God knows the difference between true service and self-centered so-called service. God knows your heart, the heart of all people.

You have free will. You can continue for as long as you want to have the experience of pursuing the quest for perfecting the separate self. This is your right, my beloved. I am not here to tell you what to choose. I am simply here to explain to you the reality of the choices you have. For so many people have come to think that they have no alternative, that the only way to enter Heaven is to perfect the separate self. For they do not see that there is more to their identity than the separate self. And thus, how can they make a free choice when they do not know their options, my beloved.

If you are standing in front of two doors, and you know what is behind the one door, and it feels safe, but you do not know what is behind the other, how can you make a free choice as to which door to enter? And so, we, of the Ascended Host, have a right – and it is our joy – to illumine people to the fact that they have other choices. They have an alternative to remaining stuck in the false sense of service, created by the separate self in order to validate itself.

The illusion that you are not free

And so, if you look at your life honestly, you might come to the realization that you have had certain relationships with other people, where you think you have to serve them or take care of them. But it is because you have created a certain image, a certain illusion, and as this messenger was inspired to say to one person, when you think you have to take care of someone else you are subconsciously saying, "I am not free to choose who and what I want to be. For I have to perform this outer service. And therefore I have to squash the free expression of my being."

Do you see, my beloved, that so many people in the world are performing acts of service but they are not doing it from the state of consciousness of true service? For they think that in order to serve others, you have to fulfill their needs or act a certain way.

Think back to what I said just a little while ago. You are walking in the streets and you meet a person. That person has a particular need, and in order to serve that person fully, you must give that person exactly what they need in order to come up higher.

The outer analytical mind will tell you that you need to establish some kind of image of how you are supposed to serve, what you are supposed to give to other people. But if you will re-read, or listen to again, my entire discourse, you will see that what I said about Being is the key to unlocking your understanding.

You see, when you meet a particular person, it is not just a matter of what that person needs. For there is an Alpha and Omega aspect. The person's needs is the Omega. The Alpha is who you are, and therefore what can be expressed through you. And I am not asking you to decide with the outer mind what kind of service to give and how to give it. I am asking you to re-establish the flow through your being, so that your own being spontaneously expresses what the other person needs. For what does the other person need, other than an example and a demonstration that there is a higher state of consciousness than the state in which the person is trapped?

And you cannot demonstrate this with the outer mind, with the separate self. You can demonstrate it only by being in the flow of life. And you will see, my beloved, that when you are in that flow, – and when you see how spontaneously your Higher Being gives another person exactly what that person needs – then you will not feel that this will restrict you and your expression. You will feel it as the most natural and joyful expression of your true Being.

Do you see the difference between trying to force yourself to give service and just walking into the flow, thereby allowing your true Being to shine through and spontaneously and creatively bring forth exactly what can help another person? This is the true joy of service. You have heard the expression by Master MORE, "The reward for service is more service." But it is because when you give true service, you feel such joy that you want to experience more of that joy. And so, you immerse yourself fully in that flow of service, where everything becomes a joy.

Your entire life becomes a joy. You are always serving in one capacity or another. Even if you are sitting alone in quiet unity and oneness with your Higher Being – simply feeling the light of your Higher Being flowing through your four-lower bodies, being radiated out into the world of form – this is also service. There are no set rules or restrictions or conditions for how to truly serve in Being. It is multi-faceted, my beloved, each one of you having a unique crystalline structure in your I AM Presence. And when the light streams through it, you bring forth a unique expression of God's being that no other being can bring forth.

And when you allow that expression to come through you, that is when God is experiencing its fullness through you. And you experience that joy that is the Creator's own joy of being expressed. You can follow that joy, merge with it, until you see that everything is joy. The underlying reality behind all form is unconditional, never-ending, ever-flowing, ever-creative, ever-self-transcending joy.

Joy is the motor of life. Life is bliss. Meaningless statements to the separate self. But once you experience being in the flow of joy, they take on ultimate meaning.

Balancing the scales of life

Lady Master Portia with Saint Germain, April 19, 2009

Both crime and punishment spring from duality

You see, my beloved, in terms of the concept of crime, it is only possible to commit any kind of crime or atrocity when one is identified with a separate self. For what is a crime? It is doing something that benefits one's self while hurting others. And so, obviously it cannot be based on oneness that seeks to raise up all life. And so, you see, then, that crime can only spring from the duality consciousness. And yet what you see on Earth is that the concept of how to deal with crime also springs from the duality consciousness.

And therefore, the human concept of justice is indeed a perversion of Divine Justice, which, as I said, should really be conceived of as balance—the balanced scales that are not pulled in either direction. Which directions am I talking about? The two extremes of duality, my beloved, where if one side of the scales is heavier, you are pulled towards one extreme. If the other side is heavier, you are pulled towards the other extreme. For example, some might be heavier on the scale of so-called selfishness, and they are therefore weighted down towards the extreme that people will call evil. But as Nada just explained, many have taken on an outer appearance of service, but they do it in order to serve the separate self and seem good. And they would then put weight on the opposite side of the scale.

Many people think that if you have committed evil in the past, even in a past life, and your scale is pulled down to one side, that if you commit good in this life, you will put weight on the opposite side of the scale and you will gradually balance them. But you see, my beloved, you may commit many good acts and raise up the other side of the scale, but you cannot hold it in balance. You cannot hold the balance; the scale will immediately begin to move down on the other side, until you have another unbalanced situation. For you are now moving from the extreme of relative evil to the opposite extreme of relative good, which is not God-good, because it is not unconditional good.

There is, of course, no unconditional evil, my beloved. And that is why, in order to balance the scales, you must empty both cups, so that you have no conditions on either side—neither the side of relative evil, nor the side of relative good.

...

Do you see, my beloved, the only way to be free of a certain state of consciousness is to let the old sense of self die and be reborn into a new sense of self? And then you do become a new being—your identity has shifted, you are reborn. Therefore, the concept of sin – the concept of karma that you must carry with you for a certain amount of time, until you have suffered enough or given enough violet flame, or done whatever else you might deem of as some kind of compensation – well that concept can only spring from the duality consciousness.

And therefore, the more you strive, the harder you strive to compensate for the past error, the more you confirm the reality of the separate self. And the more you prolong the life of that separate self, for it can only exist as long as you give it life energy through your sense of identity of being a person who deserves to be punished, perhaps by bearing a physical illness.

...

Change your mind in order to change your body
And so, should you not, then, also begin to at least contemplate that if you truly change your consciousness, you will also change your physical body and any condition in it. For that condition can only be a projec-

tion upon the Ma-ter light of a mental image. And as the movie screen itself is not changed by the movie being projected upon it, neither is the Ma-ter light. And thus, you can instantly change the image on the screen by changing the film strip in the projector, and you can instantly change the manifestation in your physical body by changing the image in your mind.

This is an absolute truth, my beloved, but it is extremely difficult for human beings to accept it. Because they are so used to looking at the material world through the filter of the separate self, which believes that matter is solid, unchangeable, permanent.

And why does the separate self believe this? Because the separate self is created out of the same frequencies as the material universe, and thus, to the separate self, to the ego, matter is unchangeable. You have heard of the concept of mind over matter—well, the ego can never have power to change matter. For that of the same vibration cannot change something else in the same frequency spectrum. A lower vibration cannot be changed by a lower vibration. A lower vibration can be changed only by being accelerated by a higher vibration. And so, where is the higher vibration to come from? Well, from your I AM Presence, but how is it going to descend into the physical body? It must descend through your four lower bodies, including what represents the physical body, which is your conscious mind.

Why do some people come to Lourdes and are healed, while others are not healed? Well, as Mother Mary said, those who are healed can make the shift by the conscious mind, of coming to accept that the disease can instantly disappear. It does not matter that they see this as a miracle from God. What matters is that they believe in it to the point, where they can shift their perception and accept the changeability of matter.

Matter is infinitely changeable, but only when you are willing to change the cause behind the effect of matter—namely the mental image, the condition of the mind. Thus, my beloved, if you have the subtle belief that your illness is a punishment for some error committed, that you deserve the punishment, and that you need to suffer for a time in order to be saved and go to heaven, well then how can you accept that you can instantly be free of the illness? How can you accept healing? How can you accept wholeness, my beloved?

Overcoming the consciousness of death

This is, indeed, a test that all must face. It is a test that Jesus had to face in order to attain that level of mastery, where he could be the open door for the light of such a high vibration that it could instantly change matter and therefore manifest what people have called the miracles of Christ. They are not miracles in the traditional sense; they are simply the out-picturing of a higher law. For as I said, it is not possible to change the vibration of matter through the dualistic consciousness. As Jesus expressed it, "With Man, this is impossible"—with the manly, the human, the dualistic, the separate, the mortal state of consciousness, it is not possible to change matter through the power of mind.

It is only possible to change matter through the force that can be exercised through the physical realm. And that is why you indeed see medical technology seeking to increase its power to change disease by force, by destroying the disease, even destroying the body in the process. And so, you need to come to that true realization that Jesus came to, towards the end of his training period, the true realization that it – truly, honestly, absolutely, realistically – is possible to change any condition in matter in an instant—when you switch the mind.

What is it that pulls you away from that knowing, that acceptance? It is the consciousness that has been called "death." Death has been called the last enemy, for death is the sense that matter is permanent, difficult to change. But behind that, the sense that matter is real, that it has some independent existence, my beloved. This, of course, is based on the illusion of the fallen beings who have rebelled against God and who have created the illusion that separated themselves from God and God's kingdom, creating a world where God is not. Therefore, they seek to spread that death consciousness to all people, so that they reinforce it. And through their acceptance of death as inevitable, the acceptance of matter as real and separated from God, they give their light to the fallen beings who have no light, for they cannot receive it from within.

Why? Because they have chosen to go into the ultimate state of separation. There are degrees of separation, and until you reach that ultimate state, you still receive some light from your I AM Presence that sustains you. But when you come to that ultimate state of separation, then you can no longer receive the light, for you are not willing to accept it. It is not that the light is not there, that God withholds his light. For I tell you that even the darkest being that you can possibly imagine, be it Lucifer,

Satan or whomever, God is not withholding light from them. For God still only desires to see them come back to oneness, but you can come to a point where you absolutely reject that you have the ability to receive light or the willingness or the worthiness or whatever it might be.

And from that point you can sustain any form of self, any form of awareness, only by taking light from others—who are still receiving it from above, but who are misqualifying it through fear, anger or whatever lower feelings that are not of love. And thus, my beloved, you will indeed see that this world is enveloped in a black cloud of the death consciousness. And that is why death is the last enemy. Because it is so difficult to overcome that illusion that matter is real.

For after all, your five senses are telling you that matter is real. And even your outer, analytical mind is telling you that matter is real. And therefore, it cannot simply be changed in an instant. For you cannot see with the outer mind and the senses that behind the matter that seems so solid, there is only light—consciousness. And consciousness can change in an instant.

This you have all experienced—how you can change your mind in an instant, from a state of sorrow, to a state of joy, or the other way around. Consider how simple it is to change your mind in an instant. Consider, my beloved, how women are often accused of changing their minds a thousand times. But realize that the reality here is that women are more in tune with the reality that you have a perfect right to change your mind at any time. For God has given you free will. So who says that because you have chosen to be in a certain state of mind – for a day, or a decade, or ten thousand embodiments – you have to continue to be in that state of mind indefinitely?

This is the death consciousness, my beloved. The death consciousness says that once you have made the mistake of eating a forbidden fruit, of partaking of the duality consciousness, you can never overcome that duality consciousness. As one person explained to this messenger yesterday, the Church of Satan says that once you have accepted membership, you can never renounce it, for you have given your soul to the devil and you can never take it back. But the reality is, of course, that there is no such thing as any permanence in the material realm. That which is unreal cannot permanently affect that which is real.

And so, when you see that you are real, you know that no promise made, no curse put upon you, no illusion can ever hold you any longer than the moment when you decide, that you are no longer the person who made the promise or made the mistake or accepted the death consciousness. You have been reborn, and thus you are free. You are free to Be what you want to be. For God within you will say, "I will be who I will be. And now I choose to be MORE than I was before." And in that choosing, you are reborn, you are free.

Freedom is not found by running away

You see, what we have told you several times now, is that you cannot overcome a condition as long as you run away from it. You cannot overcome a fear as long as you are not willing to face it. How, then, do you overcome death?

Look at how many people in the world are seeking to run away from death, either by not thinking about it, by denying it or by using all kinds of means to prolong life—as they call it. But it is truly the life of the physical body, or rather the life of the separate self, which thinks it needs that physical body. Because a part of the separate self is born to follow that particular physical body and will die when the body dies—even though part of your ego moves with you until you let it die by giving up the ghost.

So how do you overcome death? By being willing to face your fear of death. For only when you face the fear of death can you see that even death is an illusion. You will not die when your physical body dies. You will go on. Read the many near-death experiences and see how – when people let go of their attachment to the physical body – the transition out of the body was smooth, effortless, painless. And suddenly, people, or rather their beings, can find themselves in a higher space with a much expanded awareness.

What is there to fear in expanding your awareness beyond the narrow outlook on life that you have in the physical body? It is like a prisoner who has been imprisoned for so long that he clings to his bunk. And when the guards come to open the door and say, "You have served your time, get out," he says, "I don't want to leave! I can't leave! I won't know who I am once I leave this cell!"

Ah, my beloved, perhaps here we are touching upon the real issue of the death consciousness, the consciousness of punishment in order to balance the scales. For you see, as Maitreya has explained so carefully in his book, there comes a point in the spiritual sanctuary of the mystery school, where the spiritual teacher has taken you to a point where you need to become self-sufficient. So far, the teacher has given you a safe environment in which to experiment with your free will. He has taken upon himself the karma that you might have made from experimenting. So you have been free of any sense of burden, but there comes a point where you must take responsibility for experiencing the conditions that you create in the mind.

And this is truly the point, where you hopefully have attained enough oneness with the Alpha aspect of your being, your I AM Presence, that you are able and willing to fulfill the Omega aspect of deciding how you will express your Higher Being in the material realm. For as Maitreya explains, the role of your conscious self is to decide who you are, who you want to be, in expression in the matter realm.

Now, my beloved, even though you have a crystalline structure in your I AM Presence, even though you have a God Flame that gives you individual characteristics, you still have total freedom as to how you will express that in the material realm. As we have said, you have the right to have any experience you desire. And thus, the reality is that there comes a point on the spiritual path, where the teacher will step back and no longer tell you who you are, who you are supposed to be, how you are supposed to use your free will and express your creativity. And at that moment, you can either move closer, move into oneness with your Higher Being and express what Nada explained as the spontaneous flow of Being. Or you can choose to go into a vibration of fear, for you are afraid of the total freedom, and so you go into the state of duality and create the ego.

What the ego does for you

And what does the ego do for you, my beloved? It gives you the illusion that you, the conscious self, no longer has to make choices, for the ego will do it for you. But how does the ego make choices? The ego is not a self-aware being, so the ego must then look for some way that it can seemingly make choices, and how does it do this? Well, it goes into the theater of life and looks for a predefined role and it says, "Ah, this is who I am supposed to be." And it takes it on, and you must then go with it. And now you think you are a limited, mortal human being, who cannot be creative, who is supposed to be a certain way. You have accepted a set of conditions, my beloved, and you think this is who you are.

And thus, your former sense of self as a spiritual being has died, as Maitreya explains. You are now reborn into a limited being, or rather a being who thinks it is limited. And this is spiritual death.

And so, again, the ego creates the illusion that you should never look at how you came to be where you are. The fallen beings have created the false sense that you can never escape from that choice to go into duality, you can never escape from the choice not to make decisions—because they want you to permanently stay in that state of separation. But the reality is that you have a right – at any moment – to undo the choice and take back your power, your willingness to make choices as to who you are, who you want to be in this material realm, how you want to express yourself, what you want to experience.

Which is why we have said that if you desire to experience being miserable, embrace the experience, and recognize that it is a result of your own choosing. And you are doing it because you are seeking some kind of fulfillment from that experience. For I guarantee you, that the moment you fully embrace a limited experience, at that moment of fully accepting it, you will pass right through it.

You may think that by accepting death, you will move into death and die. But you will not, for by accepting death, you will move into it and see that it is an illusion. And therefore, you will emerge on the other side, seeing that what seems so real – from the viewpoint of the separate self – is completely unreal—when you know that you are an extension of the infinite Creator who can never die.

So how do you switch your perspective? Not by running away from that which you think limits you but by running right into it, by looking at it, by not seeking to hide anything from God, thereby hiding it from yourself. This is the value of the concept of confession, which, of course, has been perverted by the outer institution. But the concept is that you honestly confess to yourself, to God, that you have accepted a limited state of consciousness. And then you accept the very reality that by confessing it, by acknowledging it, you have already started separating yourself from it.

For my beloved, when you are inside a dualistic role, a dualistic sense of self, you cannot see it for what it is. But you are looking at the world from inside of it—it is as being inside a building where there is only a small opening to the outside world. And even though you can see out, you are only seeing a very small segment of the total view that is outside. And when you step outside of the building, you see the entire view. But you also see the building, and thus you see how limiting it was to your view when you were inside of it. And, of course, once you begin to see how a particular, conditioned sense of identity limits you, you are no longer completely trapped within it.

And thus, you can continue that process of separation step by step, until you get to that final point, where you realize that you have been crucified by that condition—that you cannot take yourself down from the cross by using the same state of consciousness that is nailing you to the cross. And therefore, you must give up the ghost in that final act of total, unconditional surrender that so few people on Earth have experienced. Even though it was demonstrated by Jesus on the cross, by Mother Mary when the archangel appeared to her, and by other people throughout the ages.

It is such a release, such a freedom, such a joy to go through that unconditional surrender, where you surrender any condition, any illusion. And instead of running away from that which you fear, including physical death, you embrace it. And you experience, as this messenger experienced, a sense that if you died at that moment, you could leave the Earth with no regrets, no pulls, no sense of unfulfilled work.

And of course, at that moment you can then be reborn as a Bodhisattva, who is now serving in true service to raise up all life and help them see the fruitlessness of trying to balance the scales—not by raising up one side of the scale, or by putting other dualistic conditions on the other side. Instead, helping them see that it is possible to transcend the entire consciousness represented by the scales—to transcend duality, to move out of it and into the total freedom expressed by God to Moses, "I will be who I will be."

The eighth ray of integration

Gautama Buddha, May 8, 2009.

The ego can survive the initiations of the seven rays

You see, it is indeed possible to go through the initiations of the seven rays without fully letting go of the duality consciousness. There can still be a separate self, an ego, a spiritual persona that has managed to camouflage itself and hide itself, adapting to the initiations of the first seven rays.

This is allowed. For we cannot, as spiritual teachers, demand that our students be completely ego-free. We cannot demand some state of perfection, and we do not demand any state of perfection. So indeed, you have what we might call a grace period of going through the initiations of the first seven rays, where you can still have an element of ego, you can still have a role you are playing. You can even create a role for your involvement with the spiritual path—where you seek to create that perfect persona, that perfect costume, that perfect character in the drama that fits perfectly in your particular spiritual environment.

And so, this has led some students to believe that they are on the fifth ray – or "I am on the seventh ray" or "I am on the first ray" – or "I am blue-flame" or "I am love," or I am this or I am that. And so, they have built a spiritual persona that is seemingly very strong on a particular ray. And there can even be a certain sense of pride over having these particular characteristics of a particular ray.

And so, now the student comes to the point where it needs to step up and begin the initiations of the eighth ray. But as Mother Mary stated in her discourse, what has brought you successfully through the initiations of the first four rays, will not take you into the fifth ray. You must surrender that momentum, that upward thrust and humble yourself and go back down and tie up the lose ends.

Well, so when you pass the initiation of the seventh ray of freedom, in order to go into the initiations of the eighth ray, you must again go through a complete and unconditional surrender. You cannot move into the eighth-ray initiation if you identify yourself as being on a particular ray among the first seven. So whatever momentum you might think you have on a particular ray, that momentum must be surrendered. You must lay down that life in order to climb higher and move into the eighth-ray initiations.

So this, my beloved, is an absolute necessity. For, you see, on the first seven rays, it is possible to move higher while still having ego left that you supposedly hide from the teacher. Of course, contrary to what people might think on the spiritual path, nothing is hidden from the true teachers. We of the Ascended Host are above and beyond any aspect of the duality consciousness, and what does that mean? That means, my beloved, that having seen through every aspect of the duality consciousness in our own Beings, we can, of course, see through it in your beings as well.

There are many students who have fallen prey to the illusion that Jesus has talked about: "Why is it that people believe that what they can hide from each other is also hidden from God?" There are even those who have come in contact with a true teacher – be it a messenger or another true guru – and they think they have hidden something from that guru. In some cases they might have hidden something, for the guru does not necessarily look at everything that goes on in a student's consciousness, and so the student might actually build a certain sense of the ego, a certain persona, that actually believes that it can cheat its way into heaven—that it can somehow find a way to sneak into the wedding feast without a wedding garment. It believes that it can camouflage the duality consciousness, so that it takes on the appearance of being so perfect, so in accordance with certain spiritual rules, that God simply has to let it into the kingdom.

But you see, it is not so. It is absolutely not so. You can start a new cycle of going through the initiations of the first seven rays again. You can still, then, be on the spiritual path as you are willing to pass these initiations. But there are also those who are not willing to humble themselves and go through the initiations again, thinking that should be below them because of all they have done in their outer service, or the inner initiations they have passed on the first seven rays. And so, they get stuck in a no-man's land, where they might go around strutting their stuff, so to speak, strutting their spiritual "attainment" like a peacock. And yet, they are stuck at that level and will not go beyond it until they are willing to unconditionally surrender their attainment and their perceived attainment on the path in order to go into the initiation of the eighth ray.

The initiations of the eight ray

The eighth ray is not for the faint of heart, for on the eighth ray, nothing can be hidden. You cannot even perceive what the secret rays are about through the duality consciousness. You can, of course, project a dualistic image on the secret rays, as you can project a dualistic image on everything. But you will not perceive even a glimpse of what the secret rays are about through the filter of the duality consciousness. Take note of the subtle difference here—you can gain glimpses of what the first seven rays are about even though you still have elements of the duality consciousness. You can, in glimpses, see beyond that consciousness and see what the true characteristic of a ray is—you can tune in to it. But you cannot do that beyond the seven rays, you cannot do it on the eighth ray and beyond.

Because the secret rays were named the secret rays precisely because for those in the duality consciousness, they will forever remain secret. For the ego, the secret rays will forever remain secret. For the prince of this world and the false teachers of this world, the secret rays will forever remain secret.

Why is this, my beloved? Well, when you have an element of ego left, why is it that you still have that ego? You have walked the spiritual path for lifetimes. For many years in this embodiment you have studied teachings, you have practiced various techniques, you have made real progress. Yet, there is still an element of the ego.

And why have you kept that ego around? It is, my beloved, because while you may not see this consciously, yet keeping the ego around gives you an advantage that you are not yet ready to let go of. There is something for the conscious self in keeping the ego around. There is something that the conscious self does not have to do. There is some decision that the conscious self does not have to make when the ego is around—for the ego will make those decisions for it, or make it easier for the conscious self to justify making those decisions. And so, you see, on the first seven rays, there are certain characteristics of each ray that the ego can perceive as an advantage. The ego can look at a particular ray, it can put a dualistic overlay over the characteristics of that ray, and it can see that it can use that overlay to give itself a particular advantage.

How the ego sees the first seven rays

My beloved, we have given you the concept of the duality consciousness in which there are always two polar opposites. So let me give you a very quick run-down of how this plays out when the duality consciousness perceives the first seven rays.

The first ray is the ray of will and power. The one dualistic extreme is obviously those who have a very strong will. And the ego can see that by reinforcing that strong will in a particular student, it can get the student to do almost whatever it wants in the name of some greater good. So therefore, you see some people on the spiritual path who have a very strong will, and who are willing to bend the will of others to get them to follow these strong people. They come into an organization, they think they know exactly how things should have been done all along, and they start telling the members, or even the leaders or the messengers, how they should have done things all along and how they need to do things from now on. You have people who always think they know better—who even think they know better than the Ascended Masters, for they have locked in to the very consciousness of the original fallen angels who think they know better than God.

Yet, in the opposite extreme you have those who have no will at all, and who do not want to make their own decisions, who do not want to take a stand for anything. They want to simply flow with the stream of the mass consciousness—even the mass consciousness in a spiritual organization. So, you have those in spiritual organizations who think they are very strong on the first ray, and they believe that this is a necessary and good characteristic. For, after all, someone must be the leader and tell all of these people who do not want to make decisions what to do. And so, these people exercise their power in a way that they believe is justified, yet they fail to see that they are completely out of touch with the reality of the first ray—which is powerful but never abusive, which respects free will absolutely, as the masters on all rays respect free will absolutely. And so, you see the co-dependent relationship between those who have perverted the will and made it too strong and those who have perverted it by not wanting to make any decisions.

Likewise, on the second ray you have those who think they know everything and understand everything, and they study and they can talk for hours about the smallest little details of the path; and this master said that and that master said this and this is how it really works. And then you have those who do not want to really study and know and understand but want to be told what to do. You find them even in ascended master organizations, but you find, of course, many of them in traditional religions, where they want to come to church every Sunday and have their minister or priest preach to them from the pulpit, talk down to them as if they were children who know nothing.

Likewise, on the third ray of love, you have those who have taken love to a dualistic extreme, where it has been possessive, controlling love. Where they think that it is actually good for others that they are controlled, for they know what is best for another person, and therefore in the name of loving that person, they have to control them. And of course, you have those who have perverted love to the point where they have no love for anything. And if you don't love anything – including yourself – how can you take a stand for anything? How can you take a stand for yourself?

And so, on the fourth ray of purity you have those who have become extremely judgmental, saying only these activities are pure and those who abstain from these other impure activities are the real students. Then, on the opposite extreme are those who have entered into what Jesus calls gray-thinking. Thinking, "Oh, nothing really matters, nothing is really bad. No particular form of music is worse than any other form of music. No particular food is worse than any other kind of food. I can do whatever I want. Nothing really matters." And so, they indulge themselves in whatever happens to come their way without having any standard whatsoever. Both extremes, of course, failing to see the truth in the teaching that to the pure, everything is pure.

But this does not mean that those who are pure indulge in anything that is available on this planet. They are simply not attached to it. They are not forcing themselves with the outer will to abstain from certain activities. They do not necessarily cringe when they walk into a public area where a certain type of music is playing. But they do not particularly seek it out either. They simply walk through it without letting it stick to them.

Then, of course, on the fifth ray of truth, again, there are those who believe – taking it to the dualistic extreme – that there can be only one truth—or rather, there can be only one expression of truth. Which is what you see in those who believe that there is only one particular scripture – be it the Bible or the Qur'an or the Vedas or whatever – that have the truth. But then you even have those in ascended master teachings who believe that there is only one true messenger, there is only one true ascended master organization, and that the Ascended Masters can be put in a nice little mental box and they did not speak to humankind before this particular organization and they have not spoken after.

Yet, on the other extreme, you have the perversion of truth, where there are those who say, "Oh there is nothing that is really true. Any philosophy is as good as any other." Or they take the agnostic view, "How can we know what is true? Nobody can really tell." And so, again, any religion is as good as any other, or all religions are false because they all claim to be true and that claim cannot be true for all of them.

And so, on the sixth ray of peace, you have those who have taken peace to the extreme, where they believe that peace can be attained only by suppressing all diverging viewpoints, only by suppressing differences, only by forcing all others to come into alignment with the ideal that they have espoused. And then, on the opposite side, you have what you saw in the hippie movement in the sixties, where everything is good, where nothing really matters. Or the saying that some people have, "It's all good." Well, what does that mean, my beloved? Can everything be good when two-thirds of the population live below the poverty level? How can that possibly be perceived as good? And so on and on.

And even on the seventh ray of freedom there are those who pervert freedom and believe that freedom is something that needs to be defended against all enemies of freedom. And that freedom can only be secured when you destroy your enemies, as the previous American administration – the Bush administration – believed that they could only secure the freedom of America by destroying those they had labeled as the enemies of freedom. And yet, on the other side of the spectrum, those who think that anything goes, everything is okay. You can do anything you want and get away with it, for after all, there is no life after this. It is just one lifetime, there is no purpose, you are just a sophisticated animal and you have a right to do whatever you want while you are here, your one shot at life.

The ninth ray of equilibrium

Gautama Buddha, May 9, 2009.

The underlying reality behind all appearances
When you are awake, you recognize that the fundamental underlying reality is not matter, is not energy, but is consciousness. Everything is an expression of consciousness. There is nothing in the material world that just exists. Everything is a projection upon the Ma-ter light, and that projection happens through a specific state of consciousness.

Therefore, if you try to perceive a particular material object, such as a distant star, only through the physical senses – or the extension of the senses that is what scientists have created as scientific instruments – well, then you will not truly know the object. You will know its material characteristics, but you will not know the consciousness that projected the object onto the screen of the Ma-ter light. And until you know that consciousness, you will not truly know what a star is, you will not truly know a particular star. You will not truly know the star of your own Sun and the specific consciousness of the spiritual beings who projected that image upon the Ma-ter light and who are still upholding it through their consciousness.

I would, thus, recommend that those who desire to go beyond the eighth ray, into the ninth ray, that you spend some time meditating upon the Sun, your own Sun of this particular solar system. Do not meditate on it as a physical Sun, but meditate on it as a spiritual Sun, as the expression of a spiritual being, a set of spiritual beings—an Alpha-Omega polarity. And then allow your mind to merge with the spiritual beings that occupy the space of your Sun, currently called Helios and Vesta. Merge with them, so that you know their vibration, you know their Presence.

This is the only way to know, truly know, the secret rays—which is why they have been called secret. For those still stuck in the linear mind, those wanting to objectify everything, cannot unlock the secret of the higher rays. As I said, there is nothing for the ego to magnify. There is nothing for the ego to use to confirm and validate its world-view, to raise itself up in comparison to others.

You see, my beloved, as I explained, the first seven rays are the rays that have been used to build the material universe. And thus, they have a certain expressive power, which – when perverted by the duality consciousness – the ego can then take in its perverted, unbalanced form and actually use to build its power or go into the opposite dualistic polarity of diminished power, but nevertheless thus keeping the ego alive through the dualistic struggle.

Of course, the ego can project an image onto the secret rays, creating a graven image of them, which then makes them seemingly dualistic. Yet, you need to understand that the secret rays were not used to build the material universe as such. They are higher expressions beyond the material. Which is why you must beware of the linear mind and its tendency to want to pull the secret rays down into the sphere that the linear mind can deal with and thus categorize and analyze according to its relativistic perspective on everything.

The relative mind and the dualistic mind

My beloved, let me give you a subtle distinction that few understand. We talk about the dualistic mind and we talk about the linear, analytical mind. Sometimes we even use them as interchangeable terms, but when you come to a higher understanding, you see that there is a subtle difference. The difference is that the linear mind is relative, whereas the ego mind is dualistic.

The analytical, linear mind is, in its essence, neutral. This is why scientists who are very focused on the intellect and the analytical mind have come to believe that they can achieve objectivity through the analytical mind. You see, the analytical mind will categorize everything according to a relative standard, a relative standard that has two opposite polarities. But what the analytical mind will not do is impose a value judgment on the opposite polarities. That is what the ego mind does. The ego mind is based on a value judgment. The analytical mind might say that something is this or something is that, but it will not say that this is good and this is bad—that is the ego.

And so, what you see is that the analytical mind is not necessarily your enemy—it is simply a tool. It is when the ego imposes a value judgment on top of the analytical mind—that is when people get trapped in the dualistic struggle, where they ultimately think that one side is good and the other side is evil. And therefore, they must align themselves with good and seek to destroy evil.

What you can do – when you separate the ego mind and the analytical mind – is that you can actually use the analytical mind, within certain boundaries, as a tool for exposing the ego. The analytical mind can be used to see that the value judgments of the ego are contradictory, do not make sense, will only tie you to a dualistic struggle. And so, to some degree the conscious self can use the analytical mind to expose the ego, as some of you have already done in various ways.

But you must also be aware that the analytical mind can never go beyond the level at which everything is seen in relative terms. There must be two polarities, there must be a tension between them. To the analytical mind, the tension is not necessarily a struggle, the struggle comes from the value judgment. But there is still a tension, and that tension can never be resolved through the analytical, linear mind.

For example, we have talked about the one Creator manifesting itself as two opposite polarities, the expanding force of the Father, the contracting force of the Mother. To the analytical, linear mind, expansion is an outward process, contraction is the opposite direction. And therefore, right there you have an inherent tension between the two. This cannot be resolved by the analytical mind. The linear mind cannot come up with a reasoning, with an argument, that resolves this seeming dichotomy between these two basic forces of creation. They will be seen as opposites by the linear mind.

This is why, in order to progress beyond the eighth ray and to start on the ninth ray – the first of the secret rays – you must come to that point, where you understand the limitations of the linear mind, and where you realize that you – as a conscious self – are more than the linear mind. Thus, you do not have to experience the world through the filter of the linear mind, but you can, in fact, go beyond it and have an intuitive experience – an Aha-experience – that cannot be expressed in words, that is beyond words, that is beyond concepts. But yet you know that you have experienced something that is real.

The qualities of the ninth ray

This, then, brings us to the ninth ray. What are the qualities of the ninth ray? Well, again, by putting a word upon it, I give fodder for the linear mind, so be careful not to be pulled into this. For the linear mind will do its thing and seek to analyze and categorize. But yet recognizing that, we must use words to communicate.

The word I will give you to describe the ninth ray is equilibrium. This is a concept that the linear mind finds it difficult to deal with. It is a concept that the ego does not want to deal with and does not want you to deal with. And you might recognize – if you monitor your inner state – that the ego will rebel against this, will come up with all kinds of reasonings that this cannot possibly be the case. "Why, this cannot possibly be the big secret that has been talked about by the Ascended Masters for so many years. There must be some kind of secret power in the secret rays." And there is, but it is a power that cannot be grasped by the ego. For you see, the ego can work only when there is imbalance, when there is tension. The ego cannot work unless there is tension, opposition between the two polarities, created in the act of separation from oneness. The ego cannot use oneness, and thus it cannot use equilibrium for anything.

This, then, brings us to the concept that has been known in eastern religions for centuries, for millennia, and it is becoming gradually more and more known in the West, the concept of karma. Karma is often seen in very dualistic terms, of good karma and bad karma. This is a concept very parallel to the western concept of sin, where you have sinned by doing something wrong, and then somehow the debt, the sin, must be paid before you can be free.

Thus, my beloved, you have billions of people on this planet who believe in this concept in some form, and who believe that if they do something – which according to some standard, be it religious or otherwise, is considered wrong – they must compensate for this by doing something else.

But you see, what does it mean to make karma, what does it mean to sin? It means performing an unbalanced action. Now realize something subtle, a subtle distinction. Consider what I said about the linear mind, which is relative but has no value judgment, and the ego then imposing a value judgment upon it.

If you take the ego out of the equation, the linear mind simply becomes a tool for acting in the material world. You can act through the linear mind without making karma, without sinning—when you recognize that you are more than the linear mind. But when the ego comes in and sees you as a separate individual – where you lose your sense of oneness with your own Higher Being, your sense of oneness with all life – well, then you now have the ego acting—still through the linear mind, but imposing a value judgment about what is good for you as a separate individual. Instead of the higher way of seeking only to raise the All by expressing your divine qualities, which is not unbalanced, my beloved, does not create karma, is not a sin.

This is something that both the ego and the linear mind will find it difficult to comprehend and impossible to accept. For the linear mind will say, "Well, but if two people perform the same action, then both must be sinning." But it is not so, my beloved. Two people might perform the same outer action; one is in the illusion of duality, of separation, and thus the action is unbalanced, it is aimed at raising up the separate self. Whereas another might perform the same action, but the person is beyond the dualistic mind, seeking to raise the All, and thus it is not a sin. It is a balanced action—an action that springs from equilibrium.

And thus, you see that there are certain actions that can be performed from a state that is non-dualistic, that is nonjudgmental. And therefore, through the pure intent of raising the All, there is no imbalance in the action. I am not hereby saying that this applies to all actions. Clearly, when you are beyond the dualistic mind, there are certain actions you would not even think of performing, my beloved.

In this world, action is inevitable

Yet, you recognize that even though you have attained a higher state of consciousness, as long as you are in physical embodiment, you must perform certain actions. You cannot be in embodiment and not act, in some way or another. Surely, you can do as many spiritual people have done in the past, that when they reach a certain state of consciousness – where they are above and beyond the duality that so many people are trapped in – they see the vanity, the futility of the dualistic struggle. And thus, they withdraw from it, going into a monastery or a cave in the mountains, or in other ways isolating themselves from the dualistic struggle—so as not to partake in it, so as not to add to it, so as not to feed it. And certainly, this has had some validity and still does in the sense that a few people can hold a spiritual balance for the many by remaining in this pure state of consciousness.

Yet, holding a spiritual balance only buys time. It does not actually help bring the kingdom of God or the Golden Age into manifestation. And thus, we do not need – in the Aquarian Age – more spiritual people who will withdraw and insulate themselves from society. On the contrary, we need those who will actively engage in society but do so from a state of equilibrium, where their actions are not unbalanced. And therefore, they do not add to the tension, they do not add to the struggle—they demonstrate that there is an alternative to the struggle.

This is what is needed in this age. This is what many of you have come into embodiment for the purpose of outpicturing—the possibility of being actively engaged in society while not being in duality. And how can you manifest this? You can manifest this only when you learn how to act without acting in an imbalanced manner. For obviously, you cannot engage in society without acting.

In reality, my beloved, even a person sitting in a cave in the Himalayas is acting, is taking action in the material realm. The person in most cases needs to eat. The person might eat only fruit, but that fruit has to be picked by someone and brought to the cave. If the fruit had not been picked, what would have happened? It would have been eaten by animals, by other people, by insects or it would have decayed and become part of the cycle of nature. So by taking even fruit, by drinking water, by breathing air, you are acting. You are influencing the environment. You might have a relatively small footprint – as they say – but you are still acting.

And so, why not go out in society, where your actions can serve as inspirations for other people by you demonstrating that you have risen above the state of consciousness, where you need to withdraw in order to avoid being pulled into the dualistic struggle? For you have instead come to the point, where you can engage actively in life without being pulled into the dualistic struggle—without allowing the world to pull you into the struggle, to pull you into the Sea of Samsara, the sea of suffering.

Ponder the unification of the basic forces

This is what you can attain by pondering the ninth ray of equilibrium. The Archangel for the ninth ray is Uniel, signifying unity, the unifying quality of the ninth ray that unifies the expanding and contracting forces by seeing that they are expressions of the One, of the singularity.

And as the seven rays have sprung from the singularity, so have the expanding and contracting forces. And when you see this, you recognize that the expanding and contracting forces are not opposites. They do not oppose each other, they complement each other. For if there were not forces that could interact, no distinct form could be created. That is why God manifested itself as the expanding and contracting force; there must be expansion for any form to be projected upon the screen of the Ma-ter light.

But take the scientific concept of the Big Bang. In a giant explosion, everything is hurled outward. Well, my beloved, what happens when you blow up a building with explosives? The orderly structure of the building is disintegrated, is blown apart into many bits and pieces. Thus, you see that had there only been the expanding force driving the Big Bang, no organized form could ever have been created. There must be something balancing the expanding force for a sustainable form to be created and maintained for any length of time.

The expanding force, then, is not the enemy of the contracting force. It is what starts creation and what continues to drive it to self-transcend. For again, if the contracting force is allowed to act in an unbalanced manner, it becomes what we have talked about with the second law of thermodynamics—that the structures begin to break down. Not by being blown apart by an expansive force, but by contracting so much that they are crunched into nothingness—and therefore, again, the form cannot be maintained.

And so, there is no permanence anywhere in the world of form. And this, of course, is what the ego finds it very difficult to deal with. In fact, the linear, analytical mind also finds this very difficult. For it wants to categorize everything and put everything into a box. But no sooner has it done so than reality has moved on, has transcended itself, has transcended the rules and laws, even the laws of nature that the intellect thought it had finally discovered. But in reality the intellect only defines rules that have no validity in the ongoing transcendence that is life.

The tenth ray of transparency

Gautama Buddha, May 9, 2009.

The ego cannot fathom transparency
The next ray is the tenth, which is the ray of transparency, my beloved. Again, a concept that the linear mind finds difficult, and that the ego, of course, finds completely impossible and unworkable. For how can the ego maintain an existence, when there is complete transparency?

You see, my beloved, as explained in the book of Genesis, after Adam and Eve had eaten of the forbidden fruit of the duality consciousness, they attempted to hide themselves from God. Well, my beloved, why is it possible to believe that you can actually hide?

Logically, of course, it makes no sense that you can hide from God—who is everywhere and in everything. So, in order to even believe in the concept that you can hide, you must go into the state of separation, the state of duality, where there is a distance between you and God. You can now set up the belief that there is something that is not transparent. And thus, you can hide behind that something.

My beloved, as an example, imagine that someone is playing hide and seek with a group of children and the children all go hide. One hides behind a house, one behind a bush, but another attempts to hide behind a pane of glass. Well, certainly that child cannot well hide, can it? And so, this is what you see when there is transparency—there can be nothing hidden. And the ego can exist only when there is the illusion that something is hidden—that there is a distance from the oneness of God. And, of course, what could possibly be hidden, what could be separated from oneness?

And so, this is what has happened, as Maitreya explains, after the co-creators of God separated themselves out from their spiritual teacher. For as long as they were in direct contact with the spiritual teacher, they could not forget that they are MORE, that they came from a greater source. Even if they yet had an imperfect understanding of that source and did not have a direct experience of their oneness of their source, they at least had some knowledge of this. And thus, they could not completely sink into the duality consciousness, of actually believing that there is no God, or believing that God is a remote being in the sky and not here on Earth and that they are sinners by their very existence.

You see, all of these beliefs can exist only when something has obscured the transparency that is the underlying reality of all things. Someone has thrown mud on the pane of glass of humankind's consciousness, and on the individual panes of glass in the consciousness of each person.

What obscures transparency?

So, what is it, then, that obscures transparency? In order to fully understand this, beyond what we have already given about the Ma-ter light and images projected upon it, you need to understand a concept that, again, can be difficult for the linear mind—and, again, the ego will rebel against it.

The reality is, my beloved, that everything is consciousness—everything is awareness. Thus, you are a co-creator with God. You are a self-aware being. But how do you co-create? You co-create by using the only reality there is, namely, what we have called the Ma-ter light. We have also explained that the Ma-ter light has consciousness, although few of you have truly pondered this. What exactly does this mean, my beloved? It means, that whatever is created, whatever is envisioned, whatever is imagined, is done with this basic consciousness of the Ma-ter light.

And so, that consciousness of the Ma-ter light takes on a particular form. Yet, because it is conscious, it is possible to create enough intensity that eventually that which is conscious now becomes so concentrated that it develops a rudimentary form of self-awareness. And thus, what has been created is a particular, conscious, living entity.

You have been so used to growing up in a society that presents everything in the material world as inanimate forms and objects. This, of course, is an inaccurate image, as I explained earlier, that even quantum physics itself has proven to be incomplete. Consciousness is the underlying reality, my beloved. And so, when you, as a self-aware co-creator, impose a mental image upon the Ma-ter light, you are not simply projecting an image upon the inanimate object of a movie screen. You are projecting it upon the basic awareness of the Mother light.

And when you infuse that image with enough life force, through your attention, through your awareness, well then the image will reach that intensity, that complexity, where now it begins to take on a life of its own. It is somewhat like the old dream, where people believe they can create life, out-pictured, for example, in the movie about Doctor Frankenstein—who took various body parts, stitched them together, infused them with a higher force, and then it came alive.

This is essentially what all of you do when you co-create, for that is the power of your consciousness. You have the power, through your self-awareness, to impose that self-awareness, that life-force, upon the Ma-ter light, until it takes on enough of the life force, that the image that you have imposed actually comes alive. Almost like what you see in a cartoon, where the drawings are still images, but when played in sequence it seems as if the character comes alive.

You have the power to create a living entity
But because everything is consciousness, what you create is not just an inanimate form, it is not just a dead form. It will eventually start to take on life, and the more it is infused with the life force through your attention, the more life it takes on, the more of a survival instinct it begins to develop. Which is why you can have an ego that has a survival instinct, and as such seeks to control the Conscious You. And you can have mass entities that have enough of a survival instinct to seek to control people, and pull them into an addiction – such as tobacco – that forces their light, so that the entity can absorb it and use it to survive, and even grow in intensity.

So what you see is that ever since the first beings in a previous realm descended into duality – because they were not willing to transcend themselves – they have used their co-creative abilities to co-create through the illusion – the filter, the maya – of the duality consciousness. But what they have created are these entities, these beings that do not have self-awareness as you do – as an extension of the Creator – but they have enough awareness that they exist and that they need something in order to continue to exist.

Thus, they are sort of like an animal life form that, while not having a sophisticated self-awareness that you see in humans, they have at least some rudimentary self-awareness that causes them, then, to seek to control anyone that can be controlled by their particular frequency. For all of these entities that have been created, form what Jesus called the "prince of this world."

And if they have something in you, they will pull upon it in order to force your attention into certain patterns, into certain images, so that you misqualify the light and keep feeding the life force to these entities—that have a hold on you and essentially milk you, as if you were a cow, ready to be milked twice a day by going into a certain state of consciousness.

And so, this is what you see, not only with physical addictions, but with so many people who go into anger or fear, or judgmentalness, or criticalness—of criticizing or always judging and analyzing everyone and everything, using the analytical mind, but imposing that value judgment of the ego upon it. Which then causes the misqualification of the light, causes the light to take on a lower frequency, according to this dualistic relative value judgment, where something is good and something is bad. Whereas, in the transparency – the purity of the transparency, my beloved – everything is an expression of the one, so nothing can be good in a relative sense to something that is bad. It simply IS.

The initiation of the tenth ray

So then, when you come to the tenth ray and the initiations of the tenth ray, you need to become aware of this. A topic that many people, even many spiritual people, would rather not know about, would rather not think about, would rather not talk about. For it is uncomfortable to them to recognize that perhaps they could have used their co-creative abilities to create something that has taken on a life of its own and is now seeking to control them—and is even seeking to control other people. And perhaps they could even be controlled by a mass entity created by humankind over thousands and tens of thousands and millions of years—so that that mass entity has become so strong that it is very difficult for the individual to withstand its pull.

Which, precisely, is why, as you go through the initiations of the seven rays, you need to create that momentum that keeps you going beyond the downward pull of the mass consciousness. But it is also why you need to go back, as Mother Mary explained, and recover any aspects of your being that are trapped in these lower states. But you cannot, in most cases, fully recover this until you go beyond the seven rays, go into the eighth, go into the ninth, come into that equilibrium. For you see, my beloved, the equilibrium forms a foundation. When you know that there is equilibrium beyond the struggle, well then you have a foundation for taking a closer look at the struggle. And that is when you can realize that the struggle is not really what it seems to be from a surface awareness.

It is actually a struggle between principalities and forces that are not visible to the senses and the outer mind—it is between all of these entities that have been created. And precisely because they are created out of the duality consciousness, they must be locked in a struggle with each other. For you see, the pure light of God that remains transparent, that remains at the vibration of love, is unlimited. But when the light takes on a lower vibration than love, it becomes finite, it becomes limited. So now there is only – even though six billion people on this planet are constantly misqualifying light – there is still only a finite amount. Which means that all of the entities that inhabit the forcefield, the energy field, of Earth must fight. Just like you see, when an animal dies on the African Savannah, the hyenas and the vultures immediately start fighting over the carcass, my beloved. For they know that it will only last a short time, and if they don't get it, someone else will. And this is the real cause of the struggle.

Why are people struggling

You may look at people and say, "Why are they struggling?" And you may look at what so many people that are well-meaning have done—trying to find a psychological cause, looking at the individual, looking at a particular group, looking at their beliefs. For example, you will see a wave of people who have come to conclude that the real cause of all warfare is religion and religious beliefs. And so, they think that if only we can get rid of religion and get people to disavow their belief in religion, then we will have peace.

But they fail to realize that it is not religion that is the cause of war—that religion is simply being used as a tool to agitate people, so that they misqualify their light. Whereas the real cause of the struggle and war is that there are entities beyond the physical, who need the constant misqualification of light in order to survive. And if people do not misqualify that light, well then, they will die out.

Which is why they must continue to keep people in that grip, so that they will continue to fight each other in a senseless struggle—as you see in the Middle East and elsewhere. This surely can never be construed as being the will of the real God, but could only be the will of a graven image of God, projected upon God through the duality consciousness.

And so, again, there are numerous of these living entities—born from a certain image of God, a certain image born from duality. The most dangerous of these entities are precisely the ones that relate to a graven image of God. Because those are the ones that people find it most difficult to abandon, my beloved.

You may take an entity, such as the tobacco entity, and see that it is obviously very dangerous for the people who are addicted to tobacco. Nevertheless, it is becoming increasingly easier for people in the modern world to see the dangers of smoking. Which is why more and more people have given up this habit, after realizing that it destroys their bodies and perhaps even sensing that it has negative spiritual ramifications as well. Yet, look at how many people are still trapped in believing that there has to be one superior religion and that this religion is given by God. And therefore, it is mandated by God that this religion must take over the world, for it is the only way to save people. And all non-believers will not be saved but will be condemned to live in eternity in hell.

And so, consider how difficult it is for people to give up this belief, this illusion, so that they will stop feeding their light into this mass entity—whether it be the mass entity of Christianity, the mass entity of Islam, even the mass entity of Buddhism, my beloved. For each religion, each belief system, has created such a mass entity that is struggling with the mass entities of other religions—even feeding an even greater entity that simply feeds on the struggle itself and will use anything to create the struggle. Certainly, my beloved, materialistic science has created such a mass entity that is also seeking to strengthen itself and take over, even to the point of taking the light from the mass entities of religion, by getting people to distrust religion and give up their religious beliefs.

So those scientists who believe they are working for a greater cause are simply working for the same cause that they see religious people working for. Thus, they see the fallacy of religious people, feeding their light into this beast, but they do not see that they, themselves, are doing the same thing—simply working for another beast. And that they, too, have this belief in the supremacy of their own world view and the drive to impose it and enforce it upon others—which cannot come from God, my beloved.

...

You cannot step into the same river twice
But now let us take this one step further and consider why you want permanency, my beloved? For as we have said before, the ego was created because the conscious self perceived that the ego could give it some advantage. And so, consider the saying, "You cannot step into the same river twice."

For what is a river? It is a stream of water that is constantly moving. And if you step into the river, you are stepping into certain water molecules. If you step out and step back in, other molecules have moved into the place of the previous ones. And thus, you are not – technically, in reality – stepping into the same river.

So it is with the River of Life, my beloved. The River of Life is constantly moving on. It is set up so that those who are willing to be part of that forward movement are constantly becoming MORE, instead of standing still or becoming less. Why is this so, my beloved? Well, because the goal of a self-aware being is, of course, to start out with a limited, localized self-awareness and expand it to the level of the Creator itself. We might say – by using images with which you are familiar – that God thought that you might be bored by being the same being over a long period of time. And thus, God gave you the option of being in the River of Life where everything is constantly new.

So, you will see that even though God has given you the right to create any experience you want, when you are in the River of Life, every experience is new. There is growth, there is transcendence. And so, there can be those, my beloved, who cannot fully accept or adjust to this constant flow and transcendence. They want to own something, they want to own an experience and keep it for a time, instead of transcending it.

And thus, the only place where you can own something is in the realm – the sphere, the illusion – of separation, where things can be perceived as standing still. The reality is, of course, that nothing stands still, neither in the realm of oneness, nor in the realm of separation. For in the realm of oneness, you have the constant drive to become MORE, to transcend. And in the realm of separation, you have the contracting force of the Mother – the second law of thermodynamics, the power of Shiva – that breaks down everything. And so you see, you can either transcend, which is life, or you can attempt to stand still, which is death. There is truly no other choice. Choose ye this day whom ye will serve. Choose life!

For, unless you choose life, you will choose death. And you will suffer loss. You will be less, until you eventually forget who you are and believe that you truly are a lesser being, be it a sinner or be it a sophisticated ape.

What you think you own owns you

So, the desire for ownership can be very subtle. It is what I called an attachment, when I walked the Earth. It is the desire to own or posses something, to pull it out of the constant self-transcendence of the River of Life. And you can create the illusion that you own something, but that which you own is precisely an entity created through the power of your attention. And that entity wants to survive. And how can it survive? Only when you keep feeding it your light, which means that the entity wants to own you.

And as long as you believe it is real, as long as you allow it in your sphere of identity, then it does own you. What you create in separation will own you, my beloved. You may think that you own it, but it is the other way around.

What is the beginning of the spiritual path? It is when a person comes to the point – whether it is consciously aware of this or not – but comes to the point of deciding, "I cannot do this anymore. There must be a better way. There must be more to life." And thereby essentially saying, "I do not want to be owned by my own miscreations. I want to be free. I want to be more than this." And thus, it begins the upward climb, where it gradually shakes off the snakeskins of that lesser identity, until it can stand free and recognize that, "I AM a spiritual being. I am a co-creator with my God."

The eleventh ray of transcendence

Gautama Buddha, May 9, 2009.

So you see, transcendence is, again, a concept that the linear mind finds it impossible to categorize and put in a mental box. For the linear mind wants to go to the ultimate extreme and say, "There must come a point where no more transcendence is possible. There must come some end, where you have reached a state of perfection that cannot be transcended."

Says who, my beloved? The linear mind may not be able to fathom that there is no end to self-transcendence—and that is precisely why the linear mind must be left behind by the student who comes to a point of wanting MORE, more self than what it has experienced so far.

There is no linearity in the spiritual realm; there is a spherical reality. And once you step out of the linear mind, once you transcend it, then perpetual self-transcendence becomes a living reality. You are not concerned about what might come in some future time. You are flowing with the River of Life, existing in the eternal NOW—that is perpetual self-transcendence. You are not projecting into the future what should or should not happen. You are not analyzing the past of what should or should not have happened. You are simply flowing with the River of Life. Something that the ego cannot do, for the ego wants to own and possess.

So, the question becomes, "Do you still want the experience of owning something, owning a particular experience, a particular sense of self?" And by so doing, also being owned by your own creation of that separate self, which then, in turn, wants to own you—wants you, as the unlimited, infinite spiritual being, to limit your self, your sense of self, your sense of identity to that particular limited belief from which the ego was born.

The descent into duality

How, my beloved, did all of this descent into duality begin? It began, as Maitreya explains, when a sphere had come to the point of ascension, where it could ascend and become a part of the spiritual realm. Where it had reached the critical intensity of light that made it possible to accelerate the entire sphere into the higher vibrations of the spiritual realm—the vibrations of unconditionality, of love. And yet, what was the condition for that acceleration to take place? Well, you see, my beloved, you had a great number of beings who had applied themselves in a very concentrated effort in order to raise their sphere to that level. They had made great efforts. They had truly worked selflessly, so to speak, on raising all beings in their sphere to that point.

But you see, even in so doing, some of them had retained a remnant of the separate self, thinking that by working so hard to raise up their sphere, they would receive what they perceived as some ultimate reward by God for their efforts. And so, it was a great shock to them when all of the beings who had been the forerunners for raising the sphere were called, and they were shown that the next logical step for them was not to enter the spiritual realm as some kind of superheroes – receiving position and recognition in that spiritual realm – but instead, their next logical step was to lay down their lives, their attainment, their self-awareness and give that momentum and self-awareness and attainment as the foundation for creating the next sphere that would start out as an unenlightened sphere—inhabited by beings with a limited sense of self-awareness. Thereby, the sophisticated beings in the ascending sphere would, so to speak, let their beings descend, and now they would become the ones who allowed the beings in the next sphere to do with their light according to their free will.

This was a logical step because in the sphere that was ascending, that sphere was created out of the beings of those in a higher sphere. And so, the beings who were now at the top of the ascending sphere were simply being asked to do for others what others had done for them. Many of these beings were ready to ascend – to shed the last remnants of the separate self – and gladly embraced this opportunity. Which is why the next sphere was created—leading to your own. You would not be here unless someone had volunteered to lay down their lives to give you the opportunity to have a sphere in which you could grow in self-awareness. Thus, it is only logical that as you come to having made maximum use of this opportunity, you are asked to extend that opportunity to others, my beloved.

Yet, there were a small number, among the beings that had the opportunity to ascend, who did not want to give up that last remnant of the separate self. So they rebelled against God's plan. And they wanted to keep owning what they saw as a superior position in their sphere, which they believed they had earned, and therefore they were entitled to keep experiencing that superiority for a time longer. And so, they demanded to be exempt from this—to set themselves apart as their sphere ascended. And in so doing, of course, they automatically fell into the next sphere that was created. For they could not maintain an existence in the ascended sphere, and thus could only go into the sphere that was not yet ascended and therefore had room for the separate self to continue to exist.

And yet, these beings were not stripped of their attainment. And so, they did, indeed, come into the next sphere with a far greater attainment and awareness than the beings who were just starting out in that sphere. And so, naturally, they set themselves up as leaders—as precisely what Jesus called the blind leaders of the blind followers. Some of their followers actually having followed them from the ascended sphere where they had leadership positions. And those of their followers who were not willing to let go of their obedience to their leaders, they had to fall as well.

The initiations of the eleventh ray

And so, when you come to the eleventh ray, it is indeed the challenge you face to transcend, to let go of the last remnants of the separate self. And thus come to what we might call a sense of ultimate reality, ultimate realism, of knowing that the separate self is unreal. And only when you know that your separate self is unreal – and only when you see this from within your sphere of self – can you then see that everything that was created out of duality is likewise unreal.

This, then, is the state of reality, of realism, of asking yourself, "Why am I here?" And so far, especially during the initiations of the first seven rays, you might also have asked yourself that question many times. Such as, "Why did I come to Earth? Why did I volunteer to descend here? Why did I come back to Earth?" And it is always that you are here to do something, to bring something, to achieve some kind of result. But you see, when you come to the eleventh ray, you need to transcend the very concept that you are here to achieve any particular result.

This will be a shock to the ego. It will be a shock to the remnants of the separate self. Which is precisely why I give this teaching in such a manner as to shock your separate self into objecting to the teaching, thereby giving you an opportunity to see those remnants of the separate self.

Consider how we have, several times now, said that what brings you to a certain point will not bring you beyond that point. You cannot then rise beyond the challenge of the tenth ray unless you are willing to consider the question of, "Why I am here?" from an entirely new perspective. You need to ask yourself not, "Why am I here," but, "What is the 'I' that is here?"

Is it an I that still sees itself as separate from its source, as separate from other self-aware beings? Do you think you are here to do something for God, for the Ascended Masters, or even do something for other people—saving them, setting them free, awakening them, or whatever it might be? Why do you need to consider this, my beloved? Because only the separate self can have the sense that it is doing something that affects others.

Do you see the subtlety? So many well-meaning spiritual people believe they are here to affect positive change on this planet. So many religious people believe their goal is to convert others to their religion. But even those who have transcended this need to convert others to a particular outer religion can be caught up in wanting to awaken others to the spiritual path, wanting to change them, wanting to change society, wanting to change the Earth and humankind.

But you see, my beloved, why does the world need changing? Why do people need saving? They need saving because they are trapped in the separate sense of self. The world needs changing because people have co-created numerous problems through the separate sense of self, thereby, reinforcing the illusion that the separate self has some kind of reality, some kind of permanence, some kind of real existence. And so, do you see that there comes a point on the path – when you go into the secret rays – where you need to come to the realization, the sense of ultimate realism, that you cannot fulfill the true goal of raising your sphere as long as you maintain even a faint remnant, even a shadow, of the separate self—as long as you think that you, as a separate self, are here to affect some kind of change to the separate selves of other people.

What is the Golden Age really like?

Do you see the trap? When you still have that remnant of the separate self, you think that your separate self is right and knows everything and therefore knows what should happen on this planet.

What is the plan of the Ascended Masters? You think you know what the Golden Age of Saint Germain should look like—what is God's will and God's kingdom for Earth. And so, you think that you need to go out and get other people to recognize the superiority of that view, so that they can validate it and agree with it and perhaps even raise you up to some position of leadership. Or recognize you as a spiritual teacher with more than ordinary wisdom.

But you see, the problem is the separate self and all of the entities created through those separate selves of humankind. Those separate selves will never recognize the reality of their own unreality. They will, therefore, never recognize a true teacher who speaks from the greater reality. That is why so many did not recognize the Buddha, did not recognize the Christ, but saw them as a threat to their sense of comfortability. So, if you are still dreaming of attaining some kind of public recognition, widespread recognition, for your spiritual world view or your teaching, well then that can only be a remnant of the separate self that has this dream. And thus, you are acting in an unbalanced manner, and thus, you are adding to the struggle and the energies that feed the struggle.

Take note of a subtle distinction. You are here to help in the true purpose of God – namely, to raise this sphere until it ascends and becomes part of the spiritual realm – but the challenge is to see that you cannot accomplish this goal by acting as a separate self, trying to change the separate selves of other people. You can raise this sphere only by awakening a critical mass of people to go beyond the separate self. And how can you serve in helping others come to this awakening? Well, only by first awakening yourself.

For there is, when you go into the realm of the secret rays, no hiding. How can you hide in transparency? And so, you must walk your talk. You must become your talk. Or rather, your talk must become an expression of your true Being, not an outer teaching that you have taken on and that you seek to force upon others.

What is ultimately going to change the world? Not any amount of teaching given through a separate self to other separates selves. What is ultimately going to change the world is the bringing in of light—which can only happen when your lower being becomes the open door that is transparent, so the light can shine through in its pure form to the point where the conscious selves of other people can see it. And can see that it is beyond anything they see through their own separate selves—and thus, they are awakened to the potential to be MORE.

Beware of the desire for recognition
Examine yourselves. Examine your intentions, your motives. Do you have a desire for recognition by others? Do you have a fear of being ridiculed by others or even being ignored? Do you have a fear that the planet will suffer some ultimate calamity unless people recognize your world view, your teaching?

Only the separate self can have fear. Only the separate self can have a desire that requires, that wants, something from other separate selves. Thus, if you see any elements of these vibrations in your being, then you know that they must be transcended in order for you to pass the initiations of the eleventh ray.

But what truly must be transcended is that sense of self. This, of course, is, again, a big step for those who have been on the spiritual path for many years, many lifetimes, who have built a momentum, who think they have acquired great wisdom and knowledge. And now suddenly it seems like it was all ... for nothing?—as you might feel. For you are now asked to give it all up. But you see, nothing is for nothing. Whatever you have learned, whatever you have experienced, has brought you to your present level of consciousness. There is nothing wrong with this. It is simply the progression of your personal path, where you have, for various reasons, desired to have certain experiences.

You have the free will, my beloved, to continue to have a certain experience of being a spiritual student of some status – perhaps even superiority – for as long as you desire it. I am not here to tell you that what you have done is wrong or of no value.

It is the path you have chosen, I champion your free will. I am only here to say that if you desire to pass the initiations of the eleventh ray, then you need to transcend. You need to be willing to lay down your life in order to rise higher. For you cannot rise higher with your current sense of self, whatever that sense of self might be.

Unconditional surrender

And so, on the eleventh ray, you need to very seriously ponder whether there are any remnants of a separate self that wants to accomplish something in this world—before you feel that you can leave this world behind. This was the initiation passed by this messenger, which he has described, of coming to that point of feeling that if he died at that moment, he could leave the Earth behind without any sense of regrets or unfulfilled business.

To the ego, this is the ultimate sense of loss. But to the conscious self, it is the ultimate opportunity. Does this messenger feel he lost something in that experience of complete, total surrender? No! He gained something far greater than his separate self could ever envision. And so, you see that many of you have come to a point on the path, where you are ready to step up in service to life. But you cannot see that service with your current sense of self. And in order to get beyond that sense of self, you must give up that sense of self without knowing in your outer awareness what will emerge in its place.

You see, my beloved, the eleventh ray represents an essential turning point of having to give up – being willing to give up – without seeing what will be there, what sense of self will be there, after you give up the present self. If you knew what was going to be there, you would not have the sense of giving up something, would you? When you go to buy a lottery ticket for a dollar, you give up the dollar. But if you knew with absolute certainty that you would win the grand prize, then you would not have the sense of giving up anything.

And so, the eleventh ray of transcendence represents that experience of giving up without knowing what will follow, of giving up as an ultimate expression of love—the unconditional love that is complete non-attachment. At this point on the path, my beloved, you have begun to see that you are more than the separate self. You have had glimpses of what that more is. If you took a person who had just started the spiritual path and asked him or her to go through the initiation of the eleventh ray, it would be a complete shock for such a person—which is why you are not asked to start with this initiation.

But when you come to the appropriate point on your personal path, then you know that by giving up everything, you will not end up with nothing. By giving up all sense of self, you will not end up with no sense of self. For there is a part of your self that is real. And that part that is real will come back to you. What you are giving up is the unreal part that obscures the real.

Do you see—as long as you are attached to the remnants of the separate self and the desire to accomplish something through that separate self, you cannot see the higher reality that you are and the highest potential of your divine plan. You cannot see it.

For the remnants of the separate self and the dreams of the accomplishment form a barrier that is not transparent, and thus does not allow you to see, nor does it allow the light to shine through in your outer being. And so, you cannot see at all before you give up.

That is the essential principle that you must come to realize in order to pass the initiation of the eleventh ray. You must be willing to give up the ghost, while hanging on the cross, not knowing whether you will be resurrected or not. In a sense, you can know that when you truly give up, you will be resurrected—as the real self that you are. But you cannot yet see what that real self is, and thus, you must be willing to give up—even if it means that you would disappear from the Earth and accomplish absolutely nothing on this planet.

Understanding the principle or surrender

Certainly, you can see that the Ascended Masters do not want you to leave this planet without accomplishing anything. But we want you to accomplish your highest potential—and that requires giving up your lower potential. There may be a part of your mind that says, "But I have studied the teachings of the Ascended Masters for decades, it cannot all be an illusion. I must know something that is real. I have had visions, I have had high experiences, I have had directions from this or that source, even from directly within, or directly from the masters. Some of this must be real." And it is.

But in focusing your attention on the sense of self and the vision you have right now, you are focusing your attention at that level—and there is more to your divine plan than what you see. And if you want to see it and out-picture it, then you must give up your current vision, your current sense of self. It must be let go before the new can emerge.

The ego will never, ever, understand this principle. The linear mind also finds it difficult to wrap itself around it. But you, the conscious self, can come to that point of knowing that this is the logical next step. And it can then come to the point of simply letting go, releasing it all — releasing it all. All expectations. All desires. Releasing.

The ultimate release

How can you ultimately accomplish your divine plan? Only by becoming completely non-attached to accomplishing anything whatsoever. For only in that complete non-attachment can you let go of the remnants of the separate self—which cannot let go of the desire to accomplish something. And thus, it must be exposed, whereby you can see it and let it go, for now you see that it is unreal.

This, then, is the initiation on the eleventh ray. It is not an easy one for anyone. Yet, we who have ascended, have all gone through it. We can look back – as some of my colleagues, especially, look back – at how they procrastinated this initiation, sometimes for lifetimes—hemming and hawing about the necessity of doing it, reasoning and arguing with the linear mind as to why this could possibly be necessary, when the world was in such dire straights and there was so much to be accomplished.

Do you see how easy it is to fall into this, as an ascended master student? Thinking there is so much to do to save the world and bring the Golden Age of Saint Germain. "I have to be up and doing, I cannot sit around here and contemplate letting go of everything. What would that accomplish?" But you see, it would accomplish the ultimate result of you being the open door, being transparent, so that the light of God could enter the material realm and do its work.

Yet, what is it you give up? You give up the sense that you, as a separate self, are accomplishing or contributing to God's work. But, as I have said, the problem is the sense of separation. How can the separate self do God's work when God's real work is to awaken people from the illusion of separation?

And so, you can then do God's work only by transcending the separate self—seeing that you are one with the All and that your entire purpose for coming to Earth is not to give your separate self some sense of accomplishment, even the ultimate accomplishment of feeling you have done God's work. No, your real purpose for coming is to raise up the All—that is your real self. For there is only one self that has many individual expressions. And the only way to raise up that one self is to raise the All.

And thus, as long as there are those parts of the self trapped in duality, there are parts of your self trapped in duality. And so, you desire to awaken them—not by causing a change in their separate selves, but by being who you are, being the One Self in manifestation. Knowing this, demonstrating it, letting it shine through all of your words and actions—that they may see that there is something more than the separate self. For you have happiness, joy, true peace of mind that comes from being transparent, so that nothing in this world can take you out of that state of ease, of flowing with the River of Life.

There is no shortcut

You may think, my beloved, that we of the Ascended Masters should be able to come up with a shortcut that could help you pass this initiation on the eleventh ray. But there is no shortcut.

This is the point on the path where you must face your own demons—the demons, the entities, that you have created by giving the life force to certain images that are not springing from oneness, but from separation. You must face them. You have created them.

You must face what you have created, and you must separate your real self from your own creation and the creation of others. You may think it sounds illogical that you have to give up the separate self, but at the same time I talk about you separating yourself from the mass consciousness. But they are one and the same. You separate yourself from the mass consciousness by giving up the separate self. It is the only way to separate yourself, for it is the separate self that pulls you into the mass consciousness.

And so, at the lower levels of the path, you build that upward momentum, where you actually hold on to a part of the separate self, even turning it into a spiritual persona that takes on the characteristics demanded in your spiritual environment. But that is what must go, that is what must be left behind for you to be free and be free to express your Higher Being, the being that is the real you. So there is no shortcut. You must wrestle with this, until you come to the point, where you are no longer wrestling with the demons, for you see through the illusion that created them. And you simply let it go, let it fall away from you.

What am I talking about here? There are many demons, my beloved, many entities that have been created. And you may, as ascended master students, have thought of them as being somewhat evil or dark in appearance. But it is time to face reality that there are also demons and entities that are disguised as being benevolent, spiritual, religious. What you have created, as you have walked the path up until this point, is an entity. That is what the separate self is, an entity that has spiritual characteristics, that seeks to appear so good that God simply has to accept it into its kingdom. But it can never be accepted. Only you, the real you, can be accepted. No man has ascended to Heaven, save he that descended from Heaven.

What descended from Heaven was the conscious self. And only the conscious self can ascend back. But it does not ascend back as the same that descended, but as the greater being it has become through its experiences in this world. Yet, the greater being that it has become is not the separate self. It is the being that has transcended separation by seeing through it and thus gaining a different perspective on oneness—that you could not have if you had never been outside of oneness.

Surrender whatever sense of self

And thus, ponder the need to transcend any sense of self that you have right now. For it is an eternal reality that you only grow by transcending the sense of self.

And you can come to a point, my beloved, where you realize that there is the self and there are the objects, the characteristics, of selfhood. Right now, most of you do not have a clear sense of the self as a pure state of awareness. You identify yourself with and as the characteristics, the objects.

We might say that your self is a container, and through your journey in the material realm, you have filled that container with objects and you identify yourself with and as the objects. But the real you is the self. And once you give up those remnants of the separate self, you lock in to that self—and you see that the self is more than the objects and the characteristics.

The self is a flowing stream of consciousness that is constantly transcending—and therefore never identified with any characteristic, never seeking to own or possess, never seeking to stand still at a certain level, but finding its joy and fulfillment in constantly transcending its creative expression, becoming MORE than it was a second ago. Not seeking to repeat a certain experience, not seeking to step into the same river twice.

But, instead, always seeking the newness of expression, the newness of the creative flow in which there is no separation.

And thus, there is no desire to accomplish something in order to overcome a lack. There is no sense of lack, but only fullness and the desire to express more of that fullness. And this is when you experience the joy, the transcendent, unconditional joy that can never be experienced through the filter of the separate self. And thus, when you pass that initiation on the eleventh ray, that joy will be yours—and your joy will be full.

The twelfth ray of rebirth

Jesus, May 10, 2009.

I, Jesus, come to discourse with you, making a guest appearance here in this series of discourses by the Buddha. But I do not come as the Jesus that people see in the Christian world, I come in the fullness of the being that I AM today, having attained Buddhahood after my ascension. And thus, I come to discourse with you on the twelfth ray—the twelfth ray of rebirth.

Rebirth, my beloved. For, as you have heard, the eleventh ray is the ray of the initiation of giving up, being willing to let go of the old—transcending. But you see, my beloved, giving up without knowing what comes after is a necessary initiation. But it does not mean that if you give up, then automatically a new self will emerge. For what needs to happen after you have given up the old is that you – your conscious self, your sense of self – is reborn.

And how does that happen? It happens when you, the conscious self, accepts itself as being reborn, accepts itself as a new identity, my beloved. And this can be a difficult step for many people who have been on the spiritual path for a long time. For you are so accustomed to looking at yourself, looking at the beam in your own eye, looking for something to give up, looking for what must be surrendered. And this is necessary, it is a necessary step on the path, my beloved. For if you look at many people in the world, you see that they are so identified with their egos, and so believing the lie of the ego that they do not need to give up any part of the false identity. They just need to follow the outer path, the automatic path to salvation, and then they will be guaranteed to be saved.

You, then, as the spiritual people, have risen beyond this level of consciousness. You are not in denial of the fact that there is a beam in your own eye, that there is something that must be seen and must be surrendered and must be given up before you can be free of it, my beloved. You are not in denial that you have free will, that you have used your free will to accept certain dualistic illusions, and that you must, then, see through them and give them up. But some of you still find it difficult to take that step of accepting that after you give up an element of the not-self, you, the conscious self, are reborn into a higher sense of identity. Yet you cannot accept that you are reborn—that you now are a different being.

Becoming a new being in Christ

And what trips you up in many cases is exactly your willingness to look for the beam in your own eye. Your willingness to recognize that there is something that must be given up. And therefore, you are so focused on seeing the problem, of overcoming the problem, and thinking in terms of problems, that you cannot let go of the memory of who you were in the past and how you were an imperfect being and how much you had to give up. And therefore, you cannot always accept that now that you have given it up, you are no longer that being who had that problem before.

Do you see, my beloved? When you are reborn, you become a new person, a new being in Christ. But you have free will. You cannot accept that you are a new being – you cannot accept it in your conscious mind – unless you are willing to truly acknowledge that you are not the person who made the mistake or had the belief that you discovered yesterday and gave up.

My beloved, if you look at my life as Jesus, I passed several initiations where I had to accept a higher identity. You can see this between the lines of the official scriptures, although some of them have indeed been taken out, some were never even there, because the gospel writers did not have the full understanding of my being and the path of Christhood and the initiations I went through. Nevertheless, the reality is that

I had several initiations where I had to accept a higher sense of identity in order to take my mission to the next level.

And had I not been willing to do this, then my mission would have stalled at a certain level. And I would not have gone all the way to the ultimate end of hanging on the cross and giving up the ghost of the final limitations—thereby being resurrected. So you see, my beloved, this is the initiation that all of us have faced as we walked the path and attained our ascensions.

The ascension is not automatic

What is the ascension, my beloved? What is the ascension process? Well it is that you must accept that you are no longer a mortal human being, you are now an immortal spiritual being. If you cannot accept that, you cannot ascend.

You might be used to thinking – based on past teachings given by us in other dispensations – that the ascension is a matter of fulfilling certain requirements. And once you have fulfilled those requirements – "poof" – one day you will ascend. It is not so! There are requirements to fulfill, my beloved. Certainly, that is true. But the process of ascension is not an automatic process, it is not a mechanical process—it is a creative process. Which means that it involves choices that you must make.

And what are the choices you make? What do I mean when I say "Choose life over death?" Well, "Choose life!" means that you choose to accept a new identity, a new sense of self, that is MORE than the sense of self you had before—even a second ago.

So you see, my beloved, the ego wants to pervert this entire concept of the spiritual path into thinking that you walk a long path towards an ultimate goal. And the ego has two advantages of this. By making you accept that you are walking a long path, it can make you accept that the ultimate goal is far out in the future. As you indeed have had many previous students of the Ascended Masters who have believed that they would ascend, they would become the Christ, only far into the future. But certainly not now—certainly not right now, right here. And you see, this is the ego trying to make the conscious self believe that it cannot simply shift its sense of identity in an instant and be the Christ in an instant.

And so, the other advantage that the false teachers and the ego gain from this perception is that there is this idea that there is some ultimate stage, some ultimate initiation, you go through—and then you have attained some permanent state.

Give up the dream of an ultimate initiation
You see, my beloved, give up this idea that there is some ultimate initiation, some ultimate goal that is far out there in the future. Instead, accept the reality that the River of Life is a process, an ever-moving stream of constant, on-going, perpetual self-transcendence. It is precisely, as the Buddha explained, the attempt to hold on to a particular sense of self that brings you into the consciousness of death, the consciousness of duality.

In the ascended state, you do not have a permanent, fixed, sense of identity. You are constantly ascending. In fact, it might be constructive, my beloved, instead of talking about Ascended Masters, to talk about Ascending Masters.

For we are constantly ascending, we are constantly being reborn into a higher sense of self. This is, indeed, what I represent to this Earth, having taken up a position as the representative of the twelfth ray of rebirth, my beloved. This is what I came to bring forth 2,000 years ago. And now – in the fullness that I AM now – I have taken up that position of representing this rebirth. And it is, indeed, the supreme opportunity for the more advanced spiritual seekers to accelerate their beings beyond a certain point, where they simply shed that snakeskin of the old identity and are reborn into a new sense of self.

But, my beloved, in order to be fully reborn, you have to accept that you now are that new sense of self. It is not a theoretical concept that is still "out there" in the distance and that you might someday take on. No, it is now. It is here. It is you. This is who I am.

You might have made a mistake yesterday, but if you see the mistake, see the consciousness behind it and let it go, then you are reborn into a new self. And the self that you are today was not the self that made the mistake yesterday or ten thousand embodiments ago. And therefore, you do not need to hang on to these feelings that you had in the old sense of self. In fact, you do not even need to hold on to the memory.

Guilt has no constructive purpose
And this is where many of you are tripped up. For, of course, you can remember who you were yesterday and what you did yesterday. And some

of you can even remember what you did lifetimes ago. But you see, my beloved, you are no longer that person—when you have given up the consciousness that caused you to do whatever you did in the past. And therefore, you must go through a period – like this messenger did – that when his own ego and the false teachers were projecting the memory of a mistake into his mind, he would consciously say, "But I am no longer the self that did that. I did not do that, the self that I am now did not make that mistake. And therefore, I do not need to feel guilty about it."

It is no more different than when you think back to when you learned to walk. Should you feel guilty for being clumsy and falling down when you were a few months old and trying to walk? Why on Earth would you feel guilty over this? So why would you feel guilty over mistakes you have made as an adult, or mistakes you have made in past lifetimes?

There is no constructive purpose for guilt whatsoever. It is a lower vibration, a vibration of anti-love. It is a projection of the fallen beings and of your own ego—attempting to hold you back from accepting your rebirth into a new sense of identity. It serves no constructive purpose. Just LET IT GO MY BE - LO - VED!

For you are more than this. There is no force in heaven whatsoever that wants to hold you back in a former sense of self. Therefore, any attempt to hold you back can only come from below, from the false teachers, from the fallen beings, from your own ego, from the mass consciousness, from other people. Wherever it comes from, it is unreal. And that which is unreal cannot affect that which is real—your conscious self.

Certainly, we all understand that this is not necessarily an easy transition. I can tell you this – I can tell you this with fire, in order to shake you out of your old state of consciousness – but I recognize that while you might be lifted up by my fire, you can easily go out from this environment and fall back into the old patterns. And then, what happens when you fall back into the old patterns? Are you now going to think back and say, "Oh, I just did what Jesus told me not to do. I should feel guilty for not following Jesus' instructions." And see—then you are right back in the old momentum.

The ego needs a fixed sense of identity

But you see, my beloved, the reality here is this: your ego cannot flow with the River of Life because it cannot live without – it cannot exist, it cannot maintain a sense of self, a sense of continuity – without a fixed sense of identity. The ego cannot exist when you are constantly transcending yourself. And that is what I am asking you to keep in mind. Surely, you will go out, you will be confronted with some old momentum. Simply give it up! And accept that you are reborn.

Whatever comes back to you, give it up. Accept that you are reborn. Whenever a projection comes from any lower state of consciousness, look at it if you need to look for a lie, but do not indulge in it. Do not go in and overanalyze. Look at it and see—for in many cases, my beloved, you have already seen through the lie.

You must understand that you can come to a point where your conscious self has seen through the lie. But you will still be confronted with the momentum, or even with projections from the mass consciousness. And that is why you can say to yourself, "But I thought I had given this up. And now I am experiencing it again. What is happening?"

Well, the reality is that as long as you are in embodiment – as long as you are walking these denser spheres – you will be confronted with momentums and projections from the mass consciousness. But once you have seen through the lie, what you need to do is become aware that this projection is directed at you and then simply give it up and accept that you are reborn, that this is not who you are. That you are more than this.

You see that if every time your ego projects something at you, you use it to be reborn and accept a higher sense of identity, well then your ego will eventually become so scattered – so frustrated, so blown apart by this constant self-transcendence – that it cannot maintain a grip on "reality," it cannot maintain the continuous sense of identity. And thus, you are simply accelerated beyond it. There may still be remnants of the separate self, as there will be some remnants of it as long as you are in embodiment. But your conscious self no longer identifies itself with it, because your conscious self no longer has a permanent, fixed, sense of identity that is based on the things of this world.

You realize that you are a spiritual being. And you realize that a spiritual being has no fixed sense of identity but is constantly flowing with the River of Life, is constantly transcending its sense of self. And therefore, you do not need to have that fixed permanent or semi-permanent sense of identity based on the things of this world. You see that you are MORE, and you are constantly flowing with it—you are not holding on to that sense of self. Whenever a limitation of your current sense of self becomes apparent to you, you let it go, you are reborn. You accept that you are reborn as MORE. And thus, the ego simply cannot keep up with you, the prince of this world cannot keep up, my beloved.

The prince of this world is a finite being

Do you see that the prince of this world is not an infinite being; the prince of this world is a finite being. Meaning, that even though there are some who think that the devil has great power, the devil has only finite power, because the devil has only a finite sense of self, and therefore only a finite awareness.

Do you see, my beloved, that what the devil wants is to come to you and cause you to accept the fixed sense of identity that holds you back at a certain level—so that he can now run out and start working with other people, getting them to accept the fixed sense of identity? And he wants that when he has made his rounds and comes back, you are still in that fixed sense of identity.

But you see, if you transcend that sense of identity, and the devil comes back, he will be shocked, "He is no longer there, where is he?" And now he will have to try to catch up with your new sense of identity and try to turn that into a fixed sense of identity. And that takes his attention away from all the other people that he has to entrap—and all of a sudden, when enough people transcend their former sense of self, the devil becomes so scattered, the prince of this world becomes so confused, that he can no longer keep his sense of control. And thus, even the prince of this world must somehow transcend his old sense of identity in order to keep up with the people who are accelerating, my beloved. And thus, you see, everything is pulled up.

"I, if I be lifted up, will draw all men unto me." This also means lifting up the mass consciousness—which is just one expression of what has traditionally been called the devil. For as Gautama explained last year, at New Year's, my beloved, when you go into the temple of the dark lord, you see that there is no dark lord there. It is all an empty shell, it has no ultimate reality.

But do you see that constant self-transcendence is the key to accelerating yourself out of this pull of the gravitational pull of the mass consciousness? So that you simply – whatever they send at you – you use it to transcend your sense of identity, to be reborn. You accept that you are reborn, and thus, you are a new being in Christ. And it will take time for your ego, or the false teachers, or the mass consciousness or other people to catch up with you. And when they eventually catch up with you, as they probably will while you are in a physical body, you just immediately allow yourself to be reborn again. And now they have to play catch-up.

And therefore, you come to the point where they are always playing catch-up, my beloved. For you have now turned the tables on the moneychangers, so that they are the ones that have to catch up to you. Because you are no longer allowing yourself to remain in that fixed sense of identity, where they think they have you under control.

And so you see, my beloved, that this becomes sort of a cat-and-mouse game, that you might even for a period find some enjoyment in. Where you realize that you are no longer playing the dualistic game of seeking to destroy the opposite dualistic polarity, but you are playing a sort of a higher version of the game of trying to outfox and outsmart and out-transcend the forces of this world, the prince of this world.

And you can do so very easily once you truly lock in to the process of being reborn. Of course, there will come a point where you are ultimately reborn to the point, where you do not even find enjoyment in outfoxing or outsmarting the prince of this world because that prince has simply become irrelevant to your sense of self. And you are now focused on other things, you are now focused on raising up others and awakening them from the consciousness of death by demonstrating to them how it is possible to be reborn. And by teaching them that they, too, can be reborn—challenging their present sense of self.

...

Are you willing to be reborn?

And then, my beloved, you who are the spiritual people – who see it so clearly in the world – now turn around, now look in the mirror, now look at yourself and see how you sometimes hold on to the old sense of identity. "How could I so easily be reborn and now I am no more that terrible person I was yesterday? How could that happen so easily?" You fall into that subtle reasoning of the Prince of this world and the ego. Where the ego is saying, as we have explained in previous discourses in this series, "Oh, you cannot just walk away from me. You cannot just abandon me. You cannot just give it all up." But you see, my beloved, you can.

You can – every time the ego comes at you with some lesser sense of self – you can look at it and say, "I give you up. I surrender you. And I accept that I AM reborn!" And if you will do this constantly, if you will build a habit and a momentum of surrendering and accepting your rebirth, then you will, as I said, out-pace the ego and the prince of this world.

For they cannot keep up with perpetual rebirth—they cannot keep up with it, my beloved. And thus, you will be accelerated beyond it. You will literally accelerate your sense of self beyond the ego—stop feeding it your light. Whereby it will die and be consumed. Even so, as you do with the rosaries, where you are constantly invoking the light to consume that ego and the energy that is feeding it.

And so, by taking your own personal ego out of the equation of planet Earth, you will also raise up the mass consciousness. And by showing other people that they can do the same, well then, you will become part of a new awareness – a new awakening, my beloved – that it is possible to rise above the past and to accept that not only am I reborn, but humanity is reborn, society is reborn, Planet Earth is reborn. And we can, indeed, be reborn out of this old sense of identity that causes – that manifests, that out-pictures – the current imbalance and poverty, and all of the diseases of the physical body and all of the other limitations, such as warfare and strife and conflict.

...

Do the works that I did

This is essentially the purpose of my mission—to demonstrate the lie, to challenge the lie, to demonstrate that you can rise above the lie. And when I said that those who believe on me, those who follow the path that I have followed, they shall do the works that I did and greater works shall ye do, this is precisely the highest vision that I had in mind. Not that you need to do certain miracles that are largely irrelevant in the modern, scientific age. What I need you to do is challenge the modern-day moneychangers—those who are holding back the people, the temple priests, those who are keeping the people trapped in a lie, keeping them from their God, keeping them from the kingdom of God within them.

And you, today, can do this in far greater measure than I could do 2,000 years ago. Because humankind has progressed in its awareness and understanding, and therefore a much more sophisticated teaching can be brought forth today. And therefore, you can, then, expose more of these lies, more of the lies in the psyche and how the ego is the in-road that allows the prince of this world and the external forces to control the people through that enemy within. You have so many more tools, so many more opportunities for exposing this lie.

And you all have the potential to do this. But you need to accept that you are reborn into that new level of Christhood, where you are able to challenge a particular lie and go out and demonstrate – first to a small group of people but potentially even to larger groups of people – that the lie is not real. It is a lie, and you demonstrate that you have been reborn and accelerated beyond the consciousness of the lie. For it is only the consciousness that springs from unreality—it has no life in it. For it was based on a lie from the very beginning.

And thus, this is the vision I hold for you. I already see you as reborn. Will you come to see yourselves as reborn? Will you accept it and will you then be it in action? That is the question I leave you to ponder, my beloved.

For I, Jesus, accept you for who you are right now. But I also accept you for the MORE that I see. The MORE that you already are Above. If you can only accept it here below, you can be here below all that you are Above.

Ponder this, my beloved, ponder it.

And then, come to the point where you allow yourself to be reborn and you accept that new identity, that you now are. And you accept that there is no point whatsoever in going back to the old or recreating it— for you are a new being in Christ.

The thirteenth ray of creative flow

Saint Germain, May 10, 2009.

No stillstand in the flow of life

The Creator itself was willing to let its own Being be "trapped" in the world of form, so that self-aware beings can do whatever they want with it. And so, that is the very essence of the creative flow—and you must be willing to do the same. There is no position, there is no fixed sense of self, that has any ultimate value or can even survive, my beloved. You are who you think you are at any moment—and you can change who you think you are at any moment.

The lie is that who you are at this moment must depend on who you were in the past. This is the lie, spread by Lucifer originally and by many false teachers since then. This is the lie of the ego. This is the lie that Peter presented to Jesus and then caused Jesus to say, "Get thee behind me Satan!" Again, saying that Christ should adapt to the expectations or the rules or the pre-existing conditions in this world, rather than demonstrating transcendence. This, then, is the perversion of the creative flow.

The creative flow flows. It flows. It flows. How many times have I said this? How many times do I need to say it, before something in your mind clicks? And you realize that the very essence of the consciousness of separation is an attempt to stop the flow—in order to hold on to a particular experience, state of consciousness, material condition. This is death!

Life is flow. Life is movement. Life is progression. Life is transcendence. If you will be honest – if you will look deeply into yourself and meditate on this – you will uncover, my beloved, very deep and subtle layers of your own ego that wants to maintain something, that wants to hold on to what it feels you have attained or achieved.

There will even be a subtle sense that what you have experienced and gone through on the spiritual path gives you some kind of status. And that when you attain a high enough status, suddenly angels with trumpets will appear and the pearly gates will open and you will be welcomed into the kingdom of heaven because of your status. But did not Jesus say that unless ye become as little children, ye cannot enter the kingdom. What is it about children? For them, everything is new. Do you see? In the creative flow, every day is a new day—a fresh new start. It is not a continuation of yesterday. It is a new day.

It might have elements of yesterday, but it is new. It is fresh. It is alive. And unless you are willing to flow with that, you cannot enter the kingdom. You will condemn yourself to remaining outside where you are seeking to defend some kind of position, thinking that if you attain some ultimate position in this world, it will guarantee your entry into the world beyond. But you cannot enter the world beyond as long as you hold on to the state of consciousness that is this world, the world of separation. It is not possible!

We have said this so many times, my beloved. But we keep saying it because we know that every time we say it, some will get it. But others will still have blocks in their minds that prevent them from seeing it, from truly experiencing it. So we try again. We try again, because we are transcending ourselves, seeking forever new ways of expressing it—the same thing in different contexts for different people, for different level of consciousness.

And so, once again, consider very carefully that life is a continuous flow. It is not an end result. Salvation is not an end result. The ascension is not an end result. Christhood is not an end result. Buddhahood is not an end result. And once you have attained that ultimate result, everything stands still—it is not so.

For the Creator does not stand still. And so, oneness with the River of Life means that you are not standing still. That is why you are willing to become MORE by questioning that which you thought was the highest possibility of creative expression. For unless you are willing to question what is, how can you be open to that which is MORE? How can you be open to the new unless you are willing to question the old?

Growth begins with a question. I am a master of freedom. And thus, I say, again, I welcome all students who are willing to question everything!

The fourteenth ray of sharing your Presence

Sanat Kumara, May 10, 2009.

I call for a genuine spirituality

Look at the spiritual and religious people on this planet. Turn on your television sets on a Sunday, when the preachers are on. Pay attention to when you hear other spiritual people talk about spirituality. And see how often they speak from that surface level – the linear mind – or even the ego with all of its fear or desire for control. And then, realize that if there is to be a new spiritual awakening in this age, it will not come from those who preach from the outer mind. It will come only if there are those who will be the open door for something deeper—something genuine that touches the heart.

And then recognize that this is perhaps the greatest need that you can serve to fulfill in this age—to become those who are known for speaking genuinely about their spirituality. For bringing a new voice into the spiritual debate, into the arena of spirituality and religion. Where you are not simply taking one side of defending a particular religion, or the other side of attacking all religion from a scientific, materialistic perspective. But you are going beyond it, you are finding the Middle Way of being genuine.

For you speak from the stillness. You imbue your words with the Presence that you are. For you know that you are that Presence. For you have been reborn into accepting that you are an expression of the Presence.

And thus, when you know who you are, how can you not express that in all of your words, in all of your actions, in all of your thoughts and feelings? For that is what will give you the greatest sense of joy and fulfillment.

My beloved, the ego finds a certain satisfaction in convincing someone else that it is right. But there is a far deeper joy in feeling the flow of your Presence through your outer being, and in feeling that expression, experiencing that creative flow. And also, then, in sometimes seeing how other people respond, how they are surprised, for here is a person who talks about spirituality but not in the usual way—it is a different voice.

And at first they might not know what to do with it. But you will see that many will respond in a new way, a deeper way. They will be awakened – by the sharing of your Presence – to tune in to their own Presence. And they will begin the journey, until they can come to the point, where they can share their Presence. And as this spreads as rings in the water, then there will be an entirely new spiritual movement of simply sharing the Presence, my beloved. Expressing that Presence, with no expectations of a particular result, simply the desire to share who you are, to share your Presence.

The reward for service is MORE service

This, then, is the essence of the fourteenth ray. I, Sanat Kumara, have vowed to represent this ray to the lifestreams on Earth and to serve to give you the initiations on this ray. You have now received, my beloved, a teaching beyond what has been given in any previous dispensation. Do not let it become a source of pride or superiority. It is a teaching that is not given because you are superior, but because you have been willing to humble yourselves—look for the beam in your own eye, work on the ego, look beyond the duality consciousness, and therefore, go beyond pride and elevation and superiority.

You have been willing to do with your own being, what I, Sanat Kumara, did coming to Earth—go into the depth and not shy away from getting your hands dirty. And so, you have earned the privilege of a teaching that can take you beyond and enable you to become better servants for the Ascended Host and Saint Germain, and Jesus, and the Buddha and others in the ascended realm. The reward for service is MORE service. Thus, also, the teaching on how to give better service.

Thus, there are seven rays that were used to manifest the material realm. There is one ray – the eighth – which occupies the nexus of the figure-eight flow, the first seven being in that lower part of the figure-eight. Symmetry is, of course, an inherent quality of creation. And so, there are seven rays above as well. I have talked about the fourteenth, but there is a fifteenth, completing the seven above, the seven below, and the one in the nexus.

The fifteenth is a ray that cannot, in any way shape or form, be grasped by the linear mind. It cannot truly be described with words. But

I will make you aware that it exists, and I will give you something to ponder. Ponder, therefore, "unconditionality." And beyond unconditionality, the Infinite—infinity. Infinity.

For at the top of the figure-eight is the singularity that is the Creator. The Creator is infinite, has no conditions, no form that can be captured in words or images. Yet, because your conscious self is an extension of the Creator, you can experience the Presence of the Creator by going beyond all conditions.

For the Creator, too, desires to share its Presence, which is why you exist, why the world of form exists. It is simply the Creator sharing its Presence. And you can partake of it, but the best way to partake of the Creator's Presence – the Creator's infinite Presence – is to share your finite, yet, divine, Presence with others.

It is in giving that you receive. It is in letting the light flow to others that you might have the experience of where the light comes from. So that as others experience the light coming through you, you experience where the light ultimately comes from—out of the singularity of the infinite mind, the One Mind.

Knowing your divine plan through the crystalline structure of divine direction

The Great Divine Director, December 14, 2009.

The Great Divine Director I AM, and I am a cosmic being. Do you understand, what a cosmic being is?

Now, check your reaction to that question. Were you tempted to say "Yes?" For if you were, I must tell you that one cannot "understand" what a cosmic being is. The linear analytical mind cannot fathom, cannot span the vast expanses of a cosmic being. Thus, it is not a matter of understanding, but of knowing—of experiencing, of coming into oneness with and attaining what the ancients called gnosis.

Thus, if it were possible, I would raise you up, so that you could see – even for a split second – the perspective of a cosmic being. I would raise you with me, all the way up through my Being, through that crystalline structure that I AM. I would raise you all the way up, to the very apex of the crystal pyramid of my Being. And that apex is the single point, a singularity my beloved, centered over the white cube that sits between Alpha and Omega in the Great Central Sun.

My beloved, a cosmic being is a cosmic being because it – mind you, not "he" or "she" as you conceive it on Earth – it has raised its consciousness, its self-awareness, to that point of knowing that it originated in the singularity that is, indeed, the nexus point of the figure-eight flow between Alpha and Omega. That nexus point, that singularity, is the portal, the gateway, the open door, between this world of form and the Creator who created it out of its own Being.

Certainly, you can say, "Without him was not anything made that was made." Certainly, that means that the Creator's Being is everywhere inside the world of form. Yet there is no place in the world of form, save in that central sun, where there is a direct opening to the Creator's Being. Thus, this is where the command of the Creator issued forth into the world of form: "Let there be light! Let us make man in our own image and after our own likeness, and let him have dominion over the Earth, over the world of form, over the material universe."

A cosmic perspective

If I could take you, even for a second, to sit on that white cube and look out over the vast cosmos before you – with its billions of galaxies, billions of layers and spheres and compartments – if you could see that for a split second, my beloved, your life, your perspective on life, would be instantly changed. Take note, of what I said. Your perspective on life IS your life—until you realize that you are more than your perspective, that you are more than any perspective, than any sense of self created to facilitate your expression, your experience, in the world of form.

My beloved, you cannot experience the central sun, the white cube, the comforting, healing, completely whole Presence of Alpha and Omega, you cannot experience this as a human being, seeing yourself as a human being. How then can you experience the ultimate reality, the very starting point of the world of form? You can experience it because the core of your being is an extension of the Creator's own Being.

This core of your being has been known to – or rather experienced by – the true mystics of the ages. You will see it mentioned and described in words in the ancient Vedas, you will see it described in Taoism, in Buddhism, in Christianity, sometimes veiled, sometimes more obvious. But in all the mystical, spiritual teachings of the world – Kabala, Sufism, they all have it – that description of that something that is the core of your being. That something that makes you conscious that you exist as an individual being. For indeed, you are an individual being, you are an extension, an individualization, of your Creator.

Take note, my beloved, of the subtle distinction that has given rise to a subtle lie. Individuality does not necessarily mean separation. You were not created as a separate being, as a separate self. You were created as an individual being, which has a particular perspective, seeing the world of form from a particular vantage point. That point, however, is not a separate point in space or time. It is another singularity my beloved, for truly every point in space is a singularity—if it is conscious of itself as an extension of the Creator's Being.

This, then, is your potential to raise your self-awareness, until you reach the full awareness of the Creator. Contrary to what some teachings claim, this does not mean you lose individuality. For even your Creator has individuality—although so far beyond that of any human being on Earth, even that of an ascended master, that you can scarcely fathom it.

Yet, your particular Creator created this Universe as an expression of its own creativity and individuality. There are other ways that a universe can be constructed, and your scientists have begun to realize that your particular universe depends on a series of constants that are so delicately balanced that your particular form of life – especially the carbon-based form of life that makes up your physical bodies – simply could not have existed if any of these crucial constants had been slightly different.

Well my beloved, it does not mean that had these constants been different, there would have been no life. There would have been other forms of life, but your particular Creator chose to balance the constants in this particular way in order to create this particular form of life that you see in your universe. Truth be told, you can go to other galaxies and systems of worlds, even in your world of form, where you can find other forms of life, for there, there is a slightly different balance.

Nevertheless, my point is this: Your Creator is an individual being out of the Allness of God. You are an individual being out of the All of your Creator. You have the potential to raise your self-awareness to that level of the Creator consciousness, whereby you can then qualify to create your own world of form as an expression of your being, your individuality, your creativity. That is why you are a co-creator. You learn by co-creating with your Creator, until you become a Creator who can define your own creation.

The core of your being
And what is it, then, that is the core of your being, that can grow in self-awareness? Well, it is that singularity, that point-like extension of the Creator's Being. We have called it the Conscious You or the conscious self. Other mystical teachings have called it with other names, be it the "atman" or whatever the case may be.

But you see, my beloved, unless you enjoy splitting hairs, the word is not important. What is important is the concept that, whatever you call it, there is a core of your being that makes you conscious—not conscious of a particular form of self. For this core of your being, this Conscious You, is not a self as the kind of self you have created for expression in the world of form. That self – that is meant for expression – has a form; your Conscious You has no form. It is pure awareness.

Take note, my beloved, that the linear, analytical mind cannot grasp the concept of the Conscious You. You cannot grasp the concept of the Conscious You—if you see the concept of the Conscious You as a concept. My beloved, it is not a concept. But when we give you a teaching expressed in words, we are bound by the limitations of the words themselves. And therefore, as soon as anything is described in words, the linear analytical mind can take it and turn it into a concept—that you can then describe, put words on, argue for or against, call real or unreal.

But you see, we gave the teachings on the Conscious You because we know that there are some who will understand. They understand because they have experienced themselves as the Conscious You, separated from any specific self that they have created, for the Conscious You is pure awareness. And there are those among the top 10 percent who have spontaneously – or through various practices, such as meditation or contemplation – they have experienced that pure awareness, whereby the Conscious You experiences itself as more than any self it has created in the world of form—and therefore experiences that it is free. It is not bound by anything in the world of form. It can never be bound by anything in the world of form. Unless it chooses to go inside of that self and identify itself fully with that individual self, so that it now sees the world from inside that self, sees the world through the filter of that self, and therefore can momentarily forget that it is more—that it is pure awareness.

There are indeed many people on this planet, the vast majority of them, who have never experienced pure awareness. We are quite aware, my beloved, that if you have not experienced pure awareness, then our teachings of the Conscious You will be just another concept for you—that your linear analytical mind will do its usual work with. Depending on your state of consciousness, depending on your dramas, your understanding or lack of it, you will project images upon the teachings about the Conscious You. You will do with it what you please. You might nail it to a cross, and call it this or that, turn it into a graven image—instead of doing what you ideally must do to fathom the depth of any spiritual teaching, namely, go beyond the words, my beloved, go beyond the words until you attain gnosis with the Spirit behind the words.

God is a Spirit, and they that worship him must worship him in Spirit and in truth. They that would know God must know him in Spirit, for you cannot know God through the finite mind. God is infinite—cannot be fathomed by the finite mind. It is a simple truth, my beloved, but there are those who have been embodied again and again in religious circles – even have been, for many decades, in spiritual, mystical, ascended master organizations – yet they have not understood this very basic concept of going beyond the outer teachings, going directly to the Spirit and experiencing the gnosis with the Spirit. Whereby you know – you experience – that oneness.

Pure awareness cannot be understood

My beloved, the beauty of your conscious self is that it is pure awareness. This is why your conscious self can project itself into a limited sense of self and actually believe – and experience as a believable experience – that you are a limited human being, a mortal sinner. If you desire to have that experience, you can have it, because your conscious self can go inside such a self and experience the world from inside of it.

But the beauty is that your conscious self is always just pure awareness, and thus it can also project itself the other way. Instead of projecting itself down into the lower levels of vibration, it can equally project itself up into the higher levels of vibration and therefore project itself into oneness with a spiritual being, even project itself into the Great

Central Sun—and beyond it to experience the Creator, out of which it is, after all, simply like one drop taken out of the ocean of the Creator's consciousness.

Do you see that until you go beyond the linear analytical mind, until you go beyond the separate self, then your existence as an extension of the Creator's being, as pure awareness, will be simply a theoretical concept? You can argue for or against it. My beloved, there are people who have argued for or against various spiritual concepts for lifetime after lifetime. We of the Ascended Host honor free will. If people desire to have this experience indefinitely, let them do so, within the confines of the Law of Free Will. Yet we of the Ascended Host are not using our attention to seek to help such people, for they have put themselves under the law of action and reaction—the school of hard knocks.

They may call themselves religious. They may have developed a holier-than-thou attitude, where they think they know everything better than everyone else, for they have created this perfect belief system that they believe they can fit everything into, even the Creator himself. And thus, the law was set up to make sure that these people will have reflected back to them by the cosmic mirror exactly what they send out. And they will keep reaping what they have sown until they have had enough of it and say, "There must be more life than what I am experiencing right now." And when you come to that point, of wanting more than what you have projected into the cosmic mirror, at that point you can start the spiritual path where we of the Ascended Host can help you.

We can give you teachings designed to elevate your consciousness, your understanding. We can give you techniques and tools designed to help you invoke spiritual energy. And therefore, you can start the journey of parting the veil, the veil of Maya, until you begin to see through it. But what is it you see, when you start to see through the veil of Maya? It is not, as some expect, this wonderful kingdom of heaven up there, with all of these beautiful characteristics that you might have heard or read about.

Take note of what I am saying here, that you do not confuse it with some image in the linear mind. There are indeed people on Earth who have had genuine experiences of the spiritual realms. And they have come back to tell about them. But my point is that when you start the spiritual path, when you start breaking through the veil of Maya that clouds your own particular mind, what you see is not some elevated vision of the spiritual realm with all of its beauty, although that beauty is real and it is there. No, what you see, at first, is glimpses of pure awareness, pure consciousness. Where your conscious self – which so far has been conscious of itself as a human being – starts seeing itself as more than a human being, experiencing pure awareness that makes your conscious self-conscious of the fact that it can never be confined to this world of form or any sense of self created within it.

There is nothing that can hold your conscious self, and that is what your conscious self realizes, when it experiences itself as pure awareness, beyond any self in this world—pure, unpolluted awareness. This is what you begin to see. There are spiritual traditions, such as Eastern Buddhism, where they have time-tested techniques and methods for helping people still the mind until they experience pure consciousness.

There is no room for judgment in the ascension spiral

Serapis Bey, December 18, 2009.

The ascension is transcendence

What is the ascension coil all about? It is about transcendence—transcending conditions, transcending impurities. If you have an impurity, I do not sit here, as Serapis Bey, as the master of ascension, and say, "Oh, this is bad. You must now go out into the world and get rid of your impurity and then come back to me." On the contrary, I, Serapis Bey, look at your impurity and say, "Great! What an opportunity to transcend!"

Do you see that for me an impurity is not a cause for judgment and condemnation and putting down? It is an opportunity for transcendence, for taking one more step in the ascension spiral, one more step up the spiral staircase. When you can look at it the same way – that no matter what might be exposed, it is only an opportunity for you to transcend – then you are ready to work with me in the pure white light of the Ascension Temple. Until then, it is better for you that you stay outside of that pure white light, where you can still hide that which you are not yet ready to look at without going into the negative spiral of condemning yourself.

So now what happens when you come to that point, where you are willing to look at anything without condemning yourself, for you have realized that you are a spiritual being? You have realized, as we have said, that you are a conscious self that is an extension of God's own Being, but that your conscious self is pure consciousness—and therefore cannot be a separate self, cannot be identified with a separate self. You are pure consciousness that nothing can stick to. And that is why you realize that you can look at any impurity that you have taken into your lower being, and you know that it cannot stick to the real you—for you are pure consciousness. Nothing on Earth can stick to you, nothing can color you.

And therefore, you can step out of any sense of separate self and know that you are MORE, that you can change your perspective. And thus, you realize that the ascension process is really a process whereby you – the conscious self that you are, the core of your identity – gradually shifts your perception of self. Until you get out of the polluted perception of the separate self, of any form of separate self, and get back to the pure perception of your pure identity as a spiritual being with certain divine characteristics that make you a unique individual. But those characteristics are anchored in your I AM Presence, and are not the conditions that you have taken on in your sojourn on Earth or in other realms of the material universe, the world of form.

Chapter 8: Ego Teachings, 2010-11

How a limited imagination blocks peace in the Middle East

Saint Germain, February 3, 2010.

For what is freedom? Many human beings would say, "It is the freedom to do whatever I want." But my beloved, is there – can there ever be – freedom in doing? Is there freedom in activity, or is there freedom truly in the point of stillness? So the distinction we arrive at is this: complete, total freedom is stillness. If you carry the stillness with you into activity, into doing, then you can be free in doing. But if you become so focused on the doing that you lose the stillness, then you are lost in the doing. And no matter what you do – even if you have freedom to do anything you want on Earth – you are no longer free, you are trapped by the doing. And thus, as Jesus said, what shall it profit a man, that he gains the whole world – or the freedom to do anything he wants in this world – yet loses his own soul, the point of stillness within him?

For what shall a man give in exchange for his soul? What, from Earth, can you give in exchange for stillness? For there is nothing required – no gift, no sacrifice, no suffering required – for you to experience stillness. There is only one requirement. You must give up, let go of, surrender, that which takes you out of stillness.

Some of you have become so focused on your spiritual growth – on changing your psychology, overcoming your ego, manifesting a higher state of consciousness – that this activity has become for you an act of doing. You are lost in the doing, always looking for the next thing to overcome in your psyche, the next illusion, the next aspect of your ego.

But all that is required for you is to stop doing, to stop approaching the spiritual path as a process of doing and surrender your attachment to doing—that you might experience the stillness within.

So many people on the spiritual path – especially from the West – think that the path is a matter of striving. And they think that the faster they run, the faster they get to the goal. But in reality, the faster you run – the more active and frantic you become – the faster you are running away from stillness. For in the end, what will make or break your spiritual progress is your contact with the point of stillness within you.

Stillness is a Presence. It is pure awareness. Not an awareness of this or that or the next thing on Earth, but pure awareness. If you have not experienced it or recognized it for what it is – recognized the contrast between pure awareness and what human beings call normal awareness – well, then you will not go beyond a certain level of the spiritual path. You will get stuck at that level. And therefore, you will become more and more focused on – more and more attached to – something in the material world. And you will begin to believe that that something is the key to your entering heaven—the kingdom of God, or whatever you want to call it.

You will think that perfecting this outer activity, performing it to a certain quantity – such as doing so many decrees, doing so much violet flame, doing so much meditation, prostrating yourself on the floor so many times, lighting so many candles or doing this, that or the next thing – you will think that this outer activity not only is the key to your entering heaven but in fact can guarantee your entry into the kingdom. For you have become a slave of the ancient epic drama that defines an activity on Earth as the key to heaven. And then says that when you perform that activity a certain number of times, your entry into heaven is guaranteed.

This, of course, is one of the oldest epic dramas used by the fallen beings to trap God's co-creators and prevent them from fulfilling their role to be co-creators on Earth. The effect of this drama is twofold: it focuses you on what happens after you are no longer on Earth, taking you focus away from the Earth and what you are here to accomplish in the Earth. And then it focuses you on a repetitive, mechanical activity that takes your focus away from the reality of who you are—a co-creator who has access to the infinite fount of creativity right within yourself.

And what is that fount of creativity? It is stillness—but you have no need for stillness, you think, for all you need to do is to perform this external religious activity and then you will get out of this limited realm and into this wonderful kingdom that awaits you beyond the veil. Yet why did Jesus say that the kingdom of God is within you? It is because until you find the kingdom within yourself, you will not find it. Until you find the kingdom in the present moment, you will not find it.

As long as you see the kingdom as being outside yourself, and as being achievable in some future time, you will never, ever find it. The kingdom is within you—here and now. And until you find it in the here and in the now, it will remain far from you—or so it seems to the mind that has forgotten stillness and has been trapped in doing. Even thinking it is free because it has certain powers on Earth—and can supposedly do anything it wants, which in reality means anything it can imagine from the limited human level of imagination. For if you go beyond that level and into the point of stillness, you will contact God's imagination, which is infinitely greater and can imagine things for the Earth that hardly any human being on this planet can imagine right now.

I, Jesus, withdraw my light from Christianity

Jesus, February 11, 2010.

The desire to know before you see

You all think that you have a divine plan, you all think that you have a divine individuality in your I AM Presence, but you all fail to realize that that divine individuality is beyond form. It does not have a form that you can pinpoint with your outer mind. You cannot write it down, you cannot see it in a vision. You can only let it unfold itself; you will not know what it is, my beloved, before it is manifesting itself through you. You will know it as you see it unfold; you will not know it ahead of time.

Do you see that this is precisely the Peter consciousness, the idea that there is a gap between your action and your inner knowing, so that you are supposed to know within what you will do. And then you have a space where you can decide whether you are willing to do it or not.

This is the fallen consciousness, this is the duality consciousness that wants to judge everything based on an earthly, man-made standard, even a standard of perfection—as so many have attempted to define a standard of perfection. You want to be able to judge your impulses from your I AM Presence before you allow them to manifest as actions or words. And in wanting to judge, you are not willing to let yourself die into the flow of the Spirit, where you do not know where the Holy Spirit will flow through you. But if you want to judge, you are not willing to let that Spirit blow where it listeth. You want to know ahead of time whether it will flow in an appropriate way. And therefore, you stop its flow by that very desire to know before you see.

My beloved, I have no desire for you to study even my living teachings on the AskrealJesus website, so that you become the most knowledgeable spiritual people on Earth. I have no desire for you to know everything but fail to act on anything. I desire you to become as the little child who is willing to express whatever comes through him from the Spirit. But who has, of course, gone through the learning process, the process of separating yourself from the outer identity, so that you are not expressing from the ego and the fears of the human. But you are fearless before God and fearless before men in allowing the Spirit to express itself through you. This is the Holy Spirit, this is the flow, this is the church that I came to start, and this is the church against which the gates of hell shall not prevail.

Because the gates of hell is precisely the desire to make form permanent and to enclose Spirit in form. And it cannot be done, and that is why the gates of hell will indeed prevail against any church that seeks to enclose Spirit in form, as this Catholic Church has done now for so long that everyone thinks that this is the only way to be Christian. But it is not being truly Christian, for it is not being like Christ, who expressed whatever came to me.

Do you really think that I knew everything I was going to do? My beloved, there were many times where I had no idea what God would do through me, I simply allowed it to happen. And I was as surprised when it happened as those who were looking on. There was no sense of pre-destination, of pre-definition, of premonition. My beloved, certainly I had certain inklings and visions, but I did not allow them to trap my mind into wanting to make them happen, or fearing that they would happen. I surrendered and allowed it.

Perpetual surrender

I had my moments of travail, as in the Garden of Gethsemane before my arrest. Certainly, I even had my moment on the cross, where I had to confront that last ghost and let it go, let it die, give it up to God. And this is a process that will be ongoing for you. I am not envisioning that any of you can come to a point, where you no longer have things to surrender. But what I desire to see in you is that you go into that state of consciousness that is perpetual surrender, ongoing surrender, where you do not seek to control the flow of the Spirit that cannot be controlled, but you allow it to happen.

You allow it to happen any time, in any way—as this messenger allowed this dictation to come forth, even in the midst of this busy cathedral with thousands of people buzzing around him constantly. My beloved, allow the Spirit to flow, allow yourself the joy of being surprised at what the Spirit can do through you—things you had not even been able to imagine before, because your intellect and your outer mind could not imagine them, for they did not fit in its mental box.

Surrender yourself into that flow, allow yourself to be surprised. Surprise the world, my beloved, we in the ascended realm have an infinite number of surprises that we would like to spring on this planet, in order to shake people out of their mental boxes. But we need willing minds and hearts, we need those who are willing to let themselves be surprised, instead of being so proper and planned and having everything defined ahead of time, having everything evaluated based on some human standard, that you have set up, for what will not embarrass you or what is proper in this or that context.

My beloved, the Holy Spirit will not embarrass you, for the Holy Spirit will not make a spectacle of itself—that is the ego that does that. But the Holy Spirit will surprise you and others by how it will touch people's hearts in a sincere manner, in a transformative manner, my beloved. Do you see the difference? If not, then consider surrendering into Spirit and allowing the Spirit to show you the difference. And you will be surprised, you will be overjoyed, you will be elated at what the Spirit will bring forth through you, my beloved.

You do not need to stand up and shout in any church – as I am not having this messenger shout in this church – for what is the point? But you need to be alert that when there are people who are receptive to a different message, then you allow those words to come forth that will touch their hearts. Not necessarily give them an ultimate awakening, but touch their hearts that they can take the next step, that they can begin the process that eventually will allow them to unfold, to transcend their mental box, to come up higher.

The structures in your mind

My beloved, it is only the ego that envisions some ultimate gift of the Spirit, some ultimate event that will awaken everyone. Look at the fundamentalist Christians who expect my second coming any moment. I will appear in the sky as some unmistakable manifestation that no one can deny, and therefore they can jump up and say, "We were the ones who expected this all along, look at us, look at how wise we were that we knew Christ was coming in this way." It will not happen, my beloved. This is the evil and adulterous generation that lusteth after an outer sign. I will appear like the lightning from the East to the West, in ways that you will not see because it will be gone before your eyes can even register it. I will appear through many people, through a word here, a gesture there, a cup of cold water in Christ's name that sets somebody on a different track, other than the downward track they had been on for perhaps many lifetimes.

This is how the Spirit works, not in an outer, demonstrative way, but in so many subtle ways, my beloved. Allow this flow to happen, allow it to happen by letting go of your rituals. Look at this Catholic Church and how everything is set in stone, in some ritual, in some equipment that the Pope needs in order to perform his duties, in some dogma and doctrine. Look how it has squeezed out the Spirit, but then be willing to be honest and look in the mirror. Stand in front of the mirror, at least metaphorically speaking, and look at yourself. What structures do you have, what enormous structures have you built in your own minds? For I tell you, there are some of you who have built structures in your minds – in your mental body, even in your etheric body – that are far more grandiose than this basilica of Saint Peter's.

You have built these structures thinking that one day somebody on Earth will recognize your superior wisdom, your superior intellect, your superior ego—even though you will not admit that this is what it is. Look at those structures and then allow them to crumble before the winds of the spirit. Then you will be free. You will feel such a freedom, such a joy, such an innocence. This is indeed the joy that I desire to see, this is the joy, my beloved, that I displayed in certain moments 2,000 years ago, that are not recorded in the Scriptures. This is the joy that I displayed when I was with my companion, Mary Magdalene.

The Roman Empire symbolizes your personal struggle with the structures you have created

Saint Germain, February 13, 2010.

Decoding the myth about the founding of the Roman Empire

Let me explain the significance of the entire myth about the creation of the Roman Empire. There are those who will take any myth literally, and thus will want to believe that there was a certain vestal virgin who became impregnated and gave birth to twin boys, Romulus and Remus—who were then left in the forest, raised to a certain age by a shewolf, and then raised to adulthood by a peasant. This, of course, is not reality whatsoever. There is no reality to it.

It is the myth that was given to the Roman people, as the Roman Empire was beginning to attain the power that made it clear how perverted and force-based it is. It was given to them as a symbol that could be decoded by those who were willing, those who had the awareness to see beyond the outer manifestations.

So what does the symbol represent? Well, the vestal virgin represents the feminine aspect of God that is striving for purity. Yet as Mother

Mary explained at the basilica of St. Peter's, when the female has been separated from the Creator, from the divine masculine, then the true polarities of Alpha and Omega, masculine and feminine, will become opposites. And thus, the vestal virgin does not represent one who is pure, but actually represents the female polarity to the other polarity of the Creator. And thus, the Vestal Virgin represents all of you—each human being is represented by this. The one who has gone out from oneness or who – by choosing to leave oneness to partake of the forbidden fruit – now becomes impregnated and gives birth to the twins, as the dualistic consciousness with its two opposite polarities that can only be in rivalry.

And so, when it realizes it has fallen, it wants to get rid of that division within itself, that impurity within itself. And thus, it wants to leave it; it wants to go out into the forest [representing the subconscious mind] and leave it, where it will never be seen again. And then it wants to try to return back to its normal life, instead of facing what it chose to manifest and thereby resolving it. And so, the vestal virgin represents each and every one of you, who have created the ego and thus seen it, but then trying to run away from it instead of facing it—facing yourself in the mirror and resolving the duality in your being. Instead you seek to run away from it.

And then, what you create when you run away, is that you create the ego, the ego that has two opposite polarities that are always in competition as to which one will dominate you and dominate your soul and your being. And thus, there will be the rivalry that you saw between Romulus and Remus, and out of that rivalry springs the consciousness of thinking that you cannot simply receive everything from God, but that you need to take it by force, by forcing your dualistic vision – your dualistic images, your graven images – upon the Ma-ter light. And thus, the entire desire to create an empire based on force is what you see represented in the empire supposedly founded by the twins Romulus and Remus.

And then, you see also that when you refuse to face the dichotomy, the division, in your own being, then the rivalry must continue until one of the polarities seems to kill the other polarity, as Romulus killed Remus. And then you have, supposedly, the Pax Romana, which is the peace that seemingly comes because now you have reestablished some illusion of unity in your being. Because the ego has managed to go so far into one dualistic polarity that it seemingly has suppressed the other, to where you can forget about it. And thus, you have established what we have called a state of equilibrium in your being—a false equilibrium, where you sense you have this peace, but it is a peace that is based on suppression by force of all creativity, of the life force itself.

You must face the structures in your mind

Do you not see that what has happened – precisely – is that you have done what Jesus said; you have built a structure in your mind. And that structure is symbolized, then, in the outer empire, the Roman Empire that seeks to conquer the entire world in an attempt to avoid facing the divisions within itself. And yet, even though for a time it seemed like the Roman Empire could be successful in suppressing the entire world through force, did there not come a time – inevitably – where the division from within, the insanity of the emperors and the leaders of the Roman Empire, created such corruption in the top – such divisions, such rivalry, such infighting – that eventually the empire was weakened to the point, where it was now conquered by the barbarians, so to speak, from without.

This is, indeed, a symbol for the process that is going on in the consciousness of every human being that has descended into duality. There will be times where it seems like your ego has managed to quell the division. But is a peace that is obtained only through force, and therefore it cannot last, it cannot be maintained, it cannot survive for long. And there will come a point, then, where out of the subconscious mind comes the beast of the earth or the beast of the sea, that suddenly sticks up its ugly head. And now, your peace is shattered. And now, you are in a negative spiral, as this messenger has recently described that even those who are on the spiritual path can – almost in an instant – switch from being seemingly going upward on that path, to now being caught in a negative spiral, where they are focused only on the negativity in others and in judging others. And again, not looking at themselves in the mirror.

I must tell you, as the hierarch of the Age of Aquarius, that this going from one extreme to the other, with periods of relative peace in between, can continue indefinitely, until you run out and stand before the second death. And what is it you must face at that second death? It is the death of the mortal self, and the question now is: will your conscious self, will the Conscious You, be willing to give up that mortal self? And in many cases this is extremely difficult to do, if you have been trapped by that illusion of duality for so long, and have been unwilling to question it for so many lifetimes. How can you, then, suddenly question it, when you stand before that final opportunity? Many cannot, and that is why we of the Ascended Host have done everything we can think of to give the teachings that will empower you to face it now, rather than later.

Will you wait another 2,000 years before you face the division in yourself? Will you reincarnate again and again throughout the Aquarian age with this division in your beings? For if you do, I must tell you that you will become a dead weight that will not help build the Golden Age of Saint Germain. And so, I say to you: Learn from the Roman Empire. Do not project that this was some crazy emperors that did all of this, but see the parallels to what is going on in your own being, as I have described them for you. Be willing to see it; be willing to see the structures you have built in your mind. And then, begin to question those structures. If you can, then look beyond the surface and go deeper until you reach the foundation and question that foundation—until the foundation itself begins to dissolve and the structures built upon them, then easily, easily crumble, my beloved.

Go to the core of your being

And the foundation, of course, is found in your etheric body, in your identity body. That is where you must go and question, for if you question at the higher levels [meaning the surface levels, closer to conscious awareness] then you will be confused and get nowhere for a long time. Go to the core, seek first the kingdom of God and his righteousness, the right use of your discernment, that you may see beyond the dualistic extremes—and not always find the dualistic argument that supports what you want to believe. But in reality, go beyond what you want to believe, and going into the reality of truth, as Mother Mary spoke about. The truth that will heal you, so that you can be free to again have that free imagination to imagine who you are in God and accept who you are in God. And then [you can] imagine what you can bring to this Earth as your contribution to the manifestation of the Golden Age, when you are flowing with the river of life instead of being based on force, the force that always seeks to destroy something, to put down some part of life. For it cannot conceive of raising up all life all at once.

And thus, it must seek to raise up itself by putting another part of life down. And this is the curse of duality that has been hanging over this

Earth now for so long that I would prefer not to tell you how long it has been here, for you would be discouraged and think that it could never be dissolved. Yet I tell you: with God all things are possible. With God in you, all things are possible. And thus, this is my call to you this day: Rise up and win your freedom by looking at the very thing you are not willing to look at, by looking at the very thing you are afraid to look at, by looking at what you left in the forest so many lifetimes ago, when you supposedly left the Garden of Eden."

But you were not cast out of the Garden of Eden, you left it because there was something you were not willing to look at. Look at it now, for it is only in looking at it – and going right into it – that you will be free of it. Because it is only by going into it instead of running away from it, that you will see the duality of it, that you will see the fallacy of the dualistic arguments. And therefore, you will see the reality that all life is one, you will see the one truth of Christ that will set you free, that will set you free from the dualistic illusions that have created a veil around you, so that you think what you see through the veil is reality.

I, Saint Germain, come to rend the veil, and I say, "It is not reality — it is unreality." I am outside the veil. I am free! Raise your mind so that I do not have to speak to you through a messenger who has raised his mind. Raise your mind that I may speak directly to you, in your heart, mind and being. For what one has done, all can do. If one can rend the veil and make contact with the Ascended Host, then so can everyone — if they are willing to follow the process, to see what others are not willing to look at. It is in seeing that you are set free. Look how they say that "seeing is believing." No, seeing beyond the dualistic mind is not believing; it is knowing, it is experiencing, it is being one with truth.

Don't be like the Romans—be the Christ in you

Archangel Michael, February 13, 2010.

Michael, the Archangel, I Am! Let me ask you to participate with me in a little exercise of your imagination. Even if you have not been there in person, you have certainly seen pictures, perhaps even movies about the Colosseum in Rome, and the games with gladiators and the slaughter of animals. And thus, I ask you to envision that it is a day of the games:

The Colosseum is full with tens of thousands of people, crowded in there—even more than the official numbers says that the stadium can hold. They are all ready for one thing: Blood—drama! What they desire to experience is a simulated warfare, where they can experience the drama and the bloodshed of war without being exposed to the risk that they will be maimed or killed themselves.

This is a consciousness that – although not the originator of war – is certainly the consciousness that has allowed war to continue to exist on this planet. And although it is greatly exemplified in the Roman empire, it certainly is not unique, as you even find it in the world of today.

Yet let us not get ahead of ourselves. Let us stay with the vision of the Romans sitting there, waiting for the gladiator games to begin. And for a time, they have various warm-up events: various fights among gladiators, wild animals being let loose to kill criminals or to fight against the gladiators. But everyone is waiting for the main event, which is rumored to be something special on this day. The noise is deafening, the vibration is that of a mob that is aroused to extreme anger and anxiety—and the desire for blood.

As you may know, in the later stages, the Colosseum had an elaborate system that allowed the upcoming events to be staged underneath the arena itself. And a part of the floor in the arena would then be lowered, and the next event would be raised up literally through the floor, thus appearing in the arena in front of the people.

Finally then, as the excitement reaches a crescendo, the main event is about to take place. The roar of the crowd reaches an all-time high, and now the floor moves and rises up. And what comes up through the floor is indeed myself. I come in my full stature, over 12 feet high, clad in blue armor that shines as neon lightning, an intense blue, such as no man has ever seen before with the physical eyes. I bring a sword that radiates blue flames. And suddenly the crowd falls silent—for this was not what they expected. They have never seen anything like it; they do not know what to make of it. And in their silence, they look at each other.

They start to mumble amongst themselves, as I stand there holding up my sword. And then, after a few minutes of silence, they start yelling. For now they want some action; they want some blood. They imagine that this fearsome looking creature must be able to beat any of the other gladiators. And they are expecting that all the gladiators will be let loose against me. They obviously think this is some kind of trickery, that perhaps this is a man made to look bigger, made to look more radiant.

Yet, as they begin to raise the noise level again, I point my sword against the crowd. And as I slowly turn around, blue flames, like blue laser beams, shoot out of the sword and hit all of the people in the stadium. And as they are hit by this intense light, they instantly fall silent. And as I go around the stadium, the silence follows the sword—until I have reached all the way around. And now the crowd is reduced from an angry mob lusting for blood to a silent crowd. Silent because what they are seeing is what they have not been willing to face in themselves. And suddenly, they have a sense of co-measurement, of what is the momentum, the illusion, that each person has that stands between that person and entry into heaven. They also have a sense co-measurement, that makes them realize that there is absolutely nothing they can do to cheat or force their way into heaven, as I am absolutely, completely, totally immovable.

Understanding the mob consciousness

So, what I would describe to you next is to return to the concept of the mob, the mob that sits there in the Colosseum, or that sits out there in society—even the mob that is assembled on a regular basis in front of the TV screen, where all those who watch the same program partake in that same collective state of consciousness. And what you see is that once the co-creators have been trapped in the duality consciousness – precisely because they have no inner sense of the immovability – they are susceptible to blindly following their leaders, or blindly following the mob itself, the mass consciousness itself.

This happens because when you choose not to take full responsibility for yourself, you are in reality refusing to express your individuality, your creativity. And thus, in accepting an excuse for suppressing your life force - suppressing your creativity, denying your individuality – you are creating the ego that has no creativity, has no individuality—and therefore can only follow something; it cannot create by itself. And if you are not using your individuality and creativity, you cannot create an ego that has individuality and creativity. And if you were willing to use your individuality and creativity, you would have no need to create the ego to make decisions for you.

So you see that – by definition, by its nature – the ego is neither creative nor has much individuality, certainly not the true individuality of God, given to you by God. And thus, the ego is susceptible to following either a strong leader or following the crowd, following the mob. There is nothing more destructive for spiritual growth than partaking in the mob consciousness. There is nothing more anti-spiritual on Earth than the mob consciousness. The mob consciousness is the antithesis of spiritual growth.

For what is the ascension? As we have explained recently, it is an individual process. You pass through the gate to the ascended state alone, by your own momentum—you pass through as an individual. And thus, you see, the extreme individuality that is needed to ascend is the exact antithesis to the mob consciousness, where the minds of the individuals in the mob have been taken over – have been overridden, so to speak – by the collective mind that is formed whenever a group of people come together. And with a group, I mean anything more than one person.

Do you see how the mob overrides individuality? The mob will not allow expressions of individuality. It wants all members of the mob to follow the mob and the mob consciousness. Dissent is not allowed, for then you will not only be an outcast from the mob, but it is likely that the mob will turn on you and destroy you, if they can.

And so, you see the mob that attacked Jesus, that scorned him, even as he was carrying the cross through the streets of Jerusalem. Even the mob that cried out for him to be crucified—that would rather see a convicted murderer set free than to see the living Christ set free. And this is precisely because the mob could identify with the murderer, for the murderer had the consciousness that is the consciousness behind the mob—the murder consciousness. The consciousness that wants to murder individuality and absorb the individual into the mob—and keep absorbing more and more individuals, until the mob has taken over the entire world.

How to create a mob

This is, again, a deliberate strategy by the fallen beings. How do you create a mob? There must be two elements. One is the perversion of the Father aspect, through creating and perpetrating a toxic idea that gives the mob something to focus on. A toxic idea is one that is based on duality, where there is a clear-cut division between what is right and wrong, good or evil. And now there is a division, so that there is a clear scapegoat that represents evil, and then there is the mob which is on the side of good, and therefore must take action against evil. But do you see that the deeper reality here is that the mob consciousness is that which wants to murder individuality? And thus, any individual is evil to the mob because it is a threat to the mob.

If one individual can refuse to be moved by the mob, that one individual can shatter the matrix of the mob consciousness—and therefore set people free from it, so that they suddenly switch from the mob consciousness to being individuals again. And as individuals, they have human feelings—they have a human sense of responsibility, of morals, of ethics, of right and wrong at a higher level than that defined in the mob consciousness. You see this out-pictured in the situation, where Jesus faces the angry mob who is ready to stone the woman caught in adultery. By being immovable – and by asking an awakening question – he manages to shatter the matrix of the mob and turn them back into individuals, so that they walk away one by one—instead of attacking the woman as that unity of the mob.

And so, how is the mob created? By putting out the toxic idea, and then the second element – which is a perversion of the Mother – which is the desire to create oneness in the matter realm, in the world of form. This is a subtle distinction that fools many spiritual people, for you think that oneness is supposed to be good, is supposed to be spiritual— for through oneness you can have peace. But you see, you cannot create true oneness in the material realm; you cannot create it from the duality consciousness. For you cannot create oneness through force.

True oneness through individuality
So you see, you cannot have oneness between people – true oneness between people – who deny their individuality. Oneness can only come about through individuality. Certainly, this sounds like a contradiction. But instead of seeing it as a contradiction, may I suggest that you see it as an enigma—that is an enigma only because you see through the filter of duality. For when you see beyond duality, you see that true individuality is that each self-aware being is an extension of the Creator's Being.

And so, how is true oneness achieved? By each individual being realizing its oneness with its source—and then realizing that all other self-aware beings are also extensions of that source. And that is how you have true oneness—through the connection to the one source. The fallen beings, of course, have set themselves apart from this oneness by denying their connection to their source—and by seeking to deny that every other being on Earth is connected to the source. And that is why they have attempted to create the oneness here below, the false oneness, that is created through force, namely that of the collective mind taking over and forcing into submission the individual mind.

And so, what they have done, in any number of ways, is putting out these toxic ideas, and then, as a perversion of the mother, putting out the idea that you need to accept and submit to this overall goal in order to show solidarity, to work for the greater cause, to even work for God's cause.

So you see: first you put out your overall goal, and then you put out the belief that the good people will submit to this goal, will participate in it—and will be willing to set aside their individuality in order to achieve this common goal, as it is defined. And so, once you have a population that accepts this, they have essentially become like a mob—for they are no longer thinking or feeling like individuals.

And I started out by giving you the example of the mob in the Colosseum, for I trust, that most of you will be willing and able to see this as a clear expression of the mob consciousness—that is ready to destroy, ready to destroy anything that will not submit to it. And thus, by seeing it in this extreme form, it is my hope that you will be willing to see it in its more subtle forms. For there are many of such subtle forms.

Hatred of the mother – unwillingness to face changing conditions on Earth

Portia, through Helen Michaels, February 13, 2010.

Jealousy

Behind the judgmental mindset, that the fallen ones have practiced on earth for so long, is the jealousy of the fallen consciousness. In this judgmental mindset, the emperor has the sense that he can do whatever he wants on Earth, even decide if a person on the arena will die or survive.

Yet, I have to tell you that it was not only the emperors in Rome who embodied this consciousness; it was the Roman population who magnified their emperors. Going back in world history, you see that the hatred of the mother energy did not start in Rome. It started from the fallen consciousness, which was jealous of any lifestream that had spiritual light. This light was the Presence of God that the fallen consciousness did not manifest and also could not control in any other way than by creating the structures and games on Earth, that had the purpose of taking the attention away from spirituality—and forced upon the population the standards (if in Rome, do like Romans), that if you behave like others, you are accepted in heaven.

You see, this jealousy of the fallen consciousness manifested already during Jesus' lifetime – as you see written in Mary Magdalene's gospel – namely how the other disciples were jealous of Mary Magdalene because Jesus had given her teachings that he did not give to the others. Instead of raising up all of Jesus' teachings – and raising up each other – the disciples, especially Peter, immediately went into a downward spiral, seeking to put Mary Magdalene down as they felt that she had received something that they did not.

What you have seen happen in Judea back then – and over many eons before – is that the fallen consciousness makes every possible effort to keep the illusion that God the Father is separated from God the Mother. And therefore, every situation that shatters this illusion – and every person who dares to shatter this illusion by expressing the real,

Living God – becomes a threat to the fallen consciousness—as Peter felt threatened by Mary Magdalene, who manifested a certain amount of Christ consciousness and had passed the initiations that Peter himself had not.

Thus, the threatened Peter sought to put God into his predefined limitations or structures and tried to convince everybody that if God really does not fit into those limits, then it cannot be the real God or the manifestation of the real God. Peter back then – and the Catholic Church today – outplay this gladiator game with everyone who does not fit into their limitations or predefined structures—and thus will be identified as the cause of the fighting or resistance.

In the Golden age there is no place for the hatred of mother consciousness

I myself have discoursed in Lourdes that judgment is a dualistic concept, which becomes balance and equilibrium, once it is transcended completely.

Instead of putting down another lifestream that has something that you think you don't have, realize, my beloved, that all of God's lifestreams have co-creative abilities, embodied in their individuality—which is not meant to be the same for you as for your friend or neighbor. There is no need to seek to limit the expression of God or control its manifestations, as you see in the Vatican until this day, the manifestation of the Peter consciousness and the hatred of the mother energy. What else, besides hatred of the mother, could be the reason the Vatican has to hide documents filling tens of miles of bookshelves in the Vatican Archives? It is the desire to keep even knowledge out of the reach of the masses, because it is the way to "control the mob," as it used to be said in Rome.

I, Portia, tell you that in the Golden Age there is no place for the hatred of the mother consciousness. The Golden Age is the age of unity and oneness, and the age of peace. The vibration of the hatred energy simply cannot enter this age. As my beloved Saint Germain has said – and as Jesus and Mother Mary have discoursed on – within the Golden age the Divine Father energy has to find the perfect balance with the Divine Feminine, the Mother. God can be expressed in matter only through mother. And if you really fathom this unity in yourself, you see that being within this Flow, you are one with the rest of life. How can you hate life, if you yourself are one with this life and constantly co-creating it? In the duality consciousness you might think it is possible, but in reality it simply is not possible, because you see that there is no separation between you and others.

I have to tell you, that the hatred of the mother energy has an unwillingness to look into itself, to look at what the ego has left in the forest, because the hatred of the mother consciousness cannot stand the deviation from perfection—the perfection according to its own self-defined standards, coming from duality. I, Portia, have come to say to you, "I am the Goddess of Balance, and balance can be outpictured only if you are willing to transcend the hatred of the mother energy in you, and helping therefore to raise the entire society to a new level." You find balance only by transcending the duality consciousness, so you do not seek to judge each other, or make decisions about each others lives, or put each other down—or even kill those do not submit, as seen in history.

Do you see, my beloved, that the mother plane is the expressed God, and people who cannot stand each others expressions, have to face in themselves what has made them so vulnerable to this hatred energy, and what makes them hate the creations or expressions of others. Without finding this hatred of the mother in yourself, you cannot manifest the full creativity, as Saint Germain has been talking about. Find the point of stillness in you and see from there what in this life makes you feel uncomfortable. What kind of situations, what kind of people, what kind of energy or circumstances make you feel confined or not free to have the flow of joy in you? What makes you feel uncomfortable or what makes you have negative feelings? Without looking honestly into yourself, (into the forest of your subconscious mind), you cannot embody the Mother aspect of God in full expression. In other words, God cannot express itself through you if you have set up limitations for its expression.

I withdraw space from the consciousness of anger against women

Gautama Buddha, February 14, 2010.

The Buddha I AM. Gautama is my name, space is my game. I am the Lord of the world, but what is hiding behind that title? The reality is that I am the being who is charged with holding space for planet Earth and its inhabitants.

Only some of those inhabitants are in human bodies, while some of them are spirits, or what I called beasts at Wesak, created through consciousness—not coming from God by being individualizations of the Creator's Being, but created out of the consciousness of separation by those self-aware beings who have chosen to enter into that consciousness of separation.

And in doing so they cannot shut off their co-creative abilities, their minds' abilities to impose mental images upon the Ma-ter light. And when those mental images have formed structures of a certain complexity, and have reached a certain intensity, then they are infused with enough consciousness to gain a rudimentary sense of self-awareness, a desire to survive, a desire to grow and expand.

Thus, indeed, that is why everything you see outpictured in the physical is a manifestation of consciousness, some kind of consciousness or another. And that is why it is possible that you can create – by using your co-creative abilities – a personal ego that becomes such a creation that it can take over your conscious mind and attempt to control you. Just as it is possible for a group of human beings – that form a matrix through some common characteristics – to also create a collective beast, even the mob consciousness that Archangel Michael spoke about.

Understanding space

Yet when you recognize that your physical bodies reside in the physical realm, the question then becomes, "Where do such beasts reside?" Well, they reside in space, for space is not what you commonly think of when you hear the word. For you have been so conditioned in Western culture that when you hear the words "space," you think about space travel, traveling to far-off worlds or the moon or Mars. Or you go into the sci-fi Star Wars, Star Trek – star this or star that – and you think that the salvation for humankind is to travel far away from the Earth.

Well, when you consider what Saint Germain discoursed on yesterday, do you not see that this tendency to project thought into space is nothing more but the extreme outcome of the desire to run away from that which you do not want to face in your consciousness? And that which you do not want to face then becomes something that, in your unwillingness to face it in yourself, you inevitably project it onto others. And in projecting it onto others or the world around you – always directing your consciousness outside yourself – well then you begin to create that entity on a personal level. And when many people do the same from a particular state of denial, well then they create something in the collective.

And so, that creation must then exist somewhere in space. Space then is not simply an empty area, for in reality there is no such thing as empty space. This is another fallacy, originally started by science, but then taken over by the common mind and popular culture, so that you think there is empty space outside the atmosphere of the Earth. Nothing, of course, could be further from the truth, for how would the light from distant galaxies travel to the Earth if space was indeed empty? Light is vibration, light is a wave. It must propagate through something, and thus it propagates through space. Space that has many dimensions, many frequencies of vibration.

And thus, one could – as one illustration of space – say that it is space that makes it possible for the Ma-ter light to vibrate. You may think that the Ma-ter light itself is vibration, yet this is not so. What is vibration? It is movement. Think about even the popular image of a sine wave with ups and downs, crests and troughs. Think about a wave in the ocean. Now imagine that you put a large steel plate over a part of the ocean. If the water cannot move up because of the steel plate, how could there be waves on the ocean?

So you see, the Ma-ter light itself can exist parallel to space, as both space and light are expressions of the Father, the Creator. We might say that space represents the masculine, outgoing force that makes it possible to go out, for there is space. And then the light represents the mother that can vibrate, and in vibrating taking on distinct, different forms. But if there was no room for the light to vibrate, no form would be possible. No vibration would be possible, and thus you see that space is that which allows the creation of many different forms, through the powers of the mind.

The Buddha can withdraw space

And so, we have told you that there are four distinct levels of the material universe, the etheric or identity level, the mental realm, the emotional realm and the physical realm. And thus, if there was no space beyond the physical, then obviously your minds would not be able to create the ego or these mass entities, for where could they exist? Your minds, when you go into duality, do not have the power to directly affect matter, except in special cases that are irrelevant to this discussion.

And thus, you see that it is because there are other dimensions of the material universe, other dimensions of space, other spectra of frequencies that your minds can actually create something that can have an existence that is not physical but can interact with the physical. And it is indeed the Buddha, the Lord of the World, who holds the balance for the existence of this space, these different vibratory levels, that can then be filled by some vibration or another.

Now, you will know, of course, that the primary characteristic of Buddhahood is non-attachment. You will know the story of how, before going into Nirvana, I was faced with the demons of Mara, who attempted to tempt me into reacting to them in any way. I had to demonstrate my non-attachment before I could go into Nirvana. And then, what is Nirvana? Well, it is that which is beyond space; it is the spaceless space, the timeless space beyond the material, where the lower vibrations cannot exist. And only when you demonstrate your non-attachment to these lower vibrations, can you enter that space beyond space, where there is no longer room, for the spiritual realm has ascended to a level, where there is no space for that which vibrates below the level of pure love.

That is why duality, separation, evil, even relative good cannot exist in heaven, for there is no longer space for them, as the vibrations have been raised to such a level that there is no span of space that allows these lower frequencies to even exist. Only the higher frequencies of love can exist, for they can vibrate in infinite space, whereas the lower frequencies need a finite space in which to exist. And as such, they are temporary and have no permanence in God, thus, in a sense can be said to have no reality or no real existence. For they exist only in the space that has been designed and designated as a laboratory, an experimental testing ground, a sandbox for the exercise of free will by those beings who have gone below the level of duality.

Thus, the Lord of the world holds that space, holds the balance for that space. And indeed, if I were to decide to no longer hold the balance for a certain aspect of space – a certain vibratory spectrum where a certain state of consciousness can exist – well, then there would no longer be space for that consciousness on Earth. And indeed, I do, as the Lord of the World, have this option.

I, of course, am in complete peace, in complete non-attachment. Whatever occurs on Earth, I will not be upset, I will not be disturbed. Thus, I, the Buddha, will never make the decision on my own to withdraw a certain space for a certain state of consciousness. Yet when a sufficient number of people in embodiment – or even one person reaching a certain level of consciousness – then I can indeed be moved to make the decision to withdraw a certain space, so that a certain manifestation of duality, a certain lower consciousness, can no longer exist.

Mind projections

I have described how, building on Saint Germain's discourse, that which you are not willing to look at in your own being becomes something that you – without seeing it, without seeing that you are doing it – you project upon other people. If you have anger in yourself, but you have left the twins of your anger in the forest to die – for you will not face them and deal with them – well then, that anger will grow into an angry ego. And the collective anger of a group of people will grow into a collective beast, that will eventually seek to take over their society or civilization.

As Saint Germain described, that a vestal virgin was impregnated and gave birth to Romulus and Remus, that vestal virgin was – according to the legend – impregnated by the God Mars, the God of war. And thus, Romulus and Remus represent the two dualistic polarities who are constantly warring with each other. And even though they attempted to divide Rome between them, there could be no peace, for none of them could have peace as long as there was the rivalry between them. And thus, eventually one had to kill the other, but of course that did not mean that the remaining one was in peace. For there can be no peace through this consciousness of anger and warfare.

And so, what I endeavor to explain here is that when you are still in denial of something in yourself, you are projecting it upon others. And as we have recently explained, your perception is not passive. It is an active perception that becomes a projection, and so what you are not willing to see in yourself is what you project onto others. And then, you literally see in your mind's eye that other people are angry. You see anger in them, but you fail to see that you are the one projecting it. And what you are seeing is not just their anger – even though some of them may have anger – but it is, first of all, your projection that you see. And this is, of course, why you are trapped, as we have explained here in Rome and in many other discourses, where we have approached this from different angles.

Not being willing to call a spade a spade

Yet there is another aspect that I will address here, for there are indeed those on Earth who have been willing to see something in themselves. There are millions of people who have come to the point of being willing to look at the beam in their own eye, as Christ put it, and at least see some aspect of the duality consciousness. Yet I must tell you that this awakening is being held back by a certain state of consciousness, that has been put upon humankind by the fallen angels in a last-ditch attempt to hold back a widespread awakening.

You see, when you come to acknowledge an element of duality in your own being – what you might call a fault or a flaw in your own mind or character – then, even though you work through it, surrender it and raise yourself above it, it is very easy to begin to believe in a toxic idea put out by the fallen ones. And that is that if you have had a flaw in your own mind – even though you may have raised yourself above it – you should still be tolerant towards those who have that flaw. And thus, you should not speak out against it, if you see it displayed in your society. It is, so to speak, a variant of the old saying, where you think that two wrongs can make a right. And you now think that if there is a wrong that you see in society, yet if you have had some wrong in yourself, then the wrong in you should cancel out your willingness to speak out against the wrong in society.

Thus, there are many, many people who are honestly working on themselves and have made great progress in terms of removing at least part of the beam in their own eyes. Yet these people have become so reluctant to speak out, either against other individuals or against some collective problem, that they are not having the impact upon society that they are meant to have, here in the Age of Aquarius. I must tell you straightforwardly that you will not see the manifestation of a golden age as long as those who are working on themselves are not willing to speak out and openly address what you see in other people and in society.

This is something that almost all of those who are the non-aggressive, non-forceful people – those who are the honest people, those who are the meek, that Jesus talked about – that all of you have. You can see in the description by this messenger of how he went through his transformation in Israel, of realizing that there was something that he had not been willing to see in the Jews, something he had overcome in himself and thus was able to see, but he was not willing to use that ability.

For you see, as Jesus said, first remove the beam in your own eye— and then you will see clearly. And when you have removed the beam in your eye, then you will see that beam or that splinter in the eyes of others or in society. For when you have been willing to face something in yourself, you are no longer in denial, and thus are no longer projecting that anger or whatever it may be upon others. And when you no longer project out, then your perception is not polluted by the projection, by the denial. And thus, you can see clearly what is going on in the minds of other people, what is going on in society.

How will the meek inherit the Earth?

And so, you see that Jesus said that the meek shall inherit the Earth. And the meek are those who are willing to work on themselves, who are willing to see something in themselves, to look in the mirror, to look at something in their own eye. Those are the meek, but how will they inherit the Earth? Not by God simply coming in and giving it it to them but by they being willing to overcome, and then to speak out to help others overcome.

I am not here talking about criticism. I am not talking about condemning. I am not talking about judging other people. I am not talking about accusing others of being wrong or demanding that other people change. I am talking about demonstrating that there is a higher state of consciousness, demonstrating it by living it. But also by speaking out and simply – without any accusatory energy, without any anger, without any blame – but in a straightforward, loving manner speaking out and saying: "I see this and this and this; and this just is not right, it is not necessary, it is not benefiting anyone; it is only hurting people, hurting yourself, hurting society in this way and this way and this way."

It is possible, my beloved – when you have worked on yourself so that you have overcome anger and fear to a certain level – it is possible to speak out in a very direct manner, but also in a very non-emotional – in terms of lower emotions – manner, in a very straightforward manner, where you are simply calling a spade a spade. You are being neutral and objective, and although some may take offense, you will be surprised at how many people will listen. For they are not used to this kind of energy; they are so used to the negative emotions of anger, blame and the projection.

And therefore, when someone speaks without projecting blame, or anger or negative emotions, they will listen with the heart instead of listening only with the emotions—and thus rejecting the emotional energy projected against them. For they know they have a right to live without having other people's emotions projected against them, and therefore they will not listen to the truth behind the vibration when the vibration is not pure. And in many cases, of course, they cannot listen because their own emotions are stirred by the emotional projection that comes against them. And therefore, their minds are taken over to the point where they cannot listen to what is being said behind the energy.

Those who see the least are trapped the most

And so, who are most trapped? Well, as always "those who see the least are trapped the most." That, my beloved, is a sentence that you might allow to be burned into your mind, so you can remember it, for it applies to each and every one of you. Those who see the least are trapped the most, for it is that which you do not see that imprisons you. The chains that you see are not a major concern, for they are often caused by the low state of consciousness of planet Earth and the free-will choices of other people. And although they may be unpleasant and give you certain limitations and grief, then they are not ultimately what will hold you back. For no condition on Earth can hold you back from rising to higher levels of consciousness, nothing outside of yourself can hold back your growth in consciousness.

It is that which is inside your consciousness that holds back your growth, and it holds back your growth precisely because you do not see it. That which is not seen is what imprisons you. If you will make progress towards Buddhahood, remember this. And then remember also that that which is not seen is actually seen, but it is not seen for what it is, for your perception is polluted. And thus, you will often project anger upon others and blame them for being angry, while in reality you are expressing anger but you are not able to see it, for you do not see what you do as anger—whereas you are very quick to see what others do as anger.

Everything is a matter of perspective, everything is a matter of perception. When you allow the Conscious You to enter into duality, you see everything from the perspective of duality. Thus, your perception is polluted and you do not see what you are doing. As Jesus said, "Father forgive them, for they know not what they do." They did not see what they were doing to the Living Christ.

Yet I, at the level of Buddhahood, would say, "What is the point in forgiving them if it teaches them nothing? Better that they experience the consequences of their state of consciousness, that they might actually begin to wonder why they continue to run into this or that problem, why they continue to run in to a certain kind of people—until they begin to realize that perhaps it is something in themselves that has been attracting these circumstances or people and that, in reality, it is because you need to learn the eternal lesson that what you project is what will be mirrored back to you by the cosmic mirror.

I officially inaugurate the Aquarian age—catch my enthusiasm

Saint Germain, March 22, 2010

There is a forward progression to life

For is it not so – and is it not obvious to those who have opened their minds and hearts – that the key to growth is always self-transcendence? Life is transcending itself; everything is constantly transcending itself. You may look at nature, you may look at the cycles of winter, spring, summer, fall, winter and so on, and you may think that this is but a repetitive cycle. But look at history down through the millennia, down through the eons, and see that it is not just a cycle that repeats itself, for there is a forward progression. There is a progression that brought forth, gradually, more complex life forms, until a physical body had been brought into existence with a brain and nervous system sophisticated enough to support the embodiment of the living spirits, the individualizations of the Creator's Being, the co-creators that we are.

Look even at the Earth revolving around the sun. Look how you might have grown up with the image that the Earth simply moves around the sun, and when it has moved around the sun one time, it returns to the same position that it was a year ago. This is the common perception—or rather the common misperception.

For my beloved, you do not seriously believe, do you, that the sun is stationery in space? Have not your scientists told you that the universe is constantly expanding, have they not told you that your sun is one star in a larger system, called a galaxy, and that it moves along with that galaxy? Even the entire galaxy is moving in space, so you see – when you think deeper about this – that when the Earth has revolved around the sun one time, it does not come back to the same position in space. For the sun has moved, meaning that the trajectory, the path, of the Earth around the sun is not an elliptical orbit: it is a spiral that moves in a clear direction.

And such it is with everything in the material universe. Everything is moving, not in circles but in spirals—spirals that have a clear direction. It is either upwards or downwards. It is either an expanding spiral or a collapsing spiral, for there is nothing in between. The dream of the elliptical, stationary orbit is but a dream. Where does this dream come from? It comes from the human ego, which wants to preserve itself by stopping the forward progression of the entire universe, if it could. And given that it cannot, it seeks to create the impression of something stationary. And because of free will and the density of the matter realm, it is indeed possible to create the image that something is stationary, something can be preserved, something can survive for a time in its present form. Indeed, this is the central challenge of life but it is especially the challenge faced by humankind right now.

How you can come to "know" ultimate truth

Pallas Athena, May 4, 2010.

Thus, I say to you, as spiritual students: Apply to my heart, apply to my Being. If you dare, if you dare to have your own inconsistencies, the fallacies of your beliefs, if you dare to have them exposed by the light of truth that I am. Apply to me. I am gentle, yet I am a living, breathing fire of truth. And the more you hold on to untruth, the more it will seem as if my fire is burning. But if you can let go of the untruth, then my fire will not burn.

It will instead lift you up into the heavens, where you suddenly find yourself above the human labyrinth, the human maze, the human miasma, the energy veil of Maya. You find yourself above it, that you may see the perspective you see through the eyes of Pallas Athena. You see with my perspective, and you suddenly cannot understand how you could ever have been so trapped in these philosophical systems, thinking that one of them had to be the ultimate truth, the ultimate way to heaven.

For is this not the lie: that you can follow an outer system that will guarantee your entry into heaven without having to look through the eyes of truth at your own being and the inconsistencies in your ego, and the lie that your conscious self has accepted that has served as the justification for walking away from the teacher—who also represented truth, be it Maitreya or another teacher in another mystery school in another realm.

For you see, it is not only the ego that keeps you away from oneness with truth. It is the decision you made to not go back to the teacher, as Maitreya explains in his book. There is always a decision that was not made by the ego, because the ego was made from the decision. The ego is an offspring of the decision, and the decision was made by the conscious self, the Conscious You. What folly to deny that you made that decision, for if you do not recognize that you – the core of your being, the very essence of your consciousness – made that decision, then how can you undo that decision? You cannot undo a decision through denial; only through recognition, through taking responsibility.

And thus, I admonish you: try me, try me as a guide to what is truth and untruth. And I will help you rightly divide the word of truth in your own being. And when you have divided the word of truth in your own being, then you might serve to divide the word of truth in the world and for other people. But until then, I caution you strongly not to focus on telling other people what they should be doing or what they should be believing, or what is wrong with the world. For this is another camouflage strategy of the ego, to take your attention away, to divert your attention from looking at the untruth in yourself by focusing on the untruth in others or the world.

Do you not see that there are many of the philosophies in the world that are deliberately created by the false teachers in order to fool the most spiritual people into thinking they have to focus on exposing or freeing people from the many untruths, and so that your attention is pulled into focusing on the many untruths in the world—and thereby conveniently forgetting to look at the untruth in yourself. This cannot lead to spiritual progress.

It can lead to the illusion of spiritual progress that comes from spiritual pride, because you think that by you being able to expose all these fallacies in the world, you are more sophisticated, you are more spiritual, than the people who believe in these fallacies. But it is not so; it is not so. You are, in fact, more trapped by your own ego than many of the people who believe in the false teachings but do not think they are that much better than others, as you think you are better than others for you can see all these fallacies.

Stop looking for the untruth outside yourself. Focus on the untruth in your own being. Apply to me to show you that untruth. And then, when you have gone through a period of seeing that untruth, then, when you are cleared of the untruth, you can stand naked before God, the God of Truth, the Goddess of Truth, and not feel ashamed in your nakedness. For you realize that your nakedness is a sign up your purity, a sign that you have been willing to purify your being of the artificial elements that have become an overlay that is hiding the true, spiritual individuality given to you by God before you descended into the material realm.

That purity, that pure, spiritual individuality, is still anchored in your I AM Presence, unchanged by anything that has happened to you, anything you have experienced, in the material universe. Yet your outer mind will never reconnect to that spiritual individuality, for your outer mind cannot see through the filter of duality, the filter of Maya. And thus, it will never be able to see that true individuality that is beyond duality, that is beyond the sense of identity created by both your conscious self and your ego after your conscious self decided to go into duality.

Thus, it is truly only the conscious self, the Conscious You, that can bridge the gap, that can dis-identify itself from the the worldly identity, so that it can project itself beyond the realm of Maya, the realm of duality, the material realm and realize that it is pure consciousness. And as pure consciousness, it can choose to be what it will be at any moment. No matter how elaborate a structure of a worldly identity that it has created over thousands of lifetimes, it can nevertheless choose at any moment to stop identifying itself with it, disentangle itself from this sense of identity and come back to that point of purity, where it once again recognizes and experiences itself as an extension of the pure Being of God, as pure consciousness that is not trapped in any lower sense of identity.

And at the moment your conscious self does experience itself as pure consciousness, it can then reach up and contact the individuality that is anchored in your I AM Presence. It can then contact the positive momentums that you have built in your causal body over many lifetimes. And that is when the Conscious You truly becomes the open door between that which is Above and that which is below. That is when you become the living Christ, who can then be the open door for the Spirit of Truth to flow into this world and truly challenge the untruth from a higher perspective of the Christ mind, rather than seeking to challenge or expose the untruths in the world from the level of the dualistic mind, where your challenge will only be from the duality consciousness. And therefore, it will be pitting one dualistic argument against another, which can never lead to a conclusive breakthrough, which can never lead to truly freeing people from the illusion of duality.

So, how do you want to spend the rest of this lifetime? Do you want to spend it squabbling with other people who are trapped in the duality consciousness? Or will you spend some time and effort to reconnect to the reality of your being, that you may be truly an open door for the Spirit of Truth. And so that I, Pallas Athena may thrust my Spear of Truth, first into your own being, where you are willing to let it expose anything in your being that is not truth. And then, when you are purified, the spear can be thrust through that open door into the world, where you can likewise bring forth a true challenge of the untruth.

This is the question I pose for you. If you are willing to take up my challenge, then be willing to walk right into my Spear of Truth, to let it enter your being, where at first it might be painful but then you will begin to feel how, as the Spear of Truth penetrates the veils of unreality in your being, you reconnect to something that is real. You start to feel liberated, you start to reconnect to the true joy of your being, that peaceful, blissful, bubbling joy that is God's own joy of expressing itself in form. And then, your life in the material world can also be an expression of joy, rather than you being burdened or trapped in a lesser sense of identity that sucks all joy out of your being.

For indeed, it is the illusion of the ages that your Spirit has to adapt itself to – or be limited by, or identify itself with – anything in the world of form. It is the illusion of the ages that anything in the world of form can have power over your Spirit. This is the illusion that all spiritual seekers must overcome, if they wish to manifest Christhood, rather than manifest the spiritual pride of thinking they are so advanced because they know this one true teaching and can see the fallacies of all other teachings.

So if you are willing to truly rise, then apply to me, Pallas Athena. Be willing to walk the 33 steps that I offer up in the true mystery school of the Goddess of Truth. Follow those 33 steps, as I will guide you at inner levels – and perhaps at some point even at outer levels – and then you will at one point arrive, where you have the complete non-attachment to changing or saving or battling other people. And instead, you are completely willing to be the open door for the Spirit of Truth to do its work through you, without you having to analyze or know ahead of time with the outer mind, without you having to feel that the Spirit of Truth has to conform to any structure in your mind.

My beloved, what does it take to be the open door, as Jesus said he was the open door? Well, is it not so that a door is open only when it is completely free and clear up any obstructions, any structures? And so begin by applying to me and be willing to examine and question the structures you have built in your mind, the structures that have entombed your Spirit temporarily in a prison from which the Conscious You will believe it cannot escape—until it fully and finally takes responsibility for itself and acknowledges that it was its own choices that caused it to feel entombed in matter—and that those choices can be undone in the blink of an eye.

I, Pallas Athena, await those who are willing to apply to me. I am the Goddess of Truth. Apply to me, if you will. And you will soon see what is the true vibration of the Goddess of Truth.

Can the Islamic world – starting with Turkey – be accelerated into the golden age consciousness?

Pallas Athena, May 5, 2010.

And thus, they were meant to see beyond the human idiosyncrasies of the Greek gods, to see that these were projections by the consciousness of men. But if you see beyond them, then you can indeed find something that will guide you beyond the veil of duality. But you must, of course, be willing to ask for that inner guidance, so that you may find those hidden secrets that can take you beyond, so that you can follow the epic journey described in the Odyssey, where Odysseus is truly the symbol for the spirit and its attempt to return to its kingdom, the kingdom lost when it decided to descend into duality.

And so, each and every one of the 6 billion people on this planet has a personal epic journey, but that journey is not a journey that is imposed upon you by external forces, whether it be the Greek gods or the superior God of Jehovah or Allah of whatever you may want to call it. It is a journey of your own making, for indeed, the stark reality behind all religion on Earth is that it objectifies God as some external being or beings, some external force that is forcing something upon you, whereas the essential truth, revealed in Maitreya's book, is that everything that you face in your current situation is the result of choices you made.

No one in heaven blames you for making the choices that have led you down the Primrose Path to your current situation and level of consciousness. The blame is a creation of the false teachers, but it is accepted by your ego because by accepting that you have done something that you cannot undo, you gain an excuse for maintaining the state of consciousness where you believe that you are judged by external forces and that your fate and your salvation depends on external forces and is prevented by external forces.

The reality of all true religion is that you are responsible for your state of consciousness, and that it is only your state of consciousness that keeps you outside of the kingdom of heaven. For the true kingdom of heaven is a state of consciousness—that is why Jesus said that the kingdom is within you. What is within you is your state of consciousness. You are the only authority that is responsible for it, but as Maitreya explains, there came a point where you decided you would not take that responsibility. And therefore, you turned your back upon the true teacher who was there to help you take responsibility for your path.

And in so doing, you had to justify that decision and make it seem like it was not a decision. For is it not so that the ultimate justification for turning away from the teacher is to make it seem like it was not you making the choice to turn away, but that you were forced by some punishment from this angry external God—and therefore you cannot bring yourself back by simply making a different decision. Nay, you must go through some epic journey and fulfill some external requirements defined by this external God, until you are again qualified and worthy to enter the kingdom of that God.

This is the difference between true religion and false religion. False religion will uphold the image of the external God, and the external requirements and the external path. This is the essence of false religion, whereas the true religion truly portrays the reality that the path is created by you, by the choices you have made as you journeyed away from that state of oneness that you were offered by the teacher. And therefore, the only way for you to get back to that state of oneness is that you take responsibility for your own state of consciousness, realize that it is a result of choices you made, and therefore begin to systematically unravel and undo the choices that brought you to your present position in the maze that has been created by human beings on this planet—and by the false teachers and by the egos.

You are the only one who can bring yourself back to the kingdom of God by realizing that the kingdom of God is within you and thus you have never left it. And all of these outer appearances are unreal and can be undone by you undoing the belief that they have any power over you. And thereby, you take complete command, you take back your power to change your decisions instantly, thereby bringing yourself back into oneness with the kingdom of God—in which you are also one with all life and therefore cannot indulge in the activities that can only be justified when you see yourself as a separate being, who is separate from all others. And therefore, you can uphold the illusion that you can harm another without harming yourself.

Entering the ascension spiral requires you to overcome the great projection game

Serapis Bey, June 11, 2010.

Serapis Bey I AM, and I come to discourse with you on some of the requirements for entering the ascension spiral that have not been well known and well understood, even among spiritual people or among Ascended Master students of previous dispensations.

Some of you are aware that I am called the "Hierarch of Luxor." For in the etheric plane corresponding with the physical location of the temple at Luxor in Egypt, I am the head of the Ascension Retreat. This is the retreat where people come, when they are almost ready to enter the ascension spiral. Thus, this retreat is not for newcomers on the spiritual path, it is not for beginners, it is not for kindergarten students.

Yet, there is a peculiar phenomenon that takes place at my retreat. And it is that there are indeed many of the students who need to go through a period that is almost like kindergarten. For when one sees how these students behave, one must wonder: "How did they ever graduate from kindergarten?" And this is a topic I wish to discourse on, for it is essential that those who are determined to enter the ascension spiral in this lifetime understand this concept.

It has been said in a previous dispensation that when students come to the Ascension Retreat, they are put into small groups with other people with whom they have conflicting astrology, karma, personality. Yet, not all students are put into these kindergarten groups, for those who have already overcome a certain tendency do not need to go through this initiation. So, who then are the students who are put into these groups? Well, they are the students who, although they have made progress on the spiritual path, have not yet clearly seen, understood or internalized one particular concept or necessity. And it is the necessity to overcome one of the more subtle games played by the ego, namely, the Great Projection Game, the game that causes you to project upon other people, or project upon the world, your own perception.

You see, it is entirely possible to be involved with spiritual teachings or spiritual organizations and to practice spiritual techniques for lifetimes and for decades in this lifetime. And although you make some progress, the big question is whether you come to the point of understanding the role that perception plays in your life. You see, the stark reality is that everything is perception.

What is the purpose of life? It is to expand your self-awareness. How do you expand self-awareness? By starting out with a localized, tightly-focused self-awareness, where you see yourself as a localized, individualized being—and then you expand that sense of self. But how does this expansion occur? It occurs truly by you expanding your perception, so that instead of seeing yourself as a localized being, you see yourself – eventually – as an omnipresent being, where you may say, as Mark Prophet said when he ascended, "I am everywhere in the consciousness of God."

Yet for you to expand that sense of self, you must know that the limited sense of self has no ultimate reality. It is only in your perception that you are limited, that you are localized. And thus, the process of rising towards Godhood is a process of truly overcoming the perception of being localized, giving up the perception of being a localized self, merging into the omnipresent self out of which the localized self is an extension. Yet, what happens – and what few have understood – is that when you begin to identify with a separate self – as opposed to a localized self – then your perception takes on a role of giving you a sense of identity.

You might compare this to the example given yesterday: that when you see yourself as a localized self, a localized being, it is as if you are looking at the world through your physical eyes. You will notice that your physical eyes are focused in a particular location in space. As this messenger is standing in this particular location, his eyes are looking at the material world from this vantage point. You, who are sitting in the audience facing the opposite way, are looking at the world from your individual vantage points. But as long as you realize that this is just one perspective and not the only possible or only true perspective, then you will not be fully identified with the localized view.

The Conscious You will know that it is simply looking at the material world through the binoculars of the physical body. Yet, when the Conscious You begins to identify itself as a separate being, then it forgets that it is simply looking through the perception of the body and the separate self. It now begins to feel completely convinced that that perception is not just one among many possible vantage points. No, it is somehow the ultimate one; it is reality. What the perception shows you is real. And thus you begin to feel that your perception is superior to the perception of others.

Yet, when you identify with the separate self, when you identify yourself as a separate being, there is an inevitable companion to that sense of self. And it is a very deep inner sense of aloneness. The separate self can be separate only by being set apart, being set apart from its source, being set apart from other people. And in that setting apart, there will inevitably be a sense of loneliness. This loneliness is the cosmic mirror's, the universe's, way of communicating that you have stepped into a separate self, that you have stepped away from oneness. Therefore it is, so to speak, a safety line, that – if you grasp it and are willing to look at it – then you can use the loneliness to actually climb back towards oneness. It is your lifeline that you can follow back to your source.

Yet, many lifestreams decide that they are not willing to look at the loneliness. They are not willing to acknowledge it, so they seek to cover it over by building a sense of superiority, a sense of being right. This is what was spoken about yesterday, that happened in that first sphere, where beings fell. Those that were mentioned as the ones who had set themselves up as leaders – and who had been allowed to have the experience of being leaders – those were indeed the ones who had refused to look at the loneliness and go into and through the loneliness—and who had sought to cover it over by establishing the sense of superiority. They were given the experience of being leaders for a time, that they might have an opportunity to experience being a leader, experience being superior, in the hope that they would have enough of that experience before their sphere was ready to ascend, before a critical mass of other lifestreams had chosen to go through the loneliness into oneness and thus had formed the magnet for their sphere ascending.

For, you see, you have a right to have any experience you want. You, as a separate being, have a right to have any experience you want. But you do not have the right to demand that all other beings in your sphere, on your planet, in your group, in your spiritual organization, in your family or in your relationship should follow you indefinitely into your experience. Yet, even though you do not have this right, can you see that those who build the sense of superiority come to believe that they do have this right, they do have the right to demand and expect that other people will follow them and will continue to follow them—and thereby validate their choice to go into the never-ending quest of building and maintaining the sense of superiority?

And so, what you see from this is that in that distant sphere, you did indeed have a group of beings who had been allowed to be in leadership positions and who had not been able to become the servants of all, but who were still the servants of the separate self. And they now had the perception that they were superior to those beings who were below them and who were blindly following them. Yet, this perception was, of course, unreal. It was a mental prison that kept these beings trapped in the sense of separation, which prevented them from ascending with the rest of their sphere. So, what to do to help such beings?

Well, it was determined that only the beings who had superiority had the chance of helping each other get over the superiority. You see, many of these beings had managed to isolate themselves from each other, so that they rarely met or rarely clashed. They were either separated or they had established a hierarchical order where "if you do not challenge me, I do not challenge you," and therefore they could co-exist in an uneasy peace that was not the true peace of oneness. It was a manufactured peace, an artificial peace, that was, of course, not peace at all.

And this is something you see on Earth in many cases as well among those who are part of the power elite and are not in open confrontation, because they have found some kind of equilibrium that prevents that confrontation. Yet, what was determined in that distant sphere was to break this artificial stalemate by forcing, so to speak, these beings to come together in a closed environment, where they could not run away from each other and therefore inevitably would clash. And in acting out their momentums of superiority and insensitivity to life – their momentums of seeking to force others into compliance – well then instead of being able to force each other into compliance as they could do with those below them, they could perhaps awaken each other to the futility of continuing this game of projecting your perception upon other beings with free will—who therefore have a right to grow without being burdened by the projection of your perception of how they should live and how they should grow or not grow.

This, then, is a situation that has been enacted many times throughout the spheres, many times in this sphere, on this planet. This is precisely the environment that is re-created at the Ascension Retreat. Those who have not yet overcome the projection game, those who have not yet realized that their perception is what holds them back from entering the ascension spiral, they are put into groups. And what clashes is not truly the outer personality, nor their karma, nor their astrology. For their outer personality, their karma and their astrology are not the causes, they are the effects of the perception of these beings.

Do you understand? There is the old saying "Do not put the cart before the horse." Do not confuse cause and effect, as many people do when you are in a limited perception. You think your astrology or your karma is the reason why you are behaving the way you are doing. But the reality is that the reason why you are behaving the way you are behaving is your perception. And your perception is the result of the choices you made, long ago, to go into the separate self, to refuse to question why you felt lonely as a separate self—and that perhaps this loneliness was a sign that there was something about the separate self you needed to question, namely why you perceive yourself as a separate self in the first place.

And so, the reality here is that what has caused all human beings, all co-creators, all self-aware beings to go into a negative spiral is indeed perception. And the only way to break this spiral is to come to the point where you are willing to question your perception.

Now, you may have heard from a previous dispensation that at the Ascension Retreat, these souls will stay in these groups until they have realized that harmony is more important than being right or feeling superior. This is not incorrect but it is not the full story. For what does it take for you to realize that harmony is more important than being right? It takes that you are willing to question your perception. For it is your perception that sets you apart from others, that seemingly creates this conflict and confrontation with others. Because you perceive their differences as a threat to the sense of equilibrium you have inside yourself, the sense of equilibrium that has enabled you to ignore your sense of loneliness, your sense that your separate self is superior and therefore even the sense that the loneliness is justified.

For as they say, "It is lonely at the top." And surely the one that is ultimately superior to others has no peers and therefore must feel alone—so is the justification of the ego of those people who have allowed themselves to feel superior to others. When you feel superior, you cannot relate to other people on the same level. You can relate only when you feel superior to them and when they validate your sense of superiority. And therefore, those who will not validate that – because they know they are sons and daughters of God and therefore refuse to feel inferior to you – well those people become a threat to you, so you have to ban them from your circle of influence so that you can maintain that fragile equilibrium of superiority.

...

Thus, the bottom line here is this: you will not enter the ascension spiral as long as you are not willing to question your perception. For you see, what is the ascension? The ascension is a reunion with your real Self. Do you understand, my beloved, that the Conscious You has the ability to project itself anywhere it desires? This is a form of projection, where you project yourself into a particular state of consciousness or into a physical body, in order to see the world from that vantage point. This is legitimate projection. But what happens is that when you then become identified with the perception of that limited vantage point, you create a false projection, where you now project that the perception from that limited vantage point is not limited but is somehow superior, absolute, all-encompassing.

So there are two aspects of projection. And when you begin to elevate the limited perception and project it onto the world, then you cannot at the same time realize that your perception is the result of you, the Conscious You, projecting yourself into a limited state. And therefore, you cannot project yourself back to the unlimited state. Do you see that when you are identified as a separate self, you can come to know the spiritual path, you can come to understand that you have a Higher Self, you can come to understand – theoretically and intellectually – that you need to ascend by re-uniting with that Higher Self. But you still see this as an exterior process, you still see this as a process that needs to happen according to your perception. You are still projecting an image upon your Higher Self. But do you see that you cannot re-unite with your Higher Self as long as you maintain any graven image of your Higher Self. It cannot be done.

So what I am saying here is this: the ascension is a process whereby you overcome all perception and come to a point where you are no longer perceiving reality. What do I mean?

What have I been saying? When you project the conscious self into a limited vantage point, you see the world through the perception of that limited view. Perception is per definition limited to a specific vantage point. You cannot perceive unless you are perceiving through some instrument, be it your physical eyes or a binocular or some other instrument. You are perceiving through something. When you are not perceiving, it does not mean that you lose awareness, but now your awareness is omnipresent. It is not limited by a specific viewpoint.

You are everywhere in the consciousness of God, instead of being in one place in the consciousness of God, seeing the world from there. Now when you transcend perception, you experience through oneness, you have a spherical awareness, and thus you cannot see yourself as a separate self that is somehow merging with a Higher Self. You realize that you ARE the Higher Self, you always were the Higher Self. It was only your perception that made it seem like you were separated from that self. It is all perception.

So do you then see why the souls who have not been willing to acknowledge the role of perception, who have not been willing to question their own perception – but who are still in the game of projecting that perception upon others, upon God, upon the world – well they cannot enter the ascension spiral. And thus, they must enter the kindergarten class, as we call it at the Ascension Retreat. And they must stay there until they begin to question perception, until they come to the point of saying, "I no longer want to project my perception upon reality. I want to experience reality by becoming one with it. I do not want to perceive reality, I want to know by going into gnosis with reality, by being one with reality."

But in order to go through that, you have to come to a point where you consciously and deliberately decide that you will stop projecting anything, any opinion, upon other people. You will stop judging, analyzing, feeling that you have to evaluate whether they are doing right or wrong according to your perception, which you have elevated to some ultimate system.

Look at yourselves honestly, for this is a measure I give you. This cannot be done in an instant but it can be done in a relatively short period of time. If you are willing, you can come to see how much you project upon other people, how much you project upon the world, how much you project upon God—and ultimately how much you project upon yourself. And when you see that everything you project limits you because it prevents you from experiencing oneness, well then you can very quickly come to the awareness where you simply, in an instant, see and experience the contrast between reality and the perceived "reality."

You see, as was expressed in the Bible: "the vanity of vanities, all is vanity." You see that everything that is perceived is vanity, for it is unreal, it is pointless, it is inconsequential, it makes no difference. For whatever you project upon the world will not change the world, it will only change your perception of the world.

As has already been said, the Earth was still round when most people projected the image that it was flat. Your perception will not change reality, it will only change your perceived "reality." And it is when you see this that the scales can fall from your eyes, as happened to Saint Paul on the road to Damascus, when he finally acknowledged the Christ light. This was not an outer experience, where Jesus appeared to him in some undeniable manifestation, for Jesus had appeared to Paul at inner levels many times. But it was an inner experience where Paul finally acknowledged the difference between his perception of Christians and the reality of what Jesus stood for. That was the encounter with reality that made the scales fall from his eyes, the "scales" of perception that had covered his eyes and prevented him from experiencing reality.

This can happen to anyone who is willing. It may not happen in one dramatic moment; most of you will experience it as a gradual process. Most of you have already experienced this in glimpses, in a more mild form. But by becoming aware of the process and the need to go beyond perception, you can accelerate your growth tremendously. You can experience a growth that is far quicker than anything you have dreamt of so far.

...

For do you see that when you are in the projection game, you cannot take responsibility for yourself, you must project that it is someone else who is the cause of your misery, someone else who is the cause of what seems to threaten your society, or your position as a spiritual leader, or your relationships with other people. If you project out that it is other people or dark forces that are the cause of what is happening in your life, then you are demonstrating that you are not taking responsibility. And with not taking responsibility, I mean that you are not willing to acknowledge the reality that everything in your life is a reflection coming back from the cosmic mirror of what you are projecting out. And what you are projecting out is a result of the way you look at life. It is the result of your perception of life.

Thus, for anything to change for the better, you must begin by questioning your perception. The cart cannot be put in front of the horse—if you want progress. If the cart is in front of the horse, then the horse will have to go backwards. This is the law of physics that you cannot change regardless of your perception and your projection. Thus, if you wish to make greater progress on the spiritual path, if you wish to enter the ascension spiral, stop projecting. Acknowledge when you are projecting. Look at yourself, look at the perception that causes you to feel you have to project out. And realize that the true goal is to come to the point where you have transcended perception and therefore have no need to project.

Do you honestly believe that Jesus Christ, when he walked the Earth, projected through the human ego and the separate self? Do you believe that when Gautama sat under the Bo tree and was tempted by the demons of Mara, do you believe that he was projecting images from the separate self onto those demons? For had Gautama projected such images, then the demons would have had something in him that they could use to tempt him into a reaction.

For you see, the projection is a reaction, the projection is an attachment. And as long as you react and have attachments to anything in this world, you cannot ascend, as was explained. You cannot walk through that door into the ascended state as long as you have any attachment on Earth. And as long as you have an attachment, you will feel a need to project an image onto the world that justifies your attachment, that justifies why you do not have to give up that attachment. It cannot be any other way.

Do you understand that what I am giving you here is reality, a dose of reality? It is not something that can be debated or argued against. Those who are identified with their perception will see this as just a concept. They will argue against it. They might even argue that it is a false teaching because it contradicts this or that said elsewhere. But in their arguing against it, they only prove that they are trapped in the projection game. And as long as you are trapped in the projection game, you must remain in the kindergarten classroom. And you will not go further into the Ascension Retreat no matter how advanced you think you are.

You see, my beloved, the first person who is deceived by your perception and your projection is you. You think it is real, and thus you think that you can project this upon Serapis Bey when you come to my retreat, and I am going to go into your bubble of perception and say, "Surely, you are an advanced being, come to the very heart of the Ascension Retreat." But you see, it is not so. I have risen above the projection game, and because I have been willing to see it in myself, I can easily see it in anyone else.

There is nothing that can fool me into allowing you to go on in my retreat until I know you are ready to go on. You will not move into the retreat itself until you have passed the initiations in the kindergarten classroom. You can sit there, my beloved, and feel advanced, but you are still like one of the students that can barely feed themselves without messing up their clothes, and thus you will not command my respect. For I have respect for the real you, not the projected you that you have created.

The beginning of wisdom is when you recognize a simple fact. God does not look at the world through your perception. The Ascended Masters do not look at the world through your perception. Your I AM Presence does not look at the world through your perception. You will not change us, no matter what you project out. Therefore, your only option – if you will to make progress – is to change yourself. Seeking to change all other people will not change us. You might change every human being on Earth and make them agree with you, but it will only mean that all human beings on Earth will remain outside the ascension spiral until they change their perception. You cannot force your way into Heaven. It is not possible. I could say this a million more times. But I trust that I have said enough that some will understand.

Projection is the bane of the fallen consciousness, it is the one thing that, more than anything else, prevents the manifestation of a Golden Age. For why do you not have a Golden Age? Because you are projecting images upon the Ma-ter light that are based on the separate self and its perception. How can you manifest the Golden Age? Transcend the perception until you see the images based on Oneness and then project those images. Or rather, realize what I have explained: that there is a way to transcend perception and the need to project anything.

For you see, when you do indeed transcend the entire projection game, it does not mean that you become as nothing, it does not mean that you are now a pacifist who sits in a cave in the Himalayas. You can still go out and take active part in society, but you are not doing it by projecting your perception of the separate self. You are doing it by being the open door for the perception of your I AM Presence, the vision of your I AM Presence and the light of your I AM Presence to stream through you. And this is true co-creation. You are not creating a mental image and projecting the light through that image. Your Conscious Self has no image that stands between it and the I AM Presence. You are the open door, a clear pane of glass.

But what you do do is, you focus your attention. So, you are in physical embodiment. You focus your attention in a particular location, on a particular problem or issue. You do not project an image upon it of what should happen or what is wrong. You simply focus your attention, and then you allow the light and the vision of the I AM Presence to flow through you, flow into the situation and perform whatever changes can be performed according to the Law of Free Will and the higher vision.

Do you see the essential difference between projecting and simply focusing attention, experiencing in a neutral non-attached way? You are not projecting. You are simply being the clear pane of glass that provides the frame of reference. This is what you saw when Jesus encountered and challenged the scribes and the Pharisees. He did not project, he simply allowed the light of God to flow through him and challenge their perception.

This is your ultimate role as well. We are not seeking to raise up an army of people who think they have the infallible truth and will go out there and do battle with all those who perceive the world differently and therefore have a different mental image. We are seeking to raise up the Christed ones who acknowledge that they are here to be the open door, that there is nothing to project.

There is no point, as this messenger realized years ago, of even formulating opinions. You simply focus your attention on a particular issue, then you tune in to your I AM Presence. And then, instead of having an opinion based on perception and a mental image, you sense the difference between the outer situation – the vibration of the consciousness behind that outer situation – and the vibration of your I AM Presence. And in simply sensing that difference, you know reality.

Let the cosmic wrecking ball shatter the structures that limit your Spirit

Kuan Yin, June 12, 2010.

So what you see is that the fallen angels have attempted to create a system that denies christhood, and therefore denies true individuality, but it does not deny the false individuality that comes through the ego. For it raises up the ego of certain beings to the status of a god, so that their word cannot be gainsaid, as you see in every dictator throughout the world, even in those who had risen to some power in the communist system. Even though in the communist system no individual had ultimate power, for the system itself would – at least in the time after Stalin – have power even over the supreme leader of the system.

And this, then, is a lesson to be learned. For indeed, when you create such a system, you may think that you have power over the system, but in reality, the system begins to own you as well. For the system will see any individual only as a tool to its survival, and therefore it has no room for the individuals who will not go along with the system.

...

So forgive yourselves and forgive others, and realize that what you have witnessed was a lesson for humankind, a lesson in how consciousness co-creates physical reality. And then, what you create can limit your imagination so you cannot free yourself from your own creation. In other words, when you co-create from the consciousness of separation, the consciousness of duality, you will become a slave of your own creation, as the monster created by Doctor Frankenstein turned upon him and destroyed him. This is the ancient story of the ego and what is created through the consciousness of the ego.

Imagination, acceptance, oneness: A new formula for alchemy in the Golden Age

Saint Germain, June 12, 2010.

Do you see, as Kuan Yin attempted to explain, that what was attempted in the Soviet Union was indeed to destroy the potential that someone would make this kind of unpredictable choice, this kind of creative choice. The fallen beings behind the creation of communism, especially Soviet communism, wanted to destroy individuality and creativity, so that nothing could overthrow and overturn the system, so that the system, like a machine, would keep grinding away into the distant future. They attempted to create a system that was immortal, just as individuals attempt to make their egos immortal.

This was an attempt to do on Earth what only God can do. For only God can make things permanent, and yet, that permanence cannot be manifest in the material realm, in the world of form, but only in the world beyond the material, in the ascended realm. And yet, even then things are not permanent, for they are constantly ascending, transcending themselves.

So you see, the attempt to create something permanent on Earth is the ultimate dream of the fallen beings. For they think that if they could manage to create this system that could not be overthrown – but would keep sustaining itself – then they would have created, they think, a viable alternative to God's creation. This is their logic. It is, of course, not the Christ logic, for in the Christ logic you know that nothing in the world of form can be permanent. Nevertheless, this is what they believe in their duality consciousness, in their sense of separation from the reality of God, but they cannot fathom the reality that even God is transcending itself. And therefore, they think that God is permanent. And they think that it is possible to create something in this world that is permanent, because they think that they have created a permanent graven image of God that can be maintained.

So then, what is the deeper reality? How do you break out of this closed system of the separate self? How do you become free? Well, only by realizing that you are a formless being—that therefore cannot be trapped in, cannot be limited by, any form whatsoever. For you are more than any form in this world, and therefore, you cannot be bound by any form. And therefore, no matter that you have grown up in a repressive system, such as Soviet communism – that has hammered into your mind and being that you are nothing but a material being, that you have come from dust, that you will return to dust – no matter all of this propaganda, all of this brainwashing, nevertheless, you are the Conscious You. And you can at any moment leave behind that limited sense of identity, for you have not become that identity. You have only projected your being into it, so that you look at the world through the filter of that identity.

But when you realize that you have only projected yourself into it, then you realize you can also withdraw your being from it and therefore return to that pure awareness, that pure state of consciousness that you are, that is beyond any form. And when you realize, when you re-align your attention, your focus with that formless reality, that formless pure consciousness, then you are free of that form, that form-based sense of self. Nevertheless, that does not mean that you are one with freedom. And thus, I wish to discourse with you about the possibility that you can become a representative, an example, of the Freedom Flame on Earth, that you might bring into society the Freedom Flame. So that you can give people a frame of reference, that they may see and experience that it is possible for a human being to be truly free while still expressing itself through a physical body.

For you realize, of course, that the physical body is not the same as a separate sense of identity. It is possible to be in a physical body – or rather to express yourself through a physical body – without being blinded by the illusion of duality and separation. This is what Jesus demonstrated, this is what Gautama and other spiritual teachers have demonstrated, including myself when I was given the dispensation of appearing as the Wonderman of Europe, where I took on the physical body but was not strictly speaking in physical embodiment.

So, this is then one of the ultimate forms of service you can give on this planet, that is, to withdraw your sense of identity from the dualistic identity, the separate self, to first come to the point where you know you are the formless self. Where, as Serapis Bey spoke about, you have no opinions, you have no need to project anything, you are not evaluating things in terms of good or bad, right or wrong. You are simply experiencing things as they are without any judgment, without any analysis, without any evaluation. You are just observing and focusing your consciousness.

Yet, you can then take the next step. You can take the step of becoming one with one of the flames of God, be it the Flame of Freedom or another flame, as is your individual choice, and according to your I Am Presence and the lineage out of which you have come. So you see, my beloved, I, Saint Germain, do not desire to come back into physical embodiment, or even to take on a physical body. For I desire YOU to be the embodiments of the Freedom Flame that I AM—those of you who feel this calling. And thus, this is indeed my thrust: to help you awaken to the reality that when you know you are a conscious self that is beyond form, you can then project yourself into the Freedom Flame that I AM. You can become one with that Freedom Flame, to the point where you become that Freedom Flame in embodiment. And therefore, in a very real sense you become Saint Germain in embodiment, although you still retain your individuality, but you are an extension of myself in embodiment. And that is when you become the ultimate example of freedom to the people on Earth.

...

Of course, for you to embody that Freedom Flame, you must do what other Masters have said before me. You must take a look at yourself, you must take a look at the structures in your mind. And then you must use the cosmic wrecking ball to shatter those structures, so that you can be free of the structures—for only then can you be Freedom in embodiment.

How did I become one with the Flame of Freedom? By systematically looking at the structures in my mind, seeing how they imprisoned my Spirit in a form that I thought I could not go beyond. And then, when I noticed such a structure, I would look at it with absolute honesty and determination, until I understood the belief that made me create that structure and that made me maintain it—thinking it was somehow permanent, inevitable, had power over me or that I needed it for some reason or another.

You are a god-free being. The Conscious You is a god-free being. You need no structure. You do not need a structure in order to define your identity, for you have the ability to project yourself up to the I

Am Presence and know your divine identity, your divine individuality. Neither do you have need of a structure in order to express yourself in the material world. For again, you can do what Jesus described in the Basilica of Saint Peter's: you can be in tune with the I AM Presence and allow the I Am Presence to express itself through you without knowing ahead of time what will be done.

Do you see that it is only the ego that forms the structure of what you should do or what you should not do. It is only the ego that makes you feel the need to follow some outer religious teaching, whereby you can say that if I do what this religion says, or if I do what this ascended master teaching says, then I am always good, then I am always right. And then, one day God will simply have to accept me into heaven, even though I have actually not only maintained the structures I had before I found the path, I have actually built this elaborate structure of how good and spiritual I am and how much I know, and how much I understand about the spiritual path, and how I can recite this or that teaching endlessly without seeing that the Spirit is not in the teaching, the Spirit is beyond the teaching.

...

Dare to be the Christed beings. Dare to envision, imagine and accept that you can manifest a high degree of Christhood in this lifetime. It is not an impossible goal, for those of you who are here, those of you who have gone through the initiations in Christhood that you have experienced over the past year and even beyond. For many of you have experienced throughout your lives these Christhood initiations. Do not deny your attainment.

I am not talking about being unrealistic, for many of you are able – if you are willing – to look at the difference between the pride of the ego and a realistic self-assessment. For do you understand that if you deny the attainment you have at inner levels – because your outer mind cannot accept it – then you are denying your Christhood. And that is not what will help me manifest the Golden Age.

I need those who are not jumping the gun and thinking they have Christhood before they have seen the ego. I am looking for those who will have a realistic assessment of their attainment and who will not deny it. I am not saying you have to go out and proclaim to the world: "I Am the Christ." I am just saying you need to acknowledge it in yourself, so you are not afraid to express that Christhood in whatever situations you encounter.

The choice is yours: increased resistance or increased transcendence

Gautama Buddha, January 1, 2011

The driving force is the transcendence of consciousness
And so, you see, what can make this possible is indeed the transcendence of consciousness, the acceleration of consciousness, whereby you let go of the old sense of identity that was at a certain level of density. And when this happens on a collective scale – by all of humankind raising the collective consciousness – then the entire planet will become less dense. And therefore, it can move through space at an ever accelerated pace without the application of greater and greater force.

And this will indeed bring about a revolution, not only in human thought but in society as a whole. Where you will see that you will no longer need this force, this physical, mental, emotional force to keep the old structures alive. For they will be replaced, not by new structures but by the willingness to flow with the stream of life. So that you do not seek to encage and incase the stream of light in your structure in order to give you a sense of permanence, of continuity. For you do not gain any longer your sense of identity from the structure, you gain it from seeing beyond structure, beyond even the structure of the Earth itself.

For you now see that you are an expression of the stream of consciousness. You are flowing with that stream of consciousness, and when you no longer feel like you are drowning in the stream, what is the need to hold on to a structure? Why would you seek to hold on to the banks or seek to grasp for a life-belt, if you are not afraid of drowning?

For you know that it is indeed your greatest joy to flow with the River of Life, to flow with the stream itself, to just let go and be at peace in the flow of life, rather than resisting it, rather than seeking to force it to fit into your mental boxes, to fit into the mental box created by your perception. The perception that comes from the ego, the separate self, that is afraid that at some point in time it will cease to exist.

For this is indeed the price you pay for falling behind the acceleration rate of the universe. The moment you start lagging behind the rest of the universe, there will be a gap. And this gap is what gives rise to the fear of death. The fear that there will come a point where you, as a self-aware being, are no more.

But this fear can exist only because the self-aware being that you are is now perceiving life through the filter – the structure, the perception – of the ego, rather than perceiving life through the pure awareness that you can attain when you recognize yourself as the Conscious You, as an expression of the Creator's own Being. And thus, as the Conscious You, you see yourself as the open door, as the clear pane of glass, as Jesus has so carefully explained.

And you know that the stream of life, the stream of consciousness that is your I AM Presence can flow through you unhindered, effortlessly. And thus, you do not need to exert a force to uphold the illusory existence of the separate self. For you can flow effortlessly with the stream of consciousness that is your I AM Presence, seeking expression through you.

Overcoming resistance

What is the need for force, what is the need for resistance when you recognize who you are: the open door for the I AM Presence. And you accept this, and you flow with the stream of consciousness that is the Presence, that flows through your being. And instead of hearing the roaring of the stream as a threatening noise – that you feel might one day overwhelm you and drown you – you are now flowing with that stream. And thus, you hear that it is not a roar that threatens to destroy; it is indeed the gently flowing, bubbling stream of the bliss of the Creator being expressed through you.

And thus, you would experience that bliss by simply letting go of the sense that there is anything you need to resist—or anything you need to uphold, or anything you need to destroy. It is indeed the sense that matter has reality, that matter has permanence, that trips you up, that prevents you from flowing with the stream. For you think that you need to look at matter and either accept that matter in its current form is permanent and thus has power over you. Or you need to accept that matter in its current form is wrong and thus must be changed or destroyed by you. And thus, you are here to save the world or to the destroy evil, and either way this requires you to change something outside yourself. And this is what gives rise to the dramas and the epic mindset that we have talked about now for two years.

...

Understanding the reality of time and space

What is time? What is it that time has done? What is it that the veil of matter has done, the veil of Maya has done? Well, as Jesus has explained in his latest discourse, everything – everything – follows the law of free will. What did the fallen beings say when they rebelled against God? They said: "We demand to have a place where we can feel separated from God and the stream of consciousness that is God, that is the rest of our sphere." And so, in order to give them that, there had to be created a world where there was the illusion that matter is real, that matter hides Spirit and that time exists. So that it is possible to postpone self-transcendence and uphold your current sense of self for a period of time.

When you separated yourself from the guru, when you refused to define your own role – as Jesus has explained – when you hid from Maitreya, you demanded the same as the fallen beings demanded: a place where you could believe that you were separated from the teacher, separated from your source. A place where you could believe that you could uphold your current sense of self for a length of time. This is what you demanded—not consciously, but in order to make the choices you made, you subconsciously demanded this.

If this is the way you want to continue to exist, then I, the Buddha – as all members of the Ascended Host – bow to your free will. I accept that choice, but I also say – as I said last year at new years – then you are not ready to be in the Sangha of the Buddha. And thus, I have nothing further to offer you.

I have something to offer only to those who have come to the point, where they are willing to begin to question their previous choices, their current sense of identity, their current perceptions. Those who are willing to say: "I no longer want the space where I can believe I am apart. I no longer want to uphold my current identity into the future for a period of time. I want to transcend my current identity and come closer to oneness with my source. This is my desire, this is my choice and I am willing to take responsibility for the fact that I am the one who must choose. And I am the one who must be willing to let the Wheel of the Dharma roll back that veil of illusion that has allowed me to uphold the sense of separateness, the sense of a separate self that can exist in time, or that can even exist at all.

Time is Mother; space is Buddha. Do you see that the Mother in her love allows the children to uphold the illusion that they can create something – a separate self, a form of life on a planet – and that that something can endure over time? Even the illusion that the separate self could gain some sense of permanence or immortality or be accepted into the kingdom of God. This is the illusion that the Mother allows you to uphold, so that you can experience it until you have had enough of the experience and is ready to make the choice to transcend it.

Yet on an even deeper level, how can you have the illusion that the matter world is separated from Spirit or that there is no Spirit? What allows this illusion to exist? It is the fact that the Buddha holds the balance for you. The Buddha holds the balance for space, the space between where you are now and where you would have been if you had followed the background acceleration rate of the world in which you live.

It is the Buddha consciousness that allows this to happen, again so that you may have the experience of separation until you have had enough of it. And then you desire and decide that you are willing to let it die, to let that illusory sense of self die, that you may catch up to where you could have been had you accelerated at the same rate as the rest of the universe—as indeed the Buddha has done.

But he has allowed himself to be put in between, that he might fill the space between where you are and where you could have been. Only the Buddha's love allows that space to exist. And if the space had not existed, you would either have had to follow the acceleration rate or cease to exist in the second death. And thus, the Buddha creating space is the background for the Mother giving you the illusion of time. Time truly is not.

Space is not real in the sense that the space between where you are and where you could have been is not real. But the deeper reality is that space is indeed real, as that is what allows forms to exist and what also allows them to transcend by moving closer and closer to the ultimate acceleration rate that will cause your entire sphere to ascend and become a permanent part of the spiritual realm.

Beginning to understand Hatred of the Mother

Mother Mary, January 1, 2011

And when you dare to express yourself freely, you will be able to also let other people express themselves freely. And therefore, you will begin to look at others and their diversity – their differences, their creativity – in a different way. Where you no longer look at it as a threat, where you no longer need to go through his constant, relativistic evaluation: "Is this person better than me, are they bringing forth something that I could not bring forth, will people like them more than they like me, will God love that person more than he loves me?" And all of these subtle evaluations, that you might not have been conscious of, but that nevertheless are there, running in the background, almost like this music, called Muzak, that you had in many factories or offices or stores some time ago. The music that is meant to be there without truly being noticed.

Understanding the cosmic mirror

And this is exactly how the ego and the fallen beings would like to insert themselves into your consciousness, so that they are constantly running in the background, constantly affecting your state of mind, but doing it in such a subtle way that you do not actually notice. Because there is nothing that suddenly jolts you awake and makes you realize that this noise, this background noise, is not natural and you do not want it anymore. Thus, there are people who have lived their entire lives with this background noise of the ego, constantly judging, constantly evaluating, based on a standard that they are not even aware of, that they have not created, that is truly the standard of the fallen beings, adapted to their particular society or culture or even family background.

This is one of the things that will be challenged in the year of the mother, these subtle, almost unconscious, judgments, beliefs, world views that people have accumulated individually and collectively for years, for decades, for centuries, for millennia. They will all be challenged by the Wheel of the Dharma hurled by the Buddha. And they will be challenged by the mirror of the Mother, who will mirror back to people more and more extreme expressions of what they are projecting into the cosmic mirror.

For indeed, what is it that the Mother has vowed to do? You may think that matter has vowed to give birth to your expression, to your physical body, to a planet. And while this may be so, you need to realize that there is a reason why matter has done this. It is not, as some of you may think, to allow you to create and do whatever you want. For free will, the Law of Free Will, does not exist alone. It exists in a polarity with the law that says that you will reap as you sow. You will be able to create anything you want, but you will also be required by the law to experience your own creation.

And so, matter does – as the Alpha aspect – allow you to create any mental image you want and to project that image upon the Ma-ter light. But as the Omega aspect, matter will also require that you experience what you project onto the Ma-ter light, as it is then outpictured in a physical form that you cannot escape. And this is what we have called the cosmic mirror, which through this outpicturing of your thoughts in physical form mirrors back to you what you are projecting out in the form of mental images, charged with the emotions that set the energy in motion.

And so, what is then hatred of the Mother? Well, it is indeed when you are not willing to acknowledge that what you are experiencing in the matter plane is a reflection of what exists in your own mind and that you have projected out. And thus, by not being willing to take responsibility for yourself, you project that it is matter that has created these conditions. Or it is other people who have created these conditions. Or it is the devil who has created these conditions. Or it is God who has created these conditions.

And now you begin to resent, to resist and to hate this external force, which is forcing these conditions upon you—for so you think. Yet the reality that we have attempted to explain – now for years and especially for these last couple of years with our talk about the dramas and the epic consciousness – is that what you experience in matter is not created by an external force. It is all a creation of consciousness.

Why people do not get what they say they want
When you flow with the River of Life, you are constantly projecting images that have transcended themselves and become more. And thus, the Mother reflects back abundance and nurturance. Yet when you are seeking to continue to project the same image over and over again, then the Mother also gives you back what you are projecting out. Only it is not exactly what you are projecting, as you see it in your mind.

For you see, when you are flowing with the River of Life, you do not have a mental image of what you want reality to be. Why would you have a mental image, when you are constantly transcending yourself? What is the point of having a mental image that you see as fixed, as graven, as permanent? You truly are not holding a mental image in the outer mind; you are allowing the Presence to express itself through you. And thus, the image that is being projected through the clear pane of glass of the Conscious You is not held in the outer mind, is not created in the outer mind. It is created at the level of the Presence and projected from there.

And thus you, as Jesus said in Saint Peter's, are not having a structure in your mind that you are seeking to uphold. You are allowing the Presence to express itself through you, and you are experiencing it as it is being expressed. And thus, there was no need to uphold a mental image of the world or a mental image of a separate self, that you are seeking to maintain over time. You have become as the little child, as Jesus said, for whom every new day is a new discovery, a new unfoldment of ever greater joy.

And so, it is only when you separate yourself from the flow of the River of Life that you now begin to experience the world through a mental image, created in the outer mind. And thus, you are thinking that you are projecting onto the mater light what you see from inside the separate self. But the reality, that so few spiritual seekers have understood, is that what you are seeing from inside the separate self, from inside the role, is not what you are projecting into the cosmic mirror.

My beloved, I am perfectly aware that the teachings we have given up until this point can lead some people to ask the question: "Why is it that I am seeking to project a positive image but I do not get the positive circumstances back that I envision?" Well, the reason is that you have not begun to question your perception and realize that there is a difference between what you see – what you perceive – with the conscious mind from inside your role and what you are actually projecting into the cosmic mirror through the filter of that role—much of which is below the level of conscious awareness.

Do you see that you might be thinking – as many of you have done – that at the conscious level you have adopted a positive mental attitude and you are projecting thoughts of abundance into the cosmic mirror. And then, you do this on a daily basis, and after a certain amount of days has passed, you are wondering why the universe is not showering you with abundance, as the many false or superficial teachers out there in the world are promising you will happen—if only you follow their program, their quick-fix, their guaranteed path to salvation.

The role of the subconscious mind

Yet the reality is that even though you may be projecting with the conscious mind, the conscious mind is like the tip of an iceberg. And below the threshold of conscious awareness, you do not have a positive mental attitude. For I can tell you that the ego, the separate self, can never have a positive mental attitude. For the ego can never escape the fear of death, and when you have the fear of death at subconscious levels, you will be projecting out the fear of death, the fear of lack, the fear of loss. And thus, how can you receive back what you are projecting out with the conscious level of your mind, when you have not taken responsibility for the subconscious levels?

Do you not see, my beloved, as we have now explained, when you decided to hide from your cosmic teacher, you could do this only by deciding that there was something in your own consciousness that you are not willing to look at. For you were not willing to project yourself into oneness with the teacher, so that you could see your own mind – the images in your mind – the way the teacher sees them. You decided to maintain these images, and therefore you did not want the teacher to show you their unreality.

And yet in making this decision of wanting to hide these mental images from the teacher, what did you do? Well, you also had to hide them from yourself, and this is what created some of the subconscious levels of the mind. You forced certain mental images below the threshold of conscious awareness, a threshold that was not there while you were still willing to be in oneness with the teacher. And so, that is why there is a gap between what you are perceiving and projecting out with the conscious mind and what is being reflected back to you from the cosmic mirror.

And do you not see that this is, in fact, exactly what the Mother has vowed to do? The Mother has vowed to reflect back to you whatever you are sending out through your mind. You are the one who has chosen to create a division in your mind between what is conscious – and what you like to look at – and what you have made unconscious because you do not want to look at it and take responsibility for it. You may think, in your naiveté or spiritual pride that there is nothing but what you like to look at. Nevertheless, the reality is that you are projecting the totality of your mind into the cosmic mirror. And the Divine Mother is simply reflecting back to you the totality of what you are projecting out.

And why is the Mother doing this? Out of love for you, so that the Mother can show you what is hidden beneath the threshold of conscious awareness. This is the stark truth that very, very few spiritual seekers have been willing to acknowledge. Yet I tell you that those who have been willing to acknowledge it, have attained freedom from their own subconscious prison. They are the ones who have – by being willing to look at their subconscious images and replace those decisions with better decisions – they have attained enlightenment.

This is the process that every ascended master has gone through. So many of the students who have followed a previous ascended master teaching have built this idolatrous image that those who have ascended have done so because they have always focused on the positive. But the reality is that we who have ascended, have ascended because we were willing to look at everything in our own minds—and to transcend that which is unreal. We were willing to let the old die and to be reborn so many times that there is no point in even putting a number on it, for it is the perpetual rebirth, the perpetual self-transcendence.

When you do not even consider that there is some kind of goal you have to reach; you are simply willing to die daily, as Paul said it. But not only that, you die many times a day and you are reborn over and over again. Whenever something comes up, you look at it, you see the unreality, you replace the unreal decisions – the decisions that took you away from oneness – you let that self die, and you accept that you are reborn, that you are no longer that old self.

You are a new self, and as you continue to expand that self, you will gradually rise to the point, where suddenly you cross that threshold into the ascended state. And even though it may seem like a dramatic change from a human perspective, when you actually experience it from the inside, it is only one more experience of death and rebirth.

For now you no longer fear death. For you realize that death can only happen to that which is unreal. Which means that when a part of the unreal self dies, the real self is liberated, is set free, becomes more. And so, as Paul said, death is the last enemy. It is because so few people have been willing to realize that only the separate self can die. For the Conscious You cannot die. But what can be reborn is the Conscious You's awareness that it is the open door for the Presence, and not a separate self that can act on its own, that can do things on its own.

Putting Satan behind you or putting Satan between you and God

Jesus, January 3, 2011

There is no standard for Christhood.

Why is there no standard? For a very simple reason. For you, as an individual, to be the Christ means, quite simply, that you are the open door for your I AM Presence to express itself through you. And this expression happens through the Omega aspect of the Presence, the I Will Be Who I Will Be Presence. This is where your true, God-given spiritual individuality and identity is anchored.

It is not a matter of you – with the outer mind here in embodiment – acquiring some sophisticated skill or passing a set of sophisticated initiations. This is not to say that manifesting Christhood cannot be represented as a path that leads you from a lower level towards higher levels. Certainly, the path can be pictured this way. Nevertheless, the process of acquiring, attaining, Christhood is not the same as attaining some outer skill. The process of becoming the Christ in embodiment is a process of unlearning everything you have learned with the outer mind.

Christhood is not the same as spiritualizing the ego

Why is this so? Because being the Christ means being the open door for the Presence, whereby the Presence can express itself through you, unhindered of any filter in the lower mind. Unfortunately, many ascended master students have fallen prey to the very subtle illusion promoted by the fallen beings, namely that becoming the Christ means creating a sophisticated ego that has taken on the appearance of a spiritual person.

If you look at the Christian religion, you will see that for centuries it has raised up a certain image as the ideal for how a human being should be or behave—if that human being is spiritual or saintly. Many ascended master students have built onto this and have created an image for what it means to be the Christ, to attain Christhood. They think that this can be defined through some outer standard, such as looking a certain way, walking a certain way, talking a certain way. Nevertheless, as the old song goes, "walk like the Christ, talk like the Christ" but this does not make you the Christ.

I realize there is an old book, called The Imitation of Christ. And although there can be some validity to imitating a spiritual person, I must tell you that attempting to adapt your outer behavior to a certain ideal can only take you so far on the path—and it will not take you to Christhood.

Certainly, you can look at the world today and you can find many people who have a behavior or a way of life that is not conducive to any kind of spiritual growth, because it traps them into repeating certain patterns over and over again. So there can be value in for a time imitating a higher ideal, so that you free yourself from these worldly patterns of behavior. Nevertheless, if you think that continuing to refine your behavior according to some external ideal will get you to Christhood, then you are mistaken.

For there comes a point, where you need to recognize that as long as you have an external standard, there will forever be a gap between your current state of consciousness and Christhood. For the external standard can only be a graven image that you set before the true God of your I AM Presence. And if you think that you have to adapt your behavior to this external standard, you will also automatically think that the expression of your I AM Presence through you must also be adapted to this external standard. And thus, you will not be open door for the Presence. You will not be open door for the winds of the Holy Spirit that bloweth where it listeth.

Understanding why the Spirit will not conform to matter

What is the purpose for the Holy Spirit? It is not to conform to peoples' ideas, mental images and beliefs. If the Holy Spirit were to conform, how could the Holy Spirit awaken anyone from their current state of consciousness?

The Holy Spirit has only one purpose; that is to initiate and accelerate the process of self-transcendence. For the Holy Spirit is the force that has been created by all of the self-aware beings in your current sphere that have transcended their state of consciousness. They have formed this giant force, this mighty rushing wind of the Holy Spirit, that is indeed meant to help all who have not yet awakened to awaken to their full potential as spiritual beings.

Therefore, the Holy Spirit will never conform to any mental image, any belief, any doctrine, any system, any structure that keeps you in a certain state of consciousness. So can you see why it simply is not possible that you can have a structure in your mind for how you should be as the Christ, and then at the same time be the open door for the Holy Spirit? It cannot be done. It cannot happen.

The lie of the reality of matter

There is, as I said, no standard for what a Christed being should be like, for the role of the Christed being is precisely to shock people out of their current sense of equilibrium, the false equilibrium that comes because they think their egos have managed to force the entire material universe to function according to its world view, its doctrines, its belief system, its expectations.

This is the lie of the perversion of matter. It is the lie that there is anything in the matter world that has continuity, that has permanence. You think the material universe has existed for 15 billion years, as your scientists claim. But I tell you, there is no "thing" that has existed for any length of time. For any "thing" that exists has no independent existence; it exists only because Spirit allows it to continue to exist. Yet it still has no independent existence, any more than the image on a movie screen has an independent existence. For the moment you shut down the projector, the screen goes dark.

And so it is with the material universe. What you think has permanence is simply images projected onto the screen of the Ma-ter light. It is the satanic lie that these images are not projections but are actual things that have a continued existence independently of Spirit. This is the lie of matter. This is what I meant when I said: "Judge not after the appearance but judge righteous judgment."

Question the entire idea that matter is real and that matter has power over you as Spirit. Be willing to question it continually during this Year of the Mother, and you can experience tremendous growth during this year. In fact, if you will question this illusion in its many subtle forms, you can – during this coming year – experience a growth, so that at the end of the year, you will look back and scarcely recognize yourself as you are today.

Knowing the will of God in the Year of the Mother

Master MORE, January 5, 2011

Knowing the will of God as the will of God is

The will of God is that you grow in self-awareness, and any choice you make can bring growth. Even making a choice that leads to strain or suffering can in the end bring growth. And if you made that choice, then it was because you needed to go through that strain and suffering in order to experience what you needed to experience, before you were ready to let go and transcend the old self-image.

A number of years ago, this messenger went through a period, where he contemplated the will of God. At the time, he had an inner conflict, because he had all of his life felt that there were certain decisions that he had to make. Yet because he had become a member of an organization and heard certain teachings about the will of God, he had created the mental image that perhaps his own decisions were not right or were not the highest possible. And therefore, he had come to the point where he was – reluctantly – willing to submit himself to the will of this external God, that he had a graven image of. An image that was created not exclusively because of the teachings, but because of the traditional monotheistic image of the angry being in the sky.

And so, he did not realize consciously that he was going through a process of having to let go of this mental image of the external God. Yet as he contemplated the will of God – and felt the conflict of not wanting to let go of his own will in order to blindly follow an external authority – he eventually came to a point, where he realized that a person's will can be the will of the ego. And so, he decided that because he did not want to make ego-based decisions, he was willing to submit himself without conditions to a higher authority, as he saw it.

And so, one day he came to this experience of completely letting go, of completely surrendering any predefined idea of what his own will should be or what the will of God should be. And so, in this willingness to surrender, he said: "God, show me your will and I will do it."

And the answer that came to him was this: "What if God wants you to make your own decisions?" This was a complete shock to his being, but instead of rejecting it based on a mental image, he accepted that this was indeed a message from Above that he needed to internalize. And so, he did what he has done many times in his life. He deliberately surrendered his preconceived opinions and ideas and beliefs. And he seriously pondered the answer that he received.

And after some time, he came to a higher resolution than he had before, where he realized that, yes there is indeed a will of the ego that you need to learn to see and see through. But there is also a legitimate will of your own, where you truly need to make your own decisions based on the knowledge and the perception you have at any given time. And then, you look at the results of those decisions, and then you learn from that.

He also realized that in a sense what he had done, was that he had built this image that if he submitted to the will of the external God, then he could do nothing wrong—if he always followed this will of the external God. And he then realized that this was actually not true surrender to the will of God.

For it was simply the easy way out; the easy way out for a student who has begun to realize that his will is partially colored by the ego, but he has not yet attained the Christ discernment to see what is the coloring of the ego and what is not. And so, it seems difficult to part the veil of Maya and to know what is right and what is not right. And so, it seems easier – in order to avoid making mistakes – to just say to the external deity: "'Tell me what is your will, so I can do that."

And do you see how this ties in with what I said about the mechanical mastery? For so many students think that if only they follow the will of God or the will of an ascended Master, then they will always do the right thing and produce the right result. But what is the right result? Is it that you produce a particular outcome here on Earth? Or is it that you grow in self-awareness?

What does it matter to the process of your ascension, or to the process of the ascension of the planet or the entire material universe, that you produce a particular result in a particular situation? Do you really think that the decisions you make in certain situations in your life here on Earth have an impact on the entire universe? Nay, it is not a particular outcome – whether you do this or do that, whether you run 100 m in 9.1 seconds, whether you marry this person or divorce that person or take this job or lose that job – these are not the things that matter in your ascension. What matters is how your consciousness shifts as you go through certain situations.

It is not the external outcome that is important; it is the internal outcome. If a situation reinforces your mental image, then that situation did not help your growth, regardless of the external outcome. But even if the situation has a seemingly wrong or undesirable external outcome, but the internal result is that it shifts your frame of reference and purifies your perception, well then that situation was a success in terms of bringing you closer to your ascension.

This is what this messenger realized: that there are many decisions in life that he had to make himself. Because it was the only way for him to grow in self-awareness. If he had a booming voice from heaven telling him what to do, and he did it, what would he learn from that? And so, there are many of you, who have been students of the ascended masters for years or decades, who have still not come to the point where you are willing to make your own decisions and take responsibility for your state of mind, for the way you react to the outcome of those decisions. And even then go beyond and take responsibility for the state of mind with which you make your decisions.

Understanding non-decisions

What did I say earlier through my female messenger? I said that you must be willing to be creative, to experiment, rather than always seeking to just push the button and produce a mechanical result. If you want to know ahead of time what the results of your decision will be, then you are not in the right frame of mind as a student of the ascended masters. There are many times, where you are in a particular situation on Earth, where you have a particular perception of the situation, and where you simply need to make a decision based on that perception—and then learn from the outcome. For that is how you grow—by experimenting.

Of course, as you experiment, you will learn to make better and better decisions. But if you do not experiment, how can you learn to make better decisions?

If you stand there, still, paralyzed, out of your fear of making a mistake, and you say, subconsciously: "Oh, I will not make that decision now. I will go study the teachings of the ascended Masters and give decrees or rosaries. And then, hopefully, one day I will know what is the right decision before I make it." Well, this is your right to take this approach, but then you have essentially said to me, Master MORE: "Don't bother me now, Master MORE. Let me give my decrees and study the outer teachings; don't try to tell me something from within. For am not willing to hear it; I am not willing to be your chela, for I am not willing to experiment with the creative flow."

You see, my beloved, there is a delicate balance to be found. We have talked about you being the open door for the I Will Be Presence, expressing itself through the lens of the Conscious You. We have talked about the Conscious You becoming a clear pane of glass by experiencing pure awareness, so that it knows it is not the outer personality, the separate self. But how do you come to that point of being the open door? You come to that point only by experimenting, by making decisions. You see, making a decision and learning from it is better than making no decision.

And so, the concept I wish to introduce to you here, at the beginning of the Year of the Mother is that there are decisions and there are non-decisions. A non-decision is where you want to know ahead of time what the outcome will be or what is the right decision. And therefore, you are not willing to simply make a decision and experience the outcome. You want to postpone the decision until you know what the outcome will be, so that if you do not want to experience a certain outcome, you can either refuse to make a decision or make a different decision. This is a non-decision, and you do not grow spiritually by making non-decisions.

You think you are not making a decision, but you are making a decision. It is just that it is a non-decision, which postpones your growth. People who make non-decisions are not chelas of the Ascended Master MORE, nor any other ascended master.

You will know, of course, that the first ray is the ray of the will of God. What is the will of God? It is that you make your own decisions, for it is by making decisions that you learn and grow and expand your self-awareness. So you will not move on on the spiritual path until you master the initiations of the first ray, and you will not master the initiations of the first ray until you stop making non-decisions and become willing to make true decisions. Where you make a decision regardless of whether you know the outcome, or even if you know that the outcome might not be pleasant.

For, or course, I acknowledge that there are situations on Earth, where it will seem like any decision you make will have an undesirable outcome, and thus you would rather not do anything. But you see, as I have just attempted to explain, any outcome is a potential for learning, so what does it matter whether it is pleasant or not, according to the standard, the mental image, you have created for what is pleasant or not?

If something brings you closer to your ascenscion, does it really matter whether it was pleasant or not at the moment? For certainly, it will be pleasant and when you walk through that gate into the ascended state, and I and other ascended masters will be there to greet you; not any longer as our student but as our brother and sister of Spirit. For you have become what we are, and that is the ultimate joy and the ultimate experience you can have at the end of your sojourn on Earth.

But you will not get there without making decisions, where you take responsibility for the decision, for making the decision based on what you know now, and then you take responsibility for evaluating the result, not the outer result but the effect it has on your consciousness. What will help you grow is that every time you make a decision, you evaluate: "What is my reaction and what does my reaction show me about my state of consciousness?"

If you react to a certain decision by condemning yourself because the result was not pleasant, or did not live up to some outer standard, well then you can use that reaction to see that you have taken on some worldly standard. And you have taken on the satanic tendency to judge yourself based on an external standard. Instead of being willing to be the Christ, for which there, is as Jesus said, no standard.

Why the devil cannot judge the Christ

Do you see that the devil cannot judge the Christ, for the devil can only judge – as anyone can only judge – by having a standard, by creating a standard? And a Christed being is one who has transcended all standards, all graven images. And so, when the devil comes to tempt you – by wanting you to live up to a certain standard – then you do not accept the judgment projected at you by the devil, perhaps through other people, perhaps even through those closest to you. But you can, in your own mind, say: "Get thee behind me, Satan, for you have nothing in me."

And so, do you see that any decision you make can show you something about your reaction? And when your reaction is not in peace, you know that the only thing that can take away your peace is that you have some standard in your being. And then, you should know, as an ascended master student, that any such standard will keep you out of heaven.

For it is precisely one of the more subtle satanic lies that you will get to heaven only by living up to a standard defined on Earth. And as long as you think that you will get to heaven only by living up to a standard defined on Earth, then you will not be able to step through the door that leads to heaven.

For the door that leads to heaven is the door that no man can shut. No standard on Earth can shut the door and keep you out of heaven. But how can you go through the open door to heaven? Only when you become the open door, so that you have no standard to which you are attached. And then your openness allows you to pass through the open door to heaven. For only those who are open – who have become as little children – can pass through the door to the spiritual realm.

The oldest lie, promoted by so many religions, is that you will get to heaven only by living up to a certain standard defined by that religion. It is one of the most successful plots applied by the fallen beings to keep people from attaining their ascension, or from manifesting and expressing their Christhood while still in embodiment.

This Year of the Mother is a unique opportunity for you to question whether you have such a standard to which you are attached. Those who will honestly question this, can experience a fundamental shift in their consciousness. And thus, they can truly begin to express their Christhood during this year.

These are the kind of students that I am looking for.

Will you be one of them?

The choice is yours!

Is there any injustice in the universe?

Portia, the Goddess of Justice, May 30, 2011

It is essential to understand free will

Again, of course, you cannot truly understand free will as a remote concept. You can come into oneness with the River of Life, so that you are flowing with it. And then, you will know that free will truly is free. It is free to express whatever the Presence wants to express on Earth, and it is free from all the constraints created by the fallen beings, by the mass consciousness and by your own ego.

You cannot be free to express your will freely, as long as you think you have to live up to any standard on Earth. And of course, when God first gave self-aware beings free will, it was not the Creator's intention that they live up to any standard on Earth, as the Earth was not even in existence. And as the first beings had not fallen, and so there were no beings in the fallen consciousness to impose any standard upon the beings with free will.

But do you not see, that it is only the dualistic mind that can create, that can define, a standard for what is good and evil, just and unjust? It is only the separate mind that creates a standard.

This is what we have attempted to help you see, since Mother Mary first released her wonderful book about the abundant life, where she gave the concept that you are not a self that can be defined according to any standard or mental image on Earth. You are a self that has no earthly, no worldly, no form-based definition. For, you are pure awareness. You are designed to be the open door and nothing more.

You see, my beloved, as a wise student on the path, you need to come to another turning point, where you realize that words have inherent limitations. Read the beginning of Maitreya's book if you are not fully familiar with the limitations of words. Any word can be twisted and turned, and you can use words to support just about any arguments you desire.

There are those, my beloved, who love to use words as weapons against their fellow man, playing some power game of trying to convince them or force them. You will see these throughout history, you would see Jesus being up against them, you will see the Buddha engaging them somewhat without engaging them at all. And you will see that they always come up, whenever the Living Christ appears in any form. There are the wordsmiths, the word twisters who will seek to use clever interpretations of words against the Living Christ. You find them everywhere, you find them anywhere, where the Living Christ appears.

So you have a choice to make: will you twist and turn words, or will you go beyond words? Will you become the open door, that you may experience the reality of what it is you seek to know, such as divine justice?

Is there any injustice in the universe? How can there be, when the ultimate law of the world of form is free will? Do you not understand that free will is free? And it is individual.

You are an individualized extension of the Creator—you were not created as a separate being, but as an extension of the Creator. Yet, the moment you were individualized, you were given completely free will to experience anything you desire to experience. And you were then sent into a world, that has the potential to give you any experience you desire, because the Ma-ter light can take on any form that is projected upon it. And the Mother – the Divine Mother – has vowed to take on any form, so that you can have any experience you desire. This is the simplest, the most basic form of divine justice.

No choice without consequences

You are free to create any mental image you like, and to project that image upon the mother light, and then the mother light will reflect back to you circumstances in the world of form, that reflect the image you have projected. This is the most basic form of divine justice—what you sow that shall you also reap.

Can it be any more simple? Yet, those of you who have been willing to study and apply the teachings on non-duality, that we have been giving now for several years, should be open to understanding a secret that very few people have understood. It is the essence of how the fallen beings – or should I even say: the fallen consciousness – has tricked self-aware beings into the endless struggle.

Do you not see, what I have just told you? You can take two different viewpoints, my beloved. You can look at life from the inside of your current situation, your current state of consciousness, your current perception. Or you can use your ability to return to pure awareness, so that you can see the big picture and look at life from the outside.

So let us then step outside of the mental boxes and look at the big picture! What have I just explained about how free will and the universe works? You have completely free will, but how do you actually exercise your will? You exercise your will by making choices! But what are choices? If you are walking down the road and you come to a point, where the road forks into a Y, you are now facing a choice: Should I take the right or the left road.

Yet, what if this road simply forks for a time, goes through two tunnels that are exactly alike, and then the two branches of the road merge back into the same point. In that case, do you actually have a choice, given that following either road gives you the exact same experience and brings you to the exact same place. In other words, whether you choose the right or the left, there is no difference; it has no consequence! And in that case, do you really have a choice?

Yet, if the roads now go off in different directions, give you different views, different experiences and take you to different places, then you can indeed be said to have a choice. But why do you have a choice? Because there are different consequences, depending on which road you take. So what makes it possible for you to exercise your will, is that there are consequences of whether you do this or do that. If there were no consequences, you could not exercise will!

And so, how do you produce consequences? You make the choice, to form a certain mental image, then you project it upon the Ma-ter light, and the matter light takes on the form of your image. Thus, you produce your own consequence, my beloved. This is a truth that is very difficult for most people to accept.

It is completely impossible for the ego and the separate self to accept this concept. For the ego will never – ever – take responsibility for producing consequences. And in a sense, you cannot blame the ego for this, when you understand why the ego was created. So, let us take a look at this.

How planetary units evolve
Of course, it is all well and good for me to say that you have individual free will and you produce your own consequences. Yet, as the old saying goes, no man is an island. The reality is, that you were not created

as a single individual, sent into an entire world, where you are the only being and therefore you are the only one making choices. You were created as part of a large group of beings, that were sent to some planetary system in the material world. And thus, you would exercise your free will within the context of a larger whole, where there were many other individual beings also exercising their individual will.

This is actually a mechanism that ensures more rapid growth, because if you were all alone in your own separate world, it is very possible that you would get yourself into a state of mind, where you were highly comfortable and you could stay there for an indefinite period of time. And thus, how would you fulfill the original purpose for creating you, namely that you grow in self-awareness until you reach the level of God consciousness? And so, in the infinite wisdom of the Creator, it was clear that by creating many individual beings and putting them together in some greater whole, such as on a planet, then they would make more rapid progress by observing each other or even, if they chose to enter a certain state of consciousness, clashing with each other.

And so, what has happened in most of these – should we call them planetary units – that you find in this material universe, is that after a long period of experimentation and conflict, a certain coherence has emerged. There are, of course, millions and millions of planets with intelligent life throughout the material universe. And the vast majority of them have indeed gone through this period of initial, what scientists like to call chaos. But which is truly just the outplaying of free will, until you have seen, as scientists have even observed can happen in certain gases, that the molecules, the individual molecules, gradually or even suddenly come into alignment.

And this is what has happened on most planets, where beings have experimented for a time, clashing with each other, challenging each other, conflicting each other, but then they have gradually realized, that there is greater joy in working together on a higher union, a higher vision. And so, they have come into coherence, and now they have put their planetary unit in an upward spiral, in an ascending spiral.

So you see, indeed, that the entire material universe is in an ascending spiral. Yet, when you look at this universe, you see that there are still some planets – not a large number compared to the total, but a large number if you look at just the number – that have not entered this Ascension Spiral or have not passed this point of the phase transition, where coherence emerges. Planet Earth has entered an ascending spiral, but humankind has not yet come to this point, where there is the phase transition, that aligns the consciousness of most people to a higher vision, a higher oneness, a higher unity. And so, what is it you see, then, on these planets, where there is still chaos, where there is still conflict between people?

How the ego projects responsibility

Well, what you see is this: the conflict is a product of the mental images, that the beings on the planetary system are holding in their minds and projecting upon the Ma-ter light. The Ma-ter light is simply taking on the form of what is projected upon it, and thus creates a planet with physical conditions and a society with certain conditions that outpicture these mental images.

Do you see, what I am explaining here? You, as an individual, have created a mental image in your mind. You are projecting that mental image upon the Ma-ter light and the Ma-ter light is simply reflecting back to you the consequence, that you have chosen to produce by the way you have exercised your free will.

Now, of course, you may say: "But I have not single-handedly produced the situation that exists on Earth!" And you are quite right. Humankind has collectively produced the current situation, but why are you on Earth? Well, because you have taken on the same kind of consciousness, shared by the majority of the people on this planet.

And thus, you will see that you have been part of creating the current situation on Earth. And thus, what you see on Earth is a consequence of the exercise of free will. Yet, of course, this might be possible to see when you project yourself outside of your current state of consciousness, your current sense of self as a separate being. But it is not possible to see this, when you are looking at life from inside your separate mind, your separate sense of self.

When you are looking at things from the inside, you will think that the situation you experience on Earth is not the result of your own free-will choices, or even the choices made by humankind. You will be susceptible to believing in the lie projected by the fallen beings, that what you are experiencing is something that was forced upon you by an external force—be this the angry, remote God in the sky or other people or some immutable laws of nature created by mere chance.

How the fallen beings trap you in the dualistic struggle

Do you not see, that the main thought systems – be they religious or scientific-materialist or political – found on this Earth, portrays you as a victim of circumstances beyond your control? And what does this victim consciousness cause you to do? Well, it causes you to think that the only way to improve your situation is to seek to change the outer conditions, to change the consequences.

And thus, the most simple mechanism – applied by the fallen beings in their attempt to tie you into the ongoing dualistic struggle – is indeed to get you to struggle against consequences. Yet, do you not see why this will never give you peace of mind?

My beloved, imagine that you are in a movie theater. You are looking at the movie that is playing on the screen, and you decide that you do not like the movie. But since the movie is appearing on the screen, you now get it into your head that the only way to change the movie is to change the screen. So, you get out a bucket of black paint and a paintbrush, and you start painting the screen black. And yes, that does change the movie somewhat, but it is still the same image that is being projected at the screen. So, how much can you really change the movie by changing the screen?

For is the movie not produced away from the screen? Is it not so, that the image on the screen is a consequence of a cause that is found somewhere else? And in a movie theater, that cause is the film strip in the movie projector. But, do you not see the parallel? What you experience on Earth is a consequence of a cause. And the cause is found in your consciousness and in the collective consciousness.

If you think you have to fight the consequences – instead of changing the cause – you will inevitably turn your life into an ongoing and potentially never-ending struggle. Although the struggle will certainly end at some point, as mandated by the law of free will, that although you have free will to have any experience you want, you do not have the right to have that experience, to remain in a certain experience, forever.

And so, divine justice is simply that you have free will to make choices, but that you will experience the consequences of your choices. Because when you go into a certain state of consciousness, you will magnetize yourself to a planetary unit on which a majority of the beings have that same state of consciousness. And thus, you will inevitably be tempted to go into a struggle against other people with the same state of consciousness, struggling against consequences produced by the collective state of consciousness on that planet.

How planets are pulled up by the universe
Yet, it is also divine justice that no planetary unit is an island. And therefore, the inhabitants of a planetary unit cannot do whatever they want without being connected to the whole of the material universe. And so, if the entire universe is in an accelerated Ascension Spiral, then the inhabitants of a planet like Earth, will be connected to that spiral. And thus, in order to resist the Ascension Spiral, they must exert greater and greater force. And this again intensifies the struggle.

Now, you may say – if you look at this from inside the struggle – that this is then forced upon you by this external God, who is forcing you to be connected to the Ascension Spiral. But things are not quite that simple. For the reality is this: if a planetary unit was an isolated unit, and if the inhabitants of that unit really could take their planet into a downward spiral without being connected to a greater whole, well, then that downward spiral would very quickly accelerate to the point, where the planetary unit would be destroyed. And the beings who were then responsible for that spiral, would have no other way to go than through the dissolution of their individuality in what has been called the second death.

And thus, if the Earth was not connected to the whole, then the Earth would long ago have self-destructed, and the beings who brought in into that spiral would have destructed with it. And thus, they would no longer have free will—the opportunity to choose.

And so, you see indeed, there is no self-aware being that can exist independently, for it is an expression of the Creator's own Being. And of course, the Creator prefers that all expressions of its Being go through the Ascension Spiral. The Creator has given you an incredibly long time span, and has given you free will to decide which road you want to travel on the way to the ascension point. But there is an underlying law that states, that you must go either up or down, that you cannot stand still. For that would be against the purpose of creation itself. And it would indeed be against the purpose for which you have chosen to enter this spiral that is creation, that is the world of form.

For regardless of the images created by science or various religions, the world of form is not static. It does not stand still, nor is it cyclical in nature going from one state to another of back to the first, back to the second and so forth indefinitely. The world of form is an upward spiral that has a clear direction and a clear purpose. You may fight against it – that is your choice – but you are not fighting against God or God's plan. You are fighting against the consequences that you have created and that those on your planetary unit have created collectively.

The definition of Satan

And thus, do you not see what is the simplest definition of Satan? It is the consciousness that causes you to fight against consequences, instead of taking the Christ perspective of simply changing the cause and thereby also inevitably changing the consequences.

And so, what has happened to those who have gone into this consciousness of fighting consequences, is that they inevitably get sucked into the epic mindset created by the fallen beings. Which is indeed, that something has gone wrong with God's plan, with God's original design. And this, of course, can exist only when you believe that there is a standard for evaluating what should or what should not happen. And that you are the one who can define that standard, or that those whom you consider to be the ultimate authority on Earth can define that standard for what has gone wrong with God's plan.

And once you accept that there is such a standard, you are easily sucked into the epic struggle of now seeking to change what has gone wrong according to your definition. And this inevitably leads you to the conclusion that what has gone wrong is that some people have exercised their free will in a way that threatens God's plan for the universe. And thus, it is your job to change these people, either through direct physical violence or through persuasion, of seeking to in any way persuade or manipulate them into conforming to your standard—your mental image of how the Earth should be.

This, then, is the consciousness of Satan, that Peter attempted to put on Jesus in that crucial situation described in the gospels, where Jesus turned to him, looked him sternly in the eye and said: "Get thee behind me, Satan!"

For Jesus was committed to the greater process of God's plan for the universe. Jesus had volunteered to take on the role of the Living Christ, to come into embodiment and to let people trapped in the dualistic consciousness do with him whatever they wanted, yet demonstrating that whatever they did to him, they could not change him. For he refused to see himself as being bound by consequences, ever remaining true to the reality that you as an individual being are not a consequence. You are a co-creator, which means you have the potential to be a cause and to change the consequence on Earth.

But how do you truly change the consequence on Earth? You do not change it by fighting current conditions. You change it by taking responsibility for yourself and saying "I am an individual, existing in this planetary unit. I do not have the right to violate the free will of others, but I do have the right to not let their choices violate or limit my free will. And therefore, I have a right to take responsibility for my own state of consciousness and to change my state of consciousness and to express a higher state of consciousness, regardless of what the majority on this planet are doing. So that I may be a light in the world—a light that is set on a hill and cannot be hid. So that those who are willing may see it as an example and be inspired by it, without me having to fight them or force them or persuade them in any way. I am simply the light of the world. I am the open door for the light to shine through my being, and thus I am the open door for the the flame of divine justice." Or whatever flame you desire to be the open door for that will stream through you.

And it is not that the light goes in and becomes some specific teaching that challenges other teachings. For, as I said, that which is expressed in words has its limitations. The entire teaching, given by the Ascended Host throughout the ages, has no value in itself, for once it becomes a disconnected teaching that exist only in the form of words, then it is just another teaching, and words that can be argued against indefinitely.

It has value only when people go beyond the teaching and use it as only a tool to attune themselves with the consciousness of the Ascended Host and then become the open door.

How to know divine justice

For how will you know the Goddess of Justice? Not through an outer teaching formulated in words. You will not know me as long as you see me as an object that you can know from a distance. You will know me only when you go beyond your mental images; become pure awareness, that you become the open door through which the being that I AM – the stream of consciousness I AM – may flow through you and express itself on Earth.

And then, you will know me, then you will know the Goddess of Justice. But I am an ever-flowing stream, and I will be who I will be at any moment. And in any situation, I will express something different, for my goal is not to express some ultimate truth. My goal is, in any situation where I am given an entry into this world, to challenge people to come up higher, to transcend their current state of consciousness, their current mental box.

And thus, my expression will be adapted to the current mental box and adapted in such a way that it gives them an opportunity to transcend it, to take the next step. Not some ultimate step, that they are not ready to take because it is far beyond them. This is how the Living Christ expresses itself on Earth.

Whenever someone becomes the open door, then the greater consciousness that is the Ascended Host, will express itself according to the situation, always seeking to raise up all life, never seeking to put down any form of life. Do you not see, that there are so many people who are attempting to put down others? First, they are attempting to control others, and then, when some people will not be controlled, they attempt to put them down, even destroy them or punish them. And this is, indeed, because the fallen beings have projected this false image of divine justice which says, there is a standard for how you should exercise your "free" will.

Well, if there is a standard, then your will cannot be truly free, can it? And so, they have even projected that God has set a standard for how you should exercise your free will. And thus, they say that if you do what is wrong according to the standard, then you deserve to be punished. And thus, you will see that on planet Earth the concept of justice is inextricably linked to the idea of punishment.

Yet, God has no desire to punish anyone. For God has no need to punish anyone, because God has given you free will and God has set up the Ma-ter light to reflect back to you the consequences of your own choices. So, who is punishing you, my beloved?

You are! You are punishing yourself! Who is punishing humankind? Humankind is collectively punishing itself through the choices made.

And until a critical mass of people awaken to this reality – and decide to stop fighting the consequences and instead change the cause which is their own state of consciousness – well, until that happens, humankind will not reach that coherence point, where they can unite around a higher vision. Instead, they will remain in the current state, where they will continue to struggle against each other. Only, of course, given that the entire rest of the universe is moving on, the struggle will become intensified, until it eventually becomes so much that people say: "Enough, we have had enough of this, there must be a better way."

The cause of all human conflict

And of course, many people have already reached that point. And thus, we are indeed optimistic that, as the planet moves forward in the coming years and decades, we will get ever closer to this turning point. Yet of course, there may be some very serious confrontations that will take place before then. For there certainly are many people on this planet who are blinded completely by the consciousness of Satan, where they think they have to fight the consequences of their own choices, instead of changing the consciousness that led to those choices.

And therefore, they think they have to fight other people and seek to change other people's state of mind, instead of changing their own state of mind. Do you not see, that this one mechanism is the cause of all human conflict? You think you have to change other people's minds instead of changing your own mind. Right there, my beloved, you have the cause of all conflict and the cause of all so-called injustice on this planet.

For do you not see, that the law of real free will mandates that you have no right to seek to change other people's minds? When you do so, you are violating their free will, and they will feel this as a violation of their free will, even if they do not understand the Law of Free Will. And thus, if they cannot escape your violation of their free will, then they will sense this as an injustice. And of course, this is all designed by the fallen beings to trap people in this endless struggle of fighting against each other, because they seek to force each others will, thereby violating each others free will and creating the sense of injustice. And so it goes on and on and on.

How will it ever change? Only by those who are the spiritual people, coming to see that you are not here to change the minds of anyone else. You are here to change your own state of consciousness, until you become a light that is set on a hill and cannot be hid. Let your light so shine before men, that they may see that this light cannot come from you; it must come from a greater source. You have not produced it, you have become an open door for it.

Ahh, my beloved, this is the true goal of a Christed being! It never has been and it never will be, the goal of a Christed being to fight against others, to punish others, to put down others, to expose others according to your standard, to judge them or to change their minds in any way.

If you will experience the greatest form of personal freedom that can be experienced on Earth, then you need to give up the idea that you are here to change anyone else. This is an incredible freedom, my beloved!

I give you an opportunity to escape the struggle

Do you not see that I, Portia, have also been called the Goddess of Opportunity?

What is the greatest opportunity for you? It is that you let go of the desire to change others. For when you have a desire to change others, where does your attention go? It goes outside yourself! But where did Jesus say that the kingdom of God is to be found? Did he not say that the kingdom of God is within you?

So, as long as your attention is directed out, seeking to change others, how can you find the kingdom within yourself? And thus, giving up the desire to change others is the greatest opportunity for you to go within and realize this simple fact: you have been given individual free will, and the ultimate meaning of this is that you have complete freedom to choose your state of mind. Because your state of mind does not depend on anything outside yourself!

Yes you are living on planet Earth, yes there are many things on this earth that are impinging upon you, even seeking to force your free will! But you still have the potential to go through those things and retain your peace of mind. But you cannot attain this peace of mind as long as your attention is directed outwardly, seeking to change others.

You will attain peace of mind only when you direct your attention inward and seek to change yourself—your own state of mind. That is when you have the opportunity to manifest Christhood. And then, when you become the open door for the light to shine through you, then you will give other people an opportunity to see that light and either accept it or reject it. But you are not giving other people an opportunity by going out there, trying to force them, trying to enlighten them, trying to make them see, what you think they should see.

This as not giving them an opportunity to escape the struggle, this is only enveloping them or yourself more deeply in the struggle. Become the light, become the open door, then you give people an opportunity—and then you have the opportunity to be in the world without being affected by the world but truly being the open door for the joy and the love of the Presence to flow through you, whereby you will feel at peace. You will feel fulfilled in expressing and experiencing the God quality of your Presence flowing through you. This is your greatest opportunity!

And yet, we of course know, that this is not simple to attain for people who have been in embodiment in many lifetimes in the density of this struggle consciousness. Those of us who have been in embodiment know this full well. For many ascended masters have indeed spent many lifetimes in the consciousness of the struggle, even thinking that they have to work for some ultimate good by struggling against other people, as you see in the lives of several masters. Nevertheless, how did they become ascended masters? They did so by coming to the realization, that you can never win the ultimate battle, for the struggle will never end until you transcend the consciousness that created the struggle.

And so, in order to give you an opportunity to transcend that consciousness, we have decided to release these latest four invocations. [Loving the Divine Mother, Part 1-4] Here, as we are coming to the halfway mark of the Year of the Mother, to give you an opportunity to sail through the rest of this year, without being involved with the struggle. As you may indeed likely see, that the rest of humanity will become more and more involved in the struggle in the last half of this Year the Mother.

And so, look upon these four invocations as a supreme opportunity for you to pass the initiations of the Year of the Mother, and also to make a contribution to helping the rest of humankind pass these initiations and indeed transcend the consciousness that needs to be transcended in this year. This is our hope: that you will look at them this way, that you will make use of them and that you will allow these very intricate invocations, very intricate statements, to change your state of consciousness.

For truly, it is one thing to read a book or a dictation, but it is another to have a teaching expressed in the form of an invocation, where you do not read it with the intellectual mind, but it goes into your consciousness at a deeper level, and therefore has a much more transformative effect than anything you just read.

For again, you will not be enlightened by thinking that enlightenment is some object that you can study at a distance. You will be enlightened only by becoming first pure awareness and then the open door, whereby the stream of consciousness that is enlightenment can flow through you. For enlightenment is not a static state, despite what many spiritual teachings portray it as. It is indeed the living, flowing River of Life that is ever-changing ever self-transcending, because it is always in the process of being more—at any moment being more than it was before.

This is life! Life is constant self-transcendence, death is stillstand! Therefore, I say as has been said before: CHOOSE LIFE! For if you do not choose life in the Year of the Mother, then it will become much more difficult to do so in the Year of the Holy Spirit and in succeeding years.

Thus choose wisely and use these invocations to help you transform your state of consciousness, until you are not making this choice with the outer mind—you are connecting to the deeper choice that brought you into embodiment.

And thus, you are not actually making that choice with the lower mind, you are flowing with the River of Life. You are flowing with a choice already made by your higher being and with those of your brothers and sisters in the world of form who have also joined this River of Life.

Thus, my release is complete! Make use of it as you see fit. For I give you complete freedom! Yet, I will let you know, that I have also given you – with this release and these four invocations – a complete opportunity to escape the consciousness of the struggle—the consciousness of Satan. So that you can come to the point, where you do not even need to say: "Get thee behind me, Satan!" For Satan is no longer in front of you.

For what is in front of you, is your I AM Presence and beyond that the Ascended Host and the hierarchy of beings, leading all the way to your source—the Creator itself.

Make matter real–either by materializing your perception or by seeing that all life is ONE

The Divine Mother, September 9, 2011

Everything is a spiritual activity

There are those in the spiritual and New Age movement, who are talking about a personal story, that you carry with you, even from lifetime to lifetime. This is what we have explained through this messenger as the ego, as the sense of identity that you carry with you and that colors the way you look at everything, becoming the filter that even colors your perception. So that you think, that what you see through this perception filter is not simply a perception, but it is reality.

And so, matter realization, the process of making matter real, has two aspects. If you will not question your perception of life, then your perception will become real in the sense that it will become outpictured in matter. And this will be accelerated for the last three months of the Year of the Mother but also in the coming Year of the Holy Spirit, where the Holy Spirit will accelerate the process of your perception becoming your physical reality. So that you might be forced to reconsider your perception and the power it has over your life.

And then, when you do decide to step back and look at your perception – instead of seeking mindlessly to defend your perception – then you can come to the higher understanding of materialization, of matter realization, where you make matter real in the sense that you realize – you acknowledge, you see, you experience – that matter is not separated from Spirit.

Matter is an expression of spirit, for Spirit is within everything. Without him was not anything made that was made. Do you see, the deeper reality of life is oneness? Everything is one, for everything is an expression of the one God, the One Spirit, the Creator itself.

If you do not perceive this, then your perception is not real. And thus, you have not risen to the level, where you can make matter real by realizing that every aspect of your life in matter is a spiritual activity.

Just look at traditional religion, and how many people think they can live their lives any way they want during the week, and then they go to church on Sunday and say some prayers, sing some songs, light some candles, or go into a little box and tell to the priest some glorified version of how they have supposedly sinned; not being willing to even acknowledge the sin of perception, of polluted perception. And this, then, they think is sufficient to make them right with the remote God in the sky. Yet how could it ever make them right with the God within?

Barriers exist only in the mind

Look at the New Age and spiritual movement, of how many people have made spirituality a daily part of their lives. Nevertheless, they still see a difference, a distinction, between what they call spiritual activities and everyday activities. They think they have to go to some retreat in order to be truly spiritual. They think they have to come apart from their normal lives, in order to be truly spiritual.

Or they think they have to engage in some form of meditation, or chanting, or prostrating themselves on the floor, or whatever, in order to do something spiritual, that can somehow compensate for the lack of spirituality in what they see as everyday activities.

And although this is a necessary phase to go through, if it becomes a permanent state of mind, a permanent perception, then it will hold back your growth. For what is the higher growth? It is that you accelerate to the higher level, where you break down the barrier between spiritual and everyday activities. Because you realize, that this barrier – as any barrier, as any division – is created only in your perception.

My beloved, did you notice what I just said? Any barrier, any division, can be created only in perception. For the deeper reality is that all is one, and in oneness there can be no divisions.

Life then is one. When you know that life is one, your victory is won. That, my beloved, is the thought to ponder for the rest of this Year the Mother. For I will tell you, that if you go into this physical quadrant of the Year the Mother seeking to uphold, magnify or defend the perception that creates divisions between you and other people, between you and the matter world, or between you and God, then you will experience an increasing pressure to reconsider that perception.

Look at those, wherever they are found, who have a desire to harm others, to punish others. Look at those who precipitated the event, that took place now almost 10 years ago in New York. And look how the leader of this movement had escaped capture for almost 10 years, but in the Year the Mother his own perception became realized in matter. And by the very fact that he perceived himself as an enemy, those whom he perceived as enemies caught up with him in the night—and then he was out of embodiment.

Look at your life. Do you carry resentment, do you carry anger, do you carry a desire to punish, a desire to bring justice, a desire that other people should be made to see what they have done wrong, whether to you or to the world? In that case, this then is the perception that you project onto the screen of the Ma-ter light. And what can the Ma-ter light do, but give you what you say you want?

This, of course, is always the case, but I am telling you that in these last three months of the Year the Mother, this process will be accelerated to the point, where it will challenge people who will not let go of their old momentums, their age–old momentums of seeking to control other people and resenting those, who will not be controlled.

Forcing your perception upon others

Is it not so, that the basic problem seen on earth is that there are many people who believe their perception filter is reality? And who – out of their own fear – are seeking to force others to accept their perception filter. Was it not, for example, so, that the British Empire seriously believed that its perception filter was superior to all others, and thus was seeking to force that perception filter on its colonies, or even on other nations?

Was this not the reason for the wars in Europe between Britain, France, Germany and Russia? What was communism but a perception filter, that those who thought it was reality felt compelled to seek to force upon the world?

My beloved, you who are the spiritual people must surely be able to see the vanity of this, and thus rise beyond it in your own lives, so that you no longer seek to force your personal perception filter upon others. This not only is important in your personal life; it is important for the planetary growth.

For you who are the spiritual people are the ones who have the potential to become forerunners for the process I have described, of spiritualizing western society, of helping western society make the transition from its current focus on material welfare to a new focus on psycho-spiritual welfare.

But you see, you will not be able to be the forerunners for this process, if you are attached to your perception filter. For what will you then do? You will seek to force your perception filter upon society, thinking that you have to convert other people to your particular spiritual philosophy, guru or movement, and get society to recognize this as the one superior guru, philosophy or organization.

My beloved, the spiritualization of western society will NOT happen the same way it happened in the Piscean age, where one religious organization took control of society and boxed people's minds in for over a thousand years, burning books, banning as heresy every viewpoint that challenged church doctrine. This will not be repeated in the Age of Aquarius.

Universal spirituality

There will not be one guru, organization or philosophy that will come to be seen as the primary one in the Aquarian age. It is a fallacy to believe this. What needs to happen is an awareness of what we might call a natural, a built-in, or a universal form of spirituality. This is where science has made an invaluable contribution by coming up with certain law's that are independent of the beliefs of human beings, be they political or religious beliefs.

Gravity works the same, whether you are a Hindu, a Muslim, a Christian or an atheist. Jump up in the air, and you will be pulled back down to the ground. This is, or it should be, a humbling realization.

Yet of course, you must also recognize, that science itself is in the process of acceleration. Isaac Newton was the first one to formulate a description of what he called the "force" of gravity. Of course, since time immemorial human beings have been aware, that there is something that ties them to the earth. Yet no one had to truly attempted to explain it until Newton. And what Isaac Newton did was to explain it as a force, that pulls you towards the center of gravity in the center of the earth.

Yet, as you should be aware as a spiritual person, Albert Einstein came up with a higher view of gravity, that goes beyond the force-based view. And yet, even quantum physics has indicated, although not yet fully realized, an even higher view. And so, there is room for improvement, but nevertheless the point is that spirituality must likewise become seen as a set of universal principles that guide how the human mind works.

You see that, so far, science has attempted to describe universal principles for how the material world works. And do you see, that when this is supplemented with a study of the universal principles for how the mind works, then you have a complete view of reality. And that is what can take western society to the next evolutionary level, where now society becomes able to provide all people with a sense of purpose, a sense of meaning, and a sense of how they can improve their situation by improving themselves, by working on their minds.

See yourself together with the Elohim as part of the Consciousness of the Divine Mother

Elohim Arcturus, September 12, 2011 through Helen Michaels.

Beloved beings, I wish to give you a vision of how we, the Elohim, see the matter plane. When we look at the current matter plane on planet earth with the consciousness of the Elohim, we see a large cloud, a heavy thickness that is covering the planet. We are not saying this to discourage those who are making a daily effort in giving the rosaries and invocations, giving the decrees to raise the earth and to raise all life. We only say this so that you would recognize, understand and acknowledge this heaviness that is covering the planet.

Recognize that you are not the doer!

This thick cloud has layers, hundreds of thousands of layers of negative thought patterns, mass murders, atrocities, records of wars and the records of the misuse of light. And we say that, so you can acknowledge that the most essential key to creating freely, is that you would recognize that you are not the DOER.

You are the open door for the Father's light, because no man on earth could ever clear those records, clear this heavy thickness of misusing the light through negative, heavy thoughtforms, the thoughtforms of pain, fear, anger and the sense of injustice.

The matter plane can be reborn into its original divine purity only through the Father, the Spirit being born in the consciousness of the Divine Mother. All the heaviness can be consumed in matter only with the help of the Ascended Host and higher beings, namely the beings in a higher state of consciousness, who are not part of the same plane. These beings do not have the subjective view of what happens on the matter plane, and they don't take anything on the matter plane as reality, because they see it as the temporary outpicturing of the misuse of God's light.

...

Creation is always pure, when not distorted by the consciousness of the separate self

My beloved, the mother light is always pure, as the mother light is forming the basis of matter. Why is purity the main quality of the mother light? My beloved, it is precisely because the creation of the Spirit can be pure and be outpictured in its purest form only when the Mother is pure, when the Mother does not take on any perverted forms itself but allows the Spirit of the Father to outpicture the beauty and divine geometry of God freely.

What does it mean, my beloved? It means that if we, at the level of the Elohim, look at human consciousness, the ego-based consciousness that so many people have created and are still struggling with, we see how this separate self and the ego form like a net around the matter plane. This net has all kinds of shapes, and sometimes there are only a few openings within this net that allow the Divine Father's light to be freely poured down and experienced in the matter plane.

This net is usually so thick, that the pure Light of the Father cannot just be poured down and freely manifest in the matter plane. The ego-based consciousness – all the desires and wishes, the "shoulds" and "should nots" that people have created in their separate selves – is forming a thick layer of nets that we are seeing. This layer is so thick, that no matter how much light we are pouring down, then sometimes very little of it will reach the matter plane in its purest form, as it was released by the Father.

Therefore we, the Elohim, understand very well the human dilemma, how you have to struggle with the identity of your separate self, with your ego-based desires, with your standards and judgments and evaluations in the matter plane. You have built an identity that says how your life should be, how you should be, how you should think, how you should act or how you should create. All those "shoulds" and "should nots" create another layer of obstacles for the light of the Father to reach the matter plane in its purest form.

Shattering the serpentine lie of freeing the people through Communism

Jesus, September 24, 2011.

Forgiving means giving up

And thus, let me give you a new word to ponder. You have heard of forgiveness, but I ask you to ponder a new expression: "for-give-up-ness." For you cannot forgive; you can only forgive by giving up. You cannot forgive by letting go of something—if you think that letting it go means a loss for yourself. For as long as you have remnants of the ego in your being, you cannot bear the sense of loss that the ego will have, when it feels like you are letting go of something.

And, of course, as long as you are in embodiment, you will have elements of the ego in your being, or you will not be able to stay in a physical body. I know well that people have portrayed the idolatrous image that I had no ego during the last three years of my life, or perhaps that I never had an ego in that embodiment. I know well, that there are spiritual people all over the world who believe that their guru is the only enlightened one.

Nevertheless, I tell you the truth, that I had elements of the ego with me until the moment when I gave up the ghost. And such is the case for anyone else who ever has taken embodiment and ever will take embodiment. This is part of being the meek: that you have the humble realization that you are not a perfect human being. And thus, you do indeed have need for the reality of Christ and the mercy and forgiveness of God. And therefore, you can extend that to others.

And so, you see, you cannot forgive, if you think that forgiving another means that you lose something; whether it was a desire for revenge, a desire to punish the other, a desire to prove them wrong or to prove yourself right or to prove yourself superior. But you will not be able to let it go as long as your ego thinks it will require a loss. And thus, how can you truly forgive up? Only when you realize that by forgiving, by giving up, you are not losing something, you are gaining something.

To sail into the Year of the Holy Spirit, you need to forgive up everything

You are losing what seems valuable to the ego, but you are gaining what you now see is more valuable to yourself. For you are gaining freedom from the very condition that you think you could not forgive in another. For that which you cannot forgive in another is naturally what you have not forgiven in yourself.

And therefore, I can assure you, that what you cannot forgive in another you do indeed have in yourself. For otherwise you would not even think you needed to forgive the other for that condition. And that means that what you cannot forgive in others, is what you have at hidden levels of your psychology. And it is holding you back from following Christ, for did I not say: "What is that to thee; follow thou me." Well, as long as there is something that is important to you, then you cannot give up that something and follow Christ.

And therefore, you will be able to give it up only when you see, that following Christ is more important to you than holding a grudge against your brother or sister. Only when you truly see this, can you give UP. And you will only see it, when the shaft of the Christ light touches your third eye, and therefore the scales fall from your eyes and you see the reality that I AM.

Glossary

Akasha
An energy of a higher vibration than anything else in the material realm. It serves as a recording device, recording everything that has ever happened in the material world. People with developed faculties can read the Akashic records. In the future, it will be possible to read them with technological devices.

Alchemy
In popular belief, the process of transforming base metals into gold. The deeper, mystical meaning is the transformation of the base human consciousness into the gold of a more spiritualized awareness, such as Christ consciousness.

Alpha and Omega
Two spiritual beings who reside in the central sun, the highest level of the world of form.

Angel
A self-aware being that is not created to take physical embodiment. Angels serve in a variety of capacities, the most commonly known for us is as messengers who deliver a message from the spiritual realm to human beings. Another important function is angels who protect us against lower energies or dark forces.

Anti-christ
The consciousness of separation and duality. This consciousness forms a filter that distorts perception in such a way, that it seems plausible that we are separate beings, separated from God, from each other and from the material universe. The more firmly beings are trapped in this consciousness, the more real the illusion of separation seems to them. Thus, they will be acting as if they truly are separate beings, meaning they will believe that what they do to others will not affect themselves. This is the origin of man's inhumanity to man and the origin of evil. Human beings

can be trapped in this consciousness, but so can non-material beings, forming the dark forces.

Archangel, Archeia
Angels are organized into bands, and each band is led by an archangel. Each archangel has a feminine complement, called an archeia. There is such a pair for each of the seven rays, but there are also other bands of angels.

Ascended Master
Normally refers to a being who was embodied as a human being on earth and who, often after many embodiments, qualified for the process of the ascension. The term can also be used more broadly to refer to all beings in the spiritual realm, even those who have not taken embodiment in the material world.

Ascension
A process whereby a being evolves to the self-awareness represented by the full Christ consciousness. In this state of consciousness, one can see through all of the lies created by the illusion of separation and duality. Thus, one sees the underlying reality that nothing can be separated from the Creator and that all self-aware beings are extensions of the Creator. One therefore seeks to raise all life, instead of seeking to raise oneself as a separate being. After a being ascends, it resides permanently in the spiritual realm and does not have to reembody.

Astral Plane
Everything is made from energy, and energy is a continuum of vibrations. There are certain divisions of this energy continuum, for example the material universe is made from vibrations within a certain spectrum. Yet the material universe has four divisions: the etheric (identity) level, the mental level, the emotional level and the physical level.

The emotional level itself has further divisions, and the lowest of these are created when people engage in negative emotions, such as fear, anger and hatred. The astral plane is a division within the emotional realm, and it resembles the visions of hell that people have had throughout the ages.

Atlantis

A previous civilization that inhabited a continent in the mid Atlantic. This continent disappeared around 10,000 years ago due to the actions of the inhabitants. The atlantean civilization was technologically superior to our time, but due to the lack of spiritual awareness, the inhabitants caused the civilization to self-destruct due to a misqualification of energy, which led to warfare and cataclysm.

Aquarian Age

There is a precession of astrological cycles, lasting approximately 2,150 years each. The previous age was the Age of Pisces, for which Jesus was the spiritual master. For the Aquarian age, the ascended master Saint Germain is the master. According to Saint Germain, the Aquarian age was officially inaugurated on March 22, 2010.

Aura

An energy field surrounding the human body. There are levels of the aura, corresponding to the levels of the material realm. You have an identity body, a mental body and an emotional body beyond the physical body.

Carnal mind

Sometimes used by ascended masters to refer to the entire lower consciousness, including the ego. Can also be used more specifically to refer to that part of the subconscious mind, which is designed to take care of the functions of the physical body. This includes certain basic instincts, such as protection, food and propagation. The carnal mind will seek to satisfy these needs without any regard for long-term interests and thus needs to be under the control of your conscious mind.

Causal Body

An energy "body" surrounding your I AM Presence. It stores all of the attainment gained and the lessons learned from all of your embodiments. When you raise your consciousness sufficiently, you can make use of this attainment for fulfilling your divine plan.

Catch-22

Described by the popular saying "you can't get there from here." It is a seemingly impossible situation that you cannot get out of. The ascended masters use this to refer to the mechanisms created through the illusion of separation and duality. The mind of anti-christ creates innumerable catch-22s in order to stop or slow down our spiritual growth. They are always based on an illusion, which means you can transcend them by changing your perspective. Note that a catch-22 often appears as a problem that you have to solve. Yet the problem has no solution, so the real solution is to walk away from the struggle.

Chakra
A focal point within your aura. There are seven major chakras, corresponding to each of the seven spiritual rays. If your chakras are pure, high-frequency energy from your I AM Presence can stream through them, and this gives you maximum creative powers. If your chakras are polluted, the stream of higher energies is reduced, and instead the chakras can become open doors for lower energies to enter your aura. Severely polluted chakras can open you to energies from the astral plane.

Chela, chelaship
A Sanskrit word that is often translated as "slave." This refers to Indian spiritual tradition, where a person makes him- or herself the virtual slave of a spiritual teacher, or guru, who will thereby expose the student's ego. Used by the ascended masters to refer to a sincere student, who is willing to submit to the disciplines of the spiritual path, designed to expose the ego.

Chohan
For each of the seven spiritual rays, there is an ascended master who serves as the leader or main teacher. This spiritual office is called the "chohan."

Christ
In its broadest sense, this refers to the basic consciousness out of which everything in the world of form is created. The purpose is to maintain the oneness between the Creator and its creation. This is especially relevant for beings with free will, who have the option to descend into the illusion of separation, thereby believing they are separated from their source. The Christ consciousness ensures that no matter how far you descend into separation, you always have the option to return to oneness with the Creator. Because the Christ consciousness is within everything

that is created, you can never go to a place where you are unreachable for Christ.

In a more specific sense, Christ refers to a being who has overcome the illusion of separation and has attained the Christ consciousness. There are degrees of Christ consciousness.

Christ Self
A mediator sent by ascended masters to assist beings who have become trapped in separation and duality. Most people know their Christ selves as intuition or the "still, small voice within." The Christ self does not actually tell you what choices to make. It seeks to give you a frame of reference for making better choices. The Christ self will not necessarily give you an ultimate or absolute truth. It will give you an insight that is a bit higher than your present state of consciousness.

Christ discernment
The ability to see through the innumerable illusions created through the consciousness of separation and duality. Also the ability to see the underlying oneness behind all visible phenomena.

Christhood
When a being has attained the Christ consciousness, that being is said to have put on Christhood.

Conscious You
The core of your lower being. It is the Conscious You that descends from the spiritual realm as an extension of your I AM Presence. It is the conscious you that is the seat of your free will. However, you make choices based on the perception you have. It is possible for the Conscious You to have pure perception, which means it serves as an open door for the I AM Presence. However, when beings go into separation the Conscious You projects itself into an outer self or role, and it now perceives everything through the filter of that separate self. Thus, it will often make choices as if it really were a separate being.

The important point is that the Conscious You is and will always remain pure awareness. This means that while the Conscious You can project itself into any role it chooses, it can never lose the ability to extricate itself from that role and attain the Christ consciousness in which it can say with Jesus: "I and my father (my I AM Presence) are one."

Cosmic Being
A spiritual being who holds a specific spiritual office, usually a focus of a certain divine quality. Cosmic beings have never taken embodiment on earth as they ascended in a higher sphere.

Creator
The being who created the particular world of form in which we exist. There are other worlds of forms created by other Creators. A Creator must create a world of form out of its own Being, meaning the Creator experiences everything that happens in a given world.

Dark forces
Beings who have become trapped in the illusion of separation and duality. Many such beings reside in the astral plane. Everything in the material universe is sustained by a stream of energy from a higher realm. Yet when you begin to deliberately harm other self-aware beings, you are cut off from receiving energy from a higher realm. Thus, you can sustain an existence only by stealing energy from beings in the material realm. This means that dark forces can continue to exist only by stealing energy from humans, and they do this by getting us to misqualify energy through lower emotions and selfish acts.

Dark forces can take over the minds of human beings (if people let them), and most of the warfare and crime seen on earth is caused by dark forces. They do this by agitating people to violate others, and the pain caused releases energy that the dark forces can use to sustain themselves.

Decree
A spiritual technique for invoking high-frequency energy from the spiritual realm and directing it into specific conditions on the personal or planetary level. A decree is a worded expression, usually in rhyme, that is spoken aloud with great power and authority.

Dharma
In Buddhist tradition, the sacred work that you came here to do. Also refers to your divine plan, which is the positive qualities you wanted to bring to earth before deciding to take embodiment here.

Divine Mother
A spiritual office that represents the feminine aspect of God to planet earth. Currently, this office is held by the ascended master Mother Mary.

Divine Direction
Guidance that you receive from a higher source through your Christ self. The guidance can be from your I AM Presence, an ascended master or the cosmic being known as the Great Divine Director, who represents divine direction.

Divine Plan
A plan for what you want to accomplish in this embodiment. This includes the spiritual gift you want to bring to earth, experiences you want to have, lessons you want to learn and karma you want to balance. Often, this means there are certain people you want to meet and with whom you want to engage in various types of relationships.

Duality, duality consciousness
When the Conscious You sees with pure perception, it sees the underlying reality that all life is one and came from the same source. The duality consciousness obscures this oneness, and it makes it seem like matter is separated from spirit, humans are separated from God and people are separated from each other.

Duality also implies a negative polarity between two opposites that work against each other, one seeking to annihilate the other. Thus, duality always involves two opposing sides, and there is usually a value judgment attached to them, making one good and the other evil.

Duality is always an illusion, because nothing can change or destroy the oneness of all life. Thus, duality can exist only as an illusion in the minds of self-aware beings. As long as you are blinded by duality, you cannot attain Christ consciousness and thus cannot ascend.

Eightfold path of the Buddha
Traditionally, the path prescribed by Gautama Buddha for overcoming suffering. However, a deeper mystical understanding is that it represents the path of mastering the first seven spiritual rays and the eighth ray of integration.

Elementals

The world of form is created through a hierarchy of beings that extend from the Creator. For example, planet earth was created by seven beings in the spiritual realm, called the Elohim. They envisioned the blueprint for the earth and projected it into the four levels of the material realm.

However, the blueprint is brought into physical manifestation by four classes of elemental beings. These are beings that have a lower self-awareness than humans, but who can grow by serving to help build the material world. The elementals in the four realms are named as follows:

- Etheric realm, fire elementals or salamanders
- Mental realm, air elementals or sylphs
- Emotional realm, water elementals or undines
- Physical realm, earth elementals or gnomes.

Elohim

Ascended beings with such a high level of consciousness that they have complete mastery over the creation of matter. There is a masculine/feminine polarity of Elohim for each of the seven rays.

Emotional body

An aspect of your aura/mind that houses your emotional energies.

Etheric body

An aspect of your aura/mind that houses your sense of identity.

Evil, the veil of Maya

In Buddhist tradition, the veil of Maya is what obscures reality to beings in embodiment. This reality is that everything is the Buddha nature, in other words that all life is one. This veil is actually created because the matter universe is made from energy of a certain density, which makes it impossible for the physical senses to detect that even matter is made from spiritual light. Thus, this **energy veil** is abbreviated as evil.

Fall

In its broadest sense, the term refers to the process whereby a self-aware being descends into the consciousness of separation. Before the fall, you will see yourself as a being who is not isolated but is connected to something greater than yourself. After the fall, you will be convinced that you are a separate being, who has been abandoned or punished by God.

The important distinction is that after the fall, you will find it difficult to take responsibility for your own growth. Because the fall was caused by your own choices, it can only be undone through your own choices. Yet when you think you are a separate being, you think you can do whatever you want without considering the consequences for others. This causes you to engage in an ongoing struggle against other people, which can lead to a state of mind where you think you have to fight against other people, the matter universe or even God.

This state of mind becomes a catch-22, because as long as you will not accept that you have created your own situation as a result of your own choices, you cannot change those choices. Instead, you are seeking to create a change in your situation by forcing other people, the matter world or even God to come under your control. You are seeking to change the splinter in the eyes of others while ignoring the beam in your own eye.

Fallen beings or fallen angels

In its broadest sense, refers to all beings who are blinded by the duality consciousness. Yet the masters often use this more specifically to refer to a group of beings who fell in a previous sphere. The important distinction is that these beings had attained considerable attainment before they fell, which means they are often superior to the beings who started their existence in this world.

In world history, fallen beings have often become powerful but abusive leaders, and obvious examples are Hitler, Stalin and Mao. Yet many fallen beings hold important positions without visibly abusing their power and thus have a huge influence in society. Their main characteristic is that they are absolutely sure that they are right because they feel they are superior to most people on earth. There are also fallen beings who are not in physical embodiment, but who reside in the astral plane or the mental realm.

Fallen consciousness
The consciousness of the fallen beings. In its broadest sense, the illusion of separation and duality. It can also refer more specifically to the consciousness of feeling superior to others, wanting to have special privileges or wanting others to follow you.

The main characteristic of the fallen consciousness is the belief that the ends can justify the means. This often causes people to believe they are engaged in an epic struggle and that it is their duty to use all means available to eradicate what they have defined as evil. Thus, the underlying belief is that you have the right to define what is good and evil, because you have a godlike status.

Four levels of the material realm
Everything is made from energy, so the entire world of form is made from energies of various vibrational qualities. There is a continuum of vibrations, ranging from the highest level, the level of the Creator, to the lowest. In between one can define several divisions, compartments or octaves of vibrations. For example, one major division is between the spiritual realm and the material realm.

There are several divisions in the spiritual realm, whereas in the material realm there are four divisions. They are, from higher to lower vibrations:

- the etheric or identity level
- the mental level
- the emotional level
- the physical level

Fohat
Refers to written or spoken word that is inspired from a higher source and endowed with spiritual light. Words become cups or chalices that carry spiritual light.

Four lower bodies, four levels of the mind
Corresponding to the four levels of the material universe, the masters sometimes say that we humans have four lower bodies, the identity body, the mental body, the emotional body and the physical body.

The masters also talk about four levels of the mind, where the identity mind houses our deepest sense of identity (who we are and what we can do), the mental mind houses our thoughts (how we can do things), the emotional mind houses our feelings (why we want to/have to do something) and the physical mind relates to the needs of the body.

Free will
The masters teach that it is extremely important to understand free will, especially in relation to the duality consciousness. Free will is the basic law that guides the function of the material realm. For example, the earth was created by the Elohim in a much higher state than what we see today. There was originally no lack of resources, no imbalances in nature and no diseases.

These limiting conditions have been created because a majority of human beings used their free will to descend into duality. Nature – meaning the elemental beings – had no choice but to outpicture as material conditions what was in the consciousness of a majority of the people. Human beings were created to have dominion over the earth, and the elemental beings can only take on the images we hold in our identity, mental, emotional and physical minds.

Yet the important point about free will is that we have the right to, at any time, transcend our previous choices. God and the ascended masters will never seek to stop us from transcending previous choices. It is only the ego and the dark forces who will seek to make us believe we are bound by past choices.

Guru
A Sanskrit word for teacher or master.

Garden of Eden
The deeper symbolism behind the Biblical concept of the Garden of Eden is that it represents a schoolroom in which self-aware beings are being prepared to take embodiment on earth. The "God" mentioned in the Bible was the ascended master Lord Maitreya, who was the "headmaster" of the mystery school.

Students were given graded lessons, and only more advanced students were meant to take the lesson represented by the duality consciousness. However, there was a number of beings in the mystery school, who had fallen in a previous sphere. These beings are symbolized by the Serpent, and they deceived some students into taking the initiation of duality before they were prepared by the teacher. This initiation is symbolized by the "fruit of the knowledge of good and evil," which makes beings think they are like gods and can define what is good and evil without the Christ consciousness.

The symbolism is that the fallen beings have deceived most people on earth into believing in the dualistic lies. This is what causes all conflict and struggle on earth. The only solution is that a critical mass of people follow the true path of initiation and attain Christ consciousness. The real purpose of the ascended masters is to help us do this.

God, four aspects of God

In mystical teachings, the world is seen as being made from one underlying element, called ether, which manifests as the four elements of fire, air, water and earth. One can likewise look at five aspects of God. The ether element corresponds to the original or undifferentiated Creator, which has not yet expressed itself in the world of form. As the Creator begins to express itself, it manifests itself as four aspects:

- Father, meaning the outgoing force, the will to create. For us, the ascended masters represent the father element, yet we also represent the father element on earth.

- Mother, meaning the contracting or balancing force. Compared to the Creator, everything in the world of form is the Mother. So we humans are part of the Divine Mother. Yet when we co-create by superimposing mental images upon the Ma-ter light, then this mother light represents mother for us.

- Son or Christ, meaning the consciousness that unifies the Creator (who is beyond form) with everything that has form. It is also the element that separates the real from the unreal by seeing through all dualistic illusions.

- Holy Spirit, means the force that drives all self-aware beings to return to their source. Since the beginning of the world of form, innumerable beings have gone through the process of the ascension and this has created a force or momentum that makes up the Holy Spirit.

God Flame
Your true individuality is not what we normally call your personality; it is anchored in your I AM Presence. Because your I AM Presence is made from energies of a higher vibration than anything in the material universe, it appears as a flame. Thus, your true individuality is sometimes referred to as your God flame.

Golden Age
At present, the earth is in a lower state than originally intended. This is caused by a majority of people being deceived by the duality consciousness, which inevitably leads to various conflicts and limitations. Yet the goal of the ascended masters, especially Saint Germain as the leader of the coming 2,000 year cycle, is to inspire a critical mass of people to walk the path of individual Christhood. As enough people raise their consciousness, society will begin to outpicture a much higher state than today, and this is commonly referred to as a Golden Age.

Great White Brotherhood
Another name for all ascended beings. The term "white" does not refer to race, but to the fact that ascended masters radiate a white light.

Hatred of the Mother
The Ma-ter light forms the feminine polarity to the Creator. It allows us to project any mental image upon it we want, and then it faithfully reflects back to us physical circumstances that reflect the images in our consciousness. When people enter the fallen consciousness, they cannot take responsibility for themselves, meaning they will not recognize that the Mother can only reflect back what we project upon it and is not seeking to punish us. Instead, such beings feel like victims, and they do feel like matter, the Mother element, is seeking to punish them or prevent them from doing what they want. Thus, they can develop hatred of the mother. Yet since we are all part of the mother aspect of God, hatred of the Mother is a form of self-hatred.

Human ego
An element in the psyche that is created when the Conscious You descends into the illusion of separation and duality. The Conscious You is pure awareness, so it simply cannot act as a separate being. Yet it can step into a separate sense of self, and when it perceives the world

through the perception filter of that self, it can believe that it really is a separate being. What makes this distorted perception seem real is the ego.

Human consciousness
In a general way, this refers to the consciousness that is currently considered normal for human beings. It can also be used more specifically to refer to the ego and the carnal mind.

I AM Presence
Your higher or spiritual self. The Conscious You is an extension of your I AM Presence, and your highest potential is to achieve complete identification with the Presence, so you serve as an open door for it to express itself in the material world. Your spiritual identity and individuality is anchored in your I AM Presence, which means it could never be destroyed no matter what happens to you on earth.

Identity body
An aspect of your aura/mind that houses your sense of identity.

Immaculate concept or vision
This refers to the vision of the highest potential or a pure vision that is not polluted by duality. For example, Mother Mary held the immaculate vision that Jesus would fulfill his mission.

Jesus
The ascended master Jesus was the hierarch or leader for the Age of Pisces. He holds the office of planetary Christ, and we cannot ascend without going through this office. This means that all people need to make peace with Jesus – by transcending the distorted images of Christ created on earth – in order to ascend.

Judgment
There is a group of ascended masters, called the Great Karmic Board, who oversee the overall planetary growth. One of their tasks is to determine which lifestreams are allowed to embody on earth and for how long. When a being falls into duality, it is assigned a certain time to turn around and start the path back to God. However, if a being violates the free will of other beings, this time can be shortened. The being is then

judged by its own actions. However, the ascended masters also teach that it is lawful for people in embodiment to call forth the judgment of fallen beings. If such beings will not change, then the Karmic Board can authorize their removal from embodiment.

Take note that the concept of judgment is not the same as the kind of value-laden judgment exercised by beings trapped in the duality consciousness. Such beings judge based on their own state of consciousness, often labeling as evil anything they do not understand or agree with. This is what Jesus called judging after appearances.

Initiation
A gradual process whereby you raise your consciousness towards the Christ consciousness. This can be an individual process, where you are guided from within, but it usually involves you following an outer teaching or even a guru or organization.

Karma
Everything is energy, so whatever we do – even what we think and feel – is done by using energy. We receive this energy as a gift from the I AM Presence. The energy we receive is pure, but we will qualify it according to the contents of the four levels of our minds. We are responsible for our use of energy, and misqualified energy becomes stored in both our auras and in the Akashic records as karma. In order for us to ascend, we must balance all energy by raising it to its original vibration.

The masters have also given a deeper understanding of karma, where karma is the images we hold in the four levels of our minds. Because we see everything through the filter of these energies, we are constantly qualifying energy. Yet we have the option to, at any time, examine our mental images and transcend limiting images—which is truly the path to Christhood, where we accept our divine identity.

This gives us two ways to balance karma. We can invoke spiritual energy through decrees and invocations and requalify the energy from our present level of consciousness. This is possible, but it is a slow process because we are constantly making more karma. The faster way is to work on transcending the mental images, so we stop making new karma. Once we achieve this, we can then balance all remaining karma much faster, because our higher state of consciousness allows us to invoke more energy.

Lemuria
A continent in the Pacific Ocean that had a high civilization but was destroyed about 12,000 years ago. It is often called the Mother land because it is said to have had a very high spiritual focus for the Divine Mother. The decline of Lemuria started when a group of fallen beings murdered the embodied representative of the Divine Mother.

Lifestream
A term used for an individual self-aware being. It is often used instead of "soul," as a lifestream refers to parts of our beings that are beyond the soul, including the I AM Presence and the lineage of spiritual beings leading all the way to the Creator.

Light
Usually refers to spiritual light, meaning energy that vibrates at higher levels than the energy that makes up the material realm.

Living Christ
A person who has attained some level of Christ consciousness while still in embodiment.

Living Word
Refers to written or spoken word that is inspired from a higher source and endowed with spiritual light. Words can become cups or chalices that carry spiritual light. This is also called fohat.

Lucifer
A being who rebelled against God in a previous sphere. Thus, it is considered that Lucifer was the first being to fall into the duality consciousness.

Maitreya
The ascended master who was the leader of the mystery school called the Garden of Eden. He is considered the Great Initiator, because his initiations are not obvious, and we often do not see that we are being tested. Lord Maitreya holds the office of Cosmic Christ.

God the Mother
Another word for the Divine Mother, but can also refer to the feminine aspect of God, which is the entire world of form. We are part of God the Mother.

Mass consciousness
Every human being has an aura, a personal energy field. Yet the entire planet also has an aura, and within it we find a combination of the individual energy fields of all people embodying on earth. There are certain divisions within this collective or mass consciousness, but all people are affected by the greater whole to some degree. There is a stage on the spiritual path, where our main task is to pull ourselves above the magnetic pull of the mass consciousness, so we can express our individuality.

Matter, Material Universe
Everything is made from energy, so the entire world of form is made from energies of various vibrational qualities. One can create a continuum of vibrations, ranging from the highest level, the level of the Creator, to the lowest. In between one can define several divisions, compartments or octaves of vibrations. For example, one major division is between the spiritual realm and the material realm.

There are several divisions in the spiritual realm, whereas in the material realm there are four divisions. They are, from higher to lower vibrations:

- the etheric or identity level
- the mental level
- the emotional level
- the physical level

Ma-ter Light,
The cosmic base energy out of which everything that has form is created. It has no form in itself, but has the capacity to take on any form. It also has a certain basic form of consciousness, which among other characteristics has a built-in striving for its source, the Creator.

The Ma-ter light has been stepped down in vibration to create succeeding spheres. We live in the seventh of these spheres, and the six previous ones have all ascended, becoming part of the spiritual realm.

Mental body
An aspect of your aura/mind that houses your thoughts and mental energies.

Messenger
A person who has been trained to receive teachings and dictations from the ascended realm through the agency of the Holy Spirit.

Misqualification
Everything we do, feel or think is done with energy We receive this energy from the I AM Presence and then qualify it with a certain vibration. Anything below the vibration of love is a misqualification and creates karma.

Mother, hatred of
The Ma-ter light forms the feminine polarity to the Creator. It allows us to project any mental image upon it we want, and then it faithfully reflects back to us physical circumstances that reflect the images in our consciousness. When people enter the fallen consciousness, they cannot take responsibility for themselves, meaning they will not recognize that the Mother can only reflect back what we project upon it and is not seeking to punish us. Instead, such beings feel like victims, and they do feel like matter, the Mother element, is seeking to punish them or prevent them from doing what they want. Thus, they can develop hatred of the mother. Yet since we are all part of the mother aspect of God, hatred of the Mother is a form of self-hatred.

Mother Mary
The ascended Master who was embodied as the mother of Jesus. She holds the Office of the Divine Mother for earth.

Mystery School
An environment designed to present self-aware beings with initiations aimed at raising their consciousness. It is usually overseen by an ascended master of high attainment.

Oneness

Before the Creator had created any form, there was only the Creator. Thus, a Creator cannot create anything that is separated from itself; it must create everything out of its own being. It does this by manifesting its being as the Ma-ter light and thus taking on whatever form is projected upon it by self-aware beings with free will. Thus, beneath any form, any appearance, there is still the oneness of the Creator. Separation from God is always an illusion, and it is this final illusion we must overcome before we can ascend.

Path

The masters teach that the ultimate goal of life on earth is to manifest the Christ consciousness, which allows us to permanently ascend to the spiritual realm and become ascended masters. Yet we are originally created at a much lower state of consciousness, and thus we follow a gradual path that raises our consciousness to the ultimate level. The masters say there are 144 different levels of consciousness that are possible for people on earth. You can ascend only after reaching the 144th level.

Physical body, physical mind

Obviously, this refers to the body. The physical mind is that part of the brain and nervous system that is designed to regulate the functions of the body, even prompting us to take care of the needs of the body. This is what gives us certain instinctual cravings for protection, food, sex and other physical needs.

There is nothing inherently wrong with taking care of the needs of the body, but the physical mind is not capable up limiting these needs. Thus, if we do not take command over the physical mind, all of our attention and energy can be spent on fulfilling the needs of the body, leaving nothing left over for spiritual growth.

Rays, or spiritual rays

Everything is made from energy. Even Einstein's famous equation, $E=mc^2$, says that matter is created from a very high form of energy that is reduced in vibration by a factor (the speed of light squared). The masters teach that while Einstein's theory is basically correct, there are seven of these reduction factors. In other words, the material universe is made from seven types of spiritual energy that are combined to form all phenomena in the material realm. These types of energy are called rays or spiritual rays. There is a total of 15 rays used to build the entire world of form.

Retreats
Many ascended masters have a spiritual retreat that exists in the etheric or identity realm. We can make a call to go to such retreats in our finer bodies while our physical bodies sleep at night. A retreat is usually located over a physical location on earth, yet because the retreat is in the etheric realm, it cannot be detected through physical means. A retreat focuses certain spiritual energies that are released to earth. It can also be a focus for giving specific teachings to people who are ready.

Sangha of the Buddha
The community of people dedicated to walking the path towards Christhood and Buddhahood. Not limited to a single organization.

Satan
In its most specific meaning, Satan was one of the beings who fell with Lucifer in a previous sphere. However, in a more general meaning, Satan is a state of consciousness that prompts, forces or tempts us to adapt to current conditions in the material realm.

We were created to be co-creators with God and have dominion over the earth. As Jesus said, "with God all things are possible." Satan is a consciousness that wants to prevent us from exercising our highest potential by causing us to voluntarily limit our creative powers and accepting that current conditions cannot or should not be changed.

The role of the Living Christ is to demonstrate to people that we can transcend the consciousness of Satan. That is why Jesus rebuked Peter when Peter wanted Jesus to conform to his expectations. Jesus said: "Get thee behind me, Satan."

Sanat Kumara
An ascended master of high attainment. In a previous age, so many people on earth had descended so far into the duality consciousness, that the Karmic Board and other cosmic councils had determined that the earth was no longer a viable platform for growth and thus would be allowed to self-destruct. Sanat Kumara then came with 144,000 lifestreams from Venus in order to hold the spiritual balance until enough people on earth

had been raised in consciousness, to where they could hold the balance for the planet.

Many of the 144,000 lifestreams that came with Sanat Kumara are still in embodiment and they are often very spiritual people with a great desire to help other people or improve the world. Yet there can come a point, where such people will hold back their own ascensions unless they let go of the desire to help or change others.

Serpent
A symbol for a certain state of consciousness that induces doubt into our minds. The specific purpose is to create a division in our beings, so we start to distrust our divine direction, our intuition, our own inner knowing and our spiritual teachers. Can also refer to a specific group of fallen beings.

Serpentine lie, plot
The primary serpentine lie is that the Christ consciousness either does not exist or is not attainable for us. Instead, the ultimate reality is the duality consciousness, in which we set ourselves up as gods, who believe we have the right and the capacity to define good and evil by ourselves. This inevitably causes a relative definition of good and evil, because good is seen as that which confirms our existing beliefs and desires, whereas anything that challenges them is labeled as evil.

The serpentine plot is to either get us so paralyzed by doubt that we blindly follow the fallen beings, or to get us so blinded by spiritual pride that we really do believe we are always right. In the latter case, we are also following the leadership of the fallen consciousness, which is in complete opposition to the Christ. We now seek to raise the ego to a godlike status, instead of seeking the Christ consciousness as a means to raising all life.

One aspect of the serpentine plot is to get us to believe that even God can be fit into a dualistic world view. God is portrayed as the opposite of evil or the devil. Thus, we are tempted to believe that in order to further God's cause, it is acceptable to do evil, including killing other people. History has many examples of how people have been deceived into fighting these epic battles against a self-defined evil. In order to win this final victory for good, it is necessary and justified to commit this ultimate act of destroying the enemy. In reality, such struggles only serve to misqualify more energy, that feeds the dark forces and thus give them power to deceive people into continuing the endless struggle. The only way out is the Christ consciousness that sees the oneness of all life.

Shiva
Traditionally a part of the Hindu trinity. However, the deeper meaning is that Shiva is a cosmic being who is especially helpful for cutting us free from dark forces and the astral plane. We can make a very effective call to Shiva by simply repeating his name 9, 33 or 144 times.

Sin
In ascended master terminology the same as karma, meaning misqualified energy that we need to balance before we can ascend.

Spiritual Rays
Everything is made from energy. Even Einstein's famous equation, $E=mc^2$, says that matter is created from a very high form of energy that is reduced in vibration by a factor (the speed of light squared). The masters teach that while Einstein's theory is basically correct, there are seven of these reduction factors. In other words, the material universe is made from seven types of spiritual energy that are combined to form all phenomena in the material realm. These types of energy are called rays or spiritual rays. There is a total of 15 rays used to build the entire world of form.

Soul
The ascended masters sometimes use this word as it is commonly used, namely as that part of our beings that reincarnates. However, the masters also give a deeper understanding, namely that it is the Conscious You that originally descended into embodiment. The soul is a vehicle that the Conscious You has created in order to express itself in this world, and it is often highly affected by the duality consciousness.

Jesus' crucifixion is a symbol for the fact that the Conscious You is crucified (paralyzed) by its own creation. Thus, the soul cannot be raised up or perfected. The soul is made from limiting beliefs and misqualified energies. As the energies are requalified and as the Conscious You transcends the limiting beliefs, the soul gradually dies, until the Conscious You gives up the Ghost of the final illusion of separation. The Conscious You can then claim its true identity as an extension of the I AM Presence and can ascend.

Spheres

The world of form was created by the Creator defining a spherical boundary and withdrawing its being into a singularity in the center of a void. The Creator then created a sphere in the void by using the Ma-ter light. The Creator defined structures in that sphere and projected self-aware extensions of itself into it. As these extensions grew in awareness, they raised the vibration of their sphere until it ascended and formed the first sphere in the spiritual realm. The Creator then created a second sphere, and the ascended masters from the first sphere then defined structures and sent extensions of their own beings into the second sphere.

This process of one sphere ascending and a new sphere being created has continued, so that we now exist in the seventh such sphere. In the first three spheres, all beings ascended without going into the consciousness of separation and duality. Yet in the fourth sphere, some beings refused to ascend, and they became the first fallen beings. As the fourth sphere ascended, these fallen beings could not ascend, and thus they "fell" into the sixth sphere. Because the newly created sphere had a generally lower vibration, the fallen beings could still exist there. This fact is the basic explanation for the existence of evil in our world.

Spoken word, Sacred word

The spoken word is a technique whereby we use the human voice to invoke spiritual light or energy.

Saint Germain

An ascended master who is the leader for the coming Age of Aquarius. He also represents the seventh spiritual ray, the ray of freedom. Thus, he is sometimes referred to as the "God of Freedom for the earth." Saint Germain will play an important role for the coming 2,000 years and he has a plan for taking the earth into a Golden Age.

Threefold Flame, sevenfold flame.

Everything is energy, meaning your physical body and conscious mind can survive only because you are receiving spiritual light from your I AM Presence. This light descends into your aura, into a chakra that is behind the heart chakra and called the secret chamber of the heart. The light is first manifest as a tiny white sphere, but then splits into a "flame" with three plumes, a blue representing will and power, a yellow, representing wisdom and a pink, representing love.

These three flames correspond to the first of the spiritual rays, with the white sphere corresponding to the fourth ray. When you go into duality, you begin to express the basic creative powers in an unbalanced manner, which causes your threefold flame to become unbalanced. This limits your creative powers, and you cannot grow beyond a certain level on the path to Christhood until you have balanced the threefold flame and attained the purity of motive of the fourth ray. At that point, you can begin to work on the initiations of the 5th, 6th and 7th rays, whereby you gradually develop a sevenfold flame.

Transfiguration
A spiritual initiation on the path to Christhood. It signifies that you transcend identification with the physical body and its limitations.

Twin flame
The Creator is beyond form. Yet as the first act of creation, the Creator expressed itself as two polarities, masculine or expansive and feminine or contracting. These two basic polarities are represented by two cosmic beings, called Alpha and Omega. In the spiritual realm, we find many beings, who form a polarity of masculine and feminine. For example, Elohim and Archangels all have a masculine-feminine polarity.

There is a popular belief that our souls were created in such a polarity, and thus each of us has a twin flame, who would supposedly be the perfect companion and complete us. Unfortunately, this has led to many romantic notions of finding the perfect love. It is necessary to balance this with the fact that you ascend as an individual being, not with your twin flame. Thus, the path of the ascension is a path whereby you become spiritually complete and self-sufficient, being able to ascend completely with your internal power.

Unascended being
A being that has not yet qualified for the ascension, and thus cannot abide in the spiritual realm. This does not only refer to human beings in embodiment. There are unascended beings in all four realms of the material world. For example, many souls who have ties to the astral plane can descend there between embodiments or can become permanently stuck there, not being able to reembody. We human beings can make calls for the cutting free of all unascended beings, so they can move on to the next station on their path.

Unconditionality, unconditional love

The duality consciousness operates by creating two opposites. Note that the original divine polarity of expanding and contracting are not opposite but complementary forces. Yet when these concepts are colored by the duality consciousness, they will seem like opposites. This is then coupled with a value judgment, labeling one opposite as good and the other as evil. This is what gives rise to all judgmentalness and discrimination found on earth.

When you attain Christ consciousness, you see that all this is an illusion, because the underlying reality is that all life is one and came from the same source. Thus, you see that God's reality is beyond any of the conditions and value judgments defined by the duality consciousness. It is difficult to describe the non-dual reality with words, but the most commonly used word is to say that God's qualities are unconditional, meaning beyond dualistic conditions.

For example, human love is always conditional. People have to do something right and avoid doing something wrong in order to be worthy to receive love. In God's eyes, you are worthy to receive God's love by the mere fact that you were created as an extension of the Creator's Being. Thus, you do not have to do anything to receive God's love, and nothing you do can make you unworthy of it. God's love is unconditional; beyond conditions.

Violet flame

A spiritual energy that is especially efficient for transmuting karma or misqualified energy. Saint Germain received a cosmic dispensation to reveal the violet flame in the 1930s. Since then, ascended master students have been invoking it through decrees, invocations and affirmations.

However, it is important to realize that the violet flame can be misused. Misqualified energy is caused by a limiting belief. The energy gradually accumulates in your aura, making you feel burdened. You can invoke the violet flame without changing the limiting belief, which will make you feel better in the short run. However, if you do not change the belief, you will continue to misqualify energy. And if you continue to use the violet flame to transmute the energy, you are misusing Saint Germain's dispensation, because you are not attaining long-term spiritual growth.

Word

From the Gospel of John: "In the beginning was the Word, and the Word was with God and the Word was God." This is actually a mistranslation of the Greek word Logos, which refers to an undivided whole. This is a symbol for the Christ consciousness, which is designed to maintain the oneness of all life. Thus, the Word is that which helps us see through the illusions of duality.

World teacher

An ascended being who serves the office of teaching humankind. Currently, this office is held by the ascended masters Jesus and Kuthumi. Unascended beings can also serve as world teachers in a lower capacity.

www.ingramcontent.com/pod-product-compliance
Lightning Source LLC
Chambersburg PA
CBHW050417240426
43661CB00055B/2176